I0867949

Helion & Company Limited
Unit 8 Amherst Business Centre
Budbrooke Road
Warwick
CV34 5WE
England
Tel. 01926 499 619
Fax 0121 711 4075
Email: info@helion.co.uk
Website: www.helion.co.uk
Twitter: @helionbooks
Visit our blog http://blog.helion.co.uk/

Published by Helion & Company 2016
Designed and typeset by Farr out Publications, Wokingham, Berkshire
Cover designed by Paul Hewitt, Battlefield Design (www.battlefield-design.co.uk)
Printed by Hobbs the Printers, Totton, Hampshire

Text © Santiago A. Flores 2018
Illustrations © as individually credited
Color profiles drawn by Luca Canossa © Helion & Company Limited 2018
Maps drawn by George Anderson © Helion & Company Limited 2018

Every reasonable effort has been made to trace copyright holders and to obtain their permission for the use of copyright material. The author and publisher apologize for any errors or omissions in this work, and would be grateful if notified of any corrections that should be incorporated in future reprints or editions of this book.

ISBN 978-1-912390-06-9

British Library Cataloguing-in-Publication Data
A catalogue record for this book is available from the British Library

All rights reserved. No part of this publication may be reproduced, stored in a retrieval system, or transmitted, in any form, or by any means, electronic, mechanical, photocopying, recording or otherwise, without the express written consent of Helion & Company Limited.

We always welcome receiving book proposals from prospective authors.

# CONTENTS

Introduction 2

1 Mexican Military Aviation before 1941 2
2 U-Boat attacks and the defence of the coast 24
3 The volunteers, observers and Spitfires 44
4 Evolution of the organisation of the Air Force, 1941-46 63
5 The creation of Mexican Naval Aviation 71
6 The evolution of the Mexican Military Aviation School 90
7 Training in the USA: learning new skills 97
8 Going to war I: training in the USA 109
9 Going to war II: the MEAF and the liberation of the Philippines 153

Appendices
A Combat record of the 201st Mexican Fighter Squadron 206
B Missions flown by the Mexican pilots of the 201st 207
C Missions completed by type by the 201st Mexican Fighter Squadron 209
D The replacement group of the MEAF 209
E Aircraft assigned to the *Grupo de Perfeccionamiento Aeronautica* (GPA, Aeronautical Training Group) in Idaho and Texas, 1944-45 210
F Aircraft assigned to the 201st Mexican Fighter Squadron in the Philippines 211

Bibliography 212
Acknowledgments 216
About The Author 216

# INTRODUCTION

With an expanse of more than 760,000 square miles, Mexico ranks third in size and second in population among the countries of what we often term Latin America.

Most of her mountain ranges, plateaus and lowlands are, in fact, continuations of the landforms of the south-western United States, while her demographics and patterns of historic settlement have been more akin to those of Middle America.

According to most examinations of her extremely rugged land area, only about 12 percent is arable, some 40 percent being pastoral, 22 percent forested and not less than 26 percent is occupied by other forms of utilisation or is generally described as just not usable.

Few nations of the world, let alone one with such daunting physical characteristics, have survived the torturous path that the residents of this country have experienced since proclamation as a federal republic in 1824. A measure of the internal strife during its formative period alone may be gained from the fact that the historical figure Santa Ana attained the presidency of the struggling state 11 times between 1832 and 1855.

But Mexico also proved, after the turn of the century, to be a nearly perfect laboratory for the evolving science of aeronautics, as the combinations of political power shifts, semi-isolated concentrations of authority and geographic challenges could not be serviced by the traditional railroad infrastructure alone.

The cauldron of the Mexican Revolution and, indeed, much of the first three decades of practical manned flight, saw remarkable instances of the introduction of aviation into a host of poorly understood, sparsely documented engagements – as well as the surprising emergence, in the midst of all of the turmoil, of indigenously designed and series production military aircraft.

Mexican military aeronautics, through to the end of the Second World War, somehow evolved collaterally in the midst of a nation and people inventing themselves, and the accompanying historiography to make sense of it all has required diligence, scholarship and no small degree of sheer determination and grit.

Aero-historian and friend Santiago Flores has, in these pages, crafted what is arguably the first cohesive, authoritative English-language analysis of this absolutely amazing – and yes, sometimes confusing segment of aviation history, and his carefully researched chronology will surely serve as a primer for future scholarship on the myriad of puzzles and mysteries which he has uncovered and, in many cases, corrected for history.

Many readers will be discovering this diversity for the first time. For others, some elements will be welcome additions to previously held beliefs and incomplete accounts. Through it all, Santiago has gifted us with the fruits of a life-long passion for the aeronautical heritage of his ancestry, and I warrant that one-and-all will applaud what he has accomplished herein.

Dan Hagedorn, Curator Emeritus,
The Museum of Flight, Boeing Field, Seattle

CHAPTER 1

# MEXICAN MILITARY AVIATION BEFORE 1941

Before we see how Mexican airmen could take to the skies in defence of their homeland against a foreign enemy and later fight in the liberation of the Philippines, it is necessary to give a brief history of the events that occurred in Mexico, which led to the establishment of military aviation, the Mexican revolutionary period of 1910-20 and the post-revolutionary period prior to December 1941.

### A TURBULENT PAST

After Mexico had gained its independence from Spain in September 1821, a series of governments, some modelled after its northern neighbour the United States, tried to lead the country on the road of progress and prosperity. However, due to different political parties, varying philosophies and certain individuals' actions, the young country spiralled into a series of internal strifes and suffered from foreign interventions by Spain, France and the United States.

The young Mexican republic would eventually lose some of its territory, firstly Texas, that gained its independence in 1836 after defeating the Mexican army led by General Antonio Lopez de Santa Anna (1794-1876). Santa Anna – who would govern Mexico 11 times from 1833-55 as president, and sometimes as emperor – was captured and had to recognise the independence of Texas, which later joined the growing United States in 1845. Mexico would also lose almost half its territory after the disastrous Mexican-American War of 1846-48.

The latter war was promoted by US president James Knox Polk, who believed in his country's destiny to create a bicoastal nation, taking advantage of Mexico's infighting and political upheaval. This war would have serious repercussions in the relationship between Mexico and the United States for decades to come. The post-war Mexican governments that followed had to deal with many issues, that led to a civil war, the War of the Reforms (*Guerra de la Reformas*) of 1857-60 between liberal and conservative factions. The new Constitution of 1857 stripped power from the Church and the military, officially separating the Church from the state.

Despite their defeat, the conservatives in exile gained the support of the French government of Napoleon III to intervene in Mexico in 1862, imposing a foreign emperor, Maximilian Archduke of Austria (1832-67), restoring the conservatives their lost privileges and expanding French influence into Latin America at a time when the United States was distracted by fighting its own civil war (1861-65). However, thanks to resistance headed by Mexican liberal president Benito Pablo Juarez Garcia, known as Benito Juarez (1806-72), and political pressure and military help from the United States after the Union victory over the Confederate states, Napoleon had to abandon Maximilian and his costly dream of a Mexican empire.

Despite the defeat of the conservatives and the execution of Maximilian in 1867 at Queretaro, the country would suffer from many problems. Even after Juarez had won his last re-election, he had to deal with a rebellion in 1871, which was headed by one of his former army

A Moisant Bleriot Monoplane of the Mexican Federal Army *Division del Norte* during the campaign against the Rebel General Pascual Orozco in the State of Chihuahua, 1912. (Author Collection)

generals from the days of the French intervention, Jose de la Cruz Porfirio Diaz Mori (1830-1915), commonly known as Porfirio Diaz.

Juarez would die in office in 1872, of a heart attack, and his successor, Sebastian Lerdo de Tejada (1823-89), fared no better, General Porfirio Diaz launching a rebellion against him in 1876 and forcing him into exile. Diaz was elected president for his first term from 1877-80, returned to the presidential seat in 1884 and from then ruled Mexico in a series of governments until 1910. During his time in power, Diaz's iron hand brought stability to the nation, modernising the country by inviting foreign investment, which benefited the upper class of Mexican society, while art and culture from many countries also influenced Mexican society.

Despite this progress, Mexico's economic growth did not benefit the lower class of workers and rural farmers, there was civil repression and the political opposition was attacked and its leaders sometimes jailed or forced into exile. By his final years in office Diaz had grown old, and the real power was in the hands of a group of politicians and businessmen known as *Los Cientificos* (The scientists), who oversaw the political and economic policies that ran the nation.

Anger at the unequal economic scale started to manifest itself in a number of bloody labour strikes, which the Federal Army was called to put down. There was hope that a peaceful transition of power would occur. When President Diaz was interviewed by an American newspaper in 1908, he was quoted as saying that he was ready for democracy. This launched the opposition parties into action for the upcoming elections of 1910.

The candidate who rose as the front runner was Sr Francisco Ignacio Madero (1873-1913), from a wealthy northern family and author of a book on the presidential succession, but on the eve of the election he was imprisoned and Porfirio Diaz was declared the winner. Madero escaped to the United States, and on 20 November 1910, after his return, launched the *Plan de San Luis Potosi*, starting an armed struggle that would affect Mexico for many years to come.

Madero became president from 1911-13 after Porfirio Diaz resigned from power for the good of the nation and fled to Paris, where he died in 1915. But Mexico's troubles did not end there: the Madero administration had to face many problems, challenges and insurrections from former Diaz supporters, as well as former allies such as General Emiliano Zapata (1879-1919), who was fighting for the rights of rural farmers in the south, and General Pascual Orozco Vazquez (1882-1915), who rebelled in the north.

In February 1913 a group of high-ranking army officers launched a coup in Mexico City known as the *Decena Tragica* (ten tragic days) to remove President Madero and his government. After the first clashes in front of the National Palace, the rebels retreated toward the interior of the city. Madero then appointed General Jose Victoriano Huerta Marquez (1845-1916), the victor over the rebel Orozco, to deal with the plotters.

Unknown to Madero, however, General Huerta had other plans. With the cooperation of the rebels and support of the American ambassador, Henry Lane Wilson,

Huerta overthrew the government and forced Madero and his vice-president, Jose Maria Pino Suarez (1869-1913) to resign. Both were assassinated on orders from Huerta on the night of 22 February 1913, triggering the next bloody phase of the Mexican revolution.

Among the state governors who did not recognise the new government was Don Jose Venustiano Carranza Garza (1859-1920) from the state of Coahuila, who led the combined rebel forces known as the *Constitucionalistas* (based on the principals of the Constitution of 1857) and was named *Primer Jefe del Ejercito Constitucionalista* (first chief of the Constitutional Army 1913-17), the predecessor of the modern Mexican army. The withdrawal of American support for the Huerta government facilitated the US supply of weapons to the *Constitucionalistas*.

American interference in Mexican affairs also manifested itself in helping remove Huerta from power by the takeover of the port of Veracruz to try to prevent Huerta from getting weapons and supplies from other countries, namely Germany.

With his group of able field commanders, Carranza inflicted several defeats on the Federal Army, forcing General Huerta, to resign from office and flee to the United States on 15 July 1914.

The Mexican Federal Army was disbanded and the Carranza forces occupied Mexico City on 20 August , Carranza taking over as leader of the country. However, after the defeat of Huerta, a split among the revolutionary leaders occurred. This had manifested itself in previous operations between Carranza and General Jose Doroteo Arango Arambula, better known as Francisco Pancho Villa (1878-1923), leader of the famous *Division del Norte*.

A convention was held in Aguascalientes to work out their differences, but it ended by not recognizing Carranza as leader and naming its own series of intern presidents who occupied Mexico City from November 1914 to October 1915 until elections could be organised. Carranza and his followers evacuated the capital, heading for the port of Veracruz, which had been recently evacuated by

The first five Mexican students at the Moisant Aviation school, from left to right, Alberto Salinas Carranza, Gustavo Salinas Camina, Juan Pablo Aldaroso Suarez, Horacio Ruiz Gavino and Eduardo Aldaroso Suarez. (National Archives)

The three Moisant Tandem monoplanes of the *Flotilla Aerea del Ejercito Constitucionalista* under the command of Major Alberto Salinas Carranza. (Carlos L. Vazquez)

Don Venustiano Carranza, chief of the *Constitucionalista* forces, who ordered the creation of the aviation section within the *Constitucionalista* army, sitting at his desck with an aerial bomb. (Author Collection)

United States armed forces after defeating the *convencionistas* with the destruction of the *Division del Norte* during the battles of Celaya in 1916.

The United Stated government had given its full support to the

Two Mexican pilots adjust a Madsen 7.7mm machine gun on the side of a TNCA Serie H Parasol, 4-H-56; it was tried out, but there is no information about it being used in combat operations. (Manuel Reyna Garza)

Carranza faction in October 1915, angering General Pancho Villa and causing problems with the US in the border region.

This involved the taking of properties of American citizens and in some cases even killing them, leading to a raid on Columbus, New Mexico, on 9 March 1916 that started the second American intervention into Mexico led by General John J. Pershing. The mission of Pershing's punitive expedition was to capture or kill Pancho Villa, but it failed in its primary objective, and after a series of negotiations the last American soldier crossed back to the United States on 7 February 1917.

On 30 April 1917 Don Venustiano Carranza was elected president of Mexico, but his presidency had to contend with many internal problems, including rebellions and rival warlords. During his presidency Carranza eliminated the southern leader, General Emiliano Zapata Salazar, in an ambush on 10 April 1919.

Before his election, Carranza had been an important factor in the making of a new constitution for Mexico, the *Constitucion Politica*

Two TNCA Serie A Biplanes deployed to an improvised field somewhere in northern Mexico during operations from 1918-20 against rebel and bandit forces. (Enrique Velasco Padilla)

*de los Estados Unidos Mexicanos 1917* (Political Constitution of the United Mexican States of 1917), that continued with the separation of the Church from the state and included labour and land reforms, free mandatory and secular education, and that all lands and water within Mexico was owned by the nation. Even with all this, peace was not achieved, Carranza having to deal with rebels in various part of the country. From March 1918 to early 1920, military forces were sent to fight what was left of General Pancho Villa's forces, Emiliano Zapata, the old Porfirista General Felix Diaz and Manuel Pelaez, where aviation units were used in observation, reconnaissance and even bombing missions.

Carranza tried to take the country on a different road, away from the military strongmen, but naming as his successor little-known diplomat Ignacio Bonilla Frajio (1858-1942), who had helped negotiate the withdrawal of American forces from Veracruz, instead of who was seen as his natural successor, General de Division Alvaro Obregon Salido (1880-1928), caused major divisions among the military, including the aviation branch.

Three high-profile political figures from the state of Sonora – General Alvaro Obregon, General Plutarco Elias Calles (1877-1945) and lawyer Adolfo de la Huerta (1881-1955) – launched a rebellion to oust Carranza from power, outlined in the *Plan de Agua Prieta* of 23 April 1920, forming the *Ejercito Constituacional Liberal* (Liberal Constitutionalist Army). As they advanced on Mexico City, Carranza – seeing his power erode – fled towards the port of Veracruz, using the railways to move his followers and equipment, but he didn't make it. The Liberal Constitutionalist Army attacked his rail convoys and the garrison commander of Veracruz switched sides, forcing Carranza to go into the hills with a small group of followers. He was eventually killed in an attack at Tlaxcalantongo, Puebla, on 21 May 1920. Adolfo de la Huerta was named intern president, to set up elections later that year, when General Obregon was elected president.

During de la Huerta's short term as president, he managed to get a number of rebel leaders to surrender to the government, among them General Pancho Villa, who was later compensated with money and property. De la Huerta had to contend with some Carrancista die-hards, such as the governor of the territory of Baja California, Colonel Esteban Cantu (1881-1961), who did not recognise the new government, but after a show of military force, the issue was resolved peacefully.

During Alvaro Obregon's term as president from 1920-24, Pancho Villa was murdered on 20 July 1923. His former treasury secretary de la Huerta, dissatisfied with Obregon's policies, launched a rebellion on 7 December 1923, a good part of the army and naval units joining him.

This conflict ended when de la Huerta fled to the United States and his last followers were either caught or shot by December 1924, aviation playing an important role in these events.

After Obregon left office, the next member of the Sonora group, General Plutarco Elias Calles, was elected president from 1924-28. Calles tried to impose the separation of Church from state, as marked in the Constitution of 1917, which led to a major religious conflict, with the closing down of churches, religious schools and convents. Religious marriages were thereafter carried out in secret or in the United States, for those following their religious faith.

Armed conflict broke out on 15 August 1926 and spread to 13 states. Army and aviation elements were again involved, and the conflict continued until 22 June 1929, when there were successful negotiations between the government and the Church. While these events weres occurring, other rebellions were being played out: the Yaquis Indians from the northern state of Sonora, who had previous issues with past governments, took up arms in September 1926, and army and aviation units were once more deployed to pacify the region, the conflict ending in July 1927.

Meanwhile, former general Enrique Estrada Roque (1890-1942), who had fled to the United States after the failed 1923-24 rebellion, took advantage of the situation in his homeland, attempting to seize the territories of Baja California in August 1926. Among his forces were four aircraft (Ryan M-1 parasol mail planes) from the Mahoney-Ryan Aircraft Company of San Diego, California. However, his rebellion was halted by United States border agents before they crossed the border.

Mahoney and Ryan were almost driven to bankruptcy when all the aircraft were seized as evidence, but the pair managed to convince the district attorney to release three of the four aircraft and sold them

The bomb load of a TNCA Serie A Biplane, with Mexican-built bombs, deployed to field operations during 1918-20. (Enrique Velasco Padilla)

A Douglas O-2C general purpose biplane that was used in operations during the Yaqui Indian rebellion of 1926-27. (Enrique Velasco Padilla)

to get out of their financial bind. These events happened just before a young pilot by the name of Charles A. Lindbergh enquired about them building an airplane for him, what would become the *Spirit of St Louis* in which the aviator made the first solo non-stop transatlantic flight in May 1927.

In October 1927, a former aide to General Obregon, General Francisco R. Serrano (1886-1927), and another opposition candidate, General Arnulfo R. Gomez (1890-1927), who were against Obregon's re-election for 1928, launched a rebellion that was put down within a month. Serrano and Gomez, along with some of their followers, were executed.

Obregon managed to get re-elected as president for 1928-32, but before retaking office he was assassinated by a religious zealot while guest of honour at a banquet to celebrate his electoral victory on 17 June 1928.

Intern president Emilio Portes Gil then had to contend with a short but bloody rebellion at the start of his presidency, due to the fallout from the Obregon murder. It was launched by General de Division Jose Gonzalo Escobar (1892-1969), who led a group of generals who did not recognise the new government, nor the influence of the *Jefe Maximo* military strongman, former president Plutarco Elias Calles, who became the power behind the presidential chair. Calles' influence was to be felt until 1936, when President General de Division Lazaro Cardenas del Rio (1895-1970) kicked him out of the country into exile with some of his followers.

During the presidency of Lazaro Cardenas from 1934-40, he had to deal with a second religious crisis, that led to fighting from 1935-38 in the states of Durango, Michoacán, Jalisco and Colima, when he enforced one of the articles of the Constitution of 1917, free but socialist education, that went against the Church and the conservatives.

He also met opposition in the area of land reform, leading to the uprising of General de Division Saturnino Cedillo, governor and strongman of the state of San Luis Potosi in May 1938. This revolt came about after President Cardenas had expropriated all foreign petroleum companies operating in Mexico in March that year. Army and aviation elements were again used to put down these rebellions.

Cedillo's rebellion did not last long, and he was chased into the hills, where an army patrol caught up with and killed him in January 1939, along with some of his followers.

President Cardenas also gave diplomatic and military support to the republicans fighting in the Spanish Civil War of 1936-39. Cardenas acted as middle man in arms deals for the republicans, and Mexican volunteers – some from the military – were allowed to fight in Spain. After their defeat by General Franco's nationalists, Cardenas opened Mexico for many refugees, not only those escaping Spain, but from the European war, including Jews and others persecuted by the Axis regimes.

By 1940, President Cardenas had designated General de Division Manuel Avila Camacho (1897-1955), former Secretary of War and Navy, as the next president of Mexico. But the election campaign against Avila Camacho's rival, General de Division Juan Andrew Almanza (1891-1965), turned into a bloody affair. Even after the votes were counted and Avila Camacho was declared president of the republic, there were incidents of open rebellion in Monterrey and Chihuahua, which were put down. President Avila Camacho was then faced with guiding the Mexican nation through a new storm on the horizon, and for the first time Mexican armed forces would not be facing internal threats or its northern neighbour, but an external threat beyond its shores, and aviation was about to enter a new accelerated phase of its development that would influence its present structure and policies.

## THE FIRST FLIGHTS IN MEXICO

The creative genius of native aeronautical pioneers had been at work in Mexico since the middle of the nineteenth century, with free flying balloons soaring into the sky.

Early in the twentieth century, dirigibles came into use. Pioneers like Benito Leon Acosta (1819-86), Don Joaquin de la Cantolla y Rico (1829-1914?), Alberto Braniff Ricard (1885-1966) and Miguel Lebrija Urtutegui (1887-1913) led the way with lighter-than-air craft.

Others such as Juan Guillermo Villasana (1891-1959), and the brothers Juan Pablo (1893-1962) and Eduardo Aldasoro Suarez (1894-1968) started with models and eventually built full-scales gliders.

Working in their father's mine using blacksmith tools, the Aldasoro Suarez brothers even constructed a workable two cylinder 60hp aircraft engine in 1911, while they were still in their teens. Villasana built his own aircraft that he managed to fly in his home state of Pachuca.

However, the Technical and theoretical aspect of aviation was not neglected.

Alfredo Robles Dominguez (1876-1928), an industrial engineer and later a revolutionary, wrote one of the early studies on heavier than air machines, *Teoria sobre la Locomocion aerea* (The Theory of Aerial Locomotion), that was published in Mexico in 1908.

He later worked on an actual flying machine called the *Giroplano*, that was patented, but with the outbreak of revolution in 1910 the project was discontinued.

TNCA 3-B-89 Serie B 'Puro' Biplane with a Salmon engine that was used during the De la Huertista Rebellion of 1923-24. (Tohtli)

The TNCA 3-E-130 Tololoche, an attempt to build a Mexican-built fighter aircraft for the air service. (Enrique Velasco Padilla)

A Mexican-built Avro 504 number 58-A-155, a trainer known as the 'Anahuac', that was also used for combat operations in the mid-1920s. Here a ground crewmember loads a bomb. (Enrique Velasco Padilla)

The first Mexican to fly was Alberto Braniff Ricard, who had learned to fly in France in 1909 while on a family vacation. After completing his flight instruction, he purchased an airplane that was shipped to Mexico with a French technician to help assemble it. Braniff performed a number of ground runs and made adjustments to the engine, using more high octane fuel since the high altitude of Mexico City was a serious obstacle for aircraft with low-powered engines of the period.

On 8 January 1910 he took off in the French Voisin type Canard Model XIII Pusher, from a field belonging to his family estate at Balbuena, outside Mexico City. His airplane rose to a height of 25 metres, breaking a world altitude record considering Mexico City's elevation of 2,340 metres), in the first flight of a powered aircraft in Latin America. He performed further flights before having an accident on 30 January 1910, in which his aircraft was badly damaged.

Braniff continued with his passion for aviation and ordered a new aircraft from France, a Farman MF-7 pusher type that he flew until 1911. This aircraft was stored in a hangar, which Braniff had built at Balbuena.

Before Braniff's landmark flight, news of aeronautical developments had been published in Federal Army publications that were seen by President General Porfirio Diaz, who approved the sending of Mexican military personnel to study the latest aviation developments in France.

Lieutenant of the engineer construction corps Federico Cervantes Munozcano was selected by President Diaz to go to France to undertake this important mission on 17 December 1909.

In September 1910, another Mexican officer, Major Nicolas Martinez, was sent to France on a similar mission. At first it was difficult for them to learn about French advances in military aviation, which were considered military secrets, and the Mexican officers were eventually trained in civilian aviation schools.

Martinez returned to Mexico around 27 August 1911, having learned to fly at the Farman school in France.

Braniff's first flight was followed four months later by Miguel Lebrija, who managed to coax a Bleriot Model XI monoplane into the air for the first time on 14 May, 1910. The aircraft had been imported from France in March 1910 for a failed advertisement venture for a Mexican cigarette company called *El Buen Tono* (The Good Tone).

On 27 May Lebrija was involved in a flying accident and suffered minor injuries that required a hospital stay. It has been reported that Lebrija acquired Depperdussin and Bleriot monoplanes before 1913.

Another early Mexican aviator was Martin Mendia, who had studied in France as an industrial engineer and also learned to fly there; he brought back two Deperdussin monoplanes, one a single-seater and the other a two-seater. He reportedly flew for the first time on 14 December 1911, and was later credited as the first pilot to fly across Mexico City.

He suffered an accident while landing on 24 January 1912. When he was recovering in hospital, as the story has been told, Mendia's wife, hoping her husband would leave his dangerous sport, traded his two-seater for an automobile with Miguel Lebrija, who had been to visit him and needed an aircraft. Mendia is reported to have returned to France and flew in the French air service in the First World War, but no official evidence exists. From here his trail disappears.

Having received the information they had been seeking, on or about 11 October 1910 the government announced plans for aeronautical parks for the Mexican Federal Army, one for aircraft and the other for dirigibles. It was announced in the press that many officers were being sent overseas to study aviation in various countries, including France and the United States. But on 20 November the revolution against the government of General Porfirio Diaz broke out, led by Madero, who had returned from exile and launched his 'Plan of San Luis Potosi' to remove Diaz from power.

## THE MOISANT AVIATORS IN A WAR ZONE

One repercussion of the revolution was its effect on the 'Moisant International Aviators' organised by the Moisant Aviation School of Hempstead, Garden City, Long Island, New York. The aviation school was founded in May 1911 by Alfred Moisant, whose brother John Moisant had been a well-known pioneer flyer.

Alfred and John had organised air shows with a group of

international pilots (including French, Swiss, English and American), and after the death of John in an aviation accident, Alfred continued his brother's vision of establishing not only an aviation school, but a factory to produce aircraft and eventually a plan to establish aviation schools in Cuba, Mexico, Chile and various locations in the United States.

The 'Moisant International Aviators' were doing an exhibition at El Paso, Texas, across the border from the Mexican city of Juarez, which was under attack by Madero's revolutionary army. It was proposed for the exhibition for a Moisant pilot to fly over the embattled Mexican city and the surrounding areas. Lieutenant Benjamin D. Foulouis, the fifth army officer to be rated as a military aviator of the United States signal corps, was stationed at the border, along with a large number of army troops to keep security, protect US citizens and property and prevent the fighting from spilling over the American border.

American pilot Richard K. Hamilton was asked to fly over Juarez on 10 February 1911 in a Curtiss Pusher biplane and observe what was going on. Hamilton completed his mission with no problems, with not a single shot fired at him, even though Federal Army general Juan N. Navarro (1823-1914) had ordered his troops to do so.

This was probably one of the first reconnaissance missions in the Americas over an actual war zone. Hamilton's flight was repeated by the Frenchman Roland Garros and later by his countryman Rene Simon, who on the next day flew over the rebels' camp without incident.

The Moisant Aviation School sent two flying exhibitions to Mexico City in 1911, the first in February and March of that year, visiting Monterrey, Nuevo Leon, Mexico City and the port of Veracruz. At the event in Mexico City – held from 25 February to 9 March – President Diaz and his family were present to observe the aviators in action. It is reported that Braniff stole the show when he took off first in his Farman, before any of the Moisant aviators started the event, which won approval of President Diaz.

The tour consisted of eight pilots and six aircraft (four Bleriot monoplanes, one Santos Dumont and one Curtiss biplane). On 8 March, the Moisant aviators carried out a demonstration of the military potential of their aircraft, being tasked to locate an artillery position not far from Balbuena. The first to take off was Rene Simon, who located the artillery battery position, and after his return with the information, his countryman Roland Garros took off to 'bomb' the site with oranges!

Another demonstration of the military potential of the aircraft was held at the port of Veracruz, where the international aviators held a series of exhibition flights. On 12 March, Roland Garros flew over French navy ships that were visiting the Mexican port and in a welcome gesture dropped a bunch of flowers on the deck of the French warship *Gloire*.

The second tour, visiting Mexico City, Guadalajara, Jalisco and Cuidad Leon, Guanajuato, was held in November of the same year after Madero was elected president of the country following the revolution. Before Diaz's downfall, it was reported and published in various newspapers and aviation magazines of the period that his government had placed an order for six aircraft, reported to be of the Farman or Bleriot type, with heavy engines and able to carry a crew of two and a large amount of bombs or ammunitions. The reported agent for the purchase of these aircraft was the Frenchman Roland Garros. However, with the fall of the Diaz government the plan was axed.

During the second exhibition of the Moisant aviators in Mexico City – which was held from 16 November to 3 December 1911, with seven pilots and eight aircraft (five Bleriot XI bis, one Curtiss biplane and two Deperdussin monoplanes) – Madero became the first sitting head of state in the world to fly in an airplane on 30 November. Madero bravely seated himself in a Deperdussin model B monoplane piloted by the Englishman George M. Dyott for a 12-minute flight over Balbuena and Mexico City.

The two Moisant exhibitions deeply impressed Mexican government officials, contributing to the decision to send Mexicans out of the country to study aviation.

During the second tour of the 'Moisant International Aviators', the first female pilots came with the group. Matilde Moisant, sister of Alfred and John, and Harriet Quimby were well received by the Mexican people, the latter becoming the first woman to fly over Mexico City.

## THE FIRST FIVE and THE MOISANT CONNECTION

The political situation in Mexico was extremely unstable in those early years of the twentieth century, so consequently, government officials were concerned with the internal security of the nation. President Madero set in motion the first step towards the foundation of a Mexican air service when he signed the presidential decree of 2 May 1912 to bring the armed forces up to 60,000 men (the country was not quite at peace, with a number of rebellions going on) and to better equip it with the latest technology.

Aviation elements were mentioned to be part of the Mexican Federal Army, and probably after his airplane ride President Madero authorised sending five men to the Moisant Aviation School to learn to fly. The group of aviation students selected were the Aldasoro brothers, Alberto Salinas Carranza (1892-1970), Gustavo Salinas Camina (1893-1964) and Horacio Ruiz Gavino (1893-1957), the first graduating in September 1912 and the last one in January 1913.The Mexican pilots' graduation dates were as follows:

1. Alberto Salinas Carranza graduated 25 September 1912, Aero Club licence No.170.
2. Gustavo Salinas Camina graduated 25 September 1912, Aero Club licence No.172.
3. Horacio Ruiz Gavino graduated 10 October 1912, Aero Club licence No.182.
4. Juan Pablo Aldasoro Suarez graduated 19 January 1913, Aero Club licence No.217.
5. Eduardo Aldasoro Suarez graduated 19 January 1913, Aero Club licence No.218.

On 28 January 1913, the Mexican Secretary of War and Navy paid the Moisant Aviation School $3,009 for the training of the five Mexicans. After their graduation they received the military rank of *Subtenientes Cadetes del cuerpo de Ingenieros militares* (2nd Lieutenant Cadets of the Corp of Military Engineers) from the Mexican Federal Army.

The government had also purchased two Moisant-built Bleriot monoplanes, one a single-seater with an Anzani 50hp engine and the other a side-by-side two-seater with a 100hp engine. Some sources cite the two-seater having an 80hp engine.

Mexican pilot Francisco Alvarez, who had studied at the Moisant School at his own expense, and the American Hector Worden, flew these machines for the Federal Army's Division de Norte under the command of General Victoriano Huerta against the rebel General Pascual Orozco Vazquez, who had launched his rebellion (*Plan de la Empacadora*) against the Madero government in the state of Chihuahua from 26 March. When Orozco was finally defeated in August 1912 he fled to the United States.

The two pilots took part in a series of flight demonstrations held in the *Parque Atletico* (Athletic Park) between the cities of Torreon and Gomez Palacio from 1-4 August 1912. In the last day of the

The Mexican Air Service used the Farman F50BN2 bombers, that were employed in long-distance flights and in combat operations. Here is 4-F-71, which was reported damaged on 3 August 1921. (Enrique Velasco Padilla)

One of the two Bristol Type 93B Boardhounds that were purchased in the UK around 1928. This was later assigned to the *3/o. Escuadron Aereo, 1/o. Regimiento Aereo* in 1929. (Enrique Velasco Padilla)

demonstrations, the aircraft flown by Alvarez (a single-seater) crashed after hitting power lines running between the two cities, putting his aircraft out of service. Worden could not take off, but later continued to serve in the Mexican Federal Army, carrying out reconnaissance flights in the region until the end of the campaign.

Worden returned to the United States, where he wrote about his experiences in Mexico in a number of aviation magazines before he died, reportedly of a heart attack while flying in an aviation exhibition at a state fair in Dallas, Texas, on 5 May 1916. The fate of Alvarez remains a mystery, as after his accident on 4 August nothing more is known about him.

In his writings about his adventures in Mexico, Worden mentioned that the rebels were getting weapons by air from the United States via Laredo, Texas, in a Farman biplane flown by British mercenary pilot John Lewis Longstaff, who reportedly flew at night delivering about 50 rifles and ammunition per flight, sometimes with two trips per night.

Both the Moisant Bleriots were returned to Mexico City after the defeat of the rebel Orozco and were sent to Balbuena airfield by orders of the Secretary of War and Navy to be used by officers returning from training in the United States.

## GENERAL HUERTA'S AIR SERVICE

During the Madero presidency many proposals for establishing an aviation school and for Mexico to build its own aircraft were made by various people, but none of these project came to fruition.

Among the casualties of the Orozco rebellion was Major of the Presidential Command and Staff Nicolas Martinez, who had trained as a pilot in France. He was killed in action on 22 May 1912 during the first Battle of Rellano, where the Federal Army was defeated by the rebels, and his body was not recovered.

Meanwhile, Juan Guillermo Villasana was assisting in the construction of the first Mexican-built plane, the *Latinoamerica*, with Carlos Leon, which was a copy of the Deperdussin monoplane owned by Lebrija in 1912. The only parts of the aircraft not built in Mexico were the propeller and the Anzani 80hp engine, which had to been imported into the country. The pilot was an ironmaster of French origin, Jacques Poberejsky, who was living in Mexico and had learned to fly in Belgium.

The aircraft was tested in a series of runs across Balbuena airfield, and later performed an actual flight, but on landing it was damaged. After its repair by Villasana, Poberejsky flew the *Latinoamerica* on 29 May 1912, but it was only a short flight due to engine problems. The aircraft was later destroyed when its hangar came down during a storm at Balbuena airfield.

During the tragic events of February 1913 in Mexico City, Miguel Lebrija tried to offer his services to bomb the rebels with his aircraft, but General Huerta managed to stop him. Huerta commenced building an air service by sending 30 army cadets to France to study aviation. This group left for France under the command of Captain Santiago Mendoza in May 1913.

Upon arrival, the group was put under the command of Captain Federico Cervantes, who was still in France. Of the 30 officers, five were medically disqualified, one was injured in a crash and there

A flight of three Bristol F2B fighter of the *3/o. Escuadrilla* getting ready to undertake a sortie. (Enrique Velasco Padilla)

were 15 accidents; but the last officer passed his test on 31 August 1913. After this, Captain Cervantes, who did not support the Huerta government, turn in his resignation and returned to Mexico via the United States to join the rebels.

Of this group of pilots, a few later joined the aviation service after 1915 to continue their flying careers.

Huerta's regime planned to buy about 20 Bleriot monoplanes and use the recently trained officers from France to start an aviation school, but the sale was never completed because the funds had to be diverted to the defence of his government.

A makeshift air service unit was put together on 11 April 1913 called the *Escuadrilla Aerea de la Milicia Auxiliar del Ejercito Federal* (The Auxiliary Aerial Squadron of the Militia of the Federal Army) by the Secretary of War and Navy, General de Division Manuel Mondragon (1859-1922), one of the main coup leaders against Madero, using the aircraft that had belonged to Alberto Braniff, Miguel Lebrija and Martin Mendia Tthis unit's most notable activity had been a test bombing with Lebrija's two-seater Deperdussin conducted before Federal officers on 7 April 1913 at Balbuena field.

Lebrija piloted the aircraft first and noticed the difficulty in dropping the bombs (Martin Hale rifle grenades), so when he landed he requested that Villasana fly with him as bombardier, which resulted in a more successful test.

This unit had the Bleriot XI, XI bis monoplanes, a Farman MF-7 that was Braniff's second aircraft bought from France and the Deperdussin two-seater military type. The following aviators and ground personnel were inducted into the unit:

Major Auxiliary Miguel Lebrija, Captain 1st Class Irregular Horacio Ruiz Gavino, Captain 1st Class Irregular Juan Pablo Aldaroso Suarez, Captain 1st Class Irregular Eduardo Aldaroso Suarez, Captain 2nd Class Irregular Martin Mendia, 2nd Lieutenant Irregular Juan Guillermo Villasana, Sergeant 1st Class Irregular Antonio Sanchez Saldana and Soldier Irregular Geronimo Sanchez.

All the unit's aircraft ended up in the Constitutionalists' hands when they took over the capital in 1915, and some vital parts were used later for other aircraft.

At one point the unit was about to be shipped out to fight the *Constitucionalistas* at Torreon, Coahuila, but it never left the train station, so its personnel and aircraft were sent home.

Miguel Lebrija, being an Honorary Major in the Federal Army, had been named commander of the unit. He left for France to purchase 20 aircraft and two dirigibles for the Huerta government, and to receive proper aviation training (having previously only received balloon training in Germany), but before that it is reported that he visited Hempstead Plains, New York, to test some Moisant aircraft.

During his stay in Paris, he had surgery to correct a problem with a leg, that had been damaged in an automotive or aviation accident, to be able to obtain his aviation brevet, but he passed away after the surgery on 15 December 1913, and his body was returned for burial to Mexico City.

## THE SAGA OF THE SONORA

The forces of General Alvaro Obregon, leader of the *Division del Noroeste* of the *Constitucionalistas* forces, were equipped with an American-made Martin Pusher biplane which was acquired at a time when there was a total embargo of weapons for Mexico.

Obregon agents not only acquired the aircraft in Los Angeles, California, from the Glenn L. Martin Aircraft Company, but also the services of the French/American flyer Didier Masson, a former instructor at the Martin Flying School, and Australian mechanic Thomas J. Dean. After many adventures they managed to get the aircraft to Obregon, and it was named *Sonora.*

Obregon was operating on the Pacific coast to try to isolate or pin down Huerta's forces, but the Federal forces had fire support of the Mexican Navy with a number of gunboats. Several attempts were made to carry out aerial attacks against Federal naval vessels.

In June 1913, Masson, who later flew in the *Lafayette Escadrille* N.124 in the First World War, and his mechanic Dean designed some aerial bombs, had a bomb rack built on the *Sonora* and even installed a primitive bomb sight. They tried unsuccessfully to sink Federal gunboats at the port of Guaymas, Sonora, on 21 June, targeting the *Guerrero* and *Tampico.*

On 28 July, Masson again tried to sink federal gunboats, flying three sorties over the harbour and dropping bombs, one reportedly falling so close to the *Tampico* that some though he had hit it.

With his time in Mexico almost over, Masson trained Gustavo Salinas Camina, one of the five graduates of the Moisant Aviation School of 1912, who after his return was serving in the *Constitucionalista* army command and staff, to fly the *Sonora.*

Gustavo Salinas later flew with an observer/bombardier of one of the naval gunboats that had change sides, Naval Machine-mate Teodoro Madriaga. On 14 April 1914, the *Guerrero* attacked the rebel gunboat *Tampico*, which was damaged and in a very poor position in

A typical operational scene at Balbuena airfield with DH4Bs and a Morane Saulnier MS.35 parasol aircraft. (Mexican Air Force)

the bay of Topolobampo Sinaloa from a previous engagement with the Federal gunboat.

The *Sonora*, flown by Salinas and Madriaga, intervened, attacking the *Guerrero* with homemade bombs. While they did not score a direct hit, they forced the Federal vessel to head out to sea to escape, saving the *Tampico*, its crew and the commander of the rebel forces, as General Obregon and his staff had been surveying the damage on the *Tampico* when it was attacked.

This clash is considered to be the world's first naval-aerial battle where an aircraft decided the outcome.

Gustavo Salinas continue his work as a pilot and carried out observation and bombing missions over Federal positions before he crashed the *Sonora* on 18 May, injuring himself and Madriaga, who fortunately had the safety switches on for their bombload. After his recovery, Salinas served in the command and staff of Venustiano Carranza.

The remains of the aircraft were sent to Mexico City in September of that year, and its parts were used to build a small training aircraft for cadets to practice their ground runs before mastering aircraft with greater horse power that were able to take off.

## THE FIRST AMERICAN INTERVENTION

A group of self-taught aviators in the US border state of Arizona, members of the Douglas Arizona Flying Club, started to launch bombing missions on 7/8 May 1913 against Mexican railroad tracks at Agua Prieta in the state of Sonora. They flew a locally made Douglas Bomber pusher biplane, later being reinforced with another aircraft and pilot with the support of the United States government, using locally made bombs and an improvised bombing range.

The objective was to disrupt the supplies lines of the Mexican Federal troops at Agua Prieta, who later had to evacuate to Hermosillo, Sonora, and to the port of Guaymas, Sinaloa. The pilots eventually returned to Douglas with little mention about their activities in Mexico.

The Huerta government lost the support of the Unites States. When new US president Thomas Woodrow Wilson found out how Huerta had gained power with support from Henry Lane Wilson, he sacked the American ambassador and placed an embargo on weapons and military supplies to Huerta. This led to the occupation of the port of Veracruz by US forces from 21 April to 23 November 1914 to prevent the arrival of weapons and ammunition from Germany.

During this operation, the United States naval aviation was deployed to a combat zone for the first time. The aviation naval units arrived on 24 April and flew their first mission in the combat zone that day, trying to locate the position of a reported water mine.

During a reconnaissance mission on 6 May, an AH-3 hydroplane flown by Lieutenant Patrick N.L. Bellinger and his observer Lieutenant Richard C. Saufley was struck by Mexican ground fire, being the first American aircraft to come under enemy fire.

The naval pilots continued carrying out their missions, including the first aerial photographs of the port of Veracruz. During one reconnaissance mission, as they were ordered not to discharge their revolvers against the Mexican ground forces, they instead 'bombed' Federal troops with a bar of soap!.

On some of their missions the naval aviators were accompanied by US Army observers.

The two naval aviation detachments that served at Veracruz were:

**Naval Detachment on the USS *Mississippi* (BB-23):** this detachment had gone directly to Veracruz.

4 Pilots
2 Curtiss Flying Boats
1 Curtiss Hydro

**Naval Detachment on the USS *Birmingham* (CL-2)**: this detachment was first at Tampico but later moved to Veracruz to reinforce the *Mississippi* unit.

3 pilots
10 enlisted men
2 Curtiss Flying Boats
1 hydroplane

The USS *Birmingham* had already gained fame as the first United States Navy ship on which an aircraft had taken off from its deck on 14 November 1910, flown by civilian pilot Eugene Ely.

It is reported that Lieutenant Bellinger flew for 43 days straight during his time in Veracruz in support of US forces. The initial takeover of Veracruz cost US forces 22 killed and about 70 wounded, with many more suffering sickness during the occupation.

Mexican losses were reported to be about 150-170 killed and 190-250 wounded, while local militia suffered about 150 killed and an unknown number of civilians also died during the fighting.

American personnel eventually left Veracruz in November 1914

DH-4B No.8, flown by Major Pablo L. Sidar during the De la Huertista Rebellion at Minatitlan, Veracruz, on 20 March 1924. Note his name on the propeller cover. (Enrique Velasco Padilla)

Charles A. Lindbergh with a Mexican Morane Saulnier MS.35 parasol aircraft, about to take a flight around Mexico City during his visit in December 1928. (Enrique Velasco Rojas)

after the 'ABC Group' (Argentina, Brazil and Chile) helped resolve issues between the American government and the leader of the *Constitucionalistas*, Don Venustiano Carranza, who was in power after General Huerta fled the country after his resignation in July.

## THE CONSTITUCIONALISTA'S AIR UNIT

To counter Huerta's aviation unit, the rebel forces led by Don Venustiano Carranza acquired their second aircraft, with the help of his nephew Alberto Salinas Carranza (a Moisant aviation graduate) and his brother Jesus Carranza (1863-1915).

A Kanter Moisant monoplane known as the *Bluebird* was bought in November 1913 for $8,000, including spare parts (less the engine). It was not used until the defence of the city of Matamoros in April 1915, when Villistas forces attacked the *Constitucionalista* garrison, and was damaged while taking off by pilot Pedro A. Chapa Quiroga (1890-1973), who is reported to have only just learnt to fly in Italy.

The aircraft was later recovered and sent to the newly established aviation shops at Balbuena, where its parts and engine were used for other aircraft.

Three Kanter Moisant Tandem Military monoplanes were also purchased. The first one was delivered in March 1914 at Ciudad Juarez, the other two following in May, and they formed the *Flotilla Aerea del Ejercito Constitucionalista* (Air Fleet of the Constitutionalist Army), being numbered 1, 2 and 3.

This unit included American pilots and even a Romanian-born flier.

At first these aircraft were going to be assigned to General Pancho Villa's *Division del Norte*, but due to the mounting differences between Venustiano Carranza and General Villa, this did not happen. The Italian aviation mechanic and veteran of the first Balkan Wars of 1912, Francisco Santarini Tognoli, from the Moisant Aviation School came with the aircraft, along with the aircraft designer and builder Harold D. Kantner. Kantner did the test flying and training of Alberto on the aircraft, while Santarini undertook the maintenance of the unit's aircraft.

Kantner left soon after delivering the aircraft, but Santarini stayed on, kept busy with his crew repairing the aircraft multiple times. Alberto Salinas damaged one on landing after a reconnaissance mission, and later Captain Federico Cervantes, who had returned from France, took off in another Moisant – reported to be No.3 – on 19 April 1914, armed with bombs for a practice bombing mission, and also crashed while landing; luckily for him, the bombs did not go off. Cervantes was later transferred to a ground position on the staff of General 'Pancho' Villa's *Division del Norte*.

The *Flotilla* was organised and placed on special railroad cars, with different railcars and flat cars transporting the aircraft and the personnel of the air unit, including a maintenance shop, offices, crew compartments, kitchen and radio station, giving it a mobility to move when needed to any part of the country.

The rail cars had signs painted '*Flotilla Aerea del Ejercito Constitucionalista*' and '*Division del Norte*', later changed to '*Division del N.E.*' (North East Division) due to the fallout with General Villa. Its commanding officer was Captain Alberto Salinas Carranza, nephew of the *Primer Jefe* Don Venustiano Carranza. The *Flotilla* would move to different locations as needed by the *Constitucionalista* army. After receiving all three aircraft, the *Flotilla* moved to Mexico City after the fall of Huerta, arriving on 15 August 1914 and establishing at the airfield of Balbuena.

The *Flotilla* stayed in Mexico City until November of that year, when the *Constitucionalistas* evacuated the city before the arrival of the forces of Pancho Villa and Zapata that supported the *Convencionistas*. After the fall of Huerta there was a split among the revolutionary factions; the *Convecionista* Pancho Villa and the southern revolutionary General Emiliano Zapata joined forces against Venustiano Carranza, but Carranza had the services of able leaders like Alvaro Obregon,

Pablo Gonzalez and Salvador Alvarado, who would learn the benefits of the use of aviation in their upcoming fights.

Carranza moved his forces via train to Veracruz, where he established his government. In December, the *Flotilla* was ordered to support *Constitucionalista* forces in the taking of the city of Puebla. It was here that Romanian-born pilot Jorge Puflea crashed two of the Moisants; the first after a reconnaissance mission, and the other on his return from a bombing mission when he ran out of fuel short of Panzacola, where an airfield was built.

Carranza's forces took Puebla on 5 January 1915. It was here that a young man by the name of Samuel C. Rojas joined the *Flotilla* as a *Piloto Aspirante* (pilot candidate). The *Flotilla* returned to Veracruz to rest and repair its aircraft, after which a flying exhibition was given for Venustiano Carranza and his staff which would have positive consequences for the *Flotilla*.

The next destination of the *Flotilla* was the campaigns in the far territories of Yucatan and Merida to halt a separatist movement there. After the *Flotilla* arrived at the port of Campeche, it was joined by another American pilot, Leonard Bonney, and other ground support staff. Bonney's services were used immediately, when he and the by now Major Alberto Salinas were ordered to fly over the area and drop propaganda leaflets in favour of the *Constitucionalistas*.

At this time the *Flotilla* had the following flying personnel:
pilots Leonard Bonney (American),
Charles F. Niles (American) and
Jorge Puflea (Rumanian), and
observers Major Alberto Salinas Carranza,
Candidate Salvador I Cano and
Candidate Samuel C. Rojas.

The aircraft of the *Flotilla* made a number of long-distance flights, covering all the major population areas to drop propaganda. During one flight the crew of Nile and Cano interrupted a gathering of rebel leaders with their presence over the Villa de Poc-Boc.

In a three-day battle at the hacienda of Blanca Flor that started on 14 March 1915, the *Constitucionalista* forces of General Salvador Alvarado Rubio (1890-1924) defeated the separatist and rebel forces of Colonel Abel Ortiz Argumedo (1871-1962). During the battle, pilot Jorge Puflea dropped a bomb by accident on the forces of General Heriberto Jara Corona (1879-1968), future first secretary of the independent department of the Mexican Navy (1941-46), but luckily nobody was hurt.

At the end of the battle the rebels had suffered about 450 casualties while Alvarado's forces lost some 44 men. When the *Constitucionalista* forces took over the city of Merida Yucatan, taking advantage of the break, Santarini started to tinker with the idea of converting one of the Moisant monoplanes to a biplane.

From there the *Flotilla* was moved by ship to Puerto Progreso Tamaulipas to be part of the *Ejercito del Noroeste* to stop the movement of a *Villista* force under the command of General de Brigada Tomas Urbina (1877-1915) that started the battle and siege of El Ebano, San Luis Potosi (21 March to 31 May 1915). The *Constitucionalistas* and *Convencionistas* were vying for control of the important sea port and petroleum producing area.

If the *Villistas* had gained control, they would have an outlet to receive outside help and control the oil in that area.

The *Flotilla* had in operation two of its three Moisant monoplane, the third having been damaged and being converted to a biplane by Santarini. On the eve of the siege, the *Flotilla* had the following personnel:

Commanding officer, Major Alberto Salinas Carranza;
pilots, Leonard Bonney and Jorge Pufflea; and
candidate pilots (observers), Salvador I Cano, Benjamin J. Venegas, Samuel C. Rojas, Ascencion Jimenez, Captain 1st Class Engineer Antonio Sanchez Saldana and Captain 1st Class Jose Mancillas.

The Moisants were used for reconnaissance and bombing missions. On one occasion, one of the *Constitucionalista* commanders, General Pablo Gonzales Garza (1879-1950), undertook a reconnaissance mission with Leonard Bonney, getting a good view of the battle area, after which he ordered daily reconnaissance missions to be flown with reports to assess the situation.

One of the Moisant monoplanes flown by Jorge Pufflea, who had undertaken a long-range reconnaissance mission, suffered an engine failure during its return and landed in no man's land. After walking back to *Constitucionalistas* lines, a recovery party was sent to recover some parts and the engine of Pufflea's Moisant.

After another reconnaissance flight the same afternoon, Bonney and Rojas managed to land their aircraft in the dark away from their airfield, and walked back to their own lines. The next day they located the aircraft with an armed escort, refuelled and took off to land back at base at Chila.

The *Flotilla* was in action throughout the 72 days that ended in the defeat of General Urbina, who suffered the loss of about 4,500 men while the defending forces had about 1,500 casualties. It was the defenders' use of trench fortifications and aviation that defeated their attackers.

From this important action, the *Flotilla* returned to the port of Veracruz to rest and recover, while Major Alberto Salinas and Santarini were ordered to go to the United States for a two-month tour of aviation factories and possibly to purchase aviation material. Leaving in July 1915, they returned to Mexico in September.

## 'PANCHO' VILLA'S FLYING CORPS

General Francisco 'Pancho' Villa, leader of the famous *Division del Norte* that operated in northern Mexico, purchased aircraft and employed a number of American pilots.

Firstly, around 1913-14, he had an unknown Curtiss two-seater type (probably a Curtiss Model E-4 two-seater pusher biplane) that was flown by the American Edwin C. Parsons and the mysterious Jeff de Villa. Parsons would become a notable fighter pilot in the *Lafayette Escadrille N.124/Spa 124*, and then in the famous *SPA.3* of the French Air Service in the First World War, and later served in the US Navy in the Second World War, retiring as a rear admiral.

Parsons was given the rank of captain in the *Division del Norte*, and received his first pay and money to purchase the aircraft in the United States by agents of 'Pancho' Villa, one of them the brother of the slain President Madero. His role was to fly missions for Villa's forces – reconnaissance and bombing flights – and also to try to train some of Villa*'s* men to fly the aircraft, but with no success.

Parsons and Jeff (or Jefferson) de Villa alternate roles as pilot and observer. During the campaign to take the city of Zacatecas from the Federal Army in June 1914, Parsons damaged the Curtiss, so went to El Paso to get the parts to repair it. During his stay he was warned by a German businessman that 'Pancho' Villa would cause serious problems with the United States and for Parsons. So he got the parts, sent them across the border and went back home. It was later reported that Jeff de Villa also resigned, and nothing more is known about him or the fate of the aircraft.

'Pancho' Villa later acquired the services of J.S. Berger of the Berger Aviation Company of Chicago, which had several pilots and aircraft flying for the Mexican. In April 1915, Berger sent telegrams saying that he was working for Villa, with a Standard Wright biplane and a Curtiss with a Hall Scott type A-2 engine.

By 3 May it was reported that Berger now had four Wright biplanes in the rebel camp at Ciudad Juarez for scouting on and bombing the *Carranzistas* forces. Other sources claim that Berger had ordered aircraft from the Wright Brothers Aeroplane Company since September 1914, with the order completed by 15 March 1915 when Orville Wright shipped the last aircraft.

That order was for one Wright type C, one Wright type D, one Wright type E, two Wright type Hs and a Wright type HS. In August 1915 it was reported that another type B and HS were sent to Mexico with a pilot and mechanics to assemble them there. A Model L was also reported in service.

Berger later had the services of a Lester P. Barlow, who claimed that he organised Villa's air service with a mobile train that would carry the aircraft, personnel, supplies and spare parts where needed. Barlow also flew as an observer and bombardier in some of the flights.

For the first time there were casualties among the mercenary pilots. On 3 May 1915, Jack Mayes from San Francisco was killed while making a test flight in a remodelled Curtiss biplane at Aguascalientes. It was reported that his aircraft crashed into a building and that his body was returned to California.

A second fatality was reported on 11 May when Newell 'Mickey' Mcguire crashed. After making a number of successful flights that day, he had been ordered out again on a scouting mission that evening. As he was preparing to land his Wright biplane was caught in a 50mph gale while about 300ft above the camp and crashed. 'Mickey', pinned under the engine of his aircraft, was killed. Berger arranged to ship his body back home to Chicago.

A third pilot, Farnum T. Fish, was wounded by ground fire on 15 May while flying over *Carranzistas* forces near Silas, south of Leon in Guanajuato. He returned to the United States to recover from his wounds, and did not return. Another pilot decided to quit serving Villa because of the working conditions and lateness, or lack, of pay; he flew an aircraft to the United States and left the authorities to arrange its return to Mexico.

The accuracy of some of the pilots' accounts should be treated with caution, many either making up or embellishing their stories for newspapers or aviation magazines that were hungry for news from the conflict in Mexico.

Later, some odd types such as a Driggs pusher biplane were flown by American mercenaries. The last aircraft to arrive in Mexico was a Martin TT biplane around June 1915 that was used in missions before the fall of Ciudad Juarez by *Constitucionalistas* forces in December 1915.

Some of these aircraft were later captured by Carranza forces.

A list of captured equipment that was sent to Mexico City in May 1916 included three Wright aircraft and a 'Main', which could be the Martin but was misspelled in the report.

In northern Mexico, forces under the command of Colonel Plutarco Elias Calles – a future president and military strongman (1877-1945) – had the services of American pilot Lawrence W. Brown, who flew a Christofferson two-seater aircraft. This machine was used for bombing and reconnaissance, and to enforce the law in the region.

It was about this time that American mercenary Ivan Dean Lamb claimed that he flew for the forces of 'Pancho' Villa with a mechanic named Smith, and had an aerial shoot-out with revolvers over Naco in Sonara with fellow American pilot Philip D. Rader (also flying a Christofferson biplane), who was reported to be flying with the Federal forces of Victoriano Huerta around 1913-14.

The only problem with this account is that the sole source is Lamb. The biography of Rader does not mention anything about Mexico. It records that Rader went to Europe in 1914 to offer his services, learning to fly with Britain's Royal Flying Corps. He returned to the United States in June 1916 to work as an instructor pilot, and was killed in an aviation accident on 10 June 1918.

## THE BIRTH OF AN AIR FORCE

Responding to the increasingly urgent need for an aviation force, Carranza created the *Arma de Aviacion Militar dentro del Ejercito Constitucionalista* on 5 February 1915, following the flying exhibition he witnessed at Veracruz, and placed it under the command of his nephew Alberto. To support this new unit, a military aviation school and workshops were officially established at the Balbuena airfield on 15 November the same year after the *Constitucionalistas* had taken over the capital.

'Maestro Frank', Francisco Santorini, had worked with Anzani in France and Vickers in the UK, and had served as an aviation mechanic for the Bulgarians during the Balkan Wars and later at the Moisant Aviation School, where he met the student Alberto Salinas Carranza. He came to Mexico with the Moisant monoplanes, and after a trip to Europe around 1919, he brought back his family with him to stay in Mexico.

He was in charge of the maintenance of the new unit's aircraft during this period of the revolutionary war. After the dust had settled and Alberto's uncle was in charge of the government, he helped organise the aviation shops and even trained pilots how to fly, even though he was not a pilot.

However, recent research by historians has resulted in claims that the actual founder of the Mexican air force should be the martyr President Francisco I. Madero, who on 30 November 1911 had ordered the Minister of War and Navy to buy five aircraft and arrange instruction for five pilots. This was followed by an order published in the *Diario Oficial* (Official Diary) of the nation, directing the establishment of the service on 15 May 1912.

But with the fall of the Huerta government, the Mexican Federal Army, under the *Tratados de Teoloyucan* (Treaty of Teoloyucan), was officially disbanded on 13 August 1914, leaving the *Constitucionalistas* forces with its aviation unit as the ancestors of the present day Mexican Army and Air Force.

The internal struggles of the country continued, with problems in the north with the remains of General 'Pancho' Villa's forces, and in the south with those of General Emiliano Zapata and a number of warlords and bandits.

General Villa caused the next confrontation between Mexico and the United States when he raided the border town of Columbus, New Mexico, on 9 March 1916. Some attribute the reason for this attack to the United States government's support of Villa's enemy, Venustiano Carranza, and the defeat he suffered at the hands of General Alvaro Obregon, who destroyed as a fighting force his famous *Division del Norte* during the bloody fighting for Celaya, Guanajuato, in April 1915.

It has also been claimed that Villa was seeking revenge for an arms deal that went bad, wanting to find the American responsible for it. The raid on Columbus caused the destruction of the town's commercial centre and the death of 18 American soldiers and civilians (10 civilians and eight soldiers), with 10 more wounded (two civilians, two officers and six enlisted men), while Villa lost 75-78 men killed plus 26 wounded.

Seven wounded Villistas were captured in the town, but only two survived. Later, six captured Villistas were tried and hanged.

With the backing of President Woodrow Wilson, Brigadier General John J. Pershing led a force of 6,600 American troops in the pursuit of the 'Pancho' Villa from March 1916 until 5 February 1917, when the

Another type that saw action during the Escobar Rebellion was the Douglas O2M, here in flight No.17 that was later assigned to the *2/o. Escuadron* of the *1/o. Regimiento Aereo*. (Enrique Velasco Padilla)

They were hoping to get Curtiss R-2s, but instead they got the Curtiss JN-8, which was found to be not suitable. When they did receive the R-2 in May 1916, each aircraft had to be modified and checked to be able to operate in Mexico. By August, only six R-2s were still operational.

It appears that the unit stayed at Columbus for the remainder of the campaign, trying to locate Pancho Villa. They carried out reconnaissance and photography missions, also transporting mail and official dispatches. In this, the first deployment of a US Army aviation unit to a war zone, the 1st Aero Squadron carried out 540 flights, covering 19,533 miles with 346 hours of flight time.

The 1st Aero Squadron suffered many aircraft crashes and accidents, but fortunately with no loss of life. Its experiences brought to light that the aircraft deployed to Mexico were not adequate for the task, due to altitude, power plant and field conditions, and this would serve as a lesson for the future United States Army Air Service when it fought in the First World War.

A Chance Vought O2U-2M Corsair No.2 that was used operationally during the Escobar Rebellion of March 1929. These aircraft were later assigned to the *1/o. Escuadron Aereo* of the *1/o. Regimiento Aereo* in 1929. (Archivo Torreblanca)

last US soldier left Mexico.

Among his units was the 1st Aero Squadron of the US Army Signal Corps, which used the Curtiss JN-2/3 and R-2 biplanes under the command of Captain Benjamin D. Foulois. The unit arrived at Columbus, New Mexico, on 15 March, and the next day a Curtiss JN-3, No. 44, piloted by Captain Townsend F. Dodd, with Captain Benjamin D. Foulois s observer, conducted their first reconnaissance mission, flying about 20 miles inside Mexico in the first mission of a signal corps aircraft.

On 19 March, the 1st Aero Squadron was ordered to fly to Casa Grandes to join General Pershing's headquarters, but after a troubled flight only six of the eight planes eventually made it to Casa Grande, although no crews were lost. Pershing put the 1st Aero Squadron to use in reconnaissance and courier flights.

In an incident during a flight to Chihuahua on 7 April to arrange for supplies, Captain Foulois was thrown in the local jail by the loyal *Carrancistas*, becoming the first POW (prisoner of war) of the American air service.

Luckily for Foulois, the garrison commander got him out of jail, and after some tense negotiations the Americans manage to complete their mission.

Due to the difficult field conditions and the lack of performance of the JN-3, by 20 April only two aircraft were left serviceable and the 1st Aero Squadron was ordered back to Columbus to pick up new aircraft.

## BUILDING AIRCRAFT IN MEXICO

While these events were happening, the activities of the newly founded military aviation workshops, TNCA (*Talleres Nacionales de Construcciones Aeronauticas*, National Aviation workshops), under the guidance of Santarini and Juan Guillermo Villasana, started to repair the available aircraft from parts of other aircraft found at Balbuena airfield in 1914 and later when they returned in 1915, and some recovered from other parts of the country.

The first aircraft to be ready, when the aviation school started its activities in November 1915, was a Kanter Moisant Bleriot monoplane used for the first aviation cadets' training. Other aircraft that were available on 15 November were a Nieuport biplane with a 100hp engine (Huntington), a Morane Kanter Moisant monoplane and one aircraft under construction (prototype of the Serie A biplane).

The team of Villasana and Santarini eventually led to the first aircraft design for the TNCA, a prototype biplane model Serie A, which was a Kanter Moisant monoplane that had been converted to a biplane for better flight performance at Mexico City's high altitude.

The first of these aircraft was donated to the Central American republic of El Salvador in February 1917. The original power plant was eventually replaced by a Mexican-built engine, a 60hp six-cylinder radial plant called the *Aztlalt* (Stork). Villasana produced a Mexican-built propeller called the *Anahuac*; he had built some previous ones, which had been used by Miguel Lebrija, that suited Mexico's high altitude.

Some of these propellers were later sold to Argentina and Japan.

The Serie A biplane was followed by other aircraft designed and built at the TNCA. These types included the Serie B, the first of which was designated a transport aircraft, and later a two-seater reconnaissance/light bomber, a Serie C single-seat fighter, Serie D and E (Bleriot type) trainers, a one-of-a-kind Serie F biplane trainer and

The controversial sale of the Consolidated Model 21-M, here No.1 (former No.22) that replaced the Douglas O2M in the *2/o. Escuadron Aereo* of the *1/o. Regimiento Aereo*. They would serve in the Second World War in coastal patrols. (Enrique Velasco Padilla)

the parasol Serie H.

Major Alberto Salinas was in charge of the *Departamento de Aviacion* (Department of Aviation) until 1919, when he was transferred to take charge of military industries, his place taken by Captain 2/o. Engineer Villasana, who occupied this position until May 1920.

Mexican airpower was later augmented by foreign imports.

In 1919 Alberto Salinas and Santarini visited the United States, and later Europe to acquire aircraft and engines such as the French Farman F50bn2 twin-engine bomber (a total of 13 were purchased) and single examples of the Italian Ansaldo A.1 single-seater fighter and the two-seater A.300 for possible production in Mexico. Some of the Farman bombers began to arrive in the early 1920s.

There were even plans to sell TNCA products to other Latin American countries such as Chile, and to sell some Serie H parasols on the civilian market, but they did not get any sales because after the end of the First World War there were plenty of surplus military aircraft from Europe and the United States. However, one Serie H parasol was reported sold to a civilian in Mexico.

Aviation in Mexico was continuing its development. On 6 July 1917, Lieutenant Horacio Ruiz Gavino (a Moisant graduate), flew the first air mail in the country in a TNCA Serie A biplane, No.6A19, from Pachuca to Mexico City. Seven months later, on 22 February 1918, Cadet Samuel C. Rojas (1891-1939) became the first aviation cadet to graduate in Mexico.

On 26 June he performed the first loop in the skies over Mexico in a TNCA Serie A biplane.

On 3 November 1918, Mexico suffered its first aviation fatality when Lieutenant Amado Paniagua Cortes (1897-1918), a member of the demonstration team *Flotilla de Exhibiciones Aereas* (Aerial Exhibition Unit) and one of the youngest pilots, was killed instantly when his TNCA Serie A biplane 28A43 failed to recover from an Immelmann turn over the beaches of the port of Veracruz and crashed.

His death would lead to another important event in Mexican aviation history.

One of the first people to reach Amado Paniagua after his aircraft crashed was Lola Castillo Cordera, who tried to render first aid. When Paniagua's fellow pilots went to thank her, she expressed a desire to fly in one of the aircraft. This request was approved by President Carranza.

On 9 November 1918, Lola Castillo Cordera became the first Mexican woman to fly in a Mexican military aircraft, a TNCA Serie A biplane piloted by Lieutenant Jose E. Rivera, over her hometown of Veracruz.

The Mexican air service was sent out in a number of *Flotillas Aereas de Operaciones en Campana* (Air Operations fleets in campaigns) that were equipped with Serie A and Serie H aircraft and some experimental types, and were deployed to different parts of the country to assist the army to fight rebel groups that opposed the Carranza government in 1918-19.

These units operated in many locations, carrying out bombing and reconnaissance missions and taking important messages. They were also mentioned as *Flotillas de Operaciones* or *Escuadrillas de Operaciones*, as noted in the following Air Order of Battle from this time:

***Escuadrilla de Operaciones Teniente Amado Paniagua Numero 1 Campana***
(In honour of Mexico's first fallen pilot)
Base: Fortin Veracruz
3 TNCA Serie A biplanes
1 TNCA Serie H parasol

***Escuadrilla de Operaciones del Noroeste Numero 2 en Campana***
Base: La Misa Sonora
3 TNCA Serie A biplanes

***Escuadrilla de Operaciones Número 3 en Campana***
Base: San Geronimo Oaxaca
3 TNCA Serie A biplanes
2 TNCA Serie H parasols

***Escuadrilla de Operaciones Número 4 en Campana***
Base: Torreon, Coahuila
2 TNCA Serie A biplanes
1 TNCA Serie H parasol

***Balbuena aviation airfield, for the aviation school***
Base: México City
5 TNCA Serie A biplanes (1 under repair)
1 TNCA Serie H (under repair)
1 TNCA Serie E monoplane (Bleriot type w/o engine)

***In the field of operations***
11 TNCA Serie A biplanes (2 under repair)
4 TNCA Serie H parasols (1 under repair)

About this time some 30 aircraft had already been written off in accidents or declared worn out since 1915. During these operations, the aviation service would lose its first flyer to enemy action on 8 November 1919.

Lieutenant Jose E. Rivera of the *Escuadrilla de Operaciones No.4 en Campana* was tasked to fly an important message in TNCA Serie A biplane 35A50, but due to strong winds he landed short of his objective. From a station he called for help, which arrived the next day, with mechanic Enrique Pizana, protected by a strong escort, bringing a replacement propeller.

The repairs were made, and Rivera and Pizana were about to take off, with personnel holding the aircraft, when they were attacked by a group of mounted *Villistas*. The escort was dispersed, with three killed, and Pizana and Rivera were taken prisoner. The surviving men of the escort reported their capture.

On 13 November, with a strong escort, personnel of the *Escuadrilla* recovered the aircraft, which was damaged when the *Villistas* tried to destroy it. On the 17th a citizen from a local town spotted two bodies on the road: next day the bodies of Rivera and Pizana were recovered, both showing signs of having been executed with shots to the head. They were buried in the town of Camargo, Chihuahua.

## POLITICAL INTERFERENCE OF MAY 1920

As mentioned before, in 1920 Carranza had selected his successor for the next presidential term, a civilian, and not General de Division Alvaro Obregon, who many people saw as his natural successor. Obregon, along with General Plutarco Elias Calles and lawyer Adolfo de la Huerta, had launched the *Plan of Agua Prieta*. De la Huerta, who was then governor of the state of Sonora, had some differences with the central government, which was used as a pretext for the rebellion.

The political passions, intrigues and divisions not only divided the army, but also the air service. According to many eyewitnesses, there were pilots and ground personnel who favuored Obregon and were willing to affect the performance of the air service to the point of sabotage of aircraft. These events showed the weakness of the air service at this critical time.

President Carranza had decided to evacuate to Veracruz, taking personnel, families and equipment in a series of train convoys. One of the last trains to leave Mexico City was the aviation train, which was attacked and stopped on 7 May 1920. During the attack, Colonel Alberto Salinas Carranza was wounded and evacuated to hospital, but later escape to the United States with his family, settling in San Antonio, Texas.

A number of personnel defected and aeronautical equipment was left behind, despite orders to destroy it. On the same day, three aircraft managed to leave Balbuena airfield before the rebels arrived: a Farman F-50Bn2 bomber, a Serie A biplane and a modified Serie A, which has been reported to be an early Serie B. Of the three aircraft, only the Serie B managed to reach the trains, the other two suffering engine stoppages; it is claimed, but has never been denied or confirmed, that water was poured into their gas tanks before leaving Balbuena.

One other pilot from the Farman also made it to join Carranza's forces. One of the captured pilots later committed suicide in his cell.

The Serie B was used for reconnaissance missions, first by Lieutenant Samuel C. Rojas before he was wounded by an enemy artillery shell, and later by Lieutenant Carlos Santa Ana, who in his final flight attacked rebel cavalry with his revolver, flying low to frighten the horses

until it landed, bullet-ridden and abandoned with the trains.

All the equipment was recovered by the rebels and returned to Mexico City with the aviation personnel, who after their capture returned to duty, some recovering from wounds. Some of the returning pilots later discovered that Captain 1st Class Roberto Diez Martinez, who led a pro-Obregon group within the aviation personnel, took over the school and shops on 8 May.

Diez Martinez was later confirmed as chief of the department of aviation by President de la Huerta. However, his time as air force chief was tragically cut short due to an aviation accident involving a Farman F50Bn2 that was being flown over Mexico City by a French test pilot who had arrived after the fall of Carranza, and was flying for the first time in such altitudes. The accident claimed the lives of Diez Martinez and three others, with just one survivor.

## A NEW DIRECTION

After the events of May, the Mexican air service was reduced to a few aircraft by August 1920. The interim president, de la Huerta, hired Ralph O'Neill, who served as a technical advisor from 1920-25.

Born in Mexico of an Irish-American father and Mexican mother, O'Neill became a First World War fighter ace as a lieutenant in the 147th Aero squadron of the United States Army Air Service (USAAS), flying a Nieuport 28C-1 and later Spad XIII French fighters. O'Neill claimed the destruction of 11 enemy aircraft, of which six were confirmed and the others classified as probables.

A Vought V-99M No.38 of the *1/o. Escuadron Aereo* of the *2/o. Regimiento Aereo* that was camouflaged during the General Saturnino Cedillo rebellion of May 1938. (Enrique Velasco Padilla

He also had experience of three different types of training systems before his unit flew in combat, first the American, then Canadian and finally French systems. After his appointment by de la Huerta, O'Neill rendered a report on the state of the Mexican Air Service, finding the following aircraft available:

***Active service***
- 1 Sopwith 1½ Strutter double control
- 6 TNCA Serie A biplanes with Aztatl engines
- 3 TNCA Serie H parasol aircraft with Aztatl engines
- 1 monoplane with Trebol engine

***Under Repair***
- 1 National biplane with Curtiss engine
- 2 Serie A biplanes with Aztatl engines
- 2 biplanes without engines
- 1 monoplane without engine

***In Storage***
- 6 useless antique aircraft
- 10 useless antique aircraft engines
- 3 training aircraft in bad condition

***New equipment***
- 1 Farman F50 complete
- 2 Farman F50s under construction
- 2 used Lorraine engines
- 12 new Salmon engines

In his report to the Secretary of War and Navy, General Plutarco Elias Calles, O'Neill recommended modernising the training system of the aviation school, acquiring modern training aircraft and organising the aviation units into fighter, bomber and reconnaissance units. He was the first person to call the air service the *Fuerza Aerea Mexicana* (Mexican Air Force).

O'Neill assumed command of the Mexican Air Service from September 1920 to February 1921. In this position he was sent to England to acquire the best training aircraft he could find. Next he served as chief flight instructor, introducing the Gosport dual-control training system with the Avro 504K/J biplane trainers, he bought from England.

One of the first problems that O'Neill faced was from veteran pilots he had ordered to be retrained in the new training scheme, some of whom felt insulted and downgraded and tried to block O'Neill. But O'Neill, with the backing of President Obregon and Secretary of War and Navy Calles, ensured the veteran pilots had to follow his orders.

O'Neill had good reason for insisting on this, as it was shown during the retraining that a lot of the veteran pilots had picked up bad flying habits. These veteran pilots would also become the future instructor pilots for the next generations of cadets.

Also hired alongside O'Neill to help modernise the Mexican Air Service was German pilot Fritz Bieler Doebele, a First World War reconnaissance flyer, the French-American Joe Ben Lievre, a former instructor of the USAAS and pursuit pilot, and another Frenchman by the name of Dunkerque.

At O'Neill's recommendation, the newly labelled Mexican Air Force introduced an organisation structure in line with that of other air forces of the time. A greater variety of aircraft were introduced, including such trainers as the British Avro 504 (later built in Mexico and known as Avro Anahuacs), Curtiss JN-4 Jenny and the Brown Special biplane.

Other types designed and built at the TNCA under the direction of Engineer Angel Lascurain y Osio (1882-1957) included the TNCA 3-E-130 *Toloche* fighter, 4-E-131 *Quetzalcoalt* two-seater light bomber and 2-E-98 *Sonora"*low wing monoplane.

## TROUBLED TIMES

The civil unrest of the 1920s intensified the Mexican government's need for effective airpower. Even after the fall of Carranza, the government of de la Huerta defused an intended rebellion in the northern territory of Baja California that later benefited the air service, because the forces of state governor Colonel Esteban Cantu (1881-1966) had acquired three Curtiss JN4 Jennies and a Martin Model TT, and also reportedly some American pilots to fly them.

After an agreement was concluded in favour of the central government, the Curtiss Jennies were transferred to the Air Force.

In the middle of the political strife that rocked the country at that time, Mexico managed to send Mexican pilots and aircraft in June 1922 to the centennial celebrations of Brazil, in which Mexican Air Force Morane Saulnier MS-35 parasols flew.

With the outbreak of the De la Huertista Rebellion from December 1923 to March 1924, the Obregon government acquired some combat aircraft from the United States, including the ex-USAAC de Havilland DH-4B, under the recommendations of now Colonel *Asimilado* O'Neill. Other available aircraft were used for reconnaissance and bombing missions, some, for the first time in Mexico, night bombing enemy positions, rebel gunboats and shipping.

The de Havilland DH-4B were deployed in a series of flights/*Escuadrillas* of usually three aircraft each, assigned to the different army commands in support of their missions to carry out reconnaissance and bombing or strafing of enemy forces. More modern, Mexican-built Serie B light bombers were also used, some in the south of country.

At the start of the rebellion, a flight of Farman F50Bn2s was stationed at the city of Guadalajara, which was taken over by the rebels. Some of the crews tried to resist flying against their brothers in arms, but some bombing missions were flown to attack Federal shipping, in one case forcing a ship to surrender.

Aircraft were also later used in the short rebellion of General Francisco R. Serrano and Arnulfo R. Gomez in August 1927, again against the Yaqui Indians in northern Mexico from September 1926 to July 1927, and Douglas O-2C aircraft were bought and used to counter the religious *Cristeros* in the central parts of the country from January 1927 to June 1929.

Amidst this unrest, a number of long-distance flights were undertaken within the Mexican republic, involving Farman F-50bn2 bombers and TNCA Serie B biplanes. In a gesture of good will, a number of TNCA aircraft were also donated to sister republics to the south: El Salvador received two TNCA Serie As, there was one Avro 504 for Guatemala and also one for Costa Rica.

By 1927 the Mexican Air force was organised in five *Escuadrillas* equipped with the surviving Farman F-50 bombers, de Havilland DH-4Bs, Avro 504/Anahuacs, Douglas O-2Cs and the Morane Saulnier MS 35 parasol aircraft.

In early 1928 they would be joined by British Bristol F2B fighters and two types of 93B Boardhound IIs that were used against the *Cristeros* rebels. An American intelligence report for 1 July 1927 listed the following equipment for the Mexican Air Force:

***Yaqui Territory/Sonora***
4 Douglas observation planes (Douglas O-2C)
2 Anahuacs (Avro 504)
***Balbuena Airfield, Mexico City***
2 DH-4 (ex-USAAS DH-4B)
1 Farman (Farman F-50)
3 JN-4 Lincoln-Standarts
1 privately owned Lincoln-Standart
2 Moranes (MS.35 parasols)
2 reconstructed Salmon (TNCA Serie B Puro)
14 Anahuac ships for training purpose (Avro 504s)

## THE GOLDEN YEARS AND LONG-DISTANCE FLIGHTS

Even with this number of aircraft, Mexican pilots, hearing about the feats of international pilots, wanted to plan their own flights to cover their service in glory. One flight was accomplished in a Mexican-built Sea Lefase, a two-seater biplane flown by Major Alfredo Lezama Alvarez (1901-64) and Lieutenant David J. Borja Guarjado (1902-55) in a flight from Mexico City to the border city of Laredo Tamaulipas, covering about 1,250km in 10 hours and 47 minutes.

Another young pilot by the name of Emilio Carranza Rodriguez (1905-28)flew an Angel Lascurain parasol observation aircraft named *Coahuila* in a non-stop flight from Mexico City to Ciudad Juarez, Chihuahua, in 16 hours and 48 minutes on 2 September 1927. His original plan was to land on the American side of the border, but due to the tense relations between the countries this was not allowed. However, he was invited into the US to meet Charles Lindbergh, who was in El Paso, Texas, as part of a national tour after his non-stop solo transatlantic flight in the *Spirit of St Louis* earlier that year.

Lindbergh went on to tour Mexico from 14-28 December 1927. His visit with the Ryan NYP *Spirit of St Louis* stirred interest in aviation throughout the country, and also calmed political tensions between the United States and Mexico concerning American property owners and petroleum production by foreign companies operating on Mexican soil.

American ambassador Dwight E. Morrow sponsored the visit to help forge more friendly relations with General Calles' Mexican government. During the visit, Lindbergh met his future wife, Anne Morrow, daughter of Ambassador Morrow. He also made friendships with many Mexican Air Force personnel, including Captain Carranza.

The golden age of Mexican aviation was about to open. The years 1928-30 would be a time of glory and tragedy for the Mexican military pilots, as they took their wings beyond Mexico's borders.

Captain Carranza, after being inspire by Lindbergh and with the help of public subscription, went to the Mahoney-Ryan aircraft factory and ordered a Ryan Brougham Special B-1 named *Mexico-Excelsior* that was ready in May 1928 at San Diego, California.

To test his new aircraft, Carranza flew nonstop from San Diego to Mexico City in 18 hours and five minutes on 24-25 May 1928. His goal was to return the goodwill gesture of Lindbergh's visit to Mexico City. On 11 June he took off from Mexico City for a flight direct to

One of the two Howard DGA-8 (NC-18282) aircraft that General Saturnino Cedillo had in San Luis Potosi. Found abandoned on 27 May 1938 by Federal pilots, they were later used by the *Dirreccion de Aeronautica*. (Author Collection)

A fly-by of three Fleet Model 11-32Ds of the aviation school over a line-up of Bellanca 28-90B Flashes in November 1939 at Balbuena airfield. (Enrique Velasco Padilla)

Washington, DC, but bad weather forced him to land short of his goal at Moorsville, North Carolina, after flying about 18 hours and 50 minutes.

The next day, he took off at 1:50 p.m. and landed at Bolling Field air base, Washington, at 5:15 p.m., being welcomed by high-ranking American and Mexican officials, as well as large crowds of the general public. He toured Washington and later flew to New York to prepare for his return flight to Mexico City. On 12 July, Carranza took off from Roosevelt Field, New York, after postponing his flight due to adverse weather conditions. He crashed soon after in New Jersey and his body was discovered the following day.

Another pioneering Mexican pilot of the time was Major Roberto Fierro Villalobos (1897-1985), who used a Mexican-built aircraft from the border town of Tijuana, Baja California. He first flew his Baja California No.2 (BC-2) pursuit type aircraft nonstop from Mexicali to Mexico City on 10-11 June 1928, covering a distance of 1,500 miles in 14 hours and 55 minutes.

In fine weather, he next took off from Mexico City to Havana, Cuba, on 11 August in a flight of 12 hours and 30 minutes. From there, Major Fierro would cover the whole of Central America from August to September 1928 in his BC-2. The only country he did not visit was Nicaragua, due to the Mexican government not recognising the administration of Adolfo Diaz and the American intervention that was fighting the rebel Augusto Cesar Sandino.

The next notable goodwill flight was that of Colonel Pablo L. Sidar (1897-1930) and his mechanic Sergeant Arnulfo Cortez Benavente (a reported First World War veteran) in the Douglas O2M aircraft No.18, named *Ejercito Mexicano*, covering the entire Latin American continent from 29 August to 7 November 1929.

During the flight, Sidar crossed the Andes about five times, establishing a high altitude take-off with load record at Los Altos, Bolivia.

He returned to glory and planned another long-distance flight from Mexico to Buenos Aires, Argentina, in 1930 using a high wing single-engine monoplane Emsco B-3 named *Morelos*, built in the United States.

His co-pilot was Lieutenant Carlos M. Rovirosa (1901-30). On 11 May 1930, they took off from the state of Oaxaca, close to the border with Guatemala. They had estimated a non-stop 40-hour flight, but due to bad weather conditions they crashed off the coast of Puerto Limon, Costa Rica, after flying about 11 hours. Only Sidar's remains were recovered; just a shoe belonging to Rovirosa was discovered.

Colonel Fierro Villalobos performed a long-distance flight from New York City to Mexico City in a Lockheed Sirius Model 8 called the *Anahuac* on 21 June 1930 with his faithful mechanic Capitan Arnulfo Cortez. The flight covered 2,152 miles in 12 hours and five minutes.

After this flight, President Pascual Ortiz Rubio (1877-1963) forbade any more long-distance flights following the tragic deaths of Sidar and Rovirosa. However, after 1935 smaller-scale flights were undertaken to the United States and Central America.

## INTERNAL TROUBLES CONTINUE

While theses long-distance flights went on, the Mexican Air Force was building aircraft of several types, such as the Azcarate E trainer that was designed by one of the chiefs of the air service, General de Brigada Ingeniero Juan F. Azcarate (1896-1987). Ten were built and used at the military aviation school. Azcarate also designed and built a reconnaissance and bomber version known as the Azcarate OE-1, which was used in internal flights from September to December 1928.

The service was involved in flying combat and reconnaissance missions in various parts of the country, dealing, as mentioned, with the *Cristeros* rebellion from August 1926 until June 1929 and the *Yaqui* Indians in 1926-27. Another short but serious rebellion broke out on 2 March 1929, involving General Jose Gonzalo Escobar (1892-1969) as leader of a number of disgruntled generals against the intern presidency of Emilio Portes Gil and General Plutarco Elias Calles as the *Jefe Maximo*, the power behind the presidency, after the murder of President Obregon.

During this rebellion the air service received new aircraft, the Vought O2M-2M and Douglas O2M, while a number of civilian aircraft such as the Waco ATO and Stearman C-3B were converted into bombers. Escobar acquired a number of different types of civilian aircraft and mercenary American pilots to fly them; the Federal aviation would face a more organised and better-equipped rebel force.

During the fighting, a number of Federal aircraft were shot down or badly damaged by rebel ground fire, resulting in the death or wounding of several crew. The first known official downing of a rebel aircraft by a Federal flyer was also recorded, but details are lacking. The rebel commander of Escobar's aviators was the former air service commander General Gustavo Salinas Camina, chief of the air service from 1921-25, who had moved to the United States after the failure of the Serrano/Gomez coup in 1927.

The aviation units were organized as *Escuadrillas* with a mix bag of different types of aircraft, and were assigned as follows to Mexican Army divisions that were fighting in different parts of the country:

**D*ivision del Norte of General Juan Andrew Almanza***

Operated in Colima, Chihuahua and later Sonora

**1/o. Escuadrilla Aerea**

11 pilots and 9 mechanics

5 Vought O2U-2M Corsairs

Colonel Asimilado Ralph O Neill, the Mexican-born notable First World War fighter pilot who served in the Mexican air service from 1920-25. He was instrumental in establishing a modern training programme after May 1920 and introducing the DH-4B combat aircraft in Mexico. (Archivo Casasola)

1 Waco ATO
1 Travel Air 3000
1 Stinson SM-2 Jr.

***Colunma Expedicionaria del Noroeste of General de Division Lazaro Cardenas***
Operated in Jalisco, Sinaloa and later Sonora

**2/o. Escuadrilla Aerea**
9 pilots and 10 mechanics
3 Vought O2U-2M Corsarios
1 Bristol Boardhound type 93B
1 Stinson SM-1B

***Division del General de Division Abelardo L. Rodriguez***
Operated in the Northern border

**3/o. Escuadrilla Aerea**
12 pilots, mechanics unknown
3 Douglas O2M
1 Bristol Boardhound type 93B
2 Stearman C-3B

***Division del Centro of General de Division Saturnino Cedillo***
Operated in the states of Jalisco, Guanajuato and Michoacán

**4/o.Escuadrilla Aerea**
7 pilots and 5 mechanics
2 Bristol F2B
1 Douglas O2M
1 Waco ATO
1 Stearman C-3B

***Division of General Miguel Acosta***
Operated in the state of Veracruz

**Escuadrilla Aerea**
5 pilots, mechanics unknown
3 Bristol F2B

During the fighting, a number of pilots switched sides due to their situation. When the rebellion broke out, the rebels seized two Stinson SM-1B Detroiters of the Mexican postal service, and both pilots were forced to fly for the rebels, but at the first opportunity they flew their aircraft to Fort Bliss, Texas. Both aircraft and pilots later returned to Federal control.

One of the American mercenary pilots who flew with Federal forces changed sides by flying another Stinson SM-1B to the rebels. The rebels called their aviation service 'The Yankee Doodle Squadron'. Several different sources, some of which have to be treated with caution, suggest that during the course of the uprising the rebels obtained some 16 different types of aircraft.

The only military-capable of these aircraft was a Vought O2U-2M Corsair that was captured after a forced landing by its crew when it was hit by ground fire. The rebels tried unsuccessfully to get this aircraft operational, and ended up destroying it before the rebellion collapsed. Other aircraft were flown or transported by rail back to the United States.

## THE AIR REGIMENTS

After the end of the Escobar rebellion, and with a number of aircraft now in service, the Mexican Air Force units returned to Balbuena airfield. A reorganisation of the air service was undertaken, including retiring or phasing out aircraft that were no longer needed.

On 30 May 1929, the 1/o. Regimiento Aereo (1st Air Regiment) was formed, its first commander being Colonel Pablo L. Sidar. This new unit was organised in the following manner:

***1/o.Regimiento Aereo***

**Headquarters flight**
Bristol Boardhound type 93B
1 aircraft, 1 pilot, 8 mechanics

***1/o. Escuadron***
Vought O2U-2M
10 aircraft, 20 pilots, 24 mechanics

***2/o. Escuadron***
Douglas O2M/O-2M2
10 aircraft, 20 pilots, 24 mechanics

***3/o. Escuadron***
Bristol F2B fighters (surviving examples)
10 aircraft, 20 pilots, 24 mechanics

Also added was the *Escuadron Azcarate*, a training squadron equipped with the home-made Azcarate E trainers, with 24 mechanics. At one time aviation training was undertaken at Air Regiment level. This later included surviving examples of the Bristol F2B fighters, the last ones being operational until the early 1930s.

As previously mentioned, General Azcarate wanted to build aircraft in Mexico, so he set up an aircraft factory and his first orders were for the assembly of training aircraft the air service had bought. Azcarate later undertook licensed production of the Vought O2U-4A Corsair biplane, known as the *Azcarate Corsario*. A total of 31 were built, with which the 2/o. Regimiento Aereo was formed on 1 March 1931, Colonel Gustavo G. Leon (1899-1982) serving as its first commander. It structure was along the same lines as the 1/o. Regimiento Aereo:

***2/o.Regimiento Aereo***

***Headquarters flight***
Azcarate Corsario
1 aircraft, 1 pilot and 8 mechanics

***1/o. Escuadron Aereo***

A North American AT-6 armed trainer in flight somewhere over Mexico. Note the bomb racks under the wings. (Enrique Velasco Padilla)

Azcarate Corsarios
10 aircraft, 20 pilots, 24 mechanics

***2/o. Escuadron Aereo***
Azcarate Corsarios
10 aircraft, 20 pilots, 24 mechanics

***3/o. Escuadron Aereo***
Azcarate Corsarios
10 aircraft, 20 pilots, 24 mechanics

Spanish pilots Captain Mariano Barberan and Lieutenant Joaquin Collar Sierra performed a successful long-distance flight from Spain to Cuba on 10-11 June 1933 in their CASA Breguet Super Gran Bidon named *Cuatro Vientos*, an epic flight of 40 hours and 39 minutes.

After a period of rest and maintenance, they took off from Cuba to Mexico on 20 June, heading for Balbuena airfield, where Mexican and Spanish dignitaries and a crowd of well-wishers awaited them. However, for reasons still unknown today, they never reached their destination.

General Abelardo L. Rodríguez (1899-1967), interim president of Mexico, immediately ordered air and ground units to commence a search for the missing Spanish pilots.

Even Mexican naval units were involved in the search in coastal areas where the aircraft was last reported. The search also involved both air regiments. Not only military but also civilian aviation took part in the searches, which covered the states of Puebla, Veracruz, Tabasco and Campeche.

On the ground, a reported 12,000 civilians and military personnel participated in the search. Even the mechanic of the *Cuatro Vientos* came to Mexico from Cuba and participated as an observer flying in the search. The unsuccessful search was suspended in July.

In December 1933, Comandante Aviador Ramon Franco Bahamonde, a well-known long-distance flyer, came to Mexico representing the Spanish republican government to honour and recognise the efforts to find his fellow pilots. He was given a complete report of the search and possible causes of the loss, and in the name of his government, he personally decorated a number of flying personnel from both air regiments.

Both air regiment were later involved in the second religious conflict (*La Segunda Cristiada*) between the Catholic church and the government of General Lazaro Cardenas del Rio. This began when the president implemented Article 3 of the Constitution of 1917, trying to separate the Church from education, replacing it with a socialist education, which was not welcomed by the Church, certain elements rising in armed rebellion.

The area of operations was the state of Durango, where aviation elements undertook reconnaissance, bombing and dropping supplies to advance army elements.

In 1936 there were plans to expand the air service with the proposed creation of another air regiment and acquiring more modern aircraft, but due to infighting and decisions made by high-ranking Mexican Army personnel, the project did not get off the ground.

Another view of a Mexican Armed AT-6. Note the bomb racks and the .30 cal machine gun in the rear position. (Enrique Velasco Padilla)

Colonel Roberto Fierro Villalobos, commander of the Department of Aeronautics at this time, wanted to acquire metal general purpose monoplanes, being in favour of Seversky aircraft. After an evaluation of various types, the Consolidated Model 21-M was selected, a training biplane with some limited attack capability. Colonel Fierro was not pleased with the choice, and after voicing his opposition left his post and was later named ambassador to China and Japan.

The Consolidated aircraft replaced the Douglas O2M in the second squadron of the 1st Air Regiment. The next major aircraft purchase came in 1938 when a group of pilots and mechanics of the 2nd Air Regiment travelled to the United States to bring back 10 new Vought V-99M Corsair general purpose biplanes. They were assigned to the 1/o. Escuadron Aereo of the 2/o. Regimiento Aereo, and a flight of these aircraft later took part in a goodwill trip to Cuba.

In May 1938, the strongman of the state of San Luis Potosi, General de Division Saturnino Cedillo Martinez (1890-1938), an old revolutionary and secretary of agriculture in the first cabinet of President Lazaro Cardenas, resigned from his position.

He was an ardent opponent of Cardenas' policies on land reform and the expropriation of foreign petroleum companies (from America, Britain and Holland) which were operating in Mexico. It has been reported but not confirmed that he launched his rebellion with the support of the oil companies and Axis agents trying to keep Mexico neutral or out of a future war.

Cedillo had previously established an aviation school and repair shops in his home state. Cardenas, forwarned of Cedillo's intentions, had Brigadier General Samuel C. Rojas travel to San Luis Potosi, confiscate all Cedillo's aircraft and reassign some of his military pilots.

However, Cedillo managed to acquire by way of an intermediary two Howard DGA-8 high-wing transport aircraft and a Spartan 7W-5, along with a number of civilian pilots and handmade bombs. Cedillo launched a bombing and propaganda attack on the state capital with the Howards while President Cardenas was there.

Unable to hit the seat of government or the airfield, they were pursued by a flight of Consolidated Model 21-Ms and Vought V-99Ms but managed to escape. The Department of Aeronautics deployed a mixed aviation squadron with equipment and elements of both air regiments, the secretary of communications and public works and the aviation school.

The aviation unit launched operations from 19-31 May 1938,

A Mexican-built Azcarate Corsario No.60 flying over a Mexican town, a copy of the O2U-4A built under license in Mexico. They would see service in coastal patrol operations during the war. (Enrique Velasco Padilla)

undertaking reconnaissance, bombing and strafing attacks on the rebels.Both Howards were captured and taken to Balbuena airfield, where they were incorporated into the Mexican Air Force.

With his rebellion defeated, Cedillo and some of his followers fled into the sierra. His luck ran out on 11 January 1939 when his party was found by an army patrol and during a gun fight Cedillo and two of his men were killed.

The Mexican air service received more aircraft in 1939 after the defeat of the Spanish republicans in the civil war that had started in 1936. The Spanish government had ordered 22 Bellanca 28-90B flash monoplanes, which were at the port of Veracruz getting ready to be shipped, when the fighting ended.

In a gesture of support, the Mexican government of Lazaro Cardenas bought the aircraft from the representatives of the Spanish republicans; the money was used by the republicans to help settle new refugees from Spain. The aircraft were assigned and assembled by the 1/o. Regimiento Aereo and apparently assigned to one of its squadrons.

After two fatal accidents they were withdrawal from service in August 1940, and their engines were exchanged and the airframes sold to the United States Navy for instructional purposes.

On 16 January 1940, the Mexican air service underwent another change to its operational structure when the regimental system was dropped, replaced by six individual squadrons.

This happened while Colonel Alberto Salinas Carranza was in charge of the Mexican Air Force for a second time from 1939-40. For the first time, some squadrons were assigned away from Mexico City. While the 1st, 2nd, 3rd and 4th squadrons were based at Balbuena airfield, the 5th Squadron was at Monterrey, Nuevo Leon, and the 6th Squadron at Durango.

The aviation equipment was a mixed bag of Vought O2U-2Ms, Azcarate Corsarios, Vought V-99Ms and Consolidated Model 21-M general purpose biplanes. Some of these aircraft would also serve as advance trainers in the military aviation schools.

A number of flights (*Escuadrillas*) were assigned to the headquarters of military zones; after the Cedillo rebellion, a flight was assigned to San Luis Potosi to continue the search for Cedillo and support army units dealing with local bandits.

By 1940 the country was about to elected its next president, and President Cardenas had selected General de Division Manuel Avila Camacho, his former Secretary of War and Navy. The opposition candidate was a former revolutionary, General Juan Andrew Almanza.

The campaign and election of 1940 became a violent mess. Even after the votes had been counted and Camacho was declared the winner, Almanza also claimed victory, then left the country but later came back to resign. Armed groups of Almanza supporters rose in revellion and were dealt with by army and aviation units from November to December 1940 in the states of Durango and Chihuahua. Among the pilots who participated in the campaign were future Republic P-47D pilots of the Philippines campaign.

In the same year, Major Antonio Cardenas Rodriguez and his civilian radio operator for Mexicana de Aviacion airlines, Luis Cuevas Molina, undertook a goodwill flight in the government-owned Lockheed Model 12B Electra named the *Presidente Carranza* from June to September, visiting all the countries of Latin America.

Brigadier General Roberto Fierro Villalobos returned for his second time in charge of the department of military aeronautics in 1940, implementing changes to the tactical structure of the air service by restoring the regimental system on 1 April 1941 as follows:

Vought V-99M No.40 and No.38 of the *1/o. Escuadron Aereo* of the *2/o. Regimiento Aereo* at Balbuena airfield. (Enrique Velasco Padilla)

***1/o. Regimiento Aéreo: Colonel P.A. Fernando Proal Pardo***
***Balbuena airfield, Mexico City***

1/o. Escuadrón Aéreo
2/o. Escuadrón Aéreo
3/o. Escuadrón Aéreo

***2/o. Regimiento Aéreo: Colonel P.A. Rafael Montero Ramos***
***Balbuena airfield, Mexico City***

1/o. Escuadrón Aéreo
2/o. Escuadrón Aéreo
3/o. Escuadrón Aéreo

Two flights were also stationed, one at the border city of Tijuana, Baja California, and the other at the port of La Paz on the tip of the Baja peninsula.

The aviation regiments had the following equipment: Chance Vought O2U-2Ms (surviving 1929 examples), Azcarate Corsario Model 02U-4As, Vought V-99Ms, Consolidated Model 21-Ms and Bellanca 28-90B Flashes (the type retired after the August 1940 fatal crash).

By August 1941 the *Dirrecion de Aeronautica* had also revived the aviation workshops that had been responsible for the maintenance of the aircraft. This included what was left of the Canadian Car and Foundry Co Ltd (CCFC) contract, that was set up to produce aircraft (reportedly the Grumman FF-1/G-23) during the presidency of General Lazaro Cardenas, but none were built.

Due to the outbreak of the Second World War, the CCFC could not get the materials and instruments needed to continue its work. The aviation workshops and the CCFC only repaired aircraft, and the aviation workshops, under the command of the *Dirrecion de Aeronautica*, were renamed *Talleres Generales de Aeronautica* (TGA).

By August 1941, the air service had about 140 pilot officers and 215 ground personnel (officers and enlisted), and was reporting a strength of 62 aircraft and 225 parachutes.

The aviation school reported six training aircraft on its strength, and moved from Veracruz to the military city of Monterrey, Nuevo Leon, with the proper installations to operate from there.

The *Talleres Generales de Aeronautica* was preparing to test fly the first of a series of training aircraft for the military aviation school, the Barreda Ares EP basic trainers. After the 1920s the aviation workshops had continued to produce and assemble aircraft like the Avro 504K/J (known as the *Avro Anahuac*) and produce some prototypes for training, observation and light attack that did not go into full production. During the early 1930s, General Azcarate's aircraft factory had produced some 31 Corsair general purpose biplanes that served in both air regiments.

After this there was no large-scale production of aircraft until 1941.

General Fierro had secured the approval of the *Secretaria de la Defensa Nacional* to send a number of Mexican military personnel to undertake aviation training in the United States with the US Army Air Corps.

Up to this time, Mexican military aviation had been involved in the internal security of the nation while fighting rebels and bandits across the country, it had spread its wings beyond its borders with a series of goodwill flights by noted military aviators, and now it would face its biggest challenge yet in defending its national territory on both coasts against external threats from across the oceans.

It would also bring a period of rapid modernisation and growth, not only in the tactical sense, but also in its command policies, training, and logistics. Mexican naval aviation would also be formally established during this crucial time. Mexican military aviation was about to receive a major boost in its continuing development from the United States, as for the first time both nations would work together, putting aside their long history of wars, interventions, distrust, differences and fears to fight a common enemy.

Pilots of the *1/o. Regimiento Aereo* being briefed before undertaking coastal patrols at El Cipres, Baja California, in early 1942. (National Archives)

CHAPTER 2

# U-BOAT ATTACKS AND THE DEFENCE OF THE COAST

Mexico was not on good terms with the Axis Powers of Germany, Italy and Japan because of its diplomatic opposition to the Italian invasion of Ethiopia (1935-36) and the German annexation of Austria (1938), and its support of the legal Spanish Republican government during the civil war of 1936-39. Giving open support to the Republican cause, Mexico also clashed with the United States, which was trying to enforce an arms embargo.

Mexico sent supplies and weapons to Spain, transporting them in Mexican-owned ships, and allowed volunteers to fight for the Republican side (some were professional military officers, who would return to Mexico with combat experience). Mexican diplomats in Europe acted as middle men in arms sales to the Republic, their approval of some of the weapons deals coming at a crucial time for the Spaniards.

After the fall of France in 1940, Mexico offered a home to the Spanish government in exile, which continued to function – although latterly purely symbolically – until the death of General Francisco Franco Bahamonde in 1975 and the return of democracy to Spain.

While officially opposing the Axis, the Mexican government was forced to sell its petroleum products to Germany to survive the economic embargo that was imposed by the United States, Great Britain and Holland after Cardenas had nationalized the petroleum and oil industry on 18 March 1938.

A war of intrigue and espionage was being played out on Mexican soil, where Axis agents and operatives had gained some influence with certain high-ranking Mexican government officials. Japanese agents were trying to get as many raw materials out of the country to help their war industry.

Some Mexican officials collaborated with the Axis because they still harbored a grudge against the United States. At the same time the US government and its intelligence agencies were working with their Mexican counterparts trying to stop them.

On one level, Axis agents and propaganda (in newspapers and magazines and on the radio) were trying to keep Mexico neutral and in favour of them, but on the other hand there was animosity from Germany and Italy due to the seizure by General Avila Camacho's government of nine Italian tankers and three German cargo ships in April 1940; they had sought shelter in the Mexican ports of Tampico and Veracruz to avoid being captured by allied naval forces.

These 12 ships later became part of the Mexican merchant fleet, the tankers going to the fleet of *Petroleos Mexicanos* (PEMEX, Mexican Petroleum) to replaced the three tankers *Poza Rica*, *Manititlan* and *Panuco* that had been built at the shipping yards in Genova, Italy, but were seized by the Italian government after the outbreak of war in

Lieutenant Fernando Hernandez Vega and his observer/mechanic after a forced landing in Corsario Azcarate No.46 on 9 August 1942. Vega was forced to eject his bomb load before landing. (Family of General Fernando Hernandez Vega)

September 1939.

It was an ironic twist of fate that five of the seized ships would be later sunk by German U-boats.

## December 1941: Mobilisation

After the Japanese attack on Pearl Harbor on 7 December 1941, Mexico, along with most other Latin-American nations, broke diplomatic relations with Germany, Italy and Japan. The threat of a Japanese attack on the American west coast (including the peninsula of Baja California) prompted the mobilisation of Mexican Army units and *Dirrecion de Aeronautica* elements.

Due to the urgency to get troops to Baja California, Mexican forces travelled on US soil in passenger cars on American railroads to reach the border city of Tijuana, US Army personnel present to supervise the movement.

General Fierro defined the air service mission as to patrol and safeguard the Mexican west coast. The *1/o Regimiento Aereo* was sent to Baja California, the first elements – consisting of six Corsair biplanes with their pilots and observers – arriving at Tijuana on 15 December.

They later moved south to El Cipres airfield, located south of the port city of Ensenada. Another group of five aircraft (three Corsairs and two Consolidated) and crews arrived on the 18th to undertake patrols along the peninsula, and further flights would follow to Baja California.

The *2/o. Regimiento Aereo* stayed in Mexico City but dispatched a flight of three Corsair biplanes to Merida, Yucatan, in May 1942 to establish a base of operations there. During the transfer flight, one the aircraft crashed, but fortunately there were no fatalities.

The *1/o. Regimiento Aereo* had the following units at Ensenada: *1/o. Escuadron Aereo* at El Cipres, Baja California, *2/o. Escuadron Aereo* at La Paz, Baja California, and *3/o. Escuadron Aereo* with flights or patrols located at Hermosillo Sonora, Mazatlán and Guaymas Sinaloa.

By early 1942, the regiment had mobilised the following resources to undertake its mission to protect the Pacific coast, covering the Sea of Cortez and the coastal states of Sonora and Sinaloa:

| | |
|---|---|
| Aircraft | 26 |
| Aerial machine guns | 70 |
| Mendoza machine guns | 7 |
| Mauser rifles | 54 |
| Cartridges | 300,000 |
| Bombs | 400 |
| Parachutes | 100 |

In January 1942 it was reported that the *1/o. Regimiento Aereo* had five aircraft at Ensenada, two more stationed at Rancho Hamilton (about 38km south of El Cipres) and 10 at La Paz.

Cover of the Mexican magazine *Sucesos* of May 1942, featuring an article on Mexican wings over the Pacific. (Author Collection)

On 12 March 1942, the local press in Tijuana reported that a group of fishermen had sighted a submarine getting fresh water along the peninsula of Baja California at Punta Palmilla, which resulted in three days of searching by Mexican aviation and land units, but no vessel was found.

That same month, the *Dirrecion de Aeronautica* received reinforcements of six Vought-Sikorsky OS2U-3 Kingfisher observation monoplanes, in their land configuration, as noted in a daily US tactical report dated 30 May 1942:

> The US Navy turned over six Vought Corsairs [*sic*] (obsolete attack planes) to the Mexican government in exchange for certain engines which had been purchased by the Mexican government and were located in Mexico City.
>
> These six planes are believed to be in use in the Western Defense Command of Mexico. The first Mexican air regiment, Headquarters at La Paz, BC has the paper strength of 33 aircraft but actually has only 27, plus the six Vought Corsairs [*sic*].

The engines mentioned belonged to the Bellanca 28-90B Flash monoplanes that Mexico bought from the Spanish Republic in 1939. A Mexican newspaper account of 19 March 1942 gave more details about the transaction:

> There are now in Brownsville, six observation aircraft, which were acquired by our government in exchange of 21 Bellancas,[1] which the JARE [2] [*sic*] donated to Mexico as a sign of appreciation for its policy in respect to the situation of the Spanish refugees.

A group of six Mexican pilots sent to Brownsville to receive training on the Kingfishers were led by Captain 1st Class Pablo Avelar Rubio.

1 Two aircraft had already been lost in accidents in 1939 and 1940, leaving 19 Bellanca 28-90Bs.

2 Not JARE (*Junta de Auxilio a los Republicanos Espanoles)* (the Spanish Republican Assistance Committee) but FARE (*Fuerza Aerea Republicana Espanola*), the Spanish Republican Air Force as it was commonly known.

Mexican aircrews walk toward their aircraft at El Cipres airfield, Baja California, to fly coastal patrols. Note the Azcarate Corsario No.46 in the background. (San Diego Public Library

The six Kingfishers supplied were ex-United States Navy OS2U-3 Bureau aeronautical numbers 5720-5725 in the land plane version.

These aircraft had two hard points (one in each wing) that could carry two 100lb bombs or a 325lb depth charge, and two 0.30 calibre machine guns (one for the pilot and the other for the observer). These aircraft arrived at Balbuena military airfield on 26 March. Present to receive and inspect the new aircraft at 11:00 a.m. was President Avila Camacho and high-ranking military officers including General Fierro Villalobos and the Secretary of National Defence.

The president inspected the aircraft and even sat in the cockpit of one while Captain Avelar Rubio explained its working. After seeing the aircraft and talking to the crews, the president left the airfield satisfied and told the press that this was the beginning of the delivery of many new aircraft for the air service.

The markings of the aircraft delivered were most unusual. Before leaving the United States, the regular Mexican Air Force tricolour triangle was not applied. Instead, a circular green, white and red was painted over the US star (perhaps in haste). The tricolour markings were painted on the rudder, but the fuselage and wing markings looked like the emblem of one of Mexico's political parties. While these markings were temporary, they were reported in *Jane's All the World's Aircraft* during the war years.

After some maintenance work, including changing the aircraft markings in the aviation workshops, they were allocated the Mexican air service aircraft numbers 69-74. They were flown to El Cipres in two flights of three aircraft each, leaving Mexico City on 10 April. The aircraft operated with the mixed bag of Corsair and Consolidated biplanes in coastal patrols until replaced by the North American AT-6 and some Douglas A-24B dive bombers in March 1943.

The Kingfishers flew a number of reconnaissance missions throughout the peninsula from El Cipres, and by July 1942 they were reported stationed at Mazatlán Sinaloa, while one stayed at Ensenada and later converted to the floatplane version. By early 1943, five of the six were handed over to the Mexican Navy to start their own air service.

Even before the arrival of the Kingfishers, during a patrol flight on 20 March 1942, Lieutenant Leopoldo Meza, probably from the *3/o. Escuadron Aereo* of the *1/o. Air Regiment*, reportedly attacked with machine-gun fire from his aircraft (a V-99M, Azcarate Corsario or Consolidated) a submarine that was attacking a Mexican vessel about 30 miles off the coast of Sinaloa, forcing the submarine to submerge before escaping. No more details are known about this encounter, even from personnel records.

The Imperial Japanese Navy launched long-range submarines against the American west coast in three phases, with nine submarines participating in the first phase from December 1941 to March 1942. One of the submarines, I-10, a Type A1, was stationed just outside the harbour of San Diego, very close to Mexican waters.

The second phase was launched by six submarines from May to June 1942, and the final phase in August of the same year with two submarines. During the offensive, Japanese submarines claimed to have sunk 12 merchant ships and bombarded shore installations in California, causing panic. In reality only five ships were lost, with one badly damaged with the loss 12 crew.

## LIFE IN THE FIELD IN BAJA

A report dated 26 May 1942, issued by the US Caribbean Defense Command, relates the state and disposition of Mexican aircraft and their efforts to carry out its duties with a reported 27 aircraft.

This report, provided by noted Latin American aviation historian Dan Hagedorn in his book *Texans and Harvards in Latin America* (Air Britain, 2009), provides an inside view of the problems that aviation elements had with a shortage of spare parts and support. This started to have an impact on the patrols, but the crews still carried out their missions. The report, submitted after the arrival of the Vought Kingfishers, states:

> One squadron of nine mixed types was at La Paz Baja California (supported by a battalion of army troops consisting of 40 officers and 410 other ranks).
>
> One squadron of nine mixed types was at Ensenada (otherwise) on their own, without any army support.
>
> One flight of three aircraft mixed type was at Santa Rosalia, Baja California (oddly on the inner, eastern coast of Baja California, also unsupported).
>
> One flight of three mixed types was at Hermosillo, Sonora (supported by an infantry battalion of 40 officers and 410 other ranks).
>
> One flight of three mixed types was at Guaymas, Sonora (otherwise unsupported).

Azcarate Corsario No.59 flying on a patrol. Note the way the observer's machine gun was stowed for flight. (Manuel Ruiz Romero)

Vought V-99M No.37 flown by the *2/o. Escuadron Aereo* of the *1/o. Regimiento Aereo* based a La Paz, Baja California, that was involved in a attack against a suspected target on 10 September 1942. (Enrique Velasco Padilla)

It should be noted the term 'mixed types' means that some of these units were operating Vought V-99M, O2U-2M, Mexican-built Azcarate Corsarios (O2U-4A) and Consolidated Model 21-M general purpose biplanes.

A Mexican version of life in the field at this time was published in the aviation magazine *Anahuac: Organo de la Aviacion Nacional*, which conducted an interview with Captain P.A. Juan Jose Sixto de Rio, one of the flight commanders assigned to Baja California, during a trip back to Mexico City on official business. He spoke about his experiences,

relating that life was a harsh existence. The air service was established and carried out under American and Mexican guidance, taking up all their time, with personnel always having to be ready 24 hours a day, remaining close to their aircraft, which were constantly fuelled and armed.

While the aircrews were close to their aircraft, their wings offered the only protection from the sun. Some flights deployed to other areas or had housing available, but others, like those whom Captain Sixto del Rio commanded lived in the open. During a night on the flight line they slept under the wing of their aircraft, with the pilot beneath one wing and the mechanic/observer under the other.

During the course of the day, all administrate duties and eating of meals was done close to the aircraft. Being far from home and feeling isolated, what kept up their morale was communications via radio with the outside world or news brought in by aircraft from other locations.

The crews carrying out the patrols extended their radius of action along the coastal areas.

They were well-versed in the characteristics of ships that travelled in the area. When the crews encounter a ship, they would fly toward the vessel to identify it and report its presence. If the ship had its flag up, it made the mission easier, but if it was not flying a flag and the aircraft was on a solo patrol, the aircraft would have to fly over the ship to try to ascertain its nationally, which could expose the aircrew to enemy fire.

In some instances, if the ship refused to identify itself, then the aircrew would fire warning shots to get its attention. Sometimes when a ship was spotted by aircraft, it would raise itsr flag. After returning from their patrol, the crew would report the sighting, location and type of ship to keep track of all vessels navigating in the area.

At the return of each patrol, the crew and ground personnel would also be busy preparing the aircraft for the next flight, checking its mechanics and weapons systems. After leaving the flight line, the crew and personnel would return to their camp area. In some locations the

Newspaper clipping showing the arrival of the six Vought OS2U-3 Kingfishers at Balbuena military airfield, with President Manuel Avila Camacho in attendance. (Enrique Velasco Padilla)

aircraft were out in the open, with no hangars or facilities, in which case the weather could take its toll on the aircraft.

Great care was thus taken by the ground crews to create some shelter for the aircraft and make it easy to carry out maintenance under protection from the sun. Despite these conditions, Sixto del Rio said that patrols continued with their mission to ensure protection of all shipping off the Baja California coast.

## MEXICANS IN THE FOURTH INTERCEPTOR COMMAND

As previously mentioned, General Fierro had obtained permission for a number of Mexican personnel to train in the United States with the Army Air Corps. Some were taking their initial pilot courses and others had advanced flight training.

At this time the Mexican air service, due to the nature of its experiences and doctrine, did not have a fighter aviation component, only light bombing and reconnaissance.

Many attempts were tried to establish fighter groups, either with homemade (TNCA Serie C Microplano Veloz, Serie E Sonora and Lascurain 3-E-130 parasol fighter) or imported (Ansaldo A-1 Balilla) designs, but with no success. There is the reported case of a fighter aircraft order for six Curtiss Hawk I landplane biplane fighters being cancelled in 1934 at the last moment due to the middle man trying to get a cut of the action.

On 18 December 1941, by order of the United States War Department, Lieutenant Heriberto Rodriguez Garcia and Alfonso Gandarilla Gracia were assigned to the Fourth Interceptor Command at March Field, California. They had attended a refresher course for Latin American pilots at Randolph Field, Texas, on 15 August 1941, and an advanced course at Kelly Field, Texas, on 2 October. The Mexican pilots were then assigned to Mitchell Field, New York, in December 1941, a USAAC pursuit base. Lieutenant Gandarilla Gracia remained at Mitchell Field while Heriberto Garcia went to Selfridge Field, Michigan. Gandarilla was assigned to the 36th Pursuit Squadron of the 80th Pursuit Group, where he started to fly the Bell P-39 Aircobra on 3 December, and later the Curtiss P-40C.

The 36th became the 36th Fighter Squadron of the 8th Fighter Group, during its time in the Pacific with the 5th Air Force, flying P-39s, P-47s and P-38s, claiming the destruction of 94 enemy aircraft, plus 19 probables and 11 damaged.

When both Mexican pilots were transferred to the Fourth Interceptor Command at March Field, Riverside, California, Gandarilla flew the Vultee P-66 Vanguard with the 50th. Pursuit Squadron out of Long Beach, California. The 50th became the 50th Fighter Squadron and was later equipped with the Lockheed P-38 Lightning, but was employed in the defence of Iceland from 1942-44, when it was disbanded. It was under the control of the 8th Air Force.

During his assignment, Gandarilla racked up 20 hours and 10 minutes of flying time on fighter planes. He returned to Mexico in February 1942. Gandarilla was in the first group of pilots flying the North American AT-6B armed trainers and assigned to anti-submarine patrols in the Gulf of Mexico in June 1942.

Another pilot who trained in the United States was Lieutenant Carlos Garduno Nunez, who was entirely trained in the flying schools of the USAAC, doing his primary, basic and advanced courses in Texas. After completing his training, he requested more advanced training. He reportedly requested that General Fierro send him to March Field in California to learn to fly the Lockheed P-38 Lightning, as he had undergone twin-engine training at Kelly Field, Texas, in August 1942.

He was assigned to the 14th Pursuit Group, flying P-38D/E models, but after some issues with the US War Department he was returned to Mexico. His pilot record sheet dated 30 July 1944 lists that he flew the following combat type planes: P-38, F6F (at NAS Coronado) and A-24B (in Mexico). After his return to Mexico, he helped train pilots in the North American AT-6 at Balbuena and was later assigned to anti-submarine patrols in the Gulf of Mexico out of Veracruz.

The 14th later became the 14th Fighter Group and flew the P-38 during the war, seeing service in England and later in North Africa and Italy. The group was credited with 426 enemy aircraft destroyed, plus 87 probables and 194 damaged.

## COOPERATION WITH THE UNITED STATES

Cooperation between the United States and Mexico did not have a smooth start, even with the creation of the US-Mexico Defense Commission in early 1941 that channelled all of Mexico's requests for Lend Lease and training. There were many in the Mexican Army high command who favoured a more active cooperation with their northern neighbor (mostly from the Presidential Command and Staff), while others – the old timers or *Revolucionarios* – were still suspicious of US intentions, with some concern that American troops and installations would be allowed on Mexican soil, which they felt was a violation of the Constitution of 1917 (Article 76).

Some went as far as claiming that the US wanted to take over the Baja California peninsula. More war hysteria was stirred up among the Mexican population when they saw any US troops near the border, often causing panic. The government of General Avila Camacho was trying to show its people that its armed forces could take care of the defence of the Mexican Pacific coast with no outside help, but they would gladly receive any war material needed and training to carry out missions.

In case of an emergency, they would allow US forces to help out.

There was great concern in the 4th Interceptor Command of the 4th Air Force of the United States Army Air Corps that after what

The general public checking out the Vought OS2U-3 Kingfishers after their arrival in March 1942. Note the hurried Mexican markings that were applied to the aircraft to cover over the circle, star and red dot of the US military. (Enrique Velasco Padilla)

happened at Pearl Harbor, the Japanese could launch another carrier-borne air attack from the Baja California peninsula. In such an event, San Diego or Los Angeles were a target-rich environment, not only for shipping and harbour installations, but also aircraft factories.

There was a radar coverage gap cover such an approach.

There were also concerns in the Western Defense Command (WDC) after a number of reports of sightings of Japanese submarines finding refuge in the uncharted coastal areas of Baja California and the small Japanese fishing community probably cooperating with these vessels.

The WDC, under the leadership of Lieutenant General John L. De Witt, supported the formulation of President Roosevelt's infamous Executive Order 9066 of February 1942, under which all citizens of Japanese ancestry were forcibly removed from the US west coast to internment camps in the interior of the country.

Another issue that had earlier faced the WDC was the request that a small US Army reconnaissance mission be sent into Baja California to check out reports of Japanese activities, look for sites for setting up radar stations and airfields and carry out a complete survey of the Baja peninsula.

Permission was initially given from the Mexican government for the US mission to go ahead. Yet on 16 December 1941, when the reconnaissance team of five scout cars, four trucks and two Stinson/Vultee 0-49 reconnaissance aircraft from the 115th Observations Squadron from Paso Robles, California, with all American markings painted over, were ready to cross the border,

they were told that the local Mexican commanders had no knowledge of the mission. Eventually, 'Expedition E', as it was known, went ahead on 22 December after President Camacho gave permission for the expedition to start, but with a Mexican Army escort provided in two additional trucks.

Another problem soon loomed while these events were going on. The new commander of the *Region Militar del Pacifico* (Military Region of the Pacific), General Lazaro Cardenas del Rio, the former president of Mexico, who was opposed to the presence of US troops in Mexico, was travelling to Ensenada to take over his new position and was not informed of the presence or the permission given for the American troops by the Presidential Command and Staff.

Some Mexican historians and scholars claim that Cardenas stopped the mission. Other participants made claims, which do not match US testimonies, to have captured one of the pilots of the O-49 aircraft who had flown to Ensenada to get fuel on 24 December. When the American pilot flew back he reported he was detained by Mexican Army officers who did not know anything about the mission, but he was released and as able to purchase the fuel for the aircraft.

'Expedition E' continued with its mission and returned to the border on 26 January 1942. A conference was held on 24 April 1942 at the Agua Caliente casino in Tijuana, where General De Witt and General Cardenas met and agreed to set up three radar stations. Their locations were established after a second US-Mexican Army reconnaissance was carried out from 8-27 May.

Another important development for the Mexican military, the *Compania de Deteccion Aerea No.1* (Aerial Detection Company No.1) was organised and sent to Baja California on 13 May to have a Mexican presence in the placement and operations at the radar sites. A US-Mexican Army mission carried out a reconnaissance of the Sonora-Sinaloa coastal areas to check out reports of enemy sightings.

Three SCR 270-B detector sets with equipment supplies and materials were sent to northern Baja California. At first they were manned by USAAC personnel of the 4th Interceptor Command, overseeing Mexican personnel, but later by trained Mexicans. The radar sets were used to supplement the Fourth Fighter Command Air Raid Warning system. By June 1944, two sets were discontinued, while the third remained operational to assist in locating planes downed over the sea. After the end of the war, all three sets were taken to Mexico City, but their fate after that is unknown.

The six Vought OS2U-3 Kingfishers after their arrival at El Cipres, Baja California, as reinforcement aircraft for the *1/o. Regimiento Aereo*. Note the change of markings since their arrival. (Enrique Velasco Padilla)

General Lazaro Cardenas was promoted to Secretary of National Defence in September 1942. Historian Maria Emilia Paz notes in her book *Strategy, Security and Spies* (Pennsylvania State University Press, 1997) that there was some frustration with the US military about Cardenas' influence that prevented them from stationing US troops and building installations:

> Cardenas did not reject the principal of Mexican-US collaboration and was alert on the need for some degree of rapprochement. What he objected to was the idea of stationing U.S. Troops in Mexico to carry out tasks the Mexicans were quite capable of performing, provided they were given the appropriate training and equipment.
>
> Mexico's decision not to allow U.S. troops to be stationed in Mexico, was not only a matter of ideology or nationalist zeal. As Cardenas put it, the idea was to get the most of the war experience by equipping Mexican soldiers with the best possible training and equipment under the discreet supervision of U.S. personnel.

## A STATE OF WAR DECLARED

Mexico declared a state of war against the Axis Powers on 28 May 1942, with a retroactive date of 22 May, after a number of Mexican merchant ships and tankers were attacked and sunk by German U-boats in the strait of Florida, Gulf of Mexico and off the Mexican coast.

The first victim was the tanker *Tamaulipas*, owned by PEMEX via the Mexican Trading and Shipping Company, New York, that had been reflagged under the United States flag. It was attacked and sunk by German U-boat U-552 on 10 April 1942, killing three of its crew. U-552, a Type VIIC submarine commanded by Oberleutenant Zur Erich Topp, carried out 15 patrols and sank a total of 32 ships. U-552 would survive the war to be scuttled by its crew at Wilhelmsaven, Germany, on 2 May 1945. The *Tamaulipas* is often not mentioned in Mexican accounts because it was sailing under the American flag, but it still belonged to PEMEX.

What got more attention was the sinking of the *Potrero de Llano* off the coast of Florida on 13 May 1942 by U-564, commanded by Kapitänleutnant Reinhard Suhren, causing the death of 14 of its 35-man crew, including the captain of the tanker, Lieutenant Gabriel Cruz Diaz. New information has come to light that Suhren had violated orders from Admiral Karl Donitz, commander of the U-boat fleet, not to attack Mexican shipping, since the German government was observing political developments in Mexico and intended its agents to continue to infiltrate the upper echelons of the Mexican government.

This had been demostrated on 19 January 1942, when it was reported that the former German passenger ship *Orinoco*, one of the confiscated ships and now named *Puebla,* had an encounter with a U-boat off the coast of New York. The German submarine, after checking the identity of the ship and cargo, let the *Puebla* continue unharmed.

Suhren reportedly confused the Mexican flag, which was painted on the side of the *Potrero de Llano*, for the Italian flag. Suhren reported that the vessel was sailing with blacked out lights and there were armed escorts nearby, so he could claim it as a legitimate target. The survivors of the ship reported that all the lights were on, to illuminate the flag, name and country of the ship.

A line-up of the aircraft of the *1/o. Regimiento Aereo* at El Cipres some time after April 1942. (Enrique Velasco Padilla)

The tanker was carrying around 40,000 barrels of fuel, and its captain had ordered an abandon ship drill on the day it was sunk. Some of the crew later reported that Lieutenant Cruz Diaz appeared worried and continued to be on the lookout until he retired to his quarters just before midnight. The *Potrero del Llano* was hit at 11:55 p.m. in its centre section, destroying the bridge, where a large number of casualties occurred, including the captain and majority of the officers.

The survivors were picked up by American patrol vessel USS *PC-536* and transferred them to *PC-515* to take them to Miami, Florida, for treatment. Sadly, one more member of the crew died due to his injuries. Under Mexican shipping regulations, merchant ships did not have the Mexican eagle painted in the flag, but the name of the ship and the country was painted on their side.

Due to such incidents, the efforts of German intelligence agents and spies, who were trying to keep Mexico neutral or out of the war, was derailed.

U-564 went on to complete nine patrols and was credited with 19 ships sunk and four damaged, and Shuren would survive the war. However, the U-boat later fall victim to a British air attack, by No.10 Squadron of Coastal Command, on 14 June 1943, with the loss of 28 of its crew.

The Mexican government sent a note of protest about the incident and demanded reparations, but the reply came in another attack. On 21 May 1942, U-106, commanded by Kapitänleutnant Herman Rash, sunk the tanker *Faja de Oro*, killing 10 of the crew, in the strait of Florida. U-106 was later sunk by No.461 Australian Air Force and No.228 RAF squadrons on 2 August 1943, 22 members of its crew going down with the submarine.

In 10 patrols, U-106 had sunk 22 ships.

Despite Mexico declaring a state of war after the sinking of the *Faja de Oro*, the sinkings and damages to ships continued.

On 31 May, another of PEMEX's reflagged tankers, *Cacalilao*, was damaged while berthed at the refinery in Tampico, causing the death of four of its crew. They had been flushing out the ship's tanks with a hose in preparation for the next load of gas oil for New York. The explosion caused severe damage and further reduced Mexico's tanker fleet at a critical time, but ther ship was eventually repaired and put back in service.

Mexico's merchant fleet would lose five more ships sunk by submarine attacks, two under American flag and operated by non-Mexican crews.

During 1942 the Mexican navy patrol boat *G-25* captured the Vichy French tanker *Merope*, which it suspected of acting as a supply ship for German U-boats. *Merope* was later handed over to PEMEX and renamed *Potrero del Llano II*, staying in service in Mexico until December 1968, when it was scrapped.

On 9 November 1942, President Avila Camacho declared that his government had broken diplomatic relations with Vichy France since it did not represent the spirit of the Free French of General Charles DeGaulle.

These were dangerous times in the Gulf of Mexico. From February to August 1942, 53 ships were sunk by U-boats. By 1943, with new convoy systems, improved anti-submarine weapons and aircraft, and more allied aircraft and ships patrolling the area, the U-boats were much less effective, only sinking five ships throughout that year.

Before the war was over, the Mexican tanker fleet acquired other ships to replace its losses. However, it would still suffer one more loss when, on 19 October 1944, the tanker *Juan Casiano* was sunk about 90 miles off the coast of Charleston, South Carolina, with loss of 21 crew. No official explanation has been given for the loss, but it appears it was not a U-boat attack.

Before the events in the Gulf of Mexico unfolded,

in January 1942 President Roosevelt, with the recommendation of his United States Army Air Corps (USAAC) chief General Henry 'Hap' Arnold, had authorised the delivery of 50 North American AT-6 armed trainers to Latin America – Chile, Peru, Ecuador, Venezuela, Brazil and Uruguay – but Mexico was not on the list.

Mexico was not programmed to receive its first aircraft, eight AT-6Cs, until August of that year. However, due to the critical situation in the Gulf of Mexico, the order of delivery was modified so that Mexico received the first six North American AT-6Bs (ex-USAAC stock) in June.

On 27 May, the *Dirreccion de Aeronautica* had received an order marked 'urgent' from President Camacho to send a group of Mexican pilots to San Antonio, Texas, to pick up the six North American AT-6B armed trainers. Leading these pilots was Major. Luis Noriega Medrano (1890-1979), along with

Captain 1st Class Jose Mena Barona,
Captain 1st Class. Ignacio Ortiz Diaz de Leon,
Lieutenant Alfonso Gandarilla Gracia,
Lieutenant Carlos Astorga Franco and
Lieutenant Roberto Legorreta Sicilia.

After the completion of a two-week course at Duncan Field, San Antonio, they took off for Mexico City on 13 June, arriving the next day. The American Embassy Intelligence Report of 20 June 1942 from the US naval attaché reported the importance of these aircraft to the Mexican government, and particularly President Camacho:

> The Mexicans have evidenced much interest and pride in these modern airplanes. General Fierro stated that President Avila Camacho was confined to his home with a severe cold and unable to visit the airport to see the planes. The president asked that the planes be flown over his home in order that he might see them.

Major Noriega later reported that they didn't have to pay for any

The Mexican tanker *Portero del Llano* on fire after being hit by torpedoes from German submarine U-564 on the night of 13 May 1942. (San Diego Air and Space Museum

President General Manuel Avila Camacho with the chief of the air service, General Roberto Fierro Villalobos, during the live fire demonstration of the recently arrived North American AT-6Bs on 19 June 1942. (Author Collection)

fuel for the trip down south. The aircraft received USAAC serial numbers 41-17428 to 41-17433, and were charged to Mexico's Lend Lease account. They were flown in aluminium colour scheme with the correct Mexican air service marking on the wings, but after their arrival at Balbuena underwent painting at the workshops, as noted by the American military attaché:

> The planes are painted in the usual US Army drab color with the standard Mexican army aircraft insignia on the lower side of each wing tip.
>
> This insignia is a concentric triangle with three color bands painted, green triangle inside, white triangle next and a red triangle on the outside.
>
> The rudder is painted in the three color bands from the forward edge green, white and red.

The AT-6Bss were numbered in sequence, immediately following the six Vought Kingfishers, so they received the letter and number combinations P-75, P-76, P-77, P-78, P-79 and P-80, 'P' possibly standing for *Patrulla* (Patrol).

The armed trainers had four hard points, two on each wing, and could carry up to four 100lb bombs. They were also armed with three M-2.30 calibre machine guns – one that was synchronised to fire in front of the pilot and others for the observer and on the right wing – with five 100-round ammunitions boxes, each with a capacity of 200 rounds. It appears the gun sight was the N-3B mounted in the centre, directly below the front instrument panel.

Five days after their arrival, the AT-6Bs conducted a dive bombing demonstration in a area known as Cerro del Penon, just outside Mexico City. The first to take off was Major Noriega, who within about 10 minutes dropped his first bomb on a marked target, under radio instruction from the ground from Major Alberto Najera Mercado. He was then joined by the rest of the AT-6Bs that formed two flights for the demonstration, dropping more bombs and strafing ground targets.

The combat capability of the AT-6B was witnessed by President Camacho, General Roberto Fierro and other high-ranking army and air service officers. Camacho later heard about the aircraft from the pilots and checked out the cockpits.

With the arrival of the AT-6Bs, the air order of battle of the Mexican Air Force for 31 July 1942, as given by the American military attache in Mexico City, was as follows:

***Mexican Airplane Strength***
***I. Planes***

| | |
|---|---|
| Consolidated 21-M | 10 |
| Vought Corsair O2U4 (1929) | 34 |
| Vought V-99M | 10 |
| Fleet F-11-32 | 6 |
| Ryan ST | 1 |
| Douglas O-2M | 2 |
| Fairchild 82-A | 1 |
| Stearman 81 | 1 |
| North American AT-6 (1942) | 6 |
| OS2U-3 (1942) | 6 |
| TOTAL | 77 |

Ares EP planes are being manufactured in Mexico. 11 are on order,

LUCIDAS MANIOBRAS DE LA FUERZA AEREA
El señor Presidente de la República las presenció

El señor Presidente de la República, general Manuel Avila Camacho, inspecciona los nuevos aviones adquiridos para la aviación mexicana.

Los nuevos aparatos de la fuerza aérea Mexicana, durante las maniobras del sábado pasado en Balbuena, donde se demostró la pericia de nuestros pilotos.

Newspaper cutting of the live fire demonstration of 19 June 1942 near Mexico City, with a photo of President Camacho being given an explanation of the North American AT-6B. (Enrique Velasco Padilla)

Gen. Fierro has purchased 56 motors to be used in these and additional trainers which are to be built. Lend-Lease will supply Mexico with 12 AT-6 and 2 transports by the end of August.

***II. Stations***

| | |
|---|---|
| Monterrey Aviation School | |
| Fleet F-11-32 | 6 |
| Ryan ST | 1 |
| (Ceased operations 29 January 1942)[3] | |
| Mazatlán, Sinaloa OS2U-3 | 6 |
| La Paz B.C. (Baja California) 1 Squadron | 6 |
| Ensenada B.C. (HQ) 1 Squadron | 9 |
| Sta. Rosalia B.C. 1 Flight | 3 |
| Hermosillo, Sonora 1 Flight | 3 |
| Guaymas, Sonora 1 Flight | 3 |
| Mexico City Balbuena all others | |
| Tampico East Coast Patrol to be set up | |

***III. ORGANIZATION***

*In February 1942, the Second Air Regiment [sic]* was given the mission of patrolling the West Coast from Headquarters at Ensenada B.C., they were organized into three squadrons of nine planes each divided into three flights of three planes. The 5 OS2U-3 [sic] was assigned to patrol work based at Mazatlán. The six new AT-6s are reported to be schedule for patrol on the coast, probably Tampico. The Second Air Regiment was based at Balbuena (Feb. 1942) with all its planes under repair.

3 Preparing move to Guadalajara, Jalisco.

## MEXICAN DIVE BOMBERS

These new aircraft were assigned to the *2/o.Escuadron Aereo* of the *2/o. Regimiento Aereo*, to protect Mexican and allied shipping in the Gulf of Mexico. Orders were received, dated 4 July, that a flight of three AT-6Bs (P-77, P-78 and P-80) were to establish a base at Tuxpan, Veracruz, to undertake anti-submarine patrols in the Gulf.

This unit was composed of the three AT-6Bs, three pilots and two mechanics. They were assigned to the *Region Militar del Golfo* (Gulf Military Region) with headquarters in the port of Veracruz, under the command of Major Luis Noriega Medrano. The aircraft were flown the majority of the time with only the pilots, and carried only two M-30 demolition 100lb bombs to reduce the weight and get more patrol time. Some pilots carried out up to five-hour patrols.

The first patrols were carried out on 28 June, when two AT-6Bs spotted the survivors of the *Tuxpan*. Major Noriega, flying P-80 (as he did throughout his time at Tampico), took part in a flight of two hours and 42 minutes, classified as a route and search, after the sinking of the *Las Choapas*. Flying with Noriega was Lieutenant Gandarilla in P-77 as the search for the submarine and survivors of its attacks intensified. The Mexican gunboat *G-23* (one source says it was *G-25*) was also involved in the search for three missing crew member of the *Tuxpan*, but returned to port after failing to locate any more survivors.

On 5 July Major Noriega attacked the U-boat with two M-30 demolition bombs, as he recalled in an interview during a tour of the North American Aviation plant in Texas for the plant newspaper

The arrival of the North American AT-6Bs was a great event; even the local Boy Scout organisations were given a tour of the new aircraft. (Enrique Velasco Padilla)

*Take-off* in August 1944:

> [A]nd he went on to tell, in detail, the story of the sinking which was revealed in the United States newspapers in June 1942, but which was not told in full as the NAA listeners received it from the pilot himself Tuesday.
>
> After it was learned that two oil tankers had been sunk south of Tampico, AT-6s stayed on a 24 hour patrol, he explained. 'While I was on patrol in the vicinity, I received a message from a commercial plane that the submarine had been sighted nearby.' The Major described how he spotted the partly submerged sub soon after cruising near the shore.
>
> His AT-6 had two 100 pound bombs in the wing racks. 'First getting permission to bomb it, we dropped one that hit toward the prow of the ship. Our second hit the mid-section.'
>
> The Major radioed the position of the sub and returned to base to reload, leaving a US bomber that appeared on the scene to circle the target. By the time the Major got back to the target, he said he could see nothing but a smear of oil where the sub had been.

The submarine attacked by Noriega was the Type IXC U-129, commanded by Kapitänleutnant Hans-Ludwig Witt, who had sunk the Mexican tanker *Tuxpan* on 26 June, killing four of its crew. The next day, Witt sunk the *Las Choapas*, three of the crew being lost. After his attack on U-129, Major Noriega submitted the following report of his actions:

> Luis Noriega Medrano, Pilot Aviator of the Mexican Air Force as active commander of the second squadron of the 2nd Air Regiment. On July 5, 1942, two M-30 demolition Bombs were expended when dropped in action against an Enemy Submarine.
>
> The preceding is given at the Plaza of Tampico, TampicoOn the Sixth day of July 1942.

The U-boat was initially claimed as sunk, then later as damaged, but this was not the case. U-129's diary for that day recorded that it had to dive due to enemy aircraft sightings, the first note was:

"Alarm vor Flugzeug rw. 130o Typ North American Aufgetaucht" (rough translation: Alarm aircraft 130 degrees type North American on the surface).

Witt had to dive three more times due to enemy aircraft sightings by his crew, with one identified as an 'A-20'. Major Noriega noted in his log book:

"5 Julio 1942 AT-6B P-80 5.25 Exploración, Recon, bombardeo" (5 July 1942 aircraft type AT-6B number P-80 5.25hrs flying time exploration, reconnaissance and bombing).

It is interesting to note that the Mexican press reported that Noriega had taken off with his *Escuadrilla* of Lieutenant Gandarilla Gracia in P-77 and Captain 1st Class Ignacio Ortiz Diaz de Leon in P-78, but only Noriega made the attack. The *Universal* newspaper also reported that Noriega spotted another submarine that was apparently covering the retreat of the damaged U-boat, but it was not attacked as the aircraft had already dropped their bombs.

Based on German records, two days later U-129 was forced into an emergency dive again when another North American aircraft was spotted at about 1:45 p.m.. (Lieutenant Gracia was flying P-77 that day

Another view of a recently arrived North American AT-6B armed trainer. Note the .30 cal machine gun in the rear seat. (Enrique Velasco Padilla)

on a patrol of two hours and 10 minutes).

On 6 July, but reported in a press release dated the 7th from the Presidential command and staff, it was said the Mexican ship *Cernicalo* was attacked and sunk by a submarine a short distance off the coast of Veracruz, some of the survivors reaching the small fishing town of Picolutla. However, it was later confirmed that it was not the *Cernicalo*, but a Norwegian ship reported as the "*Casmus*" (actually the Norwegian steam ship *Cadmus*) that was attacked and sunk on 1 July by U-129 in the Gulf of Mexico. Two of its crew were lost, while the 20 survivors made it to the Mexican coast in about five days, which caused the confusion over the date of the sinking.

U-129 was eventually destroyed by its crew at Bordeaux, France, on 18 August 1944 to avoid being captured by the Allies. It had sunk a total of 29 ships during 10 patrols).

Major Noriega continued to fly patrols until 24 July 1942, when sickness forced him to return to Mexico City for medical treatment. He had flown a total of 11 patrols in P-80.

By this time it was reported by the *Memorias de la Defensa Nacional* that the *2/o. Regimiento Aereo* had mobilised the following equipment:

| | |
|---|---|
| aircraft | 16 |
| parachutes | 75 |
| aerial machine guns | 32 |
| Mendoza machine gun | 1 |
| cartridges | 300,000 |
| bombs | 300 |

The regiment was put under the command of the *Region Militar del Golfo* and covered the coastal states of Tamaulipas, Veracruz, Tabasco, Campeche and Yucatan.

While these events were unfolding, by July 1942 the *1/o. Regimiento Aereo* had the following order of battle set for patrols:

| | |
|---|---|
| La Paz, Baja California 1 Squadron | 9 aircraft |
| Ensenada, BC 1 Squadron | 9 aircraft |
| Santa Rosalia, BC 1 flight | 3 aircraft |
| Mazatlan, Sinaloa 1 Patrol | 6 aircraft |
| Hermosillo, Sonora 1 flight | 3 aircraft |
| Guaymas, Sonora 1 flight | 3 aircraft |

Older aircraft such as the Azcarate Corsarios were still taking part in patrols. On 9 August 1942, Azcarate Corsario No.46 flown by Lieutenant Fernando Hernandez Vega and his observer had to drop its four MK-3/25 lb bombs due to engine problems over the state of Sonora. Hernandez Vega made an emergency landing and the bombs did not hit anything, avoiding any damage or injuries to buildings or people.

Another incident was recorded on 10 September when Vought V-99M No.37, based at La Paz, Baja California, opened machine-gun fire on an enemy submarine. The aircraft was later marked on its tail 'R.LA PAZ BC 10-IX-42'.

The Mexican air crews lacked anti-submarine warfare equipment such as radar for their aircraft.

They had to rely on their 'MK2 Eyeballs' to spot any suspicious targets, and it is possible that whales were mistaken for enemy submarines and attacked. Neither did the air crews have any survival equipment to start with if they had to ditch their aircraft in the sea. Some survival gear was later donated to the Mexican airmen via the USAAC.

The original delivery of the eight North American AT-6Cs was on 10 August 1942. Orders were issued to the *2/o. Regimiento Aereo* to send a group of eight pilots to Duncan Field, Texas, to pick up the second group of AT-6s for the Mexican air service, under the command of now Lieutenant Colonel Antonio Cardenas Rodriguez, who was assigned to the *Estado Mayor Presidencial* (Presidential Command and Staff).

After undergoing training in Texas, the group returned to Mexico on 19 August, making a stop at Monterrey, Nuevo Leon, leaving on the 23rd for Tampico and from there to Mexico City, arriving after a three-hour flight on the 24th at about 4:00 p.m. Along with the eight

One of the first six North American AT-6B trainers before being handed over to Mexican pilots at Duncan Field, Texas, in May 1942. (San Diego Air and Space Museum)

AT-6Cs, they also brought two Beechcraft AT-7 (reported in the press as Bimotore C-42) twin-engine navigator aircraft, the latter flown by additional pilots sent to pick them up.

With the additional AT-6s being flown into the country, more anti-submarine patrols were formed, as noted in another intelligence report, dated 25 September 1942. This report erroneously said the Mexican Air Force then had 10 AT-6Bs and eight AT-6Cs (there were only six AT-6Bs). It also explained how the patrols were being organized:

> Patrols along the West Coast and Lower Baja California are made each day by a flight of three planes. From Ensenada, the planes go south to the 28th parallel. This patrol covers the West Coast of Lower California and the round trip is usually made in one day.
>
> Planes from Hermosillo, cover the Gulf of California from Punta Penasco in the North to the 28th parallel in the South. Planes from Santa Rosalia and La Paz cover the rest of the Peninsula, while those from Mazatlan cover the mouth of the Gulf of California.
>
> In the Gulf of Mexico, patrols are infrequent, the aircraft being used to convoy ships running between Mexican Gulf ports and the US. The three aircraft based at Merida run one daily patrol around the Yucatan peninsula, stopping at Cozumel and Chetumal.

With these Texan planes, Major Enrique Velasco Rojas was designated as commander of the *1/o. Escuadron Aereo* of the *2/o. Regimiento Aereo*, their base of operations being Tampico, Veracruz. This squadron recorded the next Mexican Air Force attack on 22 October 1942, when Lieutenant Carlos Cervantes and his observer Cabo Jesus Vega attacked a suspicious object seen underwater.

During their first attack, they launched two 100lb bombs that did not explode. They headed back to base to reload and return to the area, where they patrolled and saw the object again and dropped two more 100lb bombs, but they too failed to explode. The squadron commander, Major Velasco, was returning from a patrol when he join the second attack, but his bomb racks did not work so he could not drop any bombs on the suspected target.

One of his pilots later accused Velasco of being too sympathetic towards the Germans in not attacking the submarine, lodging his complaints with the American liaison officer in Tampico and the Free French representative. An official report was written and sent to US military intelligence. It was suspected that the pilot's motive was to cause trouble for Velasco by labelling him pro-Nazi as revenge.

Velasco had uncovered excessive payments to ground personnel that had been transferred to them on two occasions, after which the responsible party had to reimburse the cost out of his own pocket.

In July 1943 the Air Force underwent major organisational changes, with the disbandment of the two air regiments and their replacement by individual squadrons assigned to the military zones. On 3 July, orders were issued that Major Velasco was no longer part of the *2/o. Regimiento Aereo* but was now the commander of the *3/o. Escuadron Aereo*, based at Tampico, Veracruz.

On 16 November he was assigned to the Department of Military Aeronautics, and on the 24th was put in charge of the department's Communications office.

According to Major Velasco's log book, he flew a total of 32 patrols in the Gulf of Mexico in the North American AT-6s P-85, P-86, P-87,

One of the first group of North American AT-6Bs after receiving their paint job in Mexico, in flight somewhere near Mexico City in June 1942. (Enrique Velasco Padilla)

115 and 721. He returned to Tampico to hand over the squadron to Captain 2nd Class Luis Flores Diaz on 29 December, through the intervention of Lieutenant Colonel David J. Borja. The 3rd Squadron at the time comprised the following:

Personnel:
4 Pilot Officers
1 Mechanic officer
12 Ground personnel
Equipment:
4 AT-6s (EAN-716,718,719 and 720)
3 AT-6s (EAN-715, 717 and 721, that had been transferred to Mexico City on 21 December 1943)
7 x.30 calibre flexible Browning machine guns
4 x.30 calibre fixed Browning machine guns

He returned to Mexico City to be in charge of the office of Aerial Communications on 28 January 1944, and on 7 October he was confirmed as chief of the department.

Despite their operational duties, eight AT-6C aircraft of the *2/o. Regimiento Aereo*, under the leadership of Brigadier General Miguel Molinar Simody, chief of the staff and commander of the *Region Militar del Golfo*, went on a good will visit to Havana, Cuba, on 8 October 1942.

Mexico and Cuba had signed an agreement of collaboration in anti-submarine patrols on 2 October. In February 1943, the *Cuerpo de Aviacion del Ejercito de Cuba* returned the favour with a flight of six AT-6Cs visiting Mexico, and it appears that another good will flight of Mexican AT-6s was carried out in January 1943.

In March 1943, another report on the status of aircraft shows the Mexican Air Force had 46 AT-6s of all types in service, including those that were about to be transferred under Lend Lease. The *1/o.* and *2/o. Regimiento Aereo* had the following equipment and locations:

***1/o. Regimiento Aereo:***
***Ensenada Baja California:***
3 North American AT-6s and 1 Sikorsky OS2U-3 Kingfisher
***La Paz Baja California:***
2 AT-6s and 2 O2U-4A Corsairs

***2/o. Regimiento Aereo:***
***Tampico Tamaulipas:***
2 North American AT-6s and 1 Corsario biplane
***Veracruz, Veracruz:***
5 North American AT-6s
4 Corsario biplanes
1 Consolidated Model 21-M biplane
***Merida, Yucatan:***
4 North American AT-6s

There was a further attack on a suspected enemy submarine on 22 January 1943, when Lieutenant Alfonso Gandarilla Gracia of the *2/o. Escuadron Aereo*, *2/o. Regimiento Aereo*, flying North American AT-6B P-77, attacked a suspect object following two ships, including the tanker *Potrero de Llano II*, near the port of Veracruz. He filed the following report to the regimental commander on 28 January:

> I am honoured to inform you, while undertaking my protection patrol of the tanker ship *Potrero de Llano II* and the tow boat *Pemex II*, on the 22nd of this month at the height of Laguna de Zoutecoman, I observed a suspicious submarine wake. Once I confirmed the strange wake I dropped two bombs at the head of the wake, flying over to confirm the effects of the bombs and notifying both mentioned ships so they could take necessary precautions.
>
> It was impossible to confirm if the object had been hit with the bombs. I returned to base after my relief had arrived, who I also informed what had happened so he can make his observations and take precautions.

## CONTINUING OPERATIONS

With the high tempo of operations on both coast, accidents occurred. Some were fatal, as in the case of North American AT-6C P-82 that crashed during bad weather near the town of Laja, Tamaulipas, on 7 January 1943. Lieutenant Carlos Astorga Franco and Soldier Mechanic of Aeronautics Roberto Rodriguez Bravo were killed.

The local newspaper of Tijuana reported that on 1 April 1942 a Mexican Army plane suffered an accident while landing at El Cipres airfield, giving the pilot's name as Pedro Aceves and saying the aircraft suffered damage to its propeller and engine.

2nd Lieutenant Jacobo Estrada Luna, known as 'Coca Cola', a future P-47D pilot in the Pacific war, suffered injuries in an accident on 29 November 1942 when he was taking off from El Cipres in Azcarate Corsario No.61, which was reported destroyed (there were no details whether he was flying with a crewmember or his fate).

Due to the nature of his injuries, he was reassigned back to Mexico City for medical recovery. Up until his accident, he had racked up over 171 hours flying patrols on the Pacific coast. After his recovery he was assigned to patrol duties in the Gulf Coast and later to the newly formed *Escuadron Aereo 201* in 1944 at Balbuena airfield.

Another incident was reported on 9 October 1943, an army twin engine aircraft (possibly a Beech AT-7) being forced to land due to engine trouble about 15km north of the port of Mazatlán, Sinaloa. A news report stated that one engine caught fire and lost a propeller. The crew of Major P.A. Raul Fansion and his co-pilot, 2nd Lieutenant Jesus Vazquez de Alba, made a forced landing, probably further damaging the aircraft. Major Fansion reported the aircraft and crew were heading back to base at El Cipres, Baja California, when the incident occurred.

Throughout the war years, some 48 aviation personnel lost their lives in various aviation accidents in Mexico and overseas.

Back in Mexico City at the aviation workshops, with the arrival of more North American AT-6C Texans thoughts turned to increasing the bomb load of the AT-6, as mentioned by historian Dan Hagedorn in his book *Texans and Harvards in Latin America* (Air Britain Publications Ltd, 2009):

> A request was directed to North American Aviation in early December 1942 from the CO of the FAM Gral. De Brigada Gustavo A Salinas. Oddly rather than direct the inquiry to the USAAF's Wright Field logistics centre, he requested the NAA to rush the drawings that had developed showing the preliminary design installation for the AT-6Bs and AT-6Cs to mount AN-MK-17 aircraft depth bombs.
>
> The NAA advised him that, although they were sending the drawings, they had not actually made any such installations. It is not clear if the FAM intended to fabricate such installations themselves, as their AT-6 fleet was being used entirely for such duty, or if indeed any such installations were made.

This was mentioned in the *Memorias* (annual reports published by each department of the Mexican government) of September 1943 to August 1944. Nothing more is known of the project or if it even got to a prototype phase.

With the arrival of the Texans, the *Dirrecion de Aeronautica* made the decision in 1943 to retire its general purpose biplanes from coastal patrols, since they offered little by way of safety for the crews. The surviving examples of the Vought V-99M, Azcarate Corsarios and Consolidated Model 21-M were concentrated at Balbuena airfield. Before this happened, the disposition of Mexican military aircraft in service was reported to the US military via the Mexico City military attache to be as follows:

AT-6: 46 were operational, with 30 being assigned to Mexico City (Balbuena), 3 at Ensenada, Baja California, 2 at Tampico Tamaulipas, 2 at La Paz, Baja California, 5 at Veracruz, Veracruz, and 4 at Merida, Yucatan.

Vought-OS2U-3: 1 at NAS Alameda, California, 1 at Ensenada, Baja California, and 4 at the Aviation workshops (getting ready to be transfered over to the navy).

Then Lieutenant Luis Noriega Medrano in training in the USA in the 1930s. He attacked U-129 on 5 July 1942. (via Dan Hagedorn)

Consolidated dive bombers (Model 21-M): 1 at Veracruz and 3 at Mexico City.

Corsairs O2U-4 (Azcarate Corsarios): 2 at La Paz, Baja California, 1 at Tampico, Tamaulipas, 4 at Veracruz, Veracruz, and 3 at Mexico City.

Corsairs V-99M (Vought): 2 at La Paz, Baja California, 1 at Tampico, Tamaulipas, 4 at Veracruz and 3 at Mexico City.

AT-07 (Beechcraft): 1 at Mexico City.

In reference to AT-6 operations in the far away area of the Peninsula of Yucatan that covered the states of Yucatan and Quintana Roo, a US assessment of those places reported that on 20 March 1943 a flight of three examples from the *Comandancia Central de Campos* were sent to Chetumal, Quintana Roo. This patrol connected with others from Merida, Yucatan, and helped cover the area of operations. The Yucatan flight personnel were Major Severiano Pulido Ortiz, Captain 1st Class Roberto Talamantes Corbala and Captain 2nd Class Francisco Bulnes Rivadeneira.

They had previous experience serving with the *1/o. Regimiento Aereo* on the Pacific coast and had flown biplanes. They now covered allied and Mexican shipping travelling between Chetumal and the island of Cozumel, helping the other units operating from Merida.

These pilots were operating with minimal support, flying over shark-infested waters. The Merida unit had two aircraft and crews operating between Progreso and Ciudad del Carmen. A US Navy officer detailed with this unit, flying with the Mexican pilots as an observer and gunner, reported that they would make longer flights, reaching as far as San Julian in Cuba to cover the gap, trying to locate German submarines.

## ORGANISATIONAL CHANGES

Brigadier General Gustavo Salinas Camina, who had been in charge of the *Dirreccion de Aeronautica* since December 1942, replacing General Roberto Fierro Villalobos, implemented changes to the operational

El Convoy en el Golfo de México

A newspaper report of a correspondent's participation in a coastal patrol over the Gulf of Mexico with Lieutenant Alfonso Gandarilla Gracia. (Author Collection)

structure of the air service.

On 1 July 1943, the regimental system was discarded, replaced with an initial six (later eight) individual numbered *Escuadrones Aereos*,which were located as follows:

1/o. Escuadron Aereo 2/o. Zona Militar, El Cipres, Baja California
2/o. Escuadron Aereo 3/o. Zona Militar, La Paz, Baja California
3/o. Escuadron Aereo 8/o. Zona Militar, Tampico, Tamaulipas
4/o. Escuadron Aereo 26/o. Zona Militar, Veracruz, Veracruz
5/o. Escuadron Aereo 32/o. Zona Militar, Mérida, Yucatán
(this squadron had flights stationed at Chetumal and Cozumel, Quintana Roo)
6/o. Escuadron Aereo 29/o. Zona Militar, Ciudad Ixtepec, Oaxaca
7/o. Escuadron Aereo 1/o. Zona Militar, Ciudad de México
8/o. Escuadron Aereo 1/o. Zona Militar, Ciudad de México

The 6th Squadron was moved south to a new location on the Pacific coast in the state of Oaxaca, with two new squadrons formed to receive more American-made aircraft under Lend Lease.

Another organisation that was formed at Balbuena airfield was the *Comandancia Central de Campos*, which also had the mission to train pilots on the North American AT-6 as an operational training unit (OTU). This unit had 30 AT-6s, three Consolidated model 21-Ms, three Vought O2U-4As (Azcarate), six V-99Ms and one Beech AT-7. The American report about this unit goes into more details about its activities and offers some opinions about it:

> [A] nebulous organization, having no tactical function. It is more a repository for unassigned aircraft and personnel.

In *Texans and Harvards in Latin America*, author Dan Hagedorn wrote the following on this interesting unit and the role it was playing during this time, when Mexico was getting more aircraft and replacing old machines from the units involved in patrolling the Mexican coasts:

> Meanwhile the U.S. Attache in Mexico had been directed to determine more about the 'Nebulous' *Comandancia Central de Campo* at Balbuena, and determine exactly why so many AT-6s that had been sent to Mexico were languishing there – with nothing better to do than make mass, politically motivated flights to other nations in the region.
>
> He reported on June 7th that … its main function is to see that pilots assigned to headquarters in Mexico City are kept up to date on their flying … And it is accepted that once the reorganization of the Mexican Air Force is completed, the command will disappear.
>
> He went on to say, however, that the aircraft were in fact being utilized to train pilots … who have not flown for more than a year, as well as those familiar only with biplanes and that a course of some 12 to 15 hours on AT-6s has been instituted.
>
> This involved three hours of transition training and familiarization, landing and traffic patterns, the final two hours being occupied with solo touch and go landings and take offs. This was followed by three hours of figure eights, pylon eights, lazy eights and similar co-ordination manoeuvers.
>
> Not less that two hours were devoted to discovering the stall characteristics of the AT-6 in power on, power off, turns and straight flying attitudes and finally three to five hours [to] formation flights. He observed that FAM officers giving this training had graduated recently from U.S. Flying Schools and that they were … excellent pilots and very competent instructors.

On 1 July 1943, three air groups were created to gather together the individual squadrons: *1/o. Grupo de Escuadrones Aereos*, with headquarters at Mexico City; *2/o. Grupo de Escuadrones Aereos*, with headquarters at Veracruz, Veracruz; *and 3/o. Grupo de Escuadrones Aereos*, with headquarters at El Cipres, Baja California.

A US report of 20 July 1943 stated that the squadron at Merida had grow in strength, with 12 pilots, one maintenance officer, seven AT-6s and five OS2U-1 Kingfishers, operating on wheels, replacing six OS2U-3s, of which five were being handed over to the Mexican Navy.

The squadron was commanded by Major P.A. Severiano Pulido.

By 29 July, the American report showed that Mexico now had 52 AT-6s, but 37 were assigned to the patrol squadrons.

On the Pacific coast, by August 1943 there were about 12 AT-6s to patrol the peninsula of Baja California, distributed in three areas. During operations here it was reported that a North American AT-6 piloted by Vermeda G. Rodriguez was involved in an accident due to fuel shortage, crashing near Altar Sonora.

By August, the *3/o. Grupo de Escuadrones Aereos* at Baja California had replaced its biplanes with the North American AT-6 Texan trainers, the first four having arrived in early 1943. Four were stationed at La Paz, three at Cabo San Lucas, way down on the tip of the peninsula, and five at El Cipres. Even with new aircraft now in service, there were some issues concerning maintenance support and quality of the airfields they were operating from. Dan Hagedorn wrote in his study of Mexican use of the AT-6:

> [T]he seven aircraft on the southern patrols had no spares whatsoever and, in fact the crews themselves did not even have life jackets – which must have been a matter of some concern. The sandy soil of the majority of the airfields merely aggravated the maintenance problems.
>
> The local U.S. Assistant attache at the time, Captain Paul B. Miller, AC took it upon himself to locate and present to the unit commander, five life jackets, as well as a gallon of hydraulic fluid and gaskets for the landing gear oleo struts. In spite of these conditions, the unit commander planned to extend the patrols to include the islas Tres Marias, which would mean a flight of some 170 miles over the open waters.
>
> To help keep the sand out of the aircraft, the crews has constructed shelters themselves at San Lucas, La Paz, Puerto Cortes and Ensenada.

By July 1943 it was reported that four AT-6s were out of service, with daily patrols stopped in favour of dedicated escort missions for Mexican and allied shipping passing through Mexican waters.

One squadron, the 3rd (later the *Escuadron Aereo 204*) carried patrols up to the United States to extend the coverage, the unit having acquired landing, refuelling and maintenance rights at Brownsville, Texas.

The first patrol to use the American facilities was undertaken by

A Mexican pilot with a North American AT-6 Texan armed with 100lb bombs ready for an anti-submarine patrol, probably in the Gulf of Mexico. (Enrique Velasco Padilla)

Lieutenant Fernando Hernandez Vega, a future P-47D pilot.

By 8 October 1943, the former *5/o. Escuadron Aereo*, now known as *Escuadron Aereo 206*, had two aircraft stationed at Merida, Yucatan, and four more at Cozumel; one had been damaged in an accident, but was reported repairable.

This squadron had an interesting way to maintain radio communications with it aircraft while on patrol. Using the radio set from one of the aircraft that was not flying, they performed a radio check every 15 minutes when the aircraft was flying a zig-zag course at an average speed of about 110mph over ships and convoys. The average mission time was between 90 minutes and two hours.

Other units such as the *6/o. Escuadron Aereo* (later *Escuadron Aereo 207*) at Ixtepec, Oaxaca, were responsible for flying as escorts over US Army troop transportation ships heading to the Panama Canal. This unit was supposed to have nine aircraft, but usually only had five servicable.

It would also suffered problems with spare parts and from being isolated to a far region. In its escort missions, the average radio checks were done every 30 minutes, also using as a ground station one of the unit's aircraft that was not flying that day.

By March 1944 the *3/o. Grupo de Escuadrones Aereos* on the Pacific coast was reportedly operating 18 aircraft, of which 10 were AT-6s, the remainder being the old biplanes which should have been remove from front-line service in 1943. The *Escuadron Aereo 203* at La Paz, with a detachment at Cabo San Lucas, was reported to have flown about 300 hours of patrol time in 10 months under difficult conditions, with no incidents to report.

In July 1944 the *3/o. Grupo de Escuadrones Aereos* lost one of its squadrons to the *2/o. Grupo de Escuadrones Aereos*, leaving the former with just two squadrons (202 and 203). *Escuadron Aereo 202* later operated two Douglas A-24B dive bombers.

The *2/o. Grupo de Escuadrones Aereos* had a leader who set an example to all his pilots and ground personnel.

Colonel Alfonso Cruz Rivera (a future chief of the Mexican Air Force), commander of the *2/o. Regimiento Aereo* from 1 June 1942, was named the head of the *2/o. Grupo de Escuadrones Aereos* on 1 July 1943. His headquarters were at Las Bajadas, Veracruz, and he had under his command *Escuadrones Aereos 204*, *205*, *206* and *207*, equipped with the AT-6 and Kingfishers for patrol duties in the Gulf of Mexico, part of the southern Pacific coast and the peninsula of Yucatan into the Caribbean close to Cuba.

Colonel Cruz Rivera believed in setting an example, and participated from January 1943 to August 1945 in 56 patrols, accumulating 136 hours and 45 minutes of flying time, using the aircraft of the *Escuadron Aereo 205* at Las Bajadas, Veracruz.

These squadrons later received a three-digit number, running from 201 to 209.

In June 1944 the American aviation magazine *Western Flying* published an article by Lynn Thomas, who was given permission by the Mexican military not only to report about the advances in Mexican military aviation but also to fly with them in different parts of the country.

One of the units that Thomas flew with was *Escuadron Aereo 202* out of El Cipres, after which he gave the following assessment of Mexican airmanship:

> The Mexicans make good pilots. They are alert, quick to learn and are capable of flying the hottest ships. I have flown many thousands of miles with them and they have earned my respect.
>
> In fact, I have just completed a 4,000 mile aerial tour with their Pacific patrols. This trip took me up and down Mexico's western sea frontier, over ocean, desert and mountain ranges that would mean

Two civilians standing in front of an armed AT-6 Texan trainer. Note the two 100lb bombs and .30 cal machine gun on the wing. (Enrique Velasco Padilla)

A shark's mouth painted on the cowling of the AT-6C EAN-711, probably after 1943. (Author Collection)

sure death in event of a forced landing.

One squadron with which I flew was the 202nd, patrolling Baja California. For two and a half years it was under the command of Major Raul E Foullon, setting one of the best safety records in the entire air force; no accidents to either men or planes during all this time, despite the high number of air hours flown over the difficult terrain every day.

The squadron is now commanded by Captain Roberto Talamante. Major Foullon commands a dive bombing unit which may be ready for overseas duty soon. I flew on patrol with the squadron over terrain which was about the worst I have ever seen. On these flights we flew Douglas A-24s and North American AT-6 equipped with machine guns and bomb racks, and I had to qualify as a gunner to fly as part of the crew.

We were in Baja California where the jagged peaks tower 12,000 feet into the air and all the country is strictly desert with no landing spots or water available.

Thomas also interviewed General Gustavo Salinas, who gave an assessment on his pilots, their training and equipment to meet any post-war challenges:

> Our pilots, our planes and our maintenance must be good to fly over country like this,' General Salinas said. 'Casualty figures in our air force are low, very low. We first of all insist upon taking every precaution before the plane goes on a cross country flight.
>
> 'The air force maintains a first class weather bureau and pilots in the air or on the ground know just what lies ahead. Also on a cross country flight radio contact is established and kept at all times between the aircraft and ground stations.'

By November 1944, as things were advancing in favour of the Allies in the Pacific war, a new threat had appeared on the Pacific coast. The Japanese started sending fire balloons, or *Fu-Go* (Windship Weapons), using the jet streams over the northern Pacific Ocean to launch hydrogen-filled balloons to attack and cause panic on the Canadian and American west coast.

The balloons each carried a combination of incendiary and anti-personnel devices. From November 1944 to April 1945, over 9,300 such balloons were launched, but it appears that only about 300 of them made it to the North American continent. Some were found or observed from Canada all the way down to northern Mexico (Baja California and Sonora).

One balloon landed at Sonoyta, Sonora, and another was shot down on 28 March 1945 over Laguna Salada near Mexicali, the state capital of Baja California, by a Chance Vought F4U Corsair of VBF-14, flown by Lieutenant Roland N. Kenton USNR stationed at NAAS Ream Field, Imperial Beach, California.

A view from a Mexican AT-6 flying convoy escort over an armed merchant ship. (Enrique Velasco Padilla)

Kenton was veteran naval fighter pilot who had fought in the Battle of Guadalcanal, flying F4F Wildcats and getting credit for three Japanese seaplanes on the water in 1942. This would be his only aerial kill of the war and the only kill credited to VBF-14, which did not see action, only making it to Hawaii before the war ended.

American fighter aircraft of the 4th and 11th Air Force and Royal Canadian Air Force fighters shot down about 20 of these balloons, nine over the Aleutians Islands by Lockheed P-38 Lightings of the 54th fighter squadron in April 1945.

The only casualties that these balloons caused occurred on 5 May 1945, when the pregnant wife of a pastor and five children from their Sunday school were killed on a picnic near Bly, Oregon, when they came across a fire balloon that exploded, possibly touched by one of the youngsters.

This was not reported at the time to prevent panic among the general public.

Among the accidents involving Mexican pilots reported in the last year of the war was a North American AT-6 from *Escuadron Aereo 206*, in which pilot Raul J. Escalante was killed about eight miles north of Islas de las Mujeres.

Based on available records and reports, the *2/o. Regimiento Aereo*, from 27 June 1942 until 20 June 1943, protected not only Mexican shipping, but American, Cuban, Spanish and Norwegian vessels passing through the Gulf of Mexico, compiling the following numbers:

Total flying hours 7,364 hours and 44 minutes
Hours on standby 485 hours and 30 minutes
Protected in 463 missions 1,719,733 tons of cargo (including fuel)
Total fuel consumed 738,504 litres
Total oil consumed 10,443.75 litres

These patrols were accomplished with aircraft (biplanes and the AT-6) that were not designed for such duty, flying at low altitude and up to 100 miles off the coast, with the crews initially lacking even basic survival gear. From 1 July to 31 December 1943, the *2/o. Grupo de Escuadrones Aereos* compiled the following numbers:

*Total Flying Hours 9,976 hours and 4 minutes*
*Protected in 704 missions 3,361,521 tons of cargo (including fuel)*

From September 1944 to August 1945, the Mexican Air Force reported to have flown in training more than 24,807 flight hours, plus some 8,348 in service, including patrols on both coasts and other duties.

A number of international flights were undertaken to the United States and to Central and South America, including one to take home the remains of Chilean pilots who had been killed in a crash in Mexico while flying an aircraft to their country.

A *Centro General de Entrenamiento* (General Centre of Training) was organised for flight personnel who were not assigned to the squadrons so that they could still keep up with their flight training.

The *Talleres Generales de Aeronautica* (TGA) aviation workshops was reported to have repaired 60 aircraft and 30 engines.

General Salinas was contemplating the creation of a 1,000-plane air force after the war, as he told author Lynn Thomas in 1944, predicting that Mexican aviators would have to contend with problems on the

Colonel Donovan of the 97th BG and his staff, with Colonel Antonio Cardenas Rodriguez (middle with flight jacket) when he visited the 97th in North Africa in 1943. (Mis Dos Misiones)

southern border with Guatemala:

> These planes may see services in Central America, too. For there is the possibility that Mexico may one day go to war with the little dictator country of Guatemala her neighbour to the south.
>
> There is a serious tension existing between these two countries. The Guatemalan forces stationed along the border have made provoking runs into Mexican territory. The long suffering Mexican government might conceivably lose patience and decide to put an end to the affair by taking over the country.
>
> In that event her 1,000 plane air force would be a powerful weapon indeed.

Interestingly, these words, written in 1944, would almost come true in the late 1950s when Mexican fishing boats were fired upon by the Guatemalan Air Force.

Brigadier General Gustavo A Salinas and Captain 2nd Class Radames Gaxiola Andrade during their tour of USAAF bases in the UK in 1944. (National Archives)

CHAPTER 3

# THE VOLUNTEERS, OBSERVERS AND SPITFIRES

Mexico's priorities were firstly to establish the defence of its shipping and coastal areas against any external aggression, secondly the modernisation of its armed forces and thirdly to gain experience in actual combat operations. For the latter, Mexican armed forces personnel would go to the United States and overseas as observers, with some actively participating in the war.

## THE OBSERVERS

In 1943 a group of Mexican officers went to North Africa to observe the war there against Germany and Italy up close from 28 April to 6 July. Among the officers was Lieutenant Colonel Antonio Cardenas Rodriguez of the Mexican air service. The group left Washington DC in a Boeing B-17 bomber aircraft, arriving at Aoumid airfield in Tunisia on 14 May, two days after the Allied occupation of the city of

Tunis.

Four days later the Mexican mission arrived at the headquarters of the US Fifth Army.

Here Cardenas met with Major General James H. Doolittle, commander of the Northwest African Strategic Air Force (NAAF), who assigned him to General Joseph H. Atkinson, head of the 5th Air Division, who in turn assigned him to the 97th Bomb Group (H) under the command of Colonel Stanley J. Donovan. This B-17 group had been assigned to the 8th Air Force in in England October 1942, where it had become the first combat-ready B-17 unit in the UK. On 17 August 1942, the group undertook its first combat operation, conducting a bombing mission against the Rouen-Sotteville marshalling yards in France.

After the 97th's arrival in North Africa it was first assigned to the 12th Air Force, but in November 1943 waswas transferred to the 15th Air Force. The group had four heavy bomber squadrons: the 340th, 341st, 342nd and 414th.

In his book *Mis Dos Misiones* (My Two Missions), Cardenas wrote that Doolittle assigned him to the 97th Bomb Group for three days, but that later Doolittle extended his stay for several more days to observe and participate in combat missions.

After his return to Mexico, Cardenas reported that he participated in four bombing missions, hitting the enemy airfield at Castelvetrano in Sicily, the island of Pantelleria, plus targets in Palermo, Sicily, and Naples, Italy. He wrote that he arrived at the 97th Bomb Group on 18 May and the next day flew with the mission to Castelvetrano, but the 97th's records show they did not hit Castelvetrano until the 21st. This was the only mission that Cardenas wrote about in detail in his book, only mentioning in passing his participation in the other missions.

Looking at the mission roster of the 97th, the group hit Castelvetrano on 21May, Bo Rizzo airfield, Sicily, on the 22nd, La Maddalena, Sardinia, on the 24th, Messina, Sicily, on the 25th and Naples on the 30th.

Regarding the mission to Castelvetrano, Cardenas mentions that it started with a take-off time of 0746 and involved 27 B-17s, but two returned early. At about 1010 the B-17s dropped 3,600 20lb fragmentations bombs on the airfield, which was home to about 80 enemy aircraft. Three German Me-323 'Giant' transport planes were seen burning on the ground.

The bombers came under attack from about 20German BF-109s and one Italian Macchi fighter.

The 97th Bomb Group gunners claimed eight enemy aircraft shot down, but only six were confirmed. On the return trip the 97th was again attacked by enemy fighters, which flew overhead and dropped bombs on the formation, but did not hit any of the B-17s. The group only suffered one B-17 damaged, with two wounded crewmembers. After the raid, photographs were taken and a claim for 48 enemy aircraft destroyed or damaged on the ground was submitted.

Cardenas wrote that a total of 112 B-17s participated in the raid (other groups such as the 99th also took part), with an escort of 60 Lockheed P-38 Lightning fighters from the 1st, 14th and 82nd Fighter Groups. The B-17s gunners claimed a total of 10 enemy aircraft shot down, while the escorts claimed seven, for the loss of one B-17 and another damaged, with the escort fighters losing eight P-38s.

The 97th Bomb Group continued to serve during the war, flying a total 483 combat missions and losing 114 aircraft.

After his stay with the 97th Bomb Group, Cardenas visited the Northwest African Training Command (NATC), under the command of Brigadier General John K. Cannon, in particular the Bomber Training Center. The latter was an OTU (Operational Training Unit) at Sale near Rabat in the French protectorate of Morocco for newly trained bomber crews from the United States to introduce them to actual combat theatre conditions.

This unit had B-17, B-25, B-26, A-20 and A-36 aircraft.

Cardenas reported that while participating in a training flight in a Martin B-26 as an observer, the aircraft suffered an engine failure on take-off and made an emergency landing. The aircraft was destroyed by fire but all aboard managed to get out with various injuries. Cardenas says he suffered broken ribs and wounds on both legs that required hospitalisation in Rabat, where he remained until he was able to travel back to Casablanca to rejoin the rest of the Mexican mission.

So far the author has been unable to find any further information on this incident.

The Mexican group returned to the United States, arriving in New York on 8 July. Upon his return, Cardenas reported that he had flown for 157 hours as a crewmember and observer.

In 1944, the commander of the now designated *Fuerza Aerea Mexicana* (Mexican Air Force), Brigadier General Gustavo A. Salinas, was invited by the US War Department and US Air Force to visit various combat fronts in North Africa, Italy, England and later Normandy, France. On this trip, which ran from 19 June to 28 July, Salinas was accompanied by Captain 2nd Class Radames Gaxiola Andrade (1919-66), who had trained under the USAAC system, and was a test pilot for the military aviation workshops and an aide and pilot for the general. The following news items reported General Gustavo Salinas at the different war fronts:

> The *Pittsburgh Press* and the *Chicago Imly News*. Inc. RDME, June 28 Brig. Gen. Gustavo Salinas, chief of military aviation of Mexico, has arrived in Rome as a guest of the Allied command. He will tour the Italian front as an air observer. Gen. Salinas' trip is believed to be a preliminary part of the plan to assign certain units of the Mexican Air Force to war theaters for combat duty. Capt. Raddamas Gaxiola, one of the best pilots in the Mexican Army, accompanied the general. This is the second Mexican mission to visit the Mediterranean theater within a year.

> INVASION SAVED U. S. FROM GERMAN ROBOTS, SAYS MEXICAN GENERAL
> MEXICO CITY – (UP) – August 16 1944. A Mexican air force General back from a tour of the European theatre says the invasion of Normandy prevented a possible robot bomb attack on the United States. General Gustavo Salinas says Allied troops discovered a giant launching ramp designed for the use of 16-ton flying robots. He says these were intended to travel the stratosphere to east coast seaboard cities.

Later, during his training in Texas in 1945, Captain Gaxiola Andrade was recommended for the USAAF senior wings and the European Theater Ribbon, with the following details about his qualifications:

> [S]ince Gaxiola's graduation in 1939, he has flown approximately 3,000 hours, thus becoming eligible from the flying time standpoint. Favorable consideration of this request would illustrate close friendship existing between the Mexican Air Force and the US Air Force.
>
> It is also requested that authority be granted for Captain Gaxiola to wear the European Theater Ribbon to which he is entitled in view of his service on an official war department mission in a combat theater from 19 June to 28 July 1944.
>
> During that time Captain Gaxiola was subjected to enemy bombardment as well as enemy anti-aircraft fire while acting as

[the] pilot of a U.S. Army Airplane.

This award was also considered for General Salinas and three other Mexican Army generals who went overseas to observe the conduct of the war in Europe. During Salinas and Gaxiola Andrade's visit to France they visited the headquarters of the 9th Air Force and installations in the Normandy area.

A senior military mission headed by Mexican Army General Eulogio Ortiz and Brigadier Generals Ramon Rodriguez Familiar and Beltran Moreno went to Europe to visit the different war fronts and reportedly to assist in the planning of the defeat of Axis forces.

## THE VOLUNTEERS

Meanwhile, a number of Mexican nationals or those of American, British and French descent volunteered to fight with the Allied armies during the war. In an informal talk given by Major General Guy V. Henry, US Army, before a meeting of the Offices of the Coordinator of Inter-American Affairs on 3 January 1945, he said:

> Indirectly, Mexican personnel have participated in the war effort. Approximately 6,000 individuals of Mexican birth have been inducted into the Army of the United States. Probably 4,000 of these still remain in that Army.
>
> Many of these have participated in combat overseas and have returned, and are now proudly visiting their homes in Mexico, wearing their overseas decorations, including the Purple Heart, together with their overseas service stripes.
>
> Some of these individuals were American citizens before induction; large numbers of other have acquired citizenship since induction under the law permitting this for honorable service in the armed forces of the United States.

The US War Department reported that a total of 14,849 Mexicans took part in the war under the American flag, and about 1,492 were killed or lost their lives during their service.

About half a million Latinos – including first-generation born in the United States of Mexican parents – served in the US armed forces during the Second World War. Of this total, about 9,206 were killed in action or accidents, or died from sickness, 887 were reported missing in action and 2,422 were prisoners of war. Twelve were awarded the highest US award for valour, the Medal of Honor.

A number of Mexicans, or Mexicans of European descent, joined the Royal Air Force (RAF) or Royal Canadian Air Force (RCAF), with more going to Canada due to its proximity. Some struggled to deal with the language and educational requirements, but in their quest to serve the Allies, many managed to overcome such obstacles.

Many served in the training command in Canada or in the United Kingdom, or in units tasked with the defence of Canada. Those who joined the RAF were enlisted in the RAFVR (Royal Air Force Volunteer Reserve). What follows is some of the more well-known volunteers.

## COMMONWEALTH AIR FORCES; ROYAL AIR FORCE AND ROYAL CANADIAN AIR FORCE

### 1. Pilot Officer Luis Perez Gomez, Spitfire pilot, RCAF

Pilot Officer Luis Perez Gomez of Guadalajara, Jalisco, who was born on 8 October 1922, joined the Royal Canadian Air Force on 30 June 1942. He received his wings on 6 August 1943, and was classified as a fighter pilot. He was trained in No.1 OTU (Operational Training Unit) in Bagotville, Quebec, Canada. Perez Gomez was posted to No.127 (F) Squadron at Dartmouth, Nova Scotia, in November 1943, flying patrols in the Hawker Hurricane MKXII and training in the North American Harvard.

No.127 was one of many squadrons that were formed in 1942 for the defence of the Canadian east coast. Perez Gomez flew these aircraft from November to December 1943, participating in a number of scrambles of reported unidentified aircraft, which turned out to be friendly, approaching the coast.

On 23 December 1943, Squadron Leader Henry Wallace Mcleod DFC and Bar, a notable veteran fighter pilot from Malta with 13 kills plus three probables and 12 damaged, took command of No.127. In January 1944 No.127 was among six Canadian fighter squadrons that were ordered to England to prepare for the upcoming invasion of France.

After their arrival in England it became No.443 RCAF (F) Squadron, flying Supermarine Spitfires, part of No.144 (RCAF) Wing of No.83 Group of the 2nd Tactical Air Force. No.144 Wing was under the command of Wing Commander Johnny. E. Johnson DSO and Bar, DFC and Bar, a top scoring pilot with 34 kills and seven shared victories, three probables and two shared probable, 10 damaged and three shared damaged, and one shared destroyed on the ground.

Perez Gomez saw action before and during the invasion of Normandy, escorting medium bombers to targets over France, dive bombing Noball sites (V-1 flying bomb launch sites) near the French coast and carrying out weather reconnaissance and fighter sweeps. After the start of the invasion, No.443 was involved in a number of patrols over the beachheads. He flew the majority of his combat missions in the Spitfire MK.IXB 2I-S/MK607.

On 15 June No.443, with the rest of No.144 Wing RCAF, moved from England to Ste Croix Sur Mer (B3) to start operations from French soil. The next day, in a late evening fighter sweep near Caen, Perez Gomez was part of a formation of six Spitfires MK.IXB, but due to poor weather conditions only four aircraft – including that of Perez Gomez – became involved in an aerial combat over the town of Sassy against eight FW-190s of 1/JG1. During the dogfights, all four Spitfires were shot down with three pilots killed, among them Perez Gomez, whose aircraft 2I-S went down near Sassy.

The one pilot who survived (his aircraft also crashed near Sassy) evaded capture by German ground forces and later rejoined No.443. Two FW-190s also went down during the battle, with one pilot killed and the other wounded, but since nobody claimed them, they were not included in the squadron totals.

Pilot Officer Luis Perez Gomez of Guadalajara, Jalisco, with a Spitfire of No.443 RCAF Squadron before the invasion of Europe in 1944. (RCAF)

Pilot Officer Perez Gomez flew a total of 29 combat missions before he was killed. He is considered the only Mexican to die in the service of the RCAF in the Second World War. He is buried in the cemetery at Sassy, Calvados, where he fell. Recently the town named a public square in his honour.

No.443 Squadron RCAF would finish the war with 36 enemy aircraft claimed destroyed, two probables and 12 claimed damaged, plus six enemy aircraft destroyed on the ground and 17 probably destroyed on the ground. On the debit side, No.443 lost nine pilots, plus six as prisoners of war, and five more evaded capture.

### 2. Pilot Officer Thomas Benfield Lee, Spitfire pilot, RCAF

Spitfire pilot Pilot Officer Thomas Benfield Lee of No.402 RCAF Squadron, after receiving his wings on 4 March 1941. (RCAF)

Another Mexican who flew Spitfires in combat was Thomas Benfield Lee Olmstead (known as T.B. Lee) of Pachuca, Hidalgo, born in March 1920 to a British father and American mother. He joined the RCAF in November 1939, his first job being a telephone switch operator, before he opted to become a pilot after he heard a talk from veteran fighter pilots of the Battle of Britain who were touring RCAF bases.

Going through the different stages of pilot training, including twin-engine flying, he received his wings on 4 March 1941, hoping for a combat assignment. However, he was mostly assigned to training duties in Canada until December 1942, when he was sent to England, but instead of an operational combat unit he was again assigned to training command.

Serving as a flight instructor in Scotland and around the UK, he tried to convince his superiors the weather in Scotland was not good for him and was affecting his performance. Hoping for a transfer to Italy, again he was denied operations.

In September 1944 he returned to Canada on leave to visit his family there and in Mexico. With the war progressing in favour of the Allies and some worried about their post-war positions in the RAF, many English pilots started to request posting to training command, freeing up spaces for RCAF personnel in combat duty.

After Lee return to England in December 1944 he was assigned to OTU to convert to fighter aircraft – the Supermarine Spitfire. He was later reassigned to the 83 Group Support Unit that ferried aircraft from England to the combat front.

On 14 April 1945, Flying Officer Lee was assigned to No.402 (F) RCAF Fighter Squadron, 126 RCAF Wing, 83 Group of the 2nd Tactical Air Force. This squadron had been in the UK since 1942, first as No.2 (F) Squadron RCAF flying the Hawker Hurricane MK.I/II. In December 1942 it was designated No.402 (F) Squadron 'City of Winnipeg'.

Lee finally started operational missions on 15 April 1945, flying armed reconnaissance missions with his squadron, hitting targets of opportunity in Spitfire MK.XIVcs. By this time all missions were being flown only with cannon and machine-gun ammunition, with no bombs or rockets being used against the retreating Germans.

On 20 April, the Spitfires of 126 Wing (No.402 and No.401 squadrons) were involved in a series of dogfights around Hagenow aerodrome in northern Germany. The Canadian pilots claimed 20 German aircraft shot down, plus six more damaged, for the loss of just one pilot and his aircraft to German anti-aircraft fire. Lee claimed one of the two FW-190s that No.402 was credited with, flying the Spitfire MK.XIVc AE-Y/RM651.

He wrote in his after-action report that he scored hits on the FW-190 around the cockpit area; the German pilot did not bail out, crashing into a house and causing an explosion and fire.

On 30 April, he was involved in his second aerial combat, with FW-190s and Junkers Ju-188s, above the northern German city of Schwerin. No.402 was credited with shooting down six German aircraft (four FW-190s and two Ju-188s) and damaging two more FW-190s.

They also destroyed three FW-190s on the ground and damaged two FW-190s and two more Ju-88 bombers. Lee was credited with damaging the two FW-190s as a squadron credit.

On 4 May, returning from a fighter sweep to Denmark, his formation was attacked by an Me-262 jet fighter, resulting in one aircraft being damaged but the pilot escaping unharmed.

This would be No.402's last encounter with German aircraft. The next day all operations were suspended. During his two months of operations, Lee completed 23 combat missions.

After the end of the war, he returned to Mexico to fly in commercial aviation in the peninsula of Baja California. He later moved to Canada to live in retirement, and he passed away aged 81 on 18 April 2001.

No.402 Squadron RCAF ended the war with the claimed destruction of 49½ enemy aircraft plus five V-1 flying bombs, along with 14 probables and 57½ damaged, for the loss of 49 of its pilots.

### 3. Sergeant Wireless Operator/Air Gunner Francisco Lua Manzo, RCAF

Another Mexican volunteer who flew in the Royal Canadian Air Force was Sergeant Wireless Operator/Air Gunner Francisco Lua Manzo, who was born on 11 January 1923 in Mexico.

He travelled to Vancouver, British Columbia, and enlisted in the RCAF on 18 February 1943. After his training in Canada he was posted overseas to the United Kingdom in early October, joining No.427 'Lion' Bomber Squadron RCAF on 31 October 1944, based at Leeming in Yorkshire. No.427 was part of No.6 Bomber Group, the squadron having formed in 1942 with Vickers Wellington bombers and flying its first mission in December that year. Manzo, a wireless operator, was part of a crew that also included

Flight Lieutenant Rob M. Gould (pilot),
Flying Officer R.A. Graham (navigator),
Flying Officer C.H. Robinson (bomb aimer),
Sergeant Killburn C. Embree (engineer),
Sergeant J.D. Dixon (rear gunner) and

Sergeant Wireless Operator/Air Gunner Francisco Lua Manzo RCAF, of No.427 'Lion' RCAF Bomber Squadron. (RCAF)

Sergeant Chuck H. Holmstron (mid upper gunner).

Manzo and his crewmates flew 30 combat missions, with 18 in Handley Page MK.III and 12 in Avro Lancaster MK.I heavy bombers. He left the unit on 25 April 1945, completing his tour of operations on the day that No.427 flew its last combat mission of the war. He returned first to Canada and was discharged from the RCAF on 17 August 1945, then going back to Mexico. (unknown)

During the war, No.427 flew 3,328 operational sorties and dropped 10,294 tons of bombs, claiming the destruction of 10 enemy aircraft, one probable and 10 damaged. The squadron lost 90 aircraft in operations and 522 aircrew, of which 447 were classified as missing in action and 35 killed in action; 10 became prisoners of war and 11 evaded capture and made it back to the UK.

Manzo is remembered by one of his fellow crew members:

> Frank came from the area of Mexico City to join the R.C.A.F. – where he trained in Canada I don't know. He was quite a character on the ground and [a] favorite to have on leave or at parties. (Discipline was not his strong point.)
>
> In the air on operations he was all business and dedicated to the task. I remember a contest which he won as the fastest on the squadron to send and receive on the wireless. This talent was a saving benefit to the crew on more than one occasion.

### 4. Pilot Officer Sebastian Bernardo De Mier, RAFVR

Sebastian Bernardo de Mier, who was born in Mexico City on 10 March 1912, was the son of the Mexican ambassador to the United Kingdom and France. After the death of his father and with revolutionary turmoil in Mexico, his mother married into a well-known Scottish family, and de Mier, his brother and sister remained in England, where they were brought up and educated.

In May 1940 de Mier join the Royal Air Force Volunteer Reserve and was trained as an aerial gunner, serving in No.141 Squadron, flying Boulton Defiants, from May to September 1940. He escaped his first brush with death due to emergency medical surgery, which prevented him from participating in a 19 July 1940 combat scramble that almost destroyed No.141 Squadron on its first operational sortie. It was attacked by BF-109s of III/JG51, resulting in seven Defiants lost, with four pilots and six gunners killed.

The unit managed to claim two BF-109Es shot down in return.

In September 1940 de Mier was assigned to No.68 Squadron flying Bristol Blenheims, then spending some time at No.1 Air Gunnery School as an instructor and to take an advanced course.

Pilot Officer Sebastian Bernardo de Mier RAFVR, an aerial gunner in a Defiant and later with intruder operations in 1942. (His Royal Highness Prince Bernard of the Netherlands)

No.68 Squadron would serve the rest of the war in England, flying Bristol Beaufighters and later de Havilland Mosquitos before being disbanded in April 1945. This unit was well known for a number of Czechoslvak aircrew that served in it. In total, No.68 claimed the destruction of 58½ enemy aircraft, with 12 probables and 20 damaged.

In June 1941 de Mier was assigned to No.23 Squadron, flying Douglas Havoc Mk.Is. During an intruder mission on 29 August 1941 to Evreux, France, he had his second brush with death. His Douglas Havoc YP-L/AX929 returned to base with one of the fragmentation bombs that had been stuck coming loose on landing and exploding, causing the destruction of the aircraft and the death of the observer; de Mier, pilot Flight Lieutenant P.Q.S. Andersen and another gunner were wounded.

While recovering in hospital, de Mier was visited by his friend HRH Prince Bernard of the Netherlands, who was a qualified pilot but not allowed to fly operational missions.

No.23 Squadron continued the war with Douglas Bostons and Mosquitoes in support of Bomber Command, with a detachment serving on the island of Malta. The unit, which disbanded in September 1945, finished the war with 24 kills, eight probables and 14 damaged enemy aircraft.

After his recovery, de Mier was assigned to the newly formed No.418 Night Intruder Squadron of the Royal Canadian Air Force, flying the improved Douglas Boston MK.III in the night intruder role. By this time de Mier's brother, William, a British Army officer, had been taken prisoner after the fall of Singapore. He would survive the war and return to live in Mexico.

While on his seventh intruder mission, over Holland, the Douglas Boston Mk.III W8318, in which de Mier was the gunner, went down near the town of Murmerwouden after being hit by anti-aircraft fire from Leeuwarden airfield, in the early morning of 18 May 1942. De Mier and two members of the crew were killed.

The pilot, now Squadron Leader Andersen (de Mier's old pilot from No.23 Squadron days), was thrown out of the aircraft when it exploded, and was able to employ his parachute.

Andersen was treated for his wounds and spent the rest of the war as a prisoner. After his release, he served in the post-war RAF until 1947, when he started flying for BOAC as a commercial pilot, but in 1950 he returned to the RAF.

He was an RAF exchange pilot with the USAF in 1951, but was killed in a take-off accident in a Northrop F89C at Goodfellow Air Force Base, Texas, on 9 December 1951.

De Mier and his fellow crewmembers are buried at Dantumadeel General Cemetery, along with another bomber crew of No.218 Squadron RAF.

No.418 Squadron RCAF flew the Mosquito in operations until the end of the war, flying its last mission on 3 May 1945. No.418 was credited with the destruction of 105 German aircraft in aerial combat, with nine probables and 103 damaged. The unit also destroyed 73 enemy aircraft on the ground .It participated in the anti-V-1 campaign with the destruction of 76 flying bombs over the sea and seven more over England. On the debit side, No.418 lost 59 aircraft, with 143 men killed, missing in action or prisoners of war.

### 5. Sergeant Wireless Operator/Air Gunner Harold Charles Dent Saez, RAFVR

RAF Bomber Command suffered a massive number of casualties during its bomber offensive, among those lost being Sergeant Wireless Operator/Air Gunner Harold Charles Dent Saez of Minatitlan,

Veracruz, of No.214 Bomber Squadron RAF.

Saez was posted to No.214 (Federal Malay States) Squadron on 18 March 1943 from 1651 C.U. (Conversion Unit), forming part of the crew of Pilot Officer Leslie Powell. Their first mission was on 28/29 March against St Nazaire, France and their second mission on the following night as part of Operation "Gardening Nectarines".

On 4/5 April they hit Kiel in northern Germany for their third mission, and four days later dropped bombs in Operation "Gardening Deodars. In the early morning of 15 April, on his fifth operational mission, Saez was part of the same crew under Leslie Powell, flying the Short Stirling MK.I BU-H/EF-331 on a bombing mission to Stuttgart, Germany.

They had taken off at 2126 from RAF Chedburgh, Suffolk to form part of a 462-plane raid (Lancaster, Wellington, Halifax and Stirling bombers).

The main bomber force hit the north-east of the target area. During the raid, a bomb hit an air raid shelter, killing 257 French and 143 Russian prisoners of war, bringing the number of casualties on the ground to 619, up to that time the largest total for a raid.

The bomber force lost 23 aircraft in the Stuttgart raid, while German night fighters claimed 19 RAF bombers shot down. Dent's aircraft was intercepted and shot down on the return flight by Oberleutnant Kurt Fladrich of 9/NJG4, flying a BF-110G, about 12km east of Reims in north-east France, falling from about 3,300 metres at 0159.

This was Fladrich's third kill. He would end the war with 16 kills to his credit. He passed away in Germany in 1995.

The aircraft crashed at Sept-Saulx, Marne, and all the crew were buried in the churchyard of Sept-Saulx. A propeller from the doomed bomber is used as a marker for the plot where the crew is buried.

In January 1944 No.214 Squadron, after suffering a high number of losses, was converted to the Boeing Fortress MK.II and Mk.III for an electronic countermeasure role in support of Bomber Command, being assigned to No.100 Group. No.214 carried out a total of 507 combat missions, with the loss of 112 aircraft.

Sergeant Wirless Operator/Air Gunner Charles Dent Saez of No.218 (Federal Malay State) Bomber Squadron, killed in action on 15 April 1943. (Hector Davila America Vuela)

### 6. Sergean Philip P. Pearl, anti-submarine warfare, RAFVR

Philip Pearl, whose parents lived in Mexico, was part of the crew of the Vickers Wellington MK.XIV LF-Q/HF279 of No.172 Squadron RAF that went missing on 31 January 1944 during an anti-submarine patrol that took off at 0055 that day. Sergeant Pearl was one of a six-man crew under Flight Lieutenant Charles Kirwan Fitzgerald, DFC, RAFVR.

No.172 Squadron was part of Coastal Command, No.19 Group, based at RAF Chivenor in Devon, with two other anti-submarine squadrons flying the Wellington XII and XIV models. The squadron was formed on 4 April 1942 at Chivenor, and claimed the destruction of 10 German U-boats from July 1942 to January 1944.

During January 1944, Pearl and his crew had flown six anti-submarine searches. During one anti-submarine patrol on 16 January, the crew in HF276 spotted a rubber dinghy with two survivors from a previous sinking, and remained circling the dinghy until they were relieved by two Spitfire fighters and returned to base. On 23 January, the crew attacked a reported submarine with no results. They performed other missions until they were lost without trace at the end of the month.

### 7. Captain Abelardo Rodriguez Montijo, ferry pilot, RAFVR

On 17 April 1944, a newspaper reported the son of former Mexican president Abelardo L. Rodriguez had been killed in action. Yet Captain Abelardo Rodriguez Montijo was alive and well as a North American Aviation Company test pilot, flying North American P-51 Mustang fighters and B-25 Mitchell medium bombers.

Abelardo was born in Oakland, California, in 1918, the son of General Rodriguez, then commander of the North-west Mexican military zone, and Luisa Montijo. The couple separated three years later, and he and his mother lived in Los Angeles, where he completed his education up to college level.

Abelardo learned to fly in 1939 and was a civilian contract flight instructor for the USAAF from 1941-42. He then flew in the US Army Air Corps Ferrying Command, where he delivered aircraft to Canada. It was there that he was offered a job as a ferry pilot with the RAF, with the reported rank of captain, and from 2 April to 26 June 1942 he delivered aircraft across the North Atlantic to Britain, over the South Atlantic to Africa and across North Africa and the South Pacific to Australia.

He reached the combat zone of Port Moresby, New Guinea, where he delivered aircraft and personnel to the war front. He then returned to the United States, and was hired as a test pilot for North American Aviation in California on 10 November 1942.

In 1945 he joined the Mexican Air Force as a technical advisor with the rank of lieutenant, and in November 1945 left the service. After the war he acquired a surplus North American P-51D Mustang. In June 1946, using this P-51D, he established a speed record from Los Angeles to Mexico City of six hours and 22 minutes. He flew for a short time in commercial aviation, and continued flying until 1988 when he retired.

By then he had over 15,000 hours of flight time, and was decorated for this achievement by the Mexican government. He was later involved in developing the region of Baja California Sur for tourism.

## WITH THE FREE FRENCH

Among those who served in the Free French forces of General Charles de Gaulle in Europe, Africa and Asia were a number of Mexicans of French descent, or those born in Mexico of French parents. Some took part in the liberation of Paris in 1944 with the 2nd Armoured Division under General Phillipe Leclerc.

But there were others who joined the Free French Air Force (*Forces*

*Aeriennes Francaises Libres*, FAFL), that was active from 17 June 1940 in the UK until the end of the war on 8 May 1945.

### 8. Sergent Chef Jacque Armand Crozat, reconnaissance/ bomber pilot, FAFL

*Sergent Chef* Jacque Armand Crozat, the reconnaissance and bomber pilot of the Free French Air Force. (Armee del Air Historical Dept)

Crozat was born in 1920 in Santa Rosalia, Baja California, a coastal town that was founded by a French company to exploit the copper in the region, one of the many contracts given to foreign companies during the time of General Porfirio Diaz.

He returned to France, where he joined the *Armée de l'air* in 1938 and received his wings in 1939. After the fall of France in June 1940 he went to Gibraltar to join the Free French Air Force.

From there he went to England, but was sent to Africa in October 1940. By December 1942 he was assigned to the *2. Escadrille "Rennes"* of the Bombardment Group No.2 '*Bretagne*' at Zouar in Chad, North Africa. From there on 26 December 1942 he flew the first operations of the Free French forces, an observation mission in a Westland Lysander MK.II P9181 over Italian positions in Fezzan (part of modern Libya).

He later joined Bombardment Group 1/17 '*Picardie*' (GB1/17), that was formed in Damascus, Syria, in June 1943. Initially there were two squadrons flying Bristol Blenheims and Potez Model 25s, but a third squadron was later formed with American-made Douglas A-24B dive bombers.

Their mission was to patrol the vast expanse of the Syrian Desert.

After his service in Syria, Crozat continued his wartime career in Europe with Bomber Group GBM 2/63 '*Senegal*', flying Martin B-26 Marauder medium bombers against the Germans.

He remained in the post-war air force, participating in the French involvement in Indochina. He left the service as a captain in 1954, and passed away in 1983 in France.

### 9. SM (Petty Officer, Second Master) Louis Maxime Marie Chauvet, FNFL

A Consolidated PBY-5A Catalina, BuAer No.48561/8F-2, of the *8 Flotille de Exploracion* (8F8/8FE), under Crew Officer Galliegue, disappeared on 27 July 1944 after taking off on a training mission from Norfolk Naval Air Station, Virginia, in very bad weather.

Among its nine-man crew was Marie Chauvet, who was born in Mexico on 11 December 1915 to a Mexican mother. He joined the FFL (*Forces Francaises Libres*) on 19 August 1941, was given the rank of *Caporal* (Corporal) and on 21 August 1943 transferred to the Free French Navy.

He went by the name of 'Loup Robert' or 'Wolf' from December 1942. He was officially declared dead on 2 July 1948.

8FE, also known as VFP-2 (French Patrol Squadron Two) was formed on 29 April 1944, its personnel coming from Casablanca, but was stood up on 1 July 1944 at NAS Norfolk, Virginia, with 15 Consolidated PBY-5A Catalinas. The incident was 8FE's only loss.

## WITH THE UNITED STATES: THE ENLISTED PERSONNEL, AIRCREWS AND GROUND PERSONNEL

A large number of Mexicans and Mexican-Americans served in the USAAF. Mexican volunteers did not lose their Mexican citizenships, as their government made special provisions for those serving the Allied cause. Among those who served in the bombers of the 8th Air Force were the following.

### 10. Technical Sergeant Sator S. 'Sandy' Sierra/Sanchez, aerial gunner, USAAF.

Born in Joliet, Illinois, on 11 March 1922, Sierra's mother passed away in 1924. His father remarried, but he died in 1927 and his stepmother passed away in 1939, leaving Sierra and his four sisters in the care of his grandparents, Federico and Helen Sanchez, who adopted them.

After completing his schooling in his home town and Wisconsin, Sanchez joined the US Army in 1939, later requesting and being granted a transfer to the United States Army Air Corps, where he trained as an aviation mechanic in 1941.

He was assigned to Mercer Army Air Force base in Mercer, California, where he earned his first award for bravery when he stopped a crewless runaway Vultee BT-13 trainer which was taxiing towards other aircraft and a maintenance shop. He managed to climb into the rear seat and stop the Vultee after it hit one aircraft, minimising the damage caused.

He was then trained as an aerial gunner at Las Vegas Army Air Field. He was sent overseas and assigned to the 334th Bomber Squadron of the 95th Bomb Group, flying his first combat mission on 15 September 1943 as a waist gunner. After two missions he replaced the tail gunner of the crew of Lieutenant Alden Witt before they flew their first combat mission over Europe. They were assigned to the Boeing B-17F-BO 42-29943, named '*Situation Normal*'. During their tour of combat, the crew of '*Situation Normal*' flew the mandatory 25 combat missions.

On the 10 October 1943 mission to attack Munster railroad yards in Germany, 22 bombers took off; 17 completed the mission, with nine damaged and five lost. The 95th encountered what up to that time was the fiercest Luftwaffe resistance. During the course of the air battle, two members of the crew were wounded, one losing an arm, while Sanchez would be awarded the US Silver Star for bravery. He reported:

> My tail guns were firing almost all the time. A few minutes after we bombed the target a Messerschmitt 109 attacked my position. I gave him several burst and his tail broke off. Then he exploded. A few minutes later a Junkers Ju-88 came in the same way and I shot off his left wing, so the pilot bailed out.

During this mission, the crew of '*Situation Normal*' claimed the

Technical Sergeant Sator 'Sandy' Sierra admiring his image on B-17G 42-97290, named the *'Smilling Sandy Sanchez'* after him. (Family of Sator Sierra)

Technical Sergeant Sator 'Sandy' Sierra, the most decorated enlisted man of the USAAF during the Second World War. (Family of Sator Sierra)

destruction of eight enemy aircraft, plus two more probables and two damaged. Sanchez was credited with the BF-109 and the Ju-88.

After the crew finished its combat tour, claiming the destruction of 19 German aircraft, plus two probables and six damaged, the bomber's next crew was lost on 6 March 1944, shot down by German fighters, with the death of five crewmembers and the rest taken prisoner.

Sanchez volunteered to stay longer and flew more missions with other crews, completing 44 combat missions on 1 May 1944 before he was sent home. He was a popular member of the 95th, with one of its B-17Gs, 42-97290, named *'Smiling Sandy Sanchez'* after him.

This bomber had completed 23 bombing missions when it was badly damaged during a raid over Berlin on 19 May 1944, which forced the crew to make a forced emergency landing in Sweden, where they were interned for the rest of the war. Sanchez has been generally credited with six German aircraft shot down, but so far only the following claims have been found:

10 October 1943, 1ne Ju-88 and 1 BF-109;
14 October 1943, 1 Ju-88 probable;
10 February 1944, 1 Ju-88 probable; and
6 March 1944, 1 BF-109 damaged.

The 95th Bomb Group end the war with 333 combat missions to its credit, flying its last mission on 25 May 1945. The group dropped 19,769 tons of bombs and claimed the destruction of 425 enemy aircraft, plus 117 probables and 231 damaged.

One hundred and fifty-six of its B-17s were lost in operations, plus 34 in non-operational roles. A total of 1,774 personnel were killed in action, killed in accidents, wounded, missing in action, prisoners of war or evaded capture to return to England.

Sanchez served as an instructor back in the United States, but returned for a third combat tour, flying with the 353th Squadron, 301st Bomb Group of the 15th Air Force, at Foggia, Italy, from November 1944. He was killed in combat on 15 March 1945 on his 66th mission, flying as a replacement crewmember for the crew of Lieutenant Dale Thornton in the B-17G-VE 42-97683, serving as top turret gunner and engineer.

They were hit by anti-aircraft fire on a bombing mission south-west of Berlin and were trying to reach Russian lines when the bomber lost height and started to go down. The crew started to bail out, but it appears from statements from the survivors that Sanchez stayed in his position to cover the stricken bomber from possible Me-262 jet fighter attacks.

The B-17 exploded before he had chance to bail out. After the crew was captured by the Germans, they were informed that his body was found near the wreckage of the aircraft and was buried next to it. After the war his body was not found, and there is a strong possibility that his remains were removed and buried as an unknown combatant in an Allied war cemetery.

Years later, a search was launched by former crew members and family to locate his grave. This enlisted airman, who is one of the most decorated in the USAAF – receiving the Silver Star, Distinguished Flying Cross and Purple Heart, along with an Air Force Presidential Unit citation – is honoured in an exhibit at the USAF museum at Dayton, Ohio, and a memorial park in his home town of Joliet.

The 301st Bomb Group had the unique distintion to have flown in three air forces during the war, starting with the 8th Air Force in England and later the 12th and finally the 15th Air Force in the Mediterranean and Italy. The group flew its last mission on 26 April 1945, completing 464 combat missions and losing 132 aircraft in operations.

Master Sergeant Jose Ramirez and his ground crew who helped *'Witchcraft'* to establish its combat record in the 8th Air Force. (Author Collection)

## 11. Master Sergeant Jose R. Ramirez, crew chief, USAAF

Born in Bowie, Arizona, to Mexican parents on 10 May 1915, Ramirez's father was from Aguascalientes and his mother from Leon, Guanajuato. He joined the USAAF, was trained as an aviation mechanic and was assigned to the 790th Bomber Squadron of the 467th Bomb Group (Heavy) that was formed and trained at Wendover, Utah.

When the Consolidated B-24H Liberator 42-52534 arrived at Wendover, its flight crew #Y-15 under the command of Lieutenant George W. Reed and Master Sergeant Ramirez with his team of mechanics were assigned to the aircraft, which received the name '*Witchcraft*'.

The ground elements of the group arrived at their new home of Rackheath, Norfolk, England, on 11 March 1944, and their aircraft – among them '*Witchcraft*' – followed on the 19th after a long flight from the USA via Brazil and Africa. The 467th Bomb Group (H) became part of the famed 8th Air Force, 2nd Air Division, which had been bombing targets in Europe since 1942. Ramirez took real pride in the upkeep of his aircraft, as noted by many, including 8th Air Force historian Roger A. Freeman:

> The pride of the 467th Group at Rackheath was Witchcraft .This B-24H had flown one of the Group's first mission in April 1944, and in the care of M/Sgt. Jose Ramirez continued to complete operations with near mechanical perfection.

B-24H 42-52534 *'Witchcraft'* of the 790th BS, 467th BG, which flew 130 combat mission without an abort, thanks to the efforts of crewchief Master Sergeant Ramirez. (Author Collection)

One of her pilots Lt. John Oder said of Ramirez: Joe was totally devoted to his aircraft. He keep her immaculate. To him a minor oil leak was a major disaster. Ramirez's attention was no doubt instrumental in this aircraft becoming the first B-24 in the Eighth to fly 100 missions without an abort, on the January 14th mission to Hallendorf's Steel works. During its time some 300 flak holes had been made in 'The Witch' but none of her crewmen were ever injured.

His ground crew, which was nicknamed the 'League of Nations', included Staff Sergeant George Dong, Chinese; Sergeant Raymond Belcher, German-Irish-English; Corporal Joseph Veller, German/Dutch; and Corporal Walter Elliot, American.

The ground personnel of the 467th also faced dangers, many of which were unexpected, such as on the night of 22 April 1944, when the bombers were coming back at night after a bombing mission. As the bombers of the 2nd Air Division were lining up to land back on their respective bases, unknown to them, they had been trailed by 14 Messerschmitt Me-410A-1s of II/ KG51, led by Major Dietrich Puttfarken.

Ramirez and his crew were waiting in the parking area for their aircraft to land when all hell broke loose. Roger Freeman writes:

> Meanwhile the 467th on their tenth mission were also returning in gathering darkness after an accurate bombing of the marshaling yards of Hamm. Joe Ramirez, crew chief of Witchcraft, was waiting at the dispersal for the group to return.
>
> It was dusk and he could see smaller aircraft coming with the formation. He believed them to be escorting P-51s. As the first few bombers alighted on the runway the German pilots struck, firing their machine guns and dropping bombs …
>
> A Ju-88 made a pass over the airfield at fifty feet, firing tracers and dropping two bombs.
>
> A Liberator which was undergoing repairs under the floodlights at the southern end of the airfield was hit and Joe Ramirez standing only one dispersal away, saw Private Daniel P. Miney killed while [he] cycled across the concrete. Private Michael F. Mahoney, a ground crewman working on the B-24, was wounded by the explosion. The other burst destroyed a cottage in the vicinity.

Within 30 minutes, the German airmen had shot down nine B-24s and a British Armstrong Whitworth Albermarle bomber, damaged three American aircraft that crashed on runways and two more that collided at nearby Seething, leaving some 61 airmen dead.

Two Me-410s were lost, one flown by Major Puttfarken, who had claim two Allied bombers, and the other after being hit by defensive fire from a B-24, both aircraft crashing in the same area.

'*Witchcraft*' flew its first mission on 10 April 1944 and its last on 21 April 1945, registering 137 missions, of which 130 were classified as combat without an abort. It flew for a total of 837 hours and 15 minutes of combat, using 238,683 gallons of fuel, 25 engine replacements, dropping about 304 tons of bombs and suffering about 300 flak hits. In all about 40 different crews flew the aircraft, with no fatalities or injuries.

The 467th Bomb Group, known as 'The Rackheath Aggies', flew its first mission on 10 April 1944 and last on 25 April 1945. The group dropped 13,333 tons of bombs in 212 combat missions, losing 29 aircraft in operations and 19 more in other losses, claiming the destruction of six enemy aircraft, five probables and two damaged.

The Group had an unsurpassed record for bombing accuracy in the 8th Air Force.

For his services, Ramirez received the Bronze Star with Oak Leaf Cluster. He left the USAAF after the end of the war and resided in California, where he raised his family. He passed away aged 85 on 29 January 2001 at Whittier, Los Angeles.

### 12. Sergeant Alejandro Cardenas Carranza, aerial gunner, USAAF

Sergeant Alejandro Cardenas Carranza, standing third from left, with his B-24 crew. (458th BG Association)

Cardenas Carranza was born in Piedras Negras, Coahuila, on 12 December 1922, the grandnephew of Don Venustiano Carranza, a former president of Mexico. He undertook his studies in Mexico and Corpus Christies, Texas, and in 1943 enlisted in the USAAF, being classified and trained as an aerial gunner.

He received his training in Kansas, South Carolina and Florida. He trained as part of a Consolidated B-24 Liberator bomber crew at Topeka, Kansas, with command pilot 2nd Lieutenant Henry H. Northrop. After completing their training, they left Kansas on 27 April 1944, and after a long flight arrived in the UK on 3 May.

The crew flew to Northern Ireland, where they took a training course before flying back to England and being assigned to the 754th Bombardment Squadron (Heavy) of the 458th Bomb Group at Horsham St Faith, a former RAF base near Norwich.

They flew their first combat mission on 12 June 1944 to Évreux-Fauville in northern France, followed by their second mission two days later to hit a village near Abbeville, again in northern France.

Their third mission was a bombing raid on the 18th against the airfield at Fassberg in northern Germany, flying the B-24H-10-DT 41-28733/J4P '*Rhapsody in Junk*', called aircraft #733X in their mission report. While passing over Hamburg, the B-24H took flak hits that damaged two of its engines, forcing the bomber to drop out of formation and head back to base.

Near the German naval base of Kiel they took more flak and lost another engine, forcing the crew to bail out. It appears that while they were bailing out, the flight engineer was killed, either hitting the aircraft during his escape or falling to the ground. Cardenas and the rest of the crew were taken prisoner.

After his capture, Cardenas was taken to an interrogation centre in Frankfurt and was surprised, as he wrote later, that a German officer had a personnel file on him: they knew that he was Alejandro Cardenas Carranza, a Mexican, grandson of General Jesus Carranza, grandnephew of Don Venustiano Carranza, former president of Mexico, and his maternal grandmother, Senora Florencia Stasburguer, was from Hamburg in Germany.

Cardenas ended up in *Stalag Luft* 4 at Tychovo, today in Poland. Here, to pass the time, he gave Spanish lessons to other prisoners and German guards. In 1945 the camp was evacuated due to the Soviet Army's advance, the prisoners being marched into Germany, where they were liberated by Allied forces. Cardenas return to the United States and was released from the service in December 1945.

The 458th established a combat record of 240 missions in 221 days of combat, flying its first mission on 22 February 1944 and the last on 25 April 1945. During this time it suffered 57 aircraft lost in operations and 14 in accidents. Personnel losses amounted to 539 killed in action, prisoners of war or evaded captured.

An additional 53 were killed in accidents.

Cardenas returned to Mexico, where he learned to fly and later sold surplus aircraft. He flew in commercial and private aviation. He received the Mexican aviation medal 'Emilio Carranza' for accumulating 10,000 and then 15,000 hours of flight time. He passed away on 26 August 2009, aged 86.

## FLYING PERSONNEL

### 13. Major Robert L. Cardenas, bomber pilot and test pilot, USAAF

Robert Cardenas was born in Merida, Yucatan, Mexico, on 10 March 1920, and at the age of 5 his family decided to move to the United States, settling in San Diego, California. As a child he developed an interest in aviation, building models and learning to fly gliders.

In 1936 Cardenas was naturalised as an American citizen, living with his family at El Cajon Boulevard in San Diego. He later worked for the Consolidated Aircraft Company. In 1939 he joined the California Army National Guard, while attending San Diego State University, studying engineering in his second year.

His anti-aircraft unit, the 251st Coast Artillery Regiment (Anti-aircraft), was ordered to the Philippines, and Cardenas had reached Hawaii when he received orders that he had been accepted to undertake pilot training in September 1940 due to his experience and education. This saved him from the terrible fate that later fell on this

Bomber pilot Major Robert L. Cardenas after the war, when he was involved in test flights. (National Archives)

unit, which suffered casualties during the surprise Japanese attack on Pearl Harbor on 7 December 1941 and later served in the bloody Guadalcanal, Bougainville and Luzon campaigns.

Cardenas received his commission and wings in July 1941, first serving as a flight instructor at Kelly Field, Texas, and later being instrumental in establishing the USAAC Glider School in California. He then became a flight test officer and was assigned to Wright Field, Ohio.

In 1944 Cardenas became a B-24 bomber pilot and was sent to England. In January 1944 he was assigned to the 67th (H) Bomber Squadron of the 44th (H) Bomb Group, "The Flying Eight Balls". Captain Cardenas flew his first bombing mission on 21 January 1944 in the B-24H '*Southern Comfort II*', attacking military installations in France.

On 18 March 1944, the Group bombed the Manzell air armaments factory at Friedrichshafen in southern Germany. According to the 44th Group history, this was not a good day, losing eight aircraft, six of which, due to extensive damaged from enemy fire, landed in Switzerland.

Cardenas was on his 17th bombing mission on this raid. Flying in the B-24J-65-CO s/n.42-100073, '*Sack Artists*', they were hit by German anti-aircraft fire and headed for Switzerland. With the plane damaged and on fire, the crew bailed out and the aircraft crashed on Swiss territory close to the German border. Cardenas, after bailing out, landed on the German side of Lake Constance. Not wanting to be captured, he swam the lake to the Swiss side, almost drowning but being rescued by the Swiss and interned with the rest of his crew.

He made it back to the UK in September 1944.

The 44th Bomb Group continue flying throughout the war in Europe, and according to its unit history flew 9,057 operational sorties in 343 missions. The 44th claimed the destruction of 330 enemy aircraft but lost 192 B-17s in action and suffered 186 aircraft accidents.

The 44th Group lost 854 men killed in action.

Cardenas was then sent back to the United States to Wright Field, Ohio, and his old job as a test pilot. Here he evaluated captured German jet aircraft such as the Me-262 fighter and the Arado 234 bomber, and flew the American-made Douglas XB-42 and XB-43.

In 1947 Major Cardenas was involved with the Bell X-1 project at Muroc, California, and became the command B-29 pilot who dropped Captain Chuck Yeager on 14 October 1947 in the Bell X-1, which accomplished the first supersonic flight. Cardenas was later involved in test flying the YB-49 flying wing. During the Vietman War, he flew the Republic F-105 Thunderchief in combat operations over South-East Asia with the 18th Tactical Fighter Wing.

In March 1968 Cardenas was promoted to brigadier general, serving in different locations and assigments, including as vice-commander of the 16th Air Force at Torrejon Air Force Base in Spain. General Cardenas retired from active duty in 1973, after which he worked in private industry, but also served in various organisations helping armed forces veterans in the state of California. At the time of writing, he is still living well into his 90s in San Diego, California.

### 14. Captain Luis Bonilla Coppola, bomber pilot, USAAF

Bonilla Coppola was from Arizona with an Italian father and Mexican mother. Based on available data, he seems to have lived on both sides of the Border. He completed his high school education at Tucson High School in 1938 and was an engineering student at the University of Arizona when the United States went to war in December 1941.

He enlisted in the USAAC in August 1942, having submitted to the Mexican government a request to enlist in the armed forces of the USA without losing his Mexican citizenship, which on 8 June had been approved by the Mexican Congress.

With this approval, he enlisted as an aviation cadet and undertook his training in the following locations: San Antonio, Texas; primary flight training at Muskogee, Oklahoma; basic training at Coffeyville, Kansas; and advanced training at Victoria, Texas, in the North American AT-6. He received his wings in October 1943 and the rank of 2nd lieutenant, was then selected to be a flight instructor and after training was sent back to Coffeyville.

Deciding he wanted active involvement in the war, not sitting it out Stateside, in December 1944 he complete his combat training in Boeing B-17 bombers. During his ferry flight from the US to England he read a book about the peninsula of Baja California; he fell in love with the territory, but first he needed to survive the war to explore it.

Lieutenant Bonilla Coppola and his crew were assigned to the 526th Bomber Squadron of the 379th Bomb Group, assigned to the 8th Air Force in England. By this time, with the war going well for the Allies, to complete a combat tour flying bombers involved completing 35 missions. Bonilla Coppola started his combat tour in January 1945, and three months later he and his crew had completed the required number of missions before the war ended.

The 379th Bomb Group started its war career on 29 May 1943, flying its first bombing mission to St Nazaire on the west coast of France; its final mission was on 25 April 1945 at Pilsen in Czecholovakia. The 379th flew a total of 330 bombing missions, dropped 26,460 tons of bombs on enemy targets, and its gunners claimed the destruction of 315 enemy aircraft. However, the Group lost 149 B-17s in combat, with 1,473 casualites (killed in acton, missing in action, POWs, evadees and internees).

Captain Bonilla Coppola left the service in 1945 and headed for Baja California, settling there in La Paz, where he started Trans Mar de Cortez airlines with one of the sons of former President Alvaro Obregon, with a surplus DC-3 carrying out passenger and cargo flights.

Bonilla Coppola bought into the hotel business in 1952 with the Hotel Los Arcos in La Paz, and later in Cabo San Lucas with the Hotel Finisterra.

### 15. Lieutenant Hector R. Gonzalez, photo recon pilot, USAAF

A Mexican American, Hector Gonzalez was born in Nogales, Arizona, on 28 February 1914. In 1915 his family moved to Los Angeles, where he later learned to fly and joined the Royal Canadian Air Force in 8 October 1941, training in single and multi-engine types in Canada.

After obtaining his wings, he was sent to England in October 1942, serving at No.19 Advanced Flying Unit in Scotland. In December 1942 he was serving at No.1 Bean Approach School. With the United States now in the war, in October of that year he had requested a transfer to the USAAF. Permission was granted, and

on 23 February 1943, with the rank of flight officer, he moved to the 326th Bomber Squadron of the 92nd Bomb Group to fly the B-17 bomber. He later transferred to HQ 322nd Bomb Group, where after considering his options he requested and was granted to be a photo reconnaissance pilot.

In June 1943 he was sent to the 13th Photo Reconnaissance Squadron, that was equipped with photo reconnaissance Supermarine Spitfires and Lockheed F-5s, the photo recon version of the P-38 Lightning.

The 13th Photo Reconnaissance Squadron was formed on 20 June 1942 at Colorado Springs, Colorado. After training it was sent overseas in November 1942, arriving in Scotland on 30 November 1942 and becoming the first USAAF reconnaissance squadron to serve in Europe. The unit flew its first photo reconnaissance mission on 28 March 1943, and would fly a total of 1,367 such missions before the end of the war.

On 31 August 1943, Gonzalez was promoted to 2nd lieutenant. He narrowly avoided an accident on 8 September 1943 during a long cross-country flight of 250km each way. With only about six hours in the Lockheed F-5 on local practice missions to his credit, running his engines on high he almost didn't make it back to base, both engines being dead due to lack of fuel, but he made it in with a rough but safe landing. The weather also occasionally proved a factor, and during December of that year he had to abort two missions to France.

On 22 May 1944, after flying a number of missions, Gonzalez went on leave back to the USA, returning on 21 August. He was transferred to the 27th Photo Reconnaissance Squadron, with which during one photo reconnaissance missions on 17 September he flew a number of times over the airborne landing areas at Arnhem. This mission was repeated about the 22nd of the month.

In October 1944 Lieutenant Gonzalez covered the raid on the Cologne Ford Motorworks, and on 6 February 1945, now a captain, Gonzalez flew over the Munster marshalling yards that had been hit by Allied bombers on 29 January. By March 1945 Captain Gonzalez had flown 45 photo reconnaissance missions, and would hit the 50 mark in April. He ended the war with 52 missions to his credit. On 8 April his squadron sent out 11 aircraft but three returned due to poor weather; Captain Gonzalez took photos of Ingolstadt and the city of Nurnburg and beyond, where he photographed streams of refugees .

The 7th Photographic Group, to which the 13th and 27th PRS were assigned, was assigned to the 8th Air Force in 1943. The first mission was flown by the 13th PRS on 23 March 1943 and the last on 8 May 1945. The 7th Photographic Group flew the Supermarine Spitfire XI, the Lockheed F-5A, F-5B, F-5C, F-5F and F-5G. It also flew the North American P-51D and K models.

The Group flew a total 4,247 sorties, with the loss of 58 aircraft. The P-51s of the group claimed one enemy aircraft probably destroyed and one damaged in 880 sorties.

Captain Gonzalez left the service in December 1945, went to work at Paramount Studios and later become a successful businessman in southern California. He was one of the early presidents of the P-38 National Association from 1990-2003, and was one of its founding members. He died aged 91 on 27 March 2005.

Lieutenant Hector R. Gonzalez, the F-5 photo reconnaissance pilot of the 13th PRS. (Steve Blake, P-38 National Association)

### 16. Lieutenant Richard Gomez Candelaria, fighter pilot, USAAF

Born in El Paso, Texas, on 14 July 1922, Candelaria moved to California aged 7 after his father passed away. Growing up, he developed an interest in aviation from hearing stories about the First World War.

In 1943 he joined the US Army Reserve and was accepted into the USAAF flying programme in January that year. He trained in California and Arizona, receiving his wings on 8 February 1944 at Williams Field, Arizona. He was retained for flight instructor duties at Williams and Luke Field until May, when he volunteered to join a unit overseas.

On 22 September 1944 he was assigned to the 479th Fighter Group with 463 hours of flying time. He served as a P-51D Mustang pilot in the 435th Fighter Squadron from December 1944 to April 1945.

He scored his first claim on 5 December 1944, north-west of Berlin, on a mission escorting bombers hitting targets in the Berlin and Munster area, when he shot down two FW-190s. On 13 March 1945, Candelaria and a fellow pilot attacked German aircraft on the ground at Dümmer Lake in northern Germany, where he was given credit for three damaged BF-109s.

His greatest success was on 7 April during a bomber escort into Germany, when he defended a group of heavy bombers from the German BF-109G and BF-109K fighters of *Schulungslehgang* 'Elbe' (Training Course Elbe), a volunteer unit trained to ram American bombers. At a critical moment Candelaria was left to defend a group of Liberator bombers, first from a pair of Me-262 jet fighter, when he use his drop tanks to drop them on the German fighters without success. He fired on one of the Me-262s, scoring hits on its fuselage and wings, but had to break away when the German's wingman opened fire and forced him to take evasive action.

Candelaria claimed the Me-262 as destroyed, and another pilot witnessed it going down.

He then engaged a group of about 10-15 BF-109s making a run towards the bombers, at which point Candelaria called for help from the rest of the squadron: "I have a bunch of Germans cornered!"

When the fighting ended, Candelaria claimed the destruction of four BF-109s and the Me-262 (the jet was classified later as a probable). That brought his personal score to six German aircraft destroyed.

Several days later, on 13 April, he was shot down by ground fire while strafing a German airfield.

He was taken prisoner for a short time, but managed to escape to Allied lines after 31 days in captivity, he and a fellow prisoner of war commandeering a German Army staff vehicle and its driver.

The 479th Fighter Group – known as 'Riddle's Raiders' and formed in Glendale, California, in October 1943 – flew the Lockheed P-38 Lightning in combat when it arrived in England to fly with the 8th Air Force. The group later converted to the North American P-51D and K model Mustang, going on to claim the destruction of 155 enemy aircraft, 12 probables and 39 damaged.

The 479th also claimed 166 enemy machines destroyed and 95 damaged on the ground. The unit lost 77 of its own aircraft, with 16 pilots reported killed. It was the last fighter group to join the 8th Air Force, the first USAAF unit to fight German jet fighters and claimed the last kill by the 8th Air Force during the war.

After the war Candelaria served in the USAF Reserve from 1946-50 and the California Air National Guard from 1950-64, rising to the rank of colonel before retiring on 20 October 1960, reportedly becoming a successful restaurant owner and business manager.

## THE PACIFIC WAR

### 17. 2nd Lieutenan Nicanor Zuniga Alvarez, fighter pilot, USAAF

Based on available information, it appears that Nicanor Zuniga Alvarez was born in 1921, probably in Mexico, but his family later emigrated to St Louis, Missouri, where around 1942 he enlisted in the cadet programme of the USAAC.

In 1944, 2nd Lieutenant Zuniga was assigned to the 7th Fighter Squadron of the 49th Fighter Group, which had already established a lofty reputation. It was formed in November 1940 at Selfridge Field, Michigan. In January 1942 the group was sent to Australia and participated in the defence of Darwin. Around this time the 7th Fighter Squadron was flying the Curtiss P-40N Warhawk.

On 15 May 1944, seven aircraft from the squadron were involved in escorting two or three reconnaissance B-25s to Biak, New Guinea, when they tangled with defending Japanese fighters. Zuniga was the wingman to 1st Lieutenant Lewis C. Smith, who almost brought him down, as revealed in the squadron historical records:

> Another exhibition of outstanding flying was done by Lt. Nicanor A Zuniga. He was flying the wing of Lt. Smith and was following him closely when Lt. Smith shot the wing off his first kill of the day.
>
> The Jap plane struck Lt. Zuniga's ship as it went by sheering 5 feet off the right wing. Lt. Zuniga began spinning violently but he recovered and sighted a Zero in front of him. He pulled his crippled ship into position, opened fire and the Jap Zero 'Hit the dirt'. Lt. Zuniga then flew the ship back to base landing with wheels up.

During this aerial combat, the 7th Fighter Squadron claimed a total of seven Japanese aircraft shot down, plus three more damaged. One of the top scorers was Lieutenant Smith, who claimed the destruction of two 'Zekes' (Zeroes; his only two kills of the war). Two US aircraft were damaged and one pilot wounded.

Zuniga had a take-off accident on 23 June 1944 when he wiped out P-40N 42-105896, but he escaped unhurt. By September 1944 the 7th Fighter Squadron, along with the 8th, finally converted to Lockheed P-38J Lightning twin-engine fighters.

On 15 December 1944 he was badly hit by a Japanese fighter about 5 miles south-west of the tip of Mindanao Island in the Phillipines, having to make a forced landing, but later returned to his unit. Zuniga was ordered back to the USA on 23 March 1945.

2nd Lieutenant Nicanor Zuniga Alvarez of the 49th Fighter Group, who after the war flew for the Mexican airline *Mexicana de Aviacion*. (Manuel Ruiz Romero)

The 7th Fighter Squadron of the 49th Fighter Group ended the war with the claimed destruction of 178 enemy aircraft, along with 19 probables and 24 damaged. The 49th Fighter Group totalled 639 claimed kills, plus 105 probables and 61 damaged.

After the end of the war Zuniga tried to get a job with US civilian airlines, but with no luck. It is claimed that his mother suggested he try his luck in Mexico, where Zuniga ended up being hired by the *Compania Mexicana de Aviacion*, flying with them until his retirement. He reportedly passed away in Mexico in the 1980s.

### 18. Lieutenan Arthur Van Haren, Hellcat ace, US Navy

Judging by his name, nobody would imagine that Arthur Van Haren is considered to be the highest-scoring Mexican-American pilot in the US armed forces during the Second World War.

USN naval fighter pilot Lieutenant Arthur Van Haren of VF-2. (*Latino Perspective* Magazine)

Arthur Van Haren Jr was born in Superior, Arizona, on 9 April 1920 into a pioneer Mexican-American family with Dutch ancestry. His father, Arthur Van Haren Sr, was a wounded First World War veteran who had served in the 89th Infantry Division in France and became a local sporting legend.

While studying at the University of Arizona, Van Haren was a member of the ROTC (Reserve Officer Training Corps) programme. In June 1941 he enlisted in the US Navy to enter into the Naval Aviation programme, being sent to NRAB (Naval Reserve Air Base) Long Beach, California, and from there to Jacksonville, Florida. In September of that year he was appointed an Aviation Cadet.

He received his aviation wings in 1942, but was retained for flight instructor duty at Pensacola, Florida, for about a year. In June 1943 he joined the VF-2 United States Navy Fighter Squadron.

This squadron had been disestablished on 1 July 1942 after it had fought in the Battle of the Coral Sea in May 1942, flying Grumman F4F-3 Wildcats off the USS *Lexington*. They claimed the destruction of 17 Japanese aircraft plus seven probables, but lost nine pilots and planes, and the *Lexington* was sunk.

The Second VF-2 'Rippers' was established on 1 June 1943, under the command of Commander William A. Dean, at NAS (Naval Air Station) Atlantic City, New Jersey. When Van Haven joined VF-2 he was married with one child on the way, and during his flight training at Pensacola had flown about 10 hours on the Grumman F6F Hellcat fighter. VF-2 would first serve on the carrier USS *Enterprise* (CV-6) from November 1943 to January 1944, and later on the USS *Hornet* (CV-12) from March to September 1944.

During its tour in the Pacific, VF-2 claimed the destruction of 506 enemy aircraft, of which 261 were destroyed on the ground, and the 'Rippers' produced 27 pilots who score more than five kills (a record in US military aviation history). VF-2 lost three pilots in aerial combat and four to Japanese ground fire.

Van Haren was assigned the Grumman F6F-3 'White 32', flew his first combat mission on 19 November 1943 during the invasion of the Gilbert Islands, and on 11 June 1944 he shot down two '*Zeke*' Japanese fighters around Guam Island. Eight days later he added two more '*Zekes*' to his score, and on 20 June he shot down a 'Jake' reconnaissance aircraft for his fifth kill of the war.

On 3 July, during a raid on Iwo Jima, he claimed the destruction of three '*Zekes*'. Van Haren completed his scoring on 12 September when he shot down a '*Zeke*' in the Philippines. On 28 September VF-2 started the trip home.

In the history of VF-2 there are some short biographical notes on each of the pilots that served in the unit. That for Lieutenant Arthur Van Haren Jr reads as follows:

> Address: 536 N.Hilton Dr, .San Gabriel Calif. Three years at U. of Arizona. Has the best looking wife and daughter in the U.S.A. Plans to return to school after the war, if possible. Will try for law degree. Says he must hurry up and get to school, that I would be embarrassing if his daughter were in his class – she's almost two now.

After his return from the Pacific, VanHaren went back to be a flight instructor at Glenview Naval Air Station, Chicago. He was released from the service in October 1945. His post-war career was dedicated to practicing law in his home state of Arizona, where he also took on many cases working pro bono for the Mexican American community of Mariposa. He retired from his law practice in 1985 and passed away in 1992.

## 19. THE LAST ACE: 1st Lieutenant Francis Oscar Perdomo, fighter pilot, USAAF

Born in El Paso, Texas, to Mexican parents on 14 June 1919, it has been mentioned within his family that Francis Oscar Perdomo's father was a former cavalry officer who served in the famous *Division del Norte* of General Francisco 'Pancho' Villa, who with his wife went across the border to Texas to start a new life for themselves .

Oscar was the first of five children for the Perdomos. In June 1937 the family moved to Los Angeles, where Perdomo completed his high school education. After getting the necessary education requirements, Perdomo joined the US Army in February 1943 and was appointed as an aviation cadet with a reporting date of 13 February.

He undertook his flight training in California and later in Arizona, where he received his wings on 7 January 1944. Instead of going overseas he was sent to USAAF training command in Louisiana. It was not until October 1944 that he was assigned to the newly formed 464th Fighter Squadron at Peterson Field, Colorado, later moving for training to Brunning Army Air Force Base, Nebraska.

His squadron now formed part of the 507th Fighter Group, that was along ed with the 463rd and 465th squadrons. The 507th flew Republic P-47N Thunderbolt fighter bombers and was assigned to the 20th Air Force on Okinawa, but was under the tactical direction of the 7th Air Force.

The Group started flying operations against Japan on 1 July 1945.

If the war had continued, the Group would have provided escorts for the B-29s of the 8th Air Force, which were scheduled to arrive later. The Group flew the P-47N-1-RE, which had gone through modifications for operations in the Pacific theatre. Perdomo was assigned aircraft number 146, which he named 'Lil Meaties Meat Chopper' for his first-born son.

Perdomo flew his first combat mission on 2 July, escorting bombers to Kyushu in a flight of five and a half hours. On the next day he flew in the Group's longest mission to and from the coast of China, a total of nine hours of flight time. On 9 August the second atomic bomb was dropped on Nagasaki and the Allies were waiting for a response from the Japanese Imperial Government, but the war continued.

On 13August, the 507th Fighter Group flew a fighter sweep over Keijo (Seoul) in Korea to engage Japanese aircraft in aerial combat. Fifty-three P-47Ns took off at about 0930, but after aborts and mechanical failures, only 38 reached the target area at about 1315. Some 50 enemy aircraft were sighted and the battle started, with a Japanese Mitsubishi G4M bomber going down first.

During the combat Perdomo, after making his last claim of the day, was almost shot down by an Oscar fighter, but was saved by his wingman, 2nd Lieutenant Harry M. Steinshouser (who finished the war with three kills), who shot down the fighter on Perdomo's tail. By 1345 the 507th started its flight back to Ie Shima, with the first aircraft landing back at 1755.

In the round trip of eight hours and 18 minutesp, the 507th claimed the destruction of 20 enemy aircraft, two probables in the air and one Betty bomber on the ground. The only loss was one P-47N, whose pilot had claimed two enemy fighters before going down and being capture, after his release raising the day's score to 22 for the Group.

Perdomo claimed to have shot down four Oscar fighters (Nakajima Ki-43 Hayabusa), which was confirmed by his gun camera and other pilots, but post-war research has determined that the opponents were actually Nakajima Ki-84 'Frank' fighters from the 22nd and 85th Sentais, which had been assigned to Seoul since May 1945, and a single Yokosuka Type 93 "Willow" training biplane, one of two that happened to cross into the aerial battle.

The 22nd reported the loss of six fighters, while the 85th lost five

1st Lieutenant Francis Oscar Perdomo of the 464th FS, 507th FG, after scoring his five claims on 13 August 1945. His aircraft is named after his first-born son. (San Diego Aerospace Museum)

2nd Lieutenant Harry M. Steinhouser of the 464th FS, wingman to Perdomo, who saved him from being shot down on 13 August 1945. He finished the war with three claims to his credit. (San Diego Aerospace Museum)

Lieutenant Perdomo in P-47N No.146 after having his kills painted on his aircraft following the 13 August 1945 mission. (San Diego Aerospace Museum)

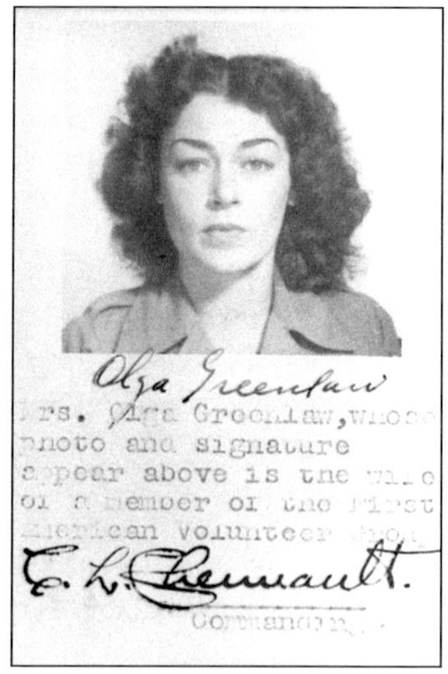

The identification card for Olga Greenlaw as a member of the first America Volunteer Group, signed by its commanding officer Claire L. Chennault. (Dan Ford)

pilots, including its commanding officer. This would be the last actions flown by all units.

The 507th Fighter Group finished the war with 40 enemy aircraft shot down, two probables and six destroyed on the ground, for the loss of 12 pilots in operations and accidents, plus two pilots taken prisoner. The Group lost a total of 19 aircraft to all causes.

Lieutenant Perdomo become the last 'Ace in a day' of the USAAF and the last ace of the Second World War. He finished the war with 10 combat sorties flown, with a total time of 56.8 hours flown in combat operations. He served in the post-war USAF, flying the F-86 and F-84, leaving the service in January 1958 with the rank of major.

He flew in commercial and civil aviation, performing some charters flights into Mexico. Two of his sons would serve in the Vietnam War, and sadly Kris was killed in action in May 1970 while serving as a door gunner onboard a US Army Bell UH-1C Huey helicopter. Perdomo passed away on 2 March 1976, at the USC Medical Center, Los Angeles, at the age of 56. His body was cremated and his ashes scattered at sea.

The cover of Olga Greenlaw's book that was published around September 1943 after her return to the United States. (Author Collection)

## A SPECIAL MENTION: THE LADY AND THE TIGERS

### 20. Miss Olga Greenlaw, the American Volunteer Group (AVG)

Among the personnel who formed the famed 1st American Volunteer Group (AVG), which was organised by Colonel Claire Lee Chennault and fought in the skies over Burma and China from December 1941 to July 1942, was a Mexican woman who was in charge of the operational diary of that unit.

Her name was Olga Clementina Sowers, who was born in El Chacala, Durango, Mexico, on 20 March 1908. Her father was an American, Edward Somer, a miner and factory owner, and her mother was Sofia, who was just 16 when they married. Olga had two other sisters, but tragically all her brothers died soon after birth.

During the Mexican Revolution, her family twice had to be evacuated by the US Navy, and her mother was wounded by a stray bullet. The family eventually decided to leave for the United States, settling first in Nogales, Arizona, and them in Los Angeles, where they settled in North Hollywood. Olga finished her education around 1929.

During her time in Los Angeles, the husband of one of her sisters had a friend who was a pilot, had been divorced and had a child, and had left the military service in 1931. They met and started seeing each other. On 23 February 1933, Olga married ex-USAAC lieutenant Harvey Greenlaw, who was born in 1897 in Superior, Wisconsin, a West Point graduate who served in the US Army for 11 years.

In the same month Harvey left for China, having acquired a job as a replacement flight instructor as part of the Colonel John H. 'Jack' Jouett's mission to help the Chinese Nationalist air force. Olga joined her husband in July 1933, and they returned to the USA in 1935 when the Jouett mission was replaced by an Italian one.

Upon their return her husband found a job at the North American Aviation Company, which sent them back to China in 1937 for him to assemble North American aircraft for the Chinese Nationalist air force. Due to the conflict between China and Japan, he was unable to complete his job. At the same time Harvey tried to sell bombers to the Dutch in the East Indies, but without success.

On 17 July 1941, they were in Hong Kong and about to return to the US when Harvey was hired as the executive officer for the 1st American Volunteer Group, later known as the 'Flying Tigers'. Olga got a job in charge of the group's operation diary, while at the same time she maintained a private diary that would later help her write about her experiences.

After the AVG ceased operations in July 1942, replaced by the 23rd

Fighter Group, Olga and Harvey returned to the USA in September that year. Olga is reported to have brought back the AVG war diary with her. Based on the group operations record book and her diary, Olga published her well-received book, *The Lady and the Tigers*, in September 1943.

In 1944 she divorced Harvey and remarried in 1946. After the death of her second husband in the 1970s she married again. Olga passed away aged 75 in Camarillo, California, on 13 August 1983. Harvey had died in Compestel, Nayarit, Mexico, on 10 January 1982.

## THE PRESENTATION SPITFIRES, MEXICO

During the Second World War, Britain established a programme in which people could donate money to finance the construction of aircraft and contribute to the defence of the Commonwealth. This programme was also run in many countries in Latin American where British subjects were living, where they contributed funds to build a Spitfire and have a name related to that country painted on it.

The 'Mexico Spitfire Fund' was started by the British Consul in Mexico City, raising money for the building of the first of four Spitfires MK.VBs that carried the following names:

'*Popocatepetl* I' (Smoking Volcano I),
'*Popocatepetl* II' (Smoking Volcano II),
'*Popocatepetl* III' (Smoking Volcano III) and
'*Iztaccihuatl*' (White Woman Volcano).

This was not an isolatde case: during the First World War, the British colony in Mexico presented one BE2C, one FK8 and two RE8s to the Royal Flying Corps.

### *Popocatepetl* I

Named after one of the volcanoes which overlooks Mexico City, this Supermarine Spitfire MK.Vb W3803, construction number 2009, was built at a factory at Chattis Hill in Hampshire. It had a long operational life, serving in a number of Royal Air Force, Czech and Free French fighter squadrons.

W3803 was first sent to the No.39 Maintenance Unit on 29 August 1941, then served in No.129 Squadron RAF that was stationed at Westhampnett in Sussex.

After flying operations with this squadron, 'Popocatepetl I' was transferred to No.154 (Motor Industries) Squadron RAF on 12 February 1942, stationed at RAF Hornchurch in Essex, where it flew on convoy escort missions and fighter sweeps into France.

From there W3803 was transferred to No.313, a Czech fighter squadron. During its service with the Czech pilots, W3803/RY-? was involved in an aerial combat. Sergeant Karel Valasek, with fellow pilot Pilot Officer Otmar Kucera DFC and a Canadian Hawker Hurricane pilot, Flight Lieutenant G.D. Robertson of No.421 RCAF Squadron, were credited with sharing a Junkers Ju-88 damaged.

Valasek was shot down by enemy ground fire over France on 21 May 1944. For a time he evaded the Germans with help from the French resistance, but was later captured and sent first to Stalag Luft VII at Bankau, Poland, and then marched to Stalag III-A in 1945 with the advance of the Russian armies.

He managed to escape and reached the American lines. Kucera became a notable fighter pilot, finishing the war with seven kills, one probable and one damaged. For Canadian pilot Robertson, the claim alongside the Czechs opened his score in the war. He finished the war with four kills, one shared kill, one probable and three damaged. He obtained the rank of squadron leader and won the DFC. He was released from the RCAF in August 1945.

From here W3803 was transferred to No.340 Free French Squadron on 29 June 1942.

On 15 September the aircraft was damaged during a heavy landing by Sergeant Robert Coly, after which it was passed to maintenance units and back to Vickers-Armstrong for modifications in December 1943.

W3803 was then prepared and packed for shipment to Portugal, where it served in the Portuguese Air Force in two of the country's fighter squadrons, first at MR-Esquadrilha at Ota air base in 1944 with the registration MR+E.

Then in January 1948 it was sent to No.1 Esquadrilha de Caca of the Esquadrilhas de Aviacao de Caca (fighting aviation group), and in April 1952 it was with No.3 Esquadrilha at Tancos in second-line duties. In 1953-54 all surviving Portuguese Spitfires were scrapped.

### *Popocatepetl* II

The Supermarine Spitfire MK.Vb W3801, with the construction number 1995, was also built at the Chattis Hill factory. It had a short operational career.

After its acceptance and test flights, it was posted first to No.39 MU (Maintenance Unit) at Colerme on 27 August 1941, then was assigned to No.71 'Eagle Squadron' on 2 September 1941.

This well-known unit, composed of American volunteer pilots, was formed in September 1940, first with American-made Brewster Buffalo fighters and later with the Hawker Hurricane MK.I. It was not until August 1941 that No.71 converted to Supermarine Spitifires, first the model MK.II and later the MK.Vb.

W3801, based upon the operational record book of No.71 Squadron, participated in its only combat mission during a fighter sweep on 7 September 1941, when 11 Spitfires of No.71 took off at 1530, although only eight aircraft made it to the French coast due to mechanical problems. They were top squadron, covering No.111 and No.222 Fighter Squadrons.

When the wing reached the area of Saint-Omer in the Pas de Calais they were attacked by BF-109Fs with yellow noses, as mentioned in the after-action report. The BF-109s were led by Oberstleutnant Adolf Galland of the Stab of JG26, with elements of 1, 3, 7, and 8/JG26. It was a bad day for No.71 Squadron, losing three aircraft, with the deaths of two pilots, one pilot becoming a prisoner of war and a fourth wounded in action and returning in a damaged aircraft.

Those killed were Flying Officer Eugene Quimby 'Red' Tobin in W3801 and Pilot Officer Hillard S. Fenlow, who was flying AB900. Pilot Officer William H. Nichols in AB909 was shot down and taken prisoner, taken to *Stalag Luft* III, while Pilot Officer Forrest P. Dowling in AB815 was the wounded pilot but managed to make it back to base.

In return one Bf-109 was claimed shot down by Flight Lieutenant C.G. Peterson, with another claimed damaged by Flying Officer Morris W. Fessler.

The JG 26 claimed six Spitfires shot down, Galland claiming his 83rd kill out of 104 during the war about 20km west of Boulogne, and *Unteroffizier* Kurt Bohn (who was killed in action on 25 April 1943) claiming a Spitfire about 10km south-east of Boulogne. The rest of the German pilots made the following claims:

*Feldwebel* Erwin Leibold of 3/JG26, one Spitfire (11 kills in all, WIA 28 March 1942); *Oberstleutnant* Joachim Muncheberg of 7/JG26, one Spitfire (135 kills, died of injuries 23 March 1943); *Unteroffizier* Emst Schick of 1/JG26, one Spitfire (1 kill, KIA 19 July 1942 by Spitfires of No.71 Squadron); *Hauptmann* Johannes Schmid of 8/JG26, one Spitfire (45 kills, KIA 6 November 1941).

It was reported that Tobin in W3801 '*Popocatepetl II*' crashed into a hill near Boulogne at about 1715. He is buried at Boulogne Eastern Cemetery.

Eugene Tobin was born in Salt Lake City, Utah, on 4 January 1917.

Flying Officer Eugene Quimby 'Red' Tobin, an American pilot of No.71 'Eagle' Squadron, who was killed in action on 7 September 1942 while flying Supermarine Spitfire MK.Vb W3801 *'Popocatepetl II'*. (USAF)

The probable victor over Flying Officer 'Red' Tobin was *Oberstleutnant* Adolf Galland, who claimed a Spitfire west of Boulogne for his 83rd kill of the war. (Author Collection)

He moved with his father to California and learned to fly in the 1930s, paying off his flight lessons while working at MGM Studios in Hollywood as a messenger and guide. During this time he met other pilots who would later be fly with the RAF in the upcoming world war.

He signed up to fight against the Russians in the Winter War of 1939-40, but didn't make it to Finland before the conflict ended. He then signed up to volunteer to fight with the French Air Force in May-June 1940, but after the fall of France he managed to escape to England with other American pilots, offering his services to the RAF on 15 July 1940.

After a spell of training at No.7 OTU, he was posted to No.609 (West Riding) Auxiliary Air Force Squadron on 8 August. He participated in the Battle of Britain, flying his first operational sortie on 16 August, reportedly engaging a BF-110 and firing all his ammunition, but with no success.

During his time with No.609, based on the Squadron Operations Record Book (ORB), on 25 August the squadron "had a big Tea-Time party with a hundred plus, mixed enemy force over Warnell". These were BF-110s of I/ZG2, V/LG1, and Bf-109s of III/JG2. During the engagement, which involved 12 No.609 Spitfires, the squadron claimed two Me-109s destroyed, six Me-110s destroyed and three Me-110 probables at a cost of two aircraft and one written off with a wounded pilot.

Tobin was credited with two Me-110 probables (although years later researchers concluded that one of the BF-110s did come down with the loss of its crew over England) but suffered a high 'G' in his Spitfire MK.I PR-K/L.1008 in an 18,000ft dive. He later reported: "I blacked out colder than a clam and realized, I was too low to be good to my motor. I came home."

The squadron ORB credited him with a Dornier Do.17Z (F1+FS) bomber of 8. /KG77 on 15 September 1941 in the Spitfire MK.I PR-C/K9997 as a sole claim. This bomber came down on English soil with three of the four crewmembers wounded and the other killed. Other sources claim it was shared with Flying Officer John C. Dundas DFC and Bar, who was born in 1915 and killed in action on 28 November 1940 after scoring his 12th individual kill. Dundas also had four shared destroyed, two probables, four damaged and one shared damaged.

Two days later Tobin and two other American pilots were transferred to the newly established No.71 Squadron, later known as 'Eagle Squadron', being the first pilots posted.

No.609 had been formed in 1936 as an Auxiliary Air Force Squadron with the Hawker Hind biplane two-seater, but in August 1939 converted to the Supermarine Spitfire MK.I monoplane fighter. The squadron participated in covering the evacuation from Dunkirk and the Battle of Britain.

On 21 October 1940, it became the first Spitfire fighter squadron to claim its 100th kill claim. No.609 converted to the Hawker Typhoon IB in 1942, claiming its first kill on 15 April. The unit had a number of notable British, American, Belgian and Polish fighters, and ended the war with 232 claimed kills to its credit. It lost 73 pilots during operations.

No.71 'Eagle Squadron' continued operations until 29 September 1942, claiming the destruction of 41 enemy aircraft, 13½ probables and 29 damaged for the loss of 40 aircraft and 24 pilots to all causes.

### *Popocatepetl* III

This Supermarine Spitfire MK-Vb was built from a batch of 450 aircraft ordered from April–October 1941 at the Supermarine Aviation (Vickers) Ltd works at Eastleigh, Hampshire. It was given the airframe number 1984 and the RAF registration W3814, and its first flight was on 21 August 1941.

W3814 was assigned to the 8th Maintenance Unit on 22 August 1941, and three days later was reassigned to No.111 Fighter Squadron RAF, a unit that would fight the war from England to Gibraltar, Algeria, Tunisia, Malta, Corsica, France and finish up on the Italian mainland, claiming the destruction of 269½ enemy aircraft.

The squadron code was the letters JU, and *'Popocatepetl III'* was assigned the individual letter 'T'. Its first flight in No.111 was on 2 September 1941, when Pilot Officer Gilbert flew it from 0745-0825 on a 20mm cannon test. Its first combat mission was flown by the same pilot on the same day during a fighter sweep over occupied France. Two days later Gilbert flew it on a bomber escort for 12

Pilot Officer Grey Stenborg, the noted New Zealander fighter pilot who scored his first two victories in *'Popocatepetl III'*. He was killed in action on 24 September 1943. (Air Force Museum of New Zealand)

Blenheims from 1530 to 1720. Through September to the beginning of October, JU-T flew a number of combat missions under different pilots, including scrambles, sweeps, bomber escorts, convoy patrols and 'rhubarbs' (low-level flights across the Channel searching for opportunity targets).

On 21 October 1941 it was damaged during a 'rhubarb', as mentioned in the squadron operations record book:

> Sgt. Smith & Hollingale took off at 0655 hrs to do an offensive patrol (rhubarb) in the Ostent-Neuport area, they crossed the Belgian coast at 0 feet, and continued up the coast toward Ostend at a very low height.
>
> They shot up a military car, and a gun post on the way, and then attacked oil storage tanks and [a] factory building at Ostend with cannon and m.g. Intense light flak was met.
>
> Sgt. Smith's machine received a bullet though one blade of his airscrew, and Sgt. Hollingdale's radiator was slightly damaged. Both pilots returned safely.

In November 1941 No.111 Squadron moved from North Weald to Debden in Essex, where with another Spitfire squadron, No.65, they began a programme to fly night missions, for which all the Spitfire MK.Vbs were painted in matt black overall. Although the national markings and squadron codes were retained on the fuselage and fin, those on the wings top and below the wings were painted over.

It was feared at this time that the *Luftwaffe* would launch a major night-time offensive.

It was during this period that *'Popocatepetl III'* suffered its first accident, on the night of 25 January 1942, while being flown by Sergeant Pilot H.R. Hollingdale during a night flying practice flight between 0105 and 0135. Hollingdale ran off the runway upon landing owing to the muddy and waterlogged state of the ground, causing some damage to the aircraft.

There is some confusion due to the handwriting on the aircraft repair form over when the aircraft returned to No.111 Squadron, but it was repaired and back in service by 3 February, and was test flown on 11 February by a young New Zealandr pilot, Pilot Officer Grey Stenborg, who took it up for a local air test between 1100 and 1110. Next day it participated in a convoy patrol being flown by Sergeant Hollingdale.

All the Spitfires in No.111 Squadron had by now been repainted in their normal daytime colour schemes. Among the pilots who flew *'Popocatepetl III'* were a number of Czechs, Norwegians and New Zealanders, including Flying Officer Josef Prihoda, who was killed in action on 6 March 1943 after scoring four enemy aircraft destroyed plus one shared, three probables and two damaged. He flew *'Popocatepetl III'* on a night flying test on 27 February 1942 between 1735 and 1800.

In March 1942 *'Popocatepetl III'* flew a number of missions and combat-related sorties. April was very interesting in the story of the aircraft. On the 26th of that month, during an escort of six bombers, Pilot Officer Grey Stenborg scored his first aerial victory in *'Popocatepetl III'*, during his second flight in the aircraft (the first was as rear support for a bomber to Saint-Omer), as noted in the squadron operational record book:

> P/O. G. Stenborg (N.Z.) distinguished himself by opening his score and shooting down the only enemy fighter which came within our range – an FW 190. He followed it down to 5000 feet [at] which height he saw it hit the ground.
>
> Stenborg's combat report reads as follows:
>
> I was Red 3, flying with 111 squadron, as part of the rear support wing. After we had crossed the French coast enemy aircraft were reported in the vicinity. Between Cassel and St. Omer, as we were turning, someone called Red 4 to look out.
>
> I did a steep turn to the left and saw an F.W.190 which had turned left as if to follow Red 4, who had done the same thing. The 190 was going very fast and I knew I could not close on him; so I fired at once from a quarter astern at about 500 yards range (estimated).
>
> I kept firing until all my cannon had gone. Just before I had finished I saw black smoke coming from the e/a. This continued and it went into a spiral and then a power dive straight down. I followed it, and from 5000 feet I saw it hit the ground and burst into flames. I then put the nose of my aircraft down and went straight home.
>
> Cine-gun camera switched on.

He used up 120 rounds of 20mm cannon and 1,400 rounds of .303 calibre ammunition.

The next day *'Popocatepetl III'* would score again, flown by the same pilot, during an escort of bombers that were attacking the *Luftwaffe* airfield at Longuenesse in the Pas de Calais, as noted in the operations record book of the squadron:

> Escort cover wing, for 8 Hurricane bombers to St. Omer, this time squadron airborne 11.21 hours, the formation was heavily engaged by enemy aircraft between St. Omer and the French coast and the wing had many victories and losses to report on its return.
>
> P/O. G. Stenborg (N.Z) shot-down an FW-190 following it down and seeing crash. Sgt. O.L. Clubb did not return from the operation. He was flying as P/O. Stenborg's No. 2 and it's believed that he had been shot-down by the FW-190 destroyed by P/O. Stenborg.
>
> Stenborg wrote in his combat report:
>
> I was Red 3, 111 sq, part of escort covering for Hurricane bombers. When approaching St. Omer there were many warnings of e/a .Suddenly I hear a yell 'Look out Gray'. I at once took the most violent evasive action, giving full right rudder and putting the stick hard over left and down in the corner with full throttle. I went down and when I realized that there was nothing behind me I pulled out and looked around, having come down from 17[000] to 7000 feet.
>
> I then saw a squadron of Spitfires ahead and made for them .On looking behind me I saw another Spit which may have been Red 4.We joined up with Blue section of this squadron and continued to weave. Shortly after I saw a FW190 turning off on my right about 50 yds away and going down slightly. Its Black crosses were very clear. Out of the corner of my eye I saw 2 more. I turned in to attack

the first which was now about 500 yds away owing to initial speed advantage.

He saw me and did a steep turn left. I pressed the boost out-out, went into fine pitch and put the throttle through the gate, at the same time opening fire from the port quarter. I saw my tracers going right at him, and he turned over on his back and went into a steep dive. I followed, also turning on my back, with my cannon still firing. We were losing height rapidly, and when my cannon was finished it stopped firing.

The 190 seemed to come out of its dive and started around at an angle of about 45 degrees. I swooped down to about 100 ft of the crashed e/a, and on looking around saw another FW190 approaching me, about 800 yards distant. I continued at full throttle at zero feet and doing everything possible to get away from him.

After about 5 mins of this [I] slowed up and climbed to about 80 ft, and on looking around I saw that the 190 had rose [*sic*]. I slowed up further and went to 0 ft and to let the compass settle. I then set course for England at 0 feet and increased speed. As I approached the [French] coast I saw a party of soldiers outside some huts but I was going too fast to do anything.

A few secs later I saw some similar huts just off the beach and fired my machine guns at them. I can only suppose that the FW190 which I destroyed had already shot down the Spitfire flying with me, which may have been Red 4, who is missing. Cine-gun switch on.

During this engagement Stenborg used up 120 rounds of 20mm cannon shells and 1,000 rounds of .303 calibre machine-gun rounds. These were the only victory and loss for No.111 Squadron suffered that day.

During the rest of the month '*Popocatepetl III*' would fly the following missions:

27 April P.O. Stenborg 1340-1400 Biggin Hill
27 April Sgt Bryson 1500-1630 Rear support to bombers
28 April Sgt Henrichsen 1035-1210 Escorting 6 Bostons to Saint-Omer
30 April Sgt Christian 1415-1555 Bomber escort to Flushing
30 April Sgt Henrichsen 1825-2010 to Abbeville Marshalling Yard

On 1 June '*Popocatepetl III*' was engaged in aerial combat during an escort of bombers, in which its Norwegian pilot, Sergeant Y. Henriksen, and another pilot opened fire against FW-190s, but no claims were submitted.

From June-August, the aircraft flew a number of combat missions, including sweeps, rodeos (sweeps over enemy territory), bomber escorts, patrols and scrambles, as well as training flights, including formation flying, air tests, exercises, flights between bases and aerobatics.

On 19 August 1942, No.111 Squadron participated in operations connected with the raid on Dieppe, during which '*Popocatepetl III*' took part in the first flight for the squadron being flown by Sergeant F.H. Tyrrell, taking off around 0930. It was to prove the aircraft's final flight, as the squadron's after-action report reveals:

The twelve Spitfires of 111 squadron down at 3,000 feet also saw the first bombers. They saw some JU-88s and Do217's escorted by 190's trying to get through to the ships.

Flight Lieutenant Vancl and his No.2 Sergeant B.A.C. Spranger attacked one of the Dornier and objects were seen to fall from it. Sergeant F.H. Tyrrel was hit by flak during the action and had to bail out.

He spent five hours in his dinghy before being rescued by an ASR [air-sea rescue] launch. This launch was strafed by German fighters on its return trip and some of the crew were wounded but Tyrrell landed safely at Dover.

During the action No.111 not only lost '*Popocatepetl III*' but another pilot, Sergeant Edward James Hendley, who, flying Spitfire P8699, was shot down after a dogfight involving Do.217 bombers and escorting FW-190s. No.111 was credited with four victories that day:

F/L. Vancl F. and Sgt. Spranger 1 Do.217 destroyed
F/L. Baraldi F.H.R 1 Do.217 destroyed
Sgt. Henrichson Y. 1 Do.217 destroyed
P/O. Gale B.E. 1 FW-190 destroyed

During its time in No.111 Squadron, '*Popocatepetl III*', JU-T W3814, flew some 189 flights, of which 59 were combat-related.

Gray Stenborg went on to claim two more victories with the squadron, a pair of FW-190s on 30 April 1942. He volunteered to go to Malta, and in May 1942 he joined No.185 Squadron and claimed a number of further victories, until he was shot down by BF-109s and bailed out on 17 August 1942.

He returned to the UK in September 1942 and was posted as a flight instructor, but in 1943 he returned to operations as a flight commander in No.91 Squadron, where he claimed a number of victories. He was killed in action on 23 September 1943 during a head-on attack on a FW-190 near Poix in France. His final wartime score was 14 destroyed enemy aircraft, one shared destroyed and three damaged.

### *Iztacchliutl*

No information is available about this Supermarine Spitifire, which may have been a model MK.Vb.

## MEXICO I FOR NORWAY

After the invasion and occupation of Norway in April-June 1940, the Norwegian government in exile based in London decided to establish a training base for the Royal Norwegian Air Force (RNAF) and Royal Norwegian Navy Air Service (RNNAS). The Norwegians also had a good number of aircraft that had been ordered and paid for before the invasion, but had not been delivered.

A location was selected in Canada – Toronto Island Airport, and later at Muskoka Airport – that would serve as a training centre for all Norwegians who wished to join the RNAF and RNNAS. This camp, later known as 'Little Norway', started operations on 10 November 1940. Its inventory of aircraft consisted of Fairchild PT-19/PT-26 Cornell trainers, Northrop N-3PBs, Curtiss Hawk 75-A8s and Douglas DB8A-5/A-33s.

Among the training aircraft a number of PT-26s were presentation aircraft that carried the names of the donors, which made possible the acquisition of aircraft for the Norwegian air arm. Among them was a Cornell PT-26-FA (42-14362) that received the number 181 (FH714) and had the name '*Mexico I*', part of the 'Wings for Norway' programme funded by Alberto J. Gundersen & Cia, probably of Mexico City.

The Norwegian training programme was moved to England before the end of the war. At the conclusion of hostilities, '*Mexico I*', with the rest of the training aircraft, was transferred to Gardermoen near Oslo, Norway, in November 1945. It continued serving in the RNAF with the registration L-BH until 1949, when it was passed down to civilian aviation with the civilian registration LN-AEW.

CHAPTER 4

# EVOLUTION OF THE ORGANISATION OF THE AIR FORCE, 1941-46

After Mexico had broken diplomatic relations with Germany, Italy and Japan in December 1941, the Mexican air service was known as the *Direccion de Aeronautica*, or *Direccion de Aeronautica Militar* (Direction of Military Aeronautics), but unofficially was known in the press and among its personnel as the *Fuerza Aerea Mexicana* (Mexican Air Force) or *Fuerza Aerea Nacional* (National Air Force).

It was a one of many branches of the Mexican Army, under the command of the *Secretaria de la Defensa Nacional* (Secretary of National Defence), which was the old *Secretaria de Guerra y Marina* (Secretary of War and Navy). In 1941 the Mexican Navy was elevated to its own *Secretaria* and was now a separate identity, so the armed forces were divided into the *Secretaria de la Defensa Nacional* and *Secretaria de Marina*.

But there is some confusion over the correct title used by 1941. Aeronautical publications in Mexico put it this way:

Dirección de Aeronáutica Militar
Director del Departamento:
Gral. P.A. Roberto Fierro Villalobos
Subdirector de Departamento:
Corl. P.A. Francisco Carrillo Torres
Comandancia General del Campo
Corl. P.A. Fernando Huerta Campuzano
Escuela Militar de Aviación
Director
Corl. P.A. Luis Farrell Cubillas
Oficinas en el Campo Aéreo Militar- Balbuena D.F.

### 1941

At this time, almost everything to do with military aviation was concentrated near Mexico City, including the military aviation workshops and the tactical units, the two air regiments.

The only component that was not there was the military aviation school, which by September 1941 was moved to Monterrey in Nuevo Leon. By the end of the year, one flight of military aircraft was stationed, as previously mentioned, at the border city of Tijuana, Baja California, under the jurisdiction of the *2/o. Zona Militar* (Military Zone), with another at the bottom tip of the peninsula of Baja California at the port of La Paz with the *3/o. Zona Militar.*

Flights of about three aircraft were deployed to different parts of Mexico as necessary to the different military zones, to help in the internal security of the state or region, dealing with rebel groups and bandits, flying reconnaissance and some bombing missions.

In other cases aircraft flew army officers to and from army outposts.

By this time some of the flights had a mix of equipment, flying Azcarate Corsarios, Vought V-99s and Consolidated Model 21-M general purpose aircraft, as noted in the pilots' flight log books.

The tactical units of the Mexican air service were the two air regiments: the *1/o. Regimiento Aereo* under the command of Colonel Fernando Proal Pardo (1891-1965) and the *2/o. Regimiento Aereo* under Colonel Rafael Montero Ramos (1895-1959), both based at Balbuena airfield.

Each regiment had three squadrons, and each squadron was organised in three flights of three aircraft each, plus a command plane, for a total of 10 aircraft for each squadron and a strength of about 30 aircraft per regiment. Due to serviceability issues there would be fewer aircraft per squadron, which affected the overall strength of the air regiment.

By August 1941, the air service had reported that they had available 12 "war" aircraft plus 52 undergoing repairs, with 225 parachutes. There were also six aircraft with the aviation school for training. In December 1941 the *1/o. Regimiento Aereo*, with headquarters at El Cipres, Baja California, comprised the *1/o. Escuadron Aereo*, *2/o. Escuadron Aereo* and *3/o. Escuadron Aereo*.

They were charge with surveillance and protection of the Pacific coast from the peninsula of Baja California to the coastal states of Sonora and Sinaloa. Its bases were in El Cipres and La Paz, Baja California, where the squadrons were deployed, while flights and patrols were deployed to Hermosillo in Sonora, and Mazatlan and Guaymas, Sinaloa.

The *2/o. Regimiento Aereo*, with headquarters at Balbuena airfield, also comprised the *1/o. Escuadrón Aéreo*, *2/o. Escuadrón Aéreo* and *3/o. Escuadrón Aéreo*.

Back in 1937, when the Consolidated Model 21-M entered service, a renumbering of Mexican military aircraft was undertaken, starting with the Consolidated Model 21Ms, receiving the numbers 1-10, then the surviving Chance Vought O2U-2Ms getting the numbers 11-20. There was then a break until number 31 for the Mexican-built Azcarate Corsarios, running through to number 63.

In 1938 the Mexican government purchased 10 Vought V-99

Balbuena military airfield, with a Douglas A-24B dive bomber and two Lockheed C-60A Lodestar transport planes. (Enrique Velasco Padilla)

Mexican pilots being briefed on their next flight, with a line-up of North American AT-6 Texans in the background. (Enrique Velasco Padilla)

Vought OS2U-3 Kingfishers that started with the number 69.

The service also had other aircraft that served in a transport role but did not receive consecutive numbers.

### 1942

This year was marked by more movement of aviation units to the Gulf coast as the German U-boat menace started to show itself, and the arrival of American-made aircraft to reinforce the Pacific and Gulf coast units.

By the end of the year there was a change of command, which would affect the direction of the *Direccion de Aeronautica Militar* in the coming years. The *2/o. Regimiento Aereo* started sending aircraft, not only to cover the Gulf region, close to the island of Cuba, but also in May it sent a flight of three aircraft to Merida in Yucatán to establish a base of operations and patrols.

In March 1942 the *1/o. Regimiento Aereo* received six Vought OS2U-3 Kingfishers. The *2/o. Regimiento Aereo*, while still based at Balbuena airfield, received the first North American AT-6B armed trainers. Due to the situation in the Gulf of Mexico, in June 1942 the *2/o. Regimiento* deployed the first three aircraft of this type establishing a base at Tuxpan, Veracruz, until July.

The presidents of the United States and Mexico at Monterrey, Nuevo Leon, before the start of a military parade in their honour. (Fuerza Aerea Mexicana)

Corsairs, which received the numbers 34, 35, 37, 38, 39, 40, 42, 43 and 44 (one aircraft was lost in a fatal accident), that seems to have caused another renumbering of aircraft in the service. The Corsairs replaced the Azcarate Corsarios that had previously been given those numbers. From there, numbers 45-68 were given to the rest of the Azcarate Corsarios. After the failed General Cedillo rebellion, two of his aircraft, DGA-8 Howards, were incorporated into the air service and received the numbers 69 and 70. The latter two were used as transports and placed in service with other federal agencies. One of the Howards was lost in a fatal accident in 1938 and the other was reportedly damaged during a landing. The next numbers for tactical aircraft would not come until March 1942, with the arrival of the

From July the *1/o. Regimiento Aereo* (headquarters at El Cipres, Baja California) was deployed as follows:

*1/o. Escuadron Aereo* at El Cipres, with one flight at Santa Rosalia, Baja California, and one flight at Hamilton Ranch, south of Ensenada;
*2/o. Escuadron Aereo* at Sonora and Sinaloa, with one flight at Hermosillo, Sonora, and one flight at Guaymas, Sinaloa;
*3/o. Escuadron Aereo* at La Paz, Baja California.

As mentioned before, this regiment had other flights at different locations in Baja California, Sonora and Sinaloa. The aviation equipment was a mix of various types of general purpose biplanes (Vought Corsair, Azcarate Corsario, Vought V-99M and Consolidated Model 21-M), while its most modern type, the Sikorsky Kingfisher, would later be sent from El Cipres to Mazatlan, Sinaloa, for patrol work.

The *2/o.Regimiento Aereo* (eadquarters at the port of Veracruz) had the following disposition of units:
*1/o. Escuadron Aéreo* at Tampico, Tamaulipas;
*2/o. Escuadron Aereo* at the port of Veracruz;
*3/o. Escuadron Aereo* at Mérida, Yucatán.

It also had flights stationed in the peninsula of Yucatán and at Campeche, Tuxpan, Veracruz and Tabasco, the only new addition being the North American AT-6B and later the AT-6C armed trainers for coastal patrols in the Gulf.

In the same year the military aviation workshops were completing

President Manuel Avila Camacho passing a review of the aerial units that participated in the live fire demonstration on 5 March 1944 near Mexico City. (Fuerza Aerea Mexicana

Brigadier General Gustavo A. Salinas chief of the Mexican air service, with a family member in front of a North American AT-6. (Fuerza Aerea Mexicana)

10 Barreda EP biplane primary trainers for the military aviation school, that would be sent there to increase its training fleet. The aviation workshop personnel increased from 125 to 178, completing 35 work orders for general repair of aircraft and 21 for partial repairs.

On 1 September 1942, General de Division Lazaro Cardenas, the former commander of the *Region Militar del Pacifico*, was designated as the Secretary of National Defense by President Manuel Avila Camacho.

In December Cardenas changed the director of the *Dirreccion de Aeronautica*, naming Brigadier General Gustavo Salinas Camina in place of General Roberto Fierro Villalobos.

With these changes, General Fernando Proal Pardo, former commander of the *1/o. Regimiento Aereo*, became the sub-director of military aviation and Colonel Francisco M. Carrillo, the former sub-director, the new commander of the *1/o. Regimiento Aereo* based at El Cipres.

## 1943

This year would see a major reorganisation in the tactical set-up of the *Dirreccion de Aeronautica militar* and the arrival of more American-made aircraft under the Lend Lease programme.

With more North American AT-6 armed trainers, the decision was made to retire from the front-line units all the general purpose biplanes, which were considered unsafe for crews to conduct patrols along the Pacific and Gulf coasts. All these biplanes were concentrated at Balbuena military airfield, where some would be retired or scrapped by 1948.

On the Pacific coast, the first four North American AT-6s arrived in March. More would later be sent to the *1/o. Regimiento Aereo* while phasing out the following biplanes:

three AT-6s and one Vought OS2U-3 Kingfisher at Ensenada, Baja California, and

two AT-6s and two Corsair biplanes at La Paz, Baja California.

On the Gulf coast, the *2/o. Regimiento* commander, Colonel Alfonso Cruz Rivera, reported by the end of the year that he had received up to 27 AT-6s, with some deployed to Ixtepec, Oaxaca, a new base on the Pacific side, and other bases in the Gulf of Mexico.

In July of that year, by the orders Director of the *Dirreccion de Aeronautica*, General Gustavo Salinas, the regimental system of the air service was abolished and replaced with six individual squadrons. The squadrons were located as follows:

*1/o. Escuadron Aereo* at El Cipres,
*2/o. Escuadron Aereo* at La Paz,
*3/o. Escuadron Aereo* at Tampico, Tamaulipas,
*4/o. Escuadron Aereo* at Veracruz,
*5/o. Escuadron Aereo* at Merida, Yucatán
(one flight at Chetumal, Quintana Roo, and one
at Cozumel, Quintana Roo) and
*6/o. Escuadron* Aereo at Ciudad Ixtepec, Oaxaca.

They flew North American AT-6B and AT-6C armed trainers, along

A Douglas A-24B Banshee dive bomber at Balbuena airfield after its arrival in 1943, receiving some maintenance. (Fuerza Aerea Mexicana)

After 1943 all biplane aircraft were removed from front-line squadrons. Here is Consolidated Model 21-M No.7/27 in the central hangar of Balbuena airfield. (Enrique Velasco Padilla)

A close-up of the marking painted on Consolidated Model 21-M No.7/27, that appears to be a horse or mule with its tongue out and the number 22,000,000. (Enrique Velasco Padilla)

with Vought OS2U-1 Kingfishers (land plane version), for patrols and convoy escort duties.

Two new squadrons also came into existence, the *7/o.* and *8/o. Escuadrones Aereos*, based at Balbuena airfield.

In July the *Grupo de Escuadrones Aereos* (Group of Aerial Squadrons) was formed, with the following units under their command:

*1/o. Grupo de Escuadrones Aéreos* (headquarters at Balbuena airfield), with *7/o. Escuadrón Aéreo* and *8/o. Escuadrón Aéreo* at Balbuena;

*2/o. Grupo de Escuadrones Aéreos* (headquarters at Veracruz, Veracruz), with *3/o. Escuadrón Aéreo* at Tampico, Tamaulipas, *4/o. Escuadrón Aéreo* at Veracruz, Veracruz, and *5/o. Escuadrón Aéreo* at Mérida, Yucatán, with one flight at Chetumal, Quintana Roo, and one flight at Cozumel, Quintana Roo; *3/o. Grupo de Escuadrones Aéreos* (headquarters at El Cipres), with *1/o. Escuadrón Aéreo* at El Ciprés, *2/o. Escuadrón Aéreo* at La Paz and *6/o. Escuadrón Aéreo* at Ciudad Ixtepec, Oaxaca.

In August 1943, after the creation of the aviation groups, the *3/o. Grupo de Escuadrones Aereos* reported that it had 12 AT-6s for

The end of the many biplanes in the Mexican Air Force after war. (Enrique Velasco Padilla)

A typical scene in the central hangar of Balbuena airfield, with Azcarate Corsario No.52 sharing it with North American AT-6s that replaced them in service. (Enrique Velasco Padilla)

patrolling the Pacific coast, with four at La Paz, three at Cabo San Lucas (at the tip of the Baja Peninsula) and five at El Cipres.

By the end of the year, new squadrons came into existence with a three-digit number, as noted in a British intelligence report and Mexican official documents:

1st Squadron at El Cipres became 202 Baja California, with three A-24Bs and four AT-6s;

2nd Squadron at La Paz became 203 Baja California, with seven AT-6s;

3rd Squadron at Rihl Field became 204 Tampico, with four AT-6s;

4th Squadron at Las Bajadas became 205 Vera Cruz, with five AT-6s;

5th Squadron at Merida, Yucatán, became 206, with six AT-6s and two OS2U-1s;

6th Squadron at Ixtepec, Oaxaca, became 207, with four AT-6s;

7th Squadron at Mexico City became 201, working on A-24Bs; and

8th Squadron at Mexico City became 101, working on AT-11s.

Due to the arrival of Lend Lease aircraft, in particular Douglas A-24B dive bombers, on 11 November 1943 the *Escuadron Aereo A-24 de Bombardeo inclinado* was formed under Major Salvador Noble Morales, with eight pilots. Previously it appears this unit was the *7/o. Escuadron Aereo*.

By December 1943 the designation was change to *Escuadron Aereo 201*, with the A-24B dive bombers and some AT-6 trainers. The *8/o. Escuadron Aereo* would later become a Beechcraft AT-11 twin-engine aircraft unit, which received the designation of *Escuadron Aereo 101*.

This renumbering system started in late 1943 and continued until 1944, when all the squadrons had received their three-digit numbers.

In August 1943 the Mexican Air Force started to receive the first of four Lockheed C-60A Lodestar transport planes. By February 1944

Armed North American AT-6Cs on standby for anti-submarine patrols and convoy escorts in the Gulf of Mexico. (Enrique Velasco Padilla)

they were all delivered. A transport flight or squadron was formed and assigned to the *1/o. Grupo de Escuadrones Aereos*.

While the aviation maintenance shops were busy with maintenance of the Lend Lease aircraft and working on some national design types, they were also correcting some issues with the Sea Tezuiltan primary trainers, a low-wing monoplane that resembled the Fairchild PT-19, and the '*Salinas*', a two-engine design. The workshops were also building replacement propellers for the Fairchild PT-19 and UC-61.

### 1944

This would be a landmark year in the history of the air service. On 10 February 1944, by presidential decree signed by President Manuel Avila Camacho, the Mexican air service received constitutional recognition as an armed force within the Mexican Army and was officially designated as the *Fuerza Aerea Mexicana* (Mexican Air Force),

thanks to the efforts of Lieutenant Colonel and lawyer Angel H. Corzo Molina (1899-1985), with the backing of General Gustavo Salinas. Since 1992, Mexican Air Force day has been celebrated on this day in Mexico.

The individual squadrons started to convert to a three-digit number, the air order of battle looking like the following circa June-August:

***1/o. Grupo de Escuadrones Aéreos,* Mexico City**
**Colonel David Chagoya Rodriguez**
*Escuadron Aereo 101* Beechcraft AT-11
*Escuadron Aéreo 201* Douglas A-24B/ AT-6
*Escuadrón Aéreo 208* Douglas A-24B/AT-6
*Escuadrilla o Escuadron de Transporte*? Lockheed C-60A
***2/o. Grupo de Escuadrones Aéreos***, port of Veracruz, Veracruz
**Colonel Alfonso Cruz Rivera**
*Escuadrón Aéreo 204* Tampico, Tamaulipas AT-6
*Escuadrón Aéreo 205* Veracruz, Veracruz AT-6/OS2U-1
*Escuadrón Aéreo 206* Mérida, Yucatán AT-6
*Escuadrilla* Cozumel, Quintana Roo AT-6

Future P-47 pilots (left to right) Lieutenants Julio Cal y Mayor Sauz and Carlos Garduno Nunez standing in front of one their AT-6s of the *3/o. Escuadron Aereo*. (Enrique Velasco Padilla)

The first transports planes the Mexican Air Force received were the Lockheed C-60A Lodestar transport, one of which is seen with a Douglas A-24B dive bomber, possibly at Balbuena airfield. (Enrique Velasco Padilla)

One of the surviving V-99Ms, No.35, after being withdrawn from front-line service after 1943 at Balbuena airfield. (Enrique Velasco Padilla)

*Escuadrilla* Chetumal, Quintana Roo AT-6

*Escuadron Aéreo 207* Ciudad de Ixtepec, Oaxaca AT-6

***3/o. Grupo de Escuadrones Aéreos*, El Cipres, Baja California**

**Colonel Francisco Carrillo T.**

*Escuadrón Aéreo 202* El Cipres, Baja California AT-6/A-24B

*Escuadrón Aéreo 203* La Paz, Baja California AT-6

***Comandancia Central de Campos*, Balbuena, Mexico City**

**Major Salvador I. Cano**

North American AT-6 and the surviving general purpose biplanes

***Grupo Aereo Mexicano*, NAS North Island, San Diego, USA**

**Colonel Antonio Cardenas Rodriguez**

Douglas SBD-5/6

As can be seen from this order of battle, several changes had been made. The *3/o. Grupo de Escuadrones Aereos* had lost one squadron to the *2/o. Grupo Escuadrones Aereos*, and a Mexican unit was operating at Naval Air Station North Island, San Diego.

A second A-24 squadron was formed in August 1944, later becoming *Escuadron Aereo 208*. It is interesting to note that the units that actually had combat planes (A-24Bs) were assigned to Mexico City under the control of the *1/o. Zona Militar.*

A reported three A-24Bs were sent to *Escuadron Aereo 202* at El Cipres around March 1944. The AT-6s and the Kingfishers were carrying out the bulk of the convoy and coastal patrols on

Another type removed from coastal patrol duties were the surviving Consolidated Model 21-Ms. Here is No.5, that continued to serve after the end of the war. (Enrique Velasco Padilla)

both coasts. All the squadrons fell under the control of the military zone commander, but still answered to the group commanders as well.

A North American AT-6C with its properly equipped pilot ready to undertake a patrol, possibly on the Mexican Pacific coast. (Enrique Velasco Padilla)

A new aircraft numbering system was established in 1944, with three letters and three to four numbers, which designated the manufacturer, the type of aircraft and its role. Forexample, the North American AT-6 under the old system had received the letters and numbers P-75 up to P-125. Under the new system, the Texans received the letters EAN (*Entrenador Avanzado North*, Advanced trainer North), the first two letters describing the function of the aircraft and the third the manufacturer, in this case North American.

The number block started at 700. Therefore AT-6 P-80 became EAN-701. The Douglas A-24B received the serial numbers BID-2501 to BID-2525 (*Bombardero Inclinado Douglas*, Dive Bomber Douglas). This numbering and letter system was used in Mexico until the 1990s.

Another change to the air order of battle happened in July 1944, when *Escuadron Aereo 201* was selected to form part of the *Grupo de Perfeccionamiento Aeronautica* (GPA, Aeronautical Training Group) to travel to the United States for training as a fighter squadron, to be eventually deployed to combat theatre of operations. In turn, *Escuadron Aereo 209* was formed to receive the Douglas A-24B and AT-6 from the 201st.

***1/o. Grupo de Escuadrones Aereos*, Balbuena, Mexico Federal District**
*Escuadron Aereo 101* AT-11
*Escuadron Aéreo 208* A-24B/AT-6
*Escuadrón Aéreo 209* A-24B/AT-6
*Escuadrilla o Escuadron de Transporte* Lockheed C-60A
***2/o. Grupo de Escuadrones Aéreos*, Veracruz, Veracruz**
*Escuadrón Aéreo 204* Tampico, Tamaulipas AT-6
*Escuadrón Aéreo 205* Veracruz, Veracruz AT-6/ OS2U-1
*Escuadrón Aéreo 206* Mérida, Yucatán AT-6
*Escuadrón Aéreo 207* Ciudad de Ixtepec, Oaxaca AT-6
***3/o. Grupo de Escuadrones Aéreos,* El Cipres, Baya California**
*Escuadrón Aéreo 202* AT-6/A-24B
*Escuadrón Aéreo 203* AT-6
**Grupo de Perfeccionamiento Aeronautica (GPA)**
*Escuadron Aereo 201* Air bases in Texas and Idaho, USA
Vultee BT-13/15, NA AT-6, Curtiss P-40 and Republic P-47

## 1945

In the final year of the Second World War, the Mexican Air Force had a large number of personnel, including pilots and ground crew, studying in various Army air bases across the United States. These included one complete fighter squadron with personnel and a replacement group for the *Fuerza Aerea Expedicionaria Mexicana* (FAEM, Mexican Expeditionary Air Force/MEAF).

Plans were discussed for a post-war air force to include an Air Division. The *Talleres Generales de Aeronautica* (TGA) was busy repairing aircraft and engines. With the number of aircraft coming

The interior of the central hangar of Balbuena airfield with the new and old aircraft of the Mexican Air Force. There is a Beechcraft AT-7, Consolidated Model 21-M and Vought V-99M general purpose biplanes. (Enrique Velasco Padilla)

from the Lend Lease programme, the air force transferred more aircraft to the new naval aviation.

The Mexican Expeditionary Air Force, with the 201st Mexican Fighter Squadron, was deployed after its completion of training to the Pacific theatre of operations. Equipped with the Republic P-47D Thunderbolt, it was involved in the liberation of the Philippines.

Patrols continued on both coasts, but on a reduced scale since by mid-1945

Germany was defeated and Japan was about to succumb to the power of the Allied forces in the Pacific.

The Mexican air order of battle for August 1945, the final wartime dispositions of the units, was as follows:

***1/o. Grupo de Escuadrones Aéreos*, Balbuena airfield, Mexico Federal District**
*Escuadrón Aéreo 101* AT-11
*Escuadrón Aéreo 208* A-24B/AT-6
*Escuadrón Aéreo 209* A-24B/AT-6
*Escuadrilla o Escuadrón de Transporte* Lockheed C-60A

Note: by the end of the year the MEAF would receive its first Douglas C-47 transport planes, and in March 1945 there were three B-25Js in

Brigadier General Gustavo A. Salinas, chief of the Mexican Air Force, undertook many trips to the United States, including to visit the chief of the USAAF, General Henry 'Hap' Arnold. (National Archives)

More than 30 years later, the same first five Mexican pilots that trained at the Moisant Aviation School in 1912 gathered for a group picture in front of a A-24B at Balbuena airfield. Left to right: Alberto Salinas Carranza, Gustavo Salinas Camina, Juan Pablo Aldaroso, Horacio Ruiz and Eduardo Aldaroso. (National Archives)

Mexico but under USAAF supervision, before being handed over in December 1945.

***2/o. Grupo de Escuadrones Aéreo*, Veracruz, Veracruz**
*Escuadrón Aéreo 204* Tampico, Tamaulipas AT-6
*Escuadrón Aéreo 205* Veracruz, Veracruz AT-6/ OS2U-1
*Escuadrón Aéreo 206* Mérida, Yucatán AT-6
*Escuadrón Aéreo 207* Ciudad Ixtepec, Oaxaca AT-6

***3/o. Grupo de Escuadrones Aéreos*, El Cipres, Baja California**
*Escuadrón Aéreo 202* El Cipres AT-6/ A-24B
*Escuadrón Aéreo 203* La Paz AT-6

***Fuerza Aérea Expedicionaria Mexicana*, Clark Field, Philippines**

Mexican ground troops in front of recently arrived Becchcraft AT-7s and North American AT-6Cs, which were later deployed to the Gulf of Mexico for anti-submarine patrols from Balbuena airfield. (Archivo Casasolas)

*Escuadrón Aéreo de Pelea 201* P-47D

From March 1944, General Gustavo Salinas, chief of the air force, was contemplating expanding the number of aircraft to over 1,000, of which 600 would be tactical types, with about 300 trainers and 100 transport and liasion types.

This would impact the number of flight crews and maintenance personnel.

General Salinas was interested in acquiring the following types: C-60s, C-53s, L-5s, helicopters, B-25s, A-26s, B-17s, A-24s, A-25s, P-51s and P-47s. However, a reduced budget for the post-war air force and a change in its command put an end to such plans. Therefore the Mexican Air Force would not be ready for the crisis of 1959 with Guatemala.

# CHAPTER 5
# THE CREATION OF MEXICAN NAVAL AVIATION

One of the repercussions of Mexico's involvement in the Second World War was the establishment of Mexican naval aviation, with the help of the Mexican air service.

There had been several attempts to create a naval aviation, going back to 1918, when a TNCA Serie A biplane was modified with floats and successfully tested at the port of Veracruz in August of that year.

But it was not until March 1926 that the Mexican Navy created the *Cuerpo de Hidroaviones* (Group of Hydroplanes) that allowed the first naval officers to attend the Military Aviation School, with the first officer graduating in August 1927. This opened the door for other naval officers to gain their wings.

Another Mexican-built aircraft was modified as a floatplane, this time one of the 10 Azcarate E trainers being equipped with floats and flown at Veracruz in March 1930.

The test pilot for the flight was Captain Carlos Castillo Brenton (1897-1935), the first naval pilot, who showed up for the test flight in his swing suit, which did not please engineer General Juan F. Azcarate, the aircraft designer. He still conducted the test flight, but on landing he flipped the aircraft over in the water. Castillo Brenton was uninjured in the incident and the Azcarate was recovered and later flown by other naval pilots.

Later a Fairchild KR-34 trainer was also modified with floats and used by the naval pilots. However, by 1940 only 11 naval officers had graduated from the military aviation school.

Plans were announced in August 1941 to start to build hydroplanes for the Mexican Navy, as reported by the US Assistant Naval Attache in Mexico City:

> SIX HYDROPLANES FOR THE MEXICAN NAVY
> In the General Aeronautics workshops, there will be started during the course of next week, the construction of 6 hydroplanes which were asked for by the Secretary of the Navy for the service of patrolling the coasts.
>
> Having checked the efficiency of the apparatus which have been constructed in said shops and the existing necessity of endowing the Navy with sufficient things to make the coastguard services in national waters more effective, the Secretary made the first request for the indicated 6 machines, which will be ready at the end of two months.

No more information has been found to determine the type of aircraft that were being built. At this time the only aircraft under

The Mexican-built Azcarate E Entrenador number 1E that was fitted with floats and test-flown at the port of Veracruz by the first Naval aviator, Captain Carlos Castillo Breton, in March 1930. (Enrique Velasco Padilla)

Another aircraft that was converted as a floatplane for the Mexican Navy before the war was this Fairchild KR-34C. (Enrique Velasco Padilla)

construction were Barreda Ares EP biplane trainers, but these ended in the service of the military aviation school, not with the Navy.

### THE WAR YEARS

In 1939, when the Mexican Navy became its own department, separate from the Army, a section of naval aviation was established. Only a small number of aircraft were being used by the naval pilots, with two civilian aircraft: a Waco model UIC open cockpit biplane, civil registration XA-AHV, and a Waco model PBF close cabin biplane, civil registration XB-BEW.

In 1943 one of the Wacos was loaned to the American Legation in Mexico.

Before General Lazaro Cardenas finished his presidential term in 1940, he signed a presidential decree on 26 August 1940 for the creation of a naval aviation school as part of the naval academy at Veracruz. The school was planned to start operations on 1 January 1941, but due to the change of administrations and the creation of the *Secretaria de Marina* in December 1940, this project was not carried out.

The director of the Mexican Navy had directed the Mexican naval attache to inform him of the cost of operations and facilities of the Fleet primary trainers with Kinner 165hp engines. The *Cuerpo de Hidroaviones* became the *Cuerpo de Aeronautica Naval*; of the 11 naval officers who had graduated as pilots, two had died and some had transferred over to the Army air service.

Mexican naval aviation was formed in 1943 with a presidential decree of 23 February that year, signed by President Avila Camacho, with the intervention of Commodore Mario Rodriguez Malpica (1893-1997). Four veteran naval flyers were ordered to form the *1/o. Escuadron Aeronaval* (1st Naval Squadron).

### THE MEXICAN NAVY, 1941

During the presidency of Lazaro Cardenas, the Mexican Navy underwent a major infusion of ships to its inventory thanks to a contract between the Mexican government and the Spanish Republic in 1932, when Cardenas was also Secretary of War and Navy, for the purchase of 15 naval units, including destroyers, transports and patrol boats, to the value of 73 million Spanish pesetas.

This deal comprised 10 patrol boats (*Guardacostas*) of 180 tons, two armed transports (*Transportes Canoneros*) of 16,000 tons and three destroyers (*Canoneros*) of 13,000 tons. Construction for the order started in 1934, with the majority delivered by 1935.

Only one armed transport was not delivered before the Spanish Civil war broke out; this ship was taken over by the nationalist forces.

Another trainer that was used initially at the Naval Aviation School in 1943 was the ex-Mexican air service Consolidated Model F-11-32. (San Diego Aerospace Museum)

Also used initially by the Naval Aviation School in 1943 were the surviving examples of the Consolidated Model 21-M, which was replaced by the Fairchild PT-19 trainers. (Enrique Velasco Padilla)

These ships were stationed in four naval zones that covered the Mexican coast. In 1941 the Navy had a total of 21 ships, and by the end of the war the number went up to 31. They undertook patrols and convoy escorts, mostly in the Gulf of Mexico.

On the Pacific coast, when Cardenas took command of the *Region Militar del Pacifico* he had at his disposal two navy infantry battalions, two patrol boats and two armed transports.

By 1942 seven of the 10 patrol boats were in American ports in California and Texas being upgraded for anti-submarine warfare, including installation of armaments.

The Mexican Navy received a total of 10 American-made patrol boats from 1941-43. The Navy only suffered one loss, when on 29 March 1944 *G-28* sunk at Veracruz due to a storm, but it was later salvaged and put back in service.

## 1/o. ESCUADRON AERONAVAL

This naval aviation unit was equipped with five of the six Vought OS2U-3 Kingfishers which had been in service with the Mexican air service since March 1942, serving with the *1/o. Regimiento Aereo* in patrols on the Pacific coast. One Kingfisher was retained at El Cipres and was later transferred.

The Mexican air service later picked up five Vought OS2U-1 Kingfishers to be used in coastal patrols in the Gulf of Mexico.

The aircraft for the Navy were flown in March 1943 to Balbuena airfield to the military aviation workshops for a complete overhaul and paint job, before being handed over to the naval personnel. As each aircraft came out of the shops, they were test flown.

The ground personnel came from different sources, some from the navy, some from the *Dirreccion de Aeronautica* and others were civilian contracted. Some of the air service personnel who transferred over were placed on temporary duty with the Navy. When the first

The first Vought OS2U-3 Kingfishers in Mexican Navy paint scheme, showing the anchor painted on the cowling after their overhaul at the military aviation workshops at Balbuena, *circa* May 1943. (Enrique Velasco Padilla)

A *1/o. Escuadron Aeronaval* Kingfisher B-02 lashed down with 55-gallon drums, probably at Tampico, Tamaulipas, in January 1944. (Enrique Velasco Padilla)

Another photo of a secured Vought OS2U-3 Kingfisher of the *1/o. Escuadron Aeronaval circa* 1943-44. (Enrique Velasco Padilla)

Side view of a reported Mexican Navy OS2U-3 Kingfisher, showing the .30 cal machine gun in the observer position. (Enrique Velasco Padilla)

Line-up of four Vought OS2U-3 Kingfishers secured with 55-gallon drums, probably at Tamaulipas *circa* 1943-44. (Jose Villela Gomez)

aircraft came out of the shops in May, an anchor wqs painted on the cowling of each to designate it as a naval aircraft.

On 1 June 1943, the *1/o. Escuadron Aeronaval* was formed with the five Vought OS2U-3 Kingfishers, that received the naval aircraft serial numbers B-01 to B-05 ('B' standing for *Busqueda*/Search). They later received the designation MB (*Marina Busqueda*/Navy search).

Its commanding officer was Navy Lieutenant Rafael Santibanez Fernandez.

In mid-July 1943 the naval squadron was divided into two flights (*Escuadrillas*) and went to Tampico, Tamaulipas. They operated from this location until January 1944, patrolling and protecting Mexican and Allied shipping between Veracruz and Port Isabel, Texas.

## THE NAVAL AVIATION SCHOOL

On 1 September 1943, by presidential decree, the *Escuela de Aviacion Naval* (Naval Aviation School) was founded. The school started its activities soon after on 5 October, with its first director Navy Lieutenant Lorenzo Egurrola Jimenez.

The school would be under the direct control of the *Secretaria de Marina, Direccion General de la Armada*. It was established at the airfield of Las Bajadas, Veracruz, and its equipment consisted of former aircraft of the Mexican air service school, that had started to receive its Lend Lease training aircraft. The Naval Aviation School is reported to have received three Consolidated Model 21-M and two Consolidated Fleet Model F-11-32 biplane trainers.

The first generation of naval cadets, instructors and ground personnel literally built the school from almost nothing. The school's first building was a wooden structure of three rooms. In one room was the office of the director, sub-director and the administrative staff, the second room was the classroom and the other one was the equipment and supply room. All the personnel were later involved in building the hangar to house the aircraft.

The first three Fairchild PT-19 primary trainers were transferred over to the Navy in 1943 to start training the first generation of naval pilots, which consisted of nine officers. The pilots were tasked to pick up the aircraft, and they had to take the bus from Veracruz to Mexico City to fly them to Las Bajadas.

Based on photographic evidence, some of the aircraft carried the Mexican Air Force aircraft serials EPF (*Entrenador Primario*

One of the two Vought OS2U-3 Kingfishers, B-05, that operated from the small beach next to the Spanish fortification of San Juan de Ulua in the port of Veracruz around 1944. (Enrique Velasco Padilla)

The last Kingfisher to be transferred over to the Navy was No.69, already converted as a floatplane in service with *Escuadron Aereo 202* at Ensenada, Baja California, in 1944. (Enrique Velasco Padilla)

Another photo of Vought OS2U-3 Kingfisher No.69 being pushed back to the beach of Ensenada after a flight, *circa* 1944. (Enrique Velasco Padilla)

*Fairchild*/Primary Trainer Fairchild). Later these aircraft received E-01(*Entrenado*r/Trainer), E-03 and still later ME-03 (*Marina Entrenador*/Navy Trainer).

Due to the lack of flight instructors, the *1/o. Escuadron Aeronaval* was ordered to Bajadas to help train the aviation naval cadets.

At about this time, the first generation of naval aviation mechanics had arrived after completing their studies at Balbuena airfield mechanics school.

By 1944, three more Fairchild PT-19s were received for the basic course, and the Fleet and Consolidated aircraft were returned to the *Dirreccion de Aeronautica*.

In late 1944 the school received two more naval pilots, who were instructor qualified, and in December the first nine naval officers completed their primary flight training at Bajadas.

With a combined 80 hours of flight time, on 15 January 1945 they were sent to NAS Corpus Christie, Texas, to complete their advanced training, returning to Mexico in 1946. The second generation of students started their training on 16 May 1945.

From September 1944 to August 1945, a total of 99 hours and 20 minutes of flight time were recorded at the school.

The official history of the development of the Mexican Navy mentions that during the war years of 1944-45, the number of

The first generation of Naval aviation cadets with the first Fairchild PT-19 trainers transferred over by the Mexican air service in 1943. One has its old EMA number 11. (*Memoria de la Secretaria de Marina Septiembre 1944-Agosto 1945*)

Group shot of the naval aviation cadets and ground personnel of the Naval Aviation School at Las Bajadas, Veracruz, *circa* 1944. (Memoria de la Secretaria de Marina Septiembre 1944-Agosto 1945)

A line-up of five of the six Fairchild PT-19s at the Naval Aviation School at Las Bajadas, Veracruz. (*Memorias de la Secretaria de Marina Septiembre 1944-Agosto 1945*)

A flight of Mexican Navy Fairchild PT-19s with the navy registration letter E-02 in a training flight. (Enrique Velasco Padilla)

personnel trained at its aviation schools were as follows: *Escuela de Aviacion Naval*, 11; *Escuela Militar de Mecanicos Especialistas de aviación*, 10; Naval Air Base Corpus Christie, Texas, nine (from the group of 11 that started their training in Mexico).

## REINFORCEMENTS FOR THE 1/o. ESCUADRON AERONAVAL

By the end of 1944, the sixth Vought OS2U-3 Kingfisher, still with its number 69 and assigned to *Escuadron Aereo 202* at El Cipres, Baja California, had been converted to a floatplane and transferred over to the navy. Before its transfer it was reported stationed in Puerto Cortez, Baja California. It arrived at the unit flown by Lieutenant Cirano Sanchez Cardenas, and received the Mexican serial number B-06/MB-06.

In 1945 the commanding officer requested that two more Kingfishers be modified with floats, B-04/MB-04 and B-05/MB-05. It was decided to move these Kingfishers to a small beach next to the fort of San Juan de Ullua inside the harbour of Veracruz.

During its flight to San Juan de Ulloa, Kingfisher B-04/MB-04 had an accident when it landed in the water, its main pontoon hitting an underwater obstacle, destroying the aircraft and injuring pilot Navy Lieutenant Carlos Cortez Cortez, to required hospital treatment. His observer, Cadet Lieutenant Joaquin Martinez Gonzalez, was uninjured. After the accident, the two Kingfishers B-05/MB-05 and B-05/MB-06 were stationed at San Juan de Ulloa, being flown by

A post-war photo of one of the Kingfishers in a very poor state at the fortification of San Juan de Ulua. (Enrique Velasco Padilla)

The post-war years were not kind to both military services, as can be seen by the state of this land-based OS2U-3 Kingfisher, probably at Las Bajadas, Veracruz. (Enrique Velasco Padilla)

Navy Lieutenant Rafael Santibanez Fernandez and Lieutenant Genaro Padilla Armegol.

Navy ground personnel built facilities where these aircraft could be housed and worked upon.

The *1/o. Escuadron Aeronaval* was recorded to have flown 91 hours and 15 minutes from September 1944 to August 1945, covering 10,037 nautical miles.

The Mexican Navy received a Beechcraft AT-7 ex-Mexican Air Force EAB-902, which was lost in a fatal accident in 1947. Here is the sister ship, EAB-901. (Enrique Velasco Padilla)

## TRANSPORT PLANES FOR THE NAVY

By 1944 the Mexican Navy had received observation and training aircraft, but on 25 November 1944 it received a Beech UC-45F, ex-USAAF 44-47466 (commonly known as '466'), from the United States. Before July 1944 the air force also transferred a Beechcraft AT-7 (42-2436) with the Mexican Air Force registration EAB-902 (*Entrenador Avanzado Beechcraft*/Advanced Trainer Beechcraft). Sadly, this AT-7 was lost in a fatal accident on 10 July 1947 in the state of Mexico.

Due to the lack of Navy pilots qualified in multi-engine types, the Mexican Air Force commissioned Captain 2nd Class Augusto Marquet Garcia (1907-1968) and Lieutenant Ernesto Hernandez to fly in the *Escuadron de Transportes* (Transport Squadron) from 10 July 1944, and by December 1945 Captain Marquet had flown about 450 hours in the UC-45 and the AT-7.

During the period September 1944 to August 1945 the transport squadron covered 40,815 miles with a flight time of 226 hours and 45 minutes.

### TRYING TO GET MORE AIRCRAFT

While these events were happening, the Mexican naval attache in the United States tried to acquire more aircraft for the Navy, and to send back to the United States the surviving Kingfishers for a major overhaul. His request was made via the Joint Mexican-American Defense Commission in Washington DC. In the request the following points were made:

> 2. These repairs will be made in the shops of the US Air Force designated by the United States.
>
> 3. The repairs include the motor, armament, equipment, and the body of each of the six planes.
>
> 4. The repairs could be made on two planes at a time.
>
> 5. The Characteristics of the Planes are:
> a. Serial No. from 5720 to 5725
> b. Number of flight hours: 1,000
> c. Armament machine guns 'Browning Colt' .30 M2."

The request was later changed to include the necessary tools and equipment to carry out the maintenance in Mexico. No information has surfaced whether the request was approved.

Arequest was also submitted for six more Fairchild PT-19 and 6 N3N basic trainers, but for reasons unknown was not approved.

By 1945 Mexican naval aviation had received the following aircraft, the majority via the Air Force: three Consolidated Model 21-Ms (returned later to the Air Force); two Fleet 11-F-32s (returned later to the Air Force); six Fairchild PT-19s; six Vought OS2U-3 Kingfishers; one Beechcraft AT-7; and one Beechcraft UC-45F from the United States.

The air order of battle for Mexican Naval Aviation by 1945 look like this:

***Cuerpo de Aeronautica Naval*:**
***Escuela de Aviacion Naval*, Las Bajadas, Veracruz**
6 Fairchild PT-19
***1/o. Escuadrón Aeronaval*, Las Bajadas, Veracruz**
3 Vought OS2U-3 Kingfishers
***1/o. Escuadrón Aeronaval*, fort of San Juan de Ulloa, port of Veracruz**
2 Vought OS2U-3 Kingfishers
***Escuadron de Transporte*, Mexico Federal District**
1 Beechcraft UC-45F
1 Beechcraft AT-7

CHAPTER 6

# LEND-LEASE TO MEXICO

One of the two major areas that would immediately impact Mexican military aviation was the amount of aircraft it received, with the repercussions of an increase in the number of pilots and ground personnel to fly and service them.

It was a challenge for the military leadership to meet the demands now put on the service. Never in its history did the Mexican air service receive such a number of aircraft as it did between 1942 and 1945.

### LEND LEASE TO MEXICO

Under the Lend Lease programme the United States sent much-needed war materials and supplies to Allied nations in exchange for different types of payments, ranging from money to the use of the nation's territory to base American troops and installations.

The programme was signed into effect on 11 March 1941 by President Roosevelt to help Britain while the US maintained its neutral stance. In the list of Latin American countries that benefitted from this programme to help modernise their armed forces, in the aviation field Mexico is ranked second to Brazil, which received over 1,000 aircraft for its navy and air force.

As more documents are studied by researchers it has been revealed that many aircraft were allocated but not taken on charge by Mexico, some due to unknown reasons and others through choice as they were not required or there were not the pilots to fly them.

Mexico's Lend Lease agreement with the United States was signed on 27 March 1942 by acting US Secretary of State Summer Welles and Doctor Francisco Castillo Najera (1886-1954), Mexican ambassador to the US from 1935-45. This agreement was later replaced with a second version signed on 18 March 1943 by Cordell Hull, US Secretary of State, and Ambassador Najera. Article I reads as follows:

A rare shot of one of the Culver LCA/LFA that Mexico received between 1940 and 1942, seen here with Mexican civil government registration XB-. (Enrique Velasco Padilla)

Among the utility aircraft that Mexico received was the Fairchild UC-61, of which three were reported sent to Mexico. This example is seen in the post-war years. (Enrique Velasco Padilla)

> The United States of America proposes to transfer to the United Mexican States under the terms of this Agreement armaments and munitions of war to a total value of about $10,000,000. In

The 25 Republic P-47D-35-RA Thunderbolts, reportedly at Bajadas, Veracruz, airport in late 1945 after their arrival in Mexico. (Enrique Velasco Padilla)

conformity, however with the act of the Congress of the United States of America of March 11, 1941, the United States of America reserves the right at any time to suspend, defer, or stop deliveries whenever, in the opinion of the President of the United States of America, further deliveries are not consistent with the needs of the Defense of the United States of America or the Western Hemisphere; and the United Mexican States similarly reserves the right to suspend, defer, or stop acceptance of deliveries under the present Agreement, when in the opinion of the President of the United Mexican States, the defense needs of the United Mexican States or the Western Hemisphere are not served by continuance of the deliveries.

Another type preferred by the Mexican Air Force was the Stinson L-5E, seen here at Balbuena airfield. (Enrique Velasco Padilla)

A scheduled payment plan was written into the agreement, started from 1 July 1943 and running to the last payment before 1 July 1948.

1942

The first aircraft that were delivered to Mexico under the Lend Lease programme were the six Vought OS2U-3 Kingfishers, which as mentioned previously were reinforcements for the Mexican air service.

They were picked up by Mexican pilots in Brownsville, Texas, in March 1942 to be flown to Mexico City. After their arrival, they were assigned to the *1/o. Regimiento Aereo* at El Cipres, Baja California. They undertook coastal and reconnaissance patrols on the Pacific coast until 1943, when they were transferred to the newly formed Mexican naval air service, to serve in their first naval squadron.

Mexico was not initially on the list of Latin American countries to receive the first 50 North American AT-6 armed trainers. But due to its situation in the Gulf of Mexico – where German U-boats had started to sink Mexican shipping – and the declaration of a state of war in May 1942,

the order of delivery was modified, with Mexico receiving six North American AT-6B armed trainers in June that year. Some believe these aircraft, the ex-USAAC 41-17428 to 41-17433, were obtained under 'Defense Aid' rather than Lend Lease. After their arrival in Mexico, three of these aircraft were deployed to start operational patrols in the Gulf of Mexico in July 1942 with the *2/o. Regimiento Aereo*.

This would be the start of a long service career for this North American trainer, which saw service not only in tactical units but also in the military aviation school. The first priority was to re-equip the aviation units with modern types and replace the old general purpose biplanes.

Another batch of eight AT-6Cs was delivered in August of that year, with a group of 12 officers commanded by Lieutenant Colonel P.A. Antonio Cardenas Rodriguez, with Major P.A. Enrique Velasco Rojas, travelling to San Antonio not only to pick up the aircraft but to tour airfields and confer with American pilots. They also flew two Beechcraft AT-7 twin engine trainers back to Mexico, that were reportedly used in Pacific coastal patrols.

The following types and number of aircraft were reported as being sent to Mexico, but no dates are given:

Culver LCA, 2;
Culver LFA, 1;
Beechcraft AT-7, 2;

Another view of a favoured Stinson L-5E, used by the Mexican Air Force and the Mexican Navy after the war. (Enrique Velasco Padilla)

A type that was received but not favoured by the Mexican Air Force was the Interstate L-6, some of which were returned to the USA for the Stinson L-5E. (Enrique Velasco Padilla)

Vought OS2U-3, 6;

North American AT-6B, 6;

North American AT-6C, 30.

In reference to the above aircraft, a memo dated 26 January 1943 for Air Corps equipment released to Mexico up to 31 December 1942 states that two Culver LCA aircraft were delivered – one in December 1940 and one in April 1942 – and a sole Culver LFC in March 1942.

North American AT-6B armed trainer spare parts including 600 100lb bombs and ammunition for both .50 and .30 calibre machine guns were sent.

A memo dated 5 June 1942 concerning the delivery of the six AT-6Bs also stated:

> Aircraft were to be accompanied by one USAAC pilot with at least two years' military flying experience since graduation from AAC flying school.
>
> Must be familiar with the use of aircraft in anti-submarine operations and speak Spanish. One aircraft and prop mechanic to act as crew chief. Desired but not necessary he speak Spanish.
>
> One radio mechanic qualified on the AT-6 radios. Desired but not necessary he speak Spanish. One armorer, same.

Also mentioned in the notes is that four AT-6Cs were delivered in July of that year before the eight that had been originally scheduled to go in August with the two Beechcraft AT-7.

As for the numbering system, the Kingfishers received the aircraft numbers 69-74, and the block of numbers for the AT-6B/Cs were from P-75 to P-110. The two Beechcraft AT-7s received the out-of-sequence aircraft numbers FAM-1 and FAM-2.

The three Culver (LFC/LFA) 'Cadets' were low-wing light aircraft, but it has proved impossible to find how they were used in Mexico.

Regarding the North American AT-6s delivered in 1942, there are some differences in accounts of their number, sub-types and dates delivered:

(1)

| | |
|---|---|
| 6 AT-6B | 14 June 1942 |
| 4 AT-6B | 23 July 1942 |
| 6 AT-6C | 24 August 1942 |
| 7 AT-6C | 27 August 1942 |
| 6 AT-6C | 14 November 1942 |
| 6 AT-6C | 9 December 1942 |

Total: 10 AT-6B+ 25 AT-6C

(2)

| | |
|---|---|
| 6 AT-6B | 14 June 1942 |
| 4 AT-6C | 23 July 1942 |
| 10 AT-6C | 24 August 1942 |
| 7 AT-6C | 27 August 1942 |
| 6 AT-6C | 14 November 1942 |
| 3 AT-6C | 9 December 1942 |

Total: 6 AT-6B + 30 AT-6C

Notes (1) Author Omar Munoz Ledo Perez in *Quauhtli* magazine of the Academia de Historia Aeronautica de Mexico (2006).

(2) Author Dan Hagedorn in *Texans and Harvards in Latin America* (Air Britain Publication Ltd, 2009).

To replace the OS2U-3s that were transferred over to the Navy, the Mexican Air Force picked up five OS2U-1 Kingfishers. Here is one example undergoing maintenance at the aviation maintenance workshops. (Enrique Velasco Padilla)

A view from the nose of a Republic P-47D-35-RA Thunderbolt after their delivery to Mexico in December 1945, showing the B-25J s in the background. (Enrique Velasco Padilla)

## 1943

This year would see a larger number of aircraft going to Mexico, but at the same time some aircraft that had been allocated were rejected, being sent to the government-sponsored civil aviation school or, if not meeting Mexican needs, returned.

Mexico was allocated fighter aircraft in 1943. Very few Latin American countries managed to get fighters under the Lend Lease programme, Brazil receiving Curtiss P-36s and P-40s, Peru some P-36s via the Norwegians, and Guatemala the Boeing P-26 or 'PT-26'. Mexico was to receive 18 Curtiss P-40 fighters, either the K or N models.

A group of nine Mexican mechanics were sent for training on the Allison engine used on the P-40 at March AAB, Riverside, California, in 1943.

However, for reasons unknown to the author, the Mexicans officials opted to receive more twin-engine Beechcraft AT-11s instead, denying the air service an early opportunity to set up its fighter aircraft component, which would have helped more in the selection of future pilots for the Mexican Expeditionary Air Force.

But the Mexicans did receive its first combat aircraft, the Douglas A-24B 'Banshee' dive-bombers. Since the air service had transferred its previous Kingfishers to the Navy, they were allocated five OS2U-1 Kingfishers, that operated in the land plane version and served on the Gulf Coast with the *2/o. Regimiento Aereo* and later the *2/o. Grupo de Escuadrones Aereos*.

Another model that did not quite meet Mexican expectations was the Interstate L-6, a liaison aircraft, 20 of which were sent to the government aviation school '5 de Mayo' at Puebla, in the state of Puebla. Fifteen of these were later returned to the United States, to be credited to Mexico's Lend Lease account, for which they later requested the Stinson L-5E liaison aircraft.

The first transport planes, Lockheed C-60As, also started arriving to form either a flight or a transport squadron. The Mexicans requested that one of the C-60As be equipped with passenger seats, since it was to be used by the president.

This particular Lockheed C-60A, registration TTL-6001 (*Transporte Tactico Lockheed*/Tactical Transport Lockheed), was later put at the disposal of the Soviet ambassador in Mexico, Constantino Oumansky, and his party for a flight from Mexico to San Jose, Costa Rica, on 25 January 1945. Oumansky had recently been named ambassador to Costa Rica as well with Mexico, and wanted to present his credentials to the Costa Rican president.

But on take-off from Mexico City airport, TTL-6001 crashed and exploded at the end of the runway, killing the ambassador, his wife, three others from the Soviet embassy and four of the five crewmembers. There were only two survivors.

This was not the last tragic accident with the C-60A, as in January 1947 another crashed, killing 21 people aboard.

A larger number of training aircraft were also sent to Mexico, that allowed the military aviation school to retire its previous inventory of biplane training aircraft for primary and advanced training.

A number of reports were generated during 1943 that highlight the movement of aircraft from the United States to Mexico, and in some cases aircraft not picked by the Mexican air service:

Memo dated 8 February 1943, Air Corps equipment release to Mexico January 1943; AT-6C 6

Memo dated 26 January 1943: Lend Lease requisition M-8 covered six AT-6B, 12 AT-6c for Mexico, Requisition M-18 was for 36 AT-6; 18 AT-6C had been delivered, six in October, six in November and six in December 1942.

Memo dated 3 March 1943: Air Corps Equipment Release to Mexico February 1943: AT-6C 6

Memo to UN Branch ASC Dayton, Ohio, dated 24 February 1943: Munitions Assignment Board (Air) case No.173 covered the

One of three North American B-25J Mitchell medium bombers that were delivered to Mexico under the USAAF Flight Demonstration program in 1945, still in USAAF markings. (Enrique Velasco Padilla)

Mexico was allocated up to 76 Douglas A-24B Banshee dive bombers, but only 30 were taken. Here some examples are ready for flight, probably from Balbuena airfield. (Enrique Velasco Padilla)

Another type received by the Mexican Air Force was the Beechcraft AT-7. EAB-901 is shown at Balbuena military airfield after the war. (Enrique Velasco Padilla)

assignment of five OS2U-1 from US Navy Inventory for delivery April 1943. This Assignment was made in lieu of performing overhaul work on seven 10-year-old Corsair aircraft of the Mexican Air Force.

Memo dated 13 July 1943: Air Corp Equipment Released to Mexico in June 1943: PT-19B 10 and BT-15 15.

The subject of Interstate L-6 Cadets are mentioned in the following memos:

Memo Dated 4 January 1943: MAC (Air) Case No.172 assigned 20 Interstate L-6 for Mexico for delivery, five in February 1943, five in March 1943, and 10 in April 1943 part of requisition M-19.

Memo dated 15 December 1943 Air Corps equipment released to Mexico November 1943: 2 PT-19, 7 AT-6, 8 A-24, 1 C-60 and 10 BT-13.

Memo dated 19 February 1944 Air Corps equipment released to Mexico December 1943: one C-60, one L-6, two AT-6 and six A-24.

The following types were delivered in 1943:

| | |
|---|---|
| Beechcraft AT-11 | 18 |
| Douglas A-24B | 21 |
| Fairchild PT-19A | 3 |
| Fairchild PT-19B | 45 |
| Interstate L-6 | 20 |
| Lockheed C-60A | 4 |
| North American AT-6C | 30 |
| North American AT-6D | 20 |
| Vought OS2U-1 | 5 |
| Vultee BT-13A | 12 |
| Vultee BT-15 | 10 |

During 1943 a number of flying accidents occurred, some fatal. For example, a North American AT-6D (construction number unknown) being delivered to Mexico crashed near Monterrey, Nuevo Leon, on 7 November, killing Mexican pilot Captain Mariano Munoz Perez. The veteran pilot was a flight instructor who had received his wings in 1929, and was said to speak excellent English.

## 1944

This year saw a decrease from 1943 in the number of aircraft being accepted and delivered. Those delivered included more basic training aircraft to supply the military aviation school and the tactical units of the Mexican Air Force.

It should be noted that not all the aircraft that were allocated to Mexico were delivered. For example, Mexico was allocated up to 76 Douglas A-24Bs, but only 30 were picked up by Mexican pilots in 1943 to equip two squadrons. Another type that was selected but rejected was the Fairchild AT-21 gunner twin-engine trainer, which was replaced by six AT-11s.

The following types were delivered in 1944:

| | |
|---|---|
| Beechcraft AT-11 | 6 |
| Beechcraft UC-45F | 2 |
| Douglas A-24B | 9 |
| Fairchild PT-19 | 26 |
| Fairchild UC-61A | 3 |
| Interstate L-6 | 15 (not picked up) |

Mexican Air Force ground personnel with a North American AT-6 Texan. (Fuerza Aerea Mexicana)

A line-up of Vultee BT-13 Valiant basic trainers of the military aviation school. (Fuerza Aerea Mexicana)

President Manuel Avila Camacho, with General Francisco L. Urquizo on his left and Brigadier General Gustavo Salinas, chief of the air service, on the right, at the start of the aerial exhibition at Penon de los Banos near Mexico City on 5 March 1944. (Fuerza Aerea Mexicana)

| | |
|---|---|
| North American AT-6D | 10 |
| Vultee BT-13A | 28 |
| Vultee BT-13B | 8 |

General Gustavo Salinas was contemplating getting more aircraft for the Mexican Air Force, which was noted in the American Assistant Military Attache for Air's report of 15 January 1944:

1. The limited size of the Mexican Air Force has thus far eliminated the development of special commands, special air commands, anti-aircraft organizations, or air infantry. It is possible, however, that within the next year, one or two special commands may develop in view of the request of General Gustavo Salinas, chief of the Mexican Air Force, that three helicopters be granted the Mexican Air Force under Lend Lease.

2. Although the Mexican Air Force has officially classified its C-60 Lockheeds as troop transports, the troops to be transported on any given maneuver or exercise will be those from branches of the Mexican Army other than the Mexican Air Force.

3. General Salinas has also requested several efficient reconnaissance aircraft for the combined purpose of air ground liaison, artillery observation, reconnaissance and aerial photography.

4. It is possible that a separate specialized command may develop within the Mexican Air Force if and when the above requested aircraft are delivered.

It has been reported that on some occasions General Salinas lost control of some of his aircraft to the chiefs of government departments, or that some requests were made by them for certain aircraft, as in the case of two UC-45Fs requested for use by the Secretary of War and the Mexican General Staff on 9 March 1944.

One of the latter aircraft was to be factory standard, but the other was to have a VIP interior to include a partition separating the cockpit and passenger compartment, and a number of creature comforts such as reclining upholstered seats, window curtains and floor rug, reading lights and ash trays, a special ventilation system, interior and entrance door upholstery, thermos bottles and holders, and a partition separating the passenger compartment from the rear of the aircraft and toilet.

By 23 November 1944, the other UC-45F, 44-47466, was ready at San Antonio Aircraft Depot on requisition M-2003 MAC (Air) case 566 for the Mexican Navy.

At the same time the Mexican Air Force was also getting picky about certain aircraft which did not meet their requirements, as was the case of the Interstate L-6 Cadets, of which they were allocated 15.

A memo dated 28 July 1944, Mexican requisition M-19-A-2, was for 15 more Interstate L-6s available for pick-up at San Antonio Air Depot, Kelly Field, Texas, on or about 30 August 1944. It appears

During the war Mexico received a reported 90 AT-6s, including different sub-types, that served in the operational squadrons and advance squadron of the military aviation. (Enrique Velasco Padilla)

One of the four Lockheed C-60A transport planes that helped form the flight/ transport squadron, based at Balbuena airfield. (Enrique Velasco Padilla)

A-24, 25 M-45-A1;
AT-11, 6 M-42-43;
AT-6, 10 M-43-A1;
BT-13, 20 M-69-A1;
L-6, 15 M-19-A2;
PT-19, 25 M-38-A1.

Memo dated 26 July 1944: 20 Vultee BT-13A for the Mexican Air Force on requisition M-69-A1 available for pick-up at San Antonio Air Depot (SAAD) on or about 10 August 1944.

The Beechcraft AT-11 Kansan bombers of *Escuadron Aereo 101* inside the main hangar at Balbuena airfield. (Enrique Velasco Padilla)

they were not collected, based on the USAAC serial numbers of the ones delivered and those that were at Kelly Field.

This was also noted in a memo dated 19 September 1944, which said that 15 L-6s on requisition M-19-A-2 (III) had not been picked up, and 19 of 20 BT-13As had also not been collected.

More training aircraft were, however, allocated, accepted and picked up, as mentioned in the following memos:

Memo dated 7 February 1944: Air Corps equipment released to Mexico January 1944 included one L-6 and one AT-6.

Memo dated 19 February 1944: Air Corps equipment released to Mexico one C-60, one L-6, two AT-6s and six A-24Bs.

Memo dated 3 March 1944: Air Corps equipment released to Mexico February 1944 included one A-24B.

Memo dated 24 May 1944: Original FAM requisition for six Fairchild AT-21a MAC (Air) substituted the final six Beech AT-11s.

Memo dated 3 June 1944: Mexican requisition for Douglas A-24s had been originally for 76 aircraft.

Memo dated 18 July 1944: MAC (Air) had approved the following aircraft for Mexico (type and requisition number):

More AT-6D were also available as per memo dated 26 July 1944, that 10 North American AT-6Ds for the Mexican Air Force per requisition M-43-A1 were ready to be picked up at San Antonio Air Depot on 4 August 1944.

1945

In the final year of the war, the *Secretaria de la Defensa Nacional* (SDN) reported that it had transferred 13 aircraft to the Mexican Navy and reported the loss of seven aircraft (one Lockheed C-60A, two Douglas A-24Bs and four AT-6 trainers) in daily operations.

This year is of interest because not all the aircraft identified for Mexico came through the Lend Lease programme. Some also came via the American Republic Programme (ARP) or the USAAF Demonstration Flight Programme (DFP), sponsored by General Henry 'Hap' Arnold, chief of the US Air Force, who wanted to create a Hemispheric Air Force to cover all of Latin America, but equipped with American-made aircraft.

Arnold had issues with the US State Department, which did not favour certain countries getting combat planes or trainers, and he also wanted to give out aircraft free. The DFP therefore became the closest thing to an American air mission in Mexico, and was also in charge of the training of Mexican personnel on the aircraft.

With Mexico's active participation in the war and the 201st Squadron about to ship out to the Pacific, they were allocated 58 Republic P-47 Thunderbolt fighter-bombers under Lend Lease, to initially equip the squadron in the Philippines and to have a number of replacements on hand for combat or operational losses. After the war ended, the 201st left its Lend Lease aircraft in the Philippines in October 1945.

In December 1945 they picked up 25 new Republic P-47D-35-RA Thunderbolts (including ground equipment) from Laredo AAFB, Texas, to be flown back to Las Bajadas, Veracruz. These Thunderbolts would serve until 1958/1959, when replaced by the North American T-28A Trojan trainer.

By the end of 1945 the first Douglas C-47B was also delivered, under the ARP programme.

The following types were delivered in 1945:

**Under Lend Lease**

| | |
|---|---|
| Beechcraft F2B | 2 |
| Republic P-47D-30-RA/35-RA | 58 |

Stinson L-5E 12
Vultee BT-13B 20
**USAAF Demostration Flight Programme (DFP)**
North American AT-6C 6
North American B-25J 3
**American Republic Programme (ARP)**
Douglas C-47B 3

Eventually all the aircraft from the DFP would be transferred over to the Mexican Air Force. Yet even by December 1945 the B-25Js (which had arrived in March) were seen and photographed still in USAAF markings, with the Mexican-marked P-47D-35-RA, at an open day for the general public at Mexico City Airport.

Another view of a Lend Lease AT-6C Texan at Balbuena airfield undergoing maintenance. (Enrique Velasco Padilla)

## PROBLEMS WITH THE NUMBERS, 1942-45

The *Secretaria de la Defensa Nacional* in its yearly report for September 1945 to August 1946 stated that the Mexican Air Force had the following aircraft in its inventory (this list is quoted exactly from the report and appears to have some errors, taking into account aircraft losses and aircraft transferred over to the Navy):

The first Douglas C-47 Transport planes arrived in Mexico after the end of the war under the American Republic Program (ARP) to reinforce the Transport squadron at Balbuena airfield. (Enrique Velasco Rojas)

North American AT-6 18 [*sic*, number was 78]
Beech AT-7 2
Beech F2 2
Douglas A-24B 26
Fairchild UC-61 3
Vultee BT-13 17
Stinson L-5 3
Douglas C-47 3
Republic P-47D 25
Beech AT-11 24
Beech UC-45 1
PT-13 47 (BT-13)
BT-19 16 (PT-19)
Sikorsky OS2U 5
North American B-25 3
Lockheed C-60 3

Based on available information and on the author's observations, the Mexican Air Force received the following number of aircraft per year: 1941, one; 1942, 46; 1943, 183; 1944, 94; and 1945, 104. This gives a total of 428 new aircraft, but we must discount the following 73 aircraft for different reasons during these years:

transferred to the Navy, 13;
returned to the US, 15;
left in the Philippines, 33;
from the DFP, 9; and
from the ARP, 3.

We are therefore left with a total of 355 extra aircraft for the Mexican Air Force by the end of 1945.

However, if we compare this figure with the numbers from noted historians Phil Butler and Dan Hagedorn, they do not match. In their book *Air Arsenal North America*, Butler and Hagedorn come up with the following numbers:

Beechcraft AT-7 2
Beechcraft AT-11 24
Beechcraft UC-45F 2
Beechcraft F2B 2
Douglas A-24B 30
Fairchild PT-19A/B 73
Interstate L-6 20
Lockheed C-60 4
North American AT-6B/C/D 70
Republic P-47D-30/35-RA 58
Vought OS2U-3 6
Vought OS2U-1 5
Stinson L-5E 12
Vultee BT-13A/B 50
Vultee BT-15 10
Grand total: 368 aircraft

Taking into account all the aircraft that have been identified as allocated to Mexico, I believe the following is a fairly comprehensive list:

**Bellezas del Aire**

Esta guapa chica que aparece en la foto de la izquierda es la "Stewardess' del poderoso avión de la American Airlines que el día 5 del próximo septiembre inaugurará un formidable servicio aéreo México-Monterrey-Laredo, para conectar con líneas internas de los Estados Unidos.

**Potencia Aérea Mexicana**

Entre los numerosos aviones que paulatinamente nos llegan de los Estados Unidos para aumentar la fortaleza aérea de nuestro país, a fin de capacitarlo a la mejor defensa de su parte correspondiente en el esfuerzo común defensivo de las Américas, figuran estos poderosos aviones de com-

During the war the Mexican press reported on the growing Mexican military aviation potential, as show here with the arrival of the Beechcraft AT-7s and North American AT-6Cs in October 1942. (Enrique Velasco Padilla)

**AIRCRAFT TOTALS, INCLUDING AIRCRAFT RETURNED OR NOT ACCEPTED, 1942-45**

Beechcraft AT-7 2
Beechcraft AT-11 24
Beechcraft UC-45F 3
Beechcraft F2B 2
Curtiss P-40 18
(not delivered, exchanged for AT-11)
Douglas RB-24B 30
(+9 not picked up, allocated up to 76 A-24B)
Fairchild AT-21 6
(not picked up, exchanged for AT-11)
3 Fairchild UC-61A
23 Fairchild PT-19B
17 Fairchild PT-19B
6 Fairchild PT-19A
6 Fairchild PT-19
13 Fairchild PT-19A
5 Fairchild PT-19
21 Interstate L-6 (15 returned
+ 15 more not picked up)
4 Lockheed C-60A
6 North American AT-6B
56 North American AT-6C
26 North American AT-6D
6 North American AT-6C
(missing data on 18 AT-6D that were delivered in 1944)
20 Republic P-47D training in the USA
22 Republic P-47D on loan from 58th FG
26 Republic P-47D-30-RA Lend Lease in P.I. 1945
7 Republic P-47D? Possibly under Lend Lease in P.I. 1945
25 Republic P-47D-35-RA to Mexico December 1945
5 Republic P-47D-35-RA not delivered, spare aircraft
6 Sikorsky OS2U-3
5 Sikorsky OS2U-1
12 Stinson L-5E
10 Vultee BT-15
10 Vultee BT-13
19 Vultee BT-13A
20 Vultee BT-13B
Total: aircraft: 425
Aircraft returned: 15
Aircraft not picked up: 84
Aircraft transferred to the Navy: 13

The table above was compiled from different sources of information. The list may not be 100 percent correct due to some aircraft being picked up while others were not, and some being lost in accidents during delivery flights and replaced by others.

Some aircraft were not accepted, or were exchanged for other types of aircraft. Some aircraft were identified for the Mexican Air Force, but not delivered. We must also take into account that some aircraft

Another type reported received under Lend Lease which had a long service life in the Mexican Air Force were two Beechcraft F2B photo aircraft, one of which is seen after the war with a line-up of Beechcraft AT-11s of *Escuadron Aereo 101*. (Author Collection)

Mexican President General Manuel Avila Camacho and American President Franklin D. Roosevelt, who were responsible for the signing of the Lend Lease agreement between Mexico and the United States in March 1942. (Fuerza Aerea Mexicana)

in Mexico were transferred to the Mexican Navy from 1943 onward.

## AMERICAN AIRCRAFT GOING SOUTH

An issue that put some strain on Mexican-American collaboration before the start of the war was the attempt to station USAAC/USAAF personnel in Mexico to service aircraft being transported from the United States to the Panama Canal Zone or later going to Latin American countries under a Lend Lease agreement.

The United States Army Air Force wanted to station maintenance personnel along the routes at Mexican airfields, as fuel and maintenance stops. During talks between Mexico and American officials of the Joint Defense Committee in June 1941, a request was made for permission to base aviation mechanics at Tampico in Tamaulipas, the port of Veracruz and Tapachula in the state of Chiapas, but Mexican official's stated a provision in the Mexican Constitution of 1917, forbidding the stationing of foreign troops in Mexico.

After some misunderstandings, the matter was resolved by placing the USAAC/USAAF personnel in the employment of Pan American Airways and working in civilian clothes or the company's uniform.

In 1943, the USAAF again proposed the sending of US personnel and equipment to Mexican airfields as Army airway control stations, to include weather and communications facilities. An agreement was

There was a sad end for many general purpose aircraft of the Mexican Air Force after the war. Some were dropped from the inventory in 1947. (Ing. Enrique Velasco)

reached that American personnel would work in civilian clothes and report to Mexican officials.

During the course of the war years, about 65 accidents occurred involving American aircraft flying from the United States to either South America or the Panama Canal Zone.

In some cases aircraft had become lost in transfer flights close to the border, as in the case of Lieutenant Richard A. 'Bud' Peterson, a member of the 364th Fighter Squadron of the 357th Fighter Group, who on 4 October 1943 crash-landed his Bell P-39Q 42-20748 in the Mexican town of El Chapo, Chihuahua. Peterson was not hurt, but his aircraft was wrecked and some rail cars were damaged. Mexican officials confiscated all the ammunition carried on the aircraft, even when a USAAF officer showed up after Peterson notified the authorities about his crash. Years later Peterson recalled:

> When the Mexican police showed up, they seized all the ammunition. The plane had a full combat load of machine gun ammunition and high explosive cannon shells.
>
> The local gendarmes thought I was something else as I ejected the 37mm shells from the nose cannon and they bounced on the ground next to me.
>
> The local gentry were wrapping the lengths of the interlocked machine gun ammunition around their shoulders and shouting to each other 'VIVA VILLA!.VIVA VILLA!' But the gendarmes quickly collected the ammo.

Lieutenant Peterson eventually rejoined his squadron in Nebraska, and his group would see action with the 8th Air Force. Peterson finished the war as a major and claimed the destruction of 15½ enemy aircraft plus one probable and two damaged. After the war he became a well-known architect in his home state of Minnesota.

Under the cover of Pan American Airways a number of Mexican airfields were also built, improved or expanded to accommodate everything from training aircraft to heavy bombers on their way to reinforce the defences of the Panama Canal, and later to be sent to the different war fronts overseas.

There was a further request from the American military authorities to base bomber and patrol aircraft at Cozumel, Quintana Roo, during the height of the U-boat campaign. However, once again Mexican officials did not permit this, only allowing 30-day stays, and all installations built by the United States in Mexican territory would be under Mexican control.

This was reinforced when General Lazaro Cardenas took over as Secretary of National Defence. This affected the conditions under which the construction or improvement of airfields in the Yucatan and Cozumel area were conducted. One proposal was for a bomber base at Tehuantepec in the state of Oaxaca. A later request to station ground troops and technical personnel there was also opposed by the Mexican government.

By 1944, with the direction of the war going in favour of the Allies, these airfields ended up only as emergency fields, and were used by the Mexican civilian and military aviation in the post-war period.

CHAPTER 7

# THE EVOLUTION OF THE MEXICAN MILITARY AVIATION SCHOOL

Another repercussion of Mexico's involvement in the Second World War, that would have a long lasting effect, was the Military Aviation School that was about to benefit from an infusion of American-made training aircraft and changes in its training doctrine.

## THE BEGINNINGS

The Military Aviation School dates back to 15 November 1915, when the school started its first day of operation, under the guidance of then Major Alberto Salinas Carranza, which also happened to be his birthday. The school was known at the *Escuela Nacional de Aviacion* (National Aviation School) and operated from the fields of Balbuena, close to the aviation workshops.

The school underwent several name changes and moves, from Mexico City to the port of Veracruz and Bajadas, until settling in Monterrey, Nuevo Leon.

## 1941

By December 1941, the *Escuela Militar de Aviacion* (Military Aviation School) was at the major military base in Monterrey, taking advantage of the installations such as the airfield and its facilities.

The director of the school at this time was Colonel Luis Farrel Cubillas (1902-77), a noted and veteran pilot of various campaigns of the 1920s, who had held the position since 16 November 1936.

In 1941, the school's flying equipment mostly consisted of biplane trainers and some general purpose biplanes, with the exception of the sole Ryan STM monoplane trainer. The latter was a survivor of six that had entered service back in 1938, but due to accidents, only one remained at the school. Based on details in some of the flight instructors' log books, the school had one Consolidated Model 21-M, one monoplane Ryan STM, one Barreda Ares biplane (a Mexican-built trainer), five Fleet Model 11-32 biplanes and one Consolidated Fleet Model 11-A.

The last class to graduate was on 15 July 1941, when 15 Mexican cadets and one Bolivian received their wings and diplomas. During the course of the year there were 40 cadets in their second year, of whom five had been dismissed due to their lack of aptitude for flight instruction and one killed in an aviation accident.

In those days, to enter the Military Aviation School a cadet had

Colonel Luis Farrell Cubillas, director of the *Escuela Militar de Aviacion* during a crucial period of growth from 1936-45. (Fuerza Aerea Mexicana)

A flight instructor with eight aviation cadets before the war. (Fuerza Aerea Mexicana

Two aviation cadets with a Barreda EP primary biplane trainer, of which 10 were used at the aviation school before the arrival of the American Lend Lease training aircraft in 1943. (Fuerza Aerea Mexicana)

to have previous service as an officer or to have enlisted first in the Mexican Army or Navy, preferably after graduation from the service academy and serving in the line units.

The average pilot graduated with between 89 and 123 hours of flight time. Based on school regulations, the first phase of training consisted of 87 hours of instruction, which was broken down as follows:

elementary phase, 10 hours;
intermediate phase, 20 hours;
advanced phase, 10 hours; and

Mexican aviation cadets in front of a visiting armed North American AT-6 trainer. (Fuerza Aerea Mexicana)

As with any training programme there were accidents, like this one involving Fairchild PT-19 EPF-18, with local people checking the scene. (Fuerza Aerea Mexicana)

Brigadier General Gustavo Salinas, chief of the air service, with the director of the school, checking out one of the first Fairchild PT-19 primary trainers. (Fuerza Aerea Mexicana)

special training, 47 hours.

The second phase of training involved a further 10 hours of instruction.

Another important development at the school was the sending of Lieutenant Alfonso Virgen Meza to Link Aviation Devices at Binghamton, New York, on 8 May 1938 to learn about the use and maintenance of Link trainers to be used for a flight instrument and blind flying course at the school.

In 1924 Meza had been a major and had gone into exile in the United States after the failure of the De la Huerta rebellion of 1923-24. He found employment at the Link factory in New York until his return to Mexico in 1936, rejoining the air service in May that year with the rank of lieutenant.

He was the only instructor from 1939-41, teaching about 1,500 hours of instrument and blind flying.

If a military pilot after his graduation wanted to get multi-engine time, he put in a request though his chain of command and if the position was available he could fly with the Compania Mexicana

One of the surviving Ryan STM monoplane trainers that was still in service at the aviation school until the school transfer to Guadalajara, Jalisco. (Fuerza Aerea Mexicana)

A group of cadets in front of PT-19 EPF-26, with an AT-11 and Vultee BT-13 in the background at Las Juntas airfield near Guadalajara. (Fuerza Aerea Mexicana)

de Aviacion S.A. (CMA) for a period of six months, flying Douglas DC-2/DC-3 passenger planes on national and international air routes.

This was possible due to a presidential decree that the national airlines had to be manned by Mexican-born personnel. For example, pilot Lieutenant Alfonso Gandarilla Gracia was granted his request to fly for CMA from April-October 1937, where he amassed a total of 299 hours and 39 minutes of flight time.

There were very few cases of civilians being accepted directly into the aviation school. This only happened if they had a higher education to their credit, as in the case of Carlos Rodriguez Corona, a student of the University of Puebla, who was given the rank of *Cabo Alumno* (Cadet Corporal) on his admission to the school on 11 February 1938. He received his wings on 16 November 1939, with about 100 hours in Fleet trainers and 50 hours in the Ryan STM monoplane trainer.

Taking advantange of the agreement with the Compania Mexicana de Aviacion, he flew with them from November 1941 to May 1942, thereafter returning to serve with the *2/o. Regimiento Aereo*.

In 1941, the world situation caused the Military Aviation School to make the first big change which would affect its future.

Civilians were allowed to compete directly for entrance to the school, a total of 1,200 applicants taking part in a series of medical

Two photographers standing with one of the Beechcraft AT-11s assigned to the *Escuadron Avanzado Bimotor* of the Military Aviation School at Guadalajara. (Fuerza Aerea Mexicana)

and educational examinations, which were held in Mexico City and Monterrey. This resulted in 76 being selected at Mexico City and another 10 at Monterrey. Five military personnel were also selected for the generation of 1941-44.

Another important development was the creation of the *Escuela Militar de Mecanicos de Aviacion* (Military Aviation Mechanics School) by presidential decree signed by General Manuel Avila Camacho. The mechanics school started operations on 5 January 1942 at Mexico City in the old Azcarate aircraft factory near the airfield. Aspiring mechanics were previously trained at the military aviation workshops.

Its first director was Lieutenant Colonel Alberto Vieytez Vieytez (1898-1971) a future chief of the Mexican Air Force from 1953-55. The age requirement for the school was between 15 and 25, candidates had to have completed the equivalent of a high school education and the course lasted for three years. The school started with a reported 263 students, and some of the graduates would eventually serve in the Philippines in 1945.

A group of flight instructors recently trained in the United States at the airfield of Las Juntas, Guadalajara, Jalisco. From left to right, standing, 2nd Lieutenant Raul Garcia Mercado, Lieutenant Reynaldo Perez Gallardo, unknown, unknown. Front row, 2nd Lieutenant Fausto Vega Santander and 2nd Lieutenant Jaime Zenizo Rojas. (Fuerza Aerea Mexicana)

A group of flight instructor of the Military Aviation School, a number of which were chosen to form part of *Escuadron Aereo 201* of the *Grupo de perfecionamiento Aeronautica* (GPA) for training in the USA. (Fuerza Aerea Mexicana)

## 1942

The Military Aviation School started its activities on 23 September 1942. A report for fiscal year September 1942 to August 1943 listed the following personnel who joined the school at this time: three chiefs pilot aviators, six officer pilot aviators, one civilian professor and 11 Army officers. There were also an initial 21 officer cadets, 70 civilian cadets and four cadets from other Central American countries.

The aviation school received more aircraft in the shape of a Bird CK biplane and the rest of the order of nine Barrera Ares EP biplane trainers, which started to arrive in July 1942.

The American community of Mexico, in a ceremony in September 1942 in the presence of General Roberto Fierro, donated an Interstate L-6 aircraft with the Mexican civil registration XA-CID, named '*Buddy*' but which later received the military number 1. This aircraft was used for training by Lieutenant Radames Gaxiola Andrade from September-December 1942.

In November, in preparation for the coming changes, the group's pilots were sent to the United States to study advanced training at Randolph Field and Kelly Field, Texas. During the same month the *Secretaria de la Defensa Nacional* announced that a number of Fairchild trainers would be acquired for the aviation school, with the sale predicted to be completed by the end of the month.

## 1943

On 12 June 1943 the school started to move to its next location, the ex-*hacienda del Espiritu Santo* in the city of Guadalajara, Jalisco. The

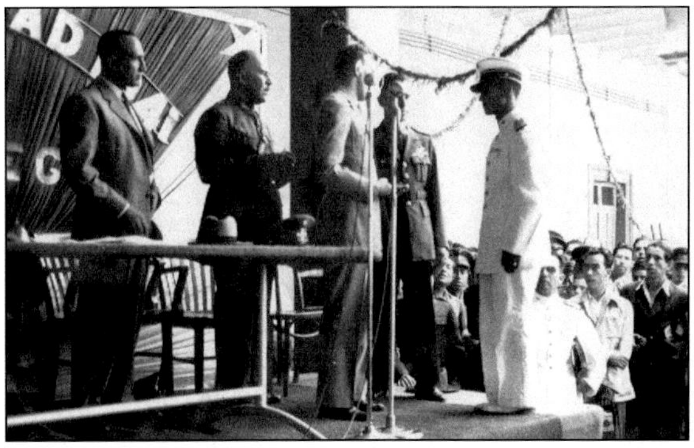

During the graduation ceremony of the generation of 1941-44, Captain Paul B. Miller USAAF, then assistance military attache in Mexico, awards the top student of the class with a .45 calibre automatic weapon. (Fuerza Aerea Mexicana)

A view of Las Juntas airfield, with a line of training aircraft of the Military Aviation School, including the Beechcraft twin-engine aircraft for advanced training. (Fuerza Aerea Mexicana)

remaining aircraft and equipment were sent to the aviation field of *Las Juntas* close to the city. Before the move a fatal accident occurred when an Ares EP biplane trainer crashed, killing Lieutenant Ranulfo Gutierrez Barragan and injuring 2nd Lieutenant Juan Perez Valadez.

This year also marked the arrival of training aircraft under the Lend Lease agreements between Mexico and the United States. In April the first of 40 Fairchild PT-19B primary trainers started to arrive, followed in August by the first of 10 Vultee BT-15 Valiant basic trainers.

In November the first North American AT-6s started to appear for the advanced squadron, and the school also received some twin-engine aircraft like the AT-11 and AT-7. Some of the retired types, the Fleet and Consolidated biplanes, were sent to the naval aviation school at Las Bajadas, Veracruz.

With these new aircraft, the Military Aviation School was organised as follows:

*Escuadron Primario* (Primary Squadron), PT-19s;
*Escuadron Basico* (Basic Squadron),BT-13/15s;
*Escuadron Avanzado* (Advanced Squadron),AT-6s; and
*Escuadron Avanzado Bimotor* (Advanced Twin-Engine Squadron), AT-7/11s.

The PT-19s were given the serials EPF-1 (*Entrenador Primario Fairchild*/Primary Trainer Fairchild) to EPF-69. The Vultee BT-13s started with EBV-401 (*Entrenador Basico Vultee*/Basic Trianer Vultee) and the BT-15s with EBV-801. The AT-6s received the letters EAN (*Entrenador Avanzado North*/Advanced Trainer North).

With the new equipment and veteran flight instructors returning from advanced training in the United States, new flight training courses were established. First-year cadets would fly 71 hours of flight instruction and solo flight, second-year cadets 40 hours and third-year cadets another 40 hours in the Advanced Squadron. Some were later selected for the twin-engine course, for which two AT-11s were

Group shot of pilots in front of one of the AT-11s of the *Escuadron Avanzado Bimotor* at the Aviation School. (Fuerza Aerea Mexicana)

A flight instructor with a North American AT-6 of the *Escuadron Avanzado*. (Fuerza Aerea Mexicana)

An instructor in front of a Vultee BT-13/15 of the *Escuadron Basico*. (Fuerza Aerea Mexicana)

Vultee BT-13 EBV-408 (*Entrenador Basico Vultee*) of the *Escuadron Basico* taxiing for a training flight. (Enrique Velasco Padilla)

The Mexican-built Barreda EP primary trainer used by the aviation school from 1941-43. (Enrique Velasco Padilla)

Another type used by the school before the arrival of the Lend Lease aircraft was the Ryan STM monoplane trainers, of which one was still in service in 1941. (Enrique Velasco Padilla)

Lend Lease aircraft arrived at the Military Aviation School in 1943, with Fairchild PT-19 primary trainers replacing biplanes there. (Enrique Velasco Padilla)

reportedly used and maybe one of the AT-7s.

With all these changes and the increase in the tempo of operations at the school, the earliest known fatal accident happened on 2 July 1943, when a Vultee BT-13 Valiant crashed near a ranch in the state of Mexico. The instructor, Lieutenant Miguel Uribe Carballeda, was killed and Cadet Amador Samano Pina was injured. This cadet would go on to earn his wings on 1 September and later flew P-47Ds in combat operations over the Philippines.

A month later, a Fairchild PT-19, number 17, was reported lost in a fatal accident near the airfield, killing Captain Carlos Zagahun Ramirez and mechanic Carlos Ortiz.

Due to the increase in the cadet population and aircraft operations, a number of well-qualified cadets and officers were selected to be sent for training in the United States at USAAF and USN installations. The

Before the war, a line-up of the aircraft of the Mexican air service, with Ryan STM trainers, fleet trainers and Bird C.K trainers, in view of the Military Aviation School. (Fuerza Aerea Mexicana)

Vultee BT-13 EBV-409 in flight. (Enrique Velasco Padilla)

Another Vultee, EBV-404 of the *Escuadron Basico* of the Military Aviation School. (Enrique Velasco Padilla)

plan was for them to return as flight instructors with the latest training techniques and help add more instructors to the school's flight roster.

In September 1943 the first aerial bombardier course was established at the school, with training starting on the first of the month. It is reported that 2nd Lieutenant Aerial Bomber Carlos Raulett Blanc received training and possibly some combat time to practice his trade in 1943 at RAF Middleton St George near Darlington in the UK. If the date is correct, Raulett probably flew with the Canadian bombers of No.6 RCAF Group, either with No. 419 or No.428 RCAF bomber squadrons flying the Handley Page Halifax over targets in Occupied Europe.

## 1944

On 1 January 1944, the first graduating class of bombardiers received their diplomas and wings in a ceremony attended by the Secretary of National Defence. All 12 graduating officers, formerly sappers, infantry or cavalry, were later assigned to *Escuadron Aereo 101* to continue with their training. One of these officers would later be selected to join *Escuadron Aereo 201*.

The Military Aviation School received back the cadets and officers who had been sent to the United States to qualify as flight instructors in single-engine and some in twin-engine aircraft with the US Navy and US Army.

The school continued to receive more Lend Lease aircraft, and with the increased tempo of training a number of accidents occurred, resulted in a number of aircraft being destroyed or damaged. Another fatal accident happened when an EPF-4 crashed, killing the two crewmembers. It is not easy to determine the names of the crew, the only information that has come to light being that during 1944 three flight instructors were killed in accidents.

On 31 May 1944, Cadet Hugo Gonzalez y Gonzalez was involved in a landing accident in the Vultee EBV-411, which resulted in the aircraft losing its landing gear. The cause of the accident was blamed on the conditions of the airfield.

Even the flight instructors were not immune to accidents. On 13 June 1944, there was a collision between two PT-19s, EPF-27 and EPF-17, while the former was taxi-ing. The pilot, Instructor Lieutenant Amadeo Castro Almanza, a future P-47 combat pilot, was not injured, but EPF-27 suffered damage to its propeller and left wing.

An event that facilitated Mexico's active participation in the Second World War happened on 5 March 1944, when an aerial exhibition was organised by the Mexican Air Force for the President Avila Camacho and the people of Mexico. The event was held at Penon de los Banos near Mexico City. Also in attendance were General Francisco Urquizo and General Gustavo Salinas. A total of 84 aircraft took part in demonstrations of the capabilities of the aircraft involved, which included the North American AT-6 and Douglas A-24B dive-bombing targets, Beechcraft AT-11s carrying out level bombing and the Lockheed C-60A landing troops on an improvised airfield so as to capture the objective.

The Military Aviation School participated with all its squadrons, with two Beechcraft AT-11s, 19 Fairchild PT-19s, 13 BT-13/15 Vultees and seven North American AT-6s.

The exhibition was held before an estimated crowd of about 100,000 people who witnesses the historic event that would facilitate General Avila Camacho's decision to select the Air Force to represent Mexico on the field of combat.

In 1944, the Military Aviation School received 25 PT-19s and 20 Vultees, and by July there were about 25 AT-6s at the school.

On 1 June 1944, the first generation of civilians (1941-44) – actually 31 civilians and three military personnel – had their graduation ceremony at Guadalajara at the *Hacienda de Espiritu Santo*, receiving their diplomas and wings as pilots of the Mexican Air Force.

Handing out their wings was General Francisco L. Urquizo, second in command of the *Secretaria de la Defensa Nacional*, with General Gustavo Salinas, chief of the Mexican Air Force, and the director of the school, Colonel Luis Farell. Among the invited guests was the American military attache with his aid, Captain Paul B. Miller, USAAF, who gave a gift to the number one student of the generation.

By 1945 the school was equipped with a good number of AT-6 Texan trainers for the advanced squadron, as well as Fairchild PT-19 primary trainers. (Memorias de la Secretaria de la Defensa Nacional Septiembre 1944-Agosto 1945)

Of the 91 cadets who had started the course, 24 were eliminated for various reasons, 34 graduated in Mexico and 33 more graduated from flight training in the United States, returning to the school to help train their fellow cadets and the next generation of 1942-45. The new pilots graduated with an average of 150 hours of flight time, with 20 hours of Link trainer time. For example, Cadet Manuel Farias Rodriguez was credited with the following training hours at the school for the period September 1943 to June 1944:

Based on evidence from pilot logbooks there were five Consolidated Model 21-Ms used at the Military Aviation School before 1942. Three of them are pictured. (Enrique Velasco Padilla)

71 hours in Fairchild PT-19s (Primary Squadron),
41.40 hours in Vultee BT-13/15s (Basic Squadron),
41.45 hours in AT-6s (Advanced Squadron) and
23 hours inLink trainers, for a
total of 176.85 hours of training.

When President Avila Camacho decided to send the Mexican Air Force to an overseas theatre of operations, the call was made for volunteers. Twelve flight instructors and 11 recently graduated pilots of generation 1941-44 were selected to join *Escuadron Aereo 201* of the *Grupo de Perfeccionamiento Aeronautica* (GPA).

From that same generation, 20 more pilots would be part of the replacement group, which headed to the United States for training.

During 1944 a number of Latin American heads of state visited Mexico. One of them, Colonel Fulgencio Batista y Zaldivar, president of Cuba, visited the Military Aviation School with General de Division Lazaro Cardenas, Secretary of National Defence, and the governor of the state of Jalisco.

The second generation of civilians graduated on 1 November 1944, consisting of two military personnel and 41 civilians, while 15 more graduated in the United States. Many from this generation were also selected to form part of the replacement group of the future Mexican Expeditionary Air Force (MEAF).

### 1945

The aviation school continued with its functions as events were developing with the MEAF, which was now about to go overseas. By 1 June 1945 the fourth generation of 54 civilians (no military personnel) had graduated and 44 of them were selected to form part of the MEAF replacement group.

By the close of 1945 the Military Aviation School had graduated a total of 339 pilots since 1939, including seven foreign pilots, and from these 47 were trained in the United States. The majority would serve as flight instructors.

By 1945 the school had about 40 flight instructors and 12 more serving as teachers. The school received 154 aircraft (69 PT-19s, 48 BT-13s, 10 BT-15s, 25 AT-6s and two AT-11s). With the end of the war, in September 1945 the government ordered the return of all personnel studying in the United States; some wished to stay to complete their course, but their request fell on deaf ears. This caused a problem at the school, since it now had an overpopulation of aviation cadets at different levels of training.

With the new post-war budgets, the school dismissed many cadets for the smallest infractions. Some continued their flight training on the civilian side, flying for private and commercial aviation.

By October 1945, Colonel Luis Farell had been promoted to a higher position, his place as school director being taken by Colonel David Chagoya Rodriguez, who oversaw the first post-war generation to graduate, with 13 new pilots (one from Costa Rica).

CHAPTER 8

# TRAINING IN THE USA: LEARNING NEW SKILLS

During the war years, a numbers of Mexican Air Force and Navy personnel were trained at various United States Army Air Force bases and Naval Stations. Grants that were given to the Mexican Military Aviation School, negotiated by school director Colonel Farell and accepted by the government, helped to decongest the aviation school at Guadalajara, which had a large number of cadets there at the same time.

The arrival of the Lend Lease training aircraft and changes to the training programme relieved the pressure on the existing training cadre, sending the most promising cadets for training in the United States.

The majority (17 cadets) ended up training at US Naval facilities, but one group of five trained with the USAAF in Texas.

## MEXICANS AT CORSICANA AAFB AND TEXAS

According to official documents, a group of the most promising cadets, under the command of an Army officer, were selected to take a *Curso de aviones de picada* (dive-bombing course) in the United States. The officer selected was 2nd Lieutenant Reynaldo Perez Gallardo, based on his previous civilian fight experience, having had a civil pilot license

The leader of the Corsicana group, Lieutenant Reynaldo Perez Gallardo, a flight instructor at the Military Aviation School, with his students in the *Escuadron Primario*. (Fuerza Aerea Mexicana)

2nd Lieutenant Jaime Zenizo Rojas, a graduate of the USAAF training system and a flight instructor at the Military Aviation School, with his students in the *Escuadron Primario*. (Fuerza Aerea Mexicana)

issued on 2 October 1940.

He had requested his transfer from the cavalry to the aviation school in October 1942, and was waiting for the training to start when he was selected to lead this group to the United States. His small group consisted of the following, all cadets 2nd class: Fausto Vega Santander, Jaime Zenizo Rojas, Raúl García Mercado and Jesus Gomez Montero.

Documents indicate the group was to be sent to train as pilots and received a dive bombing course, and on 1 January 1943 orders were issued for them to attend pilot training, leaving Monterrey for the United States. Due to delays, however, they did not leave for Waco, Texas, until March 1943.

Their first training was a six-week course in English at the University of Baylor.

It appears that the group was put up at a hotel, The Raleigh, in downtown Waco. Before the group finished their English language training, Mexico's Secretary of National Defence, General Lazaro Cardenas, authorised sending to the Mexican military attache in Washington DC $6,195 and 90 cents to cover the 65 hours of flight training for the primary school which the Mexican group would attend.

On 23 June 1943, the military attache in Washington DC sent the following information to Cardenas and the Department of Aeronautics:

> North American section, group of cadets under the orders of Subtte. Perez Gallardo will not go to Randolph field instead to Corsicana Flying School, Texas. They need to be present on the twenty fifth at said location.

The group was sent to Corsicana Army Air Field, in the Texas city of the same name, where the 301st Army Air Force Flying Training Detachment Primary was based, part of the 31st Flying Training Wing of the Central Flying Training Command.

They would form part of Class 44-A, that also had a number of Brazilian aviation cadets.

Corsicana field had been built in 1940 with private funds, and from 1941 to November 1944 there were about 500 Fairchild PT-19s stationed there. About 8,000 aviation cadets were trained there, of which only some 5,000 continued to basic flight training. During this time 14 instructors and cadets were killed in flying accidents.

As well as its main runway, Corsicana airfield also had up to six auxiliary airfields in operation at this time.

Among those who trained at Corsicana was the second top-scoring USAAF pilot of the war, Major Thomas B. McGuire, who at the time of his death in 1945 was credited with 38 enemy aircraft destroyed, plus three probables and two damaged, while flying the Lockheed P-38 with the 5th Air Force in the Pacific. Another pilot who would later make his name in the Korean War trained at Corsicana and was retained as a flight instructor during the war; Captain Manuel J. 'Pete' Fernandez became the third top-scoring USAF jet fighter pilot with 14½ kills flying the North American F-86 Sabre with the 4th Fighter Interceptor Wing.

The primary training course at Corsicana lasted for 10 weeks and each cadet received 12 hours of flight time before he flew solo and did basic manoeuvres. There was also 10 hours in Link trainers and 60 hours of classroom time.

The Mexicans arrived at Corsicana on 23 June and were assigned to V Squadron of Class 44-A, starting their instruction that same day.

Cadet Jamie Zenizo Rojas was in charge of recording information to be sent back to Mexico.

They started their flight training in the Fairchild PT-19 (Fairchild Model 62) that was being introduced to the Military Aviation School back in Guadalajara.

By 21 July the Mexicans had soloed with an average eight hours of instruction and requested, as per Mexican regulations, permission to wear their half wings. On the 30th, Colonel Farell authorised them to wear the half wings as recognition of their progress in the United States.

On the same day, Cadet Raul Garcia Mercado suffered a mishap on landing in PT-19A 41-15053 at an auxiliary field, with no injury to him, and after an investigation was allowed to continue his training.

By 5 August, Zenizo Rojas reported, the group of pilots had an average of 30 hours of flight time, performing 90, 180 and 360-degree manoeuvres, stalls and chandelles (180-degree climbing turns).

Tragedy struck the group on 20 August when Cadet Sergeant 2nd Class Jesus Gomez Montero was killed while flying PT-19A 42-33829. He had taken off at 1100 and another cadet observed his aircraft crashing at about 1145. When rescue crews arrived on the scene his body was not in the aircraft; he was found about two miles away, his parachute only having opened after impacting on the ground.

At the time of his death Montero had recorded 54.58 hours of flight training.

That same day 2nd Lieutenant Perez Gallardo submitted his report to Colonel Farell, saying that Montero had been killed when he struck his aircraft as he was ejected from it since he was found with his parachute semi-intact. Perez Gallardo claimed that Montero had been

Another member of the Corsicana group, 2nd Lieutenant Raul Garcia Mercado, with his students. (Fuerza Aerea Mexicana)

The fourth member of the Corsicana group, 2nd Lieutenant Fausto Vega Santander, with a group of cadets of the *Escuadron Primario*. (Fuerza Aerea Mexicana)

doing an acrobatic maneuver but got into trouble and tried to bail out, with fatal results.

However, years later, researchers and historians, after talking to former instructors and cadets, came up with a different cause of Montero's death. They claimed Montero was not properly strapped into his seat with his parachute pack, and when he did his high-G manoeuvres he was ejected from the aircraft and was too low to use his parachute. This type of incident had been reported by other cadets, who luckily had sufficient altitude to use their parachutes and save themselves.

In August 1943 the local press carried the following news item about Montero's death, with the headline 'Mexican cadet [at] Corsicana Field killed in crash':

> Jesus Gomez Montero 21 year old Mexican aviation cadet at Corsicana Field was killed instantly Friday while on routine solo training flight when his plane crashed approximately five miles east of the field near Eureka, according to Lt. Louis R. Renfrow, Public relations officer.
>
> The body was found two miles from the wrecked plane, will be sent to Mexico City Saturday night accompanied as far the Texas border by an officer from Corsicana Field, Lt. Renfrow said. It will be met there by a Mexican army official for the remainder of the trip. Details of the crash are being investigated by a board of Army officers, the public relations officer said. A resident of Mexico City, Aviation Cadet Montero was one of a group of Mexican Cadets sent to Corsicana Field by the Mexican Army Air Forces in Class 44-A .
>
> At the same time a group of Brazilians arrived here for their primary training. They had completed their preliminary Training at San Antonio, before coming here.

On 1 September Zenizo Rojas reported that on 29 August they had finished their primary course with about 65 hours of flight time and five hours in Link trainers, and on the 31st they were heading for basic flight training somewhere in Texas with the rest of class 44-A.

This class consisted of 432 cadets, of which 25 were Brazilian and four Mexican. Their next destination was Waco Army Airfield, home of the 54th Basic Flying Training Group, flying the Vultee BT-13/13Valiant basic trainer. This base operated from April 1942 to September 1944, and had six training squadrons with about 80 flight instructors.

Here the cadets were expected to fly 70 hours in nine weeks of training.

They also flew at night by instruments in formation and did aerial navigation. Zenizo Rojas reported that between September and November they had completed the required aerial manoeuvres, local flights and night flights. They finished the course by 30 October with the following hours for each cadet, including solo and instructional time: Jaime Zenizo Rojas, 77.45; Fausto Vega Santander, 77.40; Raul Garcia Mercado, 90.15.

The next phase of training was the advanced course at Eagle Pass AAFB, where the cadets undertook a six-week course with about 70 hours of flight time in the North American AT-6 Texan. This base was located about 10 miles from Eagle Pass, was activated in June 1942, trained cadets until April 1945 and had four squadrons. By this time class 44-A had 217 cadets, 14 of whom were Brazilian and four Mexican.

The Mexicans and Brazilians were assigned to Squadron VIII under the command of Captain A.C. Papson with his military and civilian flight instructors. The Mexicans were in 'Combat Team A', with the Brazilians in 'Combat Team B' and 'Combat Team C'.

At the end of December 1943, General Gustavo Salinas, with the approval of General Lazaro Cardenas, accepted an invitation to attend the graduation ceremony extended by Major General Gerald Clark Brant, chief of the Army Air Force Central Flying Training Command. General Salinas was accompanied to the ceremony by General Reynaldo Perez Gallardo, father of one of the pilots, and other officers. On the same day the Mexican personnel received their Mexican Air Force wings and promotion to the next rank. The four pilots – Lieutenant Reynaldo Perez Gallardo, 2nd Lieutenant Jaime Zenizo Rojas, 2nd Lieutenant Fausto Vega Santander and 2nd Lieutenant Raul Garcia Mercado – averaged over 100 hours of flight training.

Their next destination was Hondo Army Airfield in Texas, home of the Army Air Force Navigation School. This school started operations in August 1942, with 14,158 aerial navigators graduating during the war.

During a two-month course at Hondo the Mexicans flew the Beechcraft AT-7 Navigator, getting twin-engine time. They finished their transition course on 1 March 1944, and seven days later, by order of the Secretary of National Defence, the group was sent back to Mexico. They arrived at Guadalajara on 16 March, where the newly trained pilots were sworn in as pilot aviators of the Mexican Air Force with a retroactive date of 7 January 1944. The pilots returned with an average of 125 hours of flight time.

From March to July 1944 the pilots were engaged in the training

A formation of USN Douglas SBD Dauntless dive-bombers undertaking a training flight out of NAS North Island, San Diego, in 1944. It's possible that some of these were later used by the *Grupo Aereo Mexicano*. (Author Collection)

of their fellow cadets, and when the *Grupo de Perfeccionamiento Aeronautica* was formed, Perez Gallardo, Zenizo Rojas, Garcia Mercado and Vega Santander were selected to be part of it, being ordered to *Escuadron Aereo 201* on 1 July.

By this time the pilots had the following flying time to their credit:

| | |
|---|---|
| Perez Gallardo | 400 hours |
| Zenizo Rojas | 378 hours |
| Garcia Mercado | 192 hours |
| Vega Santander | 204 hours. |

## NAVAL AVIATION TRAINING IN TEXAS

Another significant group of Mexican cadets containing future members of the GPA/Squadron 201 trained at a US Naval installation, the director of the Military Aviation School, Colonel Luis Farrell, obtaining postings at the Naval Air Station at Corpus Christie, Texas, for the training of his pilots.

Corpus Christie was the largest naval flight training establishment in the United States, starting operations on 5 May 1941. Averaging 800 flight instructors, it trained nearly 600 student pilots per month, and by the end of the Second World War had trained about 35,000 naval aviators, including Allied personnel.

Intermediate flight training was taught there, training pilots in the SNJ (AT-6), SNV (BT-13/15), SNB (Beechcraft C-45), OS2U (Kingfisher), PBY (Catalina) and N3N aircraft. The naval base had almost a thousand buildings, including hangars, shops, barracks, clubs and support facilities.

Two groups of Mexican cadets and officers were sent there. The first group to go, which started its training in January 1943 with some finishing on 16 December, were (using their Mexican ranks):

Teniente de Adm. Pedro A Santillana Suarez,
Teniente de Infanteria Luis A. Orozco Hijar,
Teniente de Infanteria Delfino Flores Blanco,
Teniente de Infanteria Enrique Rodriguez Torres,
Teniente de Infanteria Jose Luis Barbosa Cerda,
Teniente de Transmisiones Jose Espinosa Fuentes,
Teniente de Artilleria Hector Espinosa Galvan,
Teniente de Caballeria Javier Martinez Valle,
Teniente de Caballeria Joaquin Ramirez Vilchis,
Teniente de Caballeria Amadeo Castro Almanza,
Teniente de Fragata Genaro Padilla Armengol (Mexican Navy) and
Pablo Herrera Perez (rank unknown).

One of the group, Joaquin Ramirez Vilchis, was a former cavalry officer who had transferred to the aviation school in 1940 as a ground instructors. In April 1941 he was assigned as a regular student, and on 15 December that year flew solo, earning the right to wear his half wings.

Cadets Raul Garcia Mercado, Fausto Vega Santander and Jaime Zenizo Rojas going over some manoeuvres during their basic flight training at Hondo AAFB. (Family of Jaime Zenizo Rojas)

He was involved in the movement of the school from Monterrey to Guadalajara.

Vilchis was ordered to Corpus Christie to attend an advanced course. Up to that time he had 56 hours and 42 minutes of flying time to his credit.

Another pilot in this group who benefited from naval aviation training was Amadeo Castro Almanza, who would have a long aviation career in Mexico with some 25,000 hours of flight time.

He suffered an aviation accident when the Vought Kingfisher floatplane he was flying suffered an engine failure that force him to land at sea; the main pontoon took in water and the aircraft started to sink, but luckily he was rescued by a PBY Catalina.

Castro Almanza graduated with his naval aviation wings, and in an interview he said that he took the opportunity to fly almost every type of American naval aircraft available, among them the

Grumman J2F Duck,
Vought OS2U Kingfisher,
Consolidated PBY Catalina flying boat,
Martin Mars patrol boat,
Grumman F6F Hellcat fighter,
Chance Vought F4U Corsair fighter and
Grumman TBF Avenger torpedo bomber.

It is mentioned but not confirmed that Castro Almanza may be the only Mexican military pilot to have flown a captured Japanese 'Zero' fighter, possibly in the US or in the Philippines.

Also among this group of officers was Hector Espinosa Galvan, who during his training at Corpus Christi managed to get married over the phone on 15 June.

He accumulated 56 hours and 58 minutes of flying time (23 hours and 33 minutes double control, and 33 hours and 25 minutes solo time), undertook a flight instrument course and was assigned as a flight instructor at the Military Aviation School, eventually being selected to form part of the GPA/Squadron 201.

While the group was training at Corpus Christie they were part of the welcoming committee at the cadet dining facility that received both President Manuel Avila Camacho and Franklin D. Roosevelt, who had their historic meeting at Monterrey on 20 April 1943.

President Camacho later had the opportunity to speak to the Mexican flyers.

All these officers returned to Mexico to serve as flight instructors at

Diputados y Aviadores Mexicanos, en San Diego, Cal.

En la base naval de San Diego, de izquierda a derecha, el subteniente Crisóforo Salido, el señor Roberto G. Hernández, del Departamento de Tesorería del Distrito Federal; el subteniente Jacobo Estrada Luna; Eliseo Russek, Cónsul de México en San Diego; el teniente Graco Ramírez Garrido; el diputado Leopoldo Hernández; el teniente F. Hernández Vega; Alfonso Hernández, consejero técnico; el capitán Carlos Cervantes Pérez; el diputado Ramón G. Bonfil; el coronel Antonio Cárdenas; el diputado Manuel Moreno Sánchez; el Teniente Carlos Garduño; Roberto Urrea, Cónsul de México en Los Angeles, Cal., y el teniente Julio Cal y Mayor.

A newspaper account of Mexican politicians visiting the Mexican airmen of the *Grupo Aereo Mexicano* at NAS North Island, San Diego, in 1944. Note the Mexican-marked SBDs in the background. (Manuel Cervantes Ramos)

the aviation school or be selected to be part of Squadron 201.

A second group of four Mexican aviation cadets also started their advanced training at Corpus Christie, of which the following three were later selected to join Squadron 201 of the GPA: Sergeant 2nd Class Cadet Roberto Urias Avelleyra, Corporal Cadet Mario Lopez Portillo and Corporal Cadet Praxedis Lopez Ramos.

This group finished their training with about 70 hours of flight time each in the SNJ-4 trainer, later also passing to fly floatplanes like the Vought OS2U Kingfisher, graduating and returning to Mexico by November 1943.

## USCG ST PETERSBURG, FLORIDA

Another group of Mexican military pilots were sent to the USCG (United States Coast Guard) Air Station at St Petersburg, Florida, to complete a four-week course of single-engine seaplane indoctrination and training. The air station was commissioned in March 1935 and was primarily used for search and rescue operations.

During the height of the U-boat menace, coast guard aircraft were not equipped for anti-submarine warfare and concentrated on locating and saving the many seamen from merchant ships attacked and sunk by U-boats. Coast guard aircraft were later armed to engage enemy submarines, but after 1943 – with the lack of presence of U-boats – USCG aircraft returned to their primary mission of search and rescue, with training for American and Mexican personnel

as part of an agreement between the governments of the United States and Mexico.

The group of eight pilots was led by Lieutenant Colonel Eliseo Martin del Campo Garcia (1900-71), who had previous trained at USAAC facilities during the 1920s. They received training in various techniques of flying.

For example, Lieutenant Graco Ramirez Garrido first received over 13 hours of flight time in the N3N-1 primary seaplane. This stage consisted of all special elements and techniques of flying as applied to seaplanes, including normal landings and take-offs, power landings, precision landings, water seamanship, taxi-ing, spin recovery, simulated emergencies and section formation tactics of naval reconnaissance squadrons.

In the next phase of training, Ramirez Garrido accumulated more than 24 hours of flight time in OS2U-3 service planes. This consisted of operational check outs, familiarisation solo flights, section formation tactics, free and fixed gunnery training and practice, low-altitude depth charge bombing and practice and dive-bombing training and practice.

Garrido and the other members of his group each completed 70

The graduation ceremony for the Mexican pilots at USCG station St Petersburg, Florida, in May 1943. (Fuerza Aerea Mexicana)

hours of ground school, which included practical aerial navigation, meteorology, radio procedures and code practice, signalling with flags and semaphore, lectures on all subjects pertaining to the usage of scout reconnaissance squadrons aircraft – including offensive and defensive tactics, convoy coverage and search procedures -and base administration, personnel, material and strategic location.

They finished their training around May 1943, and from this group of pilots the following were selected to join the GPA in July 1944:

2nd Lieutenant Crisoforo Salido Grijalva,
2nd Lieutenant Julio Cal y Mayor Sauz,
2nd Lieutenant Jacobo Estrada Luna,
2nd Lieutenant Carlos Rodriguez Corona and
Lieutenant Graco Ramirez Garrido.

These pilots, except for Rodriguez Corona, would later be sent back to their operational units in the Gulf of Mexico and were then sent for additional training at the USN Naval Air Station at Coronado, San Diego. Rodriguez Corona was sent to the Military Aviation School as a flight instructor.

## MEXICANS AT NAS NORTH ISLAND, 1944

From August 1943 to February 1944 the Mexican Air Force received under Lend Lease 30 Douglas A-24B dive-bombers, known in the USAAF as the 'Banshee'. They were first assigned to A-24 Squadron, but

on 1 December 1943 *Escuadron Aereo 201* was formed with these aircraft and some North American AT-6s at Balbuena airfield.

A memorandum directed to the Secretary of National Defence on 11 December 1943, and signed by General Gustavo Salinas, said the *Direccion de Aeronautica* wanted to send seven pilots to Ensenada, Baja California, to be assigned to the *2/o. Zona Militar* (2nd Military Zone) to participate in a joint exercise with the American Army in that region.

The pilots selected, the majority of whom had recently returned from training at the USCG station at St Petersburg, were:

Lieutenant Graco Ramirez Garrido (*Escuadron Aereo 201*),
Lieutenant Carlos Cervantez Perez (*Escuadron Aereo 201*),
Lieutenant Carlos Garduno Nunez (*4/o. Escuadron Aereo*),
Lieutenant Fernando H. Vega (*3/o. Escuadron Aereo*),
2nd Lieutenant Jacobo Estrada Luna (*Escuadron Aereo 201*),
2nd Lieutenant Crisoforo Salido Grijalva (*Escuadron Aereo 201*) and
2nd Lieutenant Julio Cal y Mayor Sauz (*Escuadorn Aereo 201*).

*Escuadron Aereo 201* was at Balbuena airfield, while the *3/o. Escuadron Aereo* was at Tampico, Tamaulipas, and the *4/o. Escuadron*

Cadet Fausto Vega Santander at Eagles Pass AAFB, Texas, in Combat Team 'A'. (*The Eagle, Forty-Four – A year book*)

Cadet Jaime Z. Rojas at Eagle Pass AAFB, Texas, in Combat Team 'A'. (*The Eagle, Forty-Four – A year book*)

*Aereo* at Las Bajadas, Veracruz, flying AT-6 Texans in anti-submarine patrols in the Gulf of Mexico. The *2/o. Zona militar* had the *1/o. Escuadron Aereo*, that would later change its name to *Escuadron Aereo 202*, under the command of Major Raul Foullon Cabrera (1907-75).

With the approval of General Lazaro Cardenas, the selected pilots were ordered on 17 December 1943 to report to the *2/o. Zona Militar* at Ensenada under the leadership of Lieutenant Cervantes Perez, (1915-93, later promoted to Captain 2nd Class), arriving on the 23rd. The local press reported the arrival of the group of pilots at Ensenada on 3 January 1944 to participate in joint exercises with American pilots.

On 16 February, the *San Diego Tribune-Sun* newspaper informed readers that seven Mexican military pilots had been assigned to Naval Air Station North Island, Coronado, California, but it appears they had arrived a little earlier since the log book of 2nd Lieutenant Estrada Luna recorded his first 90-minute flight in a US Navy Douglas SBD on 4 February.

The newspaper reported that the Mexicans would be instructed in the latest tactics and developments in dive-bombing and on their return to Mexico would impart this knowledge to their fellow pilots.

Naval Air Station North Island had a long history and was considered to be the birthplace of American naval aviation, starting as a naval station back in 1917. Pioneer pilot Glenn Curtiss had started a school to train personnel from the US Army and Navy in 1911-12. The Navy later took over, but the Army remained in North Island until 1937,when it left. The Navy has operated at North Island ever since.

When the Mexicans arrived, NAS North Island was under the command of Rear Admiral Elliot Buckmaster, who had about 12,000 military and 7,000 civilian personnel working at the base. There were also about 1,340 aircraft of different types. Twenty-eight squadrons were training there for carrier operations, with nine patrol squadrons.

The group of seven Mexican pilots were initially organised and equipped with a reported eight Douglas SBD-5/6 Dauntless dive-bombers, with seven for use and one held in reserve, but based on the flight logs it seems only four were flown by the Mexican pilots. The Mexicans were assisted by Marine Corps aviator Lieutenant Colonel Michael Sampas, who became their liaison officer.

Lieutenant Colonel Michael Sampas (1911-97) was a Guadalcanal veteran. As a major, he flew the Grumman F4F-7 Wildcat photo-reconnaissance planes of VMO-251/VMD-154, making many photo runs over enemy positions in low-level flights over the combat zone.

From 19 October to 1 November 1942, with another pilot, he took the first detailed close-up photographs of Guadalcanal.

During its time in Guadalcanal, VMO-251 not only flew photo reconnaissance missions but was also a fighter squadron, credited with 33 aerial claims, its most notable pilot being 2nd Lieutenant H.A. Peters, who had four kills to his credit.

Major Sampas later organised search and rescue operations, and was credited during a three-and-a-half month period with rescuing 39 pilots and 61 crewmen and evacuating 237 others.

At the time of the arrival of the Mexican pilots, Sampas was working in the Plans and Intelligence Department of NAVPAC.

He organised them as a squadron, with their own hangar, flight line and maintenance support from US Navy mechanics. The group was known as the 'Mexican Squadron', but official documents list them as the 'Grupo Aereo Mexicano' (Mexican Air Group).

Sampas developed a six-month US Navy-style training programme, and managed to get a US Navy dive-bomber pilot to help train the Mexican pilots in the Douglas SBDs.

As reported in the local press, the mission of the Mexican pilots was:

> Observing the latest developments in combat, training as practiced by the US Navy Air Arm. At the control of the new Douglas Dive Bombers (SBDs) and other combat type planes, the neighbor country pilots will participate in routine tactical exercises used by the US Navy in operations and combat flying.

Cadet Raul Garcia Mercado at Eagle Pass AAFB, Texas, in Combat Team 'A'. (*The Eagle, Forty-Four – A year book*)

2nd Lieutenant Reynaldo Perez Gallardo of Combat Team 'A'. (*The Eagle, Forty-Four – A year book*)

When they have completed their mission the Mexican airmen plan to return to Mexico to disseminate their newly gained technical knowledge among officers and men of the Mexican Air Force.

On 29 March 1944, the local press also reported the arrival of Colonel Antonio Cardenas Rodriguez to take over the group.

During their stay at NAS North Island, the *Grupo Aereo Mexicano* received orders and instructions from the *2/o. Zona Militar* headquarters at Ensenada and also from the US naval squadrons, which were using Mexican territorial waters to undertake their training. The *Grupo Aereo Mexicano* undertook the following missions:

1. Training in the latest tactics and developments of dive-bombing.
2. Practicing gunnery over Mexican waters.
3. Escort training formations of American aircraft that used Mexican waters for their training.
4. Flights to El Cipres airfield for simulated training over Mexican troops.

During their stay ,the *Grupo Aereo Mexicano* escorted the following US Navy aviation units that flew over Mexican waters:

Fleet Air Wing 14:
Grumman TBF Avenger, Douglas SBD dive-bomber.
CFAW-14 (Carrier Fleet Air Wing-14): VPB-104s, -106s, -117s, -118s, -119s, -152s, -153s (PBM-3D, PB2Y-3H, PB4Y-1 and PB4Y-2), VP-13s, -14s, -71s, VD-3s, -5s, VH-2s.
PTU (Photographic Training Unit): Consolidated PB2Y-1/PB4Y-1s.
Air Support Training Unit (ASTU): Curtiss SB2Cs, Douglas SBDs, Grumman TBFs.

Among the units that the Mexicans helped train, some became notable, such as the Patrol Bombing Squadron VPB-117 'Blue Raiders' (PB4Y-1 and PB4Y-2). This unit was formed at Camp Kearny, California, in February 1944 and entered combat operations in September of that year. VPB-117 became one of the most notable VPB squadrons in the Second World War. During its tour of duty, VPB-117 claimed the destruction of 210 Japanese ships, damaging another 274.

Its gunners claimed the destruction of 63 enemy aircraft plus five damaged, with 16 more destroyed on the ground and four claimed damaged. The squadron produced five PB4Y crews that shot down more than five enemy aircraft. One crew, that of Lieutenant Art Elder, established the record of the most destruction claims for a PB4Y crew with 19 ships sunk and 45 damaged, also shooting down three enemy aircraft plus nine on the ground, with three probables.

*Grupo Aereo Mexicano* also helped train VPB-116, one of whose aircraft, a PB4Y, was on 27 August 1945 considered to be the first American aircraft to land in Japan due to mechanical failure, returning that same day to Iwo Jima without incident.

Another unit the Mexican pilots helped trained that would gain fame was VC-21, a composite squadron that flew Grumman TBF torpedo bombers and Grumman FM-2 fighters. This unit was assigned onboard the escort carrier USS *Marcus Island*, which was involved in the naval battle between task force 'Taffy 3' and the Japanese task force lead by the super-battleship IJN *Yamato* on 25 October 1944, known as the naval battle of Samar Philippines. VC-21 flew in the defence of 'Taffy 3', scoring 14 hits on the attacking Japanese ships and shooting down five Japanese aircraft.

VC-21 ended the war with three Japanese ships sunk, one submarine shared with a destroyer and four ships damaged. The FM-2s claimed 18 enemy aircraft destroyed, with nine probables and five damaged, Ensign Willis N. Penney being the top pilot with three kills. VC-21 lost six aircraft in combat and two pilots.

Another notable unit the Mexicans helped train was the bombing squadron VB-84, flying Curtiss SB2C Helldivers off the USS *Bunker Hill*. VB-84 formed part of the Carrier Air Group CAG-84. Before the USS *Bunker Hill* was put out of action by two kamikaze attacks on 11

Enjoying the social life at Eagle Pass, Texas, Cadet Jaime Zenizo Rojas dancing with a local girl. (*The Eagle, Forty-Four – A year book*)

Cadet Jesus Montero Gomez, who was killed in an aviation accident at Corsicana AAFB on 20 August 1943. (Reynaldo Perez Gallardo)

May 1945, VB-84 was part of the attacking force that hit the Japanese task force lead by the IJN *Yamato* on 7 April 1945.

VB-84 sank one of the escorting destroyers. The kamikaze attack of 11 May caused the death of 21 members of VB-84, plus the loss of all its aircraft. After the fires were brought under control, the USS *Bunker Hill*, after making some stops, made it back to the United States on 3 June 1945. It was under repair when the war ended in August.

The *Grupo Aereo Mexicano* undertook active flight training on 15 April 1944, with practice dive-bombing over land targets and strafing targets in American and Mexican waters. They occasionally flew joint missions with US Navy units, as noted in the 15 April 1944 entry of the squadron diary that was kept by Lieutenant Fernando Hernandez Vega:

> One squadron of aircraft type PBY-4, from Fleet Air Wing#14 reported it was going to do the following practice flights. Over target #2, sending two aircraft per each flight.
>
> First flight from 07:00 to 10:30 hours
>
> Second flight from 10:30 to 12:00 hours
>
> Third flight from 12:45 to 15:00 hours
>
> Fourth flight from 15:00 to 18:00 hours
>
> The following pilots were named to accompany the flights mentioned: Col. Cardenas, Capt. Cervantez, Tte. Ramirez and Tte. Hernandez in Aircraft C-48, C-47, C-44 and C-43.The following gunnery training took place over Mexican waters from 11:30 to 12:30 by Tte. Garduno and Tte. Cal y Mayor in aircraft C-43 and C-44.

On 20 April the photo reconnaissance unit at NAS North Island notified that it was going to conduct a flight over Mexican waters from 0815 to 1030 with two PB4Ys, accompanied by Colonel Cardenas in SBD C-48, Captain Cervantez in C-47 and Lieutenant Ramirez in C-44.

The photo reconnaissance unit conducted more flights from 1330 to 1545 with one PB4Y, from 0730 to 1030 with another PB4Y and from 1030 to 1230 once again with a PB4Y. Lieutenant Hernandez in SBD C-43, Lieutenant Garduno in C-47and 2nd Lieutenant Cal y Mayor in C-44 accompanied these flights.

The Navy's VC-21 squadron announced it was going to conduct training over target no.2 in Mexican waters from 0900 to 1100 with four Grumman TBM Avengers, and they were accompanied by the above-mentioned Mexican pilots.

On 1 May the following mission was accomplished, as recorded by Hernandez Vega:

> The A.R.T.U. squadron communicated that it would use targets #3 in Mexican Waters from 14:30 to 15:50, using SBD type aircraft and the other type TBF. Squadron V.B. 116 communicated that they would use target #2 in Mexican Waters from 14:30 to 18:30 using B-24 type aircraft.
>
> To do the escort for the squadron the following crews were named: Tte. Hernandez in aircraft C-48, Tte. Garduno in aircraft C-47 and Tte. Cal y Mayor in aircraft C-43.
>
> No orders for the 2/o. Military Zone.

The next day no missions were flown due to bad weather in the region. On the following day, although the US naval squadrons did not train the Mexicans did, as again shown by Hernandez Vega:

> No report of flights by the North American squadrons. From 10:30 to 11:20 a dive bombing training was undertaken by Capt. Cervantez in aircraft C-47 and Tte. Garduno in aircraft C-48.
>
> No orders from the 2/o. Military Zone.

The Mexicans' conduct during the stay at NAS North Island was noted in a letter from Rear Admiral W.L. Friedell, US Navy Commandant, Eleventh Naval District, to Vice-Admiral Alfred W. Johnson USN of the joint Mexico United States Defense Commission,

North American AT-6C of the *1 /o. Escuadron Aereo* of the 2 /o. Air Regiment used to patrol the Gulf of Mexico, based at the Port of Veracruz (Las Bajadas). This aircraft carried an unusual outline of a shark panted on the nose. (Drawing by Luca Canossa).

North American AT-6B P-80 of the *2/o. Escuadron Aereo* of the *2/o. Regimiento Aereo* based at Tuxpan Veracruz used by Mayor P.A. Luis Noriega Medrano, when he attacked German U-boat U-129 on 5 July 1942. (Drawing by Luca Canossa)

The Mexican-built Azcarate Corsario No.32 of the *2/o. Regimiento Aereo*, which was based in Mexico City, surviving examples were used in coastal patrols in the Gulf of Mexico and the Pacific coast before being replaced by the AT-6s in 1943. (Drawing by Luca Canossa)

One of the 10 Consolidated Model 21-Ms which were ordered from Canada. They were used in operational units and at the military aviation school as well. Surviving examples were used by the *1/o. Regimiento Aereo* to patrol the Mexican Pacific coast. (Drawing by Luca Canossa)

The Fairchild PT-19B primary trainer that started to arrive at the *Escuela Militar de Aviacion* in 1943. The first of 45 Fairchilds used by the school, this example has the new Mexican Air Force three-letter aircraft designator EPF (*Entrenador Primario Fairchild*) (Primary trainer Fairchild) No.3. Six examples were later transferred over to the navy to their naval aviation school. (Drawing by Luca Canossa)

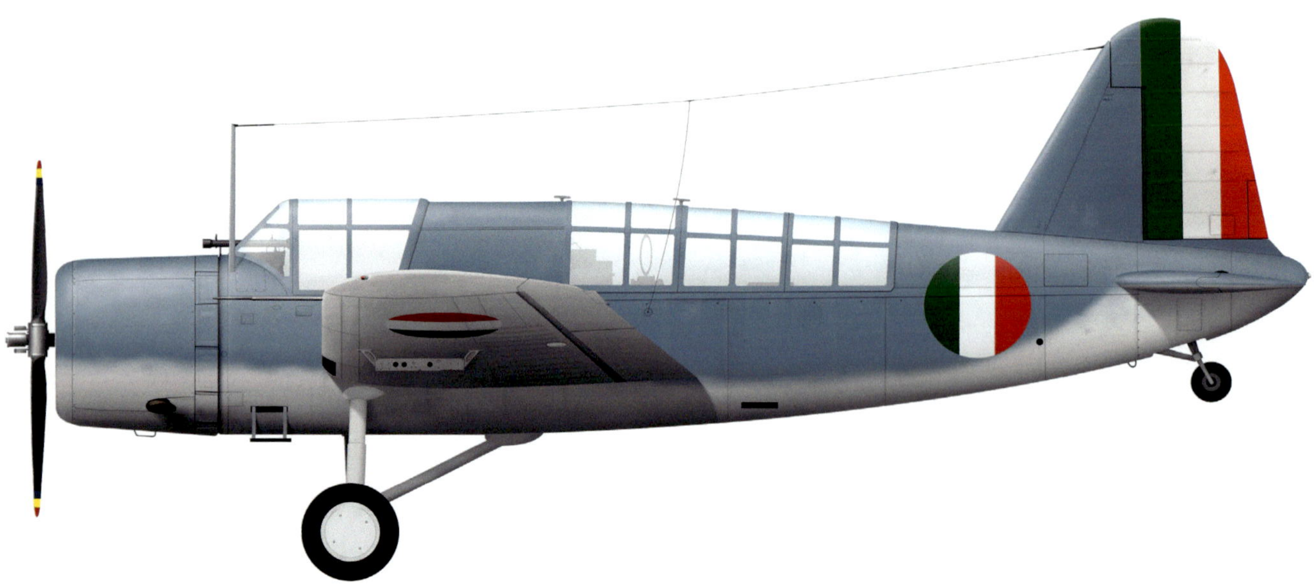

Vought OS2U-3 Kingfisher (ex-US Navy). One of six that were delivered to the Mexican Air Force in March 1942, the Mexican flag colors were painted over the US circle and star due to their urgent need. Later the markings were corrected when the aircraft were sent to the aviation workshops. (Drawing by Luca Canossa).

Vought OS2U-3 Kingfisher ANM/MB-05 in the floatplane versión of the *1/o. Escuadron Aeronaval* as it operated from the Port of Veracruz in 1944. Three of the six Kingfishers that had been transferred over to the Mexican Navy were converted to Floatplane version by 1944/1945. (Drawing by Luca Canossa)

Republic P-47D-23-RA 42-227995. One of the many former 311th Fighter squadron, 58th FG, aircraft that were loaned to the 201st Mexican Fighter Squadron in May 1945, so the squadron could complete its pre-combat training and use these aircraft to start combat operations in June 1945. (Drawing by Luca Canossa)

Republic P-47D-28-RA 42-29432/R-1 used by the *Grupo de Perfeccionamiento Aeronautico/Escuadron Aereo 201* (GPA/EA201) Pocatello AAFB Idaho and later Majors Field, Greenville Texas. The Mexican tricolor on the rudder was applied when the unit was sent to Texas. The Squadron's first casualty, SubTte .P.A.Crisoforo Salido Grijalva, was killed in this aircraft on 23 January 1945. (Drawing by Luca Canossa)

Republic P-47D-30-RA Thunderbolt No.18/ 44-33721 of the 201st Mexican Fighter Squadron of the Mexican Expeditionary Air Force, that operated first out of Porac field under the 58th FG USAAF, after June 1945 and later Clark field in August. (Drawing by Luca Canossa)

Republic P-47N-2-RE No.146/44-88211 "Lil Meaties Meat Chopper" of Lt. Oscar F. Perdomo of the 464th Fighter Squadron of the 507th Fighter Group, who on 13 August 1945 during a fighter sweep to Keiko, Korea, shot down five Japanese aircraft to become the last USAAF ace in a day during the Second World War. (Drawing by Luca Canossa)

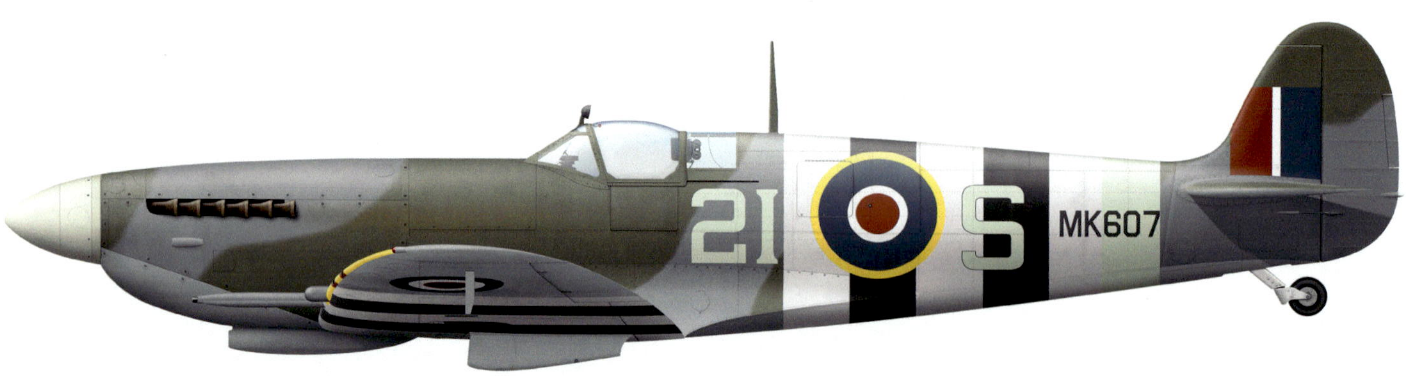


Supermarine Spitfire MK-IXB, 2I-S/MK607 of F/O. Luis Perez Gomez (Guadalajara Jalisco) of No.443 RCAF Fighter Squadron, lost his life in aerial combat with FW-190s of JG1 in this aircraft on 16 June 1944 over or near the French town of Sassy, Calvados, France. (Drawing by Luca Canossa)

Supermarine Spitfire MK-XIVC AE-Y/RM651 of F/O. Thomas Benfield Lee (Pachuca Hidalgo) of No.402 RCAF Fighter Squadron. F/O. T.B. Lee used this aircraft on 20 April 1945 to shoot down a FW-190 N.W. of Hagenow Germany. (Drawing by Luca Canossa)

Vought O2U-2M No.2 of the *1/o. Escuadron Aereo* of the *1/o. Regimiento Aereo*, one of 12 that were bought to participate in the 1929 General Jose Gonzalo Escobar rebellion. Some surviving types could still be seen in service by 1941, having been renumbered by the arrival of the Consolidated Model 21-M. fighter squadron.

Vought V-99M No.37, which was assigned to the *2/o. Escuadron Aereo*, *1/o. Regimiento Aereo* based at La Paz, Baja, California 1941-1942. This aircraft attacked an unidentified object off the coast on 10 September 1942, for which it received the inscription on the tail RLaPazBC 10-IX-42.

One of the first Vultee BT-15 Valiants assigned to the *Escuela Militar de Aviacion*; in 1943 they were assigned to the *Escuadron Basico*. They received the designation EBV 409 (*Entrenador Basico Vultee*) (Basic Trainer Vultee) 409.

## From the *Museo Militar de Aviacion*

Republic P-47D-35-RA Thunderbolt, formerly PZT-1003 44-90210, painted as No.18 44-33721 of the 201st Mexican Fighter Squadron during the liberation of the Philippines. (Author Collection)

Another view of a P-47D-35-RA, No.18 44-33721 of the 201st Mexican Fighter Squadron of the MEAF, at the *Museo Militar de Aviacion 'Teniente P.A. Jose Espinosa Fuentes'.* (Author Collection)

North American T-6G Texan EAN-796 of the Military Aviation School. (Author Collection)

Interstate L-6 Cadet LZI-609 (*Liga de Zona Interstate*), one of 20 that were delivered to the Mexican Air Force in 1943. (Author Collection)

North American B-25J Mitchell Medium bomber BMM-3503. (Author Collection)

## Emblems

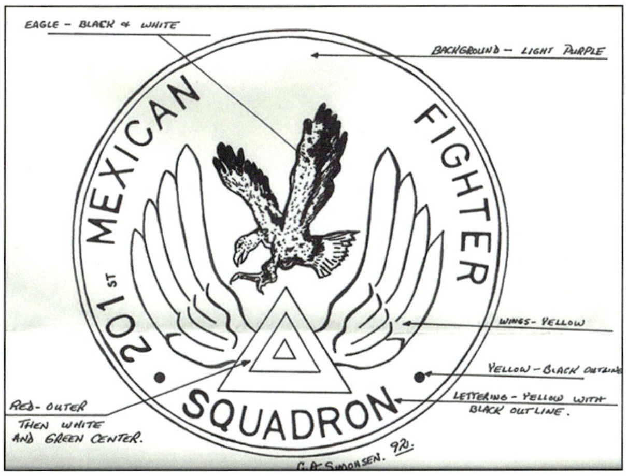


The first squadron insignia the 201st Mexican Fighter Squadron used was this design to mark the squadron area at Pocatello AAFB, Idaho, in late 1944. (Author Collection)

Picture of the squadron insignia at Pocatello AAFB, Idaho, 1944. (Manuel Cervantes Ramos)

Photo of the original drawing done by Sergeant Manuel Cervantes Ramos at Porac Field in 1945. (Manuel Cervantes Ramos)

A modern day version based on the Sergeant Manuel Cervantes drawing of 1945. (Johnny Sigmor)

Reproduction of the Panchito Pistolas wing, which is on exhibit at the *Museo Militar de Aviacion 'Teniente P.A. Jose Espinosa Fuentes'.* (Author Collection)

Reproduction of a 201st Squadron patch that was painted on some of the pilots' flight jackets during their time in the Philippines. (Johnny Sigmor)

A replica of the USAAF battle flag that was given to the 201st Mexican Fighter Squadron during its graduation ceremony at Majors Field, Texas, on 23 February 1945. (Author Collection)

The Panchito Pistolas painted on a P-47D that was flown by Lieutnant Reynaldo Perez Gallardo. (Reynaldo Perez Gallardo)

The Mexican national flag that was given to the 201st at Majors Field, Texas, on 23 February 1945, with the legend '*Ejercito Mexicano*' and '*Fuerza Aerea Expedicionaria*'. (Author Collection)

It has been reported in a internet source that Walt Disney did design a Panchito Pistolas for the 201st Mexican Fighter Squadron, but it was not used and may never have been received by them, since Sergeant Cervantes Ramos and 2nd Lieutenant Moreno Arreola had already come up with the Panchito while in the Philippines. (usmilitariaforum.com)

Today 'Panchito Pistolas' is still on active duty with the present *Escuadron Aereo 201* at Cozumel, Quintana Roo. (Captain Manuel Reyna Garza)

Another design that was used to illustrated the welcome booklet for the MEAF when it arrived back at Mexico City in November 1945. (Manuel Cervantes Ramos)

A reproduction of the *1/o. Escuadron Aeronaval* insignia that was found in a history of Mexican Naval Aviation. (Johnny Sigmor)

'A' Flight of the 201st Squadron was the only flight that produced its own insignia and the name *Aguilas Aztecas* (Aztec Eagles). (USAF)

Members of the *Escuadrilla A, Aguilas Aztecas* posing with their emblem in front of their living quarters, probably at Porac Field. (USAF)

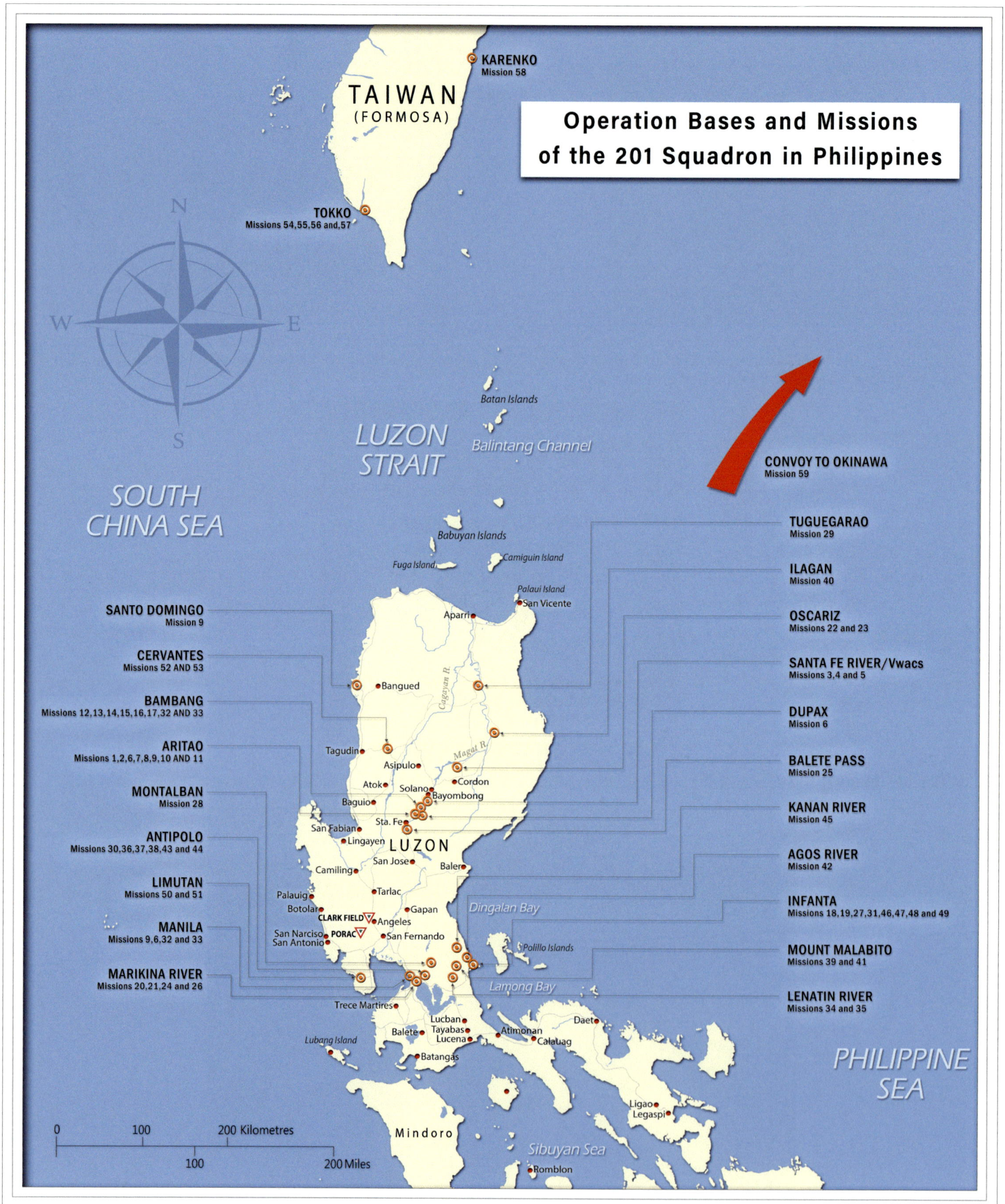


Map of the Philippines showing where the 201st Mexican Fighter Squadron of the MEAF was based and the targets they hit supporting American and Filipino units in the liberation of the Philippines, June-July 1945. (Drawing by Luca Canossa)

Map showing where Mexican shipping was attacked and sunk by German U-boats in the Gulf of Mexico and off the coast of Florida. (Drawing by Luca Canossa)

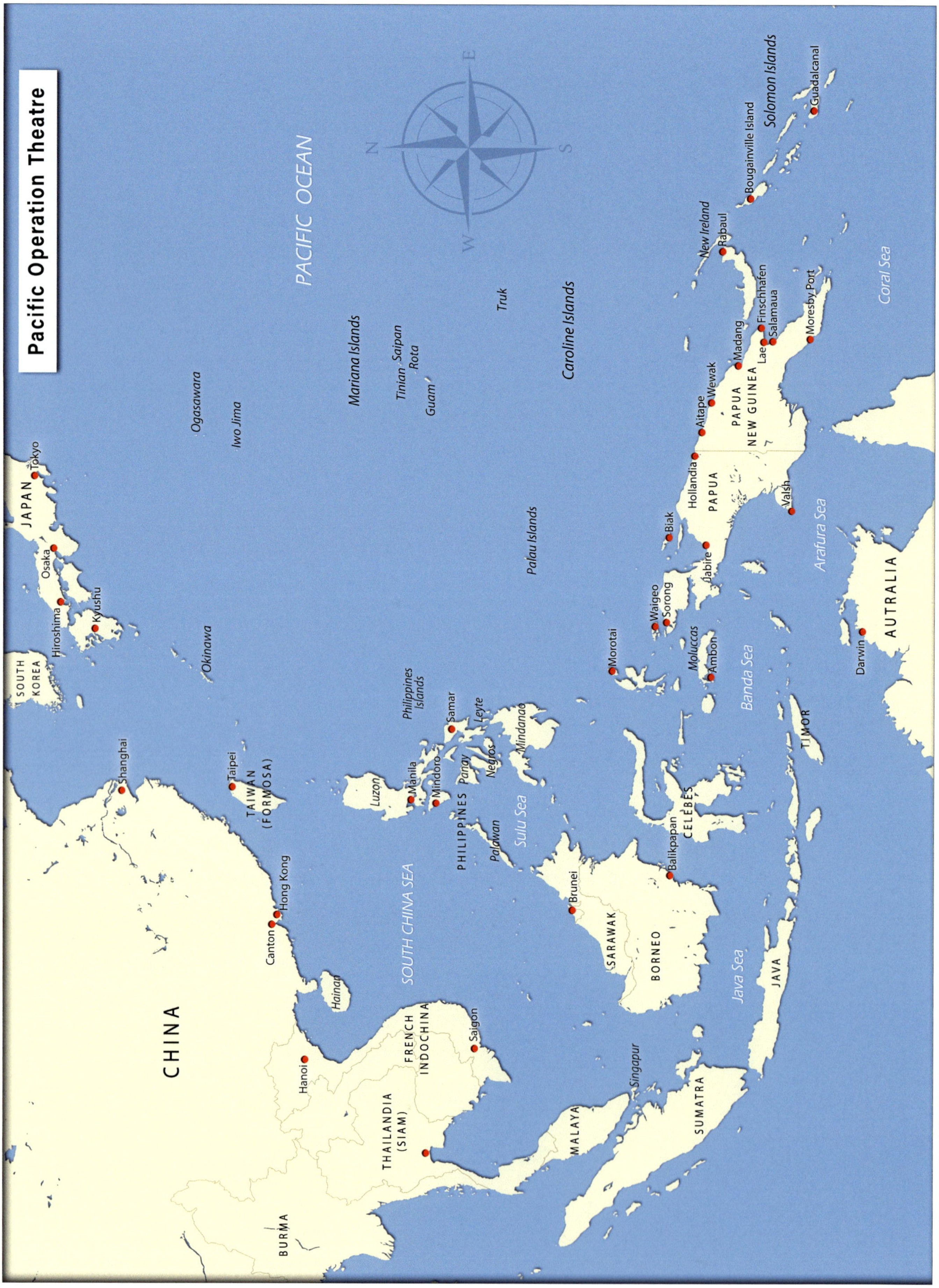


The Pacific Theatre of Operations, where the Mexican Expeditionary Air Force operated in the Philippines with flights to pick up new aircraft to Biak, New Guinea, and fighter sweeps to Formosa, July-August 1945. (Drawing by Luca Canossa)

Civilian flight instructor Boyce Dunlap explaining the next manoeuvre to Mexican pilots at Corsicana AAFB, Texas, from left to right, Fausto Vega Santander, Reynaldo Perez Gallardo, Jesus Montero Gomez, Raul Garcia Mercado and Jaime Zenizo Rojas. (Reynaldo Perez Gallardo)

Vultee BT-13/15 basic trainers at Waco AAFB, Texas, where the Mexican cadets advanced after Corsicana, Texas. (Waco Army Airfield Class 44F Cadet book)

2nd Lieutenant Reynaldo Perez Gallardo, Cadet Raul Garcia Mercado, Fausto Vega Santander and Jaime Zenizo Rojas at Waco AAFB, ready to head out to the flight line. (Family of Jaime Zenizo Rojas)

USMC Major Micheal Sampas and Colonel Antonio Cardenas Rodriguez at NAS North Island, Coronado, San Diego, when Colonel Cardenas arrived to take charge of the *Grupo Aereo Mexicano* there. (US Navy)

on 2 June 1944:

> You will be interested to know that the Fleet Air Officers who have been in charge [of] the training of the Mexican aviators at the Naval Air Station report that their charges are exceptional capable aviators and that they are making an impressive record in their operational work at the station.

The same letter gave the following information on the flight training that the Mexican pilots had in the US prior to going to NAS North Island:

> Five of the Mexican fliers (a) CERVANTES, (b) RAMIREZ, (c) CAL Y MAYOR, (d) SALIDO, and (e) ESTRADA, underwent one month of seaplane training at the U.S. Coast Guard Air Station, St. Petersburg, Florida and one month link at the U.S. Naval Station, Key West, Florida. In the later training period they operated as observers aboard PBM aircraft. Teniente GARDUNO, originally an infantry officer, obtained U.S. Army primary and basic flight training at Randolph and Kelly fields and won his wings at the latter base. No Navy training.Teniente HERNANDEZ has received no army or Navy training in the United States. All flight experience gained from military flying in Mexico. Coronel CARDENAS has received no army or Navy training in the United States. All flight experience gained from military flying in Mexico."

On the same day as Rear Admiral Friedell's letter, the Mexican group had a busy day, as noted in the operations diary by Hernandez Vega:

> Squadron VB-84 communicated that they would use target #2 from 09:00 to 10:30 hours, sending 6 aircraft type SB2-C, Capt. Cervantez in C-47 and Tte. Hernandez in C-48 was named to accompany the mission.
>
> The same squadron communicated another practice over the same target with the same number and type of aircraft from 11:00

to 12:30 hours.

SubTte. Estrada in C-43 and SubTte. Salido in C-44 were assigned to accompany the mission. At 12:15 hours they left for the airfield of Cipres, B.C. to do a demonstration of simulated strafing and dive bombing, Capt. Cervantez in C-47 and Tte. Hernandez in C-48, returning at 16:15 hours.

Squadron VB-84 communicated they would use target#2 from 14:30 to 16:00 Hours, using 6 aircraft type SB2-C. Corl Cardenas in C-44 and Tte. Ramirez in C-43 were assigned to accompany them. Fleet Air Wing 14 communicated that from 14:00 to 16:00 hours they would use target #3, with 3 aircraft typeTBF and 1 PB2Y, assigning SubTte. Estrada in C-43 and SubTte. Salido in C-44 to fly with them.

Fleet Air Wing 14 A.R.T.U. informed of another flight over the same target from 14:15 to 15:15 hours with the same number and type of aircraft, assigning the same personnel as before.

Squadron VB-84 informed that from 16:30 to 18:00 hours they would use target#2 with 6 aircraft SB2-C with Tte. Garduno in C-44 and Tte. Cal y Mayor in C-43 to accompany them.

The same squadron informed that from 16:30 to 18:00 hours they would use the same target with the same type and number of aircraft assigning Tte. Hernandez in C-47 and SubTte. Salido in C-43 to accompany them.

The same squadron with the same number of aircraft and type informed that they would use the same target from 17:30 to 19:00 hours assigning Corl. Cardenas and Capt. Cervantez in C-43 to fly with them.

Last[ly] the same squadron informed again that from 18:30 to 20:00 hours [they] would use the target with the same number and type of aircraft, assigning Tte. Garduno in C-47 and Tte. Cal y Mayor in C-48 to accompany the mission.

Cadet Jaime Zenizo Rojas about to board a BT-13/15 basic trainer at Waco AAFB. (Family of Jaime Zenizo Rojas)

Other missions were flown down to El Cipres, Ensenada, as noted in the unit diary:

May 5, 1944

0900 hours departure to Cipres B. C. Colonel Cardenas w/obs. Subtte. Cal y Mayor in C-47, Capt. Cervantez w/obs. Tte. Garduno in C-48 and Tte. Ramirez w/observer SubTte. Salido in C-43. They returned at 1745 hours.

June 2, 1944

1215 hours, departure to aviation field Cipres B. C. demonstration of simulated strafing. Captain Cervantez in SBD C-47 and Tte. Hernandez in C-48. They returned at 1615 hours.

Their last reported training mission was flown on 2 July 1944:

Two test flights were flown today, Tte. Hernandez in aircraft C-43 from 15:00 to15:45 hours and Tte. Cal y Mayor in the same aircraft from 16:00 to 16:45 hours with nothing to report over the field.

No orders from the 2/o.Military Zone.

Training flights were still undertaken by the Mexican pilots until 14 July 1944, when they were ordered back to Mexico City for the selection of personnel who would form the GPA/Squadron 201.

Cadet Raul Garcia Mercado and 2nd Lieutenant Reynaldo Perez Gallardo pointing to the sky at Waco AAFB, Texas. (Reynaldo Perez Gallardo)

During their stay at NAS North Island, the *Grupo Aereo Mexicano* was visited by high-ranking officers of the Mexican Army and US Navy, including General Juan Felipe Rico, commander of the *2/o. Zona Militar*, and Rear Admiral W.L. Friedell USN. (Carlos Garduno Nunez

Wartime publication photo of a Douglas SBD of the *Grupo Aereo Mexicano* that operated at NAS North Island, San Diego, in 1944. When the group left for Mexico City in July 1944, the aircraft were returned to the US Navy. (*Flying*, Vol.35 No.6, December 1944)

They were flown back to Mexico City on board a Lockheed C-60 transport plane.

At the end of their time in NAS North Island, the Mexican pilots had flown the following numbers of flights and hours, based on the available daily reports that were submitted by Lieutenant Hernandez Vega and some of the pilots' log books:

Rank and name No. of flights No. of hours

Colonel Antonio Cardenas Rodriguez 10 21.10

Captain Carlos Cervantez Perez 15 31.05

Lieutenent Fernando Hernandez Vega 28 52.50

Lieutenant Carlos Garduno Nunez 17 30.20

Lieutenant Graco Ramirez Garrido 56 119.01

Lieutenant Julio Cal y Mayor Sauz 66 136.24

2nd Lieutenant Crisoforo Salido Grijalva 50 103.03

2nd Lieutenant Jacobo Estrada Luna 99 191.03

Apart from Captain Cervantes, all of this group were selected to form part of the *Grupo de Perfecccionamiento Aeronautica* (GPA)/ *Escuadron Aereo 201*, with Colonel Cardenas designated as the commander of the group, that would leave later in the month for the United States, for training for eventual overseas deployment.

Note: After the war Lieutenant Fernando Hernandez Vega would claim that he flew a total OF 250 hours in the SBDs and one hour in the Grumman F6F-3 Hellcat, like other Mexican pilots who were given the chance to fly the famed US Navy fighter.

CHAPTER 9

# GOING TO WAR I: TRAINING IN THE USA

## FLIGHT TRAINING IN THE USA 1944-45 TEXAS AND IDAHO

President Camacho announced during a dinner on 8 March 1944 that Mexico would join the Allies in the war and would be represented by the Mexican Air Force. The idea originated back in 1943, when President Camacho expressed to a visiting American official his wish to see Mexican troops participate in the war.

Over time he came to consider that it was more feasible and economical for the country to send a fighter squadron rather than an infantry unit.

The personnel of the squadron that would fight overseas were already technically trained and the majority of the pilots who later formed the squadron had some training in the United States, with some also speaking English. Their impact on the battlefield would also be greater in the ratio of casualties against damage they would inflict on enemy forces compared to that of an infantry unit.

Some elements of the Army were not happy with the decision, having hoped ground forces would represent Mexico on the battlefield, but President Camacho overruled them.

After exchanges of notes and visits by American and Mexican officials, the plan was approved by both Camacho and President Roosevelt. In July 1944 a series of orders were dictated by the *Secretaria de la Defensa Nacional* (Secretary of National Defence), under the direction of General Lazaro Cardenas and his under secretary, General Francisco L. Urquizo Benavides, for organisation of the *Grupo Perfeccionamiento de Aeronautica* (GPA, Aeronautical Training Group).

The personnel who formed this group were selected from existing squadrons, the various specialtist departments of the air force and even from the Army. In the USAAF report 'American Summary History of the 201st Mexican Fighter Squadron', the following is mentioned about this selection process:

> The personnel were selected by competitive examination from all branches of the Mexican military services as well from civilian life.
>
> All walks of life were represented. Although most came from Mexico City and the vicinity, approximately two-thirds of the pilots had received previous flying experiences in the US, and had acquired considerable commercial experience, while others had received their training in Mexico City [*sic*].

What the report did not mention was that out of the 39 pilots who were eventually selected to form part of the GPA, 11 had recently graduated from the Military Aviation School at Guadalajara on 4 June 1944.

Among the high-ranking officers attending this graduation was the American military attache, General Arthur Harris, and his assistant air attache, Captain Paul B. Miller USAAF, who later during the ceremony presented the top student of the class with a semi-automatic pistol.

Fifteen instructors from the school were also selected for the GPA.

### INSTRUCTORS, MILITARY AVIATION SCHOOL

Captain Roberto Legorreta Sicilia
Captain. Pablo L. Rivas Martinez
Lieutenant Amadeo Castro Almanza
Lieutenant Hector Espinosa Galvan
Lieutenant Reynaldo Perez Gallardo
Lieutenant Joaquin Ramirez Vilchis
Lieutenant Jose Luis Barbosa Cerda
Lieutenant Carlos Rodriguez Corona
Lieutenant Jose Espinosa Fuentes
2nd Lieutenant Praxedis Lopez Ramos
2nd Lieutenant Raul Garcia Mercado
2nd Lieutenant Jaime Zenizo Rojas
2nd Lieutenant Fausto Vega Santander
2nd Lieutenant Mario Lopez Portillo
2nd Lieutenant RobertoAvelleyras Urias

From the graduating class of 4 June 1944, the following pilots were selected for the GPA:

### GRADUATING CLASS GENERATION JUNE 1944

2nd Lieutenant Miguel Uriarte Aguilar
2nd Lieutenant Angel Sanchez Rebollo
2nd Lieutenant Emilio Enrique Ruiz
2nd Lieutenant Miguel Moreno Arreola
2nd Lieutenant Miguel Mendoza Marquez
2nd Lieutenant David Ceron Bedolla
2nd Lieutenant Manuel Farias Rodriguez
2nd Lieutenant Raul Maciel Pena
2nd Lieutenant Jose Luis Pratt Ramos
2nd Lieutenant Guillermo Garcia Ramos
2nd Lieutenant Justino Reyes Retana

Other personnel were selected for the following assignments:

### *COMISION NACIONAL DE CAMPOS*

(National Commission of Fields)
Lieutenant Amador Samano Pina

### COMMANDER, ESCUADRON AEREO 101

(Commander of Squadron 101)
Captain Roberto Salido Beltran (joined the MEAF in early1945)

### DUTY AT VERACRUZ

Lieutenant Rafael Lizardi Formento

### AIDE TO AIR FORCE CHIEF GENERAL GUSTAVO SALINAS

Captain Radames Gaxiola Andrade

### DIVE-BOMBING TRAINING AT NAS NORTH ISLAND, CALIFORNIA

Colonel Antonio Cardenas Rodriguez
Lieutenant Fernando Hernandez Vega
Lieutenant Carlos Garduno Nunez
Lieutenant Graco Ramirez Garrido
2nd Lieutenant Julio Cal y Mayor Sauz
2nd Lieutenant Jacobo Estrada Luna
2nd Lieutenant Crisoforo Salido Grijalva

PRIMERA UNIDAD ME

EL SEÑOR PRESIDENTE DE LA REPUBLICA DESPIDE AL ESCUADRON

SI LAS CIRCUNSTANCIAS LO EXIGEN.- EN EL VAN 63 OBREROS DE L

Diversos aspectos de la gran revista militar efectuada en el campo aéreo de Balbuena, la mañana del 21 de julio de 1944.—1. El señor Presidente de la República y Secretario de la Defensa Nacional, despidiendo a los integrantes del Escuadrón Aéreo 201. 2.—Los mismos funcionarios con el Comité Ejecutivo de la Unión General de Trabajadores de Materiales de Guerra. 4.—El general Lázaro Cárdenas y su Jefe de Estado Mayor general Cristóbal

Coronel Piloto Aviador ANTONIO CARDENAS RODRIGUEZ digno Jefe del Escuadrón Aéreo.

The review of the *Grupo de perfeccionamiento de Aeronautica* (GPA) *Escuadron Aereo 201* being sent off by President Manuel Avila Camacho and the secretary of National Defense, General Lazaro Cardenas (continued opposite). (Manuel Cervantes Ramos)

### *DIRRECION DE AERONAUTICA MILITAR, FUERZA AEREA MEXICANA*

(Department of Military Aviation)

2nd Lieutenant Antonio Sandoval Gonzalez (did not go to USA)
2nd Lieutenant Jose M.Uriarte Aguilar
2nd Lieutenant Fernando Aviedo Rodriguez (did not go to USA)
2nd Lieutenant Miguel Romero Parra (did not go to USA)

### ESCUADRON AEREO 201

2nd Lieutenant Jose Luis Pratt Ramos

### UNKNOWN LOCATION

Lieutenant Gabriel Torres Gonzalez

The majority of the ground personnel came from the following branches and services of the Mexican armed forces:

### *DIRRECCION DE AERONAUTICA, FUERZA AEREA MEXICANA*

(Department of Aeronautics, Mexican Air Force)

3 officers and 30 enlisted men

### *PLANTA DE LA DIRRECION DE PERSONNAL DE LA SECRETARIA DE LA DEFENSA NACIONAL*

(Personnel Section of the Secretary of National Defence)

2 enlisted men

### *INTENDENCIA GENERAL DEL EJÉRCITO*

(Quartermaster General of the Army)

3 enlisted men

### *DIRECCION DE TRANSPORTE MILITARES*

(Department of Military Transports)

1 enlisted man

### *ESCUELA MILITAR DE AVIACION*

(Military Aviation School)

1 enlisted man

### *ESCUELA MILITAR DE INTENDENCIA*

(Military Quatermaster School)

1 enlisted man

XICANA DE COMBATE

201 EN EL CAMPO AEREO DE BALBUENA, QUE IRA A COMBATIR
UNION GENERAL DE TRABAJADORES DE MATERIALES DE GUERRA

Guzmán Cárdenas, presenciando la revista. 5.—Parte del Escuadrón Aéreo 201. 6.—El señor General don Manuel Avila Camacho, Primer mandatario del país, despide al Coronel Piloto Aviador Antonio Rodríguez Cárdenas. 7.—El General Cristóbal Guzmán Cárdenas Jefe de Estado Mayor de la Defensa Nacional, leyendo un mensaje de despedida a los que parten, y parte de los 63 trabajadores sumados al histórico Escuadrón 201.

***ESCUADRON AEREO 101***
(101st Squadron)
6 enlisted men

***ESCUADRON AEREO 202***
(202nd Squadron)
1 enlisted man

***ESCUADRON AEREO 208***
(208th Squadron)
3 enlisted men

***TALLERES GENERALES DE AVIACION***
(Aviation Workshops)
3 enlisted men

***DEPARTAMENTO DE MATERIALES DE GUERRA***
(Department of War Materials)
62 (civilian) enlisted men

***COMANDANCIA GENERAL DE TRANSMISIONES***
(Headquarters of the Signal Corps)
18 enlisted men

***BATALLON DE TRANSMISIONES***
(Signal Corps Battalion)
1 officer and 9 enlisted men

***COMPANIA DE DETECCION NUMERO UNO***
(Detection Company No.1)
1 officer

***1ª SECCION FIJA DE AMETRALLDORAS AA 0.50***
(1st Fixed Section of Anti-Aircraft 0.50 cal. machines guns)
1 enlisted man

***BATALLON DE TRANSPORTES***
(Transport Battalion)
2 enlisted men

***GRUPO DE AMETRALLADORAS AA 0.50***
(Group of Anti-Aircraft gachine guns 0.50 cal.)
3 enlisted men

***HOSPITAL CENTRAL MILITAR***
(Central Military Hospital)
1 enlisted man

The scene at the Buenavista train station on 24 July 1944, when the public showed up to say goodbye to *Escuadron Aereo 201* on its way to the USA for training. (Manuel Cervantes Ramos)

After his return to the United States, Torres was invited by Mexican government officials, to cooperate in the integration in the Unit of the air expeditionary force of the southern neighbor.

The last group of pilots to be selected to join the group were seven who had returned from dive-bombing training at NAS North Island, San Diego, California. Of the group of 39 pilots, 11 were replacement pilots, in case some were eliminated during the training, and to serve as a small reserve in the unit, if deployed overseas, to cover any losses.

With personnel selection completed, the GPA consisted (according to Order No.42495, 28 July 1944) of pilots, officers, specialist in armaments, meteorology, intelligence, medical, office clerks, draughtsmen, mechanics, armourers, radio operators, welders, carpenters, painters, cooks, bakers, postal clerks, drivers and soldiers.

***COMPANIA DE TRANSPORTE***

(Transport Company)

1 enlisted man

***PRIMERA INTENDENCIA REGIONAL***

(First Regional Quartermaster)

3 enlisted men

***1º. BATALLON DEL 7º REGIMIENTO DE LA* 3º DIVISION DE *INFANTERIA***

(1st Battalion, 7th Regiment of the 3rd Infantry Division)

1 enlisted man

***DE NUEVO INGRESO DEL EJÉRCITO.***

(New enlistment in the Army)

2 enlisted men

Among the personnel selected to join the GPA was a combat veteran, Corporal Manuel Alcantar Torres, who had served in an American airborne division and had made combat jumps at Casablanca, Bizerte and Sicily.

He was honourably discharged from the US Army to join the air training group. Details of his military service were later published in article written from Manila by Associated Press reporter Spencer Davis, dated 26 July 1945, with the headline Mexican paratrooper will join Squadron 201 in the Philippines':

> A paratrooper, born to the south of the border of the United States, has been discharged from the American army, with the purpose to render his services with the Mexican fighter squadron in the Philippines.
>
> Corporal Manuel Alcantar Torres, born in Mazatlan, Sinaloa and graduated from The University of Southern California, joined the American army after the attack on Pearl Harbor.
>
> He was a paratrooper that landed at Casablanca North Africa, with the first American armies that participated in the war. Later Torres landed at Messina, Sicily and helped the English and the Canadians in their operations against Saint Nazaire and Sainte Marie Eglise in France.

Colonel Antonia Cardenas Rodriguez (1903-69) was selected as the commanding officer of the GPA.

Born at Hacienda de la Trinidad, Municipio de General Zepeda, Coahuila, on 6 October 1903, his parents were Sabino Cardenas and Maria M. Rodriguez.

A civilian mechanic, he was admitted to the aviation school on 24 October 1923 and obtained his commission and wings on 1 January 1927. He fought against the Yaqui Indians in the state of Sonora from February-October 1927, then against the Cristeros in the states of Colima and Jalisco from November 1927 to October 1928.

He was commissioned to the *Secretaria de Comunicaciones y Obras Publicas* (SCOP) to fly air mail from Mexico to the United States in Stinson SM-1Bs. He was in that job at the start of the Escobar rebellion on 3 March 1929, when he was captured and forced to fly for the rebels until 6 April 1929, when he escaped with his aircraft to Fort Bliss, Texas, later returning to government forces. On 1 October 1929, he was promoted to captain 2nd classpilot aviator, and in 1930 was assigned temporary duty with the C. Mexicana de Aviacion flying Ford Trimotors in commercial routes and gaining experience in tri-motor aircraft.

During the 1930s Cardenas Rodriguez was assigned to various units and the Mexican Aviation School, and even test pilot for the Department of Aeronautics. He was a professor for aerial tactics at the aviation school and from 1932-35 was assigned to the 1st Air Regiment.

On 1 August 1935, he was promoted to captain 1st c.

In 1938 he participated in the campaign against the rebel General Saturnino Cedillo in San Luis Potosi, flying four transport and four reconnaissance missions in a Lockheed Electra Model 12-A, serial 1239, XB-ABW.

For his work in fighting this rebellion he was promoted to major on 16 October 1938. He would use the same aircraft, but named *Presidente Carranza*, for a Latin-American goodwill flight from 24 May to 16 September 1940, accompanied by C. Mexicana de Aviacion radio operator Luis Cuevas Medina. They covered more than 3,419km in over 118 flight hours, visiting every country in Latin America.

In 1941 he tried unsuccessfully to run for political office in his

A tearful goodbye for an Mexican airman from his family and baby at Buenavista train station, 24 July 1944. (Manuel Cervantes Ramos)

home state, and was promoted to lieutenant colonel. He was in charge of bringing the second group of Lend Lease aircraft on 23 July 1942, when he led a flight of eight AT-6s and two Beechcraft AT-7s to Balbuena airfield. By March 1943 it was reported that he had flown over 10,000 hours in various types of aircraft, both military and civilian, with more than 2,868 hours in the former.

From 28 April to 6 June 1943, he formed part of a group of Mexican military observers who went to North Africa to observe the conduct of the war. From 18-22 May, he was assigned to the 97th (H) Bombardment Group, XII Bomber Command, 12th Air Force, a B-17 group commanded by Colonel J. Donovan. Cardenas participated in four bombing missions, hitting targets in Sicily (including Palermo), Pantelleria and Naples. After his tour of duty with the 97th, Cadernas was injured in an aircraft accident, serving as an observer in a Martin B-26 during an in-theatre training flight, requiring hospital treatment in Morocco.

He was promoted to colonel on 1 January 1944 and was put in charge of the Mexican pilots training at NAS North Island, San Diego. He was married with three children, two girls and a boy.

His second in command selected was Captain 1st Class Radames Gaxiola Andrade (1919-66).

Born in Mazatlan, Sinaloa, on 16 December 1919, his parents were Jose Antonio Gaxiola Alcalde and Maria Andrade. His father was an officer in the Mexican Army that was involved in some of the rebellions of the 1920s and 1930s, which forced him and his family to relocate to Los Angeles, California, where his son Radames studied, graduating from high school in June 1932.

He returned to Mexico and was accepted to the Heroico Colegio Militar (Mexico's West Point) on 26 September 1932, graduating as an infantry 2nd lieutenant. He served in the 5th Infantry Battalion at Hermosillo, Sonora, until December 1936, when he requested a transfer to the Military Aviation School. After passing the entrance examinations he was accepted.

He received his wings on 1 January 1939 with 110 hours of flight instruction. After his graduation he undertook an advanced course at Kelly Field, Texas, with Class 39-D, graduating in December 1939. Upon his return he became a test pilot and instructor at the aviation school.

During this time he test flew Bellanca 28-90B Flash monoplanes, bought from the Republican government, and the Mexican-built and designed Tezuitlan primary monoplane trainer. He formed part of the formation of Mexican AT-6s in a courtesy flight to Cuba .

He was aide de camp to General Gustavo Salinas during a two-month tour of European battle fronts from 19 June to 28 July 1944. He also undertook a pilot course for Lockheed C-60 Lodestar transport aircraft, four of which were received for service by the Mexican Air Force.

When he was selected to join the GPA's 201st Squadron, he was married with two daughters.

Among the ground personnel selected were sons of former presidents, including Captain 2nd Class Jesus Carranza Hernandez (1908-65).

A 36-year-old pilot and aeronautical engineer from Mexico City, he was born on 14 June 1908, the son of Don Venustiano Carranza and Ernestina Hernandez.

His father was the President of Mexico from 1917 until his assassination in May 1920.

Carranza Hernandez undertook aeronautical engineering studies in the United States for about eight years, working with Curtiss Wright, Safair Inc and Casey Jones in New York. He completed his studies in August 1940.

He also obtained his private pilot license in the USA, No.28159, and by the time he returned to Mexico he had over 940 hours of flight time.

He joined the Mexican Air force on 16 April 1941 with the rank of lieutenant engineer and pilot aviator, and was assigned to the *Talleres Generales de Construcciones Aeronauticas* in the engineers section, where he participated in the construction of Salinas twin-engine aircraft.

He was promoted to captain 2nd class on 16 July 1944 and was assigned to the GPA's 201st Squadron. He was married with three children.

After the selection process was completed, this group took part in its activation review on 16 July 1944, and four days later was reviewed in person by President Camacho, General Cardenas and General Urquizo, with members of the military and general public, at Balbuena airfield. The GPA consisted of two high-ranking officers, 52 officers and 244 enlisted personnel on 20 July 1944. As noted by then Sergeant Manuel Cervantez Ramos:

> On the 16th of July 1944 this group passed its review of activation, heterogeneo formation, that was formed from elements of the Air Force, Medical, artillery, transports, quartermaster, signal corps, as well as civilian elements from the war materials of the military industries, these last ones, with a great effort they assimilated quickly the rules and regulations and military discipline, and due to their specialty and experience they were given a higher military rank.

In his speech to the airmen, President Camacho told them about their mission, their training in the United States, and to be prepared to go overseas if Mexico was asked to send a military force, like their Brazilian brothers who were already fighting in northern Italy. He said he had not come to say good-bye, but to greet them, and if they were deployed, he would try to be there to see them off; if not, General Lazaro Cardenas or General Urquizo would so so. He said not to worry about their love ones, as they would be taken care of.

When the president asked for any last requests from the men of the GPA, Corporal Angel Bocanegra del Castillo came forward and said, "*Una Escuela para mi pueblo, Senor Presidente*" (A school for my home town, Mr President). Since his home town did not have a school, the children had to walk to another town.

Corporal Bocanegra del Castillo (1922-92) was a 22-year-old from Tepoztlan, Morelos, born on 18 April 1922. His parents were Andres Bocanegra Martinez, who was later a brigadier general in the Army, and Dolores del Castillo Zuniga.

He was a former teacher and truck driver, who joined the Mexican Army on 10 April 1943 and was assigned due to his experience to the *Dirreccion de Transportes Militares*. He was selected to join the 201st Squadron in July 1944.

The school he requested was built while the squadron was in the Philippines and was named after the unit, *Escuadron 201*, being officially opened by President Camacho, who was joined by General Lazaro Cardenas and the Secretary of Education, Jaime Torres Bodet, on 24 November 1945.

The GPA 201st Squadron left Mexico City on 24 July 1944 by train to the US border. It was an emotional departure for their loved ones left behind, as mentioned by Sergeant Cervantez Ramos:

> The day of the 24th of July of 1944 arrived, the place was the train station of Buenavista, where the high-ranking members of the army and representatives of the congress and senate, and different representatives of different Labor organizations, family, friends and the general public were there to wish us the best as the train was leaving.
>
> I in particular did not want my family to be there to see me off, trying to save a painful moment for my mother. Slowly the sound of the train was breaking up our thoughts and little by little our sad faces changed. That started the 'Hurrays', and the old songs like 'Adelita', 'La Valentina' and the modern ones for that time 'El Cantar del Regimiento', 'Me Voy Soldado Raso', 'Despedida' etc.
>
> Thirty-six hours later we arrived at the city of Nuevo Laredo. It was already night, we were in formation when we crossed the border. Being received by the authorities of the neighboring country, we were guided to military transports, where we were given water, since the heat was hitting us hard. From there we were driven on military transports to the air base and school of Randolph Field in San Antonio, Texas, where a new selection was started, until the 3rd of August. We passed a medical exam and weapons qualifications. Randolph Field was a first-class base and clean, with strict regulations. I remember that if you threw a cigarette on the lawns you had to stomp it with your foot.

On arrival at the border, the group left the train and marched thought the town of Laredo, crossing over to the American side. They were greeted by American and Mexican officials, among them General Luis Alamillo Flores (1903-80), the Mexican military attache in Washington DC, and Colonel Leland S. Stranathan, commanding officer of the military air base at Laredo, Texas. After their arrival, the GPA Squadron 201, which numbered 299 men, was transported via train to Randolph Field, Texas. The group was prepared for medical and weapon firing testing as per American regulations. Colonel Cardenas recalled:

> From the 27th to the 30th of that same month, all members of the group were examined by the medical corps, and firing qualification was done [as] per American personnel, which resulted in the following: in the medical examination, two pilots were disqualified, as well as six enlisted personnel.
>
> The aviators not capable of the type of training they would undergo, and the enlisted [men], were rejected with the recommendation for their replacement. In the firing test all the men passed.

The two rejected pilots were Lieutenant Gabriel Torres Gonzalez and 2nd Lieutenant Emilio Enriquez Ruiz, who underwent a further test, a check ride, that was conducted on the 31st. They were returned to Mexico on 16 August.

The first two disqualified pilots at Randolph Field would continue their careers in the Mexican Air Force. By 1965, Enriquez Ruiz was a colonel and was director of the Air Force Specialist School. General Torres Gonzalez retired from the service in November 1980 after a long career in the Air Force, serving as director of the Military Aviation School from 1963-65 and in 1969.

The GPA was divided into smaller groups to undergo their specialist training at different Army Air Force bases across the country.

A group of mechanics left Randolph Field for Farmingdale, Long Island, on 31 July under the command of Captain Jesus Carranza Hernandez, to be instructed on the various systems of the Republic P-47 Thunderbolt fighter-bomber, the type chosen for the GPA. One of the instructors of this course was Sergeant Henry C. Estrada, who was in charge of the group of interpreters for the Mexican mechanics and wrote the following:

Curtiss P-40 and North American AT-6 trainers of Foster Field, Victoria, Texas, for the fighter conversion training. (San Diego Aerospace Museum)

I was with them for an eight week course which ended on Sept. 7th, 1944. The group consisted of 50 mechanics. Most of them were experienced pilots, who were given a course of maintenance & repair for the P-47, a plane the likes of which they had never seen, the first to come out with water injection, built on a frame to withstand crash-landings etc.

It was very comical to work with this group because they were not used to R & R (remove and replace) and would start taking the defective part apart to find the trouble, before they would be stopped by the instructors and told just to remove the part and replace it with a spare part. The Mexican officer in charge of the group was Capt. Carranza, a grandson of Venustiano Carranza, a former President of Mexico.

Most of the group was from well to do families in Mexico and they had a hot line to Mexico, always asking for monies from their families. After the Free French and the Brazilians groups left the school, they started to receive flights of Mexican goodies for the kitchen, which by that time was a very well equipped Mexican restaurant.

One of the Mexican mechanics, Corporal Pedro Martinez Perez, wrote about his experiences during his training at Farmingdale:

I was selected with 60 of my comrades to go to the city of Farmingdale, Long Island N. York about 30 miles from New York to one of the best military aviation schools. When we arrived we were given a tour of its installations, classrooms, sleeping quarters, library, mess hall and we were presented to our engineer instructors [who were] the very best.

Next day at about 05:30 hours a great alarm bell that made an awful sound woke us up, we dressed quickly to the sound of the polka 'Cervecinas Calientes' and we arrived at the main square with our physical instructors, which was our normal routine. After lunch [we went] to the classroom. We were in our environment, our instructor engineers showing us to work with the most modern equipment which we would use on the aircraft that we would maintain in combat, each one of us learning every word and name of the pieces that [we] were being shown in pictures or real [life].

In that same school with the same purpose were training about 100 Frenchmen. Even with a different language, we got along well with them. During our training of six weeks, we rested on Saturday and half a day on Sunday. In the night we decided to visit the city of New York [wher] in good company we danced and sang our songs 'La Adelita', 'Que Lejos Estoy' [and] 'Cielito Lindo' and sometimes we did our pranks but got out with no problems.

Near to the school was the aircraft factory for the P-47 combat plane, the same one we were training on. When we finished our training we were taken to visit the plant. We saw the big, modern

Mexican pilots being instructed by a USAAF officer. Behind is Colonel Antonio Cardenas Rodriguez. (USAF)

> and never ending lines of assembly, always in movement 24 hours a day, manned by thousands of employees, like ants, building each aircraft piece by piece until they finished building at the end of the line, every hour, an aircraft ready to fly. It was tested and sent to the flight line waiting for its test pilots, who would test fly them and were almost all women.

After completing their training, the group continued training in actual field conditions at Pocatello, Idaho, from 8 September. The administration section under Artillery Lieutenant Ignacio Salinas Ramos left for Pocatello to learn the administration functions of a fighter squadron under the USAAF system.

They completed their seven-week course and started working under actual conditions with the rest of the GPA at Pocatello. This pattern of training was applied to all the different sections which were needed to run a squadron: ordinance, motor pool, photography, chemical warfare, communications, medical, mess hall etc.

All of them completed their training, going to Pocatello to be together as a fighter squadron.

The medical section under Major Ricardo Blanco Cancino undertook an eight-week training course at the Aviation Medical School at Randolph Field.

## FOSTER FIELD, TEXAS – FIGHTER TRAINING

The flying personnel, under the command of Colonel Cardenas, were divided into three flights, 'A', 'B' and 'C'. In his book *Mis Dos Missiones* (My Two Missions), Cardenas tells of the different aspects of their flight training:

> The group of pilots under my direct orders, left for their destination, Foster Field, Victoria, Texas, [where] the flights were submitted to a transition course in the P-40 aircraft in which I participated.
>
> The course had a duration of 10 weeks, during which 40 hours were flown in the AT-6 and P-40 aircraft per pilot. The course comprised of formation flying, navigation, acrobatics etc.
>
> [There was] local night flying and simulated gunnery during the first five weeks, real gunnery with 0.50 cal. machine guns in Mata Gorda and transition in P-40 the last five weeks.

A number of American pilots helped train the Mexican pilots, who were assigned to the 2539th AAF Base unit, Section "I", to assist in the special Mexican training programme of approximately five weeks. Among them was 1st Lieutenant Octavius L. Jouffray, of a Mexican mother and French father, who wrote the following:

> On about 1 August 1944, I was sent to temporary duty to Foster Field to assist in the special training of members of the 201st Mexican Fighter Squadron in AT-6 Texan trainers, and P-40 Warhawks for fighter transition, instrument flying training and aerial gunnery.
>
> There were about eight to ten of us who were Spanish-speaking U.S. Army Air Force pilots that came from different bases on TDY to Foster to participate in this program.

The training consisted of the following phases:

1. AT-6 flying proficiency phase, the first three weeks.
2. The next four weeks were used in both instrument flying and gunnery training in the AT-6. The first two weeks, half of the instructors and half of the Mexican pilots would remain at

The group of Mexican mechanics under Capitan 2nd Class Jesus Carranza during their training at Farmindale, New York, on the Republic P-47 Thunderbolt. (Manuel Cervantes Ramos)

Foster for instrument flying training, while the others would go to Mata Gorda Island for gunnery training in specially machine-gun equipped AT-6s. For the second two weeks the instructors would remain in place but the other half of the Mexican pilots would change places.

3. The last phase of about two or three weeks was devoted to training required to transition into the P-40 fighters.

1st Lieutenant Jouffray remembers other aspects of the training:

> All the above phases required some classroom time especially the instruments blind flying and P-40 transition phases.
>
> The P-40s were the only single seaters so the instructions while flying were given while the instructors would fly in either string or echelon formation with the student.
>
> The instruction for the first solo flight in the P-40 was given on the ground. Aerial instruction [was given] for such things as demonstrations and instructions on maximum performance manuevers and acrobatic flying.

To help facilitate the training, he added:

> We Spanish-speaking instructors took turns with duty in the Foster Field control tower when the Mexican pilots were in the air without an instructor, particularly for take-off and landing instructions.
>
> I also remember we used a radio equipped jeep as a mobile control tower during the P-40 phase to allow more detailed take-off and landing instructions in Spanish in a separate channel so as not to interfere with the regular control tower.

During the course of the instruction, there were a number of accidents registered, luckily with no injuries to the Mexican pilots. The first was on 21 August 1944, when Lieutenant Joaquin Ramirez Vilchiz suffered a taxiing accident in AT-6D 42-85478 on the ramp in Foster Field AAFB.

On 10 September 2nd Lieutenant Guillermo Garcia Ramos also had a taxiing accident at Foster Field in AT-6D 42-85350, and on the next day 2nd Lieutenant Jose L. Pratt Ramos suffered a landing accident in AT-6D 41-24558.

On 9 October Lieutenant Javier Martinez Valle had a landing accident, which resulted in him ground-looping his aircraft, P-40E 41-36246. On the next day it was 2nd Lieutenant Guillermo Garcias Ramos' turn to suffer the same fate in P-40F 41-14075.

The Mexican pilots flew a mixed batch of Curtis P-40 fighters, as noted in the individual flight record (AAF Form 5) of 2nd Lieutenant Jose Luis Pratt Ramos for October 1944:

Date aircraft type flights time (hours/minutes)

2 October 1944 AT-6C 8 landings 1:00
4 October 1944 P-40F 1 landing 1:15
5 October 1944 P-40K 2 landings 2:15
6 October 1944 P-40E 1 landing 1:00
6 October 1944 P-40N 1 landing 1:10
9 October 1944 P-40F 1 landing 1:15
10 October 1944 P-40F 1 landing 1:15

10 October 1944 AT-6D 1 landing 1:00
11 October 1944 AT-6D 1 landing 1:00
11 October 1944 P-40N 1 landing 1:35

During the training, Colonel Cardenas did not take part in the gunnery training but continued to fly the P-40, reportedly passing the course. He practiced acrobatics, instruments and night flying. He joined his pilots when they arrived at Pocatello Army Air Field, Idaho, on 20 October.

## POCATELLO, IDAHO

On 6 August 1944, the first ground echelon of the 201st Mexican Fighter Squadron started to arrive at Pocatello Army Air Force Base. Their arrival was reported in the *Pocatello Tribune* on that day under the headline 'Mexican air unit to train locally':

> A group of officers and enlisted men of the Mexican air force arrived at the Pocatello army air field for a period of Training, it was announced today by
>
> Lt. Col. John L. Eaton, commanding Officer. Brigadier General George P. Tourtellet, Commanding general of the 72nd fighter Wing, under whose direct jurisdiction the Pocatello field operates, will be a frequent visitor here to watch the progress of the program.
>
> The men arrived by special train which was brought to the field. The Mexican airmen were welcomed by Col. Eaton upon their arrival and the air field band played the Mexican national anthem as the group disembarked from the train and … were making preparations to go to their new quarters.
>
> Charles Grimm, Mexican consul, and Antonio Cassillas, Mexican chancellor, of Salt Lake City visited the field and met the group. The men are all members of a Mexican Fighter squadron, and have been sent to the Pocatello field for training, under the policy agreed upon by the two nations.
>
> All of the men have been carefully selected for this training. Col. Eaton stated that the training they would receive will be typical of that given to American airmen, and that it would be of the same high standard as the training set up for members of the United States Army Air Force.
>
> Personnel of the U.S. Army Air Force who are highly skilled in many air forces jobs have been sent here from other fields and bases to aid in this training. All of these assistants have an excellent knowledge of the language of the allied nations, and in addition many of them have had a personal association with Mexican people previous to entering the U.S. Army Air Force.
>
> The program is another indication of the good neighbor policy carried on by the United States, in joining with the allied nations in the all-out campaign to win the war, Eaton said. Residents of Pocatello and vicinity, who have always been noted for their western hospitality, are already making their Mexican allies feel at home in Idaho.
>
> Civic leaders and army officials are coordinating their efforts on behalf of the newcomers.

One of the problems the Mexican personnel had during their time in the US was the language barrier, as mentioned by Sergeant Cervantez Ramos:

> The beginning of the training was not easy, since the majority of the personnel did not speak English, some could kind of speak it and some could speak it well … part of the training we were given classes in English and we had instructors that spoke some Spanish.
>
> "The major problem we had was the language, since we had to study both in English and Spanish the rules and regulations, as well as the manuals and the documentation that was necessary like orders, circulars, reports, medical records and supply etc. Both had to be maintained in both languages.

The Mexican pilots were assigned to the 265th Fighter Pilot Training Squadron, Army Air Force Base Unit, which was a P-47 operational replacement training unit (OTU/RTU). They were assigned 20 Republic P-47D-28-RA Thunderbolt fighter-bombers, which were flown in from Bruning Army Air Field, Nebraska, along with 11 flight instructors.

Some of the aircraft were reportedly flown in by female WASP (Women Air Service Pilots) pilots, which caused some surprises for the Mexicans, who were not used to seeing women flying any aircraft, let alone fighters like the P-47 Thunderbolt.

Mexican personnel carried out their own acceptance and flight tests of these aircraft, and two days later the fighter training started. The mechanics had only one P-47 assigned for their instructional maintenance work, which was not enough, considering the number and eagerness of the personnel. In the opinion of their instructors, the Mexican mechanics demonstrated a commendable seriousness of purpose, initiative and comprehension.

At the beginning of August a new section was created and added to Pocatello Army Air Field, designated Section "I", which consisted of interpreters and instructors to help in the training of the 201st. The section was initially commanded by Captain Allan F. Andrade, but on 24 August he was replaced by Captain Paul B. Miller and Andrade became executive officer of the section.

Captain Paul Miller was a 24-year-old pilot born in Los Angeles, California, on 6 August 1919. A married man, he joined the USAAC in May 1940 and was commissioned a 2nd lieutenant in December 1940. He served as a junior co-pilot with Pan American Airways, flying to Central and South America, and was detailed to PANAGRA airlines flying the route from Chile to the Panama Canal.

In 1941 he returned to the USAAC and was assigned to Ferrying Command, flying aircraft to Latin American and even to the Libyan battlefront in North Africa. He was then assigned as a military observed in Guatemala. Promoted to lieutenant in April 1942, he was instrumental in uncovering a spy ring in the Caribbean area helping the refuelling of Axis submarines.

This was accomplished after many attempts on his life, including sabotage of his aircraft. For his efforts he was promoted to captain and awarded the Air Medal. From May 1943 to August 1944 he served in the American Embassy in Mexico City . He spoke fluent Spanish, and his parents lived in Peru during the war years.

At first Captain Miller's section consisted of three officers and 20 enlisted personnel, but by the time training started in Texas it had grown to 23 officers and 31 enlisted men. Many of the enlisted personnel of Section 'I' had bilingual experience that would help in the training of the Mexican personnel. Among the enlisted men was Sergeant Fred J. Payle, who graduated from Martin High School in Laredo, Texas, in 1943, with the dream of becoming a pilot, but ended up as a NCO in the ground personnel. A specialist in instruments, he had previously served at the AAFB at Topeka, Kansas. Chosen to be an instructor and translator, he became known to the Mexican personnel as '*El Teacher*' and travelled with the squadron from Texas to Pocatello, Idaho, and later back to Texas. He put in a request to go with the squadron overseas, but was denied and ordered to stay in the US to train more Mexicans in the replacement group.

The senior enlisted trainer was Staff Sergeant Cornelius Orzatti,

Mexican and American ground personnel doing requisition training, for ordering parts under the USAAF supply system. (Manuel Cervantes Ramos)

who spoke Spanish and Portuguese fluently, having lived with his family in Argentina. He would be a great help to the squadron both in the US and later overseas.

Among the US ground personnel helping train the 201st were veterans of the early Pacific fighting, including Staff Sergeant Manuel F. Robles, who had fought and escaped from the Philippines in 1942, as noted in the following news item about his experiences in the Major Field *Flight Report* newspaper of 21 February 1945, under the headline 'Sgt Robles saw action at Manila':

> Today's news headlines, proclaiming the battle of the Philippines represent for S-Sgt. Manuel F. Robles of Section "I" the denouement of a personal drama in which ended his own first appearance on the shattered pier at Manila [on] New Year's Eve, 1941.
>
> The tall, quiet-spoken sergeant, a native of Tucson, Ariz. and serving at Majors field as an instructor with The 201st Mexican squadron, was with the 19th Bomb Group at Clark field when the Nips struck.
>
> On the morning of the first assault, he had finished chow and was crewing an Airplane. 'We had been expecting the Japs since the news of Pearl harbor', Robles says, speaking with a faint Spanish accent. 'I looked up and saw the big silver-colored Jap bombers began their run.
>
> The next thing I knew the bombs began to fall.' Robles was severely wounded sometime later. He was taken to Manila in the last week of December. 'When we reached the city the Japs were coming over. I was being carried across an open street and my litter-bearer hit the dirt. Part of the bombardment I saw from flat on my back.'
>
> With other wounded he was hospitalized in a convent in Manila. Nuns and Filipino nurses cared for the American soldiers. Shortly before Manila fell, a hospital ship slipped out of the islands carrying Robles to the Dutch East Indies and thence to Australia.
>
> After recovering from his wounds, he went back to duty. His second appearance in the drama was in the New Guinea campaigns where he served at Nadzab and Dora Dora with up front P-38 and P-63 units. His exit came months later with orders to report back to The States.

The medical section under Major MC (*Medico Cirujano*) Ricardo Blanco Cancino was set up to function as part of the unit, as mentioned in his memoirs:

> Here the personnel of the medical section were prepared by the instructors of the base hospital and I started the concept that the pillar of the military medic was preventive medicine, starting with periodical talks that would last until our return, to keep everybody informed of medical information, [and talks] to the flight personnel and ground base on first aid.
>
> During our stay in Pocatello I was assigned an excellent flight surgeon as my advisor[,] Capt. L. Amato, [who with] his vast experience showed me the basics of aviation medicine. [He] later helped in bases in Gowen, near Boise, capital of the state of Idaho, in Ogden, Utah, and in Salt Lake City [with] the practices of the

Brigadier General Gustavo Salinas, chief of the Mexican Air Force, delivers packages to Colonel Antonio Cardenas Rodriguez, chief of the GPA, at Pocatello, Idaho. In the background is one of the Mexican Lockheed C-60s. (Manuel Cervantes Ramos)

> decompression chamber, flight simulation in the link trainer and real flight to learn the maneuvers to survive in case of emergencies and the effects of speed acceleration and gravity in turns, dives. [I also had] the opportunity to visit the Neurosurgery hospital in Ogden, where all the cases came from the war fronts in a time of no more than 36 hours.

For the training on the Republic P-47 Thunderbolt, the standard 2nd Air Force flying programme included five phases and 16 components:

A. Transition (13 missions):
  1. Transition;
  2. Formation;
  3. Navigation;
  4. Acrobatics.

B. Pre-Gunnery (50 missions):
  5. Combat (individual);
  6. Combat (unit);
  7. Camera Gunnery;
  8. Ground Gunnery;
  9. Strafing;
  10. Instruments;
  11. Night transition;
  12. Night formation;
  13. Low altitude navigation;
  14. Combined training.

C. Aerial Gunnery (20 missions).

D. Post-Gunnery – Unit Training (16 missions).

E. 150 hours pilot flight (8 missions):
  15. High altitude combat;
  16. Theater tactics.

The training programme comprised 107 missions and about 120 hours to be conducted in about 12 weeks.

During their training with the P-47 Thunderbolt, only two accidents occurred involving the Mexican pilots at Pocatello. On 28 October 1944, 2nd Lieutenant Manuel Farias Rodriguez in P-47D-28-R (either B-1 or R-1) suffered a landing accident after returning from a training flight. The damage was repaired by the squadron mechanics.

The second accident occurred on 8 November 1944, when Lieutenant Amador Samano Pina ran out of fuel while waiting to land after a training flight, the pilot forgetting to change his fuel selector switch in time. The aircraft, 42-29464, Number '18', was damaged and had to remain in Pocatello for repairs until 1 January 1945 after the squadron had moved to Texas.

The flying skills of the Mexican pilots was noted in the book *The First Fifty Years: Michaud Flats US Army Base, Pocatello Regional Airport*, by Lenard J. Nelson and Bessie M. Shrontz Roberts-Wright:

> The new arrivals soon demonstrated their flying ability. In judgment and technique in take offs and landings, and in general performance they were proclaimed considerably above average by Captain Paul B. Miller, Commanding Officer, Section 'I'.
>
> At the end of the first week, all except one had been 'checked out' and were ready to begin Training Missions #6 and #7. By 10 November, the majority of them were ready for Missions #11 and #12, and Captain Miller reported that their formation flying was excellent, despite the fact that the P-47 type formation used by the 72nd Fighter Wing was completely new to them upon arrival at Pocatello.

During their training at Pocatello, they were visited twice by General Gustavo Salinas, the first time on 2 September 1944, flying in a Lockheed C-60 Lodestar which was loaded with things that the Mexican personnel missed from home, as Sergeant Cervantez Ramos recalled:

> As the Fiestas Patrias [national holidays] arrived our government put at the disposal of our families an aircraft so they could send us antojitos, mole, tacos, chilitos, tequila, Mexican cigarettes, Mexican curiosities etc.
>
> The arrival of this aircraft was a wonderful surprise and joy for everybody. With it we made a gathering and we invited our instructors and the authorities of the base and on the 16th of September we were invited to a dance in the recreation hall of the base. It was the time of 'swing' and the big bands, and on this occasion they not only played American music, but also Latin, for which the Rumba, la Conga, el meringue, the Tango and the Samba were the hits of the night.

A regular flight was established by this C-60A from Mexico City to Pocatello, with stops in San Antonio, Texas, flown by Captain 1st Class Roberto Perez Aguirre.

Many of the Mexicans' training flights could not be completed due to bad weather, so a move to another base was recommended, as described by Captain Amadeo Castro Almanza, who recalled:

> At Pocatello, Idaho, in the Rocky Mountain we could not fly much because we arrived in the winter season. The weather was bad, so we had to return to Texas to finish our training.

This is also mentioned by Sergeant Cervantez Ramos:

> The cold starts, the first snow falls, a white blanket covers the fields and the runway, the joy for seeing the snow, because the majority of us had never seen it before, but it was difficult to work in that type of weather at the runways and the training flights they are more difficult.
>
> In October in that base all the personnel that were dispersed to do their training were now one integrated unit with all its services similar to a North American squadron.

The American summary report on the 201st reported:

> Because of continuous bad weather the squadron and instructors were moved on November 27 to Majors Field, Greenville, Texas.

The USAAF Form 5 (Individual Flight Record) of 2nd Lieutenant Jose Luis Pratt Ramos shows the following training flights for October and November 1944:

Date Aircraft Time (hrs/mins)
23 October BT-13B 1.00
23 October BT-13B 1.45
24 October BT-13B 1.00
25 October Link 1.00
26 October Link 1.00
28 October P-47D 1.25
30 October P-47D 1.30
30 October P-47D 1.35
31 October Link 1.00
Total 6 flights, 8.15 flight time, and 3.00 instruments
1 November Link 1.00
2 November Link 1.00
8 November P-47D 2.00
8 November P-47D 1.30
9 November P-47D 1.30
Total 3 flights, 5.00 flight time, and 2.00 instruments

During their time in Pocatello, the Mexican personnel enjoyed their stay, without any incidents. They had fond memories of Pocatello, which went out of its way to treat them equally. When the unit arrived, the town gave them a welcome party and speeches were given in both English and Spanish. Sergeant Cervantez Ramos wrote of his time there:

> During our stay at Pocatello, we won the sympathy and the confidence of the town, and we were invited to their homes.
>
> In the streets or in the shops we would encounter uniformed personnel from the different branches and services of the Army of the United States, and in the big cities close to Pocatello we encountered military personnel from England and Australia. We also frequently saw women in uniform known as WACS (Women's Army Corps).
>
> We were a curiosity to the people of these places, because of our uniforms [which] were different from theirs and our Spanish language.
>
> When we were in a restaurant on some occasions, we were surrounded by young people, who would join us for a moment, observing us without saying anything. The songs of Consuelito Velazquez (*Besame Mucho*/Kiss me a lot) had arrived and people started to get interested in Mexican and Latin music.

As for the training, the Mexicans found it to be demanding, being woken up at 0600, with a daily routine of breakfast, classes, breaks, lunch, more classes and military instruction. There were also some English classes at night to help facilitate the training, given by American personnel fluent in Spanish. Barracks inspections were held twice a month by the chief of the barracks, failure to pass leading to cancellation of weekend passes. Cervantez Ramos recalled that people could recognise the Mexican squadron area by the flag of Mexico above it:

> In the area that the unit occupied, every day our flag was flown thanks to a friend in the war material [section of the squadron], who knows how to play the bugle.
>
> "Our flag was raised and lowered with all honors. This companion was known to everybody, his name was Pedro Guerra; his nickname was 'Pedro Amor', because he had a good voice and his favorite song he liked to sing was 'Amor, Amor'.

The big and functional mess hall also impressed the Mexican personnel, with meals served on aluminum trays and a sign overhead saying "Don't ask for more than you are going to eat". Tables were long enough to accommodate ten people, and the food was good and nutritious. As noted in the local press, the Mexican Air Force personnel were quite adjusted to living like their USAAF counterparts, but with some adjustments:

> The men are quartered in regular army barracks, and sleep in single army bunks. Each man has an individual shelf and clothes rack for his belongings and there is a window near each bunk.
>
> The neat manner in which the beds were made and the newly

> scrubbed, smart appearance of the entire barracks indicated a well-trained, well-disciplined group of soldiers.
>
> The mess hall is operated by two specially trained cooks from the Mexican squadron. First Sgt. Frederico R. Arreola is first cook, and Second Sgt. Eugenio F. Perez is second cook. Their jobs is to take U.S. army rations and convert them into Mexican style meals.
>
> Men of the squadron march to and from the mess hall for each meal. The smartness and military precision of the unit during marching and in drill formations has aroused the admiration of the American officers and men at the field.
>
> Daily classes in English and military subjects are being conducted for the men, and in addition they will receive the same basic and combat training as the soldiers in the U.S. Army Air Forces receive.
>
> A group of well trained officers of the Mexican Army are here with the squadron. Liaison Officers of the squadron is Teniente (First Lieutenant) Ignacio R. Salinas, Mayor (Major) Ricardo C. Blanco is Medical officer. Other officers are Captain Segundo (second captain) Edmundo V. Santamaria, Tenientes (First Lieutenants) Joaquin De la O. Alvarez, Cesar C. Velasco and Armando Rodriguez and SubTenientes (Second Lieutenants) Luis M. Lopez, Pablo D.Herrast and Ramon E. Caracas.

Many local families invited young Mexican airmen to their homes for meals, as noted by Jennifer Hall Levanger in her research paper 'Aztec Eagles in Pocatello':

> Other Pocatello residents invited them into their homes for home cooked meals. The Fred Quinn family had a group of 30 soldiers over for enchiladas.
>
> The Quinns were residents of Pocatello and Mr. Quinn was the assistant manager at the First Security Bank of Idaho.
>
> Carlos Martinez, a sorter for the Union Pacific Railroad in Pocatello, and his family also entertained a group. The announcement of these dinner parties tells us a lot about Pocatello in 1944. It shows that people from all levels of society got involved in attempting to make the Mexican cadets feel at home.
>
> Because they are listed in the society pages, it demonstrates perhaps that not only were the Mexican soldiers treated equally in Pocatello, but the local Hispanic families [were] also accepted as part of society.

In turn, the Mexican personnel invited American military and civilian personnel for the observance and celebration of the 134th anniversary of the start of the War of Independence from Spain. Events were held on 15/16 September 1944, as reported in the *Pocatello Tribune* of 17 September, under the headline 'Mexican fighter squadron marks Independence Day':

> Members of the Mexican fighter Squadron stationed at Pocatello Army airfield, concluded their observance of the 134th anniversary of Mexico's independence with a buffet supper and dance at the airfield officer's club Saturday night.
>
> At the opening of Friday night's celebration, a dance was held in the airfield recreation hall. Dancing was stopped shortly before 11 o'clock and short speeches of welcome were given by Cpl. Angel Bocanegra, representing the men of the squadron: Carlos Grimm, Mexican consul at Salt Lake City and Lt. John L. Eaton, commanding Officer of the field. Consul Grimm led the soldiers in the 'Cry of independence' promptly at 11 o'clock. Following the ceremony the group sang the Mexican national Anthem and the American national Anthem.

Before the squadron moved its training to Texas, a special radio broadcast was organised on 20 November as a salute to the Mexican fighter squadron, that originated from Mexico City radio station XEW and was broadcast to local station KSEI.

The personnel of the squadron were invited to use the airfield's enlisted men's service club. Since it was a general broadcast, all the southern Idaho residents had the opportunity to listen in to the Mexican broadcast. The *Pocatello Tribune* reported the content of the programme and its sponsors:

> The program will feature such musical selections as 'Rancho Grande', 'Besame Mucho', 'Maria Elena', 'Cielito Lindo', 'Perfidia', 'Amor', 'Frenesi', 'El Fuereno', 'Cuando Vuelvas', 'Santa Cuatro' and many others.
>
> The entertainers to be heard include two orchestras, one to be conducted by the author of the hit song 'Amor' Gabriel Ruiz.
>
> A second orchestra will be under the direction of the young and brilliant Juan Garcia Esquivel. At the pianos will be two famous composers, Consuelo Velasquez and Agustin Lara.
>
> Los Plateado guitar trio will be also featured.
>
> The radio program was arranged by Emilio Azcarraga, president of Radio Programas de Mexico, Latin America's largest broadcasting system. It is being produced and transmitted at considerable expense to send an atmosphere of 'home' to those Mexican soldiers who are now in Pocatello.

While at Pocatello, the GPA had completed the following between 22 October and 27 November: pilots in training, 34; total hours in BT-13s, 120.25; total hours in P-47s, 428.10; total flying hours, 548.35; hours per pilot, 16.00.

## FLIGHT TRAINING IN TEXAS

The move was made to Majors Field, Texas, due to the adverse Idaho weather, as noted in the official history of the 201st Mexican Fighter Squadron compiled by the 2nd Air Force, published in September 1945:

> The Mexican unit, including pilots, ground officers and enlisted personnel departed Pocatello by troop train on 27 November, [and] arrived at Majors field on 29 November, to receive a warm welcome from Post officials.
>
> All individual and organizational equipment was unpacked and transferred to the squadron area immediately. Twelve of the P-47 aircraft assigned to the 201st arrived the following day, and Mexican personnel were sufficiently organized to give them proper maintenance and service ... Bad weather at Pocatello, in addition to the transfer to Majors field, [had] resulted in the loss of much flying time.
>
> Furthermore adverse flying weather had delayed the transfer of approximately one-third of the airplanes belonging to the 201st.

The aircraft were all flown by the instructor pilots of Section "I", except for one, flown by a Mexican pilot who had more than 100 hours of flying experience, which departed on 23 November, making stops at Las Vegas in Nevada, Tuscon, Arizona, and Fort Worth, Texas, the next day flying to Majors Field.

Between 16 December 1944 and January 1945, Flights "A", "B" and "C" moved to Abiline Air Base to carry out their gunnery training. The training flights were broken down as follows:

'A' Flight:

Learning the role of armourers by cleaning the .50 calibre machine guns used on the P-47D, during squadron training at Majors Field, Greenville, Texas. (Manuel Cervantes Ramos)

Captain Richard S. Moore USAF,
Lieutenant Hector Espinosa Galvan,
Lieutenant Amadeo Castro Almanza,
Lieutenant Jose Espinosa Fuentes,
Lieutenant Jose Luis Barbosa Cerda,
Lieutenant Julio Cal y Mayor Sauz,
2nd Lieutenant David Ceron Bedolla,
2nd Lieutenant Jacobo Estrada Luna,
2nd Lieutenant Raul Garcia Mercado,
2nd Lieutenant Jaime Cenizo Rojas and
2nd Lieutenant Manuel Farias Rodriguez;

'B' Flight:
Captain Norman R. Hyde USAAF,
Captain 1st Class Radames Gaxiola Andrade,
Captain 2nd Class Roberto Legorreta Sicilia,
Lieutenant Fernando Hernandez Vega,
Lieutenant Reynaldo Perez Gallardo,
Lieutenant Carlos Garduno Nunez,
Lieutenant Javier Martinez Valle,
2nd Lieutenant Raul Maciel Pena,
2nd Lieutenant Praxedis Lopez Ramos,
2nd Lieutenant Miguel Moreno Arreola and
2nd Lieutenant Mario Lopez Portillo;

'C' Flight:
Captain Lowell C. Sund USAAF,
Captain 2nd Class Pablo L. Rivas Martinez,
Lieutenant Joaquin Ramirez Vilchis,
Lieutenant Amador Samano Pina,
Lieutenant Carlos Varela Landini,
Lieutenant Graco Ramirez Garrido,
2nd Lieutenant Crisoforo Salido Grijalva,
2nd Lieutenant Miguel Uriarte Aguilar,
2nd Lieutenant Justino Retana Reyes,
2nd Lieutenant Roberto Urias Aveleira,
2nd Lieutenant Fausto Vega Santander and
2nd Lieutenant Angel Sanchez Rebollo.

The official book of the MEAF (Mexican Expeditionary Air Force) noted on 2 January 1945 that the first flying elements that transferred to Abiline Army Air Base consisted of five lieutenants, six 2nd lieutenants, about 13 mechanics and two signal corps personnel, with eight more personnel joining the group later, all of them returning to Majors Field on 19 January.

During the stay at Abiline, Lieutenant Joaquin Ramirez Vilchis heard some interesting comments on the flying ability of the Mexican pilots:

"In Abiline, Texas one of the two Americans that were near me said in English 'Dammitt these Mexicans fly the P-47s like they were SNJs' [the North American trainer]."

Mexican personnel were transferred over from the 256th to the 266th AAFBU (CCTS (F)) at Majors Field, under the command of the 72nd Fighter Wing, 2nd Air Force. The training of the Mexican squadron continued with more combat veterans assigned to pass down their knowledge, among them Lieutenant William L. Kester,

The American pilots of Section I under the command of Captain Paul B. Miller, seated in the center, who helped train the Mexicans from Pocatello to Majors Field in 1944-45. (Lowell Sund)

who received the Distinguished Flying Cross while at Pocatello, as noted in the base newspaper *The Fighter Pilot*:

> Lieutenant Kester, 25, of Chicago, is the son of Mr. and Mrs. Richard B. Kester, now residing at Caripito, Venezuela. A veteran of 95 missions in the South Pacific Theater, he received the Distinguished Flying Cross for extraordinary achievement while participating in aerial combat from October 17 to October 23, 1943, [during] which time he destroyed an enemy plane.

Lieutenant Kester was credited with a total of one Japanese aircraft destroyed and one shared while assigned to the 44th Fighter Squadron, 18th Fighter Group of the 13th Air Force, flying the Curtiss P-40F in the South Pacific.

His squadron, known as the 'Vampires', would later convert to the Lockheed P-38 and finish the war with 163½ kills, 33½ probables and 15 enemy aircraft damaged. Later promoted to captain, Kester would return to combat duty in the Pacific with the 45th Fighter Squadron of the 15th Fighter Group, flying Very Long Range (VLR) missions in the North American P-51D from Iwo Jima to Japan, being credited with the shared damage of an enemy aircraft.

Another notable pilot assigned to the training of the Mexican pilots was 1st Lieutenant Robert H. Knapp, a veteran ETO fighter pilot who was assigned to the 83rd Fighter Squadron, 78th Fighter Group, and was reported to have done a 840mph dive in a Republic P-47D Thunderbolt during a combat mission. During his tour with the 78th Fighter Group, Knapp flew a total of 119 missions and claimed a single aerial victory against an FW-190 on 24 January 1944 while flying P-47D-1 42-7914 HL-P.

His unit, the 83rd Fighter Squadron, would finish the war with 118½ aerial kills, 11 probables and 54 enemy aircraft damaged. The squadron was also credited with 112 aircraft destroyed on the ground and 65 damaged.

Another instructor was Captain Lowell C. Sund, who saw action in North Africa and the Mediterranean, flying mostly ground support missions in the Bell P-39 Aircobra with the 81st Fighter Group. Captain Sund completed 80 combat missions. His unit later moved its operations to Sicily, Italy, India and finally to China, where it ended the war there. During the training of the Mexican airmen, Sund remembers one particular incident:

> There were some interesting things that happened in training the Mexican pilots, most of which are not really worth mentioning. One exciting thing that happened [was] on a routine flight at Majors Field. We were doing various maneuvers when I noticed one of the planes was for some reason losing altitude.
>
> I tried to contact him by radio without success so I flew as near to him as I could and got his attention. I them realized that he was coasting and his propeller was dead so I tried to figure out what I could do to help him. All of a sudden I remembered that I had just switched my fuel tanks so I tried by sign language to tell him to check his gas tank.
>
> Suddenly he realized what I was telling him and he reached down and turned to his other tank. There was a spurt of smoke from the engine and he was back [in] business.

During the training in Texas, three more pilots were eliminated, the first one being 2nd Lieutenant Raul Maciel Pena, who after transitioning to the P-47 was found not suitable for this type of aircraft, and was suspended from training on 10 November.

During aerial gunnery training at Matagorda in September he had a run-in with Lieutenant Joaquin Ramirez Vilchis that caught the attention of some of the American pilots and his instructor:

> During an aerial gunnery mission I was upset with Maciel Pena, because he came from below, without warning. After firing all my blue colored rounds I landed and while discussing with Maciel my instructor took me by my arm to show me the big white tow sheet where there were many blue impacts, and one of the American students said in English, 'dammit I don't want to face this pilot in the air'.

A Republic P-47D-28-RA Thunderbolt assigned to the 201st Squadron at Pocatello AAFB, Idaho, during the winter months. (Manuel Cervantes Ramos)

The other two pilots to be dismissed were Lieutenant Rafael Lizardi Formento and 2nd Lieutenant Miguel Mendoza Marquez, who were informed they were disqualified on 20 October but remained at Foster Field awaiting orders from Mexico City. Mendoza Marquez, after his return to Mexico, continue to serve in the Mexican Air Force and eventually obtained the rank of general de division, being named commander of the Mexican Air Force from 1982-88.

As in any training programme, a number of accidents occurred during this period, two proving to be fatal for Mexican pilots.

The first accident at Majors Field happenedon 18 December, when Lieutenant Carlos Rodriguez Corona, flying in P-47D-28-RA 42-29441 'R10', ran off the runway after landing from a training mission, in which the flight leader was Captain Lowell C. Sund. Corona's aircraft got stuck in the soft ground, caused by recent rain. He tried to get the aircraft out by applying some power, but it remained stuck. He wrote in his report:

> While the control tower was giving instructions to the other aircraft to turn to [the] left and circle, I made another attempt to make the ship function by giving it more power but it was impossible and then I decided to stop the engine, waiting to be towed in.
>
> Approximately two minutes later I looked to the right and saw plane M-2 [P-47D-26-RA 42-28228 flown by 2nd Lieutenant Robert W. Grimm, another trainee pilot) coming very near and directly towards where I was parked. When the pilot of M-2 saw me, he applied both his brakes to prevent the collision, thus hitting the ground with his propeller and slightly hitting with his propeller the tip of my right wing.

Lieutenant Grimm wrote in his report:

> After rolling about three-quarters of the way down the runway, after landing, I noticed a ship stalled off the runway. In order to avoid contact, I jammed on the brakes, causing the plane to nose-up, with resulting damage to the prop. The tower had not advised that the ship was stalled on the runway. Damage was caused to the wing of the other ship.

Lieutenant Grimm later served with the 406th Fighter Group of the 9th Air Force in Europe, and was killed in Germany on 27 June 1945 after the war was over while serving with the occupation forces in Germany.

On 14 January 1945, 2nd Lieutenant Manuel Farias Rodriguez, flying in P-47D-28-RA 42-29442 'R11', was involved in an accident after landing from a training flight. The control tower had directed him to clear straight ahead to the taxi strip:

> Then I speeded up. As I was almost to the end of the runway I became aware of the red line which marks the end of the runway. Quickly, I cut the throttle and started to put the brakes on, but it was too late and I went off the E W [east to west] runway. When I hit the soft dirt at the end of the runway, the aircraft stopped, causing damage to two propeller blades.

The next accident that occurred caused the first fatality for the squadron, this sad distinction falling to 2nd Lieutenant Crisoforo Salido Grijalva on 23 January 1945. The accident report gave the following details:

> On 23 January 1945, 2Lt. Crisoforo G. Salido was scheduled to lead a camera gunnery mission. The other member of the flight [was] 1st Lt. Carlos Rodriguez Corona. The flight left the parking area and taxied down E-W (8-26) runway. At the East end of the runway the flight parked and completed the pre-take-off run up. Lt. Salido taxied out on the taxi strip between runway 26 and 30 and called for take off instructions.
>
> The tower instructed him to the end of runway 30. Lt. Salido started taxiing down the taxiway, stopped and turned around,

starting back to runway #26. The tower called him and instructed him to make another 180 turn and continue taxiing to #30. This message the pilots 'Rogered'. The pilot turned as instructed, but lined up on the taxi strip, attempted to take off, running off the end of the taxi strip into the mud and flipping over on his back.

The runway control truck with Lt. Egelhoff on duty was parked on the taxi strip which intersects 12-30 runways, instead of the usual position due to the soft shoulder off the runway. The rolling terrain and the distance from the end of runway 30 prevented Lt. Egerhoff from observing all that occurred, but he heard the radio conversation and also repeated some of the instructions in attempting to get the pilot oriented.

When the pilot attempted to take off, neither the tower nor runway control officers could determine if he was taxiing faster or attempting to take off.

The radio had not been written up in the Form 1A since 5 December 1944. However, investigation revealed that the radio was out approximately 1400 that same day as the accident and was corrected. Lt. M. A. Moreno flew the plane from 1500 to 1630 and found some interference in the radio which he told the radio maintenance man about.

The radio man Sgt. 2/o. Francisco Rodriguez Castaneda, made test calls from R-1 (P-47D-28-RA s/n. 42-29432) to the tower and other planes on the field and released the plane for flight. This evidence, coupled with the fact that the pilot did 'Roger' his instructions from the tower, and the fact that he had been briefed never to take off when his radio was out, is evidence that the pilot's radio was operating.

Attempting to take off, he ran off the end of the taxi strip into the soft mud causing the aircraft to nose over on its back. The canopy (Bubble type) collapsed on the pilot forcing his head forward into such a position as to restrict air from his lungs causing suffocation. The accident was fatal to the pilot, the aircraft did not burn.

Every effort was made to save Crisoforo Salido's life, as detailed in the sworn affidavit given by Captain Joseph I. Wosanchuk, Medical Officer of Section 'M':

When we reached the plane the firemen were digging underneath the cockpit and stated that they could see the pilot's head but I could not see it at the time of arrival.

The first time I saw the body in the plane the head of Lieutenant Salido was facing the tail of the P-47. The mud was very tenacious and it had to be scraped away manually [with] shovels. [After] about two minutes I was able to go down into the pit underneath the cockpit on my hands and knees and palpate [examine by touch] the area about the mandibular artery and no pulsation was felt.

Ephedrine sulphate hype, one ampule was given into the Massete muscle. The head and lips were marked blue. I requested that the fuselage be cut and Colonel Kellond stated that the instruments on the crash truck such as I described to him, namely, metal cutting power shears and axes, were not adequate enough to cut out the fuselage and further stated that he thought there was a directive against cutting the fuselage.

He also stated the even though the fuselage would be cut the body would be, more or less inaccessible due to the multifold cables and pipes. About ten minutes after my arrival at the scene of the crash the body was removed and plasma was immediately given intravenously and artificial respiration and oxygen were immediately given.

Putting my ear to the … area no heart sounds were audible. After giving plasma, artificial respiration and caffeine into the rubber connecting the plasma set a period of ten minutes elapsed and I again listened for heart tone and none were audible.

It was the opinion of Captain Kira who was also at the scene and I that, after fifteen to twenty minutes of artificial respiration and oxygen, no further benefit could be obtained by continuing … the patient was pronounced dead at about 1820.

The news of the death was reported in the local press, under the headline 'Mexican Lieutenant first casualty at Majors Field':

Second Lieutenant Crisoforo Salido Grijalva, of the 201st Mexican Air Force Squadron taking advance training at Majors field was killed at 5:35 o'clock Tuesday afternoon when his plane crashed in a takeoff. [It was] the first fatal accident at the local field, since it was changed to the Second Air Force some weeks back, when the Mexican group was assigned to the local field.

Announcement of the accident was made by Colonel Herbert M. Newstrom, field commandant Tuesday night. Lieutenant Salido was the son of General Conrado Salido, Comandancia de Zimapan, Hidalgo of Mexican Republic. The Mexican Military Attache in Washington was notified of the fatal accident by Colonel Newstrom and was advised that the young Lieutenant would be buried in the national cemetery at San Antonio.

At first his body was planned to be interned in a US cemetery, but it was eventually returned to Mexico City by train from Nuevo Laredo. A group of Mexican Air Force personnel were at the train station to meet the body and take it to the Salon de las Aguilas at Balbuena airfield until the afternoon, when it was buried at the Panteon Civil in Mexico City.

After Crisoforo Salido's death his half-brother, Captain 1st Class Roberto Salido Beltran, asked to replace him.

The 32-year-old pilot, from Los Alamos, Sonora, was born on 8 October 1912, the son of army general Conrado C. Salido and Altagracia Beltran. After doing his studies in Mexico City, he graduated on 1 January 1932 as an artillery officer with the rank of 2nd lieutenant.

From 1932-35 he served in the 1st Regiment of Artillery, and on 1 November 1936 was promoted to 1st lieutenant. From January 1935 to March 1937 he undertook training as a pilot, graduating as a lieutenant with 105.35 hours of flight training.

Roberto Salido was posted to the 1st Air Regiment from March 1937 to February 1940. He was sent for advanced training to Randolph Field, Texas, from February-October 1940. He was promoted to Captain 2nd Class on 16 August 1938 after his participation in the Cedillista rebellion, in which he flew 10 combat missions from 19-31 May, flying Consolidated Model 21-Ms and Vought Corairs V-99Ms.

He was sent to the state of Durango to keep an eye on rebel activities from August 1938 to June 1939, flying Consolidated and Azcarate Corsair general purpose biplanes.

He was posted to the 2nd Air Squadron from October-August 1941, and was later assigned as a instructor at the Escuela Superior de Guerra.

He undertook an advanced twin-engine course with several Mexican pilots at El Hondo, Texas, from December 1943 to January 1944, having been promoted to Captain 1st Class on 23 November 1943. After more postings he was given command of the 101st Air Squadron at Mexico City on 1 May 1944, having amassed about 1,185 hours of flight time.

His request to replace his half-brother was granted, but due to the stage of the unit's training, he was assigned to the command and staff of the MEAF.

The next mishap to affect the Mexican pilots occurred on 6 February1945, when Lieutenant Julio Cal y Mayor Sauz, flying P-47D-28-RA 42-29449 'R15', suffered an accident on landing. He stated:

> After making a normal peel off and having checked my approach with runway control I landed the plane P-47, R-15 on runway 13R, landing with both wheels on the right side of the runway.
>
> After my right wheel got … on to the mud my tailwheel hit one of the runway lights, causing the tail to rise and [damaging] one of the prop tips and motor.

This photo caption tells it all: "Brrrrr … that's cold!". Mexican mechanics working in the snow of Pocatello AAFB, Idaho. (Manuel Cervantes Ramos)

The next accident would be the second fatal one for the Mexican squadron. It occurred during final gunnery training, after the 201st had received its battle flags. On 10 March 1945, Lieutenant Javier Martinez Valle was killed when his P-47D -28-RA 42-29463 'R17' collided with the tow target.

His plane hit the target while making a 90-degree side approach. The P-47 made a snap roll to the left and started to climb up and over the tow cable. It rolled over on its back and dived into the ground. One witness to the accident was the American instructor, 1st Lieutenant Harold V. Johnson, who was leading the gunnery mission and gave the following statement:

Lieutenant Fernando Hernandez Vega ready to take off on another training flight in one of the P-47D-28-RAs in sunny Texas at Majors Field, Greenville. (Family of General Fernando Hernandez Vega)

> I saw him pull over the other side of the tow ship [do] a flip or snap to the left and seem to wobble in the air. As it began to climb over the tow ship I started to call to him on the radio and to direct him not to do acrobatics on the gunnery range. At this moment R11 (Tte. P. A. Reynaldo Perez Gallardo) called and said 'R17 hit the target'.
>
> R17 pulled over or soared over the tow ship in a climbing turn to the left,and them his nose dipped [in] about [a] 30 degree dive. I called R17 from R8 'Are you in trouble' … There was no answer.
>
> The ship leveled out at about 2,000 ft, and began to climb or zoom and I called 'R17 if you are in trouble bail out – R17 bail out'. There was no response. The ship climbed to 2500 ft and rolled over to the left on its back. I called again to bail out. Then R17 began to dive to the deck and went straight in at about an angle of 80 degrees.
>
> The ship hit the sand about 5 miles NNE of Green Island. The tide was going out and the area was draining. R17 burst into flames as soon as it hit. At no time did he transmit after hitting the target, and [I] did not see any object leaving the ship. The accident occurred at approximately 1735 CWT [unofficial time zone].

Lieutenant Johnson recalled the rest of the flight, sending the tow ship and two of the Mexican pilots back to base, and called for a crash boat. R11 (Gallardo) stayed with him circling the crash site until

they were relieved by an AT-6 that remained on site to guide the rescue boats and water sleds. The location of the crash site was on the beach of Padre Island, Port Isabel, about 30 miles north-east of Harlingen Army Airfield, Texas.

Martinez's remains were returned to Mexico with the disqualified

Mexican radio personnel working on one of the P-47D-28RAs on the flight line at Majors Field, Texas, in 1945. (Manuel Cervantes Ramos)

pilots. Both Salido Grijalva and Martinez Valle were buried in Mexico City in the cemetery of *Panteon de Dolores* in a section known as the *Lote de las Aguilas Caidas* (Plot of the Fallen Eagles).

Doctor Major Ricardo Blanco Cancino was not there to deal with either of the fatal accidents as he was completing his training at the Aviation Medical School, at the end of which Captain Amato awarded him his medical aviation wings.

In Texas, the Mexican airmen also faced the ugly face of discrimination, against them and their fellow countrymen who were living in Greenville. In Fred Allison's 1998 conference paper on the 201st in Texas, 'The Fighting Eagles, Mexico's Squadron 201 in World War II', he wrote:

> A significant aspect of their training experience in Texas had nothing to do with flying or learning combat skills, but rather exposure to a culture that had preconceived and often negative notions concerning Mexicans.
>
> Resultantly, although nearer to their home country, the Mexicans of the 201st felt less comfortable training and living in Texas than in Pocatello. Angel Rebollo (a pilot) noticed a 'big difference' in the attitude of the townspeople in Greenville compared to those in Pocatello.
>
> The citizens of Greenville seemed to be much more 'suspicious' of the Mexicans, he noted. The culture of Greenville, and Texas in general, which at this time had neatly defined rules of racial segregation regarding African-Americans, found that these rules were hazy concerning the Mexican squadron members.
>
> These Mexicans were native Mexicans, allies in the war effort, and seemed to be articulate and well-educated. Therefore, the citizens might be suspicious, but it was probably because the Mexicans of Squadron 201 did not fit the mould, and Texans were not sure which of the rules of race, class or diplomacy applied.

One of the first problems encountered was locating housing off base for the wives of some of the Mexican officers, some landlords refusing to rent to Mexicans. This matter was resolved when Captains Paul Miller and Radames Gaxiola Andrade went to the Greenville Chamber of Commerce, asking for help from city officials.

This issue appears to have been resolved by the city and Air Force officials and was given some press in the local papers, such as the *Greenville Morning Herald* of 22 February 1945:

> "U.S. Customs are easy for Mexicans'
>
> With a few exceptions Mexican Military personnel here and their Family's [sic] have had little difficulty in adjusting themselves to American Customs after being transplanted from a lifetime of Mexican customs.
>
> With fully 10 per cent of the Mexican military maintaining homes in Greenville for their wives and families, entertainment and parties have been as frequently as the training program has permitted. Natural language-barriers between Americans and Mexicans have been overcome through the ability of many Mexicans to speak English as well as many Greenville stores employing interpreters for the convenience of their Mexican customers.
>
> It has been no uncommon sight to see Mexicans seated in cafes in this area, ordering dinner from a Spanish English Dictionary.

Another incident that occurred would have some far-reaching consequences. When a restaurant refused to serve Lieutenant Joaquin Ramirez Vilchis, his wife and fellow pilot 2nd Lieutenant Jose Miguel Uriarte Aguilar, Ramirez Vilchis wrote a report on what had happened, with the help of Senor Obregon, the Mexican Consul at Brownsville.

Days later, while on a training flight, he was ordered to land because he had an important phone call from New York City. A jeep was waiting to take him over to the operations base; on the line was the Mexican Ambassador to the United States, Dr Francisco Castillo Najera, who had received the report from Brownsville. Dr Castillo Najera asked Lieutenant Ramirez Vilchis what happened and what he did. Dr Castillo Najera then told Vilchis to look out for the San Antonio newspapers over the next month.

An article was published in the papers that a new law had come into effect, under which it was considered a criminal offence to discriminate against Mexicans at restaurants, with a fine of $500 or 15 days in jail. Lieutenant Ramirez Vilchis later received a personal letter from the governor of Texas, apologising for what had happened to him, his wife and fellow pilot.

Before this incident, there had been another one in which a coffee shop in the downtown area refused to serve some of the squadron's mechanics.

It was reported that the base commander of Majors Field, Colonel Herbert Newstrom, went to the coffee shop in question and had it 'closed down', or more likely placed 'off limits' to all military personnel. This affected its business to such an extent that it was forced to close down, reopening later with no discrimination policy.

Word of these incidents got back to Mexico City, where they appeared in the local press and in the news magazine *Jueves del Excelsior*, which wrote:

> Amparo Aroznema tells us, that during her recent theater tour through our brother or stepbrother territory of Texas … so hard is the discrimination in the land of the cowboys.
>
> That Squadron 201 during their training there had to dedicate itself to destroying cafes and restaurants … when it was known that somebody from the squadron or a fellow countryman had been discriminated by its service.
>
> The pilots from the democracy would arrive and didn't leave any glass untouched … [It was only through the use] of their fists [that] they gained admission without restrictions [for those] that Mexico sent to shed their blood next to Uncle Sam's flag.

A reported large-scale fight was avoided at the base's enlisted men's club when some of the Mexican airmen got too friendly with some of the American airmen's girlfriends. Only the timely intervention of duty officers and military police prevented a major incident.

Another fight occurred between Mexican and American airmen at the Mess Hall, when one of the Mexican sergeants played a joke on the squadron's youngest soldier which started a fight in which American personnel, trying to break it up, got involved. The MPs were called in and separated the belligerents. It was later discovered that the 'soldier', Fernando Nava Musa, was not officially in the squadron. He had left Mexico City to see a friend who was in the squadron and decided to stay. When Colonel Cardenas found out that he had a stowaway in his unit, since Nava Musa had previous military experience and had attended all training, the Mexicans' commander requested that the youngster be added to the unit.

It appears that steps were taken to remedy some of the tense situations between American and Mexican servicemen. A Mexican Military Police unit was assigned to Majors Field to assist their American counterparts and the Greenville police force, as noted in the following newspaper article from 13 December 1944 under the headline 'Mexican MPs are on duty in area':

> Soldiers from the Greenville area though long accustomed to the sight of GI policemen, did a fast double take this week after glimpsing the purple and yellow Insignia 'MP' on members of the Policia Militar law enforcing unit of the Mexican Armed forces now stationed at Majors field.
>
> Assigned for supervision of Personnel in the Mexican fighter squadron, the Mexican police are on duty at Majors field, and in Greenville on weekends, according to Capt. L.L. Van Sttarven, provost Marshal.

During their time training in Texas a small number of the Mexican pilots were engaged and married to some of the local girls, as in the case of Lieutenant Angel Sanchez Rebollo. A book about the history of the Army Air Force airfields in Texas mentions his efforts to win the heart of the young lady:

> One such officer in fact dated a local girl, whose father operated a service station in town. When not on duty, the pilot charmed the station's patrons by washing their car windows and checking the air in their tires.

A study about the squadron's relations with the town of Greenville gives more details of this young pilot's amorous conquest:

Mexican markings were painted on the P-47D-28-RA Thunderbolts during their training in Texas. This member of the ground personnel cleans up the tricolor rudder. (Manuel Cervantes Ramos)

> The young fighter pilot, Rebollo, was not much daunted by the townspeople's suspicions as he met, and married, a young anglo woman from Greensville during his short period of duty there. The whirlwind romance and wedding however had the town abuzz.
>
> This gossip eventually subsided when the marriage proved succesfull and Rebollo, after the war, climbed in rank in the Mexican Air Force [and] attained the rank of Major General and indeed, became the personal pilot of Mexico's president Lic. Gustavo Diaz Ordaz. Rebollo became popular among the citizens of Greensville as he made frequent family visits and attended numerous social functions.

Others also married, besides Rebollo. Lieutenant Reynaldo Perez Gallardo later took his young wife to live in Mexico among the other pilot wives, while Lieutenant Joaquin Ramirez Vilchis' wife, Trinidad, gave birth to a girl in Greenville on 19 February 1945; little Eva Ramirez Santana, their third child, became a favourite of the pilots and was given the nickname 'Evita Peligros' (avoid danger).

Even with the changes in the law, many people living close to the base still held negative views of the Mexicans, as Fred Allison noted in his research paper:

> Although the loss of two pilots from [a] 30-pilot squadron in a three-month span seems terribly costly, by World War II standards, these two losses were not exceptionally high.
>
> Indeed, until the crash of Salido in late January, the Mexicans were the only squadron among the four P-47 squadrons stationed at Majors Field that had obtained 1,000 hours of flight time without an incident of any sort.

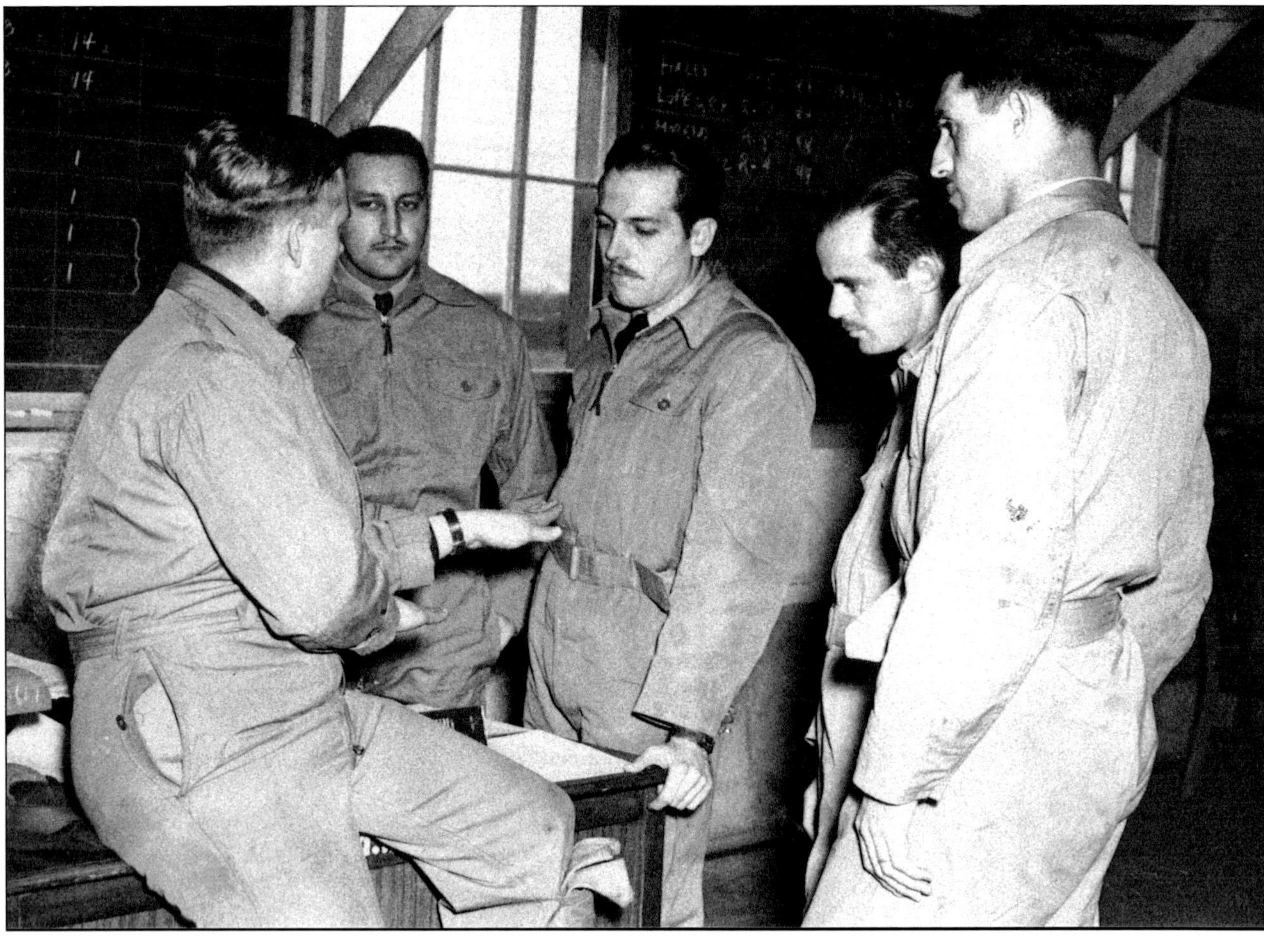

An American instructor explains the next aerial manoeuvre to a group of Mexican pilots, from left to right, 2nd Lieutenant Crisoforo Salido, 2nd Lieutenant Justino Retana, Lieutenant Graco Garrido and Lieutenant Joaquin Ramirez Vilchiz. (Manuel Cervantes Ramos)

Despite their credible flying the Americans in town on the base had a negative impression of the Mexicans' piloting abilities. Witnesses of any P-47 crash seemed to assume that it was one of the Mexicans that crashed. One young man who lived near the field claimed witnessing two P-47s crash land. Both aircraft he asserted were flown by Mexican pilots.

An ex-soldier who assisted at the scene of aircraft accidents, had come to believe that the Mexican 'pilots couldn't fly'. He described one aircraft wreck in which the pilot landed upside down, decapitating the pilot. He assumed that it was one of the Mexicans.

The records, as mentioned earlier, do not bear out these assumptions, most obviously because that one Mexican fatality at Majors Field was a take off accident. These assumptions are a reflection of the American stereotype of Mexico and Mexicans as technologically unsophisticated and backwards.

## CONFLICT OF COMMAND

Before completion of the training of the 201st, Captain Paul B. Miller was relieved as head of Section 'I', as requested by the Mexican Government on the recommendation of Colonel Cardenas. Since Pocatello, a rift existed between Cardenas and Miller, due to a misunderstanding. The young 25-year-old captain told the senior Mexican Air Force colonel (who had been flying since 1926)

that he was too old to fly fighter planes and reportedly had not taken part in the P-40 conversion course at Victoria Field, Texas (which Cardenas claims he did). The American captain did not realise that Cardenas had good relations with the President and the Secretary of National Defense, General Lazaro Cardenas del Rio, who was President of the Republic when Cardenas took part in his Latin American good-will flight in 1940.

That Cardenas was the fighter squadron commander was something that American USAAF officials did not understand, as such positions would normally be filled by a younger captain or major. Yet a mixed squadron that was used during the Cedillo rebellion of San Luis Potosi in May 1938 had been commanded by Brigadier General Alfredo Lezama Alvarez.

The Americans, however, felt that Colonel Cardenas' position should be that of a group commander.

The American command and Captain Miller believed that Cardenas' main role was one of liaison, rather than squadron commander, and they wanted his deputy, Captain Radames Gaxiola Andrade, to lead the squadron due to his age, experience and having trained in the USA.

In a confidential letter dated 26 December 1944 from Colonel Cardenas to the military attache, Brigadier General Luis Alamillo Flores, in Washington DC, he cites a number of complaints in the way he was being treated with the full knowledge of the commander of the Mexican Air Force, Brigadier General Gustavo Salinas Camina. In the letter Cardenas said:

> During the stay at Pocatello the writer flew the AT-6 for transition and the P-40 fighter, going to the ground school as an extra member. Later we were sent to the Pocatello air base where we found Captain Paul B. Miller who had instructions to take charge of our training of the group of pilots (said Captain made a trip to Foster field to take care of issues with Captain Gaxiola). Since no orders existed for me, I waited for the visit that you made to Pocatello, taking this issue to the command and resolving it accordingly.

> I was permitted to fly [after] delaying my training due to medical examinations [and] I came out successfully. During my stay at Pocatello I received many complaints against Captain P. Miller who dared to get the ground personnel together and expressed ill will torwards [my] lack of work and patriotism and he finished by saying your Colonel does not order here, just him.
>
> Knowing his lack of tact in dealing and working with our people, I talked to him and called his attention by way of Capt. Gaxiola Andrade [to] what had happened. I informed you, that this officer in all cases [did not take into consideration] any defence of any Mexican officer or ground personnel.
>
> I did not propose the [replacement] of Capt. Paul Miller because he had the support of the Mexican Command, who had requested he be the squadron liaison officer … I did not request that he be removed … After flying one time in Pocatello, I joined the group at Majors field where we were located. I was called to fly a test flight blind flying, this time with a Colonel sent by the American command who had been presented to me by Capt. Miller.
>
> Without knowing the results of the examination until the arrival of General Salinas in company of General Tourteollet I was called to his temporary office to be told the following: 'Colonel I need to tell [you] that we don't send to the front, squadron commanders over 26 to 30 years old … It is better that you come to the wing to be shown the organisation of major units; the squadron is a minor unit, [to which] we only send boys aged 26. Even if you can fly fighter aircraft it's not a job for you but a 20 year old. We want to avoid you getting killed on these flights etc etc …

The 201st Mexican Fighter Squadron area at Pocatello AAFB, Idaho, with the Mexican flag and the first squadron insignia that was used to mark the area, *circa* 1944. (Manuel Cervantes Ramos)

After receiving the letter, General Alamillo Flores made the case to the Mexican high command that neither Colonel Cardenas nor Captain Gaxiola Andrade should be relieved from their duties. He asked that the problem be corrected by the Secretary of National Defense, avoiding other agencies not involved in the issue.

In William Tudor 1997 dissertation 'Flight of Eagles: The Mexican Expeditionary Air Force Escuadron 201 in World War II', he mentions other incidents in which Colonel Cardenas would not support or cooperate with Captain Miller:

> A controversy arose between Captain Miller and the Mexican enlisted men that added to the breach between him and Cardenas. Because Miller wanted to generate a top-notch program, he initiated certain duties and procedures for the Mexican enlisted personnel to follow.
>
> In particular, he believed that they should perform KP (Kitchen Police – mess hall workers) services. Mexican enlisted men balked at performing work considered beneath their station and they considered KP duty to be degrading. They protested and Colonel Cardenas supported them.
>
> Already at odds with Miller from the prior rift, Cardenas wrote a letter asking that Miller be removed. Approximately sixty enlisted men signed the letter. Another incident that further acerbated the breech between them came about because Cardenas decline to support Miller when the Mexican airmen refused to salute him.

While some of the Mexican pilots did not like Captain Miller, Lieutenant Reynaldo Perez Gallardo mentioned to the author that Miller did not get along with the majority of the pilots and ground personnel. One incident that came to mind was when Perez Gallardo was scheduled to fly a mock combat with Miller to check the progress of each pilot.

They took off and started the dogfight and at one point Miller lost sight of him, yelling on the radio: "Where the hell are you?" Perez Gallardo answered: "Here I am." He was under Miller's aircraft, then came up on one side and pointed at him with his fingers like he was shooting at him. Perez Gallardo realised years later that was the wrong thing to do, as after they landed Miller never spoke to him again.

What finally sealed the breakdown in their relationship was that at about 8:15 p.m. on 3 January 1945, Perez Gallardo buzzed the town of Greenville in a low-flying Vultee BT-13, to the intense annoyance of Miller, who had been at the cinema with his wife.

This incident almost ended Perez Gallardo's dream of serving overseas.

During his free weekends, Perez Gallardo had been in the habit of going to Dallas for some R&R. It was during one of those weekends that he meet Miss Audry Denton; they had a good time together, dancing and drinking.

He returned the next weekend to spend more time with her, but on the Saturday night, instead of taking her home, they drove back to Greenville and the next day Perez Gallardo managed to find a Justice of the Peace and they were married that same day.

That evening, Perez Gallardo had night flying training so went back to Majors Field. But after completing his training flight, instead of heading back to base to land, he decided to fly over the town of Greenville and the hotel where his young bride was staying. Being young and impulsive, and something of a risk-taker, Perez Gallardo decided to buzz the town, flying at low level over the main street and doing barrel rolls as he went by to impress his new wife.

On his second pass he saw people coming out of the buildings to see what was going on. He did not realise at the time that Captain Miller and his wife, Marjorie Jean, were at the movie theatre, enjoying a film that was interrupted by the loud sound of the buzzing Vultee BT-13, according to the recollections of Mrs Miller. (Years later, Mrs Miller would claim in a documentary about the 201st that the offending pilot was sent back to Mexico, but this was not the case.)

The Mexican administrative personnel at Pocatello AAFB, Idaho, training with the 265th Base Unit and one of the USAAF instructors. (Manuel Cervantes Ramos)

Miller suspected that it was one of the Mexican pilots under his command and headed back to Majors Field, mad as hell, to find the culprit. When Perez Gallardo landed at Majors Field and taxied back to the parking area, the American MPs were waiting for him, and as soon as he shut down the engine and got out of the aircraft he was placed under arrest.

Miller requested to Colonel Cardenas that Lieutenant Perez Gallardo be dismissed from the squadron and sent back to Mexico City. In a confidential letter, dated 6 January 1945, to the Director of Training, Majors Field, Miller made the following points against Perez Gallardo:

> This incident demonstrates complete lack of discipline and sense of responsibility, judgement and consideration for the well being of others.
>
> Since the buzzing occurred at approximately 8.15 P.M. on the night of 3 January 1945, investigation has brought to light several other incidents of violations of air regulations by Lt. Gallardo since his arrival at this base, in addition to attempting to talk some of his fellow Mexican pilots into participating in these violations.
>
> In the light of the above facts the undersigned believes that the continuation of Lt. Gallardo's training in fighter aircraft would be [prejudicial] to the welfare of the 201st Mexican fighter squadron from the point of unity, discipline and justness.

However, Perez Gallardo's father was a general in the Mexican Army and had been governor of the state of San Luis Potosi, and with such influence Cardenas, against Miller's recommendations, helped keep Perez Gallardo in the squadron as a maintenance test pilot.

Years later in an interview with Perez Gallardo, he said he was brought before an American officers' board to answer the charge of buzzing the town. He believed that they were using him as an excuse to show that the Mexican pilots could not be trained or disciplined to USAAF standards.

Perez Gallardo argued the point to the board that he was just following his instincts as a fighter pilot, the same instincts that the American instructors were trying to instil in the Mexican pilots, and which were needed to become a good and aggressive fighter pilot. Using these arguments, Perez Gallardo was saved from being sent home but was not permitted to fly in the squadron, being removed from flight status for six months and assigned to work in the engineering section of the squadron under Captain Jesus Carranza. He was put in charge of the squadron's mechanics, as related in an article about him more than 30 years later:

> Youth and impulsive personality brought an abrupt change in Mr. Gallardo assignment. Because he disobeyed orders and 'Buzzed' (flew low) over the city, Mr. Gallardo was restricted from flying and given temporary assignment as the officer in charge of the squadron's mechanics.
>
> Mr. Gallardo remembers this experience. 'This was helpful to me because I was able to learn a lot,' he says. 'I was in charge of the ground services. I felt very sad but I knew I would one day fly again and I did.'

The issue of Lieutenant Perez Gallardo went to Mexico City, where it was taken to the Subsecretary of National Defense, General Francisco L. Urquizo, who ordered that Perez Gallardo continue his training.

In the end Captain Miller requested to his superiors that he wanted

The fatal accident of 2nd Lieutenant Crisoforo Salido Grijalva. (HQ Air Force Safety Agency)

Colonel Cardenas removed as head of the squadron. His request went back to Mexico City, where General Gustavo Salinas, head of the Air Force, was notified of the American wishes and he in turn notified the President and named Colonel Eliseo Martin del Campo Garcia (1900-71) as Cardenas' replacement, being expected to take command in February 1945. But Cardenas flew back to Mexico City, and the following American Intelligence report records what happened next:

> AMERICAN EMBASSY
> Office of the Military Air Attache
> Mexico City, Mexico
> No. A-78-45 30 January 1945
> SUBJECT: Return of Colonel Antonio CARDENAS Rodriguez to Command of 201st Fighter Squadron, Mexican Air Force.
> TO: Chief, Military Intelligence Service, War Department, Washington, D. C.
>
> 1.- On 24 January 1945, the undersigned notified your office of the appointment of Colonel Eliseo MARTIN DEL CAMPO as commanding officer, 201st Fighter Squadron, M. A. F., now in training at Majors Field, Greenville, Texas, who was to relieve Colonel Antonio CARDENAS. General SALINAS, chief of the Mexican Air Force, had notified the undersigned of the change on that date; however, the evening of 24 January General SALINAS stated that Colonel CARDENAS was to be reinstated as the Commanding Officer of the Squadron upon the direction of the President of Mexico.
>
> 2.- President CAMACHO had been informed by General SALINAS of the desire of Army Air Forces Officers in charge of the training of the squadron to have Colonel CARDENAS relieved for incompetency and uncooperativeness in the training program being given by Army Air Forces, and had asked General SALINAS to submit the names of three officers, one whom was to be selected. Colonel CARDENAS returned to Mexico, and without obtaining permission from General SALINAS, succeeded in seeing the President. General SALINAS states that Colonel CARDENAS stated to the President that if he (CARDENAS) was relieved that it would indicate that Mexico was not able to run its own organization, but that it was entirely controlled by the United States Government.

2nd Lieutennt Crisoforo Salido Grijalva, killed while taking off at Majors Field, Texas, on 23 January 1945. (Manuel Cervantes Ramos)

> He is reported to have further stated that there were numerous occasions of racial prejudice shown by A. A. F. personnel against the Mexicans. As a result, the President directed that Colonel CARDENAS return as commanding officer of the squadron.
>
> 3.- General SALINAS is in quite an embarrassing predicament. He is faced with the fact that although he is appointed chief of the Air Force, he cannot, in reality, command it. He stated to the undersigned that he was in ill favor with the President as a result of the incident, and that it would be no surprise to him if he were relieved from command in the near future.
>
> 4.- In the opinion of the undersigned, this places our government in a rather Embarrasing situation. Our Air Forces have asked for the relief of an officer who has proven incompetent and uncooperative, yet the President of Mexico refuses to concur in this request. It is the recommendation of the undersigned that nothing more be done by Army Air Force towards effecting the relief of Colonel CARDENAS until the squadron reaches a combat theater. Under the provisions of section I (b) (4) the agreement entered into between the United Mexican States and the U. S. War Department 15 January 1945, the theater commander may return Mexican personnel to Mexico for any reason he might deem advisable. This would be the least embarrassing method of effecting the removal of Colonel CARDENAS and certainly one that could not be contested by Mexico.
> GEORGE P. CHAMPION
> Colonel, Air Corps,
> Military Air Attache
> Approved and forwarded for and
> in the absense of the Military

An autographed picture of the pilots of the 201st Mexican Fighter Squadron to one of their instructors, Captain Lowell Sund USAAF, a veteran of the North Africa campaign. (Lowell Sund)

The accident scene of Lieutenant Javier Martinez Valle. (HQ Air Force Safety Agency)

Lieutenant Javier Martinez Valle, killed during aerial gunnery training on 10 March 1945, after the unit graduation. (Manuel Cervantes Ramos)

Attache, by:
CANTWELL C. BROWN
Lieutenant Colonel, G. S. C.
Asst. Military Attache

As a result of all these moves, Captain Miller was eventually replaced by Lieutenant Colonel Arthur W. Kellond.

Born in Honolulu, Hawaii, in 1916, Arthur W. Kellond graduated from high school in 1935 at Texas Military Institute, San Antonio. He enlisted in the Army Signal Corps on 25 June 1939, became a flying cadet on 29 June 1936 and received his pilot wings on 9 June 1937.

After being commissioned in July 1937, 2nd Lieutenant Kellond's first assignment was to the 34th Attack Squadron, 17th Attack Group, at March Field, California. He was later transferred to the 38th Reconnaissance Squadron at the same base. In August 1939 he received his regular Army commission in the Air Corps. In 1940, Lieutenant Kellond was ordered to Panama, where he rose to the rank of lieutenant colonel in assignments to the 6th Bomb Group, 19th Bomb Wing, IV Bomber Command and Sixth Air Force Headquarters.

He returned to the United States in 1943 and was assigned to Headquarters Second Air Force and Headquarters 72nd Fighter Wing in Colorado and Wendover, Utah, where he commanded the base, before his eventual assignment to the 201st Mexican Fighter Ssquadron.

On 14 January 1945, Kellond took over Section 'I' and continued with some of Captain Miller's training policies. Two days earlier, a memo concerning the assignment of the US liaison officer with the 201st Mexican Fighter Squadron was signed by Brigadier General Frederic H. Smith Jr, Deputy Chief of Air Staff, US Army, that detailed the qualifications of the liaison officer:

> 1. The 201st Mexican Fighter Squadron has been organized and trained by the USAAF in exactly the same manner as one of our own squadrons. This squadron is scheduled for overseas shipment (South Pacific) about the middle of March 1945. This squadron will to all intents and purposes be handled as an integral part of the Army of the United States, with the exception that the actual tactical commander of the squadron will be a Mexican officer. Subject squadron will be accompanied by a Senior Mexican officer in rank not to exceed Colonel accompanied by a very small commissioned and enlisted staff. The Duties of this Senior Mexican officer will be limited to those pertaining to supervision, liaison and administration.
>
> 2. The above information is given to permit your officer to select a qualified U.S. Army Air Forces officer to accompany subject squadron overseas as liaison officer and not in a command capacity. This U.S. officer must be a fighter pilot, have seen service overseas, and should speak and write fluent Spanish. In addition to this, subject liaison officer must be possessed of unusual tact and be capable of dealing smoothly with the higher ranking Mexican officers and U.S. officers with whom he may often have to handle delicate diplomatic and other problems.
>
> 3. It is directed that immediate action be taken to select and assign preferably a Lt. Colonel meeting with the above qualifications to duty as liaison officer with the 201st Mexican Fighter Squadron. This U.S. liaison officer will be under the jurisdiction of the American command to which the squadron is attached.

General Francisco L. Urquizo, under secretary of the *Defensa Nacional*, leading the delegation to present the national flag and battle flag to the 201st Mexican Fighter Squadron of the Mexican Expeditionary Air Force, during the graduation ceremony at Majors Field, Texas, on 23 February 1945. (Manuel Cervantes Ramos)

On 29 January the following memorandum signed by US Brigadier General Joe L. Loutzenheisser, Chief Operational Plans Division, designated Lieutenant Colonel Kellond as the liaison officer:

> It has now been decided to designate Lt. Colonel A. W. Kellond 0-22520 as the U.S. Liaison officer to accompany subject squadron overseas. This officer is at present the Director of Training for the 201st Mexican Fighter Squadron stationed at Majors Field, Texas under the jurisdiction of the 72nd Fighter Wing, Second Air Force. Both General Tourtellet and Colonel Branch, his successor as Commanding Officer of the 72nd Fighter Wing have informally concurred in this assignment.

As for Captain Miller, he was transferred to the 260th AAF BU (FW) at Peterson AAFB, Colorado, where he was named assistant director of flight training with effect from 23 January 1945.

He travelled to Mexico City in February, leaving his wife there with some family, and attended the 201st's graduation at Majors Field, Texas. He later served overseas in China, with the 81st Fighter Group, surviving the war and staying in the USAAF.

After the war the Mexican government recognised Miller's efforts by awarding him the *Merito Militar 2/o.Clase* and *Merito Aeronautico 3/o. Clase* medals on 12 February 1949 at Mexico City, for meritorious performance as chief instructor to the 201st Mexican Fighter Squadron during the war. He also received letters of commendation from the USAAF for his work with the 201st. Miller stayed in the air force, only to be killed in action in the Korean conflict on 16 June 1951 during a ground support mission, while assigned to temporary duty as a lieutenant colonel with the 27th Fighter Escort Wing, flying Republic F-84E Thunderjets.. After the end of the war his remains were recovered and buried in Los Angeles.

Mexican records state that their 33 pilots in training at Majors Field had flown 469.15 hours in P-47s since 2 December 1944, each pilot having an average flying time of 14 hours.

From 16 December 1944 to 6 January 1945, the 32 Mexican pilots in training flew 291.45 hours in P-47s at Majors Field, 178 hours at Abiline and 38.15 hours in BT-13 night flights for a total hours flown of 508.10, each pilot averaging 16 hours.

With their training reaching its conclusion, in February 1945 the Mexican pilots flew for 782.50 hours with an average of 23.40 hours, while the instructors flew for 149.40 hours (average 9.20 hours). The following month the Mexican pilots recorded 363.10 flight hours (average 11.20 hours) and the instructors 109.15 hours (average 6.48 hours).

Throughout their training in Idaho and Texas, the Mexican pilots flew a total of 1,017.50 hours, an average per pilot of 31 hours.

Eighteen P-47s were assigned to the squadron in February, with 17 in March. The P-47s assigned to the 201st had the individual number letter combinations 'R1' to "'R20' painted on the fuselage, and towards end of the training some of the aircraft received Mexican Air Force markings, in the form of the Mexican Air Force tricolour (red, white and green) on their rudders.

As for the maintenance of these aircraft, the engineering section received letters of commendation, including the following from the commander of Brownsville Army Air Field in Texas, Colonel Arthur G. Salisbury, on 18 February 1945:

> SUBJECT: Commendation to the Engineering Section, 201st Mexican Fighter Squadron
>
> TO: Commanding Officer, 201st Mexican Fighter Squadron, Brownsville Army Air Field, Brownsville, Texas
>
> 1. It has been brought to my attention, both by status reports as well as by personal observation, that since the arrival of the 201st

Mexican Fighter Squadron to this station, the high standard of maintenance set by the Engineering Section has been particularly outstanding.

2. In maintaining an average of over 90% of assigned airplanes in Commission at all times, your Engineering Section has set a standard of which you can be justly proud, and which is so vitally essential in a theater of war.

3. It is with the greatest of pleasure that I have written this Letter and please accept the wishes of myself as well as my staff, for your continued success and good hunting in your forthcoming operations.

The engineers were also praised by the field service representative of Republic Aviation Corporation, W.J. Knight, who wrote to the 201st's commanding officer at Brownsville on 26 February 1945:

It has been my extreme pleasure to work with 1st Capt. Carranza R., the maintenance officer of the 201st Mexican Fighter Squadron. Your personnel have been extremely cooperative thus earning a maintenance record of 90.6% aircraft in commission.

The maintenance record is far higher than any squadron I have worked with in the past.

The crew chiefs have made many suggestions and improvements in aircraft maintenance procedure on P-47s. I found these improvements worthy of mention to the Republic Aviation Factory for improved production and maintenance of the P-47 aircraft.

I know the long hours and hard work your men have spent on these aircraft will benefit them greatly in combat. The 201st will make their mark in this war.

With the completion of the Mexicans' training on 14 March 1945, members of Section 'I' were reassigned to different units across the base, except for 10 members – five officers and five enlisted men – under the command of Lieutenant Colonel Kellond. These were directed by higher headquarters on 21 March to be placed on TDY (temporary duty) with the Mexican squadron to act as a liaison group when the 201st was deployed overseas.

## THE CREATION OF THE MEXICAN EXPEDITONARY FORCE, 1945

When Colonel Cardenas returned to Mexico City to see the President on the matter of Captain Miller, he also attended meetings that would organise the sending of the squadron overseas.

With the assent of the US and Mexican governments the following was agreed, as noted in a study of the MEAF by Colonel Vega Rivera:

The agreement established the participation of the Mexican squadron, accompanied by a senior officer and a small staff group. The Squadron and adjuntant personnel were to be handled as an integral part of the US Army, with exceptions in the command, administration, expenses and equipment and supply.

The command and control coordination are particularly important due to the terms of the agreement. The commander of the squadron had been a Mexican Colonel, and it did not represent any problem during training. However, the Mexican congress approval for the participation of a force overseas and the terms of the agreement for such participation required changes.

The regular command line for a US P-47 squadron, normally commanded by a Major or Captain, was a Fighter Group headed

The Mexican national flag that was presented to the Mexican Expeditionary Air Force at Majors Field, Texas, on 23 February 1945. (Manuel Cervantes Ramos)

usually by a Colonel or Lieutenant Colonel. The rank of the commander of the 201st Squadron was higher than usual, a normal designation for independent forces, but unnecessary for the agreed structure.

Since the squadron would be operating under tactical tasking from a US fighter group, it was necessary to appoint a new commander. A Mexican officer, qualified to command in accordance with the standards applied for selection of a commander for a fighter squadron in the US Army, was to be in command of the Squadron. As a result, Captain Radames Gaxiola was appointed for the position after the creation of the MEAF.

The Mexican government [recognised] the importance that this force represented for Mexico and in accordance to the nature of its mission, created the MEAF … The commander of the MEAF was the senior Mexican officer accompanying the Squadron, and he represented the Mexican Army in matters pertaining the squadron.

The Mexican government appointed for this position Col. Antonio Cardenas Rodriguez, the previous commander of the 201st Squadron. His responsibility included to further the administrative efficiency of the MEAF, and foster good relations with United Nations troops.

He disposed of a small staff group to assist the training and operations of the 201st Squadron. Col Cardenas received instructions from Mexico's Secretary of Defense on March 1945 regarding the MEAF performance overseas. The American side in a memorandum of the senior U.S. Army member of the joint Mexican United States Defense Commission dated January 11th 1945, represented the American reason for the squadron commander to be of the rank of Captain or Major: It is felt that the present commanding officer of the squadron Colonel Antonio Cardenas, though an outstanding officer of sound military experience has not due to his age and lack of experience in USAAF fighter squadron operations, been able to readily adapt himself to the task of commading this squadron.

It will be noted that such [a] position in the USAAF is held by a very young officer qualified to lead his men in actual combat operations. Reference is made to the letter addressed to the military attaché Mexican Embassy, Washington, D.C. from the foreign Liaison Officer of the war department military intelligence division, dated 2 October 1944 in which attention was invited to the necessity of making a definite changes in the command of the squadron, and in which it was pointed out that Captain Gaxiola had demonstrated that he is well qualified to assume the tactical command of the squadron.

The Mexican government may desire to send an older and more mature officer with the squadron. This officer would assume the duties indicate in Paragaph 1 (a) "Command" in the agreement

The pilots of the 201st Mexican Fighter Squadron march past the newly received national and battle flag during the graduation ceremony of 23 February 1945. (Manuel Cervantes Ramos)

recently presented by the War department to the Mexican government. In this case, it would be advantageous to expedite the selection of this officer.

However, because of the proximity of the date that the 201st Mexican Fighter Squadron is to go overseas, it is deemed essential that immediate action be taken to relieve Colonel Cardenas of command of the subject squadron as it is inadvisable for this officer to accompany the squadron overseas.

For the Commanding General, Army Air Force
L.S. KUTER, Major General, U.S.A.,
Asst Chief of Air Staff Plans"

By Order No.8606, dated 27 December 1944, from the *Secretaria de la Defensa Nacional, Dirrecion de Aeronautica*, the *Grupo de Perfeccionamiento De Aeronautica* (GPA, 201st Squadron) was designated as the *Fuerza Aerea Expedicionaria Mexicana* (FAEM/MEAF, Mexican Expeditionary Air Force).

This arrangement created a command and staff and the designation of Colonel Cardenas as commander of the MEAF, handing over the squadron to the newly promoted Captain 1st Class Radames Gaxiola Andrade. The Mexican Expeditionary Air Force consisted of a Command and Staff and a Replacement Group of pilots and enlisted personnel, which was manned by the following personnel:

## MEXICAN EXPEDITIONARY AIR FORCE

Commanding Officer
Colonel Antonio Cardernas Rodriguez
Staff
Lieutenant Colonel Alfonso Gurzan Farfan
Major Enrique Sandoval Castarrica
Captain 1st Class Roberto Salido Beltran
Lieutenant Colonel Arthur B. Kellond (USAAF)
Major Ricardo Blanco Cancino
Major Guillermo Linage Olguin
201st Fighter Squadron
Captain 1st Class Radames Gaxiola Andrade
Replacement Group
Major Rafael J. Suarez Peralta

Before the completion of their training, pilots and personnel of the MEAF were given a graduation and battle flag presentation at Majors Field on 23 February 1945, in a ceremony attended by high-ranking military and civilian officials from both sides of the border.

It had been originally planned for 20 February, but was postponed twice by torrential rains. The preparations had been announced before the squadron had moved to its gunnery training, as noted in an article that appeared in the air base newspaper, *Flight Report*, of 31 January 1945, under the headline 'Plans laid for Mexican flag rites':

> While prodigious plans for the impending flag-presentation ceremony to the 201st Mexican Fighter squadron for February 20 were being developed this week on and off Majors Field, pilot trainees of the Mexican unit planned to slip quietly from their south stage operations rooms Wednesday or Thursday for a two week training session at Brownsville Army Air Base, Texas.
>
> At Brownsville, situated on the very tip of the Rio Grande section of Texas, Mexican pilots will spend some two weeks in aerial gunnery training, stressing air-to-air tactics with B-26s handling two-targets. Under the command of Lt. Col. Arthur B. Kellond, a group of Section I, American EM and pilot instructors will accompany the trainees. Mexican enlisted personnel too, will lend a hand in the training activities.
>
> Upon returning to Majors Field, the 201st will begin the last

The ground personnel of the 201st FS passing in review of both flags at the graduation ceremony at Majors Field on 23 February 1945. (Manuel Cervantes Ramos)

lap of training before officials from Mexico and the United States arrive here for the battle-flag presentation in February. General H. H. Arnold is scheduled to present the flag to Mexican President Representative, General Francisco L. Urquizo, under secretary of war.

Other celebrities will be at the ceremony. Col. Herbert M. Newstrom, Majors Field's commanding officer, said Lieutenant Colonel Martin Del Campo, named in Mexico to replace Col. Antonio Cardenas Rodriguez last week as CO of the 201st, has not arrived. At the helm of the Mexican fighter unit until the arrival of Col. del Campo is Capt. Radames Gaxiola, senior pilot.

Sergeant Cervantez Ramos remembered that the training still continued:

Last flights, last exams for all the personnel and the satisfaction to know that the Headquarters of the 2/o. Air Force was giving the end of our training and they grade the squadron as a unit ready to enter combat as soon as the Mexican government decided.

At the same time arriving in the United States was more personnel of the Air Force and different branches and services, which would receive the same training as we, so when the moment arrived or the circumstance dictated they would be our future replacements.

The postponement of the graduation event gave time for NBC International staff to interview about 30 pilots and some of the instructors. Among them were Colonel Cardenas and Lieutenant Colonel Kellond, the latter saying:

It has been a privilege and a pleasure for the personnel of the Army Air Force to work with the men and officers of the 201st Mexican Fighter Squadron. Everybody knows the 201st, feels certain that it will establish a brilliant record in combat and will be a great credit to Mexico.

Leading the Mexican delegation at the ceremony was General de Division Francisco L. Urquizo, the Undersecretary of National Defense, who was designated by President Camacho, in the name of the nation, to give the battle flag to the MEAF.

It was a standard Mexican national flag that on the top had the inscription *Ejercito Mexicano* (Mexican Army) and on the bottom *Fuerza Aerea Expedicionaria* (Expeditionary Air Force). The flag bearer was Urquizo's aide de camp, Captain Mardonio Berlanga Gonzalez. The group also included General Gustavo Salinas and Brigadier General Luis Alamillo Flores, the Mexican military attache in Washington DC. There was also a Mexican marching band, as recalled by Sergeant Cervantez Ramos:

A marching band belonging to an infantry battalion … stationed in Monterrey, was transferred to Major's field …

When they got off the plane which brought them, and once in formation, they started to march, playing drums and bugles. [They played] 'Diana' and later 'Las Margaritas', with [such spirit] and enthusiasm that it appeared they would break the skins of their drums, and the bugles were playing to the max. It was [such] a pleasure for us that we ran over to applaud them what great emotion.

On the American side, Lieutenant General Barton K. Yount, commanding general of the Army Air Force training command, was to present a second flag to the MEAF, a squadron guidon, on behalf of General "Hap" Arnold, chief of the USAAF. This guidon was in the colours of the Mexican flag, with the inscription in Spanish *201*

Mexican newspaper editorial cartoon on the deployment of the Mexican Expeditionary Air Force to the Pacific. (Manuel Cervantes Ramos)

*Escuadron de Caza* (201st Fighter Squadron).

Others present were Major General Robert B. Williams, commanding officer of the 2nd Air Force; Major General Richard F. Donovan, commanding officer of the 8th Service Command; Brigadier General Richard A. McGinnis, Assistant Chief of Staff of the 2nd Air Force; and Colonel I.L. Branch, commanding officer of the 72nd Fighter Wing.

The flag ceremony started at 11:00 a.m. in the presence of family members and friends of the Mexican personnel. General Urquizo, before handing the battle flag to Colonel Cardenas, read out the oath of loyalty:

> Citizens, Commanders, Officers and Enlisted [men] of the Mexican Expeditionary Air Force; I come here in the name of the country to trust our valour and patriotism, and strict discipline.
>
> This flag symbolizes its independence, its institutions, the integrity of her territory and her military honor. Do you swear to follow her with vigor and perserverance and defend her in combat until obtaining victory or die trying?

After receiving the answer 'Yes' from the men of the MEAF, Urquizo handed the flag to Cardenas, who in turn gave it to the squadron flag bearer. The squadron then received the guidon from Lieutenant General Yount. After the flags were presented, Senator Pentose Metcalf of San Angelo, Texas, with fellow senators C.G. Morris and Howard Carney and three other members of the state House of Representatives, read a resolution recently passed by the Texas Legislature, praising the Mexican Fighter Squadron, which had received much of its training in Texas. The final event of the ceremonies was a fly-past by the Mexican pilots.

The formal training of theMEAF came to an end soon after on 14 March. The American summary report on the unit's training included the following:

> The Squadron finished all phases of its training by early March 1945, with a record slightly better than of the average U. S. fighter squadron. Only two pilots had been killed in training, Lt. G.E. Salido and Lt. Javier V. Martinez, and the overall accident ratio was average.

Even before the flag ceremony, a major question remained over what the Mexican government was to do with the MEAF after the completion of its training. It had been determined that if the Mexican government had not decided the fate of the 201st Squadron of the GPA by December 1944, it would return to Mexico after completing its training.

Part of the issue was resolved on 29 December 1944, when the Mexican Senate authorised President Camacho to send troops overseas and fight outside of Mexico. But the question was, where would they fight? The Mexican military attache, General Luis Alamillo Flores, suggested the use of the Mexican squadron in the Pacific theatre of pperations. He felt

the presence of Mexican personnel there would be more significant than if sending them to Europe, where they would be with the big Allied armies fighting their way into Germany. By the time the unit would have reached France, the war would have been practically over before it was ready for combat operations. (The war in Europe ended on 7 May 1945, at which time the 201st was in pre-combat training in the Philippines).

Another issue was that General Douglas MacArthur was already fighting with US forces in the Philippines, and it was felt perfect for the MEAF to help liberate a nation common in its Spanish heritage. President Camacho was an admirer of General MacArthur, who visited Mexico with Filipino President Manuel L. Queson in April 1937. The following memos about the use of the Mexican squadron were exchanged between MacArthur and General George Marshall, US Chief of Staff, and 'Hap' Arnold in December 1944 and January 1945:

> NOTE: Message 80442 of December 21, Marshall to MacArthur, informed that one Mexican P-47 Fighter Squadron would be ready for overseas shipment about March 1, 1945, having been organized and trained by the Army Air Forces under standard organization and equipment.
>
> The President of Mexico is anxious that the squadron be stationed in your theater, with background of your
>
> visits to Mexico, close personal friendship with late President Quezon including radio
>
> broadcast with President Roosevelt participating and President of Mexico promising assisntance to Philippines.
>
> Assigment to your theater has political implications. Subject was taken up by President [who] favors assignment. Request your reaction.
>
> Message C-55289 of December 29, Arnold from MacArthur, stated would be delighted to receive the Mexican P-47 Squadron.
>
> No. WAR-85672, 1 January 1945, to Messersmith [American ambassador to Mexico] from Arnold signed Bissell.
>
> Elaborating conversation with you during visit to Washington,

The arrival of the Mexican Expeditionary Air Force at Manila on 1 May 1945. From left to right, Lieutenant Colonel Alfonso Gurza, General George C. Kenney, commander of the FEAF, Miss Conchita Carmelo, Colonel Antonio Cardenas Rodriguez, Alfredo Carmelo and Miss Leonor Carmelo. (MacArthur Memorial)

> General MacArthur has replied to inquiry that he would be delighted to have Mexican P-47 Squadron assigned to his command. Now making necessary arrangements to process this project and for Squadron to be ready to leave United States about March 15 is now uur general plan.

The conditions for sending the MEAF overseas was decided in an agreement by members of the US Mexico Defense Commission that included the following points:

> A. – The Internal administration with Mexican personnel would be under the command of Mexican Officers and subject to Mexican regulations.
>
> B. – All aircraft used by the MEAF would carry regular Army Air Forces insignias and Mexican insignias would be carried on the aircraft, but the positions of these would be subject to the approval of the commanding officer of the theater of operations.
>
> C. – All Mexican personnel would be subjected to Mexican military law.
>
> D. – Mexican government will provide a replacement group.
>
> E. – All communications between the unit and the Mexican government would be via the department of war in the United States.
>
> F. – Salaries of the Mexican personnel were to be paid in dollars by the paymaster general helped by the MEAF."

The Mexican unit's main equipment, the Republic P-47D-30-RA Thunderbolt fighter bomber, would be supplied in the following manner, as per a US War Department memo from General 'Hap' Arnold to the commander of the SWPA (South West Pacific Area), General Kenny, dated 30 January 1945:

> Initial equipment of 25 P-47 aircraft will be shipped from United States with arrangements made for you to supply at a later date when needed 17 additional such aircraft for reserve plus four aircraft per month for attrition requirements, both from theater stocks at your disposal.

Another memorandum regarding equipment for the 201st Fighter Squadron, dated 9 January 1945, made the following observations:

> Beginning about June 1945, according to information informally

Mexican pilots and ground personnel greeted by Miss Conchita Carmelo, dressed in a traditional Mexican costume, on the pier at the port Manila on 1 May 1945. (MacArthur Memorial)

> received from OCAR, P-47N may be furnished the Mexican Squadron instead of P-47D D-30. The P-47N series is a longer range version of the same model aircraft and it is anticipated that General Kenny's remaining P-47 squadron will by then be receciving P-47N as replacements. At present that theater has seven P-47 squadrons, three of which are currently being converted to P-51 aircraft.

A request to provide a Beech C-45 transport aircraft for the staff of the MEAF was not accepted, as it was said the particular theatre to which the squadron was being assigned would not readily permit the use of such aircraft for the purpose indicated.

Back in Mexico City, a church service was held on 2 April 1945 to bless a special banner from family members of the MEAF, the ceremony being conducted by the monsignor of the Basilica de Guadalupe, Luis M. Martinez.

This banner was bought at the Majors Field base by Sofia Mercado Vda de Garcia, the mother of 2nd Lieutenant Raul Garcia Mercado, and was signed by a number of squadron personnel, from Colonel Cardenas to the cooks. In the centre of a Mexican flag, at the top, was written '*A LA SRA. VIRGEN DE GUADALUPE*' (to the Virgin of Guadalupe) and at the bottom '*DEL ESCUADRON 201, ABRIL 2, 1945*' (from Squadron 201, 2 April 1945).

However, the actions of Sra Mercado Vda de Garcia, later known as *Mama 201* (Mother 201), would almost cause her son to be dismissed from the squadron and sent back to Mexico.

Having links with the secret police, she had supplied information about an attempt on the life of President Camacho in April 1944.

On 10 April, when President Camacho arrived at the National Palace and was about to take the lift to his office, Mexican Army Lieutenant Antonio de la Lama Rojas saluted him and then opened fire on the president. The shot missed Camacho by inches, and he grabbed Lama Rojas so he didn't get a chance to fire again. A lieutenant and soldier then subdued the attacker, who died of a bullet wound two days later while trying to escape custody.

Although Sra Vda de Garcia was behind getting the special church service for the families of the personnel of the 201st, and also the blessing of the flag, her actions were later criticised by other family members. She had asked for money from family members and even movie stars for this event, and when it was found that the service was free, the family members went to see General Cristobal Guzman, chief of the Command and Staff, to complain about 'Mama 201'. She had also openly criticised the military for sending their sons and husbands to war for miserable pay. This caused some anger among higher-ranked military officers, including the Secretary of National Defense, General Lazaro Cardenas del Rio, who on 28 March 1945 issued a directive that 2nd Lieutenant Garcia Mercado be dropped from the 201st.

Following the directive, General Gustavo Salinas issued orders on 12 April that Garcia Mercado be sent as a flight instructor to the Military Aviation School. Yet by the time the order reached the 201st on 15 May, the unit was at Porac Field in the Philippines, and

Colonel Antonio Cardenas Rodriguez meets General Douglas MacArthur in his offices in Manila after his arrival on the same day. With them are Lieutenant Colonel Alfonso Garfan and General George C. Kenney, commanding officer of the FEAF. (MacArthur Memorial)

commanding officers Cardenas, Radames Gaxiola and Captain Rivas Martinez requested that it be cancelled due to the need to retain the valuable services of Garcia Mercado and that his dismissal would affect the morale of the squadron.

Even the wife of Mercado Garcia, Maria Yolanda Gutierrez Quintanilla de Garcia Mercado, sent a letter, dated 5 May, to the Secretary of National Defense defending her husband, saying the actions of her mother-in-law should not affect the good name of her husband, who had volunteered of his free will to fight in the war. Thereafter tempers appear to have calmed, as on 12 June the orders were rescinded and Garcia Mercado remained with the 201st.

The MEAF had left Majors Field on 18 March, as recalled by Corporal mechanic Pedro Martinez Perez:

> We left on March 18 from Dallas, Texas to the Port of Pittsburg, California where we arrived on [the] 21st. When we boarded the train we were prohibited from speaking to civilians, [or to] send letters or telegrams to our families and each time we arrived at a station, we had to close the windows so nobody could see who we were traveling in the train convoy. Our uniforms had been changed to the American one and [there was] nothing in sight to identify us.

After receiving American equipment, the Mexicans moved to Camp Stoneman, California, for preparation for the movement overseas. Major Blanco Cancino of the MEAF staff recalled that the last medical examinations were conducted for the Mexican personnel before boarding the Liberty ship *Fairisle*, and two members of the unit were found with medical problems; one was sent home but the other remained with the MEAF.

The Mexicans boarded the *Fairisle* on 27 March at San Francisco and set sail that same evening on a 33-day voyage across the Pacific. The ship was crowded with other US military units, as observed by Sergeant Cervantez Ramos:

> This boat, along with us was transporting approximately 2,800 US soldiers from different units. In the afternoon on the deck we were given lectures about the war in the Pacific, the way of living of the Philippinos [*sic*], the mind and way of fighting of the Japanese, their threats, their lies, their fanaticism, as well as [the] friendly troops and enemy [we would find] at the war theater we were headed to.

To combat some of the boredom of the trip, the Mexican personnel found ways to try to make it livelier, that include performing for an audience of American soldiers, as Cervantez Ramos also recalled:

> Also at night we gathered on the deck to remember our country [and] home. [For us] Mexicans the guitar was not missing and [with] a pair of buckets or cans to accompany we would sing 'El Cantar del Regimiento', 'Me voy Soldado Raso', 'Nochecita', 'Despedida', 'Que Lejos Estoy', 'Amor, Amor', 'Babalu', this last song magnifcently sung by our comrade named Bernandino Mendoza, alias *El Verde* (The Green), and other songs remembering each region or state of our republic.
>
> Many times we were joined by the Americans [who] enjoyed our serenade, asking [us] to sing 'Cielito Lindo' and 'Alla en el Rancho Grande'.

From San Francisco the ship sailed through the north and south Pacific, to the Coral Sea, New Guinea, the islands of Palau, Leyte Gulf, Strait of Surigao, the sea of Mindanao, the sea of Sulu, the China Sea and finally to Manila Bay in the Philippines.

In New Guinea the ship joined a convoy of some 40 ships, including the *Mexico* and *Monterrey*, the latter catching the Mexicans' attention when it was discovered the ship was transporting a contingent of Women Army Corps Services (WACS) women who were on the decks sunbathing and could be seen with binoculars.

The Mexicans had to get used to the practice alarms, held in case of attacks. Everybody had to carry their life vest with them at all times, it serving many purposes, in some cases a pillow to aid sleep. The first practice alert for the ship's crew to man their anti-aircraft guns caught many of the Mexican personnel off guard, as remembered by Sergeant Cervantez Ramos:

> I have to confess that the first occasion that we were warned that a practice alert was going to be conducted, almost none of us Mexicans paid any attention, because we were talking or playing cards. Sometimes we would not pay any attention to the voice over the speakers that said 'Now Hear This'.
>
> But when we heard the first shots of the machines guns and

cannons, the stairs got a bit narrow to get quickly up to the deck and take our places. This [made] us pay more attention to the speakers.

Major Edward F. Roddy, commanding officer of the 58th Fighter Group, to which the Mexican squadron was assigned for prep combat training and combat operations in the Philippines on 2 May 1945. Roddy was a notable fighter pilot with eight kills to his credit from his days in the 348th Fighter Group. (Edward F. Roddy)

## DEPLOYMENT OVERSEAS AND ARRIVAL, APRIL-MAY 1945

When the MEAF arrived in Manila Bay on 30 April 1945, already waiting for them were Lieutenant Colonel Gurza Farfan and Lieutenant Colonel Kellond, both having arrived by air on 8 April. Their mission was to prepare for the arrival of the MEAF in the Philippines, as Farfan recalled:

> Having landed at the island of Leyte, and in the absence of the commander of the Far Eastern Air Forces, General Kenney, I got in touch with the headquarters of this air force, having taken cognizance of the fact that our elements would be assigned to the 5th Air Force, with headquarters on Clark Field, Island of Luzon, [to] which I proceeded on the 8th inst. and where I at once got in touch with the commander of said air force, General Whitehead, and with the commander of the 5th Fighter Command, General Smith, as well as with the headquarters of both outfits.

After a conversation between General George C. Kenney, Commanding Officer of the Far East Air Force (FEAF), and General Ennis C. Whitehead, Commanding Officer of the 5th Air Force,

it was decided to assign the 201st Squadron to the 5th Air Force, 5th Fighter Command, in General Order No.67, dated 5 April. It was also agreed that before the squadron started combat operations it would undergo pre-combat training to adapt the Mexican pilots to the theatre of operations.

When the MEAF arrived in Manila, it was greeted by General Kenney and the Honourable Consul of Mexico in the Philippines, Alfredo Carmelo.

Born in 1896, Alfredo Carmelo was the first Filipino to fly solo in his country (as well as being the first licensed pilot) in a Curtiss Seagull flying boat on 9 January 1920.

He had taken his first flying lesson in a Rumpler Taube in Germany in 1914 before the start of the First World War. He had been in Germany because his family printing company had sent him to Leipzig. He returned to the Philippines in 1916.

He then tried to apply for flight training in the Philippine National Guard, but was turned down due to his height. When two Americans opened the Curtiss flying school in the Philippines he was one of the first civilians to enrol. Carmelo held the No.1 pilot certificate from the Curtiss flying school and later the Filipino CAA license No.622. During a trip to Paris after the war he bought a surplus Nieuport Model 17 fighter, but sold it before returning home in 1927.

Carmelo specialised in acrobatic performances in a Curtiss JN4 Jenny he owned later. He then launched his business venture, the Carmelo & Bauermann Company, and continued his aviation activities up to the outbreak of the war in the Pacific.

When the Mexican 201st Fighter Squadron came to the Philippines he assisted them in many ways, acting as a facilitator in their operations, assuming the role of translator and even opening his family home to the squadron.

Colonel Cardenas made him an honorary member of the squadron and awarded him with his 'wings'.

The Republic P-47D-23 42-27995 of the 311th Fighter Squadron of the 58th Fighter Group returning from a mission over the Philippines. This aircraft was loaned to the 201st Mexican Fighter Squadron. (USAF)

With Carmelo were his two daughters, Leonor and Conchita, the latter dressed in a traditional Mexican 'China Poblana' outfit, which attracted the attentions of the Mexican airmen. A story or myth has since arisen about the 'Kiss of Death'", a photograph taken of Captain. 2nd Class Pablo L. Rivas Martinez and Lieutenant Jose Espinoza Fuentes each giving a kiss on the cheek of Conchita.

Both would die during operations in the Philippines.

General Kenney's impressions of the MEAF upon its arrival are found in his book *General Kenney Reports: A Personal History of the Pacific War*, in which he writes:

> That afternoon Colonel Cardenas of the MEAF landed at Manila with the 201st Mexican fighter squadron.
>
> After a reception at the pier, I took Cardenas over to see General MacArthur after the official exchange of greetings. The Mexicans were officially assigned to my command. They then proceeded to Clark Field where I turned them over to Brigadier General Freddy Smith with instructions to outfit them with P-47s and give them a course of advanced Combat training before putting them into action.
>
> "Both officers and enlisted were a fine-looking lot and seemed anxious to get to work against the Japs as soon as possible.

Sergeant Cervantez Ramos also gave his impressions of their

Nose art in the form of Disney's Panchito Pistolas on a loaned P-47D Razorback of the 311th FS of the 58th FG, flown by Lieutenant Reynaldo Perez Gallardo. This photograph was found in his personal collection. (Reynaldo Perez Gallardo)

arrival at Manila Bay:

> We left the ship, the next day, 1 May, the sad irony being that in Mexico it was 'workers' day' when nobody works.
>
> But we left the ship with our rucksack, weapons and our baggage on our shoulders, in infernal humid heat, in silence … our faces dripping in sweat … the landing barges took us to the beach where we were received by General George Kenney, chief of the allied air forces in the Pacific theater, Lt. Col. Kellond of the American Air Forces and Mr Alfredo Carmelo our honorary Consul of Mexico.
>
> A small music band not knowing the Mexican national anthem played the 'Marcha Zacateca'.

Major Blanco Cancino made the following observations of their arrival:

> Immediately we received of portion of K rations and a small train took us to Porac, [in the] province of Pamganga, Island of Luzon, at the foot of the Zambales mountains. The Squadron is now part of the 58th Fighter Group, 5th Fighter command, of the 5th Air Force.

While the unit was being transported to its camp, a detail of about 30 enlisted men from the squadron was formed under the command of Lieutenant of Administration Luis Alvarez Maytorena, to see to the off-loading of supplies and materials that the MEAF brought with them on the boat. One of the detail's members was Sergeant 2nd Class Armourer Carlos Ortiz Moreno, who commented on the assignment:

> We had to obey the order, stay with the detail until the job was completed, not with great enthusiasm …
>
> We stayed in a tent, close to the place where we had to do our jobs, it was a big tent that could accommodate about 100 people, [who] like us had to complete their details, they were all Americans and we had to wait for the arrival of our supplies.
>
> We noted some fires in the city and we heared some isolated shots, like machine gun fire, that indicated some resistance by some remaining Japanese troops.
>
> Our food consisted of dry rations … known as the K ration, which was normal in the American army when there was no food service around. Since the boxes that were waiting to classify to be sent to our base in the North part of the island were being delayed, we spent the time exploring around and we discovered about 50 meters from our tent an excavation with regular dimensions, in which we observed a fire with many containers around it.
>
> But at close inspection we saw that what was burning were human remains, which were no doubt Japanese. We saw arms, legs and other human parts, some of the legs still had the Japanese field boots, like a baseball catcher glove, that covered all the [toes] except the big toe.
>
> The strange thing was that with the burning of the bodies, there was no odor that emanated from the cremation; probably they used some chemicals to accelerate the process and at the same time eliminate the odor that … is not very agreeable and sometimes produces nausea.
>
> After two days of waiting we received orders to move to the airfield at Manila to be transported to our base, because the boxes that we were waiting [for] would take longer to be off loaded.
>
> Tte.de Admo. Maytorena ordered us to prepare for the move with our war equipment, our helmet, M-1 rifle, belt with water canteen, and our back pack. We formed up in a column of twos and with the Tte. leading … we started our march towards the airport, which was about 3 kilometers away. We were walking straight to cut the distance when we were approached by two MPs (Military Police) on motorcycles, [who] yelled at us to stop and slowly do an about face and return the same way by the road that we had taken, because we were in a field full of land mines.
>
> We … slowy retraced our steps in the road until the MPs escorted us to the place where a C-47 aircraft was waiting for us, which would take us to our base at Porac, to be reunited with the rest of our buddies.
>
> We took off and landed after a short flight to our base.With the recent experiences in our minds we didn't mind that the landing was a bit rough, since the runway was in the process of construction … the runway consisted of metal planks with holes about 20 cm [apart] in the surface ….
>
> But we arrived happy and with the satisfaction that … we [had] avoided [the] land mines.

The command and staff of the MEAF was established at Fort Stotsenburg. Colonel Cardenas assigned the following officers of his staff for liasion duty with the Headquarters of 5th Fighter Command:

Major Sandoval Castarrica, Intelligence A-2;
Captain Salido Beltran, Plans and Training A-3;
Major Linage, Maintenance and Supply A-4;
Lieutenant Colonel Gurzan Farfan, Confidential Business.

Upon arrival, the 201st was assigned as the fourth squadron of the 58th Fighter Group (the others were the 69th, 310th and 311th Fighter Squadrons), commanded by Major Edward F. Roddy.

Major Edward Roddy, a pilot from Cleveland, Ohio, was 25 at the time of the 201st's arrival in the Philippines. Born on 29 June 1919, he entered the USAAC as a flying cadet in April 1941 and was trained at Sikeston, Missouri; Randolph Field, Texas; and Foster Field, Texas. He flew P-36s, P-38s and P-47s, and was first assigned to the 56th Fighter Group on the East Coast, but was transferred to the 348th Fighter Group and sent to Australia. As a member of the 342nd Fighter Squadron he shot down eight Japanese aircraft between November 1943 and February 1944.

On 23 April 1944, promoted to captain, he was transferred to the 58th Fighter Group as the Operations Officer. In May he was promoted to major, and in February 1945 became Deputy Group Commander.

On 12 March he replaced Colonel Gwen G. Atkison as Group Commander. Major Roddy spent two years in the SWPA command, with 225 combat missions, and racked up over 1,500 flight hours in his P-47D over New Guinea, the Philippines, Okinawa and Japan.

Mexican ground personnel with another loaned P-47D Razorback from the 40th FS, the 35th FG which had converted to the P-51 Mustang and passed down their P-47Ds to the 58th FG. (Reynaldo Perez Gallardo)

## THE 58TH FIGHTER GROUP

The 58th Fighter Group began its life as the 58th Pursuit Group on 15 January 1941 at Selfridge Field, Michigan. It then moveding, from base to base, started training Chinese pilots and lost a couple of squadrons to overseas duty with other groups.

The 58th started training on P-47s in 1943 and arrived in the SWPAS in November that year, flying its first mission in February 1944. The unit was used as a fighter-bomber outfit; rumour had it that Colonel Neel E. Kearby of the 348th Fighter Group didn't want competition from the 58th, and had the power to give it ground support missions instead.

The 58th served from New Guinea through the Philippines to Okinawa, earning the DUC (Distinguished Unit Citation) on the night of 26 December 1944, when two of its squadrons (the 69th and 311th) attacked a Japanese surface fleet that was heading to shell Mindoro.

Attacking this fleet with only machine-gun fire, the 58th saved the forces on Mindoro from a serious Japanese naval bombardment, losing 11 P-47s and five pilots listed as MIA (missing in action).

On 3 January 1945, during a fighter sweep in the Clark Field area, four P-47s from the 58th Fighter Group destroyed between 16 and 20 enemy fighters on the ground, lined up in preparation to escort a suicide mission. The Japanese aircraft were identified as Kawanishi N1K Shiden "George" fighters. Two P-47s were shot down, one of whose pilots was Colonel G.G. Atkinson, the group commander, who had shot down a "Dinah" twin-engine fighter before falling victim to ground fire. He evaded capture by the Japanese, and with the help of Filipinos he returned to the unit on 14 January. The other 58th pilot shot down, Lieutenant Roy 'Tex' Kindred of the 311th Fighter Squadron, was killed.

It appears that these 'George'" fighters belonged to the 341st Air Group of the Imperial Japanese Air Force, some of whose pilots flew *kamikaze* missions. This unit was reported as destroyed in the Philippines in January 1945.

The 58th was the last unit in the 5th Air Force to continue flying the P-47 in operations. At one time the 5th Air Force operated four P-47 groups, while another group, the 49th, had a single P-47 squadron.

The 5th Air Force P-47 pilots would eventually be credited with 511 aerial victories against Japanese aircraft. The top-scoring group was the 348th Fighter Group with 326 claimed victories, followed by the 35th with 165 claims, the 58th with 14 and the 9th Fighter Squadron of the 49th Fighter Group with eight.

The top-scoring pilot was Colonel Neel Kearby (who was killed in action on 6 March 1944) with 22 victories, followed by Major William Dunham with 16, Lieutenant Colonel William M. Banks with nine and Captain Walter G. Benz with eight kills, all these pilots from the 348th Fighter Group.

Later in the war, other groups such as the 35th and 348th exchanged their P-47s for the North American P-51D Mustangs. Some of those ex-35/348th P-47s were handed down to the 58th, and some of them were subsequently handed over to the 201st Fighter Squadron.

During the course of its service in the Pacific, the 58th Fighter Group flew around 2,645 combat missions and over 13,559 combat sorties, losing a total of 30 pilots killed or missing in action, with 17 more killed in operational flights not related to combat duties (including two Mexican pilots).

Its best month was January 1945, when the 58th shot down eight Japanese planes and probably destroyed between 20 and 30 on the ground, from 1,420 combat sorties flown.

The Mexican 201st Fighter Squadron was assigned to the 58th Fighter Group as per General Order No. 19, dated 2 May 1945. The 201st established its camp at Porac Field, about30 km from Manila. On the morning of 2 May, the squadron held a special presentation where the flag of the MEAF was unfurled from its protective case. Thus for the first time, a Mexican flag flew in a foreign theatre of operations at Porac, as noted in Sergeant Cervantez Ramos' memoirs:

> Once we arrived at Porac airbase within the limits of Clark Field, we proceded to put up our tents, construct our latrines, as well as septic wells, baths, headquarters, operations office, supplies, medic station etc.
>
> Our field tents accomodated four to six people and we were given field cots, as well as mosquito nets, which were mandatory to put up. Everbody worked to put up our camp, to include a small *glorieta* with a flag pole, where our flag flew every day.
>
> We gave our camp a happy touch, with flowers and pathways between the tents, which we gave names of streets like '16 de Septiembre' [and] 'Madero "o" Bolivar', [and] we also put a sign saying 'To Zocalo [the main square in Mexico City] 10,000 Km'.

At this point the organisation and the building of the 201st's camp were under the direction of Lieutenant Joaquin Ramirez Vilchis, who wrote:

> On April 30, 1945 we arrived in Manila, after the official welcome, we were taken to Porac, a place where we lived for about 4 months … We received food for a couple of days for another unit. We had to walk a distance to be able to eat.
>
> After the 3rd day I told Capt. Rivas Martinez we should already have our messhall and chowhall and the other services for the personnel and he told me 'What do you suggest?' He named me as assistant to start to organize what we need – I was made a helper and started to use the troop building latrines, fixing the kitchen, the mess hall, building the tables and the counters.
>
> The area where the squadron gathered was fixed, to be able to have roll call and read the orders of the day. At the center a flag pole was installed and around the flag pole a circle with pieces of bamboo was built and some grass was put in and a path, to be able to raise and lower the flag daily.
>
> There was plenty of help from everybody and quickly our camp became noticed. Arreola P.A (Miguel Moreno Arreola pilot) put at the entrance of the camp a big drawing of Panchito Pistolas.
>
> The orders of the day were read with other information. When we arrived it was already the raining season and the ground was not level and the tents were not properly line up, so to avoid the water from coming into the tents, dirt was put around each tent.

The Mexican personnel used wood, bamboo and other materials to build a movie house and recreation centre, with a ping-pong table and a volleyball court in which a number of matches were played when the weather permitted and the work was done for the day.

A number of interesting games were played with teams by such names as *Los Tlacuaches Del Norte* and *Los Carabaos Del Sur*. As for the movie house, it would have some impact on the security of the camp, as some of the veteran pilots remembered:

> Periodically we had a movie house on the air base, and as soon as the sun went down we [were] shown movies brought from the United States.
>
> When there was a show by magic the attacks from the enemy would stop. We didn't know the cause of that until we discovered that the Japanese would be in the jungle to watch the movies [before] later return[ing] to their trenches.

Sergeant 2nd Class Mechanic Carlos Colin Portilla recalled that the movie house had a projector mounted in the back of one of the squadron's ambulances, with two wings of an aircraft to hold up the screen. Even in the rain, the Mexicans would watch movies, wearing their steel helmets and their ponchos.

Alo Mexican personnel also undertook patrols around the camp, in case of attack by Japanese troops that were still hiding around the area, on some occasions capturing Japanese soldiers. These were luckly to be captured by the Mexicans rather than the Filipinos, as one of the ground personnel remembered:

> When we arrived at Clark Field … the Japanese kept fighting hard against the 'Gueritos' (Americans). At night the Japanese would attack the camps.
>
> We had to sleep with a pistol in our hands and having a foot outside the cot, ready to jump and defend ourselves. In the area of Clark Field, our people found a large number of Japanese cadavers; two skeletons were given as trophies to the medics of the unit, which were taken back to Mexico as sourvernirs.

Sergeant 2nd Class Gilberto de la Rosa remembered what precautions the squadron personnel took at night in the camp:

> "I was in the service, in an aviation Mexican fighter squadron in the 58th Fighter Group, Fifth Air Force. We lived in tents, which held about thirty persons each, near the airstrip in the jungle where our planes were parked ready to start daily missions.
>
> We had to sleep with our clothes on and only our boots off, the M-1 rifle beside the light bedstead. There were too many mosquitoes and snakes and there was fauna in accordance with the tropical latitude.

The alarm was sounded at night in the Mexican camp on two occasions, which sent the Mexicans to search for Japanese soldiers who had entered into the flight line, but none were found. Those Japanese soldier that were captured by Allied personnel would become the first enemy that the Mexicans saw up close, as remembered by Sergeant De La Rosa:

> He was there; standing in the middle of the hall, between two armed guards with his eyes looking at the floor … I was in my tent when suddenly I notice[d] some people who were going to the mess hall.
>
> I followed them and I saw for the first time, the enemy in front of me. His hair was black, his eyebrows heavy and his face enlarged. He had a beard. When he lifted his head up, we inspected his black eyes – like two hazelnuts, characteristic of the Asian people. He was barefoot.
>
> Probably the guards had taken his shoes to prevent escape. He wore a shirt and pants that previously had been white, but now they were gray. He had no belt around his waist. I think he felt like an animal in a zoo cage, because all of us were looking at him. In military training we saw many films to teach us to hate the enemy. They pictured the enemy as monkeys with ridiculous hats on their heads and showing big teeth like a horse.
>
> But what a deception. This man was normal! He was more or less the same age as I (20 years) and both of us had left our countries with the same thing in mind – to win the war. Life had appointed us the same place, face to face. I stopped hating him, instead thinking of his family.
>
> Probably he had a mother, a father and siblings expecting some good news of the son in the service, but now he was the representative of the Rising Sun Empire, a prisoner. When I was thinking about my relatives, the guards took the prisoner to a table

and he filled his empty stomach.

After he was finished he started to look from one side to the other. We thought, 'He is trying to escape'. He said something in Japanese but nobody knew the language. At last he asked for a piece of paper and wrote 'WC' and they took him to the rest room.

Afterwards he sat down to wait for the intelligence officers to handle the situation, and then they went away with the prisoner. For him the war was over. But war is like this: some win and some lose.

The Republic P-47D-23 42-27615 from the 35th FG and later the 58th FG, loaned to the 201st Mexican Fighter Squadron, was badly damaged by Japanese ground fire on 20 June 1945. (San Diego Aerospace Museum)

The Mexicans also witnessed the hatred the Filipinos had against any Japanese they captured:

> When the Filipino guerrillas captured Japanese, before killing him, they would torture him. They would wound him first, with a bullet in the leg, then the other, they would leave him for about two hours and later kill him with a knife.

The Filipino guerrillas showed the Mexicans the source for their hatred towards the Japanese. The story goes that a group of Mexican officers were shown a house in which the Japanese used to kill Filipino civilians, including women and children. They saw hundreds of bodies in the house. The Japanese would tell the people that at night they were giving out food in that house, but when the people got there they were killed.

## STORY OF PANCHITO PISTOLAS

While the Mexicans were setting up their camp, waiting for their aircraft and starting their pre-combat training, the squadron commander's secretary, Sergeant 2nd Class Manuel Cervantes Ramos was making trips around Porac to help get the 201st organised getting supplies, filling requisitions and getting used to the field conditions. In his many wandering through Porac, he saw USAAF aircraft painted with squadron markings, pin-ups and cartoons.

This gave Sergeant Cervantes the idea to create a unit marking for the Mexicans, and his inspiration was a Christmas card he had received from his family in December 1944, when the squadron was stationed at Pocatello.

The card featured Disney's *The Three Caballeros* (featuring the characters Donald Duck, Pedro Carioca and Panchito Pistolas) riding on a flying carpet over the Mexican countryside. At his desk he started working on a drawing, hoping that it would be applied to the squadron's aircraft. When the squadron commander, Captain Gaxiola Andrade, caught sight of this, at first he told Cervantes to put it away as there were more important issues to address.

But as the days went by and the unit was getting settled in, Gaxiola asked Cervantes to continue with the drawing. However, unknown to Cervantes and maybe even Gaxiola, one of the pilots, 2nd Lieutenant Miguel Moreno Arreola, had also hit on the idea of a squadron insignia with Panchito Pistolas.

Moreno Arreola and some of the pilots went around the wrecked Japanese aircraft that were at Porac Field and selected part of a wing of a KI-84 "Frank" fighter, and they agreed that Panchito be selected as the squadron mascot and painted on the wing to mark the entrance to the Mexican camp in Porac, and later when the 201st moved to Clark Field in August 1945.

Researching the history of the 201st, it appears that Panchito was not initially applied to the aircraft, since the first group of P-47Ds used by the squadron was loaned from the 58th Fighter Group and the aircraft were eventually returned when the Lend Lease P-47D-30-RAs started to arrive in late June 1945.

It seems these aircraft also did not have Panchito painted on them. But new information has come to light, that back in 1993 one of the former members of the squadron and president of the *Asociacion Mexicana de Veteranos de la II Guerra Mundial A.C.*, former armourer Alfonso Cuellar Ponce de Leon, replied to a Canadian aircraft researcher that Panchito 'nose art' was painted on the aircraft flown by Lieutenant Reynaldo Perez Gallardo, a natural fighter pilot, by his armourer, Sergeant 2nd Class Pedro Guerra Garcia:

> I have to make clear that the only 'nose art', as you name it, was painted by 2nd Sergeant Pedro Guerra Garcia who happened to be the armorer of the P.47 piloted by Lieutenant Reynaldo Perez Gallardo, both assigned to '*Escuadrilla* B', according to the Squadron organization.

It appears that Perez Gallardo was assigned a Republic P-47D Razorback that came from the 310th Fighter Squadron of the 58th Fighter Group, and based on photographic evidence he was probably assigned an aircraft numbered between H60 and H66. The cowlings of the 310$^{th}$'s aircraft were painted in yellow.

It is possible that Perez Gallardo used this plane for pre-combat training and later in actual combat operations until the arrival of the Lend Lease P-47D-30-RA bubble canopy aircraft.

When the war ended and the MEAF was going home in October 1945, the Panchito wing marking the entrance to the camp was not among the squadron items shipped home and was left behind at Clark Field; when the unit was based for a time at Mexico City International Airport it had to paint a new one. However, Panchito did not appear painted on the unit's aircraft until almost the end of the operational life of the P-47D-35-RA in 1958. Since then, the 201st has painted different variations of Panchito Pistolas on its aircraft, right up to the current one that graces the Beechcraft T-6C+ Texan II.

## OTHER COMFORTS

Regarding the medical service of the 201st Fighter Squadron, Major. Ricardo Blanco Cancino would later write:

> In Porac, the medical service was installed in a tent. We had shifts on duty, but a couple of kilometers away.
>
> We were prohibited to use the international red cross emblem, or any similar identification. I was even given a weapon in case of self-defense. Our [facilities were] similar to those that I [had] in the medical section of the 18th Cavalry Regiment, when this unit was in pursuit of 'El Culiche' [a bandit) in the sierra of Durango in 1939, but with more elements: with 2 ambulances and a jeep, plus equipment and material for curing [conditions] and sufficient medications.

A lot of the sick and injured Mexican personnel, including the pilots, were sent to the US medical unit at Santa Rita, where the major would make his rounds. He also visited the American field hospitals of the Sixth American Army around Baguio.

The squadron would lose the services of one of its pilots during May 1945 when 2nd Lieutenant Justino Retana Reyes was injured in a road accident, that resulted in a fractured arm, on a bridge between Manila and Angeles. The vehicle carrying Retana Reyes turned over in low visibility during torrential rain.

As for the spiritual needs of their personnel, since the Mexican armed forces did not have their own chaplains, they received visits from those of the American forces. No matter what the denomination of these chaplains (Catholic, Protestant or Jewish), the men welcomed their services and a chance to chat with the visiting priest.

Another service that would win the admiration of the Mexican personnel was the Mess Hall section. The Mexican cooks had to use all their imagination to try to convert the standard American rations, into something more flavourable and to Mexican taste. On an average day the meals consisted of the following: a breakfast: of butter, cereal, toasted bread, powdered eggs, coffee, powered milk, sugar and tomato juice; a lunch of cooked meat, vegetables, onions, mashed potatoes, cheese, apples, condiments, tea and bread; and a dinne of cooked meat, vegetables, fried potatoes, bread, cocoa, and apple pie.

The food was not great, but edible. Even some of the hungry and desperate Japanese soldiers would come out of their hiding places to sample the food, as recalled by pilots and ground personnel:

> [On] occasions we would discover them in the chow line (*Rancho*) in between the Filipinos. In some cases we shared, without knowing, the bread and salt with the enemy at the same table. Later when we found out, hell would break loose!

Three days after their arrival, while listening to the radio, which was tuned to Radio Tokyo, the Mexicans were surprised when 'Tokyo Rose' welcomed them to the Pacific with the following message, and after that played them some Mexican music:

> Welcome those of the Mexican squadron, we hope that you have many successes, but remember that you are going to have losses and they are waiting for you at home.

## PREPARATION FOR COMBAT, MAY 1945

The 201st underwent pre-combat training under the responsibility of the 58th Fighter Group, with the assistance of the 5th Fighter Command. This started on 7 May 1945 with two days of lectures. On 7 May there were lectures on the overall picture on the war fronts, SWPA forces, weather in the SWPA and fighter sector orientation, followed on the 8th by air sea rescue, escape and evasion, zones of action, the friendly ground situation and support air party.

From 9-12 May, eight Mexican pilots reported every day to the 51st Fighter Sector for practical demnostration coordination by Captain M. Williams. Other pilots received ground pre-combat training under the supervision of the operations officers of the 58th Fighter Group.

Back in the United States, the following *Associated Press* news report on 12 May, headlined 'Mexicans wait chance at Japs', reflected on the Mexican pilots waiting to fly combat operations:

> Members of the Mexican air force's 201st fighter Squadron are anxiously awaiting the arrival of Thunderbolt planes so they can get busy on the Japs said Capt. Jesus Blanco of Mexico City. Most of the squadron now housed.
>
> In a tent camp eagerly await the 'Great opportunity for the Mexican Army'.
>
> The pilots have an average of 500 hours in the air and are tired of being on the ground. The majority of the unit is from the regular army, including enlisted men.
>
> Some of them have already seen combat in Mexico.
>
> First Sgt. Miguel Castillo of Mexico City has served 24 years in the Mexican air Force. The airmen find the Philippine climate hotter than at home. Most Of them are from Mexico City.
>
> 'The training there is tougher than this' said Lt. Raul Garcia of Monterrey. One of the busiest men in the Camp is Corp. Antonio Enriquez of Mexico City, who is accustoming himself to the American army system of making combat reports.
>
> Most of the Mexicans speak fair English. One Corp. Manuel Alcantar attended the University of Southern California and lived in Los Angeles when the war started.

In a more detail newspaper article about the squadron's wait for its aircraft, mention was made of the postman, who was now handling thousands of pieces of mailthat had started to arrive for the Mexican personnel when the unit stopped at Finschhafen in New Guinea, and more mail was waiting for them in Manila.

In his civilian life the postman had a literary calling, as noted in the following Associated Press newspaper account from Clark Field that was published on 23 July under the headline 'Mexican poet in Air Force':

> One of Mexico's well-known writers and poets has put down his pen and is helping the Mexican Expeditionary air force take part in the final air blows against Japan.
>
> He's Cpl. Hugo Seaman Jimenez, formerly of Avenue Beethoven, Numero 23, Colonia Peralville, Mexico D.F. and he's assigned as a unit mail clerk in the headquarters of the 201st Fighter Squadron of the Mexican Expeditionary air force. Seaman is a graduate of the School of Arts and Professions at Guadalajara and formerly was the Director of the 'Hospital Invisible' a literary publication in Mexico City.

Mexican mechanics working on a P-47D Thunderbolt. (Manuel Cervantes Ramos)

Back on the home front, on 10 May 1945, Mother's Day in Mexico, a special ceremony was held at the Balbuena military airfield, where all the mothers and wives of the members of the MEAF were invited.

The ceremony was hosted by air force chief General Gustavo Salinas Camina and the Secretary of Public Education Jaime Torres Bodet. One person not attending the event was the mother of 2nd Lieutenant Crisoforo Salido (the 201st's first fatality back in January), but the mother of Lieutenant Javier Martinez Valle (who had died in a flying accident in March) did attend, dressed in mourning black and seated next to General Salinas.

All the attending mothers received flowers and a diploma, while a line of beauty products was offered free to all the mothers and wives by one of the department stores in the city.

The 201st was expected to complete its training between 12 May and 7 June and be ready for commitment as a combat unit. On 12 May the air training phase started, but since the Mexicans' own Lend-Lease P-47D-30-RAs had not arrived, they were allocated about a mixed bag of 20 borrowed P-47s, including some Razorback models. Lieutenant Ramirez Vilchis would write years later about these borrowed aircraft:

> The command and staff and the captains made possible the loan of 18 aircraft for the FAEM, which our mechanics started to work on … to put them back in service and test fly them.
>
> These 18 aircraft that were selected by our mechanics and by some of the pilots were in an area where they were parked, after completing their flight time and [being] flown until they were declared fatigued.

The 310th Fighter Squadron reportedly transferred over one P-47D-23 and 11 P-47D-28s (in July they would get three P-47D-28-RAs back), while the 69th Fighter Squadron reported 14 of their aircraft transferred (possibly to the 201st?). Only twenty-three aircraft have been positively identified as going to the Mexicans.

These transfers of aircraft to the 201st caused some mixed feelings for ground personnel and pilots of the 58th Fighter Group, as noted by Anthony J. Kupferer in his history of the 58th:

> The fact that the pilots and crews of the 58th Group were jealous of the preferences given to the Mexicans in supplying the best of the planes and equipment is quite evident.
>
> It had long been a standard practice that the newer aircraft were assigned to more important combat roles and the older aircraft used by the newer pilots for orientation and training flights.
>
> This practice was denied in the case of the 201st pilots. They were given new D-28 'Bubble Canopy' versions of the Thunderbolt while the squadrons were still using the old D-15 version which had now been in combat for well over a year, with hundreds of hours logged.

In fairness, however, the 201st did not receive all D-28 versions, but a mixed bag, as shown in this listing of types compiled from the squadron's records:

Model Number Type
*P-47D-11-RA 1 Razorback Version*
*P-47D-15-RA 5 " " "*
*P-47D-16-RE 2 " " "*
*P-47D-21-RA 3 " " "*
*P-47D-22-RE 1 " ' '*
*P-47D-23-RA 4 " " "*
*P-47D-28-RA 7 Bubble Canopy Version*
*Total 23*

Crew chief Staff Sergeant Ned Ailes of the 69th Fighter Squadron remembers:

> We had to give them four of our best planes – mine was one of them. It had a perculiarty [in that] the cylinder head temperature hand would hang near the 'red line', while in flight, but never go over.
>
> Guess they didn't like that. They raised such a fuss about us giving them junk that a 5th Air Force Inspector came down and personally checked out the next batch.
>
> The flight chief asked if I wanted my old plane back and I said sure. I then had two planes to take care of [for] quite a while.

Another observation comes from Staff Sergeant George E. Mayers of the same unit:

> At first they [had] no aircraft so some were selected from our outfit and transferred to the Mexicans for use until they received their own aircraft.
>
> They had American Army Air Force personnel with them acting as advisors and these people performed the acceptance inspections. For some reason, they were extremely meticulous and we really had to work to get this equipment ready for the Mexicans.
>
> As it was, the Mexican squadron had nothing but nice, shiny new vehicles and lots of equipment that we wouldn't have and then to add further insult, we were tagged with these fanatical inspectors.
>
> Then when the Mexicans got their nice, shiny new aircraft, with bubble canopies, the equipment that had been [on] loan was returned to us.
>
> The cockpit of the interiors of the returned aircraft had been changed somewhat, a very expensive and elaborate paint scheme

had been added. It served to color code various controls and systems and was quite well planned.

Even some of the veteran pilots voiced their opinion, such as Joe Madison of the 311th Fighter Squadron:

> In the Philippines, when we had the 201st Mexican Fighter squadron attached to us, though the Lend-Lease program, we had to supply planes to them, and gave them our worst planes, which they wouldn't accept. We were forced to give them our best planes.

From the 201st, 2nd Lieutenant Zenizo Rojas had the following to say about the borrowed aircraft from the 58th Fighter Group:

> When we arrived, different units of the U.S. which were operating loaned us temporarily some of their aircraft, while we awaited the arrival of the new P-47s that the Mexican government bought.
>
> By the way they didn't lend us their best aircraft, [but] later our mechanics left them in such perfect order, that the commanders of the different units would fight who would get these aircraft when we returned them.

For the Mexican mechanics, these borrowed aircraft presented a technical nightmare. The mechanics working on the flight line were exposed to the tropical heat, as Sergeant Genaro Romero Parra recalls:

> Our objective was to maintain in [as] peak efficiency as possible these machines. Many times the cowling of the engine was so hot we could not touch them, but we had to do a good job.

Another Mexican veteran, Sergeant 2nd Class Alfonso Cuellar Ponce de Leon, one of the armourers, mentioned that 15 old P-47s were given to the squadron, but the talents of mechanics like Blanco Talavera, Spindola Miranda and Galvez Perez, sergeant mechanics under the orders of Captain Jesus Carranza, left the aircraft practically new. Lieutenant Fernando Hernandez Vega would later write that the ground crew were more magicians than mechanics: "They were used to working practically with nails and they [performed] miracles, which [surprised] the Americans."

Lieutenant Reynaldo Perez Gallardo, working as a test pilot for the engineering section, test flying aircraft after they were fixed, remembers it was difficult period to get the borrowed aircraft back in flying condition and to obtain spare parts for them.

Perez Gallardo had to see Captain Radames Gaxiola or Colonel Cardenas to see what could be done about the mechanical situation of the aircraft, but did not receive a positive response from them. Perez Gallardo therefore went out at night in a jeep with some of the squadron's most trusted mechanics to remove parts from other aircraft at the field, or they would trade spare parts for their beer rations with other squadrons stationed at Porac.

Years later Perez Gallardo mentioned the role of the mechanics in getting these aircraft operational again:

> When we got there I felt the Americans looking down on us. Nothing was ever said, [but] you felt it. Our first planes were out of commission.
>
> They were mechanically unfit or damaged. Our mechanics were marvellous to get them ready. I always told my men we were not to say a word. Our time would come, and we'd show them what we could do.

Mexican ground personnel also manned anti-aircraft positions at Porac and later at Clark Field, Philippines. (Manuel Cervantes Ramos)

Some of the veteran pilots of the 58th Fighter Group had concerns about the Mexican pilots and their understanding of English in communications with ground support elements, directing the strikes against Japanese positions. Another un-named 58th pilot remarked on their struggles during missions:.

> The Mexicans at Porac had better ships than we did and did some flying as individuals with us. They lived in a separate camp some distance away and we didn't have much contact with them.
>
> They had a fair amount of trouble completing missions as I remembered and lost a fair number of men on missions.

But other pilots, like Captain Art Marston, expressed a different opinion:

> While at Porac, we had the 201st Mexican Fighter Squadron attached to our group for orientation. About half could speak English well and … the other half were weak in the use of English.
>
> We had many dive bombing missions in the Balete Pass under ground control, bombing or [dropping] smoke shells on fortified positions in front of the troops. The Japanese would shoot smoke shells into our lines, so the controller would time their targets markers.
>
> There was some concern whether the Mexicans could understand this without hitting our troops, but they apparently did well.

Mexican pilots started to fly training missions in the theatre of operations from 17 May. Flying first in American formations over the combat zone, they learned the following: familiarisation and orientation (six hours), aerial tactics and techniques of aerial combat (four hours), simulated combat missions (four hours), dive-bombing training and skip bombing, interception missions and combat missions (12 hours).

Captain 2nd Class Pablo Rivas Martinez, the executive officer, maintained a squadron diary in which he reported that from 18-20 May the squadron's pilots flew their P-47Ds for 26 hours and 20 minutes, 17 hours and 15 minutes, and 31 hours and 58 minutes respectively.

As with any training programme, a number of accidents occurred during this phase, with several aircraft damaged or destroyed due to engine or mechanical failures. Lieutenant Ramirez Vilchis noted some of the probable causes:

Mexican pilots being briefed before a flight over the Philippines. From left to right, 2nd Lieutenant Raul Garcia Mercado, Captain 1st Class Radames Gaxiola Andrade, 2nd Lieutenant Mario Lopez Portillo, Captain 2nd Class Pablo L. Martinez and 2nd Lieutenant Roberto Urias. It appears that the photo was taken at Porac Field, when the 201st still operated loan aircraft from the 58th FG. (Manuel Cervantes Ramos)

> In the second phase of our pre-combat training from May 17th, [we had] borrowed aircraft from two units that had really flown their P-47s …
>
> These aircraft were [left] out in the open and probably when they were refuelled they didn't clean their tanks well, or they were clean but the water did not [fully] evaporate in the tanks [when] they were in storage and when the fuel was being used up, and a small amount of water entered into the carburettors and the failures occurred.

The 201st did inherit a number of aircraft that had been flown in combat, which combined with normal wear and tear took its toll on the airframes, and causing engine failures. This is no criticism of the Mexican or American mechanics, who did a heck of a job to maintain the equipment under difficult working conditions, not least the weather, in the SWPA.

These borrowed P-47s kept the same markings of the 35th, 58th and 34th Fighter Groups with which they were received. Since they did not belong to the Mexicans, no Mexican markings were applied to the aircraft, except for Perez Gallardo's *Panchito Pistolas*, until the arrival of their own Lend Lease P-47D-30-RAs.

The first accident with these planes occurred on 21 May, when Lieutenant Graco Ramirez Garrido was flying the P-47D-28-RA 42-280505 at about 1230 in a training flight of five aircraft flying south-east, heading towards Porac Field at about 5,000ft. He noticed his oil pressure drop to zero, flames and smoke were coming out of the cowling and his rpm indicator was out of control. The engine started to vibrate and then stopped completely. Ramirez Garrido carried out a text book forced-landing about 3 miles north of Bagio. The pilot was unhurt, but the aircraft suffered damage to its underside, cowling, propeller blades and flaps.

The cause of the accident was determined to be mechanical failure, although an American report listed the cause as a forced-landing due to fuel shortage.

On that same day, three P-47s flown by Lieutenant Jose Luis Barbosa Cerda, Lieutenant Julio Cal Y Mayor Sauz and 2nd Lieutenant David Ceron Bedolla landed during a training flight at Camp Cringer on the island of Mondoro, but did not take off because all three aircraft suffered engine problems. The pilots returned to base until the problems were corrected.

On that day, Lieutenant Jose Espinosa Fuentes, assistant to Captain Rivas Martinez, reported that the squadron flew 18.20 hours in training.

Two days later, 2nd Lieutenant Guillermo Garcia Ramos suffered a forced-landing, about 2½ miles east of Villa de San Manuel, and east of the towns of Tarlac and San Miguel, at about 0915. His P-47D-28-RA 42- 29051 had damage to its underside, cowling, propellers and engine.

He was part of a training flight flying north of Luzon. Fifty minutes into the flight, he noticed the temperature rising in his cylinder heads, which he reported to his flight leader. After two hours of flying, and heading back to Porac, his oil pressure dropped to 50lb and the propeller control malfunctioned, oil pressure continuing to fall to 10lb and then zero, when his engine stopped. Notifying his flight leader of the problem, he made a forced-landing, escaping unhurt.

He checked the oil tank and found it empty. Mexican records list the accident cause as a mechanical failure, while the Americans record a power failure.

That same day, P-47D-15-RE 42-23225 was damaged while preparing to take off for a training mission. Both American and Mexican reports agree on the causes of the accident, which happened at about1130 when 2nd Lieutenant David Ceron Bedolla was taxiing and collided with a steamroller "due to poor visibility caused by excessive dust and carelessness".

Ceron Bedolla was unhurt, but the aircraft required a new engine and propeller. Since it was determined that pilot error played a part, Ceron Bedolla was suspended from flying for eight days.

The next day, 24 May, 2nd Lieutenant Mario Lopez Portillo became the first Mexican pilot to be rescued by the SAR (Search and Rescue) service when his P-47D-15-RE 27877 (American sources say it was a D-25) went down in Manila Bay. There are different accounts of what happened, one from 1st Lieutenant Ken G. Larson of the 69th Fighter Squadron, who was the flight leader, given in William Tudor's dissertation on the history of the 201st:

> On May 24 Larson and his wingman, 201 pilot Lopez Portillo, came down into the Bay to kick up a little spray.
>
> As they thundered across the bay, Portillo positioned his plane slightly below Larson. When Larson brought his plane closer to the

The Christmas postcard that Sergeant 2nd Class J-62 Manuel Cervantes Ramos received from his family while at Pocatello AAFB, Idaho, that gave him the idea to make Panchito Pistolas the squadron mascot. (Manuel Cervantes Ramos)

white caps, Portillo as if challenged, dropped still closer.

Finally Portillo dropped so low that he flew his plane into the water. Fortunately it did not kill him and he was rescued, but he lost a valuable plane.

For whatever reason, Lieutenant Hector Espinoza Galvan believed that the Portillo accident came about because of engine problems. There are no accident reports to verify this supposition however.

There is an accident report on the Portillo crash from squadron records that states that during a low navigation flight over Manila Bay by a formation of four aircraft, Portillo's P-47's engine coughed several times; he checked his instruments and fuel, and found that both pressure and temperature of the oil were high.

As he was about to notify his flight leader of his intention to return back to Porac to make an emergency landing, he heard an explosion, his engine stopped and he tried to restart it with no success. He made a forced-landing in the bay, got out of the aircraft and dived into the water, but his lifeboat failed to inflate. While in the water he saw the other three P-47s of his flight circling above him, along with a Stinson L-5. There was also a Douglas C-47 of the 3rd Emergency Rescue Squadron; its navigator, Don W.Campbell, wrote the following about the incident:

> In June 1945, flying from Mindoro to Floridablanca, P.I. I observed a P-47 crash into Manila Bay.
>
> The parachute from the plane was also observed. My home base unit was the 3rd emergency rescue squadron. Had we been in an OA-10 (PBY) we could have effected the fastest rescue on record.
>
> However [we were] in a C-47 [so] we circled the pilot who was in a life raft until rescue boats from shore arrived. The pilot of the C-47 (I was the navigator) did call the rescue boat people and then learned it was a Mexican Air Force plane. I understood the Mexican pilot was rescued O.K.

Lopez Portillo was in the water about 15 minutes before he was picked up by a rescue boat and taken to Manila to a US military hospital for treatment for some minor injuries.

Colonel Cardenas reported the loss of the P-47 as follows:

> Total loss, fell into the sea could not be recovered. According to the declarations of the pilot which appears in the report, the crash was due to failure and stoppage of the motor while flying above the water.

Lieutenant Ramirez Vilchis later added his observations of this incident:

> On the 24 of May SubTte. Mario Lopez Portillo force landed away from the coast due to engine failure. Luckly for him where he fell in the sea there was a wooden box and holding to it he was rescued by the Rescue Squadron. The aircraft had the three digits 877 in its long number.

That day in question, Ramirez Vilchis recalled he had problems with another aircraft after landing from a training mission, which proved the last straw for him:

> [A]fter a training flight and landing and testing the brakes one by one he noted that the right brake did not respond and the left one [only] did by gradual pressure.
>
> Joaquin Ramirez Vilchis decided to stop the engine and gradually step on the left brake to climb an incline in the terrain on that side of the aircraft that stopped the aircraft by itself, and the mechanics from the squadron came for the aircraft to take it back to the flight line.
>
> [ … A]fter the accidents [that] had occurred Vilchis decided to get admitted to the hospital in Clark Field and stay until the aircraft were checked. Daily he was visited by the commander of Flight 'C' and the chief of flight operations P. Rivas to ask him to leave the hospital.
>
> His answer was I didn't come here to die like that! When he

The inside of the Christmas card that Sergeant Cervantes received at Pocatello AAFB, Idaho. (Manuel Cervantes Ramos)

left the hospital to do his missions, the status of the aircraft had improved due to the changes in parts; the training had been suspended for four days, flights [starting] again on the 29 of May.

After these accidents, all fighter training was suspended on 25th May to give time for a complete check-over and maintenance of the remaining P-47s, which lasted about four days. As for the lost aircraft, Colonel Cardenas wrote:

> The materiel which suffered damage as well as that which was lost belongs to the lot assigned to the squadron for its training and operations.
>
> Therefore the plane losses have been placed on the Lend Lease account to be charged to Mexico, but not the replaced motors, which as was stated, have been returned and have to be considered as exchanges, the same as planes in similar conditions.

Flying was resumed on the 30th, on which day the Mexican pilots flew a total of 59 hours and 35 minutes. The total flying hours for the whole of May was 281 hours and 16 minutes.

CHAPTER 10

# GOING TO WAR II: THE MEAF AND THE LIBERATION OF THE PHILIPPINES

## INTO COMBAT, JUNE 1945

This month started badly for the 201st, when on the first day they lost their first pilot. This tragic honour fell to 2nd Lieutenant Fausto Vega Santander, who was killed in a dive-bombing training mission off the coast of Subic Bay.

His death that was reported as a training accident, but years later some pilots claimed that he was killed in the unit's first combat mission.

## THE DEATH OF A MEXICAN PILOT

The story of Vega Santander losing his life in combat, circulated by some of the surviving Mexican pilots, has received attention from American writers and was published in various aviation magazines, including the *Air Force Times* in the United States, also being repeated in a number of documentaries.

Since this story contradicts published accounts of the unit's history, the author was moved to search for information from the United States, Mexico and even Japan.

The story goes that the squadron's first casualty in the Philippines theatre of operations was killed during the unit's first combat mission on 1 June 1945, while dive-bombing a Japanese ammunition dump at Vigan on the west coast of northern Luzon.

The story tells of a mission lead by Lieutenant Carlos Garduno Nunez (B Flight leader), with 2nd Lieutenant Miguel Moreno Arreola, 2nd Lieutenant Praxedis Lopez Ramos and 2nd Lieutenant Vega Santander. This account begins with the 201st Mexican Fighter Squadron commander, Captain 1st Class Radames Gaxiola Andrade, requesting that a special mission be assigned to his unit. Supposedly, an order came down from General George C. Kenney, Commander of the Far Eastern Air Forces, to hit the Japanese ammunition dump protected by anti-aircraft guns at Vigan.

This particular target had been giving the USAAF a hard time since it was located on a beach surrounded by steep ridges. This mission was assigned to the Mexicans because a number of them, including

Lieutenant Garduno, had received dive-bombing training in Douglas SBD dive-bombers at North Island Naval Air Station, San Diego, back in 1944.

Since the American command felt the Mexicans could do the job, Garduno was approached by Captain Gaxiola, who asked if it was possible to carry out the mission using the P-47 as a dive-bomber. At first Garduno said it was impossible, but after some simulated dive-bombing runs he returned and informed Gaxiola the mission could be done. Garduno selected three pilots and reportely they were briefed by a 5th Air Force A-2 (Intelligence) officer before and after the mission. The *Air Force Times* picks up the story:

> The target, a Japanese ammunition dump well protected by anti-aircraft guns was surrounded on three sides by steep ridges, and on the fourth by the sea near Subic bay on the west coast of Luzon, a Philippine island.
>
> As 1st Lt. Carlos Garduno crossed the steep ridges while leading his flight of four P-47s, he rolled his Thunderbolt over, put the nose down into a steep dive and then leveled his wings.
>
> With the target in his sights, his airspeed at virtual terminal velocity and the altimeter unwinding, he [released] his two 1,000 pound bombs over the Japanese warehouse. With both hands, Garduno pulled the stick back into his lap, his plane clearing the water at the bottom of his dive with 500 feet to spare.
>
> As he climbed back to altitude, he looked over his shoulder delighted to see columns of black smoke shooting up from the target. Unexpectedly, he also noticed a roiling ring of white water on the Vigan beach 300 feet from the shore.
>
> A Japanese antiaircraft gunner had claimed his wingman Fausto Vega, on his 20th and last birthday. It was June 1, 1945 and 'Cacho' [Vega Santander], the youngest pilot in the squadron, was the first and only Mexican Air Force pilot to lose his life by direct enemy action in World War II.

The third pilot in the formation, 2nd Lieutenant Moreno Arreola, who was behind 'Cacho', gave the following account to the Mexican aviation magazine *America Vuela* (No.12, November 1993):

> I was behind 'Cachito' in the middle of the strong antiaircraft fire, when his aircraft was hit near the cockpit.
>
> I thought that something came out of the wounded P-47 which pulled to the right to crash into the sea. Garduno reprimanded me for leaving the formation, to fly over the area of the crash, while the Japanese were still firing at us, but only saw the yellow Mae West [life jacket] of my friend floating.

But there is another key eyewitnesses to these events who is not mentioned by Garduno and Moreno Arreola, the overall leader of the mission, who was killed in a flying accident just four days later.

Lieutenant Jose Espinosa Fuentes told a diferent version of that day's events when he made a written statement to Captain 2nd Class Pablo L. Rivas Martinez, the 201st's executive and intelligence officer. He writes that the 201st was still in its pre-combat training period, undertaking dive-bombing practice missions as outlined in the American training programme, carried out under the supervision of the 58th Fighter Group. Espinosa Fuentes reported as follows:

> On today's date, at 10:40 hours, we took off from Porac Field in a formation of two sections (8 aircraft) on a dive bombing training mission.
>
> After making the second pass at the target, I observed one of the aircraft of the 2nd section in a dive. I lost sight of him near the surface of the water, but this was followed immediately by an explosion.
>
> The time was 11:15 hours. I ordered the aircraft to form up and received the report from Lt. P. A. Carlos Garduno Nunez who was in charge of the 2nd section, that 2Lt. Fausto Vega Santander was missing.
>
> I put into operation the emergency radar and contacted Fighter Control Station WEWAK to report the accident and gave them the position of the crash which was about 2 miles SW of the Tabones Islands (Lat. 120 63' E Long. 14 49' N).
>
> I ordered Lt. Garduno to take command of the flight while I circled the area until the arrival of a P-51. I indicated where the aircraft fell and gave him the information on what I had seen.
>
> He replied that the only thing he saw was a small oxygen tank and oil slick. I got in contact with the Fighter Control Station telling them of the presence of the P-51 and they informed me that a rescue boat had been sent out.
>
> In my personal opinion, the cause of the accident was [a] high velocity stall while recovering abruptly from a dive. The lost machine was a P-47D serial number 42-232228.

Moreno Arreola gave the following statement after his return from this mission, which conflicts with the quote attributed to him in the aviation magazine:

> Today, 1 June 1945 at 10:40 A. M. I took off on a training flight as No. 3 man in the flight lead by 1st Lt. CARLOS GARDUNO NUNEZ. Upon arriving at the zone where our dive bombing practice was to take place, and when going thru my second dive at the target, I noticed that the ship ahead of me piloted by 2nd Lt. FAUSTO VEGA SANTANDER was going thru a barrell roll to the left, immediately after attempting to pull out of his dive [and the] next thing I saw was the ship crashing in the water in a inverted position and exploding.

When Lieutenant Raul Rodriguez Corona returned to Mexico City early due to sickness, in a newspaper interview he told the following story about the death of Fausto Vega Santander:

> They left early in a bombing mission. During breakfast Vega's [birthday] party was organized – that day was his first as a pilot – there was beer, whiskey, mole and Enchiladas Mexicanas.
>
> 'We will celebrate when I return,' said Vega Santander. Hours later the flight returned, one machine was missing. Everybody went to the flight line, and the men that were flying the Mexican P-47s were crying.
>
> Vega Santander ... could not celebrate his party. 'Charro' Cardenas ordered that everything proceed as if nothing happened. It was hard but we did it and they kept doing it every time a plane did not return, doing it up to six times more.
>
> This was important to us, for each one in particular. It's horrible to think about a friend who was having breakfast with us, and by midday he wasn't [returning] to eat [with us] because he was in the middle of the ocean in his tomb of a seven ton aircraft.

Lieutenant Fernando Hernandez Vega later made the following entry in his diary (in English) for 1 June:

> Today was a terrible bad day for us in general. During a dive bombing mission Lt. F. Vega S. did a high speed stall into the ocean.

At the suggestion of Sergeant Cervantes and 2nd Lieutenant Miguel Moreno Arreola, Panchito Pistolas was painted on the wing of a Japanese fighter to mark the entrance to the Mexican squadron at Porac Field. (Family of Captain Paul B. Miller)

When the 201st moved to Clark Field in August 1945, Panchito was moved there to mark the Mexican area. From left to right, Colonel Antonio Cardenas Rodriguez, Alfredo Carmelo and Captain 1st Class Radames Gaxiola Andrade. (Enrique Velasco Padilla)

> His plane exploded. Up to this afternoon his body hadn't been found … I didn't get to fly.

Another surviving member of 'B' Flight that took part in that day's mission mentioned to the author that the whole flight flew that day. Lieutenant Reynaldo Perez Gallardo said that he witnessed Fausto Vega's fatal crash into the water off the Tabones Islands and recalled the cries of his fellow flight members that 'Cachito' had gone down.

Lieutenant Perez Gallardo overflew the area where the plane of 'Cachito' crashed into the sea, seeing only debris and bubbles and sensing that the pilot had not survived the crash. As this was seen as an open and shut case of an accident, only the statements of Espinosa Fuentes and Miguel Moreno Arreola were used to complete the paperwork submitted to American and Mexican officials.

Another of the Mexican pilots, Lieutenant Joaquin Ramirez Vilchis, added his own opinion concerning the probable causes of the accidental death of Fausto Vega Santander:

> On June 1, 1945 a fatal accident occurred [involving] SubTte. P.A. Fausto Vega S. when [he] drop[ped] his bombs on a point over the sea near an island, where supposedly [there] was a submarine.
>
> [It was a] maneuver we had practiced during our training in the USA. The pilot aviators who had been in the naval base of Corpus Christie and others knew how to do the dive and at what altitude to let go of the bombs to [ensure] the splinters would not damage the aircraft or kill the pilot.
>
> In these cases [there are several] probable causes [of an accident]: if a one thousand pound bomb stays attached to the aircraft, the plane has the tendency to fall in that direction; [it is] also very important for the pilot to have a clear view outside [the aircraft] and a short pilot could not see the proximity to the surface of the water; or if the aircraft is heavy on that side and [the] pilot does not have sufficient strength [it is] very dangerous to dive too low.

On the day of the incident, the 201st's Engineering Section, headed by Captain Jesus Carranza Hernandez, made a report which included the following:

> TO: Operations Officers, 201st Mexican Fighter Squadron,
> A. P. O. 74.
>
> 1.- In compliance with the operations memorandum 54, 19 July 1944, the following information is submitted:
> A. – DATE OF ACCIDENT: st June 1945
> B. – TYPE OF AIRCRAFT AND SERIAL NUMBER: P-47D-15 A. C. S. 42-23228
> C. – EXTENT OF DAMAGE: Aircraft completely lost, airplane crashed in sea.
> D. – DISPOSITION: No Disposition
> E. – ANALYSIS OF EVIDENCE INDICATING MATERIAL FAILURE OR LACK OF SUCH FAILURE: No Material Failure.

At about 1:00 p.m., a Military Judicial Affidavit was prepared by Captain 2nd Class Quartermaster Samuel Rafeal Pacheco, along with Signal Corps Lieutenant Samuel Raul Rodriguez Carreon and Infantry Lieutenant Jesus Tapia Estrada.

Taken under oath, the statements of Espinosa Fuentes and Moreno Arreola were written in the affidavit and signed by both pilots, and later sent to Mexico City.

On 2 June, the American report of the accident, marked 'Priority Secret' and signed by United States Air Corps 1st Lieutenant Charles J. Fly, was published by the 58th Fighter Group for inclusion in their records, which included the following:

> IN COMPLIANCE WITH V FIGHTER COMMAND MENO 62-1 DATED 11 OCTOBER 1944 THE FOLLOWING AIRCRAFT ACCIDENT REPORT ISSUBMITTED:
>
> A. P-47D-15 42-23228
> B. TRAINING Mission
> C. 201st MEXICAN FIGHTER SQUADRON, 58TH FIGHTER GROUP
> D. ½ MILE SW TABONES ISLAND 1 JUNE 1945 1115 HOURS
> E. 2nd LT VEGA S FAUSTO 313437. FATAL COM TIME: NONE
> F. PILOT TRIED TO RECOVER FROM HIGH SPEED STALL. AIRCRAFT EXPLODED UPON CRASHING INTO THE WATER.
> G. COMPLETE LOSS"

On that same day, Captain Radames Gaxiola signed and submitted the following statement, again marked 'Secret':

> RADAMES GAXIOLA ANDRADE, serial number 259974 Capt. 1/o. P. A. of the Mexican Army and commander of the 201st Squadron of the Mexican Expeditionary Air Force. Certify that 2nd Lt. P. A. FAUSTO VEGA SANTANDER, serial number 313437, killed in a aerial accident near the coast of the Philippines was receiving from the pay officer of the MEAF, the amount of $366.89 (USD) corresponding to his wages of a 2nd Lt. P. A. authorized to the pilots of his rank, serving in my command. At the same time same officer received via the Dept. of Aeronautics the sum of $560.00 pesos corresponding to his salary and extra benefits financed by the pay officer of the MEAF until June 30 of this year. Unknown is the status of payments to his family in Mexico City. In view that no proof has been sent to this squadron.

Attempts were made to recover the body, but without success, as noted in a message sent from Colonel Cardenas to General Luis Alamillo Flores, Mexican military attache in Washington DC, dated 6 June:

> Second Lieutenant Fausto Vega Santander, serial number 313453, killed in course of mission. It has not been possible to locate remains. Necessary reports will be sent soon as possible.

In his monthly report to the Secretary of National Defense, Mexico City, dated 1 July, Cardenas also noted:

> June 1, P-47 D-15 serial number 42-23228 completely destroyed and lost in the sea when it did not come out of a dive made in bombing practice. The pilot, 2nd Lt. P. A. Fausto Vega Santander, was killed.

In March 1946, Captain 2nd Class Amadeo Castro Almanza, operations officer and acting 201st Squadron commander, submitted a report on all combat missions flown by the Mexican pilots. These were just short summaries with no pilot's names. This report was later sent to the United States Embassy in Mexico City, and is now part of the historical records of the USAF.

They indicate that the actual start of combat missions was on 4 June 1945, when the Mexican pilots were attached to every flight of the 69th, 310th and 311th Fighter Squadrons for them to start gaining first-hand experience, since their pre-combat training had not ended until the previous day.

Japanese Army forces around Vigan recorded no details of any incident which could match the suggested operation which led to the death of Fausto Vega Santander. The National Institute for Defence Studies in Tokyo wrote to the author with the following:

> With regards to your inquiries, I could not find any records of USAF bombing attack against [the] Japanese Army in the area of Vigan, Northern Luzon. The area of Vigan [on the] Northwestern coast of Luzon, fell into the hands of U. S. Armed forces on 19th April.
>
> In the begining of February, Japanese 19th Division placed their fortified positions in the area of TANGADO about 20 – 30 km [east inland] from Vigan. On the 19th April, this division received the orders from Headquarters of the 14th Army to abandon their positions and retreat [inland].
>
> According to the book titled *General Kenney Report, A Personal History of the Pacific War*, the Commander of The MEAF with the 201st Mexican Fighter Squadron landed at Manila in the afternoon of May 1st. That is to say, [the] Mexican Air Force arrived in Luzon after the fall of Vigan. [The] Mexican Fighter Squadron proceeded to Clark Field and they underwent a course of Advanced combat training before getting into combat action.

The 58th Fighter Group did carry out a mission to Vigan on 19 April, involving four Thunderbolts of the 311th Fighter Squadron, each carrying two 1,000lb bombs (although one P-47 did not complete the mission due to blown tyre on take-off). The remaining three P-47s were directed to bomb a large warehouse building on the north bank off the Abra River about 4 miles east of Vigan city. Some of the bombs fell short of the target, while others overshot, causing little or no damage to the building, the pilots reporting it as an unsuccessful mission.

Another point that warrants consideration is that US Marine Corps dive-bomber groups were based in the Philippines at this time, MAG (Marine Air Group) 24 and 32 operating Douglas SBD-6 Dauntless and later Curtiss SB2C Helldiver dive-bombers. These US units could have carried out the dive-bombing mission against the ammunition dump at Vigan that Lieutenant Garduno claims was handed down to him.

Noted Filipino aviation historian Albert Anido (a reserve captain in the Philippine Air Force) also casts doubt on Garduno's story, writing:

> Tabones Island is off Subic Bay, and was used as a target range. Perharps this is where Lt. Vega lost his life, as Vigan is too far away north and was liberated by U. S. Forces in the middle of April.

Fausto Vega Santander's death cerificate lists his death as an aviation accident, and was registered in Mexico City civil registry book #640, Foja 130, on 6 June 1946. There is no grave for Vega Santander, but there are a number of monuments to him. One of them is in his home town of Tuxpan, Veracruz, where in 1946 the local airport was named in his honour 'Teniente Vega Santander'.

## OPERATIONAL SITUATION IN NORTHERN LUZON

The official history of the 58th Fighter Group has the following to say about its operations at the beginning of June:

> Operationally, the early part of the month of June was merely a continuation of the past month. The 58th continued to strike designated targets in both the Ipo Dam area and along the northern front.
>
> The 25th and 32nd Divisions had overrun the Santa Fe Area north of Balete Pass by the last of May and were now moving rapidly up the Cagayan Valley.
>
> Missions on this northern front could no longer be termed as close ground support, but rather were really armed reconnaissance, as the infantry was advancing so rapidly that close support could not be given in safety. In many instances 58th Group planes ranged several miles ahead of our forward positions, knocking out gun positions, caves, bridges, armor concentrations and strafing all buildings and transportations along the roads.

The SAP (Support Aircraft Party) had several teams out in the field at this time liaising between ground and aerial units and had many different code names, as revealed by the 201st Squadron's mission reports.

Lieutenant Dryden E. Moon, a SAP controller known by the code name 'ZOMBIE', was with the 25th Infantry Division. The following describes the role he played as SAP:

> SAP ZOMBIE recommends that pilots continue to follow the instructions of the SAP implicitly as he knows the exact location of enemy troops as well as those of our most advanced patrols.
>
> The angle of turn or direction after the bomb run has been made should be as nearly as possible to that angle or direction designated by the SAP because it takes into consideration the possibility of hang up bombs etc. ZOMBIE cleary points out that his job is to help the pilots. If the SAP gives a suggested bombing run but the flight leader feels it endangers pilots' safety notify the SAP and he will suggest another angle for the bomb run or assign another target.
>
> ZOMBIE points out those flights should be over the target area at designated times [and] no later. Many of these attacks are closely coordinated with the infantry, and the doughboys come in right after our bombing. A timetable is set up for the infantry to take the objective and is coordinated with simultaneous attacks by other

infantry units in the area. Thus if our planes are late in getting to the target the entire timetable is thrown off and confusion results.

This SAP states that information relative to new targets is gathered from POWs and observations made by our infantry patrols. He says also that an accurate estimate of enemy troops killed by our bombing attack is just about impossible as the Japs bury their dead immediately.

It is also hard to determine whether out bombs [or] artillery shells are the exact cause of enemy killed. It is known however that our attacks have accounted for many enemy dead. ZOMBIE says that SAP will not give favorable comments after an attack unless it is deserved and also states that if the bombing is 'lousy' flight leaders will be told it is 'lousy'.

As a final statement the SAP ZOMBIE says that flight leaders must always clear with him before making a strafing pass and that on all missions to date cooperation between the 58th Fighter Group and SAP has been remarkable.

Meanwhile, training continued for the 201st on 2 June, as reported by Captain Rivas Marinez, who wrote:

I have the honour to inform you that on today's date, a total of 42 hours and 10 minutes were flown by the pilot personnel of the squadron.

Lieutenant Fernando Hernandez Vega also wrote of the activities for that day in his diary:

Flew an early morning mission [with] 2x 250 lb bombs – made fair hits on water target – 2 hrs. Lt. R.P.G made a force landing at Erqruse [*sic*] and almost crashed into 2 P-51s taking off.

During the afternoon I set up the private shower. The 'summer house' was finished today. Had a cloud burst tonight … our place is [okay].

The pilot that Hernandez Vega was referring to in his diary was Lieutenant Reynaldo Perez Gallardo, but nothing is noted in the squadron reports about his forced landing. On 3 June, Lieutenant Graco Ramirez Garrido, who joined the squadron two days later, was forced to land on Nielson Field on account of bad weather, but was unhurt.

On the same day at about 8:45 a.m. Lieutenant Carlos Rodriguez Corona nosed over P-47D-11-RE 42-23109 after landing from a dive-bombing training mission. The accident happened due to his sudden application of the brakes to avoid a collision with a truck full of troops on the taxiway. It was determined that the incident's blame was equally shared between the pilot and the truck driver, but Rodriguez Corona was suspended from flying for three days.

The second fatality suffered by the Mexicans occurred on 5 June, when Lieutenant Jose Espinosa Fuentes was killed. He was the assistant to Captain 2nd Class Pablo L. Rivas Martinez in the Operations, Intelligence and Flights section and was tasked to test fly P-47D-28-RA 42-28528. This aircraft had been flown in a previous training mission by Lieutenant Joaquin Ramirez Vilchis, who reported in notes supplied by his family that the engine overheated and he was forced to land on an emergency airstrip:

There the mechanics filled the engine with oil and indicated that the last flight of this aircraft would be back to Porac.

Tte. Ramirez Vilchis made it back to Porac, with the engine almost to the point of exploding; he reported the problem to engineering.

Later on June 5, when he was preparing for another mission, he found his friend Tte. Jose Espinosa Fuentes: 'Whats new compadre?' asked Ramirez. 'I am going to test fly 528,' responded Espinosa, as he headed for the flight line. 'That cannot be, that aircraft has a bad engine, reported as inservicible,' warned Ramirez Vilchis, before boarding his plane.

Another witness to Espinosa Fuentes taking off was Major Ed Roddy, who recalled:

At Porac (I don't remember who was with me) I was near the ramp area at the end of the runway, and one of the 201st birds was checking his mags.

The drop in the RPM was obvious to me and I mentioned that this was the place to find engine problems – not after you got in the air.

Well I was dumfounded when the plane taxied into position and started its takeoff, still missing badly. This was Espinosa and he died when his plane hit the sugar mill.

Another pilot, Lieutenant Samano Pina, wrote the following about the Espinosa crash, which happened at 5:16 p.m.:

On take-off, his engine failed. He could have save himself, if he had gone straight in a forced landing without turning as specified in the aviation manuals. But in front of him was a military camp and instead of crashing on the troops Tte. Espinosa turned to the right, crashing into various obstacles (the Pampanga Sugar Mills) [and] he burned to death, near the town of Florida Blanca, Luzon June 5, 1945.

Captain Gaxiola immediately sent Captain 2nd Class Roberto Legorreta Sicilia and Lieutenant Hector Espinosa Galvan to the 58th Fighter Group operations centre and control tower to confirm this tragic event and recover the personal effects of the pilot.

An accident investigation team was formed and was sent to the crash site. When Captain Legorreta Sicilia and Lieutenant Espinosa Galvan arrived at the scene, the team was composed of Lieutenant William W. Kester, Lieutenant Sheridan Kenny of USAAF ground liaision and Sergeant 1st Class Aurelio Becerra Suarez, chief mechanic for 'B' flight. American ground troops stationed around the sugar mill, who witnessed the crash, told the team what they saw:

They saw an aircraft coming from the northeast, observing said aircraft 'derrapando' (skidding) and the engine working, then the engine cut and the aircraft fell crashing into three railroad cars [and] exploding.

Interviewing other personnel they said they noted fire on the top part of the engine and [the aircraft] was completely stopped, 'derrapando' to the right, [then] suddenly the aircraft stalled falling on its nose and right wing, did a bounce and then exploded …

The central section where the gas tanks were located was completely burned; they were informed that [it] was necessary to remove that section to rescue the remains of Teniente Piloto Aviador Jose Espinosa Fuentes, whose body had been removed when they arrived at the scene of the accident … Tte.P.A. Hector Espinosa Galvan [recovered] a boxed clock that said officer carried, the hands on the clock stopped exactly at 17.16 hours.

Lieutenant Jacobo Estrada Luna was then tasked to arrange the

Mexican ground personnel on guard duty at the entrance to the Mexican camp at Clark Field with a disarmed Japanese bomb. (Manuel Cervantes Ramos)

funeral at the distribution point of the 6th Infantry Division, with Major Ricardo Blanco Cancino carrying out the medical report, Lieutenant Jesus Tapia Estrada going with a platoon of troops to the American cemetary No.2 in Manila, and

Captain 2nd Class Jesus Carranza Hernandez to do the accident report. The medical report, signed by Major Blanco Cancino on that same day, gave the cause of death as fractures to the spine and general third-degree burns and incineration below the knees and hands.

Ramirez Vilchis did not know about the fatal accident until returning from his mission:

> After a five hour flight we returned to base and went to eat. I found the crowd was small and very quiet. I asked 'why so quiet?' 'Didn't you know...' He didn't finish talking, because I knew that Jose Espinosa had fallen, [and] 528 had crashed.
>
> "'Did you know about it?' I didn't answer, [and] without eating I went to maintenance and I was told that the squadron commander had ordered 528 to be test flown [taking] no regard [of] my report, [and] on take-off he had lost power and Tte. J. Espinosa had lost his life.

Colonel Cardenas mentioned the accident in his monthly report to Mexico:

> June 5. P-47D-28, serial number 42-28528, completely destroyed, having caught fire, probably because of loss of power in the motor during take-off. The pilot, Lt. P. A. Jose Espinosa Fuentes was killed.

After the death of Espinosa Fuentes, Major Roddy went to see Captain Gaxiola:

> I looked up Gaxiola to express my condolences, and noticed that the Mexican flag was still at the top of the flagpole.
>
> I questioned him about this, explaining him what our procedure was. He told me he would call Col. Cardenas and let me know.
>
> About an hour later, he stopped by to tell me that the Mexican flag [did not] come down half-mast unless some great statesman died.
>
> I told him since the 201st was part of our outfit we were going to lower the Stars and Stripes as a tribute to our fallen comrade. It was his turn to be awed.

Lieutenant Carlos Garduno Nunez later claimed that he and Radames Gaxiola visited the crash site that same night. After checking what was left of '528', Garduno claimed the following:

> The trim tab on the vertical part of the aircraft rudder was positioned to the extreme right, an abnormal and critically unsafe position. Either the pilot, in error, used the trim tab incorrectly and created an extremely dangerous flying condition or a mechanic had reversed the control mechanism of the trim tab.

So far there are no official documents, either Mexican or American, to support this claim. All witnesses said that the probable cause of the accident was engine failure.

The remains of Espinosa Fuentes, having been recovered, were buried at the No.2 American cemetery in Manila. After the end of the war his remains were taken back to Mexico City.

It should be noted that on the same day as his fatal crash, Espinosa Fuentes had flown a combat mission in the morning, a two-hour flight in the Aritao region.

His recently discovered flight record shows he had a total of four hours and 30 minutes in combat missions, and he had flown a total of 23 hours in the Philippines.

The day after the funeral, Captain Carranza, the squadron's chief of engineering, wrote his accident report, which included the following:

> SUBJECT: Statement of Accident
> TO: Operations Officer, 201st Mexican Fighter Squadron A.P.O. 74
>
> 1. – In compliance with Operations Memorandun 5A, 19-July 1944, the following information is submitted.
>
> A. – Date of accident – 5 June 1945
> B. – Aircraft type and ser. No. – P-47D-28, 42-28528.
> C. – Extent of damage – Aircraft burned, completely lost.
> D. – Disposition – Aircraft burned.
> E. – Analysis of evidence indicating material failure or lack of such failure. – Investigation reveals no failure of movable or fixed surfaces, probable cause of failure due to lack of engine power.

The Mexican pilots officially started to participate in actual combat missions on 4 June with the 58th Fighter Group, as noted in the history of the 311th Fighter Squadron:

> On the 4th June, the 201st Mexican Fighter Squadron, which up to this time had flown only local training missions, began assigning one pilot per flight to fly combat missions with the other squadrons in the group, to gain the experience necessary for handling the operations of their own missions. The 201st flew with the 311th on missions into the Cagayen Valley for approximately three days.

By this time the 201st Squadron was organised in four flights, composed as follows:

'A' Flight '*Aguilas Aztecas*' (Aztec Eagles):
Captain 2nd Class Roberto Legorreta Sicilia, with six pilots.
Lieutenant Fernando Hernandez Vega
Lieutenant Carlos Varela Landini
Lieutenant Graco Ramirez Garrido
2nd Lieutenant Jose Luis Pratt Ramos
2nd Lieutenant Miguel Uriarte Aguilar
2nd Lieutenant David Ceron Bedolla
'B' Flight '*Condores*' (Condors):
Lieutenant Carlos Garduno Nunez, with six pilots.

Lieutenant Julio Cal y Mayor Sauz
Lieutenant Reynaldo Perez Gallardo
2nd Lieutenant Miguel Moreno Arreola
2nd Lieutenant Praxedis Lopez Ramos
2nd Lieutenant Fausto Vega Santander
2nd Lieutenant Angel Sanchez Rebollo

'C' Flight '*Gavilanes*' (Sparrow Hawks):
Lieutenant Hector Espinoza Galvan, with seven pilots.
Lieutenant Joaquin Ramirez Vilchis
Lieutenant Carlos Rodriguez Corona
Lieutenant Amador Samano Pina
2nd Lieutenant Raul Garcia Mercado
2nd Lieutenant Guillermo Garcia Ramos
2nd Lieutenant Manuel Farias Rodriguez

'D' Flight (name unknown):
Lieutenant Amadeo Castro Almanza, with six pilots.
Lieutenant Jacobo Estrada Luna
Lieutenant Jose Luis Barbosa Cerda
2nd Lieutenant Mario Lopez Portillo
2nd Lieutenant Roberto Urias Aveleyra
2nd Lieutenant Jaime Zenizo Rojas
2nd Lieutenant Justino Retana Reyes

Among the Mexican flight crews, one tent was known unofficially as the '*Acuario*' (Aquarium), based on the nicknames of some of the pilots based there: Lieutenant Amadeo Castro Almanza, known as '*Camaron*' (Shrimp); 2nd Lieutenant Manuel Farias Rodriguez, '*Pescado*' (Fish); 2nd Lieutenant Angel Sanchez Rebollo, '*Sapo*' (Frog); and 2nd Lieutenant Jaime Zenizo Rojas, '*Pato*' (Duck).

On 4 June, about 20 Mexican pilots participated in five combat missions, as shown in the mission reports. In the first ones, there is no mention of the Mexican pilots' participation.

The first day of combat for the Mexicans started early at 6:20 a.m., continuing through five missions until 1:00 p.m.

**Mission No.1**: 4 June 1945
FFO 155-B-6 Mission Number 9-879
4 June 1945 69th Fighter Squadron
11 P-47s
Bomb and strafe target #6, Artillery and mortar positions in the Aritao area. Mission completed.
TO 0620/ I TOT 0650/I – 0750/I. Altitude from deck up to 6,000.
Landed 0815/I
11 aircraft dropped 22x1,000lb bombs on hillside and in ravine designated as target #6 , located on west side of Highway 5, two miles south of ARITAO. Bombing was done through low hanging thin scud which prevented close observation of results.
Wooded area (targets 19, 20 and 21) on hills along eastside of Santa Fe RIVER, 2 miles south of ARITAO, was thoroughly strafed with results unobserved due to trees. Upon entering target area flights contacted SAP BUNNY who gave clearance for attack. Because of ground fog, flight had to circle for 20 minutes until it burned off sufficiently to spot target.
Bombs were released at 2,000ft. on south to north run. 22x1,000lb bombs ANM-65 GP with ANM-103A1 instantaneous nose fuse and ANM-102A2 instantaneous tail fuse. Expended on target. 4,200 rounds of .50 caliber ammunition expended.

The Mexican weekly report compiled by Capitan Rivas Martinez mentions the following results:

Mexican ground personnel with one of their USAAF advisors, probably at Porac Field. (Family of Lieutenant Mechanic Jesus Gutierrez Figueroa)

Artillery positions thoroly [*sic*] strafed – results of bombing unobserved due to nature of terrain [with] thick foliage.

Four Mexican P-47Ds participated in this mission, carrying 500lb ANM-64 GP bombs, all eight bombs hitting the target area, although this is not mentioned in the 69th Fighter Squadron's final mission report.

**Mission No.2**: 4 June 1945
FF0 155-B-6 Mission Number 0-821
4 June 1945 310th Fighter Squadron
16 P-47s
Bomb and strafe target #18, tanks and trucks, in ARITAO area. Mission completed.
TO 0722/I for 15 a/c 1 a/c TO 0732/I TOT 0800/I – 0820/I. Altitude 8,000ft 1 a/c landed 0855/I due to fuel shortage. 2 a/c 1 snafu due to mechanical trouble and 1 escort landed 0907/I. 13 a/c landed at 0930/I.
Flight identified target #18 and made bomb run from NW to SE releasing bombs 1,500 ft above terrain scoring 31x1,000lb bomb hits in south eastern ⅔ of target with good coverage. All a/c strafed on bomb run. 1 bomb hung up temporarily and fell off 1,500-2,000 yards east of the target area.
Flights them made 2 strafing passes on wooded hill designated as target areas #19, 20, and 21 (artillery positions). Due to wooded terrain assessment of bombing and strafing results were impossible, however the targets were covered.
31x1,000 lb ANM-65 GP bombs with ANM103A1 instantaneous nose fuse and ANM102A2 instantaneous tail fuse expended on target. 1x1,000lb bomb fell in enemy territory. 13,743 rounds of .50 caliber ammunition expended.

Again the final mission report fails to mention the 201st Squadron's participation, but the Mexican report gave the following short account:

Area well covered by bombs, assessment of bombing and strafing results not possible due to wooded terrain.

On the ground, Japanese forces had assembled a combined force of about 10 light tanks with a number of 47mm and 75mm guns, along with some 250 men, deployed on 1 June along Route 5 just south of Aritao, as noted in the US Army history of the liberation of the Philippines:

> In a running fight during the period 1-4 June, the Japanese antitank unit south of Aritao, now reinforced by a few pieces of artillery from the 2nd Tank and 10th Divisions as well as some rear service troops, destroyed two tanks and damaged another of the 775th Tank Battalion, a company of which reinforced the 129th Infantry. The fight scarcely slowed the 129th Infantry, which entered Aritao on 5 June. Bambang fell bloodlessly the next day.

**Mission No.3:** 4 June 1945

FF0 155-B-6 Mission Number 9-881

4 June 1945 69th Fighter Squadron

15 P-47s

Bomb and strafe target #22 (Bivouac area) in ARITAO area.

Mission completed. 2 snafus due to mechanical trouble landed 1245/I.

TO 1110/I TOT 1140/I – 1235/I Altitude from deck uo to 6,000ft.

Landed 1300/I.

13 a/c with 26x1,000lb bombs attacked enemy bivouac area in woods on west side of Highway 5, 2 miles north of ARITAO.

23 Bombs fell in the target area and 3 dropped out of the woods on the side of the hill. Results were unobserved due to trees. 12 a/c strafed wooded area (artillery positions in target #19, 20, and 21) on side of hill along east bank of Santa Fe RIVER.

Area was well covered starting a small fire and damaging a building at tree line on northeast side of hill. Active machine gun position among the destroyed huts 2 miles south of ARITAO on east bank of Santa Fe RIVER was strafed with no visible damage.

Moderate inaccurate M/G fire from destroyed huts, 2 miles south of ARITAO on east bank of SANTA FE RIVER and from woods on the west side of hills 2 miles south of ARITAO on east side of SANTA FE RIVER. Results of bombing was reported to SAP BUNNY.

White phosphorous smoke south of ARITAO believed to be a Jap because BUNNY reported friendly artillery was not firing. 2 planes returning early jettisoned bombs safe in North MANILA BAY. Mechanical difficulty prevented reaching TABONES ISLANDS. Pilots believe wooded area (target #19, 20, and 21) on west side of Hill 2 miles south of ARITAO along Santa Fe RIVER would be excellent target for napalm.

26x1,000lb ANM65 GP bombs with ANM103A1 instantaneous nose fuse and ANM102A2 instantaneous tail fuse expended on target area. 4x1,000lb bombs jettisoned in MANILA BAY. 3,205 rounds of .50 caliber ammunition expended.

Once again the final mission report did not mention the presence of the Mexican pilots, three of whom flew their P-47s and dropped a reported six 500lb ANM64 GP bombs. The Mexican weekly status and operations report recorded the result of their mission as follows:

> Area well-covered – fired strafed building [which was] damaged … results unobserved due to terrain.

In the next two mission reports for the day, mention is finally made of the Mexican presence with the 311th Fighter Squadron by the type of bombs dropped on the target area:

**Mission No.4:** 4 June 1945

FFo No.155-B-6 Mission No. 1-837

4 June 1945 311th Fighter

Squadron 16 P-47s

Ground support in the ARITAO area. Mission completed.

TO 1145/I TOT 1230/I to 1315/I Altitude 1,200 to 8,000ft. Landed 1420/I.

20x1,000lb bombs and 5x500lb bombs were direct hits on target number 14, 4x1,000lb bombs fell just east of target area in a heavily wooded area at base of hills, 3x500lb bombs under shot and were dropped at western approach to bridge.

Results could not be ascertained due to heavily wooded terrain. Target was also strafed on bomb run. Bridge crossing river near target number 14 was definitely unserviceable.

Planes did not strafe targets 19, 20, and 21 due to fuel shortage. 24x1,000lb GP ANM-65 bombs with ANM103A1 nose fuses and ANM102A2 tail fuses. 8x500lb GP ANM-43 bombs with ANM103A1 nose fuses and ANM102A2 tail fuse. 800 rounds .50 caliber ammunition expended.

**Mission No.5:** 4 June 1945

FFO 155-B-6 Mission Number 0-822

4 June 1945 310th Fighter

Squadron 14 P-47s

Bomb and Strafe target #16 (bivouac area) at ARITAO. Mission Complete.

TO 1229 /I TOT 1305/I – 1325/I Altitude 6,000ft. Landed 1405/I.

SAP (Support Aircraft Party) BUNNY cleared flight to designated target #16 and flight proceeded to make bomb run from NW to SE releasing bombs at 1,500ft above the terrain.

24x1,000lb bombs and 3x500lb bombs were dropped in northern part of the target area. All a/c strafed on bomb run. 1x500lb bomb hung up and later fell off north of target in mountains. 2 strafing passes then made from W to E on target 19, 20, and 21 (artillery positions). Due to character of terrain, results of bombing and strafing not observed.

Slight, light, innaccurate A/A appeared to come from small shack in northern part of target area No.20. 24x1,000lb ANM-65 GP bombs with ANM103A1 instantaneous nose fuse and ANM102A2 instantaneous tail fuse expended on target. 4x500lb.ANM65 GP bombs with ANM103A1 instantaneous nose fuse and ANM102A2 instantaneous tail fuses expended on target. 5,537 rounds of .50 caliber ammunition expended.

The Mexican operations report says:

> Strafed during bomb run – 2 passes strafing at artillery positions. Results not observed ([due to] Character of Terrain).

Back in Mexico, a delayed press release wrongly dated 3 June by Russel Brines, a reporter for the Associated Press, under the headline 'Capt. Gaxiola led the Squadron', stated that about 20 fighter pilots of the 201st received their baptism of fire in the sector of "Ararao" [*sic*] in the Cagayan valley:

> Captain Radames Gaxiola of Mexico City, commander of the squadron led the Mexican pilots in combat. They flew besides the combat experienced 58th American group. The Mexicans [were] flying P-47 aircraft each carrying 2 demolition 500 pound bombs and 250 [rounds] of 0.50 caliber ammo.
>
> The Japanese responded with 50 shots of 20 mm anti-aircraft fire, when the Mexicans passed by flying at low altitude to drop their

> bombs on the objective. The Latinos left in flames many tanks and trucks, [and] they proceeded to do low level strafing operations.
>
> Lt. Carlos Diernos [*sic*] of Mexico City, returned to base, with two holes in the wings of his aircraft produced by anti-aircraft grenades. The ground fire was described as 'light but innacurate'

'Lt. Carlos Diernos' was actually Lieutenant Carlos Garduno Nunez, leader of 'B' Flight, who on 5 June was part of a 14-plane formation of the 311th Fighter Squadron which attacked targets around Aritao.

The wise decision to equip the Mexican squadron with the Republic P-47D Thunderbolt is shown in the official history of the MEAF, which says that the P-47 had a great advantage over other types of fighter aircraft operating over the Philippines, its strong structure being best suited for its role as a fighter bomber.

That was demonstrated when during one week in June the 35th Fighter Group reportedly lost three North American P-51D Mustangs to Japanese ground fire in the Santa Fe valley. This was mentioned in the official book of the MEAF that was published after the war, but in reality just one P-51D was lost on 10 June with its pilot after strafing an enemy convoy and another was lost, again with its pilot, in a collision at Clark Field on 3 June.

During the course of the month many Mexican P-47s were hit by anti-aircraft fire, but they all managed to return to base with no pilot loss.

While the Mexican pilots were flying with the American formations they felt some resentment from the American pilots, as mentioned by Lieutenant Reynaldo Perez Gallardo:

> When we first went into action, we were serving with three U.S. squadrons (and taking orders from American Officers). The Americans looked down on us at least a little bit. They didn't say so, but I noticed it.
>
> We made up our minds that we wouldn't say anything, but instead would show these people what we had. Not long after that I had my first incident.

Perez Gallardo was anxious to flying combat missions to able to prove to himself, and to the Americans, that Mexican pilots had the 'right stuff'. He initially felt the American pilots did not trust them, and there were fears among some US pilots that language would be problem, as was noted by Perez Gallardo.

He told his fellow pilots that they were going to show the American pilots what they were capable of:

> I would tell my companions – because I could speak English, I could translate – 'look we have to be patient, we have to endure it … When we get the chance to fly, we'll show 'em. For the time being let's just be patient'.

During these early missions Perez Gallardo came up with a way to show the American pilots what he could do, as he later explained in a interview in Austin, Texas:

"My tactic after a bombing or strafing was to come from the target and roll my plane over the enemy so that the Americans pilots could see me. Later I heard comments like 'Look at that crazy Mexican, they're bulls, they're pretty good.'"

On a combined US-Mexican sortie in which Perez Gallardo's mission was to disrupt the flow of Japanese troops and vehicles along a frequently used road, he pulled his victory roll stuntc, which got him noticed and into a confrontation with an American pilot from the 58th Fighter Group, as the following report reveals:

> [Perez Gallardo recalled:] 'We strafed a column of Japanese vehicles and after I made my pass, I got a little crazy and maneuvered my plane into a [celebratory] roll.'
>
> One of the U.S. pilots chastised Gallardo over the on board intercom saying 'look at the crazy Mexican!' Gallardo was offended by the comments. Their ensuing in flight communications led to a challenge to settle the argument behind the hangar once they landed.
>
> Gallardo had no idea which of the Americans he would soon be fighting. 'When we met, I realized that he was about 3 times as big and 4 times as heavy as I was,' Gallardo recalled. 'He looked at me, and grinned and asked if I still wanted to fight. I said "I'll fight you, you son of a gun."'
>
> Fortunately for Gallardo, the fight turned out to be a minor tussle. Afterwards the two pilots shook hands and [with the American] impressed by Gallardo's spunk in a situation where he was hopelessly overmatched, the two became friends.
>
> In fact, the incident broke the ice and reduced the tension between the two groups. From them on, the American and Mexicans directed their wrath at the Japanese rather than each other.

On another mission, Perez Gallardo's unusual tactic was noticed by one of the squadron commanders of the 58th when part of a formation of American and Mexican pilots bombed a bridge over the Marikina River. Ignoring anti-aircraft fire, he dropped his two 500lb bombs, which hit the bridge, bringing down one of the steel spans into the river and blocking a key link in the Japanese transportation network. After releasing his bombs, he was seen performing his signature manoeuvre over the target area.

By the end of 4 June, US Army Intelligence summary No.276 noted that a total of 88 P-47 sorties were flown in the Aritao area, causing several fires and numerous machine gun positions being silenced.

More missions were flown by the Mexican pilots the next day, again starting early in the morning.

> **Mission No.6**: 5 June 1945
>
> FF0 No. 156-B-7 Mission No. 0-823
>
> 5 June 1945
>
> 310th Fighter Squadron 16 P-47s
>
> Air Alert over ARITAO. Mission completed on town of DUPAX at request of controller.
>
> TO 0650/I. TOT 0710 to 0750/I. Altitude 7,000 ft. Landed 0830/I.
>
> 1 snafu and escort landed 0800/I.
>
> SAP BUNNY had no close support targets and requested flight to bomb town of DUPAX (16.17N-121.05E).
>
> All a/c made bomb run from south to north with bombs released approximately 2,000ft above terrain. 18x1,000lb and 6x500lb bombs were well scattered throughout western part of town.
>
> 2 hits were scored on building described in Paragraph I. These hits however, were on SW corner of building and did not completely destroy it, although a small amount of fire and white smoke were momentarily observed at point of impact. 2 a/c strafed on bomb run.
>
> Further results of the bombing and strafing not observed. 2x1,000lb bombs were released approximately 5,000 yards south of DUPAX as described in paragraph K. Entire town of DUPAX appeared to [be] void of lucrative targets, with possible exception being one large building located just south of intersection of two main highways leading north and west of DUPAX.
>
> Friendly forces and vehicles observed on Highway 5, just south

of main bridge crossing into SW part of ARITAO town. Mission leader, as he broke away for bomb run, found himself in a rudder lock. The nose of his a/c slipped into vertical position and the controls were frozen. In order to decrease weight on wing surface, he pulled bomb releases dropping bombs approximately 5,000 yards south of DUPAX.

This action on his part enabled him finally to pull out of rudder lock at minimum altitude. SAP BUNNY was questioned three separate times concerning effect of bombs, but he said that to the best of his knowledge no friendly troops had been hit.

22x1,000lb, GP AN-M65 bombs with AN-M103A1 nose fuse and AN -M103A1 nose fuse and AN-M102A2 tail fuse. 6x500lb GP AN-M64A1 bombs with AN-M103A1 nose fuse and AN -M101A2 tail fuse. 2x1,000lb bombs and 2x500lb bombs jettisoned in LINGAYEN GULF.

The mission leader was Major Howard Tuman of the 310th Fighter Squadron, whose aircraft suffered the rudder lock during the mission. The 310th's summary for this mission noted:

15 a/c bombed and strafed town of Dupax, Luzon. 18x1,000lb bombs and 6x500lb bombs were hits in western part of the town. 1 building partially destroyed. Further results were unobserved.

The weekly Mexican operational report noted:

SAP had no support target & requested bombing of Dupax. Bombs well scattered throughout W. part [of] town. 2 hits on building.

**Mission No.7**: 5 June 1945

FFO No.156-B-7 Mission No. 9-882

5 June 1945 69th

Fighter Squadron 16 P-47s

Air Alert over ARITAO. Mission completed.

TO 0715/I TOT 0755/I to 0825/I Altitude – from deck to 6,000ft Landed 0910/I.

As directed by SAP BUNNY, 12 a/c with 24x1,000lb bombs and 4 a/c with 8x500lb bombs attacked enemy positions in the draw on north side of highway 5, at BANGANAN, 4,000 yards above ARITAO.

22x1,000lb bombs and 7x500lb bombs fell in target area, 2x1,000lb bombs dropped long and 1x500lb bomb hung up falling off in the mountains to northeast. Target area and both sides of highway 5 between BANGANAN and INDIANA thoroughly strafed at request of SAP. All results were unobserved due to trees and thick underbrush.

Slight, inaccurate M/G fire received from south side of small bridge 300 yards north of MAGINANG (1:50,000, DUPAX, 89.2-74.0) 24x1,000lb GP AN-M65 bombs with AN-M103A1 nose fuse and AN-M102A2 tail fuse. 8x500lb GP AN-M64A1 bombs with AN-103A1 nose fuse and AN-M101A2 tail fuse. 7,338 rounds of .50 caliber ammunition expended.

**Mission No.8**: 5 June 1945

FFO No.156-B-7 Mission No. 1-840

5 June 1945

311th Fighter Squadron 14 P-47s

Ground support in ARITAO area. Mission Complete.

TO 0745/I TOT 0830 to 0900/I Altitude 1,200 to 6,000 ft Landed 0950/I.

As directed by SAP BUNNY planes bombed and strafed enemy gun positions and possible tank concentrations in a ravine on west side of Highway 5 about 1 mile north of INDIANA TOWN (90.6-76.8 sheet 3460-III, 1, 50:000) and troops concentrations on west side of highway 5 at INDIANA TOWN.

24x1,000lb bombs and 4x500lb bombs were dropped in target area with excellent coverage reported by SAP BUNNY. Results difficult to observe due to foliage and dust over the target area. Planes also strafed both target areas and INDIANA TOWN starting numerous fires of short duration and silencing small arms fire from buildings in town.

Slight, light and possible mortar fire, accurate to inaccurate. Small arms and M/G fire from buildings in INDIANA TOWN holed one a/c once in wings, puncturing hydraulic system. Pilot Lt. C.N. GARDUNO, 261829, 201st Mexican fighter squadron, uninjured. Damage to plane minor.

Also observed two pinkish-white burst at 3,000ft above 100ft from left wing of second plane in first flight. No a/c holed by these bursts, which were possibly mortar fire believed to have come from wooded area at 89.4-69.3, sheet 3459-IV, 1:50,000.

SAP BUNNY reported friendly forces now in ARITAO. 24x1,000lb AN-M65 bombs with AN-M103A1 nose fuses and AN-M102A2 tail fuses, both instantaneous. 4x500lb AN-M64 bombs with AN-M103A1 nose fuses and AN-M101A2 tail fuses, both instantaneous. 17,255 rounds of .50 caliber ammunition expended.

The Mexican report stated that 4x1,000lb bombs were used by the two Mexican pilots on this raid. The following short report was given about Lieutenant Garduno sustaining combat damage during the mission:

5 June Combat Mission #840

14 aircraft

Ground strafe Aritao area

Lt. C. N. Garduno 261629, 201st Mexican was holed in the wing by A/A puncturing hydraulic system. Minor damage.

Garduno made it back to Porac unhurt. Years later, he remembered the feeling of being hit by enemy ground fire during this mission:

One time I was hit with cannons and machine guns. I felt like I passed through turbulence ... I saw that my instruments and engine were working, but I had problems with the landing gear, which lowered with gravity, if not I would have made a belly landing.

After landing not only did I notice that the hydraulic system from my aircraft was damaged but one of the wings was scratched and was leaking oil. Also my parachute showed damage from bullets.

**Mission No.9**: 5 June 1945

FFO No. 156-B-7 Mission Number 0-824

5 June 1945

310th Fighter Squadron 10 P-47s

Air Alert over ARITAO. Mission completed on SANTO DOMINGO AREA.

TO 1149/I TOT 1215 to 1255/I Altitude 8,000 ft. Landed 1345/I 1 a/c returned early due to oil leak landing at 1330/I.

Target assigned by SAP BUNNY was southwest side of hill located vicinity 97.1-88.1 on BAYOMBONG map no. 3460-III of 1:50,000 series. Area to be bombed was NE of highway 5 and parallel to the road. Bomb run made from south to north with bombs released approximately 1,500ft above terrain, scoring 14x1,000lb bombs and

The entire ground element of the 201st Mexican Fighter Squadron on the parade ground at their camp at Porac Field. (USAF)

4x500lb bombs in target area obtaining overall coverage.

2x1,000lb bombs fell short and hit just south of highway in creek bed. Two strafing passes made on target area by 9 a/c. Only visible results of bombing and strafing were several grass fires that were still burning as flight left the area. Slight, light, inaccurate s/a fire from both sides of hwy 5 from grid point 96.0-88.1 to 97.4-87.0 on BAYOMBONG map No. 3460-III. Entire hill where our flight bombed was covered with vehicle tracks that appear well used and possibly newly made.

16x1,000lb AN-M65 bombs, AN-M103A1 nose fuse, AN-M102A3 tail fuse. 4x500lb AN-M64A1 bombs, AN-M103A1 nose fuse, AN-M102A2 tail fuse, 5,280 rds of .50 cal. ammo expended.

**Mission No.10**: 5 June 1945

FFO No. 156-B-7 Mission No. 9-884

5 June 1945

69th Fighter Squadron 15 P-47s

Air Alert over ARITAO. Mission complete.

TO 1215/I TOT 1245 to 1345/I Altitude from deck to 6,000ft. Landed 1415/I.

As directed by SAP BUNNY, 12 a/c with 26x1,000lb bombs and 2 a/c with 4x500lb bombs attacked enemy positions on hill, east side of Hwy 5 1,000 yards south of BAMBANG (1:50,000 BAYOMBANG BLOCK 95-80).

24x1,000lb bombs and 4x500lb bombs fell in target area covering the southern slope and top of the hill. 2x1,000lb bombs hit 2,000 yards NW of target on west side of road. Same area was thoroughly strafed by 15 a/c. Results were unobserved due to trees and thick foliage.

At request of SAP BUNNY 4 a/c strafed either side of road between BAMBANG and BAYOMBONG or 8 a/c strafed from BAYOMBONG north along Hwy 5 for 6 miles. 8 to 18 metal roofed buildings were damaged.

Many Filipinos were seen in fields between BAMBANG and BAYOMBONG. In one field 3 miles NW of BAYOMBONG 20-25 people appearing to be nuns or sisters were kneeling as though in prayer. SAP BUNNY assigned target by description using BAMBANG as reference point.

Bombs were released at 2,000ft on south to north run. 26x1,000lb AN-M65 bombs with AN-M103A1 nose fuse and AN-M 102A2 tail fuse. 4x500lb AN-M64A1 bombs, AN-M103A1 nose fuse and AN-M 101A2 tail fuse. 9,315 rds of .50 cal. ammo expended.

**Mission No.11**: 6 June 1945

FFO No.156-B-7 Mission No. 1-842

6 June 1945

311th Fighter Squadron 13 P-47s

Ground Support in the ARITAO area. Mission complete.

TO 1245/I TOT 1330/I to 1400/I Altitude 1,000ft to 7,000ft. Landed 1530/I.

As directed by SAP BUNNY, planes bombed enemy gun positions in a ravine about 500 yards west of Highway 5, at 94.4-80.9, sheet 3460-III, 1:50,000, approximately 1 mile southwest of Bambang.

22x1,000lb and 3x500lb bombs were dropped in target area with results unobserved due to foliage. At SAP BUNNY's request planes also strafed target of opportunity along highway 5. A building in northwestern part of BAMBANG town was left burning, and ravines and ridges east of Highway 5 were strafed.

Strafing passes on a machine gun emplacement located at 94.4-80.0, same map reference, resulted in a large explosion followed by fire. The gun did not continue firing.

1x500lb bomb was accidentally released in mountainous country about 10 miles east of SANTA FE, but did not explode. Slight, light, inaccurate machine gun and small arms fire was received from a position located at 94.4-80.0, same map reference.

This position was silenced by strafing. 22x1,000lb GP AN-M65 bombs with ANM103A1 nose fuse and ANM102A2 tail fuse, both instantaneous.

3x500lb GP AN-M64A1 bombs with ANM103A1 nose fuse and ANM101A2 tail fuse, accidentally dropped in probable enemy territory. 17,220 rounds .50 caliber ammunition expended.

**Mission No.12**: 6 June 1945

FFo 157-B-8 Mission No. 9-885

6 June 1945

69th Fighter Squadron 14 P-47s

Air Alert over BAMBANG. Mission complete.

TO 0620/I TOT 0650/I – 0755/I

Altitude from deck up to 6,000ft. Landed 0820/I.

As directed by SAP BUNNY, 12 aircraft with 24x1,000lb bombs and 2 aircraft with 4x500lb bombs attacked enemy positions in wooded draw east side of highway 5, 1,000 yards south of BAMBANG.

24x1,000lb bombs were in the target area marked by smoke. 4x500lb bombs fell long, dropping near BAMBANG. Building in target was destroyed with debris and smoke visible. Same area was thoroughly strafed with results obscured by foliage and low hanging fog.

Ground forces patrols reported to BUNNY that bombs fell exactly where needed. Our tanks and motorized equipment were proceeding north along Highway 5, 4,000 yards below BAMBANG. Flashes like exploding shells were seen in BAMBANG during attack.

SAP BUNNY reported friendly troops accepted to occupy BAMBANG today. Flashes in BAMBANG while planes were bombing and strafing appeared to be artillery. Bombs were dropped from 2,000ft from south to north run. 24x1,000lb ANM-65 bombs with ANM103A1 instantaneous nose fuse and ANM102A2 instantaneous tail fuse. 4x500lb GP ANM-64 bombs with ANM103A1 instantaneous nose fuse and ANM102A2 instantaneous tail fuse. 9,530 .50 caliber rounds of ammunitions expended.

**Mission No.13**: 6 June 1945

FFO 157-B-8 Mission No. 1-843

6 June 1945

311th Fighter Squadron 14 P-47s

Ground support in the BAMBANG area. Mission complete.

TO 0715/I TOT 0800/I – 0830/I Altitude 1,000ft to 8,000 ft.

Landed 1000/I.

As directed by SAP BUNNY, planes bombed and strafed enemy gun positions and concentrations on east slope of hill about 2 miles West of BAMBANG at 91.2-81, sheet 3460-III, 1:50,000 map series.

20x1,000lb bombs and 2x500lb bombs were dropped in target area, and 4x1,000lb bombs and 1x500lb bomb under shot and fell in ravine at bottom of hill. 1x500lb bomb hung up and was jettisoned at sea west of TABONES ISLAND. Target area was also strafed starting numerous small grass fires. SAP BUNNY reported bombing as very well [targeted] although results were unobserved by pilots due to heavy foliage.

Friendly forces were observed on highway 5 about 5 miles north of ARITAO. SAP BUNNY marked target with white smoke. 24x1,000lb GP ANM65 bombs with ANM103A1 instantaneous nose fuse and ANM102A2 instantaneous tail fuse. 3x500lb GP ANM64A1 bombs with ANM103A1 instantaneous nose fuse and ANM 101A2 instantaneous tail fuse. 1x500lb bomb jettisoned. 9,120 rounds of .50 caliber ammunition expended.

**Mission No.14**: 6 June 1945

FFO 157-B-8 Mission No. 0-826

6 June 1945

310th Fighter Squadron 16 P-47s

Air Alert over BAMBANG. Mission completed.

TO 0750/I TOT 0815/I – 0920/I Altitude 8,000 ft. Landed 0950/I.

1 aircraft landed CLARK FIELD.

Target assigned by SAP BUNNY was eastern slope of mountain located 1,000 to 1,500 yards west southwest of BAMBANG (16.23 north-121.06 east) which was reported to contain enemy positions dug in there.

Bomb run made southeast to northwest with bombs released approximately 1,500ft above terrain scoring 23x1,000lb bombs and 8x500lb bombs well dispersed throughout area. 1x1,000lb bomb hung up and was jettisoned unarmed in LINGAYEN GULF. Due to wooded terrain, no results observed, but SAP commented that results were very good.

Numerous fox-holes of apparently new construction, located in foot hills northwest of BAMBANG (16.23 north -121.06 east). SAP BUNNY informed flight leader that friendly troops were 4,000 yards south of BAMBANG along Highway 5. 23x1,000lb GP ANM65 bombs with ANM103A1 instantaneous nose fuse and ANM102A2 instantaneous tail fuse. 8x500lb GP ANM64A1 bombs with ANM103A1 instantaneous nose fuse and ANM101A2 instantaneous tail fuse. 1x1,000lb bomb jettisoned in LINGAYEN GULF.

**Mission No.15**: 6 June 1945

FFO No. 157-B-8 Mission No. 9-887

6 June 1945

69th Fighter Squadron 15 P-47s

Air Alert over BAMBANG area. Mission complete.

TO 1110/I TOT 1140 to 1230 /I Altitude from deck to 6,000ft. Landed 1300/I

As directed by SAP BUNNY, 15 a/c with 24x1,000lb bombs and 6x500lb bombs attacked enemy positions along wooded ridge on south side of Hwy 5 1,000 yards west of BAYOMBONG.

All the bombs fell in the target area covering the ridge and side of hill for ½ mile with results unobserved due to trees. 12 a/c, at request of SAP BUNNY, strafed same area setting a small house afire.

Wooded area on west side of Hwy 5, 4 miles north of SOLANO was also strafed with results unobserved due to trees. Well worn paths leading from road to woods indicated activity.

Friendly troops and vehicles were seen along Hwy 5 just outside of BAMBANG. SAP BUNNY who was still south of BAMBANG said our troops were being held up by minefields. Target was assigned by description. Bombs were released from 2,000 ft. on east to west run. 24x1,000lb AN-M65 bombs with AN-M103A1 nose fuse, AN-M102A2 tail fuse, 6x500lb AN-M65A1 bombs with AN-M103A1 nose fuse and AN-M101A2 tail fuse. 4,300 rounds of .50 caliber ammunition expended.

**Mission No.16**: 6 June 1945

FFO No. 157-B-8 Mission No.0-827

Sergeant 2nd Class Mechanic Jesus Gutierrez Figueroa and a buddy with Republic P-47D-30-RA No.23 44-33727, a Lend Lease aircraft, at Clark Field. (Family of Lieutenant Mechanic Jesus Gutierrez Figueroa)

> 6 June 1945
> 310th Fighter Squadron 15 P-47s
> Air Alert over BAMBANG. Mission completed.
> TO 1208/I TOT 1245/I – 1315/I Altitude 9,000ft. 3 a/c landed 1400 /I 1 a/c landed BORAX strip due to mechanical trouble 11 a/c landed 1415/I.
>
> Target assigned by SAP BUNNY was last slope of hill NW of SANTO DOMINGO consisting of ravines in area between grid coordinates 95.0-88.1 and 95.0-88.9 on BAYOMBONG map No. 3460-III of 1:50,000 series.
>
> Bomb run made from east to west with bombs released approximately 2,000ft above terrain. 22x1,000lb and 8x500lb bombs were dropped in target area obtaining excellent coverage. Due to terrain being heavily wooded results were unobserved.
>
> No comment was made by SAP as he was not in sight of target area. Advance elements of our friendly forces are reported by SAP BUNNY to be in BAMBANG (16.23 N – 121.06 E). 22x1,000lb GP AN-M65 bombs, AN-M103A1 nose fuse, AN-M102A2 tail fuse, 8x500lb GP AN-M64 bombs, AN-M103A1 nose fuse, AN-M101A2 tail fuse.

A summary of the Mexican pilots' participation in 311th Fighter Squadron missions to this point was given as follows:

> 4-5 [June]: 6 sorties Weather Reccos, ARITAO AND CAGAYAN Valley. 58 sorties – ground support, ARITAO area Luzon. 500 and 1000 pounders were dropped at point requested by the controller. Results of the bombing was generally unobserved due to trees and foliage. Strafing attacks started many fires, caused one large explosion and knocked out gun position.
>
> 6 [June]: 2 sorties Weather Reccos. To SANTA FE-ARITAO area. 23 sorties – ground support to BAMBANG area Luzon. 1000 pound bombs were dropped and area was strafed. Controller reported good result.

On that same day, Lieutenant Fernando Hernandez Vega made a forced landing on Clark Field and joined the squadron the next day. No information has been found to explain the cause of his forced landing.

During the period from 4-6 June, the Mexican pilots flew a total 16 combat missions (six with the 69th FS, six with the 310th FS and four with the 311th FS), flying about 47 sorties, dropping 88x500lb and 4x1,000lb bombs and reportedly firing about 7,880 rounds of .50 calibre ammunition, for one aircraft that was damaged by enemy ground fire with no injury to the pilot (Lieutenant Carlos Garduno Nunez).

Before he passed away in 2003, Lieutenant Colonel Joaquin Ramirez Vilchiz left behind some written accounts of the combat missions he flew in the Philippines. His log book describes a combat mission of 5 June at Bambang, involving dive-bombing, as follows:

> 2nd combat mission strafing against Japanese troops ordered by the American command against a convoy of ground units that was transporting troops on road that followed the course of the Magallanes river [*sic*].
>
> The point to attack was a wide curve close to the river and the road, and we arrived at that grand curve where the enemy was descending with trucks full with troops … the commander of these units was very astute. He placed a machine gun nest that fired with tracer rounds that we could see from the air. I was the second plane that was trying to dodge the enemy bullets by moving side to side in the same horizontal plane.
>
> I passed the machine gun nest in the direction of the middle of the curve and didn't see any trucks due to the heavy foliage of the tress, but I saw running on the beach of the river that was wide, 8 soldiers that were standing and kneeling firing at us; in a millisecond my eight machine guns reached the group.
>
> A hill was coming up on me and I rapidly pulled the stick heading the aircraft to the pass that was on the left side of the curve. I felt the blindness of the blackout …
>
> I recovered rapidly and moved the stick forward so the blood would reach my eyes. I passed close to the top of the trees, my only thing was to form up with Hector (Tte. Espinosa Galvan) I could not see the eight Japanese. I do believe they were good soldiers.

At the start of the 201st's operations as a unit, the ground situation in Luzon was described by Colonel Cardenas in his report to Mexico:

> The situation in Luzon where the missions took place has not changed appreciably from that indicated in the last report, but there are to be noted deep penetrations of U. S. forces towards the Northeast in the region of Baguis.
>
> Active operations also took place in the Cagayan Valley with a deep penetration across the river of the same name, and two further penetrations diverging from it which judged to the former seem to have the aim of surrounding the enemy in separate, isolated pockets.
>
> With the exception of one enemy plane over Clark Field, which did not make any attack against the ground, enemy planes have not made any appearances in the air above the island.

The 201st was supporting the advance of the Sixth US Army under the command of Lieutenant General Walter Krueger, who led a number of infantry divisions, among them the 25th 'Tropic Lightning', 37th, 40th, 6th and 43rd.

Facing the Americans and organised Filipino guerrillas were the Japanese forces under the overall command of General Tomoyuki Yamashita, known as the 'Tiger of Malaya'. After the end of the war, he was tried for war crimes against humanity and executed on 23 February 1946.

Yamashita's command in Luzon consisted of remnants of the 2nd

Armoured, 19th, 23rd and 105th Divisions and the 58th Independent Mixed Brigade. His forces had lost men and equipment to the American and Filipino advance. It has been estimated that from 18 October 1944 to the end of the war, the total number of Japanese forces (including naval and air force personnel) in the Philippines was about 529,800.

The type of operations that the Mexican pilots in the 201st undertook against these Japanese forces was described years later by Lieutenant Amadeo Castro Almanza:

> The missions consisted essentially in escorting bombers and strafing and bombing troops.
>
> Our main operations were against the troops of General Yamasita [*sic*], known as the Japanese equivalent of the famous German General Rommel. The tactic employed by him was difficult for the ground troops, since he mined almost all the hills.
>
> In the island of Luzon, he had fortified the 'Cordillera' which divides it, constructing caves with internal passeges, which had all kinds of armaments, hospitals, supplies.
>
> He had made big rooms inside those caves. When they were attacked, they hid or they pulled out troops or artillery out of these caves making it impossible to cross to the North part of the island, which had not yet been taken … we participated fully to get them out.

Lieutenant Carlos Rodriguez Corona remembered:

> Our mission consisted in strafing and bombing the Japanese army and its tanks, so the allied infantry could advance. Each one of us carried 2,000 rounds and two one thousand [pound] demolition bombs to support the ground forces.
>
> To the north the Japanese occupied the island … while to the south there were American, Australian, Filipino and Mexican troops. At the beginning of each mission, our principal operational officer Capt. Amadeo Castro Almanza would explain what formation we would use, which where the code words, which was our primary target, in case of bad weather and we could not find the target, where we could drop the bombs, with the safety on so they would not explode. After executing the mission, we had to return flying low so not to be seen by enemy radars.

It should be mentioned that not only US forces and Filipino ground troops operated in northern Luzon: there were British Army, Royal Australian Air Force and even Dutch naval units at Subic Bay. There were also a good number of Mexican-Americans or Mexican nationals fighting with the US ground forces. Four Mexican-Americans won the Congressional Medal of Honor for acts of valour that went beyond the call of duty in the liberation of the Philippines.

They were Private Cleto Rodriguez, Private Manuel Perez Jr (posthumously), Staff Sergeant Ysmael R. Villegas (posthumously) and Private First Class David Gonzalez (posthumously).

On 7 June, the Mexican pilots started to fly combat missions as a unit, two missions being flown that day.

The first one (No.1-1, #17) was from 9:30-11:30 a.m. by five Mexican pilots and two American pilots. One of them was Lieutenant Max Itzkowitz of the 311th FS, who later wrote:

> I think I led the first combat mission flown by the 201st in the spring of 1945 on Luzon in the Philippines.
>
> We were assigned to dive-bomb enemy gun positions in the mountains. Our Infantry ground control advised that they would fire a smoke flare to pinpoint enemy positions for our bombing run.
>
> However after ground control advised they had fired their flare, I could see at least a dozen similar smoke puffs curling up in the same area. My Mexican Jug jockeys were only too eager to bomb everything in sight, but my pre-flight orders were not to drop even a coke bottle until I dropped my eggs on the target.
>
> After 130 or so missions, I wasn't about to risk obliterating a platoon of hapless G. I.s brewing their morning coffee. After several fruitless runs, and unable to distinguish between ground control's smoke flares and ordinary fires by either Japanese, Filipino or American, I decide to abort.
>
> We flew out over the Pacific, in lovely formation I must say, and dropped our bombs in the deep forever.

Lieutenant Itzkowitz flew a total of 154 combat missions in the Pacific with the 58th FG and accumulated about 700 hours of combat time in the P-47D Thunderbolt. He had the experience of being shot down by ground fire on a raid to Timor in the Celebes Island, ditching in the sea off the south-east tip of Dutch New Guinea on 20 October 1944, and was picked up an hour later by a rescue PBY Catalina. He left the service as a captain in December 1945 to work in private industry.

Thirteen 1,000lb ANM-63 GP bombs were dropped in Lanan Bay, with one bomb returned to base still on its aircraft. The Mexican pilots who participated in their first mission were:

Captain 1st Class Radames Gaxiola Andrade,
Lieutenant Jacobo Estrada Luna,
2nd Lieutenant Raul Garcia Mercado,
2nd Lieutenant Roberto Urias Avelleyra
and 2nd Lieutenant Jose Luis Pratt Ramos.

The second mission of the day (1-2, #18) was flown at 2:00 p.m., with five Mexican and two American pilots. One of them was Major Harry M. 'Ody' Odren, deputy commander of the 58th FG, who led the mission, as noted in the following final mission report from US Air Corps intelligence officer Major Arnold F. Schoen Jr:

> A. FFO 158-B-4 Mission Number 1-2 7 June 1945 201st Mexican Fighter Squadron 7 P-47s
>
> B. Bomb Enemy Concentrations in INFANTA area. Mission complete.
>
> C. TO 1400/I TOT 1430/I – 1530/I Altitude 5,000ft. landed 1600/I.
>
> D. As assigned by SAP 'OUTLIVE', 14x1,000lbs bombs were directed at enemy troop concentrations at 52.2 – 30.3 INFANTA map No. 3556-II, 1:50,000 series. 13x1,000lb bombs fell directly in target area and 1x1,000lb bomb fell approximately 300 yards SE of target area. Heavy foilage obscured results …
>
> J. 5/10 scattered to broken clouds enroute. 8/10 to 10/10 clouds at 1,000ft over target. 7/10s to 9/10s scattered to broken on return.
>
> K. 58th Fighter Group Deputy Commander who led the flight commented that the bombing was excellent.
>
> L. 14x1,000lb SP ANM65 bombs with ANM103A1 instantaneous nose fuses and ANM 102A2 instantaneous tail fuses expended.

The Mexican pilots participating in this mission with Major Odren were:

Captain Pablo L. Rivas Martinez,
Lieutenant Amadeo Castro Almanza,
Lieutenant Jose Luis Barbosa Cerda,
Lieutenant Reynaldo Perez Gallardo
and 2nd Lieutenant Mario Lopez Portillo.

During the rest of June the 201st continued flying its missions as

Mexican ground personnel loading a 1,000lb ANM-65 general purpose bomb on a Lend Lease Republic P-47D-30-RA Thunderbolt for its next combat mission. (Enrique Velasco Padilla)

a unit, accompanied by American pilots from the 58th FG and the liasion group, providing ground support to the American and Filipino troops fighting their way through northern Luzon.

By this time the squadron had developed a routine for days with missions to be flown. They started with an early morning wake-up for all the pilots, then breakfast and reporting to the operations tent, where the mission of the day was posted on a blackboard, with what flight would be involved and take-off time. During the briefing pilots received the latest intelligence information and the targets they would be hitting that day, some of which would become routine, such as a highway or a river crossing. The order of attack was also discussed among the pilots, for example the first section would strafe first, while the second would drop their bombs first.

After the briefing, some pilots returned to their tents to pick up anything they needed or would board the jeeps to take them to the flight line. The maintenance officer, Captain 'Chucho' Carranza, would know how many aircraft were needed, so when the pilots arrived at the flight line all aircraft would be ready for the mission, with bombs and ammunition loaded and final checks being made. When the pilot arrived at his assigned aircraft, he would carry out his visual inspection and receive any information from the crew chief.

The pilots would board their aircraft and wait for the flare or signal to start their engines, report via radio the aircraft condition and be ready to start taxiing over to the runway.

After returning from a mission, the gun camera film was collected from all the aircraft and taken to be developed in the squadron laboratory, which was set up in a tent. Sometimes pilots were shown these films, when the results of a mission were not good or an error had been committed by the squadron or the other squadrons from the 58th FG.

As for the mechanics, Corporal Pedro Martinez Perez, who was assigned to 'A' flight as an assistant mechanic, noted that they too had fallen into a routine:

> Our routine was a constant monotony and our jobs were [only] over when everything was in order, the aircraft engines operating with all precision, the aircraft loaded to the max with fuel, machine guns and armed bombs, gun cameras in their wings, radios ready, oxygen etc.
>
> When the pilots arrived to occupy their cockpits we helped them connect the radio and oxygen, while he regulated and put on his oxygen mask, with the engine running making a loud sound. We would put on their belts and the ones to their seats, they would visually check their instruments, then they would put out their left arm outside the cockpit and give us a thumb up and we would replay the same, which signified everything clear, good, good luck. Increasing the speed of their machines they would head to the end of the runway to take off and do their missions.

Meanwhile, back in Mexico the following news item was published about the squadron's actions by Reuters reporter James Henry in Manila. It appeared in the Mexico City newspaper *Novedades* with the date 9 June 1945 and the headline 'Great Mexican victory':

> The pilots of the Mexican Expeditionary Air Force flew combat missions against the Japanese for the first time on June third, when 20 combat aircraft of Squadron 201 lead by Captain Radames Gaxiola attacked and bombed with machine guns and bombs, tanks and trucks in the area of Amaratao in Central Luzon.
>
> The town of Aritao was captured the next day by American Ground troops. The Mexican aviators flew coordinated operations with the fighters of the 5th American Air Force. In this way they received their baptism of fire, under the proctection of pilots forged in hundreds of combats. Each Mexican aircraft carried two 250 kilogram bombs and more than 25 thousand rounds for the machine guns. The Mexican pilots dropped their bombs on Japanese vehicles with mathematical precision and later strafed them in passes so low that they touched the tops of the threes.
>
> Many tanks and trucks were left in flames, as a result of the brilliant performance of the aviators from Mexico. The Mexicans had arrived in the Philippines on the first of May.

The following missions are summarised from the squadron records from American and Mexican sources:

**Mission No.1-3(#19):** 10 June 1945

Support to ground forces in the area of Mariquina – Watershed.

Captain Roberto Legorreta Sicilia, Lieutenant Hector Espinosa Galvan, Lieutenant Joaquin Ramirez Vilchis, Lieutenant Amador Samano Pina, 2nd Lieutenant Miguel Uriarte Aguilar and 2nd Lieutenant Jose Luis Pratt Ramos, accompanied by one US pilot.

Take-off time 0710, time over target 0740 to 0910, return to base at 0940. Results: the 7 P-47s directed by SAP Coyote bombed enemy troop in the western part of a narrow section, west of the Panas Mountain.

They could not observe the results of the bombing, due to vegetation covering the target area. Two aircraft strafed target as directed by SAP Coyote. Two aircraft did not complete the mission, due to fuel shortage.

Twelve bombs were dropped over the target area and four more in the security zone east of Manila Bay. 840 rounds of 0.50 cal. expended.

**Mission No.1-4 (#20):** 10 June 1945

Support to ground troops in the area of Mariquina – Watershed.

Lieutenant Amadeo Castro Almanza, Lieutenant Jose Luis Barbosa Cerda, Lieutenant Julio Cal y Mayor Sauz, 2nd Lieutenant Praxedis Lopez Ramos, 2nd Lieutenant Jaime Zenizo Rojas, 2nd Lieutenant Angel Sanchez Rebollo and 2nd Lieutenant Mario Lopez Portillo, accompanied by one American pilot.

Take-off time 1220, time over target 1250 to 1400, return to base at 1430.

Results: the mission was not completed, due to failure to locate the Stinson L-5 liaison aircraft of the 25th Liaison Squadron, which would mark the target. The American report mentions failure due to weather. All 16 bombs were dropped in the safety zone of Tabones Island.

A Mexican armourer working on .50 calibre machine guns, using a 55-gallon drum for his work area. (Manuel Cervantes Ramos)

Mechanics working on one of the 201st's P-47D Thunderbolts. (Family of Lieutenant Mechanic Jesus Gutierrez Figueroa)

**Mission No.1-5 (#21):** 11 June 1945

Air alert over Oscariz (completed on Lamut).

Captain Pablo L. Rivas Martinez, Lieutenant Carlos Varela Landini, Lieutenant Graco Ramirez Garrido, Lieutenant Julio Cal y Mayor Sauz and 2nd Lieutenant Jose Luis Pratt Ramos, accompanied by three American pilots.

Take-off time 0800, time over target 0830 to 0945, return to base 1025.

Results: as directed by 'Bunny 2' planes were to bomb area north of intersection of Hwy 4 and LAMUT RIVER (09.6-13-8 on sheet No.3460-I, 1:50,000).

Leader made dry run over the target from NNW to SSE to get SAP's OK, and after receiving verification, flight made two more consecutive passes. 8 a/c bombed and strafed area along Hwy 4 south of bridge.

15x1,000lb bombs hit along Hwy 4 on south bank of LAMUT RIVER, 1x1,000lb bomb hit at 11.5-12.7 probably near friendly troops. SAP reported no damage. Due to trees bombing results unobserved. A/A reported over LAMUT TOWN. Height undetermined. Calibre 37mm and smaller.

1 a/c holed by two bursts. Pilot uninjured. [2nd Lieutenant Ramos was the pilot hit.]

Motor columns sighted moving south from LAMUT to BAGABAG. Vehicles parked along Hwy 4 near LAMUT to the SW on the E side of Hwy. Fires sighted in BAGABAG and area 1,200-2,000 yards south of LAMUT along Hwy.

16x1,000lb AN-M65 bombs and 540 rounds of 0.50 cal. ammunition expended.

It appears that on this mission the Mexican and American pilots were supporting the 148th Infantry Regiment of the 37th Infantry Division, whose 1st battalion attacked near the neighbourhood of Lantap on the Lamuet River northwest of Bagabag on 10-11 June, as mentioned in the following account taken from the book *Combat Stories* written by Charles Henne, who was an officer in the battalion:

Ahead of our battalion on the road (Highway 4), the 1/148th was given the mission of blocking route 4 and securing a bridgehead over the Lamuet River. Upon reaching the near bank of the Lamuet, the leading elements of the Battalion ran into heavy 47 mm mortar, and machine gun fire from across the river.

Dug in on the far bank [was] an estimated rifle company, reinforced, occupying good positions controlling the old bridge site. After pounding the Japs with air and artillery, the battalion held on the south bank for the night. During the night the 1/148 prepared to cross the fordable river at first light, and called on supporting air and artillery to hit the Jap positions.

At dawn after the air strike and artillery preparation, Company C charged across the river and overran the battered Japanese positions. The resistance on the far bank was light to moderate and it was evident that many of the Japs had been killed in the open – out of their holes. The battalions attack was not only successful, [but] casualties light, … [and] the body count totalled 103 dead Japs. Among the battle debris were 10 light Tanks, 10 trucks and several 20 mm antiaircraft cannon. The Battalion held at Lantap until relieved by the 20th Infantry.

Although the fight was won by the 1/148th, most of the men occupying forward positions were anything but happy about their air support. From what I was told later, the original strike was executed by American P-51 pilots and on target. However, as they were finishing a flight of Mexican P-47s in the area wanted a piece of the action.

The Division's air controller operating aloft in an L-5 had innocently vectored them onto the targets. Their first run was close to the [friendly] troops but not dangerously close, but each following run was closer and then too close. Screaming Yankee to stop the Spanish speaking Mexican pilots was futile, for the airwaves were filled with Spanish and the air controller was no linguist.

Relief came when the Mexican warriors ran out of munitions and headed for home, chased by a lot of cussing by 1/148th ground pounders. For some time after that air mission requests went in with the stipulation – American pilots only.

At the time of this incident, Henne was the Executive Officer of the 148th's 3rd battalion, located several miles away.

Since his knowledge of the episode is based largely on what he was told later, the possibility exists that the GIs' complaints were associated with the wrong ground action and thus involved an incident on 20 June (as related below).

**Mission No.1-6 (#22):** 11 June 1945

Air alert over Oscariz, mission completed on Payawan Rest House area

Lieutenant Joaquin Ramirez Vilchis, Lieutenant Carlos Rodriguez Corona, 2nd Lieutenant Mario Lopez Portillo, 2nd Lieutenant Angel Sanchez Rebollo and 2nd Lieutenant Miguel

Moreno Arreola.

Take-off time 1130, time over target 1200 to 1300, return to base 1335.

Results: as directed by SAP Bunny 2, 5 a/c bombed and strafed enemy troop concentrations blocking Hwy 4 aproximately 2,200 yards WNW of PAYAWAN (05.2-19.1, sheet No.3461-II, 1:50,000).

Leader made dry run from SE to NW to get the SAP's OK, and in two subsequent passes the 5 a/c dropped 10x1,000lb bombs and strafed both sides of Hwy. SAP Bunny said artillery observers reported impacts on both sides of Hwy with excellent results.

A/C attacked in string formation from 8,000ft. Troops observed camped in tents on hills at 05.2-25.5, 05.0-25.3 and 03.1-24.4. Extensive traffic from BAGABAG to points approximately 8,000 yards to NW on Hwy 4.

Troops sighted 4,000 yards SE of PAYAWAN on Hwy 4. Movement of troops toward CORDON on Hwy 5 NE from BAGABAG.

10x1,000lb GP AN-M65 bombs and 3,330 rounds of .50 cal. ammunition expended.

**Mission No.1-7 (#23):** 12 June 1945

Air alert over Mariquina – Watershed. Mission completed on hill approximately 2,000 yards NE MT MAPATAD and area approximately 1,500 yards NE MT CAMPANA.

Captain Roberto Legorreta Sicilia, Lieutenant Carlos Varela Landini, Lieutenant Fernando Hernandez Vega, 2nd Lieutenant David Ceron Bedolla and 2nd Lieutenant Jose Luis Pratt Ramos, accompanied by one American pilot.

Take-off time 0900, time over target 0930 – 1015, return to base 1100.

Results: as directed by SAP TROPHY 7, a/c bombed and strafed enemy troop concentrations in MT MAPATAD-MT CAMPANA area.

Leader made dry run from W to E to identify bombing objective, and in two successive passes the two flights dropped 11 bombs in target area. SAP TROPHY reported excellent results to flight leader. The first flight, after bombing enemy troop concentrations at 15.3-77.8 on sheet No.3455-II strafed positions marked by L-5 between 16.7-76.3 and 17.0-76.6, making run from NE to SW.

The second flight did not strafe. Pilots observed bomb striking in area marked by WP. 1x1,000lb bomb stuck approximately 400 yards NW of target on E bank of MANADLAN RIVER. Friendly artillery fire observed NE of fork of PURAY RIVER at 07.3-88.2 and also on MT PANAS, MT CARIBA and MT MALAC. Friendly artillery fire noticed over target strafed.

C-47 sighted flying S over MT MAPATAD area. One bomb on 1 a/c hung up, later jettisoned off TABONES ISLAND. One a/c without radio contact jettisoned bombs off TABONES IS.

11x1,000lb AN-M65 bombs and 1,300 rounds of .50 cal. ammunition expended.

**Mission No.1-8 (#24):** 12 June 1945

Air alert over Balete Pass.

Lieutenant Amadeo Castro Almanza, Lieutenant Jacobo Estrada Luna, Lieutenant Reynaldo Perez Gallardo, 2nd Lieutenant Angel Sanchez Rebollo, 2nd Lieutenant Miguel Moreno Arreola and 2nd Lieutenant David Ceron Bedolla, accompanied by one American pilot.

Take-off time 1430, time over target 1535 – 1555, return to base at 1630.

Results: this mission was not completed due to bad weather and lack of targets. When the leader was flying over the target he asked the controller for instructions (SAP RUMBLER) but the objective was very overcast and as the controller SAP BUNNY had no alternatives, SAP DOODLEBUG ordered the bombs to be dropped at the security zone. All P-47s jettisoned their bombs in the security zone of Tabone Island.

In the United States, a UP report filed from Manila on 12 June appeared in the *New York Times* under the headline 'Mexican fliers score – Blast Japanese in caves on independent mission':

> Mexican Expeditionary Air Force pilots, now operating on their own, blasted Japanese troops holed up in caves in the Sierra Madre Mountains east of Manila Sunday. In close support of American infantry, the Mexicans flying Thunderbolts, bombed and strafed caves within 1,000 yards of American front lines. All flights returned and reported no ack-ack fire .The Mexicans got their first taste of combat flying as wingmen to battle-wise American fighter pilots, but have been operating independently since June 7.

Back in Mexico City, a 12 June United Press news release from Manila, headlined 'Squadron 201 covers itself in glory', was published in *Universal*, including some details of the 201st's first day of actual combat operations as a squadron:

> The operations being done by the Mexican contingent of Squadron 201 have been distinguished by their efficiency and precision in their attacks in support of the activities of the ground forces; this was informed by Maj. Harry N. Oden of Duncenter, Dakota, second in command of the 58th Fighter Group, 5th Fighter Command of combat aircraft, the one American to fly with the Mexicans in their first independent mission last Sunday. 'They did a magnificent job and they obtained magnify results,' he said.
>
> The Mexicans operated for the first time in combat forming as wingmen to American pilots committed to the fight, but they had been operating ndependently since 7 June.
>
> Their first independent attack was directed towards a concentration of Japanese troops, about 12 kilometres towards the interior of the south- west coast of Luzon in the zone of Islanda. The American infantry forces, that were seven thousand metres away, oriented the Mexicans towards the objective, Japanese-occupied prepared positions in a heavy wooded area. The Mexican pilots reported that they saw the whole zone of the objective being shaken by explosions and covered by dense smoke when they left.
>
> Six pilots distinguished themselves, all are from Mexico City: Capt. Pablo Rivas and Lt. Amadeo Castro, Reynaldo Perez Gallardo, Luis Barbosa Cerda, Manuel Farias and Mario Lopez.
>
> Operating in support of American infantry forces, the Mexicans drove their Thunderbolts over difficult objectives, bombing and strafing the caves where the Japanese were hiding, about a thousand metres from the American forward lines. Following their regular tactics, the Japanese would fire their artillery or machine guns from the mouth of the caves or hiding places. They would hide in the interior of these, which was important to attack with speed as the positions were located … in wooded areas.
>
> There was the added difficulty of low clouds by the sides of the mountains of the Sierra Madre, forcing them to find the route guided by signals launched by the American artillery with phosphorus white smoke.
>
> Each Thunderbolt carried two bombs, which made impact in the zone of the objective, but the trees of this wooded area didn't

permit observeration of results after the bombing. All the aircraft returned to base, after dropping their explosives over the zone … and strafing enemy positions.

United Press also reported mission 1-7 (#23) of 12 June in a release dated 14 June, headed 'They bombed with success – They suffered no losses over the Philippines':

> Six Thunderbolts piloted by Mexicans bombed and strafed Japanese positions in the area of Marikina [*sic*] Dam, to the east of Manila, guided by an American pilot of the 58th Group of the Vth fighter command of the 5th Air Force.
>
> The Mexicans hit the target on the objectives which were assigned with eleven [460kg] bombs out of the twelve that they dropped and later strafed the Japanese positions which were marked by an observer who was flying a small aircraft for that purpose. They didn't encounter any anti-aircraft fire [and] all the pilots returned safely to their bases.

**Mission No.1-9 (#25):** 13 June 1945

Air Support to ground troops in the area of Mariquina.

Captain Pablo L. Rivas Martinez, Lieutenant Graco Ramirez Garrido, 2nd Lieutenant David Ceron Bedolla and 2nd Lieutenant Miguel Uriarte Aguilar, accompanied by two American pilots.

Take-off time 0830, time over target 0910 – 0930, return to base at 1030.

Results: as directed by SAP TROPHY, 6 a/c bombed ravine marked by WP at 14.5-77.9 (sheet 3455-II, 1:50,000) with the second aircraft of second element strafing during the bomb run.

9x1,000lb bombs fell directly in target area, 1 bomb fell 400 yards NNW of marked target and 2 bombs hung up and were jettisoned in LAGUNA DE BAY. Results unobserved due to heavy foliage. C-47 sighted flying west to east vicinity target area.

10x1,000lb GP AN-M65 bombs dropped on target and 16 rounds of 0.50 cal. Ammunition expended, 2x1,000lb bombs jettisoned LAGUNA DE BAY.

**Mission No.1-10 (#26):** 13 June 1945

Air alert over Infanta.

2nd Lieutenant Raul Garcia Mercado, 2nd Lieutenant Jaime Zenizo Rojas, 2nd Lieutenant Roberto Urias Avelleyra, 2nd Lieutenant David Ceron Bedolla and 2nd Lieutenant Praxedis Lopez Ramos, accompanied by two American pilots.

Take-off time 1240, time over target 1320 – 1325, landed at 1500.

Results: the mission was not completed due to the lack of targets. The leader contacted the controller SAP CURLESS 2 and they notified him that there was no target in that area.

The controller told him that the previous night the command had been informed that said mission was ineffective. The 7 P-47s dropped their bombs in the security zone of Bagac Bay.

**Mission No.1-11 (#27):** 14 June 1945

Air alert over Montalban.

Captain Roberto Legorreta Sicilia, Lieutenant Carlos Varela Landini, Lieutenant Amador Samano Pina, Lieutenant Graco Ramirez Garrido, Lieutenant Fernando Hernandez Vega, Lieutenant Carlos Rodriguez Corona2nd Lieutenant Manuel Farias Rodriguez, 2nd Lieutenant David Ceron Bedolla, 2nd Lieutenant Guillermo Garcia Ramos and 2nd Lieutenant Miguel Uriarte Aguilar, accompanied by one American pilot.

Take-off time 0730, time over target 0800 – 0845, return to base 0915.

Results: the mission was not completed due to communications problems with the ground units.

The leader contacted controller TROPHY when arriving at Montalban area. The controller ordered that he contact the controller in the area; the leader contacted controller TROPHY 2 who indicated to him the target, but the leader could not find the designation to the target.

The leader tried to contact Controller TROPHY but radio contact was nil.

The 11 P-47s did not bomb any targets. 3 P-47s flown by Lieutenant Carlos Rodriguez Corona, 2nd Lieutenant Manuel Farias Rodriguez and Lieutenant Amador Samano Pina turned back early to base due to engine problems. Their bombs were dropped in the security zone of Manila Bay, while the remainder were dropped at Tabone Island.

One bomb hung up, and it finally fell outside the security zone of Laguna Bay, hitting the water and causing no damage.

**Mission No.1-12 (#28):** 15 June 1945

Bombing and strafing of enemy troop concentrations, supplies and ammunition dump at Tuguegarao.

Captain Radames Gaxiola Andrade, Lieutenant Hector Espinosa Galvan, Lieutenant Joaquin Ramirez Vilchis, Lieutenant Amadeo Castro Almanza, 2nd Lieutenant Guillermo Garcia Ramos, 2nd Lieutenant Roberto Urias Avelleyra and 2nd Lieutenant Jaime Zenizo Rojas, accompanied by two American pilots.

Take-off time 0800, time over target 0900 – 0930 at altitude of 5,000ft, return to base 1030.

One aircraft landed back at 0820 due to mechanical trouble.

The flight leader made two dry runs from E to W over the target and on the following pass bombed and strafed the objective.

One aircraft failed to release bombs over the target due to mechanical failure and two 1,000lb bombs were jettisoned in the Gulf of Lingayen. One direct hit with attendant explosion was observed on W building of two designated as target. Another explosion was observed upon the impact of a bomb which hung over target and hit approximately on the SW corner of intersection at point … 900 yards N from W bank(.

Five minutes later the strike leader noticed blue smoke approximately 1,500ft over area where the two larger explosions were reported. The controller reported two prolonged explosions in the target area.

One building of two designated as target observed almost demolished prior to attack.

One aircraft delayed in take off and snafued, two 1,000lb bombs dropped in the vicinity of Tabone Island. A total of 14 1,000lb bombs and 480 rounds of 0.50 cal. ammunition expended over the target.

During this mission, the 201st was credited with the probable destruction of a small ship, which has still to be officially confirmed. One of the pilots taking part would later be mentioned by one of the squadron's personnel, 2nd Lieutenant David Ceron Bedolla, who was interviewed in a Mexico City newspaper in August 1945 after his return home:

> He refers to a historical act of a comrade, who is known by the entire squadron; his name is Zenizo Rojas, who has received the nickname of 'Donald Duck' (*Pato Pascual*).
>
> This officer with others from the squadron was ordered to bomb

Ground personnel taking a break under the wing of a 201st P-47D Thunderbolt. (Family of Lieutenant Mechanic Jesus Gutierrez Figueroa)

The squadron jeep picking up three pilots and ground crews after their return from a mission. In the background is P-47D-30-RA No.21 44-33737. (Enrique Velasco Padilla)

a concentration of Japanese troops. He dropped his first bomb without any problems, but the second one did not drop. This able pilot entered on a horizontal flight, to be able to observe the trouble when he was raising the aircraft up, and in that precise moment the bomb dropped ....

This pilot had some tremedous luck, that later everybody found out about ... 'Donald Duck' told his comrades and some who witnessed in the field of operations, that the 'stuck bomb' fell on a Japanese ammo dump. This caused heavy casualties and he received commendations from the American high command.

The 201st and other USAAF units hit Tuguegarao the day before a major offensive was launched by the 3rd Battalion of the 11th Infantry of the US Army Forces in the Philippines to take the town.

The Filipino guerrilla force had been received a major reorganisation in 1943 and was now was a major unit in the fight in northern Luzon. Tuguegarao was taken the next day after a fight with continuing air support, with no artillery used in the action.

**Mission No.1-13 (#29):** 15 June 1945

Air alert over Antipolo.

Lieutenant Carlos Garduno Nunez, Lieutenant Reynaldo Perez Gallardo, Liutenant Julio Cal y Mayor Sauz, Lieutenant Amador Samano Pina, 2nd Lieutenant Angel Sanchez Rebollo and 2nd Lieutenant Miguel Moreno Arreola, accompanied by two American pilots.

Take-off time 1230, time over target 1320 – 1400, return to base 1430.

Results: 9 P-47s took off (including two American pilots) but two aircraft flown by Lieutenant Amador Samano Pina and 2nd Lieutenant Angel Sanchez Rebollo returned to Porac without completing the mission.

The remaining aircraft bombed and strafed enemy positions 1,200 metres south-east of San Andres, which the controller SAP CURLESS 1 had directed the leader to bomb and strafe at approximately 1,200ft. They strafed the east side of the gorge of said town. The results of the bombing could not be observed due to the vegetation in the area.

The ground observers reported the bombing as very good.

12 bombs and 3,720 rounds of 0.50 cal. were expended. Four bombs were dropped at the security zone of Laguna de Bay and two more at Tabones Island (by one of the American pilots?).

## COMBAT TIME MID-JUNE 1945

Not only were the pilots were getting to see action, but also some of the ground personnel of the MEAF. Lieutenant Colonel Alfonso Gurza Farfan and Major Enrique Sandoval of the command and staff visited the general headquarters and subordinated units of the 33rd Infantry Division of the I US Army Corps, which was part of the US Sixth Army, from 15-16 June. The division operated in Baguio, Luzon.

**Mission No.1-14 (#30):** 16 June 1945

Air alert over Infanta.

(Target to bomb and strafe enemy concentrations at 44.6-77.3 not attacked; area occupied by friendly troops.) Completed.

Captain Pablo L. Rivas Martinez, Captain Roberto Legorreta Sicilia, Lieutenant ReynaldoPerez Gallardo, Lieutenant Jacobo Estrada Luna, Lieutenant Hector Espinosa Galvan, Lieutenant Jose L.Barbosa Cerda, 2nd Lieutenant Jose L. Pratt Ramos, 2nd Lieutenant Guillermo Garcia Ramos, 2nd Lieutenant Mario Lopez Portillo and 2nd Lieutenant Manuel Farias Rodriguez, accompanied by one American pilot.

Take-off time 1145, time over target 1235 – 1315, return to base 1350.

Results: As directed by SAP CURLESS 2 the first target was not attacked, since American troops had captured it.

They were ordered to attack enemy concentrations along Ikdan Creek. 11 P-47s (including one American pilot) bombed in the first pass and in three more passes strafed the same area. The Mexican pilots observed two larger explosions that produced brown smoke. The controller reported good results on this mission. Enemy anti-aircraft fire was encountered, moderate, medium accurate from 500-700ft. Mortar fire and machine-gun fire with large volumes of small arms fire. This came from both sides, to the south of Irdan Creek and along the beach.

Two aircraft hit, one by mortar and machine-gun fire at approximately 500ft, and the second received three hits of small arms fire.

A total of 22 bombs and 13,520 rounds of 0.50 cal. ammunition expended.

It was reported, but without confirmation, that the Mexican and American pilots destroyed a column of Japanese tanks that were threatening a US advance in the area. On that same day, the 310th Squadron of the 58th FG flew a ground support mission with the following results:

4 A/C bombed and strafed enemy bivouac area east of IGUIG Luzon. 8x500lb bombs were direct hits in target. 1 large building was completely destroyed. Numerous shacks were holed by strafing, but no resulting fires.

**Mission No.1-15 (#31):** 17 June 1945

Bomb enemy concentrations, mission completed on alternative target in the area of Bangong.

Lieutenant Amadeo Castro Almanza, Lieutenant Carlos Garduno Nunez, Lieutenant Jacobo Estrada Luna, 2nd Lieutenant Jaime Zenizo Rojas, 2nd Lieutenant Praxedis Lopez Ramos and 2nd Lieutenant Roberto Urias Avelleyra.

Take-off time 0730, time over target 0920 – 0930, return to base 1000.

Results: As directed by SAP BYGONE 1 the mission was completed on an alternative target.

On take-off the P-47D-16-RA 42-75894 caught fire and was completely destroyed. The plane left the runway during take-off and the pilot, Lieutenant Carlos Garduno Nunez, received burns to his neck and was taken to SANTA RITA hospital.

The aircraft flown by 2nd Lieutenant Jaime Zenizo Rojas returned early due to mechanical problems.

The target was located 6,500 metres South West of Bangong. With the help of ground controller BYGONE 1 four P-47s dropped eight bombs over the target area. The results could not be observed due to the vegetation covering the area. SAP BYGONE 1 reported first 2x1,000lb bombs long, but into the target area, and 6x1,000lb bombs direct on target.

8x1,000lb ANM65 bombs expended on target; 2 bombs returned to base by snafu.

Information for the 201st Squadron's activities that day given by Captain Pablo L. Rivas Martinez includes the following:

During the day … 28 hours and 55 minutes were flown in P-47D aircraft in combat missions by the pilots of the squadron. 30 more minutes were flown in test flights. Lieutenant Carlos Garduno Nunez suffered an accident on the runway while attempting to take off, in which the aircraft burned, 42-75894. He suffered burns, being transferred over to the 894th Hospital Clearing Co. (Sta. Rita). The pilots 2nd Lieutenants Jose Luis Pratt Ramos and Guillermo Garcia Ramos left for Manila City with permission.

The aircraft accident report for 17 June, signed by Captain Pablo Rivas Martinez, the operations officer, states the nature of the accident and probable causes:

A/C seemed to lack enough power for take off and engine started a fire setting off the belly tank, which exploded. A/c carried 2x1,000lb Bombs, both recovered.

The aircraft was a complete loss. The summary of the accident report says the responsibilty was 80 percent pilot error and 20 percent mechanical failure. Reportedly one of the pilots who didn't take off due to the accident was Lieutenant Reynaldo Perez Gallardo, who got out of his aircraft and took pictures of what was left of Carlos Garduno's aircraft.

**Mission No.1-16 (#32):** 17 June 1945

Bomb enemy concentrations in Payawan Rest House, north central Luzon.

This mission is best described by Lieutenant Samano Pina, who recalled:

One important mission was number 1-16 of June (17th) in the region of Payawan Rest House (Chart 3641-16) led by by the controller BYGONE. Our flight leader discovered an enemy convoy on a secondary road and notified us to strafe it, and you can imagine, we strafed the hell of it!

The flight headed for the target, I had a truck right in front of me. We rapidly closed in, I let go two bursts. After the second one, I saw flames rising from the vehicle, and we gained altitude to avoid any explosions, while the others were doing the same to the convoy.

Enemy anti-aircraft fire was light and [inaccurate]. Two aircraft of our flight were hit by machine-gun fire. With the strafing we dropped fourteen 1,000lb bombs. With this mission our leader Lieutenant Hector Espinosa Galvan showed [himself] to be precise and effective, having obtained good results in all the missions he led.

In this instance, we took off at 1330 hours and landed back at 1545 hours.

This mission involved eight P-47s flown by Lieutenant Hector Espinosa Galvan, Lieutenant Carlos Varela Landini, Lieutenant Fernando Hernandez Vega, Lieutenant Amador Samano Pina, Lieutenant Joaquin Ramirez Vilchis,2nd Lieutenant Miguel Uriarte Aguilar,2nd Lieutenant Manuel Farias Ramos and 2nd Lieutenant Raul Garcia Mercado.

The aircraft flown by Hernandez Vega and his wingman Uriarte Aguilar returned early. A total of 14 bombs were dropped and 6,900 rounds of 0.50 calibre ammunition used, with two 1,000lb bombs dropped safely on a hill in the Balete Pass area – the pilot reported they did not explode. The official summary of the mission reads as follows:

Bombardment of enemy concentration in the vicinity of Payawan (north and centre of Luzon). Nine planes took off at 1315, flew over the target at 5,000ft from 1430 to 1500; landed at 1545. (One aircraft returned due to mechanical problems.)

Controller BYGONE with the help of controller DAISY BLUE directed them to bomb and strafe enemy concentrations and a convoy, located approximately 6,000 yards NE of Payawan. The pilots saw the bombs fall on the objective. After making strafing passes on the convoy they saw two trucks catch fire. The airplanes were fired at by large mortars and close-range guns. Two planes were hit but suffered only slight damage.

After the successful mission, the members of the flight received a surprise day's leave, as recalled by Lieutenant Amador Samano Pina:

The next day we were notified that the pilots of 'C' flight had the day off. We were loaned two light vehicles to go into Manila. Our medic Major Ricardo Blanco Cancino recommended caution on our day off – not to eat fruits, to avoid stomach problems be careful with the water, with this and that!

When we arrived in Manila, we found a Spanish colony, where we made friends due to our facility to understand the same language. We enquired about a good restaurant, and we were recommend 'Ciros', where we found high-ranking American officers and well-accommodated Filipino families.

I ordered a dish of white rice with a fillet, which was the best thing on the menu. The fillet was microcsopic due to the war but I was charged 10 Filipino pesos, which was about five U.S. dollars and about $24.00 Mexican pesos. Which made me remember, when I was stationed in Zacatecas, the '*Madre* [Mother] *Maria*' of the infantry batallion would feed us for about $1.50 pesos daily! …

After that we went to visit Sr Alfredo Carmelo, the Mexican

Consul in Manila, who treated us well and invited us to dinner. After the war Sr Carmelo and his family moved back to Mexico, where he frequently gave receptions to the members of the squadron.

After dinner we returned to Porac, having our .45s ready, because on the roads there were still enemy guerrillas. Luckily nothing happened. We went to bed, to be ready for the next day.

**Mission No.1-17 (#33):** 17 June 1945

Bomb enemy concentrations, Lenatin River.

Lieutenant Amadeo Castro Almanza, Lieutenant Julio Cal y Mayor Sauz, Lieutenant Jose Luis Barbosa Cerda, 2nd Lieutenant Miguel Moreno Arreola, 2nd Lieutenant Jaime Zenizo Rojas, 2nd Lieutenant Mario Lopez Portillo and 2nd Lieutenant Angel Sanchez Rebollo, accompanied by one American pilot.

Take-off time 0730, time over target 0805 – 0845, return to base 0930.

Results: As directed by SAP CURLESS 1 8 P-47s (including one American pilot), led by Lieutenant Castro Almanza, bombed and strafed enemy positions to the West of the Lenatin River.

The objective was marked by an L-5 aircraft, which dropped a smoke flare on the target. The fight leader first made a recon pass from S to N. In the following pass he dropped his bombs and strafed the target.

All 16 bombs struck the target. The flight made two more passes strafing the target. The ground controller CURLESS reported excellent results.

Anti-aircraft fire, light but effective, was encountered at 2,000ft. Four anti-aircraft machine gun positions reported in four locations. A total of 4,360 rounds of 0.50 cal. ammunition used. 1 aircraft landed with flat tyre upon return to base.

**Mission No.1-18 (#34):** 18 June 1945

Bomb enemy concentrations, Lenatin River.

Lieutenant Hector Espinosa Galvan, Lieutenant Graco Ramirez Garrido, 2nd Lieutenant Guillermo Garcia Ramos and 2nd Lieutenant Manuel Farias Rodriguez, accompanied by one American pilot.

Results: The mission was completed on both sides of the Lenatin River. The five P-47s led by Lieutenant Hector Espinosa Galvan (including one American pilot), were led by the ground controller CURLESS 1 to attack enemy troop concentrations near the river bed in two passes and then procceded to strafe both sides of the shore and river beds. An L-5 aircraft marked an initial point for straffing passes aproximately 1 mile south of bomb objective.

Two m/g positions were silenced during the first strafing pass. No m/g fire encountered on the second strafing pass. A total of 10 bombs and 6,180 rounds of 0.50 cal. ammunition used. CURLESS 1 reported the strafing as good, and bombing as excellent.

During take-off for this mission, the aircraft flown by 2nd Lieutenant Ceron Bedolla suffered an accident, as he did not reach sufficient speed. His P-47D-23-RA 42-27995 suffered propeller and engine damage, necessitating a complete change of engine and repairs to the flight controls and tail landing gear. Ceron Bedolla was unhurt in the incident.

Mission No.1-19 (#35): 19 June 1945

Air alert over Antipolo.

Captain Pablo L. Rivas Martinez, Captain. .Roberto Legorreta Sicilia, Lieutenant Reynaldo Perez Gallardo, Lieutenant Carlos Rodriguez Corona and 2nd Lieutenant Guillermo Garcia Ramos, accompanied by one American pilot.

Take-off time 0800, time over target 0845 – 0915, return to base at 1000.

Results: As directed by SAP CURLESS 1 the mission was cancelled by orders of the ground controller, due to radio communications failure with the L-5 aircraft. The six P-47s (including an American pilot) dropped their bombs in the security zone of Laguna del Bay.

One phosphorous shell of undetermined calibre was fired at the formation over the target area, exploding at approximatly 2,000-3,000f. and about 500 yards from the formation. SAP CURLESS 1 ordered the leader to return flight to base and not to jettison bombs in the area.

MANGOS could not be contacted. 12x1,000lb bombs jettisoned LAGUNA DE BAY upon direction of SAP DOODLE BUG.

On this day another of the squadron's ground personnel participated in a combat mission when Captain 2nd Class Jesus Blanco Ledesma, the intelligence officer, took part in a bombing mission to the island of Formosa by elements of the 5th Bomber Command. He returned to the unit the next day, and news of his feat was published on 23 July in an Associated Press report from Clark Field, Luzon, under the headline 'First Mexican pilot hits Japs':

> Capt. Jesus Blanco Ledesma, one of Mexico's veteran pilots, now holds the distinction of being the first member of the Mexican Expeditionary Air Force to hit Japanese territory.
>
> Blanco flew with the famous 'Red Raiders' heavy bomber group of the American Fifth air force in a Liberator strike at Japanese shipping and shore installations on Formosa. Blanco has other 'famous firsts' to his record.
>
> He was the first member to join Mexico's first expeditionary air force and activated the 201st fighter squadron at Mexico City last year. He also was the first bombardier to win wings with the Mexican air Force.

Captain Blanco Ledesma's mission was flown with the Consolidated B-24J Liberators of the 22nd Bomber Group, which hit the docks, warehouses and rail yards at Kiirun, Formosa.

The 27-year-old married officer from Tacubaya, Mexico, was born on 22 January 1917. His parents were Brigadier General Joaquin Victor Blanco, who was killed in action during the Mexican revolutionary period soon after his birth in 1917, and Flora Ledesma.

After completing his education, he participated and was admitted to the *Heroico Colegio Militar* on 21 June 1933, graduating on 1 January 1939 as an artillery 2nd Lieutenant, being assigned to the 2nd Artillery Regiment.

In that same year he requested to join and was admitted to the Military Aviation School to train as a pilot, but was eliminated from the course in June 1940 and sent to the 1st Artillery Regiment at Acapulco, Guerrero, being promoted to Lieutenant on 16 November 1940.

He was promoted to Captain 2nd Class on 1 July 1943.

Blanco Ledesma had requested to be sent back to the Military Aviation School in July 1941, but ended up serving as a instructor at the *Escuela Superior de Guerra* from 1942-43, when he was selected to be part of the first generation of the bombardier and navigator course in the Mexican Air Force in 1944.

After graduating he was assigned to the 101st Squadron equipped with the Beech AT-11 from January to March 1944, and from there to the *Direccion de Aeronautica* until assigned on 4 July 1944 to the 201st

Mexican ground personnel on a mission outside the airfield have their weapons ready in case of a surprise attack by any Japanese soldiers still left in the area. Notice the vehicle is marked as belonging to the MEAF. (Manuel Cervantes Ramos)

Squadron.

**Mission No.1-20 (#36):** 20 June 1945

This mission was an air alert over Antipolo. The leader was the squadron Commander, Captain Gaxiola Andrade, with five Mexican pilots and two American pilots who accompanied the flight. But the final mission report submitted by Captain Radames Gaxiola Andrade lists a total of eight pilots participating in this mission, not mentioning 2nd Lieutenant David Ceron Bedolla (who crashed after landing), and with possibly only one American pilot joining them: Captain Radames Gaxiola Andrade, Lieutenant Jacobo Estrada Luna, Lieutenant Graco Ramirez Garrido, Lieutenant Fernando Hernandez Vega, Lieutenant Amador Samano Pina and 2nd Lieutenant Jose L. Pratt Ramos, accompanied by two American pilots.

Take-off time 0730, time over target 0830 – 0850, return to base at 0930.

Led by elements of liaision detachment SAP CURLESS 1, the leader was to make contact with an L-5 aircraft.

Captain Gaxiola reported he made contact with the liaison aircraft, which marked the target with smoke bombs. The formation bombed the target and two additional strafing passes were made. The pilots observed all bombs exploded on the target area. The leader observed two red bombs (smoke) to the side of the target. The ground controller CURLESS 1 reported the results satisfactory.

Later reports were received in the 5th Fighter Command that the formation had carried out the attack in the vicinity of Purro Mountain, where American troops were operating and had been hit. It was later found out there was a misunderstanding between the leader of the formation and the ground support, and there were many L-5 aircraft operating in the area, adding to the confusion.

Sixteen bombs and 5,260 rounds of .50 cal ammunition were fired.

During this mission the aircraft of 2nd Lieutenant Jose Luis Pratt Ramos, P-47D-23-RA 42-27615, was damaged by anti-aircraft fire, suffering a damaged left wing and perforated air connection to the carburettor. It was sent for repairs to the 2nd Aerodrome Squadron but was later dropped from the inventory, which was not mentioned in the final mission report.

2nd Lieutenant David Ceron Bedolla's P-47 D-21-RA 42-25412 was damaged when it nosed over while taxiing back to the squadron flight line. He did not notice the wooden tower with personnel working around it until the last moment, hitting the brakes which nosed over the aircraft. It was determined that pilot error was to blame, and Ceron Bedolla was suspended from flying indefinitely.

The other aircraft that did not take off due to brake failure may have been piloted by Lieutenant Joaquin Ramirez Vilchis.

Both incidents are mentioned in the combat report for this mission by Captain Jesus Blanco Ledesma, which included the following:

A. FF0 171-B-6 Mission number 1-20, 20 June 1945. 201st Mexican fighter Sq.8 P-47s
B. Air Alert over ANTIPOLO. Bombed and strafed enemy concentrations at 11.5-85.5 Sheet 3455-II. Mission completed.
C. TO 0730/I TOT 0839 to 0850/I Altitude 2,000ft landed 0930/I.
D. As directed by SAP CURLESS 1 and an L-5, 8 a/c bombed and strafed enemy concentrations on E bank of MONTALBAN RIVER at 11.5-85.5 (1:50,000). Objective was spotted perfectly by L-5 which dropped two white smoke bombs. Pilots observed all bombs strike target area, but were unable to observe results due to heavy foliage. Flight Leader observed two red smoke bombs on side of target. Formation made two strafing passes at target. SAP CURLES 1 reported SATISFACTORY results. ...
G. Slight, light inaccurate [enemy fire] at 500ft. Enemy positions reported firing at 11.3-84.7 from 0835/I to 0850/I. ...
I. Pilots observed possible barracks of enemy troops on E bank MONTALA RIVER at 11.0-85.0.
J. CAVU to target: 4/10s cover from 2,000 to 4,000ft over target; 5/10s cover from 2,000 to 4,000ft on return.
K. 1 a/c failed to take off due to mechanical failure of brakes. Pilot uninjured. No damage to a/c. 1 a/c. taxiing on return from mission, nosed over and damaged propeller.
L. 16x1,000lb GP AN-M65 bombs with AN-M103A1 nose fuse and AN-M102A2 tail fuse, both instantaneous, expended; 5,960 rounds of Cal. 50 ammo expended.

In Colonel Cardenas' report to Mexico City, he mentions the following about this incident:

On June 20 as elements of the 201st Squadron were on a bombing and machine-gunning mission against enemy troops ,weather conditions and signalling of the target resulted in a confusion of the target which affected friendly troops. Investigation made it possible to attribute the confusion to the means of signalling the target, as the formation which was performing the mission was acting under the direction of a ground controller of friendly troops, over a target signalled by the smoke of a liaison plane of these troops.

In his dissertation about the 201st, William Tudor claims that this incident actually occurred a day later on 21 June:

On June 21-22, 1945, unidentified allied fighter planes strafed and killed a number of US Infantry soldiers near the Payawan Rest House on Luzon. Russel E. McLogan, then a scout with Company K, 63rd Infantry, fought in this area just before and during one of the allied fighter raids. A Japanese machine gunner seriously wounded him on the afternoon of June 21, putting him out of action.

While he convalesced in a Bagabag hospital, reports reached him that the pilots of these planes were Mexican and that a language problem had caused the mishap. Although this 'Friendly fire' incident did not involve the 201st, McLogan later wrote a book which made this unsubstantiated assertation.

Republic P-47D-30-RA Thunderbolt No.1 44-33721 ready to undertake another mission over the Philippines. (Enrique Velasco Padilla)

In his book *Boy Soldier: Coming of Age during World War II* McLogan wrote that between June 21 and 22 the first battalion continued guarding the supply route to the forward elements. At the close of the period, Company A was moving to the vicinity of the Payawan Rest House. 'Friendly planes, strafing in front of our troops caused some eight casualties among our men.'... An Officer in his company, Lieutenant Tom Atchley, wrote [to] McLogan concerning the June 22 incident.

'All of a sudden here came three fighter planes, they made a circle around us tilting their wings, I suppose to tell where we were. I told Capt. Fleming that they were going to strafe or bomb us – maybe both. The lead plane had its nose down. They made three runs over us shooting fifty-caliber machine guns.

'About 12 or 18 of our men got wounded,' Atchely continued. 'Those planes were flown by Mexican pilots, they were supposed to be on recon patrol. They weren't supposed to do any shooting or bombing. We didn't have any way of contacting them.'

Mr Tudor is quite correct to mention that the 201st did not conduct any reconaissance missions, while the sister squadrons of the 58th did carry out weather reconaissance in the region. But the actual date of the incident was 20 June, not the 21st and the location was in the region of the Antipolo and Puro Mountains, as recorded in official Mexican documents and by the 5th Fighter Command, as well as several pilots' diaries.

For the next two days, pilots from the 58th Fighter Group replaced the American pilots of the liaison group and accompanied the squadron flights. This mission highlights the fears that some of the pilots and 'ground pounders' had that a strike would go wrong and hit friendly troops.

Historian Terrill Clements wrote about this very problem:

Readers may also be interested to know that in addition to the occasional 'friendly' fire problem, P-38 Lightnings were unpopular providers of air support for US troops on Luzon.

All too often these aircraft experienced hung up bombs that the pilot tried to shake off without much regard for the forces they were flying above.

After an errant bomb destroyed one of the 148th Infantry HQ jeeps during the battle of Baguio in April, Regimental command asked that only P-51 units fly air support in their sector. Combat was difficult enough without such unnecessary dangers.

This issue was obviously a major concern among American pilots, as noted in the history of the 311th Fighter Squadron covering events in July 1945:

The missions into the Cagayen Valley could be termed armed reccos rather than close ground support, as the infantry was advancing so rapidly that close support could not be given safely. Therefore, our planes would hit several miles ahead of the forward lines, knocking out gun positions, caves, bridges and tank concentrations and strafing buildings and transportation along the roads.

The North American P-51 Mustang also ran into the same problem in January 1945, when reports were received that some P-51s shot up friendly troops along the Pampanga River. General Whitehead could not find the guilty pilots and began to suspect Japanese Tony (KI-61) fighter planes painted with American insignias had been responsible, so he grounded all Mustang fighters for about 10 days and sent out patrols to shoot down any suspect aircraft they found.

Another problem was artillery rounds that landed short on American and Filipino positions, although not many unit histories mention their errors that occurred during the fighting in northern Luzon.

Meanwhile, some Mexican pilots tried to prevent any unnecessary destruction of churches in some of the towns they attacked, as highlighted in a story that was published on a Hispano-Filipino website. It told of the Catholic church in the town of Manaoag in Pangasinan province, the sanctuary of the Lady of Manaoag, today

A picture of the flight line showing the Lend Lease Republic P-47D-30-RAs, probably at Clark Field. (Manuel Cervantes Ramos)

an important cultural and spiritual centre and popular pilgrimage site in the Philippines. Years after the war, a Mexican tourist visited the church and talked to the priest there, telling him he was a fighter pilot with the 201st Mexican Fighter Squadron who, while leading a flight of four aircraft, had been ordered to bomb Manaoag in 1945. It had been reported that a Japanese force was in the town halting the advance of American troops.

The Mexican officer told the priest that he overflew the town many times to try to see any activities of Japanese forces, but the only thing he saw was local people coming and going around the church. He reported back his findings but was told to carry out the original plan and bomb the town. The Mexican officer, being a Catholic, felt he could not endanger the town and church, so instead he ordered his flight to bomb the outskirts of the town and return to base. His actions thus spared this important church and the town of Manaoag. So far the author has not been able to determine in what mission this incident happened.

However, recent research has been able to locate the US Army unit that was involved in the incident of 20 June 1945; it was the 1st Battalion, 151st Infantry Regiment of the 38th Infantry Division, as noted in the unit history:

> On 20 May [*sic*] the 1st battalion 151st Infantry while awaiting a C-47 air drop was accidently attacked by 7 P-47s which dropped 10 bombs and made 13 strafing attacks. Casualties numbered about 30 men but fortunately no one was killed. Two litter cases were evacuated by Helicopter.

This highlights part of the Philippines campaign story that is not widely known: that Sikorsky R-4B helicopters were deployed to the combat zone, part of the 5th Aircraft Repair Unit. This unit evacuated between 75 and 80 wounded soldiers from 15 June to 29 July 1945.

**Mission No.1-21 (#37):** 20 June 1945

Air alert over Antipolo.

Lieutenant Amadeo Castro Almanza, Lieutenant Jose L. Barbosa Cerda, 2nd Lieutenant Praxedis Lopez Ramos, 2nd Lieutenant Miguel Moreno Arreolla, 2nd Lieutenant Roberto Urias Avelleyra and 2nd Lieutenant Mario Lopez Portillo, accompanied by one American pilot.

Take-off time 1300, time over target 1345 – 1414, return to base 1500.

Results: As directed by SAP CURLESS 1 leader proceeded on vector 50-16 Mi. CURLESS 1 ordered return to ANTIPOLO to wait for L-5 who spotted target with WP.

One dry run was made by leader and on following pass 14x1,000lb bombs were dropped on target area, 1 on N bank of river. Bomb run made S to NE. Upon order of SAP CURLESS 1, a/c strafed, made passes SW to NE. Results unobserved due to heavy foliage. SAP reported bombing 'OK' and that all but 1 bomb struck in target area.

Slight, light, inaccurate [enemy fire] at 500ft. Pilots report having silenced MG position at 29.0-79.5. Mortar fire bursts from 29.2-80.1. Heavy s/a fire from area. SAP CURLESS 1 advised leader that mission tomorrow would probably be in the same place as today's second mission. 1 a/c did not take off, pilot reported high oil consumption and leak. 14x1,000lb GP bombs and 8,880 rounds of .50 cal ammunition expended.

**Mission No.1-22 (#38):** 21 June 1945

Bomb enemy troop concentrations near Malabito Mountain.

Captain Pablo L. Rivas Martinez, Captain Roberto Legorreta Sicilia, Lieutenant Hector Espinosa Galvan, Lieutenant Carlos Rodriguez Corona, Lieutenant Joaquin Ramirez Vilchis and 2nd Lieutenant Jaime Zenizo Rojas, accompanied by one pilot 58th FG.

Take-off time 0830, time over target 0935 – 1000, back to base 1030.

Results: As directed by SAP CURLESS 1, 7 aircraft bombed and strafed an area within approximately 150 yards radius of point at 30.1-78.7 photomap MT MALABITO SW 3555-III, 1:50.000.

Leader made dry run and on second pass 14x1,000lb bombs were dropped in target area on both E and W banks of river. 1 large explosion reported near machine gun emplacement at 30.2-78.7. 4 strafing passes were made.

SAP CURLESS 1 reported results of bombing and strafing good. Slight, light, inaccurate [enemy fire] at 100 to 500ft. Concentrated machine-gun and small arms fire received from 29.8-49.1.

Machine gun emplacement at 30.2-78.7. L-5 identified self with white flare and rocked wings, led mission to target and spotted objective with WP. 14x1,000lb GP AN-M65 bombs and 8,860 rounds .50 cal. ammunition expended.

**Mission No.1-23 (#39):** 21 June 1945

Air alert over Ilagan.

Lieutenant Amadeo Castro Almanza, Lieutenant Julio Cal y Mayor Sauz, 2nd Lieutenant Roberto Urias Avelleyra, 2nd Lieutenant Miguel Moreno Arreolla, 2nd Lieutenant Angel Sanchez Rebollo and 2nd Lieutenant Miguel Uriarte Aguilar, accompanied by one pilot 58th FG.

Take-off time 1300, time over target 1400 – 1500, return to base at 1600.

Results: 7 P-47s (including one from the 58th FG), led by Lieutenant Amadeo Castro, were directed by ground controller BUNNY to get in contact with NEWPHEW 2, who directed the formation towards Alcala and later to the South of Tuguegarao.

NEWPHEW 2 ordered the American pilot from the 58th FG to drop a bomb on an undentified town, with the objective of recognising the target. The controller informed the leader not to attack this particular town, and directed the formation over Pena Blanca, warning them that American troops were operating about five miles from the town.

With the help of another ground controller MOKO, the formation dropped 13 bombs, setting several buildings afire. The ground controller could not observe the results of the bombing. No .50 cal. ammunition was used or expended. Two aircraft assigned to this mission could not take off due to mechanical problems.

**Mission No.1-24 (#40):** 22 June 1945

Bomb enemy concentrations, Monte Malabito.

Mission completed on alternative target.

Lieutenant Amadeo Castro Almanza, Lieutenant Reynaldo

Republic P-47D-30-RA 44-33679, later to receive the number 22, taxis out of the 201st flight line. The aircraft has not yet received its Mexican markings. (Enrique Velasco Padilla)

Perez Gallardo, Lieutenant Jose L. Barbosa Cerda, 2nd Lieutenant Roberto Urias Avelleyra, 2nd Lieutenant Mario Lopez Portillo and 2nd Lieutenant Jose L. Pratt Ramos, accompanied by two pilots 58th FG.

Take-off time 0800, time over target 0840 – 0920, return to base 1000.

Results: 8 P-47s (including two aircraft from the 58th FG) bombed and strafed enemy positions in a ravine, approx. 12,000 metres West of Infanta, this being an alternative target.

SAP CURLESS ordered leader contact SAP CURLESS 2 over Infanta. Leader made dry run over target marked by artillery WP. One bombing run and three strafing passes were made from S to N on both banks of creek and on stream bed. Slight, light, inaccurate small arms fire reported from both E and W banks of ravines.

15x1,000lb GP AN-M65 bombs and 13,500 rounds of .50 cal. ammunition used. One bomb dropped outside of target. Ground controllers reported very good results.

**Mission No.1-25 (#41):** 22 June 1945

Bombing and strafing enemy troops, AGOS River area.

Captain Radames Gaxiola Andrade, Captain Roberto Legorreta Sicilia, Lieutenant Carlos Varela Landini, Lieutenant Joaquin Ramirez Vilchis, Lieutenant Julio Cal y Mayor Sauz, Lieutenant Graco Ramirez Garrido, 2nd Lieutenant Raul Garcia Mercado and 2nd Lieutenant Miguel Uriarte Aguilar, accompanied by one pilot 58th FG.

Take-off time 1245, time over target 1330 – 1350, landing 1445.

Results: As directed by SAP CURLESS 2 the formation of 9 P-47s (one from the 58th FG) attacked enemy positions marked by artillery. Results could not be observed due to vegetation covering the target.

Three strafing passes were made on a summit, newly made trail observed on hill bombed and strafed running N from N bank of AGOS RIVER. Three strafing passes were made on military crest of hill.

White phosphorous grenade was fired at the formation from area of enemy positions, with no results. Total of 17x1,000lb GP AN-M65 bombs and 8,732 rounds of .50 cal. ammunition used. One 1,000lb bomb jettisoned at LAGUNA DE BAY.

The last combat mission to be flown by the 310th Fighter Squadron of the 58th Fighter Group in the Philippines was flown on 22 June, when eight aircraft bombed Basco Airstrip on Batan Island in the north of Luzon. All bombs were placed on the strip and in the parking areas, cratering the strip.

During June the 310th Fighter Squadron flew 193 combat sorties, dropping 432 bombs (212x1,000lb, 16x500lb and 204x260lb) and 62 napalm bombs, and firing 40,869 rounds of .50 calibre machine-gun ammunition.

**Mission No.1-26 (#42):** 23 June 1945

Bomb enemy troops in the Antipolo area.

Captain Pablo L. Rivas Martinez, Lieutenant Hector Espinosa Galvan, Lieutenant Carlos Rodriguez Corona, Lieutenant Amador SamanoPina, 2nd Lieutenant Miguel Moreno Arreola, 2nd Lieutenant Manuel Farias Rodriguez and 2nd Lieutenant Guillermo Garcia Ramos, accompanied by one American pilot.

Take-off time 0730, time over target 0900 – 0930, return to base at 1000.

Results: As directed by SAP CURLESS 2 the mission was completed on an alternative target. The 8 P-47s (including an American pilot) bombed and strafed enemy positions marked by the ground controller, making one bomb and one strafing run. Four great explosions were observed to the North of the secondary road. Ground controllers reported the attack as very good.

A secondary road reported in target area apparently in use for movements and supply by enemy. SAP reported its bombing and strafing as 'very good' except for two bombs which were long, striking approximately at 52.1-81.2. 16 bombs and 5,730 rounds of .50 cal. ammunition used.

Two aircraft were slightly damaged on landing. While taxiing, P-47D-21-RA 42-25395, being flown by 2nd Lieutenant Manuel Farias Rodriguez, ran into another plane which was off the runway. Mexican records mention that this accident was pilot error, Farias suffering an arm facture. His

aircraft had a damaged left wing, bent propeller and possible damage inside the engine. The aircraft was sent for repairs to the 2nd Aerodrome Squadron. The P-47D-28-RA 42-28504 suffered wing damage, broken landing gear and damaged propeller and engine, pilot error while taxiing causing a tail skid.

The pilot, 2nd Lieutenant Miguel Moreno Arreola, was unhurt but

Mexican ground personnel would return from patrols around the airfield with war trophies like this sword and Japanese flag. (Manuel Cervantes Ramos)

his aircraft was also sent to the 2nd Aerodrome Squadron for repairs.

**Mission No.1-27 (#43):** 23 June 1945

Bombing enemy concentrations, area of Antipolo.

Mission completed on alternative target at 48.8-81.0 Ref. 3555-II.

Captain Radames Gaxiola Andrade, Lieutenant Julio Cal y Mayor Sauz, 2nd Lieutenant Jaime Zenizo Rojas, 2nd Lieutenant .Jose L. Pratt Ramos and 2nd Lieutenant Mario Lopez Portillo.

Take-off time 1130, time over target 1220 – 1250, return to base 1330.

Results: As directed by SAP CURLESS 2, 5 P-47s bombed and strafed an alternative target. Led by the squadron commander Capt. Gaxiola Andrade, they attacked enemy positions on a topographic summit.

Leader was ordered by CURLESS to contact CURLESS SPECIAL (L-5 aircraft). No radio contact with L-5. CURLESS ordered the leader to check in with CURLESS 2 who designated target.

On first pass 10x1,000lb bombs were dropped on target area, the pass being made from SE to NW. 2x1,000lb bombs jettisoned safely in LAMON BAY (an aircraft that probably returned early). SAP CURLESS reported very good results.

The last mission by the 311th Fighter Squadron in the Philippines was flown on 23 June. Eight aircraft bombed Basco Airstrip on Batan Island with 1,000lb bombs, cratering the runway and revetment area. The squadron was non operational for the remainder of the month.

During June the 311th flew 29 combat missions with 220 sorties, dropped a total of 187 tons of bombs (222x1,000lb, 16x500lb, 210x260lb frags and 86x165 gallon napalm tanks) and expended 77,583 rounds of .50 calibre machine-gun ammunition.

**Mission No.1-28 (#44):** 24 June 1945

Bomb enemy troop concentrations, Kanan River.

Captain Pablo L. Rivas Martinez, Captain Roberto Legorreta Sicilia, Lieutenant Amadeo Castro Almanza, 2nd Lieutenant Angel Sanchez Rebollo and 2nd Lieutenant Mario Lopez Portillo, accompanied by one American pilot.

Take-off time 0730, time over target 0815 – 0945, return to base at 1045.

Results: As directed by SAP CURLESS 1, the mission was completed on alternative target. One aircraft, that flown by 2nd Lieutenant Angel Sanchez Rebollo, returned to base 30 minutes after take-off due to high oil pressure at 0755 hours.

The 5 P-47s (including one American pilot who joined the flight) bombed and strafed enemy concentrations located on both sides of ravine, with results unobserved by pilots due to heavy foliage.

Leader made dry run and 1 bombing pass and 3 strafing passes using .50 cal. ammunition on target. SAP CURLESS 1 unable to observe results from his position. US pilot on mission reported very good bomb pattern. Slight, light inaccurate small arms fire received from 46.4-82.1, alt. 3,000ft. Artillery fire, probably friendly, on E bank of KANAN RIVER between points 1,200 yards SW of target and 500 yards W of target. 1 aircraft (Rebollo's) jettisoned bombs on dry wash approximately 5 miles S of PORAC upon the direction of SAP DOODLEBUG.

After strike SAP CURLESS 2 ordered leader to proceed 13° 56'N – 121° 36'E and report bombing results to LUCENA.

10x1,000lb GP AN-M65 bombs and 10,060 rounds of .50 cal. ammunition expended.

**Mission No.1-29 (#45):** 24 June 1945

Bombing enemy troop concentrations, area of Infanta.

Lieutenant Amador Samano Pina, Lieutenant Graco Ramirez Garrido, 2nd Lieutenant .Mario Lopez Portillo, 2nd Lieutenant Jose L. Pratt Ramos and 2nd Lieutenant Angel Sanchez Rebollo, accompanied by one American pilot.

Take-off time 1245, time over target 1320 – 1345, return to base 1445.

Results: Directed by ground control group CURLESS 2, the six P-47s (including one American pilot), led by 2nd Lieutenant Mario Lopez Portillo, bombed enemy positions marked by white phosphorus on the East bank of a ravine.

Due to poor weather conditions the bombing was made in close formation diving through a hole in the overcast.

Ground observers reported the bombing as OK. All 12x1,000lb AN-M65 bombs struck the target. No .50 cal. ammunition used. One aircraft failed to take off due to broken belly tank hose.

The 69th Fighter Squadron flew its last mission in the Philippines on 24 June, sending eight P-47s to bomb Basco airdrome. This was the 69th's 898th combat mission during the war. During June the squadron flew 14 combat missions with 220 sorties, dropping over 117 tons of bombs (207x1,000lb, 8x250lb and 132x260lb frags) and 82 napalm tanks, and firing 65,578 rounds of .50 calibre ammunition.

On 24 June the 201st Mexican Fighter Squadron started to receive its Lend-Lease aircraft, the first five Mexican-owned Republic P-47D-30-RAs arriving. Four more were received on 30 June, which led to four of the borrowed P-47s being returned to the 58th Fighter Group. By the end of the month, the squadron had 18 aircraft (nine Mexican and nine borrowed). These aircraft were applied with Mexican Air

Force markings on the wings and rudder. In his weekly report to Mexico City, Colonel Cardenas gave the following aircraft strengtht for the week 24-30 June:

average airplanes loaned to 201st, 11;
average airplanes property of 201st, 5;
average airplanes assigned to 201st, 16;
average airplanes available daily for operational flights, 11;
average airplanes in repair, 5.

**Mission No.1-30 (#46):** 25 June 1945

Bomb enemy troops, area of Infanta.

Captain Pablo L. Rivas Martinez, Lieutenant Hector Espinosa Galvan, Lieutenant Joaquin Ramirez Vilchis, Lieutenant Carlos Rodriguez Corona, Lieutenant Amador Samano Pina, Lieutenant Jose L. Barbosa Cerda, 2nd Lieutenant Guillermo Garcia Ramos, 2nd Lieutenant Jaime Zenizo Rojas, 2nd Lieutenant Mario Lopez Portillo, 2nd Lieutenant Roberto Urias Avelleyra and 2nd Lieutenant Angel Sanchez Rebollo, accompanied by one American pilot.

Take-off time 0915, time over target 0920 – 0945, return to base 1045.

Results: As directed by SAP CURLESS 2, the formation of 12 P-47s (including one American pilot), led by Lieutenant Hector Espinosa Galvan, attacked a ravine, located between the hills.

The leader made one reconnaissance pass from North to South, dropping his two bombs. He ordered the rest of the formation to attack from South to North for bomb run and strafing passes. 23x1,000lb bombs dropped directly on target and 1x1,000lb bomb was accidentally dropped, unarmed, approximately at 50.0-75.9 S of AGOS RIVER.

SAP CURLESS 2 reported bombing and strafing as very good, and the bomb dropped S of river did not explode and did no damage. Ground observers reported the bombing and strafing as very good. A total of 23x1,000lb AN-M65 bombs and 9,200 rounds of .50 cal. ammunition was used.

It was probably after this mission that Lieutenant Joaquin Ramirez Vilchis had an incident that, while not reported in the records of the 201st, would later affect the performance of his duties. He wrote about it years later:

> [I was] wingman to Hector Espinosa Galvan. For this mission the armourers helped instal gasoline tanks in the form of zeppelins hanging one each side, with a capacity of 300 litres each to prolong the reach of the aircraft.
>
> The situation was that during the mission while changing the auxiliary tanks (Zeppelin form) the left one did not work. We finished the mission and on the return my aircraft was unbalanced. The left auxiliary tank could not be used, if I tried the engine would stop. I was carrying all tanks empty, except for the few gallons that I left on the main tank for landing.
>
> On my return to Porak … the aircraft was heavy on the left wing. The wind was blowing 20 knots from the right side and close to the ground I felt a strong wind that lifted the right wing, almost at the speed of a stall I saw the tip of the wing hit the ground and it broke and immediately the other wing fell with speed and also broke. There was no fire because the aircraft was out of fuel, and guiding the aircraft over the strip I arrived at the end …
>
> I took my charts and my parachute, got out and started walking, very angry. A few minutes later I saw a jeep coming at full speed, he almost stopped and asked me what happened to the pilot? 'Nothing,' I answered and he took off to the aircraft immediately. He came back again and asked me 'Are you the Pilot?' 'Yes,' I answered. 'Climb on board,' he told me … once in a while he would look at me without saying a word. He took me to the hospital.
>
> For two long hours every 15 minutes they would look at my eyes, took my blood pressure and felt the beating of my heart. At the end they told me to write a report about what happened in English. Later I was taken to the squadron, made my report in Spanish and H. Espinosa translated it in English.

Mexican personnel besides P-47D-30-RA 44-33737 No.21 showing the full Mexican and American markings. (Manuel Cervantes Ramos)

About three days later Ramirez Vilchis was scheduled to fly a combat mission when the following happened, that almost got him grounded, as revealed in his personal notes, provided by his family:

> On the third day it was JRV's turn to fly, everything was normal, but when he was assigned to an aircraft that he would use in the bombing mission, Surprise! JRV forgot how to fly! They took him to the aircraft and the mechanic received him with the same humour as always and asked him 'what happened, you look pale?'
>
> He answered: 'I forgot how to fly after the accident, I was normal and when they told me which aircraft I was to fly in the mission briefing, my memory failed and I don't know how to start it.' 'Don't go!' [the mechanic said]. 'No, if I don't do it I will be useless. Start the engine, but tell me three times what you are doing, also tell me three times the names of the instruments.'
>
> They started to report to the leader and the mechanic told JRV, 'they are calling you'. JRV reported and asked to be the last one to take off, which was approved by the leader. The aircraft started to vibrate, with the brakes on, and JRV said 'God help me. I want to go with the squadron. Help me.'
>
> He made the sign of the cross on his chest and let go of the brakes, put more power to the engine and forced the tail of the aircraft up, pushing the stick down and in that position the aircraft went up in the air. In that moment JRV recovered his memory and started to climb, and tried to do a barrel roll but the officer in the control tower yelled at him, 'you last one remember you are carrying 1,000lb bombs.' JRV returned to normal flight and formed up … They dropped their bombs and returned to Clark Field. JRV asked again to be the last one to land, [which was] approved [and] he landed perfectly. He had killed his fear!

**Mission No.1-31 (#47):** 25 June 1945

Attack enemy positions, area of Infanta.

Captain Radames Gaxiola Andrade, Captain Roberto Legorreta Sicilia, Lieutenant Jose L. Barbosa Cerda, Lieutenant Amadeo

Mexican mechanics working on a P-47D. (Manuel Cervantes Ramos)

Castro Almanza, Lieutenant Carlos Varela Landini, Lieutenant Carlos Rodriguez Corona, 2nd Lieutenant Praxedis Lopez Ramos, 2nd Lieutenant Miguel Moreno Arreola, 2nd Lieutenant Miguel Uriarte Aguilar, 2nd Lieutenant Jose Luis Pratt Ramos and 2nd Lieutenant Angel Sanchez Rebollo, accompanied by one American pilot.

Take-off time 0730, time over target 0815 – 0850, return to base 0930.

Results: As directed by SAP CURLESS 2, 12 P-47s (including one American pilot) led by Captain Gaxiola Andrade bombed and strafed enemy positions. Ground observer CURLESS 2 reported the results as good.

Two bombs fell long. A total of 24x1,000lb bombs were dropped and 12,290 rounds of .50 cal. Ammunition expended.

**Mission No.1-32 (#48):** 26 June 1945

Attack enemy positions in the area of Infanta.

Captain Pablo L. Rivas Martinez, Captain Roberto Legorreta Sicilia, Lieutenant Hector Espinosa Galvan, Lieutenant Fernando Hernandez Vega, Lieutenant Graco Ramirez Garrido, Lieutenant Julio Cal y Mayor Sauz, Lieutenant Carlos Varela Landini, Lieutenant Jacobo Estrada Luna, 2nd Lieutenant Miguel Uriarte Aguilar, 2nd Lieutenant Jose L. Pratt Ramos and 2nd Lieutenant Jaime Zenizo Rojas.

Take-off time 0730, time over target 0815 – 0850, return to base 0930.

Results: 11 P-47s led by ground observer CURLESS 2 bombed and strafed enemy positions. The target was marked by smoke markers, the results were reported as good.

A total of 21 bombs and 8,750 rounds of .50 cal. ammunition were used in this mission. One bomb hung up, over target, and was jettisoned in LAMON BAY by direction of SAP CURLESS 2.

No combat missions were flown on 27 June, allowing the squadron to dedicate its time to maintenance. During the course of the day, the Mexican pilots flew a total of eight hours and 30 minutes in test flights.

**Mission No.1-33 (#49):** 28 June 1945

Attack enemy troop concentrations, Limutan area.

Captain Radames Gaxiola Andrade, Lieutenant Carlos Varela Landini, Lieutenant Jacobo Estrada Luna, Lieutenant Graco Ramirez Garrido, Lieutenant Jose L. Barbosa Cerda, 2nd Lieutenant Raul Garcia Mercado, 2nd Lieutenant Roberto Urias Avelleyra, 2nd Lieutenant Jaime Zenizo Rojas and 2nd Lieutenant Manuel Farias Ramos, accompanied by one American pilot.

Take-off time 1300, time over target 1330 – 1345, return to base 1420.

Results: As directed by SAP CURLESS SPECIAL, 10 pilots vector bombed and strafed enemy positions at 29.2-79.4 (Map reference 3555-III), making one bomb run from N to S and three strafing passes from S to N. 18x1,000lb bombs were dropped on target area, leaving several fires with black smoke.

SAP did not report results due to poor radio contact. Pilots sighted two excavations or caves covered with bamboo lattice work in target area. SAP CURLESS ordered the leader to contact CURLESS SPECIAL, who marked target with WP. Radio contact poor but target was marked satisfactorily after dry run.

Pilots reported two bombs long.

2x1,000lb bombs jettisoned in SUBIC BAY after hanging on two different a/c over target. 18x1,000lb GP AN-M65 bombs and 9,290 rounds of .50 cal. ammunition expended.

Back in Mexico City, the latest news reports covering the squadron's activities in the Philippines included one by United Press correspondent Manuel Navareno, headed 'The 201 in its glorious day':"With the 201st Squadron, Philippines June 28 – The Mexican Expeditionary aviation has had today an intensive day until now of more intense combats.

The squadron sent its units in twenty-four flights of bombing and strafing in two groups of twelve Thunderbolts against the area of Infanta in the eastern part of Luzon. They dropped twenty three tons of explosives in the zones of their objectives, as informed by the American observers that have accompanied them in every flight.

In the morning the mission to bomb as well strafe was 'Marvelously precise', informs Captain Pablo Rivas 'Cocalito' of Monterrey. Captain Radames Gaxiola, commander of the squadron, led personally the afternoon mission, and later declared it a complete success.

Gaxiola, who lived eleven years in Los Angeles, and [with] his family now resides in Mexico City, described the raid as 'Especially lucky' for the squadron. Gaxiola was repeating his favourite expression when I greeted him after the mission '*Les Sacamos el Diablo a Bombazos*' (We removed the devil with bombs), and he added that the operations were 'simply perfect'.

**Mission No.1-34 (#50):** 29 June 1945

Attack enemy positions, Malabito Mountains.

Lieutenant Hector Espinosa Galvan, Lieutenant Carlos Varela Landini, Lieutenant Joaquin Ramirez Vilchis, Lieutenant Jacobo Estrada Luna, 2nd Lieutenant Miguel Uriarte Aguilar, 2nd Lieutenant Mario Lopez Portillo, 2nd Lieutenant Manuel Farias Rodriguez and 2nd Lieutenant Raul Garcia Mercado, accompanied by two American pilots.

Results: As directed by SAP CURLESS SPECIAL, 10 P-47s led by Lieutenant Hector Espinosa Galvan (including two American pilots) attacked Japanese positions by bombing and strafing.

They set off two explosions and fires by strafing. The 1st and 7th plane of the flight strafed approx. 25 Japanese soldiers who were lined up across the LIMUTAN river, firing at the Mexicans with machine gun and small arms fire.

The ground observers reported that the 4th aircraft of the first flight dropped two bombs directly on a heavy troop concentration, and grade both the bombing and strafing as excellent with good coverage. Slight, light inaccurate concentrated small arms fire. Troops sighted in target area on E bank of LIMUTAN RIVER, two bamboo-covered excavations reported in target area.

SAP CURLESS directed leader to contact CURLESS SPECIAL who tried to mark target with white phosphrorus with poor results. L-5 directed leader by radio with excellent results according to mission leader. Bomb run and strafing passes were made S to N. 20x1,000lb AN-M65 bombs and 15,910 rounds of .50 cal. ammunition were used.

During this mission, Lieutenant Ramirez Vilchis saw the commitment of Japanese troops in defending their positions. He spotted a number of Japanese soldiers go down to the beach and start firing at the Mexican aircraft. During his pass, they opened fire on him,

forcing him to move his P-47 around so as not to get hit. At about 700-750ft he positioned his P-47 directly at them and opened fire with his eight .50 calibre machine guns, making short work of them. He pulled up and turned, seeing the dead Japanese soldiers. He later said he imagined they were ordered to defend their position at all costs.

Mission No.1-35 (#51): 30 June 1945

Bomb enemy troop concentrations in the area of Cervantes.

Lieutenant Amadeo Castro Almanza, Lieutenant Reynaldo Perez Gallardo, Lieutenant Julio Cal y Mayor Sauz, 2nd Lieutenant Praxedis Lopez Ramos, 2nd Lieutenant Jaime Zenizo Rojas, 2nd Lieutenant Raul Garcia Mercado, 2nd Lieutenant Angel Sanchez Rebollo, 2nd Lieutenant Roberto Urias Avelleyra and 2nd Lieutenant Miguel Moreno Arreola.

Take-off time 0800, time over target 0830 – 0915, altitude 3,000ft, landed back at base at 1000/I.

Results: The mission to bomb enemy concentrations at 12.1-89.4 map reference (3455-II) was cancelled due to bad weather over the primary target and no alternative target was on hand.

Leader directed by SAP CURLESS to contact CURLESS SPECIAL, who assigned target which was closed by overcast. Contact was made with SAP TROPHY who reported no targets available.

All 18x160lb FS-M81 fragmentation bombs jettisoned vicinity of security zone of TABONES ISLAND.

After the completion of this mission, the 201st flew no more ground support missions until 4 July.

**Mission No.1-36 (#52):** 4 July 1945

Air alert over Cervantes.

Captain Radames Gaxiola Andrade, Captain Pablo L. Rivas Martinez, Lieutenant Jacobo Estrada Luna, Lieutenant Jose L. Barbosa Cerda, Lieutenant Joaquin Ramirez Vilchis, Lieutenant Carlos Rodriguez Corona, Lieutenant Reynaldo Perez Gallardo, 2nd Lieutenant Raul Garcia Mercado, 2nd Lieutenant Justino Reyes Retana and 2nd Lieutenant Jaime Zenizo Rojas, accompanied by one American pilot.

Take-off time 0700, time over target 0800 – 0815, return to base at 1000.

Results: 11 P-47s (including one American pilot) did not

Two pilots and their ground personnel with P-47D-30-RA No.21, possibly at Porac Field, with other P-47Ds in the background. (Manuel Cervantes Ramos)

complete the mission due to failure to contact the L-5 spotter aircraft. All 22x1,000lb bombs were dropped in the security zone in the SOUTH CHINA SEA 3 miles from LUNA by SAP TROPHY orders.

From 27 June to the last day of July, the 201st put two aircraft on 'Ready Alert' and two on '30 Minute Alert' for any missions needed to support ground troops. By the end of the month, the 35th and 348th Fighter Groups that had converted to the North American P-51D Mustangs were moving to their new bases at IeShima.

General Douglas MacArthur had declared the end of operations in Luzon on 28 June,

announcing that the entire island – embracing 40,420 square miles with a population of 8 million – was now liberated. The only Japanese strongholds left were in the Kiangan pocket, which elements of the 6th US Division and Filipino guerrilla units were tasked to eliminate. The 37th US.Division and Filipino guerrillas meanwhile mopped up any Japanese that were left in the Sierra Madre Mountains.

However, American intelligence had underestimated the situation, as by the end of June about 65,000 Japanese troops remained alive in northern Luzon, 13,000 of them in the Sierra Madre; 52,000 would make a last stand between Route 4 and 11. Fighting would continue right up to the formal surrender of Japan in September. During this period two intercept practice missions were undertaken by the Mexican pilots, with good results.

The medical and mental state of the pilots of the unit at this time was praised. The squadron's medical officer, Major Ricardo Blanco Cancino, wrote years later:

> In the unit there never existed a 'SNAFU' [Situation Normal: All Fucked Up] pilot, which was observed in other units. After their baptism of fire, they undertook combat missions day after day, accumulating ounces and ounces of whiskey, of which the majority received more than a bottle from the medical services.

Among the ground personnel, Sergeant 2nd Class Radio Operator Francisco Rodriguez Castaneda of 'A' flight was evacuated back to the United States, to Letterman Army Hospital in San Francisco, when it was discovered that he had pulmonary tuberculosis.

Republic P-47D-30-RA Thunderbolt 44-33718, later No.10, flying with No.23 over the Philippines. (via Jose Antonio Quevedo)

During the period from 4 June to 4 July 1945, the 201st Mexican Fighter Squadron flew a total of 52 ground support missions, with a reported flying time of 818 hours and four minutes. The unit was praised for its work, as highlighted in the summary report:

> The squadron flew right along with the 58th Group the rest of the month in ground support missions – often two per day – helping the 25th Division in its breakthrough from the Balete Pass and Marikina Watershed area into the Cagayan Valley.
>
> They carried two 1,000 pound bombs and strafed when called on. They attacked every type of target marked in various manners, i.e., by map co-ordinates, by dry run vectoring by SAPs, by bombing on White Phosphorous artillery or mortar shells, by vectoring by L-5 spotters, etc.
>
> Their missions were aborted on four or five occasions due to weather, failure of SAP to have a target, failure of radio communications with L-5 etc. The Group's work which included the missions run by the 201st in support of the 25th Division was highly commended by the Commanding General of that division.
>
> There was no separation of Mexican missions from an American mission as far the ground forces were concerned, and that is sufficient praise in itself.

The 58th Fighter Group history for June 1945 noted the following activities of the 201st:

> From the 7th thru the 25th of June, the 201st flew 31 missions with the 58th Fighter Group. The results of the various missions ran the scale from good to excellent, with results of some missions not reported by SAP. During this period some 461 x 1,000 pound bombs were dropped and 113,592 rounds of .50 caliber ammunition expended in a total of 232 sorties."

As for the effectiveness of the Mexican squadron, the following averages were figured from 5th Fighter Command statistics for June 1945 for the 58th Fighter Group, which was flying the same type of aircraft and missions as the 201st. One third of the groups figures were used as an average for a squadron.

| Average 58th FG Fighter Group Sqdn | Average 201st MEAF |
|---|---|
| 27.4 | 17 |
| 10.2 | 9.8 |
| 40.8 | 32 |
| 10.2 | 9.8 |
| 307 | 293 |
| 630.5 | 794 |
| 32 | 40 |
| 197 | 181 |
| 117,053 | 104,000 |

The figures above are of necessity approximations and interpolations, but considering that the 201st was new to combat its record compares favourably with that of the veteran pilots of the 58th FG.

The best compliments that the Mexican pilots received were from the ground troops, as experienced by Lieutenant Reynaldo Perez Gallardo:

> The North Americans used to call us the 'White Noses' because our mechanics painted the nose of our aircraft white ... We became very popular.
>
> On one occasion I was in the hospital getting treated for little things that happened to us over there, when a wounded soldier that was next to me noticed that I wasn't North American.
>
> He was very injured but got up and came to the bed [in which] I was lying. He asked me 'Do you fly a white nose?' and I said 'yes'. He embraced me and said: 'You cannot imagine how much we love you, because you have helped us so much.'

## FIGHTER SWEEP AND TRAGEDIES, JULY 1945

By the time the 201st had flown its last ground support mission, it was operating by itself. On 26 June it had separated from the 58th Fighter Group, which moved to the island of Okinawa for the next stage in its war against Japan.

Operating by itself, the 201st flew long-range missions in the form of fighter sweeps to the island of Formosa (modern Taiwan) at the beginning of July. Four such missions were flown. The remaining USAAF units in the Philippines continued their operations in support of Allied ground forces against pockets of resistance, fighter bombers hitting targets around Kiangan, Mankayan, the Cagayan valley and Batan between 2-5 July.

The Mexican pilots wanted to find aerial targets and did not strafe any ground targets. This was a wise move, as the Japanese set up 'flak traps', leaving non-operational aircraft out in the open and siting a number of anti-aircraft guns ready to shot down Allied aircraft strafing these aircraft.

Before the start of their latest missions, the following report by a United Press correspondent was published in Mexico City about the 201st's commanding officer, under the headline 'How Mexican Eagles fight':

> With the Mexican Expeditionary Force, Philippines July 2. – 'First we bomb them and later we strafed them with our machine guns'. This is the job of Squadron 201 based on the description given by Radames Gaxiola Andrade, 29 year old commander of the squadron and a veteran of aviation with 3,800 hours of flight time.
>
> Gaxiola speaks English perfectly without a foreign accent. He did his primary and secondary studies in Los Angeles, because his father Doctor Jose Antonio Gaxiola, General in the Mexican army, was involved in a revolutionary plot and had to live for a time in the United States.
>
> The wife and two kids of commander Gaxiola live in Mexico City.
>
> The officers and the rest of the personnel call him '*El Turco*' (The Turk) and he gives his time to participate in flights even with his administrative duties as a squadron commander.

There was still some Japanese aerial opposition in the Philippines, with a number of aviation units of the Imperial Japanese Army Air Forces (IJAAF) stationed at Formosa.

However, little was left of the 13th, 19th, 21st, 26th, 29th, 50th, 54th, 105th and 204th Sentais (squadrons) after being mauled by American airpower. All these groups were disbanded in Formosa after the end of the war.

The first Mexican fighter sweep was flown on 6 July. Reports of these missions were sent to the commanding generals of the Fifth Air Force, 5th Fighter Command and Sixth Army, with copies also going to the 58th Fighter Group.

> **Mission No.1-37 (#53):** 6 July 1945
>
> Long-range training to Toko, Formosa.
>
> Captain Radames Gaxiola Andrade, Lieutenant Amadeo Castro Almanza, Lieutenant Reynaldo Perez Gallardo, Lieutenant Jacobo Estrada Luna, 2nd Lieutenant Miguel Moreno Arreola, 2nd Lieutenant Praxedis Lopez Ramos, 2nd Lieutenant Mario Lopez Portillo and 2nd Lieutenant Jaime Zenizo Rojas.
>
> Results: Mission was completed by 8 P-47s, led by Captain Radames Gaxiola Andrade. Take-off was at 0830, with time over the target from 1053 – 1105 at an altitude of 10,000ft, the formation landing back at Porac at 1330.
>
> On this mission nothing was observed due to poor meteorological conditions, with no enemies encountered to attack. One aircraft landed at Lingayen on the return due to shortage of fuel at approximately 1300.

The P-47 which landed at Lingayen was Lieutenant Reynaldo Perez Gallardo's 44-337722. He experienced his most difficult mission due to a fuel leak and the distance he had to travel back to the Philippines; to conserve fuel he had to reduce speed, being left behind by the formation after receiving words of encouragement. With his fuel level getting more critical and not seeing land, Perez Gallardo prepared mentally and physically for a possible forced landing at sea, with little chance of being picked up and saved.

However, at the last moment he spotted land, the coast of Lingayen, where he made contact with the tower and received permission to land straight in. He made his landing with the last of his fuel, and his aircraft had to be towed to the parking apron to be fixed and refuelled for his short hop back to Porac field.

When Perez Gallardo landed at Lingayan, he was met by an American serviceman, communications officer Lieutenant James P. Gallapher of the 7th Fighter Squadron, 49th FG. Gallapher later recalled the incident:

> As the P-47 taxied off the strip towards the parking apron, near the control tower, I got a different [view] of it. This was a different breed of bird. I grabbed my 7th Fighter Squadron communication jeep and off I sped to get my camera from my foot locker at our 49th FG camp.
>
> Our campsite was less than a mile a away.
>
> I snapped the photos for my collection. As it turned out this was the only MEAF plane we ground crewmen of the 49th would see, as this P-47 made its brief maintenance and refueling stop at our base at Lingayen. It was a pleasure spending some time with the pilot whose name has slipped away with time. He told me about how anxious he was to see and take on enemy aircraft and that the squadron had not scored any air victories.
>
> He told me that the only purpose for this particular Formosa sweep, had been to seek out airborne Japanese planes, [but] none were encountered.

The squadron report submitted by Captain Pablo L. Rivas Martinez noted the next day's activities as follows:

> On today's date, 40 hours were flown in combat missions by the pilots of the squadron, plus 1 hour in the combat zone.

A line-up of the 201st Squadron's P-47D-30-RA Thunderbolts, probably at Clark Field after the unit moved from Porac Field in early August 1945. (via Jose Antonio Quevedo)

**Mission No.1-38 (#54):** 7 July 1945

Long-range reconnaissance training mission to Toko, Formosa; mission completed.

Captain Pablo L. Rivas Martinez, Captain Roberto Legorreta Sicilia, Lieutenant Hector Espinosa Galvan, Lieutenant Joaquin Ramirez Vilchis, Lieutenant Jose L. Barbosa Cerda, 2nd Lieutenant Guillermo Garcia Ramos, 2nd Lieutenant Raul Garcia Mercado and 2nd Lieutenant Roberto Urias Avelleyra.

Results: There was an incursion mission over Formosa Island. The purpose was to attack all enemy aerial objectives.

Ten airplanes took off at 0900, flew over Formosa Island from 1120 to 1140, and landed back at 1415.

Four unidentified aircraft sighted head-on at 8,000ft at 1045 approximately 125 miles from north coast of LUZON. Unidentified aircraft without wing tanks turned back immediately gaining altitude.

Leader could not overtake because of wing tank load with speed 200 miles per hour. Over SHO-KOTO-SHO island fires covering Empire Island sighted.

Four unidentified seaplanes sighted from 10,000ft anchored on TOKO BAY. Airfield between GARAMBI PT and TOKO appears to have been repaired. Bomb craters filled. No aircraft nor equipment in sight. 2 small auxiliary craft and junks sighted TOKO BAY.

Back in the Philippines, the aviation units of the Far East Air Force, including the Thirteenth Air Force, was still busy attacking Japanese ground forces on 7 July.

B-25s and fighter bombers struck at remanants of the Japanese army in the Laguna de Bay and Marikina areas, while fighter bombers also hit areas of resistance near Kiangan, Penablanca and Mankayan.

In his weekly report to the *Secretaria de la Defensa Nacional*, Colonel Cardenas said that from 1-7 July the MEAF had flown three combat missions with 16 sorties, plus 11 aborted sorties. Two of the missions were completed: the long-range fighter sweeps over Formosa. A total of 22 bombs were dropped during these missions.

Twenty-eight training sorties were also completed, and the number of pilots assigned to the squadron was also 28. He reported that an average of four aircraft were still loaned to the squadron, with 10 P-47s belonging to the Mexicans, giving the squadron a total strength of 14 aircraft, 11 being available for operations and three under repair. The 201st had received five new aircraft and returned five to the 58th FG.

During that week the Mexicans also received five jeeps, five trucks, two ambulances and two water trailers.

**Mission No.1-39 (#55):** 8 July 1945

Long-range reconnaissance training mission to Toko, Formosa.

Lieutenant Carlos Varela Landini, Lieutenant Fernando Hernandez Vega, Lieutenant Graco Ramirez Garrido, Lieutenant Julio Cal y Mayor Sauz, Lieutenant Amador Samano Pina, Lieutenant Carlos Garduno Nunez, 2nd Lieutenant Jose L. Pratt Ramos, 2nd Lieutenant Miguel Uriarte Aguilar and 2nd Lieutenant Manuel Farias Rodriguez.

Results: Mission completed. 10 P-47s under the command of Lieutenant Carlos Varela Landini took off at 0925, time over Formosa 1115 to 1210 at an altitude of 10,000ft,

landed back at Porac at 1425. One P-47 SNAFU landed back at base at 1040 due to failure of left wing tank to feed.

During the mission four unidentified aircraft were sighted on return north of Ryukyu Island,

flying north at an altitude of 1,000ft. Jabber leader lost them under the overcast. One squadron of P-38s and one squadron of P-51s sighted south of Formosa, flying towards Luzon. One pilot reported a submarine approximately 22° 10' N, 120° 30' E.

Years later in an interview, by then General Julio Cal y Mayor remembered that the most difficult part of these missions was fuel consumption. If the Mexican pilots had engaged in any aerial combat they would have to drop their external fuel tanks, reducing their chances of returning to the Philippines.

It was Cal y Mayor's intention to fly to the Chinese mainland and try to force land, hopefully in areas that were under control of the Chinese Nationalist Army and so avoid being captured by the Japanese.

It appears that some of the Mexican pilots managed to get some 'Blood Chits' that were worn by the American pilots of the Fourteenth Air Force in China: one was seen in the house of the family of Lieutenant Fernando Hernandez Vega.

The 201st daily reports for 8 July mention that 45 hours and 30 minutes were flown in P-47D-30s by the pilots of the squadron, plus 30 minutes in the combat zone. They also show that 2nd Lieutenants Guillermo Garcia Ramos, Raul Garcia Mercado and Justino Reyes Retana were granted permission to leave for Manila.

**Mission No.1-40 (#56):** 9 July 1945

Long-range reconnaissance training mission to Toko, Formosa.

Captain Pablo L. Rivas Martinez, Lieutenant Amador Samano Pina, Lieutenant Fernando Hernandez Vega, Lieutenant Reynaldo Perez Gallardo, 2nd Lieutenant Guillermo Garcia Ramos, 2nd Lieutenant Manuel Farias Rodriguez, 2nd Lieutenant .Angel Sanchez Rebollo and 2nd Lieutenant Raul Garcia Mercado,

flight of Mexican P-47D-30RAs about to peel off to start their landing approach to Clark Field, Philippines. (via Jose Antonio Quevedo)

accompanied by two American pilots.

Results: Mission completed. Ten P-47s (including two American pilots), under the leadership of Captain Pablo L. Rivas Martinez, took off at 0900, time over Toko was about 1130 at 12,000ft, landing back at 1415.

Numerous flights of B-24s, B-32s, P-51s and P-38s seen flying north over South Formosa. Two one-engine aluminium coloured aircraft sighted parked at Heito North a/d. Two destroyers and 7 larger craft sighted anchored in Toko Bay from 10,000ft at 1130. Three seaplanes sighted in Toko Bay with hanger facilities and service machinery.

Flight leader did not attack ships in Toko Bay, since mission was only to attack enemy airborne a/c intercepted.

Squadron daily reports for 9 July showed that 42 hours and 45 minutes were flown in combat missions in P-47D-30s, along with two hours and 30 minutes in the combat zone. Other USAAF units were keeping the pressure on the Japanese ground forces in the Philippines, P-38s and P-51s flying ground support missions in the Iguig area of the Cagayan River valley and hitting Sabangan.

No flights were carried out on 10 July, but Lieutenant Amadeo Castro Almanza and 2nd Lieutenant Mario Lopez Portillo left on a detail for Biak, New Guinea, first going to Clark Field, probably to start transferring borrowed aircraft for new aircraft. Fighting continued, with P-38s and P-51s supporting ground action in the northern Cagayan Valley and hitting enemy pockets east of Manila.

On 11 July there was an accident during a training flight, in which 2nd Lieutenant Jaime Zenizo Rojas was involved in an emergency forced landing at Florida Blanca due to fuel shortage. Although it is reported that his borrowed Republic P-47D-16 42-75889 engine burst into flames, Zenizo Rojas managed to escape with a fractured arm, which required a stay at the hospital. However, in Mexico he was mistakenly reported killed until things were cleared up, to his relief and that of his family.

On the same day as Zenizo Rojas' accident, fighter bombers pounded troop concentrations and defences in the Cayagan valley, while on the 12th they hit pillboxes east of Iguig, attacked troop concentrations in the Bontoc-Kiangan area and supported ground forces east of Manila. Although Kiangan fell to the 6th Infantry Division, resistance in the area continued.

On 13 July medium bombers and fighter bombers hit the Kiangan area, attacked Japanese pockets east of Iguig and north of Tuguegarao, pounded pillboxes, an ammunition dump and vehicles around Cervantes and raided near Siniloan, north-east of Laguna de Bay.

The operations of the Fifth Air Force continued until 26 July, when Thirteenth Air Force B-25s and P-38 started providing ground support missions until the end of the war.

It was not until 16 July that news reached Mexico City about the Mexican flights over Formosa. A United Press report from Manila, headed

'Squadron 201 attacks Formosa', said:

> General Headquarters of the 5th Air Force said today, that elements of the Mexican Expeditionary Force, of the 201st Squadron had taken part in raids over the island of Formosa, [which is] still in Japanese hands.
>
> The Mexican combat group, which helped effectively in the cleaning up of Japanese units which continued to resist in the jungles of Luzon, a couple of days ago participated in bombing and strafing. The Mexican pilots formed part of an attacking force of American combat planes, bombers and light bombers which are neutralizing Japanese positions in Formosa.
>
> Details of the Mexican participation in the assault over Formosa could not be obtained immediately in accordance with the communique from General Douglas MacArthur.

During the week of 15-21 July, the Mexican pilots started to fly their borrowed P-47s to Biak, New Guinea, and pick up their Lend-Lease P-47D-30-RAs. Twenty-five had been allocated, but only 23 have been confirmed as received via their serial numbers. On 17 July the following pilots were detailed to the transfer of aircraft: Captain Pablo L. Rivas Martinez, Lieutenant Hector Espinosa Galvan, Lieutenant Joaquin Ramirez Vilchiz, 2nd Lieutenant Raul Garcia Mercado, 2nd Lieutenant Praxedis Lopez Ramos and 2nd Lieutenant Guillermo Garcia Ramos.

Another group of three pilots went to Tacloban on Leyte to pick up some of the new aircraft that had arrived there. One of these pilots was Lieutenant Samano Pina, who later wrote:

> We received the good news that our new aircraft had arrived and we had to pick them up from the island of Biak, New Guinea and at Tacloban on Leyte. I went to the latter, which was much closer, with Lieutenant Fernando Hernandez Vega and 2nd Lieutenant Manuel Farias Rodriguez.
>
> We were transported in a B-25 Mitchell medium bomber – I took the tail gunner position – and upon arriving at Leyte, I saw crashed aircraft on the side of the airstrip, about 30 types, A-24s and F-4 Wildcats of the U.S. Navy … I was told that before the base was finished, the Japanese had sunk a carrier, while the planes were in flight.
>
> They went to the island and finding the runways not yet

completed they crashed.

Later on another air strip, there were hundreds and hundreds of new types of P-47s and P-51s, which conviced me that the Japanese didn't have the remote chance to win the war. Their armed forces would succumb to the impresive air supremacy. It would serve nothing to get out their obsolete weapons and conduct their 'Banzai' charges – their bravery could only serve to delay a little their final defeat.

Here we inspected the new aircraft which we were supplied and they had many new things like the bubble canopies that permitted a visibility of 360 degrees; and a device with the letters I. F. F. (Identification Friend or Foe) that when connected, would send waves to the radar sets, to advise that it was a friendly aircraft, avoiding the waste of fuel on intercepting unidentified aircraft.

We flight tested the new aircraft for about an hour. I felt very proud to fly this modern fighter, that our leaders had put us in … to support our unit … with these experiences passed down to the new pilots. Our element returned without incident to Luzon.

The official history of the MEAF list these transport flights, undertaken on 13 July, when a formation of eight P-47s flown by four Mexican and four American pilots flew to Biak, New Guinea, to pick up new P-47Ds. webeing The Mexican pilots were Lieutenant Hector Espinosa Galvan, Lieutenant Amador Samano Pina, 2nd Lieutenant Praxedis Lopez Ramos and 2nd Lieutenant Justino Retana Reyes, while the known American pilots were Lieutenant Gus T. Roberts (leader), 310th Fighter Squadron, 58th FG; Lieutenant Fred J. Clark, 69th FS, 58th FG; and Flying Officer William C. Meeks, 310th FS, 58th FG.

This transport mission, which would end in tragedy for one of the Mexican pilots, had a bad start when one of the American-flown P-47s could not take off due to engine problems.

After take-off, the P-47 flown by Samano Pina had to return to Porac due to engine problems, then Retana Reyes also turned back after losing the formation while flying on instruments. That left only five P-47s in the formation that reached the Vista air strip on Zamboanga and staying there due to bad weather until 16 July, taking off at about 9:30 a.m. The following official report of the incident describes what happened next:

> Hector Espinoza [*sic*] Galvan and SubTte. Praxedis Lopez R. went to base operations to check on the weather and departure time. They took off at 0930 in a flight of 5 aircraft led by Lt. G. Roberts, their destination Biak base. After three hours of flying, they saw the island of Morotai, in which Tte. Espinoza asked the leader of the fight if they were going to land at Morotai, receiving a negative.
>
> They contiuned flying, the weather conditions were reported as good [and] they encountered a storm in which they detoured, a little to the South; reaching the coast of New Guinea. The fuel in the wing tanks got used up. The leader ordered the flight to drop the wing tanks.
>
> SubTte. Praxedis informed Tte. Espinoza that his left wing tank had not dropped, he tried many times with no success. They continued to fly by the coast of New Guinea and the leader tried to contact Biak base, because they were lost .Since Tte. Espinoza and SubTte. Praxedis did not carry any maps of the region, they could do nothing, and they were lost [for] about an hour.
>
> The problem with the fuel was getting serious. Tte. Espinoza and SubTte. Praxedis spotted an emergency field on the island of Newfort … Tte. Espinoza told the flight leader, why not land there. Lt. Roberts flew down to check the field. When he was about to land a C-46 aircraft called them by radio and told them if they wanted to go to Biak he would lead them. Tte. Espinoza and Lt. Clark told the flight leader, that they were going to land in that field, since both had little fuel left.
>
> The C-46 told them, it would be 15 minutes to arrive at Biak. SubTte. Praxedis decided to go with them, now having the route to return and the time in case they could not find Biak. After a couple of minutes flying towards Biak, Tte. Espinoza reported back to the flight leader and continued flying with the formation. After 15 minutes of flying Tte. Espinoza reported in with 5 gallons of fuel; 5 minutes later, he reported that his engine had stopped and he was descending, he was about 900 feet in altitude, it was raining and the weather was bad.
>
> Tte. Espinoza did a good job ditching even with the left wing tank on. He dropped his flaps, touched the water and sank [but it is not known] why Tte. Espinoza did not get out of the cockpit. As [the rest] were short of fuel, they kept flying towards the island of Biak, doing a landing pattern. In the approach SubTte. Praxedis saw that he had only 15 gallons of fuel left and decided to land.
>
> Lt. Roberts left in a C-47 to look for Tte. Espinoza [but] did not find him. Next day SubTte. Lopez Praxedis with the hope of finding Tte. Espinoza went personally in a C-47 aircraft that flew in the area where his plane went down … for about two and a half hours without finding a trace of Tte. Espinoza.

The flight leader, Lieutenant Roberts, also made a report on the incident:

> We were on a flight from Zamboanga, Mindanao P. I. to Biak, New Guinea. As we approached Neomfoor, New Guinea I asked the flight if anyone was low on fuel. Two reported they were, Tte. Galvan was one of the two. We flew over Neomfoor, and the two planes left our formation to land.
>
> We then proceeded on to Biak. As we neared Biak, I saw a plane coming from the rear, this was Tte. Galvan. He still had his wing tanks; I advised him to drop his tanks, this he attempted to do, but was out of fuel. I advised him to bail out of the plane.
>
> He decided to make a forced landing in the water. As he landed the wing tanks must have made the plane 'cart wheel'. It sank almost immediately. Tte. Galvan was not observed in the water.

It appears that the aircraft that Espinosa Galvan was flying was a P-47D-21-RE listed in the records as No. 034 (possibly 42-25629 ex-460th FS/348th FG). At the time of his death he had about 27.30 hours flying in the combat zone and 36.15 in combat missions, a total of 63.45 hours of flight time.

On 19 July, 2nd Lieutenant Praxedis Lopez Ramos returned to Porac with a P-47D-30RA with one of the American pilots delivering another new P-47D to the 201st. On the 16th four more Mexican pilots had left Porac field on the same type of mission to Biak. Part of a formation with four other American pilots, the Mexican flyers were Captain 2nd Class Pablo Luis Rivas Martinez, Lieutenant Joaquin Ramirez Vilchiz, 2nd Lieutenant Raul Garcia Mercado and 2nd Lieutenant Guillermo Garcia Ramos.

They flew from Porac to Zamboanga, a three-hour flight, and from there to Morotai on a two-and-a-half-hour flight, and then Biak.

They remained there until 19 July, when they received their new P-47D-30-RA aircraft and started the journey back to Porac field that would end badly for another Mexican pilot. One of the American pilots who was part of the formation, Lieutenant Roger Fox of the 69th Fighter Squadron, wrote the following on the incident and the dangers of long-distance flights over water:

> I also made the trip to Biak with 'War wearies' to park them in the jungle and bring back new ones. The trip to Biak was very memorable. I believe we had 8 planes and 4 were flown by pilots from the 201st [Pablo Rivas Martinez, Joaquin Ramirez Vilchiz, Raul Garcia Mercado and Guillermo Garcia Ramos].
>
> The plane I flew had radio connections for the pilot Jerry-rigged but the radio did not work. The gear did not always retract the first time, but if [retried] it would come up. We had no maps with us so we checked the weather map and calculated a heading that would bring us to the next island and we would follow that around to an airfield. Heading south, the landing at Zamboanga was interesting. As I was coming in on final [approach], wheels and flaps were down, I was indicating 130 mph, but the seat of my pants told me the plane was losing altitude too fast so I added throttle and eyeballed it for a safe landing.
>
> When I peeked in a revetment the indicator was still reading 50 mph. A crew chief checked it and drained the water out of the pitot line and then it indicated ok. On our return from Biak, our flight leader whose name I don't remenber, asked the ATC if we could have a map for our return. They … couldn't imagine anyone flying all that way without a map. So they loaded him down with maps, radio charts, let down charts etc. He took one map and the rest was 'safely' stored in the rear of the aircraft.
>
> When taking off from Biak, two of the Mexican pilots were delayed for some reason. They did eventually get airborne but we never did see or hear from them. They were probably … [Rivas Martinez and Garcia Ramos]. Two others of the 201st did stay with us on take-off [Garcia Mercado and Ramirez Vilchiz]. Midway to Zamboanga we were flying in comfortable formation and we hit a cloud bank. Immediately we were forced on instruments on our own. After several minutes we broke out into the clear and regrouped except for one of the 201st pilots [Ramirez Vilchiz].
>
> We found Zamboanga and just as we landed a tropical cloudburst hit the field. In the parking revetment I sat in the plane waiting for the downpour to stop and I saw our last plane buzzing the runway. In the opposite direction there was a C-47 also dragging the runway. He must have been waved off by the tower, but our P-47 came around to …
>
> He had both wing tanks still on and his gear was up. I remenber sitting there shouting 'OH NO! OH NO!' but he made a very smooth landing, not wavering but straight down the runway with sparks flying from his prop tips and the tanks. However there wasn't a whiff of smoke [or] fire.
>
> I guess the rain helped out. Of course the prop and engine were unflyable so the pilot was told he had to stay with the aircraft until a replacement engine arrived. I never did hear of the follow up on that. We did strongly urge the one remaining 201st pilot [Garcia Mercado] to stay close and out of trouble. The rest of us did return safely to the P.I.

Garcia Mercado gave the following account of the events:

> On the 19th of July we received the new airplanes, P-47D-30s. Also the flight leader gave each one of us maps for our return trip, but we were not briefed as to weather, nor were we told which islands were enemy held. Capt. Pablo L. Rivas Martinez and Lt. Guillermo Garcia Ramos remained on the ground so our flight was composed of six airplanes.
>
> We took a heading toward Morotai. After approximately 40 minutes of flying we encountered a storm and flew on instruments approximately for 30 minutes. Upon arriving at Morotai the visibility was very poor and the ceiling was about 500 feet. Due to that we were unable to locate the airstrip so the leader requested a homing and the station gave us a wrong steer of 40 degrees which took us away from the island. After 15 minutes on this course the leader was aware of the erroneous heading so he worked any orientation problem on the beam and got us over the field.
>
> Before landing I heard Lt. Guillermo Garcia Ramos call our flight and ask for our position. He stated he was lost and if he was unable to orient himself he would bale out. Upon landing we were informed that Capt. Rivas and [Ramos] had taken off 30 minutes after us.
>
> That is the last I heard of the two above-mentioned pilots.
>
> On the 20th we took off from Morotai to Zamboanga and as usual we were not briefed on anything before take-off. About thirty minutes after take-off we encountered a storm with strong turbulence which [meant we were] unable to maintain our positions in the formation so the formation split up and each of us flew independently on instruments for about 45 minutes. When we entered the bad weather, our leader did not give us any orders as to what to do so I kept the same heading which was 220 degrees and 9,000 feet of altitude.
>
> As soon as I broke out of the storm I saw two airplanes, P-47s, so I joined up with them … later two more airplanes of the flight joined up. The airplane missing in the flight was that of Lt. Joaquin Ramirez, whom I contacted by radio and the leader told me to give him the heading that would take him to Zamboanga …
>
> Upon arrival at Zamboanga there was a heavy shower over the field but [I] landed safely. A few minutes later Vichis arrived over the field [and] after circling … he landed wheels up. That day we did not continue our flight on account of weather.
>
> On the 21st in the morning five airplanes took off from Zamboanga to Porac airstrip and encountered very bad weather and were on instruments for 1 hour, landing at Porac at 1130 that same day.

2nd Lieutenant Garcia Mercado returned on the 21st and Lieutenant Ramirez Vilchiz on some later date, since his pilot log book lists no more flights until 26 August.

But Captain Rivas Martinez was not lucky, and the same fate almost fell on his wingman, 2nd Lieutenant Garcia Ramos. They took off from Biak from Morotai on the 19th at about 3:30 p.m. for Porac field in two new P-47D-30-RAs. Rivas Martinez was flying 44-90058 and Garcia Ramos 44-33711. While flying between Biak and Morotai Island, they encountered bad weather, with storm clouds and scattered rains that formed a weather front from sea level to 15,000ft.

They entered the storm front flying on instruments. Garcia Ramos lost sight of Captain Rivas Martinez at about 6:00 p.m., which was the last time he was seen alive. Garcia Ramos, still flying by instrument,s was trying hard to find a place to land and tried to reach the control tower at Biak, Morotai, with no success. After reaching the New Guinea coast, and finding no place to land, he climbed to 12,500ft and bailed out, as he later reported:

> Inverting my aircraft in a roll, I fell into the sea a short distance from an island. Next day using my life boat I made it to the beach on the coast. I heard a bomber but could not signal it because the sun had not come out. At about 1030 I saw a plane on the horizon flying circles over the ocean.
>
> I flashed for a long time with my mirrow, [but] it appears he

didn't see it, [as] he climbed and flew away. By the afternoon a PBY Catalina appeared flying over me in a circle and finally landed in the sea. I swam to it with my life boat. To reach it [I had] to avoid coming close to some rocks that border the coast. The sea was [rough].

I was helped on board the flying boat and told them about my situation. They in turn informed me that the pilot Major Larry D. Dennis (U.S.A.A.F.) was a test pilot from Biak and didn't know anything about me. In the morning they were flying casually by the place and saw my signals with my mirror. But due to Japanese positions they thought of the possibility of a Japanese trick. They returned to base to render a report and in the afternoon they returned to rescue me.

They informed me that I had bailed out on the West coast of New Guinea about 10 miles from Sarong Bay, where the Japanese had anti-aircraft guns. They took me to Biak where I stayed two days at Maj. Dennis' house. On July 22 I took off in a B-24 bomber back to my base at Porac.

The search for Captain Rivas Martinez was undertaken by the Fifth Air Force, but no trace of him was found and he was officially declared missing.

On 18 July 2nd Lieutenant Roberto Urias Avelleyra and 2nd Lieutenant Mario Lopez Portillo flew the same type of mission. Urias Avelleyra returned safely on the 20th. Lopez Portillo left Biak with two American pilots flying three new P-47D-30-RAs. The Americans, 2nd Lieutenant Lee A. Houck of the 311th Fighter Squadron and Lieutenant Alex Z. Harris of the 69th FS, were both from the 58th Fighter Group. However, only Harris made it to Porac airstrip, the other two being killed when their aircraft crashed. An initial accident report written by Captain Radames Gaxiola and the operations officer, Lieutenant Amadeo Castro Almanza, included the following:

On July 21, 1945, SubTte. Mario Lopez Portillo serial number 3133434 did a flight from Tacloban airport, destination Porac field, as part of a formation of three P-47D-30 airplanes. At the height of Downtown Manila, they encountered bad weather conditions, detoured from their route, and they went back to a point between the island of Corregidor and the Bataan peninsula.

Based on the accounts of Lt. A. Z. Harris, who was part of the formation, Lt. Houck and SubTte. Lopez Portillo, No. 2 wingman, started to climb with a course of 5 degrees, and Lt. A. Z. Harris got separated from the formation. He radioed Lt. Houck that they could retrace their course under the clouds.

Lt. Houck answered back that they were at 600 feet and due to the rains, he could not find Corregidor Island. This was the last comunications with Lt. Houck's flight; it was approximately 11:30 hours.

A search was conducted by the 58th and the 201st during that afternoon and on the following two days, with negative results. It wasn't until 26 July that the 201st got word that the planes had crashed into a mountain on the Bataan peninsula, killing both pilots.

Both aircraft were found by the 1575th Engineer Company, US Army, under the command of Lieutenant Burvier, which was working in the forest on the peninsula. The location of the crash site was about six miles south-west of Laman. It was the conclusion of an investigation board that a 60km wind blew the pilots off course and Lieutenant Houck did not correct it, causing them to crash into the mountain.

Lopez Portillo's remains were not recovered until 3 August, when a 20-man expedition led by Lieutenant Reynaldo Perez Gallardo was sent to retrieve what was left in P-47D-30-RA 44-90149.

He was at first buried at the US Military Cemetery No.2 in Manila, then his remains and those of Hector Espinosa Fuentes were sent back to Mexico after the end of the war.

The 58th Fighter Group history mentions the circumstances of 2nd Lieutenant Houck's death without mentioning that he was flying with Lopez Portillo:

The 311th Fighter Squadron lost a pilot on 21 July, but not while operating from Porac. 2nd Lt. Lee A. Houck was reported missing on a ferry flight.

Houck had been sent to Biak Island, New Guinea to ferry new aircraft to Luzon. On the return trip Houck last contacted the controller as he approached Luzon. He reported that he had encountered a severe storm and his last radio transmission stated that he would attempt to climb over the storm, which was in the vicinity of the Bataan Peninsula. The pilots at Porac were busy on search missions during the remaining days in the Philippines but no trace of Houck was found.

Hopes were high that Houck had landed safely or had bailed out and that he would be rescued. These hopes were not realized as sometime later [there was] a report that Houck had been found, having been killed in the crash of his plane.

The week of 15-21 July 1945 had been a bad one for the Mexican squadron, with the loss of two pilots killed, one missing and another rescued. Three aircraft were lost and one damaged. Colonel Cardenas' weekly report to the *Secretaria de la Defensa Nacional* included the following:

3. A) – Training sorties flown: 37.

B) – There were 9 pilots on Ferry Missions during the week.

4. A) – Pilots assigned: 28.

B) – Airplanes property of 201st Mexican Fighter Squadron: 15. Average airplanes available for operational flights daily: 11. Average airplanes in repair: 4.

6. Aircraft received: 4 airplanes.Ground material received: 4 new ¼ [ton] trucks and 2 used ¼ [ton] trucks.

With Rivas Martinez missing, Lieutenant Amadeo Castro Almanza from 'D' flight was named assistant to the operations officer from 23 July. Castro Almanza was now wearing two hats, running his own flight and taking on Rivas Martinez's role. On the 24th he sent the following daily operational report to the squadron commander:

This is to inform you that yesterday, 15 hours were flown in P-47D-30 aircraft in observation missions, but nothing was found of the missing pilots. Yesterday SubTte. Guillermo Garcia Ramos returned to [the] squadron coming from New Guinea. Yesterday P-47D-30 aircraft serial numbers 44-33717 and 44-33711 were assigned to the squadron, at the same time 44-33717 was removed and sent to the 15th Airdrome Squadron and 44-33711 was removed from the squadron per Reg. 55-25 dated September 1944.

During the ferrying missions, Mexican pilots also helped out the 58th Fighter Group by flying some of their aircraft to Biak for the new ones, as one mechanic, Sergeant George Meyer of the 69th Fighter Squadron, recalled:

2nd Lieutenant Jaime Zenizo Rojas with a captured Japanese soldier brought to the Mexicans before being turned over to the US Army. (Mis Dos Misiones)

> As the old aircraft were transferred out, the Mexican pilots would help ferry them with an American pilot as a navigator.
>
> When we were to get rid of an airplane with a terrible stench, a Mexican pilot came out to fly it. His entire English technical vocabulary consisted of 'Fuel Pump'. Apparently he was trying to make sure the fuel pump worked. So I used an affirmative head shake and sign language to assure him that the fuel pump and everything else was in good working order.
>
> He didn't seem to notice the smell in the cockpit, just grinned, cranked up the engine and taxied off for take off. In 20 or 30 minutes he was back, the windshield covered with oil as one of the gaskets on the rocker box cover on a top cylinder had blown out.
>
> This was a fairly frequent occurrence and we had a lot of new gaskets available so I installed one, but in the process I dropped one of the small hold-down nuts that held the rocker box cover in place.
>
> This was also a fairly frequent occurrance so we had extra nuts available – I got another one and finished the job. The next day the same pilot showed up. He inquired about the fuel pump and flew away. In about 20 minutes he was back, oil all over the windshield once again.
>
> I took off the piece of engine cowling, [and] found out what happened to the nut that I had dropped the day before. It had fallen down into the cylinder head and when the engine was running, the action of the rocker arm punched it out through the top of the aluminum cast rocker box cover, resulting in a second oil bath for the poor Mexican pilot.
>
> The third day that same pilot was on hand and asked if the fuel pump was okay and flew away. This time he apparently didn't experience any problems and that was the last we saw of the airplane with the unbelievably bad odor.

From squadron records for the 201st, some 15 pilots were involved in this ferry flights. They were Captain 2nd Class Pablo Luis Rivas Martinez, Lieutenant Amadeo Castro Almanza, Lieutenant Hector Espinosa Galvan, Lieutenant Amador Samano Pina, Lieutenant Fernando Hernandez Vega, Lieutenant Joaquin Ramirez Vilchiz, Lieutenant Carlos Varela Landini, Lieutenant Jacobo Estrada Luna, 2nd Lieutenant Praxedis Lopez Ramos, 2nd Lieutenant Raul Garcia Mercado, 2nd Lieutenant Guillermo Garcia Ramos, 2nd Lieutenant Roberto Urias Aveleyra, 2nd Lieutenant Manuel Farias Rodriguez, 2nd Lieutenant Justino Retana Reyes and 2nd Lieutenant Mario Lopez Portillo.

At the same time, a detachment of 58th Fighter Group personnel remained at Porac field when the unit was preparing its move to Okinawa and helped train new replacement pilots that were coming from the States.

They made sure that all of the 58th FG aircraft flew out to Okinawa. Some of the Americans had the opportunity to use the Mexican mess hall facilities and taste Mexican food, prepared from American standard rations. Among those tasting the Mexican food was Lieutenant Joe Madison, who said:

> I stayed with the planes until they flew off, and ate with the Mexican Air Force … they ate true Mexican food – mainly pepper.
>
> The worst meal I had with them though was their chicken soup. My mess kit on that trip through the chow line was filled with broth and three chicken feet from the claws to the knees – that was all. No meat, no vegetables, nothing but water and yellow chicken legs.
>
> I had never seen this before, and haven't seen it since. Needless to say, my soup went directly to a garbage can.

During July three officers were relieved of duty in the squadron as excess personnel and sent back to Mexico for reassignment, while one officer and three enlisted men were hurt in a vehicle accident.

On 15 July Major Guillermo Linage Olguin, the pay officer of the MEAF, was sent to hospital with an injured shoulder that later required him returning to Mexico.

His place was over by Lieutenant Carlos Varela Landini.

Some of the 201st's ground personnel would get a chance to meet the enemy face to face. Some had felt the frustration of being in an aviation unit but being unable to engage the enemy on the ground if the unit was attacked.

The chance to encounter Japanese soldiers would come in an unexpected moment, as related by 2nd Lieutenant Guillermo Albert Robles, who led a detail to the peninsula of Bataan to pick up wood for the squadron:

> On the night of July 22nd the squadron commader called me and ordered me to leave the next day to the Peninsula of Bataan to an engineer company that operated a mill, to bring back wood needed to make boxes since we had a preparatory order for a forthcoming move.
>
> The next day early in the morning with a detail with Sgt. First Class Jesus Herrera Zayas, Jose Gutierrez Gallegos, Agustin Velasco

Alegria, Luis Mondragon Hoyos, Sgt. Second Class Jose Torres Vara, and Francisco Baustista Gonzalez and as a driver Soldier Enrique Moedano Gomez, we left towards the mill located in the middle of the jungle in the Peninsula.

The road was dirt and there were some small wooden bridges in bad conditions. We arrived at our destination at about 13:30 hours, which was lunch time, and the commader of the mill invited us to lunch, while his personnel loaded the truck. During lunch the commander, who was a Lt. in the American Army, told me that in that area there were many mango trees and avocado, and that we should take advantange and take some back to the camp and at the same time pick up some pulleys to reinforce the bridges on the road.

I told him that by orders of the American commander, when traveling in the communications zone it was without weapons … the only [weapon was] my carbine in the Jeep but he also told me that the area was clear of Japanese. With that situation I told the men not to go far, and bring back some fruit and the pulleys we were going to use.

About 20 minutes later they returned running. Torres Vara and Zayas, with their uniforms in a mess, told me that Moedano had been killed. Immediately I took the carbine and told them to show me the road. It was a small one of about 200 meters and turned to the right onto another bigger road bordered with bamboo … small bushes did not provide any cover or concealment.

Looking at the situation, I ordered Torres Vara and Zayas, who had acquired weapons, to follow me trying not to ocuppy places I had left. Some American soldiers had joined us with the Lieutenant and were following at a prudent distance.

They moved through the terrain, where they found a wooden hut where they discovered an injured Moedano.

I was awaiting at any moment for [the Japanese to fire on us] because the path was not more than a meter and a half wide, which would permit a sniper to have an easy target. With this fear and sweating profusely, with even the Lieutenant asking me not to go further, we arrived at the area and surprisingly didn't find anybody, but there were many foxholes with signs that they had been occupied days before, covered with sheets and grass, leaving a space for the weapon, so that from afar you could not see anything.

After walking around the area, I found between the foxholes, two empty cartridges that looked like they were recently fired of 0.30 cal. carbine used by American troops. The search was suspended, because an incident occurred that made me realize that everybody was nervous, a twig broke and the American personnel opened fire in the direction of the sound. The Lt. agreed with me.

We returned to the mill and found the rest of the personnel, who informe me what had happened. They were going on the trail, and arriving at the Plazoleta, Moedano saw some Japanese shoes and said 'Look at these Japanese shoes'. When he got close to take them, a Japanese soldier popped up. Thinking that he was Filipino they yelled 'Don't shoot, Mexican Army!!'.

In that moment he opened fire, wounding Moedano in the elbow. At the shot everybody fled, including possibly the Japanese, who had also been surprised. The Lt. informed me that Moedano was taken to the 894th Hospital. When we returned to camp I immediately informed Capt. Gaxiola what had happened, rendering a report.

News about Moedano's treatment for his wound and recovery was published in Mexico in a UP report from Manila, dated 5 September, under the headline 'In better condition – Corporal J. Moedano of the 201st Squadron':

Col. Cardenas commander of the MEAF states that Corporal Moedano who was wounded in an encounter with Japanese while on a mission to collect wood about a month ago, is recovering from his wound in the arm in a hospital close to the base of squadron 201: 'He is Okay, no need to worry.'

Moedano was later evacuated to the United States to continue his recovery.

While all these activities were going on, the 5th Fighter Command was moving from the Philippines to Okinawa to better carry out its operations against the Japanese homeland. The MEAF was notified of the move via Lieutenant Colonel Arthur W. Kellond, the senior liaison officer, and preparations for the move were carried out.

But nothing more was heard from the 5th FC, as the headquarters had already moved and General Frederick H. Smith, its commander, had not decided to order the 201st to Okinawa, postponing the move until the situation in Okinawa was more stable for operations by the MEAF. This decision was based on a report submitted by Lieutenant Colonel Kellond (who had been involved in the training of the MEAF in the USA), and comments on by General George C. Kenney (Allied air commander in the south-west Pacific), that outlined a number of problem areas in the operations of the 201st. One of the issues was the pilots of the 201st:

Your attention is particularly invited to paragraphs 2 and 3 of this report which reflects an unprecedented number of non-combat losses of personnel and aircraft, crash landings and taxiing accidents during a relatively short period of time. To date six pilots have been lost and fourteen aircraft have been wrecked.

One pilot has been grounded and two [are] recovering from injuries incurred in accidents, one of these may eventually be permanently grounded. As a results of the attrition the effective [strength] of the unit has been reduced to twenty-three active pilots, of the remaining pilots there are two can be called satisfactory leaders, a fact which in itself has probably been [the] most important cause of the marked decline in efficiency of this organization.

In all fairness to the Mexican squadron, by July they had lost five pilots, in the theatre of operations, not six. As for the aircraft wrecked, taking the number lost to all causes (combat, accidents, damaged etc) the total for the 201st at that point was 18. By comparison, the 58th Fighter Group for the same period, from May to July, had 18 aircraft wrecked with the loss of three pilots (none in combat).

Another fighter group in the Pacific region, the 348th, had 14 operational accidents in January 1945, in which nine aircraft were destroyed and six more damaged.

Of this number, six were take-off accidents, four were landing accidents and four various other causes. These figures include five P-51D Mustangs lost in accidents. The losses can be broken down to the following squadrons: 340th FS, 4; 341st FS, 6; 342nd FS, 2; and 460th FS, 2.

Five pilots were lost by the 348th in January, with three MIA during missions and two killed in flying accidents.

The following table shows the comparison of aircraft losses and pilots between the 201st Mexican Fighter Squadron and the 58th Fighter Group:.

### Aircraft destroyed or Damaged to all causes, including Pilot losses

| | 201st MEAF | | 58th FG USAAF | |
|---|---|---|---|---|
| | a/c | Pilots | a/c | Pilots |
| May | 4 | 0 | 7 | 1 |
| | | | (69th: 2, 310th:1, 311th:4) | |
| June | 9 | 2 | 3 | 0 |
| | | | (69th:2, 310th:1) | |
| July | 5 | 3 | 8 | 2 |
| | | | (69th: 4, 311th: 4) | |
| Aug | 3 | 0 | 19 | 8* |
| | | | (69th: 5, 310th: 7, 311th: 7) | |
| Sept | 0 | 0 | 1 | 1 |
| | | | (311th:1) | |
| TOTAL: | 21 | 5 | 38 | 12 |

* Four pilots of the 311th were killed when the bomb bay door of a converted B-24 transport gave way, dropping them while making a pass over a runway on Iwo Jima on 26 August 1945.

## CONFLICT OF COMMAND AGAIN

The three Mexican pilots lost in July were considered some of the best leaders seen in recent missions. For example, Lieutenant Espinoza Galvan was recognised by his fellow pilots as a very good flight leader.

The American command considered that the 201st squadron's strength should be brought up to 40 pilots, and was awaiting the arrival of 10 replacement pilots who were expected to arrive in early August (but did not due to the end of the war).

Their training and indoctrination was to take place in the Philippines, not on Okinawa.

Another problem noted in the report by Lieutenant Colonel Kellond was the functioning of the command and staff of the MEAF, and its tactical unit the 201st. The report noted:

> It is believed that certain of the dificulties which have become apparent in the functioning of the organization are and will remain incapable of solution as long as the Mexican Liaison component is in position to interfere with the internal administration of the tactical squadron.

The role of Colonel Cardenas as commander of the MEAF, as seen by the US Military, was to attend to other matters as the senior representative Mexican officer in the Philippines, to look out for the general welfare of his troops and not to interfere with his squadron commander, as noted in the same report:

> "When this officer interferes with the squadron commander's exercise of his command functions by countermanding his orders with respect to internal administration of the unit, the net result can only be lessened efficiency in its general operations.
>
> "The squadron commander then finds himself accountable to two superiors and the divided control makes it extremely difficult for him to be able to carry out the operational missions which are assigned to him."

Colonel Cardenas, in his book *Mis Dos Missiones* (My Two Missions), published after the war, gave his own views of his responsibilities as commander in the theatre of operations:

> Outside the American continent, the commander of the Mexican Expeditionary Air Force is the representative of the Mexican Army to whom will be subordinate all the elements integrated in the squadron, both in its relations with the American Army and in those aspects that affect its combat capacity and the general welfare of the personnel under his orders.
>
> Assisting the commanding group, the commander of the Mexican ExpeditionryAir Force will determine all those affairs related to military justice, pay and allowances, affairs derived from the laws of Lend Lease, unit history, administration aspects and correspondence with the Mexican Army and North American authorities, and in accordance with the legislation of the United States, it will have the power to censure correspondence and information in general.
>
> He will cooperate in a special manner with North American authorities to maintain cordial relations with the troops of other United Nations.

It should be noted that the command structure of the Brazilian fighter squadron, which had been operating in Italy since late 1944, was that of an American fighter squadron, with a strength of 43 pilots, and its commanding officer was a lieutenent colonel, not a major or a captain as the Americans requested for the Mexican squadron. Lieutenant Colonel Nero Moura flew a total of 65 combat missions. He was selected to command the Brazilian unit while a major. He was the personal pilot to President Getulio Vargas and was promoted to lieutenant colonel, but still remained commander of the Brazilian fighter squadron.

His second in command was Major Oswaldo Pamplona Pinto, who flew 47 combat missions in Italy.

The Brazilian fighter squadron, which was part of the 350th Fighter Group, XXII Tactical Air Command, Twelfth Air Force, also had some problems getting replacement pilots to make up their losses, but had a group of medical doctors and female nurses. The Brazilian squadron only had one American pilot assigned to it, Captain John W. Buyers, who flew 21 combat missions while attached to it.

The US report also noted:

> It is further recommended that a study be made of the necessity for the liaison group in view of the fact that the squadron has been thoroughly trained in all matters normally pertaining to a similar squadron in the United States Army Air Forces.

Brigadier General F.H. Smith of 5th Fighter Command made the following recommendations in the report:

> 2. It is strongly felt that the indoctrination and training of the new replacements cannot be efficiently accomplished at Okinawa because of the congested dromes, airpace and the necessity for an all out concentration on future commitments. The inherent handicaps to be overcome, such as speech difficulties, mental temperament and difference in experience level between U. S. units now operating in Okinawa and the Mexican Sq. as it now stands, precludes the possibility of minimizing operational accidents at Okinawa.
>
> 3. It is therefore urgently requested that the 201st Mexican Fighter Sq. be retained in the Philippines until such a time as its operational efficiency is brought to a higher level in order to ensure reasonable success in combat operations.

This finding was also endorsed by General Ennis C. Whitehead, commanding officer of the Fifth Air Force, who made the following recommendation:

> It is suggested that pending the completion of necessary training

and the receipt and absorbtion of replacement crews, the 201st Mexican Fighter Squadron be attached to either the Combat Replacement Training Center or the Air Defense Commnand.

On 24 July, Lieutenant Colonel Kellond delivered the following document to General Smith:

MEXICAN EXPEDITIONARY AIR FORCE
LIAISON GROUP OF THE UNITED STATES ARMY
APO 710 JULY 24, 1945.
SUBJECT; Movement of Mexican Fighter Squadron.
TO; The Commanding General of the 5th Fighter Command APO 710 – By way of the Official Commander Expeditionary Air Force MEAF APO 710.

1. – Since the issue of the order for the movement of the Mexican Fighter Squadron 201 to Okinawa, certain changes have come about in the combat effectiveness of the squadron. These changes have been presented in virtue of the loss of the three best pilots the squadron had.

Before the squadron is in condition to engage in combat operations, on the scale foreseen in Okinawa, it is necessary to obtain and indoctrinate new pilots to replace the ones lost.

2. – With the object to help the squadron in the work it has before it, it is recommended that the move to Okinawa be put off for much later.

A.W. KELLOND Lt. Col. Air Corps. – Liaison Officer of the United States Army (Signed)
FIRST ENDORSEMENT – MEAF
APO 710 July 24, 1945.
TO; The Commanding Officer of the 5th Fighter Command, APO 710.
I agree with the recommendations in this basic official letter and recommended that they are followed – ANTONIO CARDENAS R. (signed), Col. of the Mexican Army, Commander of the MEAF.

This opinion was also shared by Captain Radames Gaxiola, who sent a similar letter to Colonel Cardenas addressing the issue.

## REPLACEMENT GROUP MEAF

When the MEAF was formed a group of replacement pilots and ground personnel was under training in the US, and while the above events were unfolding none of them had yet graduated.

Since early 1945, the *Grupo de Reemplazos* of the MEAF was being trained in various bases across the United States, including Foster Field, Texas; Chanute Field, Rantoul, Illinois; Napier Field, Dotham, Alabama; and San Antonio Cadet Center, Texas.

The Mexican Air Force had started to send groups of recent graduate pilots to the United States for training as part of the replacement group. This had been announced in the Mexican press on 9 May, under the headline '58 new pilots at Guadalajara – some will be replacements for Squadron 201':

During a brief interview with the representatives of the press General Gustavo Salinas Camina, Director of military aeronautics informed yesterday that in the first days of next June in Guadalajara, Jalisco, 58 new pilots will be graduating, that are presently doing their flight training in the Port of Veracruz.

From this group 16 will leave in the month of June with destination the USA to take a course of advanced training, to be part of the reserve of squadron 201 of the Mexican Expeditionary Air Force in case of a vacant slot in the squadron.

A second group of 16 pilots will leave with the same destination in the month of November and 26 will stay in Mexico so they can fill any vacant slots during the training in North America.

The selection of the new pilots will be made via lottery in which representatives of the press of Mexico will be part of, because some problems have presented since all the young pilots have presented their request to be taken into consideration and all their requests cannot be granted.

The replacement group would suffer two fatal aviation accidents. The first occurred on 9 July 1945, when 2nd Lieutenant Hugo Gonzalez y Gonzalez was flying a 'round robin' navigational flight with three other Mexicans pilots. Gonzalez was flying the P-47D-40-RA serial number 45-49290, assigned to the 269th AAFBU CCTS (F) at Strother Field, Kansas, II Squadron of the 72nd Fighter Wing.

His aircraft crashed and exploded in bad weather about two miles south-west of Arkansas City, Kansas. He was part of a formation of four P-47Ds, the other members of the flight being Lieutenant Jose Gonzalez del Rio, 2nd Lieutenant Jose Gomez Ignorosa and 2nd Lieutenant Cesar Gomez Amador. The official accident report read as follows:

On 9 July 1945 at approximately 1850 hours a Mexican air force pilot crashed a P-47 aircraft two miles southwest of Arkansas City, Kansas. It was a fatal accident. The aircraft exploded and burned upon contact with the ground, and wreckage was thrown over [a] 500 yard area.

Prior to the accident the pilot was one of four flying a round robin navigation flight. The flight plans were made out individually, with an ETA of two hours after take-off. The forecast weather for the route was above marginal for CFR. The cold front was plotted on the synoptic map but little activity was accompanying it at the time the weather was given to the pilots. As the weather conditions grew worse in the vicinity of the field, Army Flight service was contacted by Base operations and the base route were notified to contact the aircraft to have them land, but due to language difficulties, contact was not made.

As the four aircraft came within approximately 25 miles of the field, each tuned to 'C' (homing) channel and called for homing. The first aircraft flew within five miles of the field but turned back and circled outside the squall.

While the first aircraft was circling, two of the remaining aircraft came within sight and were contacted by the pilot in an attempt to have them join and return south to Ponca City Municipal Airport to land. One of the aircraft joined but the third aircraft was going to try to make the field and continued into the weather.

All conversation was in Spanish and reception was poor due to weather conditions. Two interpreters were on duty in the control tower, but were not able to contact the aircraft. The Homer on duty was unable to receive a 'count' from the pilots, but took a fix by getting a null in the continuous conversation.

Two ships landed safely at Ponca City Municipal Airport but the third ship crashed to the ground and exploded and burned within one half mile of a farmhouse. The fire that occurred in the crash was of minor importance and it was immediately quenched by the heavy rain. They only part that burned was one tire.

In the Mexican report of the accident, one of Gonzalez's wingmen, Cesar Gomez Amador, said he believed the radio in the aircraft of

Gonzalez had failed before they encountered the bad weather, as no reply could be got from him when the decision was made to land at Ponca City.

After being notified of the location of the crash site, 2nd Lieutenant Enrique Zapata Buttner immediately went there with the base adjutant, but found that 2nd Lieutenant Gonzalez had been killed in his aircraft, which was destroyed. He was identified by the name on his parachute and his dog tags. From observing the scene, Zapata Buttner believed that the aircraft fell in a left turn at a speed of about 350mph.

The second fatal crash was on 26 September 1945, after the end of the war. Lieutenant Roberto Gomez Moreno, of the 2116th AAFBU, X squadron, 29th Fighter Training Wing, was killed flying the North American P-51D-NA Mustang 44-74935 while on a local transition flight. He had flown for about two-and-a-half hours in this type of aircraft. Witnesses on the ground revealed that his aircraft was in a spin, and at one time a partial recovery was made, but it began spinning again and crashed about 14 miles north-east of Napier Field, Alabama.

His crash was reported in the local paper, the *Dothan Eagle*, on the afternoon of Thursday 27 September, with a small article under the headline 'Mexican flier killed in crash':

> A Mexican student officer from Napier Field was killed yesterday when a P-51 crashed about five miles south of Abbeville, it was announced today by the public relations office.
>
> Cause of the crash has not been determined, it was announced, and identification of the officer is being withheld pending notification of next of kin. A board of qualified Army Officers has been appointed to investigate the crash in which the plane was completely demolished, the public relations office said.

The 24 July document from Kellond on the state of training of the replacement group was the only information the MEAF received from the US, and even that was delayed. Colonel Cardenas felt they had lost control over the replacement group when his command went overseas, with a breakdown in communication between the two units.

Officially Major Suarez was in charge, but this role was handed down to the Mexican military attache in Washington DC and later to Captain Salido Beltran in the Philippines. Many consider that this breakdown in communications caused the problem of receiving the necessary replacements in time for the squadron to be able to move with the 58th to Okinawa.

With the end of the war, pilot training at Napier field was temporarily inactivated on 31 October 1945 by order of the US War Department. The base had been training 40 Mexican cadets, with 16 of them scheduled to complete their training on 26 October. It is possible that the training was moved to other USAAF bases, and by the end of the year all Mexican replacement personnel had returned to Mexico.

With the end of the war, all the pilots and ground personnel training in the USA were ordered to return to Mexico. While some of the students requested to stay to complete their training, these requests fell on deaf ears.

Colonel Cardenas' weekly report to Mexico City for 22-28 July stated:

> 3 A) – The squadron flew two interception missions with 8 sorties.
> B) – Training sorties flown: 31.
> 4. A) – Pilots assigned: 26.
> B) – Airplanes property of 201st Mexican Fighter
> Squadron: 16.
> Average airplanes available for operational flights daily: 12.
> Average airplanes in repair: 4.
> 5. Personnel
> A) – On July 23 2ndLt. Guillermo Garcia Ramos joined his squadron. This pilot was rescued from New Guinea, and is unhurt.
> B) – On July 27 was found the body of the late 2nd Lt. Mario Lopez Portillo. This pilot was killed on July 21 when his plane crashed against a mountain in Bataan peninsula.
> C) – 2nd Captain Pablo Rivas Matinez is still missing.
> D) – On trial: 6 enlisted men.
> E) – Average hospitalised personnel: 4 officers and 8 enlisted men.

Among other administrative actions on 30 July, Colonel Cardenas signed requests for promotion for several officers, among whom were two pilots: Lieutenant Carlos Varela Landini, who had commanded 'A' fight since 1 June and had flown 12 combat missions with 28.5 hours and 16 missions in the combat zone with 27.25 hours; and Lieutenant Amadeo Castro Almanza, flight commander and Adjuntant of the Operations Officer, who had flown 14 combat missions with 33.00 hours and 17 missions in the combat zone with 30.45 hours.

Ground personnel to be promoted included 2nd Lieutenant Samuel Cueto R., a mechanic who worked in the engineering section of the squadron under Captain Jesus Carranza, and 2nd Lieutenant Guillermo Albert R., who worked in the headquarters section.

## THE RESCUE OF 2nd LIEUTENANT GARCIA RAMOS

One bright note in the bad month of July for the 201st was the rescue of one of the Mexican pilots. A story that often circulates at reunions of surviving veterans of the MEAF (and is referred to in several articles about the 201st, is the rescue of 2nd Lieutenant Guillermo Garcia Ramos by an American pilot on 20 July 1945.

The story goes that after bailing out, Garcia Ramos was rescued by Major Larry D. Dennis, a test pilot based at Biak, New Guinea, with the help of two Australian Catalina flying-boat rescue pilots. The rescue was accomplished under enemy fire, Garcia Ramos paddling his dingy to the Catalina while Major Dennis and one of the Australians pulled him in.

After returning to base, Dennis presented the Mexican pilot to his commanding officer, who had refused to let him join the rescue attempt because of fears of a Japanese trick. Nineteen years later, as the by then Colonel Dennis was about to retire from the US Air Force, he was invited to Mexico by the Mexican Air Force to receive the Mexican Army Medal of Merit First Class for his actions.

However, the above events are not historically correct. After much research and contacting people who knew Colonel Dennis, a different picture has emerged. Even his brother Bob, years later, would comment to the author on the errors of the accepted version of events back in July 1945:

> Glad to learn that your version of Garcia's rescue was published. I do not think much of the second version, not very factual; Larry was in the depot, not a B-25 bomb squadron.
>
> He may have been flying a B-25 the day he spotted Garcia. Coming back from Holandia, New Guinea, his log book shows a B-25 on or about that date. His log also shows a ten hour flight in an OA-10, the air force designation for the Catalina and it says 'rescue'. All aircraft that were in the depot became the jurisdiction of the depot and were not released back to their unit until the depot repaired and test flew the aircraft.
>
> Larry didn't have to ask permission to use any aircraft in the depot, nor did he have to ask any commanding officer, as his only commanding officer was Fifth Air Force Headquarters Material

2nd Lieutenant Jose Luis Pratt Ramos outside the grounds of the Imperial Palace in Tokyo. He was part of the group that accompanied Colonel Cardenas to Japan to thank General MacArthur for his support of the MEAF. (Jose Luis Pratt Ramos)

Command Division under the jurisdiction of Wright Field. Fifth Air Force Headquarters at that time I believe were still in Hollandia, New Guinea.

Larry Dennis (who received his wings on 15 November 1940) was born in Cedar Rapids, Iowa, in 1915, a graduate of the University of Iowa with a Major in Business and Economics and was married.

He was one of three test pilots and the commanding officer of the 374th Service Squadron (from 26 April to 24 September 1945) at Biak with a large amount of experience in flight testing work at Wright Field, Ohio. At the time of the rescue he had about 4,020.40 hours of flight time (based on his Form 5details).

Also stationed at Biak was No.120 (Dutch) Fighter Squadron, equipped with the Curtiss P-40N for ground attack missions against the Japanese. On 19 July, flying a Vickers built OA-10A Catalina flying boat, shown on his flight records as a 'search', Dennis thought he saw a flash of a signal mirror and hunted around but saw no one, and as it was getting dark he returned to Biak. There was no formal air/sea rescue operation in the area, so when a Dutch pilot failed to return from a mission

they called Major Dennis, who was anxious to have some combat experience, as mentioned by his brother Bob, who was also serving in the air force and stationed at Tacloban:

> Biak was actually in a combat zone, but the air fighting had moved to the Celebes and the Philippines. Larry would often take a fighter plane that the depot had repaired and deliver it back to the fighter command unit, and always had a fighter pilot wingman along beside him and both planes armed and combat ready.
>
> At that time I was stationed in Tacloban air base right in the center of the fighting, and Larry and Jim Watson, a fighter pilot, came in delivering the two P-38 aircraft, and they were looking for a fight, but said they didn't see any Jap aircraft.

The next day Dennis told the other two test pilots, Lieutenant Paul L. Chell and Lieutenant Joe Lynch (Chell was a former A-20 bomber pilot from the 417th Bomb Group and Lynch a former fighter pilot from the 68th Fighter Squadron, 347th Fighter Group of the Thirteenth Air Force, credited with one kill in a P-40F), that he was going back to look for the Dutch pilot.

Dennis used one of the USAAF OA-10As that were available at the depot (at any time there would be three or four of them). He recruited a crew of a flight engineer from the unit and an Australian non-pilot who was walking by and was probably from the replacement depot at Biak.

Since many Allied personnel would be waiting to be assigned to a unit, they would often be around the flight line, and some were offered rides in the American aircraft. Because of the lack of personnel, all the depot aircraft, including four-engine types, were operated with only one pilot and an engineer.

Major Dennis thus had the minimum crew to operate the OA-10A – a non pilot Australian in the co-pilot position and the flight engineer.

It was the Australian on the blister position who threw the rope to Garcia Ramos, since Dennis had to be at the controls, with the OA-10A going about 10-15 knots. As these aircraft were flown by a skeleton crew, such equipment as sea anchors, used to slow down the aircraft on the water during a rescue, were stored in a warehouse back at the base.

The flight engineer at his station controlled the electrical switches and mixture control.

While pulling Garcia in, the Australian fell out of the aircraft and was being dragged in the water. Finally the Australian was pulled in by the engineer and Garcia Ramos. Then, being only a few miles from an active Japanese base, Dennis was anxious to take off before they encountered any Japanese.

It was dark when the OA-10 made it back to Biak. The aircraft was heard returning by Chell and Lynch in Dennis' quarters, which they all shared. Both were having 'cold' beers when Dennis pulled up in a jeep. They were ready to kid Dennis about 'another wild goose chase', when Dennis came in, pulling Garcia by the hand, the Mexican with one shoe missing, a two-day beard, in his tan flight suit, wet, cold and shivering.

Dennis thrust Garcia in front of him and said to Chell and Lynch, 'Now.don't say I don't do anything', and for the next 15 minutes told them the story of the rescue, while Garcia sat shivering, after which Chell and Lynch asked who the pilot was he rescued. They were introduced to Garcia Ramos, who told them his story in his broken English.

Garcia had been so afraid of the Japanese that he thought any noise he heard, even that made by wild pigs, was evidence of a Japanese patrol, so he kept heading back out into the water in his dinghy. Dennis gave Garcia a pair of shoes, and he stayed in their quarters until he returned to his unit two days later. Chell and Dennis got to know Garcia well; he was a personable person and well liked.

After Garcia returned to his unit and informed Colonel Cardenas and Captain Radames Gaxiola Andrade about what had happened, Major Dennis received a translated copy a couple of days later of a request by Cardenas to the Secretary of National Defense in Mexico City that he should be decorated:

Republic P-47D-30-RA Thunderbolts reportedly during one of four fighter sweeps to Formosa to seek aerial targets. (Family of General Fernando Hernandez Vega)

> This is to inform you that on 20 July 1945 2nd Lt. Guillermo Garcia Ramos, P. A., who was lost the day before, was rescued under circumstances that constitute a highly meritorious deed by Major Larry D. Dennis, North American Air Force.
>
> Lt. Garcia Ramos, after having made a parachute jump, landed on the Northwest coast of New Guinea about 10 miles from Sarong, in which neighborhood are Japanese troops. In spite of this, and being informed that in the mentioned area were enemy anti-aircraft positions, Major Dennis landed a flying-boat 'Catalina' in the waters near the shore to save an officer of the Mexican Army.
>
> Considering that the deed should be rewarded by the Military Authorities of Mexico, I request that the High Command grant to the above-mentioned American officer the decoration or citation that is fitting.

News of the rescue of Garcia was also published in the USA, with one undated clipping supplied to the author by the brother of Major Dennis reading, under the headline 'Maj. Larry Dennis of Osborn rescues flyer from island':

> Major Larry Dennis, [of] 220 Wallace Dr. Osbron, a former Patterson Field pilot was credited this week with braving rough waters around [a] Jap-infested ssland to save a Mexican air force flyer.
>
> The major's wife, the former Kathryn E. Alexander, lives at their home in Osborn. They have been married since April 3, 1943, when they were married in the Patterson Field chapel.
>
> Lt. Guillermo Garcia Ramos of the 201st Mexican air force, fighting Japs in the Pacific, had taken off in a P-47 from Biak, off the coast of New Guinea, for the Philippines. A sudden tropical storm swept Lt. Ramos over [an] enemy held island near the coast of New Guinea, the Associated Press reported from Manila.
>
> With visibility zero and landing impossible the Mexican pilot fought the storm until his fuel ran low. Then he soared up to 12,000 feet and bailed out. After inflating his life raft, he maneuvered it into a small bay where he hid 48 hours from Jap patrols.
>
> Major Dennis, on a test flight from Biak, saw the flash of a mirror. He swooped low, spotted the Allied pilot and returned to his base. Five hours later Major Dennis was back with a Catalina flying boat, which he set down in a small lagoon hemmed by coral reef and churned by a heavy cross wind. "It was a miracle we were able to take off in such a sea," said Lt. Ramos.
>
> Major Dennis received a commendation from Col. Antonio Cardenas Rodriguez, commander of the Mexican air expeditionary force.

Bob Dennis would later comment on his brother's rescue mission:

> I was there in New Guinea and Biak when Larry made the rescue flight, but he didn't tell me much about it, other than the weather was bad and no one else wanted to go with him and winds were pretty bad.

Nothing more was heard about any award for Major Dennis until 1948, when he was back at Wright Field carrying out cargo aircraft testing with Chell in the Fighter Test Department. He was ordered to fly to Detroit, Michigan, in a Beechcraft C-45 to receive the *Medalla Del Merito Militar, Primera Clase* (Military Merit Medal, First Class) from the Mexican Consul, Fernando Rueda, on 11 February.

The offices of the Mexican Consul were a one room affair, and his staff a single secretary.

The Consul became emotional during the ceremony because of the humble circumstances in which his country's highest military award was being presented, and Major Dennis was not getting a three-day celebration in Mexico City, as was usually the case for recipients. The only thing he could offer after the ceremony was drinks at a local bar.

The Consul lamented that the award should have been presented by the President of Mexico, not a humble official such as he. The reason for this was the refusal of the USAF to let Major Dennis travel to Mexico, due to severe budget cuts during the Truman administration.

A couple of days later, Major Dennis received the following letter from Fernando Rueda:

> Dear Major Dennis:
> It is with pleasure that I am sending to you with this note, several clippings in which appear photograhs taken on the occasion of the presentation to you, of the medal of 'Military Merit, First Class', from the local newspapers of February the 11th 1948. I already contacted General Ruiz, our Military Attache at Washigton, D.C., in connection with the obtaining of the ribbon of the medal and the address of Lt. Guillermo Garcia Ramos. As soon as I receive the ribbon and the address I will be very glad to forward them to you.

It was not until 1963 that the then Lieutenant Colonel Dennis, who was about to retire from the air force after having served in various units and commands after the war, finally got to go to Mexico City

with his family and the Secretary of the Air Force, Eugene M. Zuckert. Dennis was honoured in person by the Mexican government, the Mexican Air Force and veterans of the 201st Mexican Fighter Squadron.Dduring a meeting of the 'Mexico Squadron' of the Air Force Association, contact was made with former Lieutenant Guillermo Garcia Ramos, who wrote the following to Dennis:

> Every time I look back at the years that have passed since that heroic deed where you, exposing your life, saved mine, one of a modest and unknown Lt. of the Mexican Air Force, I recall that all these years since that period are owed to you, and my gratitude is renewed time and again. I sincerely believe that every opportunity should be taken to let you know my endless gratefulness, as I am doing now. Many, many thanks again, my dear Colonel.
>
> Dennis replied to him:
>
> Your gratefulness in very much appreciated. However, just to keep the records straight your astute action was the most important factor in your rescue. The clarity of your mirror communications and the unmistakable sincerity of your 'all-out' effort in paddling that dingy into the open sea convinced us that you were not a trap set by the Japanese and that we should go in after you.
>
> Although we earnestly would like to locate the other members of the crew (Co-pilot RAAF and engineer USAF) such an undertaking would be difficult. To my knowledge, no United States Air Force recording of this mission was ever accomplished. The Expeditionary Report [of] your Colonel Cardenas and the examplary action taken by the Mexican National Army and Government, in presenting the Mexican Military Medal in 1948 are the only records believed available.
>
> Queries to Headquarters, United States Air Force and the United States Inspector General Historical Records were negative. It would be a pleasure indeed to see you in Mexico.

Larry Dennis did finally meet Guillermo Garcia Ramos again, who was now a captain for Mexicana Airlines, with a large family of seven children. As Dennis and Garcia met for the first time since the rescue, Garcia embraced him and pointed to his wife and seven children, saying: "This is the result of my being saved." Garcia would go on to have an eighth child in March 1965.

Dennis received a symbolic gesture of thanks from Garcia Ramos, a pair of shoes, as a token for the ones Dennis had given him back in Biak in July 1945.

On the afternoon of his arrival in Mexico, Dennis received the *Servicio en el Lejano Oriente* medal (Medal for Service in the Far East) from the Secretary of National Defense, General Agustin Olachea Avila, with a certificate which read:

> The *Servicio en el Lejano Oriente* medal is awarded to Lt. Col. of the American Air Forces Larry D. Dennis as recognition of his valor and spirit of comradeship, demonstrated in rescuing 2nd Lt. Guillermo Garcia Ramos from the waters of the Pacific during World War II.

General Roberto Fierro Villalobos, chief of the Mexican Air Force, also made Dennis an honorary member of the Mexican Air Force, pinning Mexican Air Force wings on his uniform, while

Garcia Ramos presented him with a pin from the *Compania Mexicana de Aviacion* (CMA). Dennis and his family spent three weeks in Mexico courtesy of the Mexican government.

Captain Garcia Ramos lost his life in tragic circumstances six years later, on 4 June 1969, when the Boeing 727-64, XA-SEL (19256/355) he was piloting hit a mountain near Monterrey City airport during a thunderstorm, killing him and 78 others aboard.

Six years later, retired Lieutenant Colonel Dennis died of a heart attack on a tennis court on 23 November 1975. He is buried in his home town of Cedar Rapids, Iowa.

## STAND DOWN, AUGUST-OCTOBER 1945

During August 1945 the MEAF was no longer part of the 5th Fighter Command, initially being transferred from Porac Field to Clark Field (code name Borax), establishing its camp to the north of the field. The 201st had reported to the Center of Training Combat Replacement at Clark Field since 30 July.

On 2 August the squadron's pilots had 30 minutes of flying time in their P-47D-30 aircraft, and one pilot returned from hospital. During the early part of the month, the squadron undertook several missions, including a practice intercept mission on the 7th. Despite being 'disenfranchised', the 201st was not idle, undertaking a long-range combat mission on 8 August.

> **Mission No.1-41 (#57):** 8 August 1945
> Long-range bombing mission to Karenko, Formosa.
> Results: 9 P-47s took off for the mission at 0745, time over target was 1130 to 1140, and they returned to base at 1345. Only 6 bombed the target, the other 2 aircraft turning back before reaching Formosa, due to lack of fuel.
>
> The P-47s flew over the objective at 12,000ft, dive-bombing the buildings designated as primary target [2nd Lieutenant Moreno Arreola said it was a turbo-electric plant], according to references from a photograph of Karenko, Formosa. The bombs fell between the river and the highway which runs from north to south, causing two fires but no damage to the buildings.
>
> The bombing did not have complete results, due to the use of just one 1,000lb bomb per aircraft. 7x1,000lb GP AN-M65 bombs were expended on the target area.

There were great dangers to this mission, as discovered by Lieutenant Amadeo Castro:

> The mission was a long range [one] to Formosa, what is today Taiwan, about 600 miles from our base in Luzon, Philippines, a 600-mile flight in single-engine aircraft, for which we required a large amount of fuel.
>
> We carried an additional external central tank, plus one on the wing and on the other a 1,000lb bomb. During the trip, the consumption of fuel made the wing carrying the bomb heavy and we needed to compensate the aircraft on its longitude axis continually. We arrived at the objective and I dived against it. A couple of tracers crossed the skies, while one of my pilots dived against the objective.
>
> I took aim and dropped the bomb, and instantly my P-47 did a terrible 'Alazo'. The lack of weight on the wing that released the bomb caused a 'barrell roll' that caught me by surprise. I [only] managed to control the aircraft a couple of metres from the ground.
>
> Immediately I warned the others to be ready for the reaction of their aircraft. Our mission accomplished, an almost 700-mile trip home was waiting for us.

The Mexican pilots who reportedly participated in this mission were Captain 1st Class Radames Gaxiola Andrade, Lieutenant Amadeo Castro Almanza, Lieutenant Carlos Garduno Nunez, Lieutenant Reynaldo Perez Gallardo, Lieutenant Julio Cal y Mayor Sauz, 2nd Lieutenant Justino Reyes Retana, 2nd Lieutenant Miguel Moreno Arreola, 2nd Lieutenant Praxedis Lopez Ramos and 2nd Lieutenant Angel Sanchez Rebollo.

One of the squadron's ground personnel, mechanic Corporal Martinez Perez, wrote about the long wait they had to endure for the pilots' return:

> When all the aircraft took off for the mission, the base was now quiet. The attack to the island would take them about seven and a half hours of flying time coming and going, it was too much time for a medium fighter bomber, single seater and a drain to the pilot.
>
> After three hours and forty five minutes had passed, we [were] imagining that it was the exact time they would arrive over the enemy target and do their bombing dives on it to destroy the objective, without worrying about the enemy anti-aircraft fire trying to shoot them down. After seven hours and forty five minutes had passed after their departure, it was time for them to arrive [back] at our base.
>
> All the personnel were scanning the sky, some with their hands covering their eyes to see better the horizon, others with binoculars, and the administrative staff would ask us every minute if they had arrived. The aircraft arrived in formation even with the physical fatigue the pilots had, all complete, no losses to worry about. They made their entrance lightly flying about 350 kilometers per hour and they broke up the formation to the left in ones like a giant fan, separated by seconds, circled the field, lowered their landing gears and flaps and aligned themselves to the runway to land.
>
> To us to hear the screeching of the tyres of each aircraft on the asphalt at 200 kilometers per hour, marked another mission completed by the pilots. The tension is over, we do the normal inspection and carefully after every mission check the engines and correct any reported problems, we change some parts if it's necessary and leave the aircraft ready for the next mission.
>
> The radio operators go up and down each piece of radio and radars. The armourers had to remove the machine guns, the eight empty, and mount others and load them with ammo and check the bombing mechanisms.
>
> The intelligence personnel were receiving the individual reports from each pilot and picked up their gun cameras from the aircraft and installed others. In the office they would interpret the film taken and inform the commander the results of the mission and wait orders for the next one.

There is some confusion in the after-action report for this mission about the two aircraft that returned early, Lieutenant Garduno and 2nd Lieutenant Justino Reyes Retana not being mentioned in the above account.

An interesting side note to this mission is that years later, former Staff Sergeant Cornelius Orsatti of the USAAF liaision group would claim the 201st probably sank a Japanese destroyer. He wrote the following to the author in January 1980:

> [During the] next to the last mission over Formosa by the 201st, a Jap destroyer was sunk at the Port of TOKO, August 8, 1945. The report of this mission was held back by Air Intelligence for not knowing exactly the name of the destroyer. Air Intelligence mentioned the name of the destroyer was 'HONSHU or HOKKADO', but as they did not know which of the two, the report of the mission was not released.

So far research has not been able to confirm any Japanese shipping lost in the port of Toko on the day the 201st carried out their dive-bombing mission.

The accident report for 9August 1945, states that 2nd Lieutenant Angel Sanchez Rebollo, flying P-47D-30-RA s/n. 44-33715, on his return from the bombing mission was ordered to land in Lingaye with his flight leader, because of lack of fuel.

After both aircraft were refuelled, Sanchez Rebollo suffered a mechanical problem which forced him to stay overnight. The next morning, after the problem was fixed, during take-off run his left landing gear wheel burst, which carried the P-47 to the left and off the runway. He tried to correct it by applying his right brake, but his left wheel hit some rocks on the side of the strip. The P-47 was so badly damaged that it could only be used for spare parts. Sanchez Rebollo suffered injuries to both arms and his right ear.

On the same day as the dive-bombing mission to Formosa, the other pilots from the squadron flew 10.15 hours in the combat zone. The previous day, Lieutenant Joaquin Ramirez Vilchis suffered a landing accident at Borax Field in P-47D-30-RA 44-33728, after which the aircraft could also only be used for spare parts. Ramirez Vilchis, who escaped unhurt, was blamed for causing the crash.

For the rest of the FEAF (Far East Air Force), the fighting continued in the Phillipine Islands during the first week of August, with P-38s, B-25s and B-24s supporting ground forces on Luzon and targeting pockets of Japanese resistance.

On 2 August bad weather cancelled all FEAF missions from Okinawa. Thirteenth Air Force P-38s supported Allied ground forces in northern Luzon, hitting pockets of resistance west of Kiangan and blasting enemy-occupied caves on ridges north-west of Bontoc. The following day, P-38s and B-25s again provided support for ground forces in northern Luzon, targeting buildings in Apunan and Japanese positions at various locations, including ridges south-west of Kiangan and west of Banaue.

On 4 August B-25s and P-38s hit Japanese forces on Luzon near Santa Ines and in the Butitio area near Mount Obundan, while B-24s were in action south of Fabrica. The next day, P-38s attacked several enemy concentrations, including north-east of Naguilian, near Mount Data, and B-24s pounded Japanese positions south of Fabrica. Then on 7 August, B-25s and P-38s launched several ground support missions against Japanese forces near Ambuclao, Kiangan, Batangan, Aparri, Malikayan, Bontoc, Tabayoc and in the Palugloko Mountains.

On 8 August, B-24s were in action in the Lenatin River valley, south-east of Mankayan and near Kiangan and Bagabag. The day after, more ground support missions were launched by P-38s and B-24s of the Thirteenth Air Force around Baguio, Manakayan, Cervantes, Kiangan and Infanta.

Three days after the Mexicans' Karenko mission, the MEAF received notofication that it was now assigned to the 360th Air Service Group (Combat Replacement & Traning Center). That same day, the *New York Times* carried the story of the Mexican attack on Formosa, with the headline 'Mexicans bomb Formosa – Fliers aiding Americans start fires in enemy port':

> Two flights of Thunderbolts, manned by the 201st Mexican Expeditionary Air Force, made a long-range fighter sweep Wednesday, the United States Fifth Air Force announced today.
>
> Operating from a base to which the force moved intact overnight recently the white nose Thunderbolts dive-bombed and started fires in the enemy port of Karenko. The Mexican pilots joined the Far East Air Forces in May and flew their first combat mission on June 7. In recent weeks they had been furnishing ground support for American troops in Northern Luzon.

On 12 August, Lieutenant Jacobo Estrada Luna and Lieutenant Carlos Varela Landini completed another ferrying mission from Biak, New Guinea, bringing two new P-47D-30-Rs, 44-33725 and 44-90062, handing them over to the engineering section of the squadron.

While returning from a training flight on 15 August, Captain 2nd Class Roberto Legorreta Sicilia suffered an accident on landing in P-47D-30-RA 44-33733 due to excess speed, damaging the propeller blades of his aircraft.

On 24 August, an American transport plane, while taxiing too close to the Mexican flight line, damaged two Mexican P-47s.

Two days later, the 201st undertook its final combat mission of the war:

> **Mission No.1-42 (#58):** 26 August 1945
>
> Escort mission for naval convoy north of the Philippines.
>
> Results: All the pilots of the 201st participated in this mission to escort a naval convoy from 0600 until they were relieved by USAAF Northrop P-61 Black Widows at 1800. The mission took place because it was feared there would be an attack of [*kamikaze*] suicide aircraft based at Formosa.

It appears that all available Mexican pilots participated in the day-long mission, some of the pilots even flying twice. For example, 2nd Lieutenant Jose Luis Pratt Ramos' individual flight record shows that he flew for three and then four hours,

as did Lieutenant Jacobo Estrada Luna.

In the weekly operational report, Colonel Cardenas mentions the squadron flew one escort mission for surface forces, with 26 sorties and a possible total time of 89.30 hours for the mission.

On 27 August, the Thirteenth Air Force's XIII Bomber Command moved from Morotai to Clark Field. While the pilots were busy with that mission, a group of Mexican ground personnel had another chance encounter with Japanese troops when a 12-man detail (two officers and 10 enlisted men) left the camp on a patrol. What happened was described by 2nd Lieutenant Guillermo Alberto Robles, who went with the group:

> On the 26 of August the commander of the squadron, Capt. Gaxiola, ordered Tte. de Aeronautica (Meteorologista) Jose Cruz Abundis Cano, with [other] personnel to leave on a patrol close to the base, information having been received that a group of Japanese soldiers were about (going on such missions was called 'Looking for trouble', and the nightly guard duty to safeguard the aircraft on the flight line was known as 'Going to a party').
>
> Abundis invited me to accompany them, [along] with Sgt. 1/o. Class Eusebio Alvarez Huerta, Sgt. 2/o. Class Jose Maria Hernandez Bailon, David Lozano Hernandez, Hector Gomez Oaxaca, Jose Luis Trejo Patino, Corporals Fernando Miranda Gomez, Ricardo Quintal Pinzon, Olegario Gomez Rodriguez, Rafael Valdez Balleza and soldier Vieyra Pozos.
>
> We left the base on a truck and we headed … to the northwest, until we found the warning sign that indicated … 'NO MAN'S LAND'. We walked about 3 kilometres more [and] arrived at the end of the road where there was a drop off – at the bottom was the beginning of a river, but on those dry days it was [just] small puddles.
>
> Abundis told me he was staying there. If I wanted to go down he would wait for me up here. I went to the bottom of the cliff with David Lozano, Hector Gomez Oaxaca, Quintal Pinzon, Olegario Gomez and Vieyra Pozos. We covered the area with all the security measures, when somebody called my attention that in one of the puddles was … the print of a Japanese shoe. Japanese shoes were made of lona on the upper part and the shoe was like a tennis shoe but with the big toe separate (like a baseball glove). I told the guys we were going to follow him, but after walking about a mile we saw a cave with many antennas, that indicated a radio there. We entered with caution and there was a radio [that was] turned off. Due to its size I ordered it destroyed and we removed some identification plaques with Japanese symbols.
>
> … We returned to the place we had climbed down, … [where] somebody [told us] … that the clearing at the foot of the ravine formed by the river was full of Japs. … We got close [behind] the protection of some big rocks that closed the access … [and saw] eight Japanese in different activities, some walking, some seated and others on their knees.

2nd Lieutenant Robles told his men to fire on the Japanese soldiers when he yelled "Surrender", as he felt the Japanese were sure to then grab their weapons. One of his men then told him that one of the Japanese was behind him, and as Robles made for his carbine that he had left against a rock, a shot rang out as the enemy soldier had grabbed a hand grenade and tried to remove the safety pin.

> In that moment I yelled 'FIRE', and the firing started. I ran to the wounded Japanese … Once I had the grenade in my hands, I put the safety pin back in its normal position. The fire fight had finished and I yelled to [my comrades up on the cliff] 'Why didn't you intervene?' … They indicated there were [more Japanese] in a cave to the front about 50 metres from where we were.
>
> I asked for a volunteer to get close to the cave and throw the hand grenade under the protection of our fire, but nobody came forward, because nobody had thrown a hand grenade [before]. I did it personally, with the fear that at any moment I could be killed or wounded.
>
> Once I threw the grenade into the cave, it exploded and we all ran

into the cave [but there was nobody there]. I ordered a good search … and saw a Japanese in the foetal position, and with the mouth of my carbine stuck in his ribs he looked up and said 'Surrender'.

Once on his feet I searched him for weapons and asked him who he was, from what branch he was etc. He answered in [poor] English that he was a shot down Zero pilot and he had joined the Navy Infantry. I gave him some rations and water, which he ate, and I went to see the wounded [Japanese soldier]. He turned out to be a Sergeant in the Imperial Japanese Navy … around his waist he carried a Japanese flag with some Japanese writing on it, a samurai sword and some identification tags … Since we didn't have a stretcher, I ordered one made from shirts and sticks We climbed [up the cliff] with both prisoners but on the climb the improvised stretcher broke and the wounded Japanese fell into a crack. I thought that the wound was mortal and asked for a volunteer to put an end to this man's life. Nobody wanted to do it, so I decided to. I dispatched the men and I was alone with him. I pointed with the carbine and in that moment I realised I was going to commit a cruel crime and it was my obligation to turn him in whatever state he was in. I was thinking he maybe had a wife, kids and family and they were waiting for his return like mine.

Since there was nobody to help me, I threw him on my shoulders and I climbed with him to where the truck was waiting. A little later an ambulance arrived with Tte. P.A. Amadeo Castro Almanza and I turned over to him the prisoners. After interrogation they were handed over to provost marshal of the base.

In the official report, even though Abundis did not participate in the firefight, he signed it since he was a Lieutenant and by his rank he gave orders and was in charge.

A different view of these events was given by four of those who took part: Sergeant Jose Maria Hernandez Bailon and Corporals Ricardo Quintal Pinzon, Olegario Gomez Rodriguez and Fernando Miranda Gomez. They said they discovered a group of eight Japanese soldiers around a campfire by a river, preparing their food. Quintal Pinzon gave his version of the events that followed:

They were armed with large calibre weapons, and they were talking, moving side to side and gesturing. We didn't know what they were saying. After we confirmed their numbers I moved to get my friends on the other side. I got down from the rock and moved silently, but as I turned back I discovered not far from me, by the road, the silhouette of a man who was coming to the spot where we were. I thought that he saw me, so I ran across the hillside to warn my friends. I dropped my rucksack and readied my weapon. I ducked as much as I could and with my weapon ready I moved quietly to encounter him. I knew if I let him past, he could warn his friends. I had told my friends, that at the first shot they should open fire on the Japanese group, which was on the other side. I waited for him in the crouched position.

A couple of seconds passed, that felt like hours, because no doubt he had seen me. He was hiding between the rocks and the trees and I had lost sight of him. I retreated some steps back and hid again, when all of a sudden appeared a figure of a man 15 metres from where I was. He had a sword in his left hand and a hand grenade in his right. He yelled in a high voice, who knows what.

Rapidly I got up and fired five shots and I saw him fall on the ground, which started the fire-fight. My friends were attacking the group. I joined them, running over the fallen man. Later there was a brief silence. No doubt surprised, they had run into a cave on the side of the mountain.

We gathered and got to the man I had fired on seconds ago. He was lying on the ground bleeding everywhere, but showing signs of life. We were going to finish him off, but we decided against it. To make any noise would uncover our position. Corporal Olegario climbed a mound to observe those that had disappeared into the cave. A couple of moments later he saw a man running out, he open fired and he saw him fall. He went and got him, bringing him to us. He was perfectly alive, but was bleeding from his foot. With our two prisoners of war, we left one of our group to guard them, and the rest of us headed for the cave to get the rest of them.

"At the entrance there was a rifle on the ground and on the point of the bayonet was a Japanese flag, which I took and put away. With the grenades we had taken from one of them, we threw them [in], some blew up [and] some did not, because some were wet, but nobody came out, it was quiet. Cautiously we approached the entrance and looked inside …

We saw many sacks of rice and sugar and many small bags of tea, also many bodies with a bad odour. We waited for a couple of minutes, [then] we got out of the cave and joined everybody. We didn't know what to do, since we were in an area of fugitive Japanese soldiers, who could easily surprise us. Our only hope was that some Filipino soldiers might have heard the shots and were coming looking for us.

… about an hour later, a large group appeared, and we ran to them and told them what had happened. With them came some of our officers, whom we informed about our adventure, carrying the wounded and the other Japanese soldier prisoners.

Hours later we arrived at the base with our prisoners of war, and like four Mexicans in search of adventure, obtained a small reward to add to the exploit of our brave pilots in the war front.

Years later, Alberto Robles would wonder who had fired the warning shots at the start of the fire fight:

I never wondered to ask who had alerted us and fired during the event. It was 50 years later when we celebrated the anniversary of the squadron departure that I asked Capt. Cervantes if he was there and fired. He said no but he told me it was Quintal Pinzon.

I went to the rail car where all the personnel were. It was here that I found him and told him, 'Pinzon I come to give you an apology for not thanking you for others there in the Philippines for having given the alarm and fired at an opportune moment. Certainly if you had not none of us who were there would be alive. Thank you Pinzon.' I gave him a hug.

During the course of the action against the Japanese fugitives, about 40 rounds of .30 calibre ammunition were expended by the Mexicans. Upon their arrival at Clark Field, both POWs were taken to the squadron medical station, were they were treated for their wounds.

After being interrogated by squadron personnel, they were handed over to the US Military Police at Clark Field.

One of the pilots who saw the arrival of the POWs was Lieutenant Samano Pina, who would later write:

I was in the camp when Corporal Olegario Gomez Rodriguez arrived with the two POWs, one of them wounded. They looked thin and dirty, reflecting the suffering of their defeat.

We gave them food and cigarettes and later handed them over to the US Military Police. I realised out of combat, all military personnel are almost friends. That we had the idea to serve our country, to sacrifice our lives.

> That the propaganda had not affected me with hatred towards the enemy. Either way we are professional soldiers, and we are ordered to bomb and strafe them. Since man tragically was born to fight. They say many don't withstand war, but many others can't withstand peace, mostly the young ones with much energy. I remember many soldiers of our unit wanted to go into combat, and they felt disappointed, because as a fighter squadron, they didn't fight like an infantry battalion.
>
> Mostly everybody wanted to fight, but being an aviation specialist their mission was to maintain the aircraft and pilots in perfect conditions. We had mechanics, armourers, clerks, medics, drivers, and cooks, mail clerks, orderlies etc, etc. for a pilot needs the support of ten to eleven … other specialists.

In a separate incident, another Japanese soldier who had been captured in or near Clark Field or Porac Field was about to be killed by his captors when 2nd Lieytenant Miguel Moreno Arreola intervened and saved the Japanese prisoner. Not understanding any Spanish, as a token of his gratitude the Japanese soldier gave Moreno Arreola a large dirty silk handkerchief. At first Moreno Arreola had wanted to throw it away, but after cleaning it he found it to be a beautifully made one, which he kept as a souvenir.

The squadron's Medical Officer, Major Blanco Cancino, had the opportunity to visit what was left of the Japanese positions, finding among them a military hospital:

> The Japanese Army built caves and tunnels in the mountains. In one of those was the burned out remains of a hospital, burned and twisted beds, medical supplies, patients' charts, manuals for first aid etc. In other caves small Japanese flags were found and other articles. In other excursions some members of the unit had a scare with dispersed Japanese and in others were found and rescued enemy soldiers that were frankly sick and in bad shape.

In his weekly report to the *Secretaria de la Defensa Nacional* for the period 26 August to 1 September 1945, Colonel Cardenas said the squadron flew 27 training sorties and had 16 P-47s, with an average of 14 ready for operational daily flights and two in repairs.

Captain Pablo Rivas Martinez was still reported missing, two officers and 11 enlisted men were at the hospital and on 26 August two Japanese soldiers had been captured by squadron personnel.

On 1 September 1945, the 201st with the 360th Air Service Group was assigned to the 13th Bomber Command of the Thirteenth Air Force. Before that moved occurred, rumours had been circulating about the end of the war, notably after the two atomic bomb attacks on Japan and Russia's entry into the Pacific conflict.

Sergeant Cervantez Ramos recalled the announcement being made to the squadron about Japan's surrender:

> I remember we were watching a movie that night, when all of a sudden the movie was stopped [and] the lights were turned on in our improvised movie theater. Our squadron commander was in front of us and ordered silence to tell us: 'I want to give the good news, it has not been yet confirmed, but appears to be true and is the following. I have received from Headquarters a communique, in which a radio operator has intercepted the news, which they are trying to confirm as official, that Japan has surrendered to the Allies. I don't want to raise your hopes, until the news is officially confirmed. Just take it with caution, meanwhile our operations continue as always, that is all.

Everybody in the audience went crazy with joy. The squadron's youngest soldier, Fernando Nava Musa, also remembered that night's events:

> It was about 7:30 at night and was getting dark. I was seated and taking care of the radio communications, when a call came into the camp and told me in English that a powerful bomb had fallen on Japan and that country had surrendered. I thought at first [it was] a joke and I ignored it, [but] the phone rang again, and it was the operator who had called before, he thought I didn't understand the message in English so he repeated the message in Spanish referring to the dropping of the atomic bomb in Nagasaki on August 10, 1945.
>
> Nobody knew about the first atomic bomb dropped on Hiroshima 4 days before, because there was no access to the radio and news were generally four days late.

Nava Musa immediately headed over to the movie theatre to inform the unit, but first he had to convince the projector operator to stop the film, which was not easy as he was known as the squadron joker:

> Since I had the fame of being a comedian, the operator did not believe me and refused to stop the film, until [I spoke] to him very firmly. When he stopped the film the cries of protest started. He asked for a moment of silence and headed to Capt. Radames Gaxiola, the squadron commander of the 201. I told him [of the call I received] that a powerful bomb had been dropped on Japan and possibly the war would end.

Captain Gaxiola went and confirmed the news and came back to tell the crowd the following:

> *Senores*, a message has been received in the sense that apparently Japan has surrendered and that the war is about to end. But don't throw caution to the winds until we have official confirmation, our operations will continue as normal.

In an undated Texas newspaper interview, Lieutenant Perez Gallardo remembers that day in a different way:

> 'We were watching a movie at Clark Field when the film was stopped. A high ranking officer stepped in and said that all aerial operations were suspended and we are now on the red maximum alert.'
>
> Perez said everyone in headquarters was expecting a mass Japanese attack. Aircraft remained fuelled and combat ready Perez said, recalling it as the longest and perhaps the most difficult day of the campaign. 'The following day, all the pilots were gathered at the mission control and told we just dropped a new type of bomb on Japanese territory and we expected a death defying counter attack,' explained Perez.
>
> The Captain said they expected nothing less than suicide attacks on the part of the Japanese. Perez said Mexican communications officers had rigged up a radio that enabled them to hear American newscasts.
>
> [That] was how they found out that an atomic bomb had been dropped on Hiroshima. After news broke that the Japanese intended to surrender, those at the camp exploded into feelings of bliss because the war was ending.

Even after the announcement of the possible ending of the war, there are unconfirmed reports that the 201st pilots flew six more missions to help capture or neutralise pockets of Japanese soldiers that did not know about the surrender of their government to the Allies and were conducting guerrilla warfare in the countryside. On this subject, Sergeant Manuel Cervantez said:

> Still in the month of September, squadron 201 was on Alert condition with other units and some flights were [made] due to the existence of some groups of enemy troops that ignored the surrender [and] were still showing hostile signs.

The official history of the US Army campaign in Luzon mentions that the Japanese still had forces keeping up the struggle:

> By the end of the war, the Japanese were still holding out in the rugged Asin Valley of the Sierra Madre in North Central Luzon, enduring the drenching summer Monsoons. Nevertheless, General Yamashita and about 55,500 of his men surrendered only after the close of hostilities on 15 August.

During the liberation of the Philippines, American and Allied forces had destroyed nine of Japan's best divisions and rendered six more combat-ineffective. Japan lost or had rendered unavailable for the defence of its homeland over 380,000 military personnel, numbers it could not replace.

Casualties for the American forces were high. The Sixth and Eighth Armies lost around 47,000 men, with some 10,380 killed and 36,550 wounded. Non-battle casualties were higher; for example, the Sixth Army from the period of 9 January to 30 June 1945 reported over 93,000 non-combat casualties, including 260 deaths, most related to diseases.

Japanese losses were reported to be around 230,000 personnel on Luzon alone.

On 15 August it was confirmed that the Japanese had accepted the surrender terms put by the Allies. The war in the Pacific officially ended in Tokyo Bay on board the US Navy battleship USS *Missouri* on 2 September. The Mexicans, as well as other units in the Philippines, were informed that at noon on 3 September, the Philippines campaign was officially over.

On that day, Lieutenant Joaquin Ramirez Vilchis flew as commander of 'C' Flight in ready alert status with fellow pilots Lieutenant Reynaldo Perez Gallardo, Lieutenant Sheridan Kenny and 2nd Lieutenant Graco Ramirez. He would later say about that flight:

> I flew over Clark with the shock that the war was over.

Despite the end of the conflict, the 201st still carried out training missions, and had a flight ready in case of any trouble with hostile Japanese forces that might refuse to surrender.

On the night of 15 September, the Mexican personnel celebrated *El Grito de la Independencia*, the anniversary of the start of their country's war of independence from Spain, with events presided over by Colonel Cardenas. On the same day, back in Mexico it been announced that all the members of the MEAF were promoted to the next grade by presidential order, as reported:

> Via radiotelegraph, the Secretary of National Defence communicated to the members of the glorious Squadron 201 their promotion in favour of them by the message sent by the President of the Republic. The official message says the following: 'General Antonio Cardenas Rodriguez, commander of the MEAF, it is a pleasure to notify you that by Presidential order, from the first of this month, all the personnel of the MEAF under your command have been promoted to the next rank immediatly please accept my personal congratulation.'

The return of the 201st Mexican Fighter Squadron, marching to the centre of the city (the Zocalo). The escort with the flag bearer, Lieutenant Miguel Moreno Arreola. (Author Collection)

The next day, five members of the 201st were selected to be awarded the Liberation of the Philippines' medal in the name of the MEAF by Major General Basilio J. Valdez, chief of the Philippine army.

This medal was to be given to the families of the fallen pilots, when Alfredo Carmelo, the Mexican Consul, visited Mexico. Colonel Cardenas and Captain Gaxiola were also recommended by General Douglas MacArthur for the US Legion of Merit medal for their work with the Mexican squadron in the Philippines.

In September 1947, while serving as a military attache in Canada, the by then Colonel Alfonso Gurzan Farfan received the unit's third US Legion of Merit medal in the grade of officer.

Before the MEAF left the Philippines, a monument was designed and built to honour their fallen comrades by Lieutenant Miguel Moreno Arreola, with the help of Alfredo Carmelo and the artist known as Tolentino, who helped create the eagle for it. The monument was erected at Paseo Bonifacio in the city of Manila and dedicated on 25 September 1945 in a ceremony that was attended by Mexican and Filipino military and civil officials. During the ceremony, Colonel Cardenas and Captain Gaxiola Andrade received from Alfredo Montelibano, the Secretary of National Defence of the Philippines, a Japanese *Samurai* sword and a Japanese Navy dagger respectively as war souvernirs. The monument was unveiled and had the following inscription:

> The components of the Mexican Expeditionary Air Force, Squadron 201 erect this monument to their fallen brothers in the commitment of their duty.
> Cap. 2/o. P.A. P. Rivas Martinez
> Tte. P.A. J. Espinoza Fuentes
> Tte. P.A. H. Espinoza Galvan
> SubTte. P.A. M. Lopez Portillo
> SubTte. P.A. F. Vega Santander
> Glory to them.
> Luzon, Philippines Sep 1945

The monument was later moved to a city park, named 'Mexico', near to the statute of Don Miguel Hidalgo y Costilla, the father of the Philippine war of independence against Spain in 1810.

## GOING HOME, OCTOBER-NOVEMBER 1945

The objective of the MEAF was now to go home to Mexico. But the 201st kept on flying, as Colonel Cardenas noted in his report of the week of 7-13 October, which recorded that the

Major Larry D. Dennis USAF receives from the Mexican consul, Fernando Rueda, of Detroit, Michigan, the Mexican military decoration *Medalla de Merito Militar, Primera Clase* on 11 February 1948 for the rescue of 2nd Lieutenant Guillermo Garcias Ramos. (Family of Lieutenant Colonel Larry D Dennis)

squadron accomplished two ferry missions and three training missions, along with a test flight, with a total of 28 sorties comprising 48 hours and 14 minutes of flight time. The squadron had 26 pilots and 17 aircraft (including one brought from Zamboanga), with a daily average of 14 available for service and three under repair and inspection.

The Mexicans were looking forward to seeing their love ones again, and on 30 September received orders for the unit's movement back to America. At first the MEAF wanted to return with all its equipment, but that would have required the use of a US Navy 'Jeep' carrier for the journey to a Mexican port.

As a result, this plan was not carried out. Upon the suggestion of the Mexican military attache, General Alamillo Flores, the MEAF would turn in its equipment, and when the unit arrived back in Mexico it would be re-equipped by the US government.

Seventeen P-47s were thus turned over to the 45th Air Service Group on 12 October (there were still four P-47Ds at Biak). All heavy equipment went to the 570th Group.

While work was in progress for the return of the equipment and preparing the unit for deployment back to Mexico, Colonel Cardenas left in a Douglas C-47 for Tokyo, along with Lieutenant Amadeo Castro Almanza, 2nd Lieutenant Guillermo Garcia Ramos and 2nd Lieutenant Jose Luis Pratt Ramos, for one last visit to General MacArthur to thank him for his support for the MEAF. They left on 19 October, returning to the Philippines on the 29th.

Pratt Ramos remembered that when they were loaned the Douglas C-47 with crew, many American personnel thought they were part of a Command staff of a three-star general, since the rank of a Mexican Army colonel also consisted of three stars. They made a stop on the island of Okinawa, where they slept for the first time in comfortable beds and went to the officers' club, where he remembered seeing the Esther Williams film *School for Mermaids*.

They flew over the cities of Hiroshima and Nagasaki and took pictures of the destruction, and during their trip they saw what was left of Japan after all the raids it had endured. There was an unexpected encounter during their stop at Nagoya airport, waiting for the weather report under the wing of their C-47.

A Japanese merchant offered the group some fine silk kimonos in exchange for cigarettes, negotiating the price with them. The Japanese spoke some English, but when the Mexicans were about to close the deal he asked in perfect Spanish if they were Spaniards or Mexicans, which caught the group off guard. They asked him where he learned to speak such good Spanish, and he told them that he used to live in California, where he had the opportunity to meet and get to know many Mexicans, who had made a good impression on him.

What really shocked the group was when he asked why Mexicans had fought against Japan when the Japanese had been good friends and had done them no harm. They could not answer him, giving an excuse that they had to close the deal due to time and handing him more cigarettes than he had asked for.

As they arrived in Tokyo, 2nd Lieutenant Pratt Ramos could see from the air many burned-out plots with metal boxes, being told this used to be the small business area of the city, but everything had burned down during US air raids except for the companies' strong boxes.

They saw only three buildings that were still standing, and these were being used by American occupation forces. The group stayed in a big room with comfortable beds. Their meals were served in a dining room attended by gracious Japanese girls dressed in kimonos, who had learned that Americans loved coffee and would always refill their cups; the only way to tell the girls they wanted no more coffee was to turn the cup over.

When people left the dining area, the girls would bow to them, including to the Mexicans. When Colonel Cardenas returned the gesture by bowing to them, Pratt Ramos joked to the MEAF commander: "Hey Colonel, we are the conquerors, why are you bowing to them?"

The Imperial Palace was nearby, and the Mexicans were impressed that neither the Palace nor its grounds had been touched by the American bombing campaign, which had respected the site. While Colonel Cardenas went to see General MacArthur, Pratt Ramos, Garcia Ramos and Castro Almanza visited the gardens around the Imperial Palace, where with their American-supplied Japanese phrasebook they tried to speak to Japanese girls, who laughed out loud to hear the Mexicans speaking Japanese.

Pratt Ramos said that it was at such moments that he realised the ordinary people had not been at war, just their leaders; there was a fraternity, not hatred, between them and the Japanese. Years later, Pratt Ramos paid a return visit to Tokyo to see the changes that had occurred after the war.

The MEAF left the Philippines on 23 October 1945 onboard the American transport ship *Sea Marlin*, for a 23-day voyage to the United States. On 25 October the Associated Press reported from Manila of their departure, under the headline 'Mexico's 201st on the way home':

> Mexico's contribution to the Pacific war, the 201st Fighter Squadron, left yesterday for California aboard the Transport *Sea Marlin*. Four of their comrades – Lts. Fausto Vegas, Jose Espinosa and Mario Lopez and Capt. Pablo Rivas – paid with their lives while fighting the Japanese on northern Luzon and Formosa.
>
> The pilots had renewed a century old [relationship] of Filipinos and Mexicans at Clark Field, a short distance from a town named Mexico. The town still is inhabited by descendants of Spaniards [who] in the 17th Century helped to defend the island against Malay pirates.

During the voyage home, sad news was received that on 2 November radio operator Sergeant 2nd Class Francisco Rodriguez Castaneda, who had been evacuated back to the States with tuberculosis, had died in a US military hospital in Santa Fe, New Mexico.

On 3 November, during a visit to Mexico City, General H.H. 'Hap' Arnold, commander of the United States Army Air Force, was decorated by the Mexican government and gave a speech about the performance of the Mexican Expeditionary Air Force. His speech was reportedly written by Staff Sergeant Cornelius Orzatti of the Liasion Group, who wrote to the author:

> This picture shows Gen Hap Arnold making a speech I wrote for him on the last days of October 1945 … The reason that I had to give Gen Arnold a brief of what the 201st had done, was because the Air Force in the Pentagon did not have one stitch of information concerning training and missions overseas.
>
> Since training started with the 201st, and overseas afterwards, I was in charge of sending to the Air Force in Washington DC weekly reports (confidential) concerning their training, and once overseas, once a week I used to send everything pertaining to the 201st, including every combat mission. But when I arrived at Washington DC Gen Arnold told me that they didn't have one single report of mine. I think that when the Statistical Section received my reports, for sure they threw them in the waste basket or probably they used to destroy them being that they always excited the usual professional jealousy, because the 201st turned out to be very good. But who knows what happened.

Arnold spoke about the achievements of the 201st Mexican Fighter Squadron after being decorated with the Mexican order of *Aguila Azteca* (Aztec Eagle) and the Military Merit Medal.

> Finally landing in the Philippines, after a short period of orientation and training, they participated in a major way in the Luzon campaign, cooperating with the ground troops against the Japanese troops in the Cagayan valley, using their machine guns and fragmentation bombs against enemy columns of soldiers on the march, against artillery, against tanks and vehicles, and we must recognise the merit to have put out of action about 30,000 Japanese.

The press at this time was still reporting the possible arrival date of the MEAF at the port of San Pedro in California and the estimated date of arrival back in Mexico City. Under the headline '300 Mexican flyers honored', the Associated Press reported on 6 November:

> The Medal for service in the Far East, newly created by the Mexican Government, will be presented to the 300 members of the 201st Air Force Squadron who fought in the Pacific, Secretary of War Francisco Urquizo said today. General Urquizo said the exact date of the squadron's arrival had not been determined, but added it will be here by Nov. 18 to participate in a holiday parade the next day. Urquizo and other officers will go to Laredo, Tex., by train to meet the flyers, and accompany them to Mexico City in army trucks.

The *Sea Marlin* docked at the port of San Pedro on 13 November. Waiting for them on the dock was General Cardenas with the pilots who had gone to Tokyo, having travelled by air to catch up with the unit.

The MEAF crossed the border back into Mexico three days later at Laredo, from there travelling by train to Mexico City. During its stops at major cities they were welcomed as heroes, with ceremonies and awards given in their honour,

on some occasions events getting out of hand. In Monterrey, Nuevo Leon, the unit marched to a military field for a welcoming ceremony, but the public broke down the barriers, resulting in chaos and the event having to be cancelled. When the order was given to march back to the train station, only the flag bearer appeared, the rest of the unit being mixed up with the crowd, and it took a lot of effort by officers and officials to get everybody on the train again.

Their next stop was Saltillo, the home town of General Cardenas, where he ordered all personnel to stay in the train so the events of Monterrey would not be repeated. But Cardenas was not prepared for the reception he received, being taken from the train on the shoulders of the happy townsfolk. It took the commander of the MEAF a long time to get back on the train.

They arrived at Mexico City train station on 17 November. Due to their arrival, the traditional 20 November parade to commemorate the start of the Mexican Revolution of 1910 was moved forward two days, the only time this has happened. Members of the MEAF drove down part of the parade route, then paraded to the National Palace, where they were welcomed by President Avila Camacho, who gave a

General Francisco L. Urquizo awards the *Merito Militar 2/o. Clase* and *Merito Aeronautica 3/o.Clase* to Captain Paul B. Miller for his work in the training of the 201st. Both medals were awarded on 12 February 1949. Brigadier General Gustavo Salinas looks on. (Family of Lieutenant Colonel Paul B. Miller)

The monument that was designed by 2nd Lieutenant Miguel Moreno Arreola and built to remember the five fallen pilots of the 201st Mexican Fighter Squadron. Today the monument is located at the Don Miguel Hidalgo y Costilla monument, Intramuros, Manila. (Manuel Cervantes Ramos)

short but emotional speech welcoming them back home:

> You have returned with glory because you have discharged brilliantly your duty and in these moments, in this our historic plaza, heart of the republic, received the thanks of our people. Your companions 2nd Lieutenant Fausto Vega Santander, Lieutenant Jose Espinosa Fuentes, 2nd Lieutenant Mario Lopez Portillo, Captain 2nd Class Pablo Rivas Martinez, 2nd Lieutenant Crisoforo Salido Grijalva, Lieutenant Javier Martinez Valle, Lieutenant Hector Espinoza Galvan, 2nd Lieutenant Hugo Gonzalez y Gonzalez and Lieutenant Roberto Gomez Moreno are missing from your ranks, because they have passed to the eternal veneration and the memory and honour of our people. You remain to live with that honour of our people to conserve it with that devotion that today we render to you.

After the ceremonies all the personnel were reunited with their love ones. All members of the force were awarded the *Servicio en el Lejano Oriente* (Far East Service) medal and promoted one rank, as promised.

Among those receiving awards were Lieutenant Colonel Kellond, who accompanied the squadron back to Mexico. He received the *Servicio en el Lejano Oriente* medal from the hands of President Camacho during an open air event with all members of the MEAF, and would later receive the *Merito Militar 2nd Clase* (Military Merit, 2nd Class).

On 27 December 1951, Kellond wrote to the then General Cardenas concerning the Filipino government's General Order No.116 issued on 30 April 1950, by the Headquarters of the National Defense Forces in Quezon City, that did not mention the award of the Philippine Presidential Unit citation to the MEAF:

> I am very disappointed to know that the Mexican Expeditionary Air Force is not included in this list, I feel sure that a mistake has been made and I would like to assist in correcting it. I believe that we can work out this matter in two ways. First I think it is important that you request the Mexican diplomatic representative in Manila to bring this matter to the attention of the headquarters of the National Forces of the Philippines.
>
> I am certain that the Filipinos fully appreciate the very valuable assistance given them by your organization. They cannot overlook the fact that many brave Mexican pilots lost their lives fighting for the liberation of the Philippine Islands. As soon as I hear from you telling me that you have notified the Mexican diplomatic representative, I will fly to the Philippines to assist in any way possible to rectify this error.
>
> I have in my possession a complete list of the Mexicans who served in the Philippines. I also have other papers to confirm the dates and deeds accomplished. Please write to me as soon [as possible] and let me know if I can help you in this matter.
>
> Please say hello to my good friends in Mexico. Best wishes for a prosperous New Year.

It appears that the error was corrected, as in General Order No.380, dated 30 September 1953, Filipino President Elpidio Quirino awarded the Presidential Unit citation to the Mexican Expeditionary Air Force.

Another honour that was given to the MEAF was from its former enemy, Japan. On 16 November 1952, at the military field in Balbuena, a ceremony was held in honour of the fallen pilots, organised by the senior Japanese diplomat in Mexico, Koy Ciba.

His speech was answered by General Cardenas as commanding officer of the Mexican Air Force, while a company of cadets from the military specialist mechanics fired a rifle salute in honour of the fallen.

The 10 members of the MEAF who lost their lives while serving in 1945 are, from the top row,
Captain 2nd Class Pablo L. Rivas Martinez,
Lieutenant Hector Espinosa Galvan,
Lieutenant Jose Espinosa Fuentes,
Lieutenant Javier Martinez Valle,
2nd Lieutenant Fausto Vega Santander,
2nd Lieutenant Mario Lopez Portillo,
2nd Lieutenant Crisoforo Salido Grijalva,
Lieutenant Roberto Gomez Moreno (Replacement Group, MEAF),
2nd Lieutenant Hugo Gonzalez y Gonzalez (Replacement Group, MEAF), and
Sergeant 2nd Class Francisco Rodriguez Castaneda. (Fuerza Aerea Mexicana)

Later, the entire Japanese diplomatic corps performed a guard of honour at the monument of independence with many former veteran pilots.

The MEAF had also received an honour in June 1946, when its battle flag, with a small contingent of members, participated in the Victory Parade that was held in London before the Royal Family, wartime Prime Minister Winston Churchill and current Prime Minister Clement Attlee. Mexico and Brazil were the only Latin American countries that took part in this grand parade.

The Mexican flag bearer was Lieutenant Justino Retana Reyes.

On 12 June 1950, General George C. Kenney, then chief of the Caribbean Air Command, awarded Air Medals to 22 pilots of the former MEAF who were present during his visit to Mexico City. They were presented in the reception room of the *Secretaria de la Defensa Nacional*.

All the citations to accompany the award of the Air Medal were signed by President Harry S. Truman at the White House. The citation reads, as for example in that given to Lieutenant Manuel Farias Rodriguez:

> Citation to accompany the award of the Air Medal to Lieutenant Manuel Farias Rodriguez, Mexican Air Force.
>
> For meritorious achievement while participating in aerial flight in the Philippine Islands during the period 1 May 1945 to 1 August 1945. As a Pilot in the 201st Fighter Squadron, Mexican Air Force, attached to the Far East Air Forces, this Officer executed numerous flights which contributed to the success of both air and ground operations during the Luzon Campaign. The high degree of competence and exceptional courage which he displayed in the performance of a hazardous and difficult Task reflect credit upon himself, his organization, and the Mexican Air Force.

On 1 December 1945, by presidential order, and since their services were no longer needed, the *Fuerza Aerea Expedicionaria Mexicana*/ Mexican Expeditionary Air Force was disbanded and became another proud chapter in the history of the Mexican Air Force.

*Escuadron Aereo de Pelea 201* was returned to the control of the *Fuerza Aerea Mexicana*. The *Escuadron Aereo 201* still continues today as an operational squadron, now based at Military Air Base No.4 at Cozumel, Quintana Roo. At the time of writing, the 201st was exchanging its Pilatus PC-7 COIN/ trainers for the Beechcraft T-6C+ Texan II.

Today in Mexico, and even in some places in the United States, there are numerous monuments and streets named for the 201st Squadron and its fallen pilots.

To remember and honour the activities of the *Dirreccion de Aeronautica*, later the *Fuerza Aerea Mexicana*, during the Second World War, the Museo Militar de Aviacion 'Teniente P.A. Jose Espinosa Fuentes' at Military Air Base No.1 has in its collection, for public viewing, aircraft that were flown during the conflict; not only the Republic P-47D Thunderbolt, but the North American B-25J, AT-6, Interstate L-6 and hopefully in the future a restored Vought OS2U-3 Kingfisher, to represent and honour the memories of those aircrews who had to make a quantum leap from biplanes to the very latest aircraft in the defence of the Mexican Republic.

## APPENDIX A

# COMBAT RECORD OF THE 201ST MEXICAN FIGHTER SQUADRON

| | |
|---|---|
| Missions flown | 96 |
| Offensive sorties flown | 785 |
| Defensive sorties flown | 6 |
| Hours flown in combat | 1,966.15 |
| Hours flown in the combat zone | 591.00 |
| Hours flown in pre-combat training | 281:00 |
| Hours average per pilot | 86:00 |
| Total hours flown | 2,842.00 |
| Bombs dropped 1,000lb (453kg) | 957 |
| Bombs dropped 500lb (226kg) | 500 |
| Bombs dropped 250lb (training) | unknown |
| Frag. bombs dropped 160lb | 18 |
| Total rounds of .50 cal. expended | 166,922 |
| Aircraft lost in combat | 0 |
| Aircraft damaged in combat | 6 |
| Aircraft lost in accidents | 11 |
| Aircraft damaged in accidents | 11 |
| Pilots killed in combat | 0 |
| Pilots killed in flying accidents | 4 |
| Pilots missing | 1 |

NOTE: There is a discrepancy among the American and Mexican records on the type and amount of bombs dropped by the squadron. A translated copy of a summary of all combat missions by the 201st submitted by Captain 2nd Class Amadeo Castro Almanza, to the American Embassy in Mexico City on 12 March 1946 shows the following bombs dropped by the unit:

| | |
|---|---|
| 1,000lb | 530; |
| 500lb | 500. |

The information taken from the Weekly Status and Operations Reports USAAF Form No.34 for the period 11 May to 31 August 1945, prepared by the squadron's Operations Officer – firstly Captain Pablo Rivas Martinez, and after he went missing Lieutenant. Amadeo Castro Almanza – shows the following information, although there are no suchreports for the months of September and October

| | |
|---|---|
| Combat missions | 58 |
| Combat sorties | 360 |
| Effective combat sorties | 284 |
| Hours flown in combat | 832.6 |
| Hours flown in combat zone | 1,862.3 |
| Total hours flown | 2,694.9 |
| Bombs dropped (1,000lb) | 514 |
| Bombs dropped (500lb) | 91 |
| Bombs dropped (160lb) | 18 |
| Total rounds of .50 cal. expended | 165,138 |
| Total rounds of .50 cal. expended in training | 3,260 |
| Total gallons of fuel consumed | 158,063.75 |
| Total quarts of oil consumed | 43,458 |
| Aircraft damaged in combat | 5 |

It appears that during their training the Mexicans used 250lb bombs, but their number is unknown at this time.
It has been reported, but not confirmed, that the 201st flew six more missions in support of American troops capturing Japanese soldiers who were engaged in guerrilla warfare after the surrender was announced in August 1945.

## APPENDIX B

# MISSIONS FLOWN BY THE MEXICAN PILOTS OF THE 201ST

A list of the number of missions flown by the 201st's pilots was found in the personnel file of General Antonio Cardenas Rodriguez, Chief of the Mexican Air Force, based on a request from the US military attache in Mexico.

However, this document, signed on 19 May 1950, does not come close to the total numbers and hours flown in combat missions by the pilots of the 201st. The following listing is compiled from various sources, including personal log books, AAF Form 5, Mexican Air Force flight logs, orders, accident reports and testimony from various pilots. This list is not 100 percent complete, and any additional information would be most welcome.

Some of the figures in missions, combat hours and combat zone hours do not match those found in the some of the pilots' personal logbooks or AAF Form 5 flight records. The document of 19 May 1950 gives most surviving pilots 33.30 hours in the combat zone.

This list excluded the five Mexican pilots who died in the Philippines, but they have been added in the following author listing:

### HQ FLIGHT 201st Mexican Fighter Squadron

Captain 1st Class Radames Gaxiola Andrade
Known total missions: 20 (11 were combat missions)
Combat hours: 79.00
Combat zone hours: 33.30
(other sources list his combat zone hours as 27.30)

Captain 2nd Class Pablo L. Rivas Martínez
Known total missions: 16 (13 were combat missions)
Combat hours: 34.15
Combat zone hours: 8.00

Lieutenant José Espinosa Fuentes
Known total missions 15 (2 were combat missions)
Combat hours: 4.30
Combat zone hours: 18.30
(These figures are from his AAF Form 5)

### 'A' FLIGHT

Captain 2nd Class Roberto Legorreta Sicilia
Known total missions: 22 (11 were combat missions)
Combat hours: 79.50
Combat zone hours: 33.30
(other sources list his combat hours as 29.35)

Lieutenant Fernando Hernández Vega
Know total missions: 16 (7 were combat missions)
Combat hours: 69.35
Combat zone hours: 33.30
(other sources list his combat hours as 20.15 and combat zone hours as 2.00)

Lieutenant Carlos Varela Landini
Known total missions: 22 (12 were combat missions)
Combat hours: 81.00
Combat zone hours: 33.30
(by 30 July 1945, Landini had flown 12 combat missions with 28.05 combat hours, plus 27.25 combat zone hours)

Lieutenant Graco Ramírez Garrido
Known total missions: 22 (10 were combat missions)
Combat hours: 79.50
Combat zone hours: 33.30 (other sources give him 20.30 combat hours)

2nd Lieutenant Jose Luis Pratt Ramos
Known total missions: 25 (14 were combat missions)
Combat hours: 36.00
Combat zone hours: 22.30 (
these figures are from his AAF Form 5, while the May 1950 list credits him with 79.00 combat hours and 33.30 combat zone hours)

2nd Lieutenant Miguel Uriarte Aguilar
Known total missions: 21 (10 were combat missions)
Combat hours: 73.00
Combat zone hours: 33.30
(another source puts his combat hours at 21.30)

2nd Lieutenant David Ceron Bedolla
Known total missions: 14 (6 were combat missions)
Combat hours: 61.00
Combat zone hours: 33.30
(another source puts his combat hours at 9.45)

### 'B' FLIGHT

Lieutenant Carlos Garduño Núñez
Known total missions: 12 (5 were combat missions)
Combat hours: 57.20
Combat zone hours: 33.30
(other sources credit him with 17.05 hours of combat missions)

Lieutenant Julio Cal y Mayor Sauz
Known total missions: 24 (13 were combat missions)
Combat hours: 34.00
Combat zone hours: 26.00
(information from his AAF Form 5; the 1950 list gives him 78.20 combat hours and 33.30 combat zone hours)

Lieutenant. Reynaldo Pérez Gallardo
Known total missions: 20 (11 were combat missions)
Combat hours: 71.00
Combat zone hours: 33.30
(other sources credit him with 30.20 combat hours)

2nd Lieutenant Miguel Moreno Arreola
Known total missions: 23 (11 were combat missions)
Combat hours: 77.45
Combat zone hours: 33.30
(other sources give him 30.45 combat hours)

2nd Lieutenant Praxedis Lopez Ramos
Known total missions: 20 (8 were combat missions)
Combat hours: 78.20
Combat zone hours: 33.30 (other sources give him 24.00 combat hours and 5.30 combat zone hours)

2nd Lieutenant Fausto Vega Santander
Known total missions: ?
Combat hours: ?
Combat zone hours: ? (
probably had some hours flying in the combat zone, but unknown at this time)

2nd Lieutenant Angel Sanchez Rebollo
Known total missions: 32 (13 were combat missions)
Combat hours: 32.20
Combat zone hours: 29.20 (information from his AAF Form 5; the 1950 list credits him with 78.20 combat hours and 33.30 combat zone hours)

### 'C' FLIGHT

Lieutenant Hector Espinosa Galvan
Known total missions: 14 (11 were combat missions)
Combat hours: 36.15
Combat zone hours: 27.30
(based on known information)

Lieutenant Joaquin Ramirez Vilchiz
Known total missions: 31 (14 were combat missions)
Combat hours: 38.15
Combat zone hours: 34.40
(based on his logbook; the 1950 list gives him 79.00 combat hours and 33.30 combat zone hours)

Lieutenant Carlos Rodríguez Corona
Known total missions: 20 (8 were combat missions)
Combat hours: 17.50
Combat zone hours: 1.30
(based on known information; the 1950 list credits him with 79.00 combat hours and 33.30 combat zone hours)

Lieutenant Amador Sámano Pina
Known total missions: 32 (12 were combat missions)
Combat hours: 32.20
Combat zone hours: 41.45
(information from his AAF Form 5/logbook; the 1950 list gives him 70.00 combat hours and 33.30 combat zone hours)

2nd Lieutenant Raúl García Mercado
Known total missions: 20 (10 were combat missions)
Combat hours: 27.25
Combat zone hours: 9.25
(based on known information; the 1950 list gives him 77.20 combat hours and 33.30 combat zone hours)

2nd Lieutenant Guillermo García Ramos
Known total missions: 22 (9 were combat missions)
Combat hours: 25.50
Combat zone hours: 7.45
(based on known information; the 1950 list gives him 77.30 combat hours and 33.30 combat zone hours)

2nd Lieutenant Manuel Farías Rodríguez
Known total missions: 31 (12 were combat missions)
Combat hours: 31.30
Combat zone hours: 47.05 (based on his logbook; the 1950 list gives him 77.20 combat hours and 33.30 combat zone hours)

### 'D' FLIGHT

Lieutenant Amadeo Castro Almanza
Known total missions: 31 (15 were combat missions)
Combat hours: 36.20
Combat zone hours: 30.45
(based on known information by 30 July 1945 he had flown 14 combat missions with 33.00 hours and 17 missions in the combat zone with 30.45 hours; the 1950 list credits him with 27 missions, 88.30 combat hours and 33.20 combat zone hours)

Lieutenant Jacobo Estrada Luna
Known total missions: 34 (14 were combat missions)
Combat hours: 35.15
Combat zone hours: 36.35
(Information based on his Mexican AF logbook; the 1950 list gives him 79.50 combat hours and 33.30 combat zone hours)

Lieutenant José Luis Barbosa Cerda
Known total missions: 20 (12 were combat missions)
Combat hours: 25.50
Combat zone hours: ?
(information based on different sources; the 1950 list credits him with 79.35 combat hours and 33.30 combat zone hours.)

2nd Lieutenant Mario López Portillo
Known total missions: 16 (13 were combat missions)
Combat hours: 30.05
Combat zone hours: ?

2nd Lieutenant Roberto Urias Aveleyra
Known total missions: 23 (11 were combat missions)
Combat hours: 26.25
Combat zone hours: 2.30
(from known sources; the 1950 list gives him 79.35 combat hours and 33.30 combat zone hours)

2nd Lieutenant Jaime Zenizo Rojas
Known total missions: 22 (13 were combat missions)
Combat hours: 30.20
Combat zone hours: ?
(from known sources; the 1950 list credits him with 78.30 combat hours and 33.30 combat zone hours)

2nd Lieutenant Justino Retana Reyes
Known total missions: 13 (2 were combat missions)
Combat hours: 8.00
Combat zone hours: ?
(from known sources; the 1950 list credits him with 59.30 combat

hours and 33.30 combat zone hours)

**Notes**

Captain 1st Class Fernando Hernandez Vega, in a letter to the Foreign Liaison Office in Washington DC dated 10 May 1946, submitted the following flight hours he flew in the Philippines:

Republic P-47D-30 Thunderbolt:Asiatic-Pacific Theatre, 200 hours
Stinson L-5: Clark Field, Luzon, 60 hours
North American P-51E: Clark Field, Luzon, 1 hour

## APPENDIX C

# MISSIONS COMPLETED BY TYPE BY THE 201ST MEXICAN FIGHTER SQUADRON

| Number | Type of Mission |
|---|---|
| 52 | Ground support missions for American troops in Luzon from 4 June to 4 July 1945. |
| 37 | Training missions from 15-21 July 1945 (including ferry missions of new aircraft from Biak, New Guinea, to the Philippines; the 201st carried out two practice intercept missions in July 1945, with about eight sorties). |
| 4 | Fighter sweeps to the island of Formosa, from 6-9 July 1945. |
| 1 | Dive-bombing mission against the port of Karenko, Formosa, On 8 August 1945. |
| 1 | Convoy escort mission in the north of the Philippines, 26 August 1945, with 26 sorties. |

## APPENDIX D

# THE REPLACEMENT GROUP OF THE MEAF

According to the official book of the MEAF published in 1946, the first group of replacements began their training at Napier Field, Dotham, Alabama, in February 1945, but this is not correct. Based on photographic evidence and information known, the first groups of replacements for the MEAF began arriving in February 1945 at Majors Field, Texas, with ground personnel also sent to various American airbases for armaments and mechanics courses.

On 1 October 1945, according to the official book of the MEAF, the following replacement personnel were studying in the United States: 22 lieutenants, 112 2nd lieutenants, nine sergeants, 16 corporals and seventeen cadets. It should also be noted that when *Escuadron Aereo 201* went to the Philippines, it took a group of replacements; there had been 11 of these 2nd lieutenants who were pilots, of which three were eliminated during training in the United States for various reasons.

This group of replacements (all 2nd lieutenants) comprised
Emilio Enrique Ruiz (elimínated),
Jaime Zenizo Rojas,
Justino Retana Reyes,
Jose Miguel Uriarte Aguilar,
Angel Sanchez Rebollo,
Miguel Moreno Arreola,
David Mendoza Marquez (eliminated),
David Ceron Bedolla,
Guillermo Garcia Ramos,
Manuel Farias Rodriguez and
Raul Maciel Pena (elimínated).

Mexican air force historian Captain 2nd Class Manuel Reyna Garza, has reported it was planned that if the war had continued, a 1st Mexican Fighter Group would have been created, featuring the 201st Mexican Fighter Squadron (flying P-47Ns),
202nd Mexican Fighter Squadron (P-47Ns) and
203rd Mexican Fighter Squadron (P-51Ds).

This group would have been stationed on Okinawa to participate in the projected invasion of Japan in 1946, with its commander being Colonel Antonio Cardenas Rodriguez.

The Replacement Group of the MEAF was under the command of Major Rafael Suarez Peralta, who was stationed at Maxwell AFB, Alabama, with his counterpart Captain 1st Class Roberto Salido Beltrán of the Command and Staff acting as Liaison officer.

The different pilot groups of the Replacement Group between February and October 1945 were as follows:

1st Replacement Group:

This group of 10 pilots started its training in February 1945 at Majors Field, Greenville, Texas, with the 266th AAFBU (CCTS) (f), and at Foster Field, Victoria, Texas, with the 2539th AAFBU.

2nd Replacement Group:

This group of six pilots started its training at Majors Field and Foster Field in March 1945.

3rd Replacement Group:

This group of 11 pilots started its training at Majors Field and Foster Field on 1 April 1945.

4th Replacement Group:

This group of 20 pilots started its training on 6 April 1945 at Majors Field and Foster Field.

5th Replacement Group:

This group of eight pilots started its training at Majors Field and Foster Field on 16 April 1945.

6th Group of Replacements:

This group of 10 pilots started its training on 1 May 1945 at Majors

Field and Foster Field.

(In June 1945, the training programme for the Mexican pilots was moved from Majors Field and Foster Field to Napier Field, Alabama.
7th Replacement Group:
This group of 26 pilots started its training at Napier Field, Alabama, with the 2166th AAFBU.
8th Replacement Group:
This group of 16 pilots started its training on 16 July 1945 at Napier Field, Alabama.

During their training, there were a reported 20 aviation accidents involving landing problems, engine failures and collisions with other aircraft. Only two were fatal, with the complete loss of a Republic P-47D Thunderbolt and North American P-51D Mustang.
Ground personnel training was undertaken as follows:
Training Chanute Field, Rantoul, Illinois: mechanics course for Republic P-47 aircraft run by the 3502nd AAFBU Technical School. This group of two officer and nine enlisted men started its training on 1 June 1945.

Majors Field, Greenville, Texas: USAAF administration course that started on 1 June 1945 with three officers.

Truax AAFB, Madison, Wisconsin: course on radio maintenance that started in June 1945 with the 3508th AAFBU, with nine enlisted personnel.

Lowry AAFB, Denver, Colorado: armaments course that started on 1 June 1945 with two officers and six enlisted men.

San Antonio Aviation Cadet Center, San Antonio, Texas: course started in February 1945 with 19 officers and 16 cadets.

## APPENDIX E

# AIRCRAFT ASSIGNED TO THE GRUPO DE PERFECCIONAMIENTO AERONAUTICA (GPA, AERONAUTICAL TRAINING GROUP) IN IDAHO AND TEXAS, 1944-45

**Foster Field AAFB, Victoria, Texas:**
2539th AAFBU, Section I
AIRCRAFT:
North American AT-6A, AT-6B, AT-6C and AT-6D Texan advance trainer.
Curtiss P-40E, P-40F, P-40K and P-40N Warhawks.

Known Curtiss P-40 fighters:
P-40E 41-36246, damaged 9 October 1944;
P-40F 41-14075, damaged 10 October 1944.

**Pocatello AAFB, Idaho:**
265th AAFBU (FPTS) Section I
AIRCRAFT:
Vultee BT-15B Valiant Trainer.
Republic P-47D-28-RA Thunderbolt.

**'A' FLIGHT**
Line Chief: Sergeant 1st Class mechanic Manuel Espinosa Gonzalez

| AAF Number | Individual No. | Remarks |
|---|---|---|
| 42-29432 | R-1 | severely damaged 23 Jan 1945. Pilot killed. |
| 42-29433 | | |
| 42-29434 | | |
| 42-29435 | | |
| 42-29436 | | |
| 42-29438 | | |
| 42-29439 | R-8 | |

**'B' FLIGHT**
Line Chief: Sergeant 1st Class mechanic Jesús Herrera Zayas

| | | |
|---|---|---|
| 42-29440 | | |
| 42-29441 | R-10 | accident 8 Dec 1944. Pilot unhurt. |
| 42-29443 | | |
| 42-29444 | | |
| 42-29445 | | |
| 42-29449 | R-15 | accident 6 Feb 1945. Pilot unhurt. |

**'C' FLIGHT**
Line Chief: Sergeant 1st Class mechanic Aurelio Becerra Suarez

| | | |
|---|---|---|
| 42-29437 | R-6 | |
| 42-29442 | | |
| 42-29446 | | |
| 42-29462 | R-17 | accident 10 Mar 1945. Pilot killed. |
| 42-29463 | R-18 | accident 8 Nov 1944. Pilot unhurt. |
| 42-29464 | | |

Known individual R numbers used by the GPA/ Squadron 201, based on photos and accident reports: R-1, R-5, R-8, R-9, R-10, R-11, R-12, R-13, R-14, R-15, R-16, R-17, R-18 and R-19.

16RE: 42-75889 lost in landing accident 21 July 1945, pilot hurt.

Note: These code numbers were not applied to borrowed aircraft but were noted in an official document.

APPENDIX F

# AIRCRAFT ASSIGNED TO THE 201ST MEXICAN FIGHTER SQUADRON IN THE PHILIPPINES

**1. Known Republic P-47Ds supplied to the 201st via the 58th Fighter Group, May 1945:**

| Sub-type | Serial | Code | Remarks |
|---|---|---|---|
| -28-RA | 42-29052 | '1' | CO's machine. |
| -28-RA | 42-29077 | '2' | CO's machine. Ex-58th FG aircraft |
| -21-RE | 42-25395 | '3' | Ex-460th FS, 348th FG, to 58th FG, March 1945 to 201st, damaged 23 June 1945 |
| -21-RE | 42-25412 | '4' | Ex-460th FS, 348th FG, to 58th FG, March 1945 to 201st, damaged 20 June 1945. |
| -15-RA | 42-22212 | '5' | |
| -28-RA | 42-28523 | '6' | Ex-41st FS, 35th FG 'Me Darling' of Captain Morgan R. Beamer, 1 'kill' marking for a Japanese Zero 23 Nov 1944 , 10 miles SE of Cadiz, Negros, Philippines. |
| -16-RA | 42-75894 | '7' | Ex-39th FS, 35th FG, later 311th FS, 58th FG, to 201st. Destroyed during take-off accident, 17 June 1945. Pilot hurt. |
| -15-RA | 42-23225 | '8' | Damaged 24 May 1945. |
| -11-RA | 42-23109 | '9' | Damaged 3 June 1945. |
| -21-RA | 42-25629 | '10' | Ex-460th FS, 348th FG, to 58th FG, March 1945 to 201st. Possibly lost 16 July 1945. Pilot killed. |
| -16-RE | 42-75889 | '11' | |
| -28-RA | 42-28504 | '12' | Ex-310th FS, 58th FG, damaged 19 April 1945 in landing accident, repaired, to 201st. |
| -23-RA | 42-27904 | '13' | |
| -23-RA | 42-27615 | '14' | Ex-35th FG, 58th FG to 201st damaged by enemy AA fire 20 June 1945. Pilot unhurt. Struck off inventory same day. |
| -23-RA | 42-27995 | '15' | Ex-35th FG, 58th FG, to 201st, damaged 18 June 1945. Later repaired. |
| -15-RA | 42-23225 | '15'? | Damaged 24 May 1945. |
| -28-RA | 42-28505 | ? | Ex-40th FS, 35th FG, No. 64 of Captain Álvaro Jay Hunter Oct-Dec 1944. 'My Baby', five 'kill' markings. To 58th FG, to 201st. Destroyed 21 May 1945. Pilot unhurt. |
| -28-RA | 42-29051 | ? | Damaged 23 May 1945. Pilot safe. |
| -23-RA | 42-27877 | ? | Destroyed 24 May 1945. Pilot safe. This aircraft was probably that of Captain Leroy Grossheusch, CO of 39th FS/35th FG, with six 'kill' markings. |
| -15-RA | 42-23228 | ? | Destroyed 1 June 1945. Pilot killed. |
| -15-RA | 42-23216 | '5'? | |
| -16 RE | 42-75889 | "11" | lost in landing accident 21 July 1945 pilot safe but hurt. |
| -22-RE | 42-25629 | ? | |
| -28-RA | 42-28528 | ? | Destroyed 5 June 1945. Pilot killed |

**2. Known Republic P-47D-30-RAs supplied under Lend-Lease to the 201st Mexican Fighter Squadron, based on record and photo evidence:**

| Sub-type | Serial | Code | Remarks |
|---|---|---|---|
| -30-RA | 44-33721 | '1' | '1' At some point also '18' |
| -30-RA | 44-33710 | '2' | |
| -30-RA | 44-33713 | '3' | |
| -30-RA | 44-33717 | '4' | Aircraft damaged 20 July 20 1945, replaced by 44-33715. |
| -30-RA | 44-33720 | '5' | Reported as '12', replaced by 44-33728. |
| -30-RA | 44-33523 | '6' | |
| -30-RA | 44-33730 | '7' | |
| -30-RA | 44-33732 | '8' | |
| -30-RA | 44-33738 | '9' | |
| -30-RA | 44-33718 | '10' | |
| -30-RA | 44-33711 | '11'? | Lost 19 July 1945. Pilot later rescued. |
| -30RA | 44-33720 | '12' | Replacement aircraft for 44-33728 |
| -30-RA | 44-33728 | '12'? | Accident 8 Aug 1945, replaced by 44-33720 |
| -30-RA | 44-33715 | '13'? | Replacement aircraft for 44-33717, lost in accident 9 Aug 1945. |

| | | | |
|---|---|---|---|
| -30-RA | 44-33716 | '16' | |
| -30-RA | 44-33735 | '17' | |
| -30-RA | 44-33721 | '18' | Aircraft at one time '1'. |
| -30-RA | 44-33733 | '19' | Damaged 15 Aug 1945. |
| -30-RA | 44-33722 | '20' | Mission to Formosa 6 July 1945. |
| -30-RA | 44-33737 | '21' | |
| -30-RA | 44-33679 | '22' | |
| -30-RA | 44-33727 | '23' | |
| -30-RA | 44-33725 | '25' | Delivered 12 August1945. |
| -30-RA | 44-90149 | | |
| -30-RA | 44-90058 | | |
| -30-RA | 44-90062 | | |

The Code Numbers were not applied to these borrowed aircraft even after they were assigned.
Missing candidates, who cannot be positively accounted for:

- 44-33712, 44-33714, 44-33719, 44-33723, 44-33724, 44-33726 and 44-33729.
- P-47D-30-RAs damaged in the Philippines by datesDATES:
- 20 July 20, Lieutenant Joaquin Ramirez Vilchis, wheel ups landing after mission, pilot not hurt. 44-33717.
- 8 Aug 1945, Lieutenant Joaquin Ramirez Vilchis, landing accident, pilot not hurt. 44-33728, aircraft reduced for spare parts.
- 9 Aug 1945, 2nd Lieutenant Angel Sanchez Rebollo, take-off accident, pilot not hurt. 44-33715, aircraft reduced for spare parts.
- 15 August 1945, Captain 2nd Class Roberto Legorreta Sicilia, damaged during training flight, pilot not hurt. 44-33733
- 24 August1945, two P-47Ds damaged by American transport plane taxiing close to the Mexican flight line.

## BIBLIOGRAPHY FOR CHAPTER 1


Casasola, Gustavo, *Historia Gráfica de la Revolución Mexicana 1900-1970, Volumen 7* (Mexico: Editorial Trillas, 1992).

Cassagneres, Ev, *Ambassador of Air Travel, The Untold Story of Lindbergh's 1927-1928 Good Will Tours, 80 Cities in the United States, Canada & 15 Countries South of the Border* (Missoula, Montana: Pictorial Histories Publishing Co. Inc., 2006).

Del Campo, Eliseo Martin, *40 Anos y Siempre con la Aviación Mexicana* (Durango, México: 1964).

Duran, Pablo Larumbe, *Aviación Mexicana 1910-1924* (Mexico: Grupo Editorial Albatros S.A. de C.V., 2008).

Gallardo, Raúl Pérez, Águilas de Anáhuac, Historia de la Aviación Mexicana Tomo I, (Mexico D.F., 1974).

Gordon, Dennis, *Lafayette Escadrille Pilot Biographies* (Missoula, Montana: The Doughboy Historical Society, 1991).

Hagedorn, Dan, *Conquistadors of the Sky, A History of Aviation in Latin America* (Washington DC: Smithsonian National Air and Space Museum/University Press of Florida, 2008).

Hagedorn, Dan, *Latin American Air Wars and Aircraft 1912-1969* (Manchester: Hikoki Publications, 2006).

*Kukulcan* magazine, Órgano Mensual de la Fuerza Aérea Mexicana, 15 Nov 1939, 15 Dec 1939, 15 Jan 1940, 15 Feb 1940, 15 Mar 1940, 15 Apr 1940, 15 May 1940, 15 Jun 1940 (Mexico D.F.).

Larumbe, Prof. Pablo, *Larumbe Los Inicios de la Aviación Mexicana 1910-1919 Tomo I* (Editor José Serur Cababie, Albatros Grupo Editorial).

Morales, Armando Cruz, *Caballero Águila, Historia Militar del General de División Piloto Aviador Alfonso Cruz Rivera* (Mexico: Primera Edición, 2009).

Negrete, Doroteo, Director General del Tothli, *Historia de la Aeronáutica en México* (Mexico D.F.: Una publicación del Antiguo Tothli, 1918).

Osio, Ingeniero Ángel Lascurain y, *Historia de la Aviación en México* (Mexico: Departamento de Aviación, 10 March 1925).

Reinhold, Ruth M., Sky Pioneering, Arizona in Aviation History (Tucson, Arizona: University of Arizona Press, 1982).

Rich, Doris L., *The Magnificent Moisants, Champions of Early Flight* (Washington & London: Smithsonian Institution Press, 1998).

Romero, Manuel Ruiz, *Aviación Militar, Historia de la Fuerza Aérea y de la Aviación* (Mexico: Biblioteca de la Historia Aeronáutica de México, 2004).

Romero, Manuel Ruiz, *Diccionario Biográfico Aeronáutico de México* (Mexico: Biblioteca de la Historia Aeronáutica de México, October 2002; El Ejército y Fuerza Aérea mexicanos Tomo II Secretaria de la Defensa Nacional México, 1979).

Romero, Manuel Ruiz, *La Aviación Durante la Revolución Mexicana* (Mexico: Soporte Aeronáutico S.A de C.V., 1998).

Romero, Manuel Ruiz, *Legendarios en la Aeronáutica de México* (Mexico D.F.: Reaseguros Alianza S.A., 1997).

Romero, Manuel Ruiz, *Los Orígenes Volumen 1 Biblioteca de la Historia Aeronáutica de México* (Mexico, 1996).

Rosas, Alejandro, and Villalpando, José Manuel, *Los Presidentes de México, La Historia de los gobernantes de la nación (1821-2000) narrada para los lectores de hoy* (Mexico D.F.: Editorial Planeta Mexicana S.A de C.V., 2001).

Taylor, Lawrence, *La Gran Aventura en México, El papel de los voluntarios extranjeros en los ejércitos revolucionarios mexicanos 1910-1915 Tomo. I Tomo. II* (Mexico: Consejo Nacional para la Cultura y las Artes, 1993, 1994).

*Tohtli* magazine, Revista de Aeronautica Militar, Oct, Nov and Dec 1938 (Mexico D.F.).

*Tohtli* magazine, Revista de Aeronáutica Militar, Jan, Feb and Mar 1939, Nos 1, 2 & 3 (México D.F.).

Torres, Medardo Córdova, Secretaria de la Defensa Nacional, Estado Mayor, *Historia de la Iniciación del Fuerza Aérea Mexicana* (Mexico D.F.: Sección Segunda).

Valenzuela, Pablo Macias, el C. Secretario del Ramo Gral. De División, *Memoria de la Secretaria de la Defensa Nacional Septiembre de 1940-Agosto de 1941* (Mexico: Presentada al H. Congreso de la Union, 1941).

Wagner, William, in collaboration with Dye, Lee, *Ryan The Aviator, Being the adventures and ventures of Pioneer Airman and*

*Businessman T. Claude Ryan* (New York: McGraw-Hill Books, 1971).
Walker, Dale L., *Only the Clouds Remain, Ted Parson of the Lafayette Escadrille* (Amsterdam, New York: Allandale Press, 1980).
Welsome, Eileen, *The General & The Jaguar, Pershing's Hunt for Pancho Villa, a True Story of Revolution & Revenge* (New York & Boston: Little Brown and Company, 2006).

## BIBLIOGRAPHY FOR CHAPTER 2

'Air Intelligence Information Report IR-162-56', 16 August 1956, Mexican Air Force History and Relations with USAF. Biographical data of General Alfonso Cruz Rivera.
Baumann, Gerold Gino, *Los Voluntarios Latinoamericanos en la Guerra Civil Española, en las Brigadas Internacionales, las milicias, la retaguardia y el ejército popular* (San José, Costa Rica: Editorial Guayacan S.A., 1997).
Benítez, Fernando, *Lazaro Cárdenas y la Revolución Mexicana III. Cardenismo* (Mexico: Fondo de Cultura Económica).
Bishop, Chris, *Kriegsmarine U-Boats 1939-45, the Essential Submarine Identification Guide* (London: Amber Books, 2006).
Blair, Clay, *Hitler's U-Boat War, the Hunters, 1939-1942* (NewYork: Random House, 1996).
Cedillo, Juan Alberto, *Los Nazis en México* (Mexico: Editorial Random House Mondadori S.A de C.V., 2007).
'Constitucion Política de los Estados Unidos Mexicanos Edición 2003 Actualizada', Editores Mexicanos Unidos S.A. Enero (Mexico, 2003).
Dean, Francis H., and Hagedorn, Dan, *Curtiss Fighter Aircraft, A Photographic History 1917-1948* (Pennsylvania: Schiffer Military History Books, 2007).
De la Pena, Enrique Cárdenas, *Gesta en el Golfo, La Segunda Guerra Mundial y México* (Mexico D.F.: Editorial Primicias S.A., 1966).
Departamento de Archivo, Correspondencia & Historia, 'Archivo de la Plana Mayor Gral. Alfonso Cruz Rivera'. Tomo Cuarto. Informe de actividades del 2/o. Regimiento Aereo y Comandancia de Grupos Aéreos. Fojas 784-787, 788.
Palencia, Mario Moya, *1942 Mexicanos al Grito de Guerra!* (Mexico: Grupo Editorial Miguel Ángel Porrúa, 1992).
Hagedorn, Dan, *Texans and Harvards in Latin America* (Air Britain Publication Ltd, 2009).
Intelligence Report, Office of Chief of Naval Operations, Navy Department Serial 153-R-43, MEXICO – AVIATION LESS COMMUNICATIONS -MILITARY PLANES OF ALL TYPES, 7 May 1943.
'Memorias de la Secretaria de la Defensa Nacional, Septiembre de 1941 a Agosto de 1942'. Presentada al H. Congreso de la Unión por el C. Secretario del Ramo Gral. De Div. Pablo E. Macías Valenzuela (Mexico: 1942).
'Memorias de la Secretaria de la Defensa Nacional Septiembre de 1942 a Agosto de 1943', por la Secretaria de la Defensa Nacional, Estado Mayor, Taller Autográfico (Mexico D.F., 1943).
'Memorias de la Secretaria de la Defensa Nacional, Septiembre de 1943 a Agosto de 1944', por la Secretaria de la Defensa Nacional, Estado Mayor, Taller Autografico (México D.F., 1944).
Mikesh, Robert C., *Japan's World War II Balloon Bomb Attacks on North America* (Washington DC: Smithsonian Annals of Flight, National Air and Space Museum, Smithsonian Institution Press, 1982).
Morales, Antonio Campuzano, 'Teniente Coronel de Caballeria D.E.M. Luis Alamillo Flores', *Revista Armas*, May/June 2012 (Mexico D.F.).
'No Pasaron Soldados de E.U.', *El Heraldo* (newspaper), Tijuana, B. Cfa., Vol.1 Ano.1, Wednesday 17 Dec 1941, No.156.
Olynyk, Frank, *Stars and Bars, A Tribute to the American Fighter Ace 1920-1973* (London: Grubb Street Books, 1995)
Paz, Maria Emilia, *Strategy, Security and Spies. Mexico and the U.S. as Allies in World War II* (University Park, Pennsylvania: Pennsylvania University State Press, 1997).
Perez, Omar Munoz Ledo, *El North American AT-6 'Texan' en Mexico* (Quauhtli Edicion Ano 2006, Publicacion del Academia de Historia Aeronautica de Mexico.
Revah, Mario Ojeda, *México y la Guerra Civil Española* (Madrid: D.R. Turner publicaciones, 2004).
Shrader, Grahame F., *The Phantom War in the Northwest, Account of Japanese Submarine Operations on the West Coast 1941-1942* (self-published, 1969, second edition 1970).
Torres, Blanca, *Historia de la Revolución Mexicana 1940-1952, México en la Segunda Guerra Mundial* (Mexico: El Colegio de México Volumen 19, 1988).
Uboat.net (website).
Urquizo, Francisco L., *Tres de Diana* (Mexico: Dirección de Comunicación Social, Secretaria de la Defensa Nacional, 2015).
Wagner, Ray, *History of the Western Defense Command Vol. I* (San Diego, California: San Diego Aerospace Museum).
Warnock, Timothy, *The U.S. Army Air Forces in World War II, The Battle Against The U-Boat in the American Theater* (Maxwell AFB, Alabama: Air Force Historical Research Agency, United States Air Force, 1991).

## BIBLIOGRAPHY FOR CHAPTER 3

*421 Squadron History*, Canadian Armed Forces (Canadian Wings Inc., 1982).
Alison, Les, and Hayward, Harry, *They Shall Grow Not Old, A Book of Remembrance* (Manitoba, Canada: Commonwealth Air Training Plan Museum, 1992).
Boot, Henry, and Sturtivant, Ray, *Gifts of War, Spitfires and other presentation aircraft in World War II* (Tonbridge, Kent: Air Britain, 2005).
Cleaver, Thomas McKelvey, *F4F Wildcat and F6F Hellcat Aces of VF-2*, Osprey Aircraft of the Aces No.125 (Oxford: Osprey Publications, 2015).
Fairfield, Terry A., *The 479th Fighter Group in World War II: In Action over Europe with the P-38 and P-51* (Atglen, Pennsylvania: Schiffer Military History, 2004).
Fernandez, Virgil, *Hispanic Military Heroes* (Austin, Texas: VFJ Publishing, 2006).
Foreman, John, *RAF Fighter Command Victory Claims of World War Two. Part Two: 1 January 1941 to 30 June 1943* (Walton on Thames, Surrey: Red Kite Books, 2005).
Foreman, John, Matthews, Johannes, and Parry, Simon, *Luftwaffe Night Fighter Claims 1939-1945* (Walton on Thames, Surrey: Red Kite Books, 2004).
Freeman, Roger A., *The Mighty Eighth, A History of the U.S. 8th Army Air Force* (London: Macdonald, 1970).
Greenlaw, Olga S., *The Lady and the Tigers* (New York: E.P. Dutton, 1943).
Greenlaw, Olga, *The Lady and the Tigers. Remembering the Flying Tigers of World War II* (ed. Daniel Ford) (Writers Club Press, 2002).
Kershaw, Alex, *The Few: The American 'Knights of the Air' Who Risked Everything to Fight in the Battle of Britain* (Boston, Mass: Da Capo Press, 2006).

Kostenuk, S., and Griffin, J., *RCAF Squadrons and Aircraft, Squadron Histories and aircraft 1924-1968* (Ottawa, Canada: National Museum of Man, National Museums of Canada, 1977).

Listemann, Phil H., *No.443 (RCAF) Squadron 1944-1946. RAF, Dominion & Allied Squadrons at War: Study, History and Statistics* (Philedition, 2012).

Listemann, Phil, *No.71 (Eagle) Squadron 1940-1942. RAF, Dominion & Allied Squadrons at War: Study, History and Statistics* (Philedition, 2013).

Lloyd, A.T., 'The Hour Has Come: History of the 97th Bomb Group', *Journal of the American Aviation Historical Society* (spring 1992).

'Memorias de la Secretaria de la Defensa nacional. Septiembre 1944 – Agosto 1945', Taller Autográfico (Mexico D.F., 1945)

Morin, Raul, *Among The Valiant, Mexican-Americans in WWII and Korea*, Introduction by Lyndon B. Johnson (Alhambra, California: Borden Publishing Co., 1963).

'No.71 (Eagle) Squadron Operational Record Book, September 1941', National Archives, Kent, UK.

'No.609 Squadron Operational Record Book, August and September 1940', National Archives, Kent, UK.

Olynyk, Frank, *Stars and Bars, a tribute to the American Fighter Ace 1920-1973* (London: Grub Street Publishing, 1995).

Olynyk, Frank J., *Victory List No.7. RAF 400 Series Squadron Credits for the destruction of enemy aircraft in air to air combat, World War 2* (November 1989).

P-38 National Association, *Lightning Strikes* (March 2011).

Parry, Simon W., *Intruders Over Britain, The Luftwaffe Night Fighter Offensive 1940 to 1945* (Walton on Thames, Surrey: Air Research Publications, 1987).

Reynolds, Jean, *A Legacy of Courage: The Story of Arthur Van Haren Jr., Arizona WWII Ace Fighter Pilot* (Phoenix, Arizona: Latino Perspective Media, 2011).

Rodríguez, General Antonio Cárdenas, *Mis Dos Misiones, Monografía Aérea* (Mexico: Talleres Graficos de la Nacion, 1949).

Rodriguez, Maggie Rivas, Torres, Juliana, Dipiero-D'sa, Melissa, and Fitzpatrick, Lindsay, *A Legacy Greater Than Words. Stories of U.S. Latinos and Latinas of the World War II Generation* (US Latino and Latina WWII oral history project, 2006).

Shores, Christopher, and Thomas, Chris, *2nd Tactical Air Force, Volume One, Spartan to Normandy, June 1943 to June 1944* (Air War Classics, 2004).

Shores, Christopher, and Thomas, Chris, *2nd Tactical Air Force, Volume Three, From the Rhine to Victory, January to May 1945* (Air War Classics, 2005).

Shores, Christopher, and Williams, Clive, *Aces High, A Tribute to the Most Notable Fighter Pilots of the British and Commonwealth Forces in WWII* (Grub Street Books, 1994).

Stanaway, John, *479th Fighter Group, 'Riddle's Raiders'*, Osprey Aviation Elite Units No.32 (Oxford: Osprey Publications, 2009).

Thomas, Andrew, *American Spitfire Aces of World War 2*, Osprey Aircraft of the Aces No.80 (Oxford: Osprey Publications, 2007).

Tillman, Barrett, *U.S. Navy Fighter Squadrons in World War II* (Forest Lake, Minnesota: Specialty Press, 1997).

Various, *From White-Caps to Contrails, A History of a Modern Air Formation* (Shearwater, Nova Scotia: 1981).

Villarreal, Rudolph C., *Arizona's Hispanic Flyboys 1941-1945* (New York, Lincoln, Shanghai: Writers Club Press, 2002).

Watts, Perry, *The Famous B-24 Witchcraft, the Enchanted Liberator, a Unique U.S. Bomber's Experiences During WWII* (Schiffer Military History, 2015).

## BIBLIOGRAPHY FOR CHAPTER 4

Flores, Santiago A., 'Mexican Air Force Serials 1937-1943 Part 1', *Small Air Forces Observer* Vol.37 No.1 (145), July 2013.

Flores, Santiago A., 'Mexican Air Force Serials 1937-1943 Part 2', *Small Air Forces Observer* Vol.37 No.2 (146) October 2013.

'Memorias de la Secretaria de la Defensa Nacional, Septiembre de 1944 a Agosto de 1945', Taller Autografico (Mexico D.F.).

'Memorias de la Secretaria de la Defensa Nacional, Septiembre de 1945 a Agosto de 1946', Taller Autografico (Mexico D.F.).

## BIBLIOGRAPHY FOR CHAPTER 5

Argudin, Mario Lavalle, Vicealmirante IMN, *1821-1991 Memorias de Marina, Buques de la Armada de México, Acaecimientos Notables*, Vol.1 and 2 (Mexico, 1991).

de la Pena, Enrique Cárdenas, *Semblanza Marítima de México Independiente y Revolucionario No.2* (Mexico: 1970).

Gómez, Ingeniero José Villela, *Breve Historia de la Aviación en México* (Mexico: 1971).

Historia General de la Secretaria de Marina-Armada de México, Las Políticas Navales 1940-2012 Tomo. II, SEMAR, INDEHRM, SEP (Mexico, 2012).

Lavalle, el Vicealmirante I.M.N. Mario, *La Armada en el Mexico Independiente* (Mexico: INEHRM, 1985).

'Memorias de la Secretaria de la Defensa Nacional, Septiembre de 1945 a Agosto de 1946' (Mexico: 1946).

'Memorias de la Secretaria de Marina, Septiembre de 1944 a Agosto de 1945' (Mexico: 1946).

## BIBLIOGRAPHY FOR CHAPTER 6

Arnold, General of the Air Force H.H., *Global Mission* (New York: Harper & Brother Publishers, 1949).

Butler, Phil, and Hagedorn, Dan, *Air Arsenal North America, Aircraft for the Allies 1938-1945, Purchases and Lend Leases* (Midland Press, 2004).

Conn, Stetson, and Fairchild, Byron, *United States Army in World War II. The Western Hemisphere. The Framework of Hemisphere Defense* (Washington DC, Center of Military History, United States Army, 1989).

'Expediente Cancelado General de División P.A. Gustavo Salinas Camina, Secretaria de la Defensa Nacional', Dirección de Archivo & Historia, Mexico D.F.

Hagedorn, Dan, 'Lend Lease to Latin America, Part I, Army Aircraft', *AAHS*, Vol.34, No.2, Summer 1989.

Hagedorn, Dan, 'Notes Pertaining to Mexico, National Archives at College Park, RG 18 October 1943-1944, Foreign Sales files Japan to Mexico Box 937'.

'Memorias de la Secretaria de la Defensa Nacional, Septiembre 1944 a Agosto de 1945', Taller Autográfico (Mexico D.F., 1945).

'Memorias de la Secretaria de la Defensa Nacional, Septiembre 1945 a Agosto de 1946', Taller Autográfico (Mexico, 1946).

Peterson, Richard A. 'Bud', 'Holiday in Mexico', *American Fighter Aces and Friends Bulletin*, Vol.14, No.1, Spring 1997.

Romero, Manuel Ruiz, *Capitulo IV; De 1940 a 1949: La Segunda Guerra Mundial, Aviación Militar, Historia de la Fuerza Aérea Mexicana y de la Aviación Naval* (Mexico, 2004).

## BIBLIOGRAPHY FOR CHAPTER 7

*El Heraldo* newspaper, Tijuana, Baja California, 17 November 1942.

*El Heraldo* newspaper, Tijuana, Baja California, 19 November 1942.

Osuna, Cap. P.A. Enrique Guerrero, *Alas Para México, Edición Conmemorativa del 80 aniversario de la Escuela Militar de*

*Aviación. Historia Extra Oficial de la Escuela Militar de Aviación y otros Relatos* (Mexico, 1995).

## BIBLIOGRAPHY FOR CHAPTER 8

*Air View News*, July 1944.
*El Heraldo* newspaper, Tijuana, Baja California, 3 January 1944.
*Flying*, Vol.35, No.6, December 1944.
Hornfischer, James D., *The Last Stand of the Tin Can Sailors: the Extraordinary World War II Story of the U.S. Navy's Finest Hour* (New York: Bantam Books, 2004).
Jacobs, Jan, and Tillman, Barrett, 'The Wolf Gang: A History of Carrier Air Group 84', *Hook Journal of Carrier Aviation* (Special Issue 45th Anniversary of VJ Day: the Carrier War in the Pacific), Vol.18, August 1990.
Kennedy, Maxwell Taylor, *Danger's Hour, The Story of the USS Bunker Hill and the Kamikaze Pilot who Crippled Her* (New York: Simon & Schuster, 2008).
Operational Daily Reports of the Grupo Aereo Mexicano April-July 1944, submitted by then Teniente P.A. Fernando Hernandez Vega, copies provided by his family.
Sampas, Colonel (Ret.) Michael, USMC, interview 10 October 1991.
Spurr, Russell, *A Glorious Way to Die, the Kamikaze Mission of the Battleship Yamato* (New York: Newmarket Press, 1981).
*The San Diego Tribune Sun*, San Diego, California, 16 February 1944.
*The San Diego Tribune Sun*, San Diego, California, 29 March 1944.

## BIBLIOGRAPHY FOR CHAPTERS 9 & 10

Aviation Archaeological Investigation & Research website for Foster Field, Texas.
Cardenas R., General Antonio, *Mis Dos Misiones, Monografia Aerea* (Mexico D.F., 1949).
'Fondo Historico Escuadron Aereo 201', Archivo de Historia, Secretaria de la Defensa Nacional, Mexico D.F.
Gallagher, James P., *With the Fifth Army Air Force: Photos from the Pacific Theater* (Baltimore & London: The John Hopkins University Press, 2001).
Gallardo, Reynaldo Perez, *Sangre Mexicana en el Pacifico, Fuerza Aerea Expedicionaria Mexicana Escuadron 201*, 2nd edition (Mexico D.F.: 1945).
'Historial Oficial de la Fuerza Aerea Expedicionaria Mexican por el Teniente Coronel de Estado Mayor Enrique Sandoval Castarrica, Secretaria de la Defensa Nacional' (Mexico: 1946).
Lagunes, Rolando Niquet, *Escuadron 201, Mexico en la Segunda Guerra Mundial* (Mexico D.F.: Editorial Trillas, August 2015).
'Los Aguiluchos Mexicanos: El Escuadron 201, Una Historia Olvidada, Tesis de Antonio Campuzano Rosales', Universidad Nacional Autonoma de Mexico, Naucalpan, Edo de Mexico (October 1995).
Mendoza, Captain CAC, P.A. Reynaldo A., '1948 – A Military Monograph, Air Support for Guerrillas on Northern Luzon'. Philippine Army, Instructor Training Division General Instruction Department, the Armored School, Fort Knox, Kentucky. Advance Officers Class No.2. (1 May 1948).
Narro, Alfredo Macias, *Aguilas Sobre Filipinas, Fuerza Aerea Expedicionaria Mexicana, Escuadron Aereo de Pelea 201* (Mexico, 2013).
Nelson, Lenard J., and Roberts-Wright, Bessie M. Shrontz, *The First Fifty Years: Michaud Flats US Army Base, Pocatello Regional Airport* (1993).
Perez, Pedro Martinez, 'Mexico en la II Guerra Mundial, Fuerza Aerea Expedicionaria Mexicana, Escuadron de Pelea 201' (Monterrey, Nuevo Leon, Mexico).
Pinzon, Captain Ricardo Quintal, *Presencia de Mexico en la II Guerra Mundial 'Escuadron 201' Una narración Historica, Tercera Edicion (Aumentada) Porque se desmembró el Escuadron 201?* (Merida, Yucatan: February 2000).
Ramos, Manuel Cervantes, Capitán 2/o. FAEAA (Ret.), 201st Squadron veteran, personal archive (Mexico City).
Rivera, Lieutenant Colonel Jose G. Vega, 'The Mexican Expeditionary Air Force in World War II: the Organization, Training and Operations of the 201st Squadron', research paper presented to the Research Department, Air Command and Staff College, March 1997.
Tudor, William G., *Flight of Eagles: The Mexican Expeditionary Air Force 'Escuadron 201' in World War II* (UMI Dissertation Services, 1997).

## GENERAL BIBLIOGRAPHY

Pilot log books and general information for the following pilots of the Mexican Air Force, personnel files from the Secretaria de la Defensa Nacional (SEDENA), Archivos de Cancelados, Mexico D.F.:
General Gustavo Salinas Camina
General (Ret.) Jesús Blanco Ledezma
General Antonio Cardenas Rodriguez
Brigadier General Radames Gaxiola Andrade
Brigadier General Enrique Velasco Rojas
Colonel Alfonso Gandarilla Gracia
Colonel Luis Noriega Medrano
Captain Roberto Salido Beltrán
Captain 1st Class Reynaldo Perez Gallardo
Captain 2nd Class Pablo L. Rivas Martínez
Captain Luis Noriega Medrano
Captain Roberto Legorreta Sicilia
Lieutenant Carlos Rodriguez Corona
Lieutenant Graco Ramirez Garrido
Lieutenant Alfonso Gandarilla Gracia
Lieutenant Carlos Varela Landini
Lieutenant Jacobo Estrada Luna
Lieutenant Julio Cal y Mayor Sauz
Lieutenant Fernando Hernandez Vega
2nd Lieutenant Crisoforo Salido Grijalva
2nd Lieutenant Fausto Vega Santander

# ACKNOWLEDGMENTS

As the author I would first of all like to thank Mr Duncan Rogers of Helion Press 'Latin America @ War' series for launching this series, that has allowed me and my fellow historians to tell the history of Latin American warfare to the world. Since the beginning of this journey to learn about Mexican military aviation history, I have encountered the following people and organisations which have given me valuable help in my research activities, and I know that a simple 'thank you' is not enough for all the help and advice they have provided me:

The publishers wish to acknowledge the great assistance of Tony Walton in the preparation of this manuscript for publication.

Ingeniero Adolfo Villasenor Mancias
Ingeniero Enrique Velasco Padilla
Sr Carlos L. Vazquez
Sr Hector Davila Cornejo
Sr Manuel Ruiz Romero
Sr Mardonio Islas Perez
Sr Jose Antonio Quevedo
Sr Luis Gutierrez
Sr Armando Cruz Morales
Sr Corneluis Orzatti, 201st Squadron veteran
Sr Fernando Nava Musa, 201st Squadron veteran
Capitán 2/o. FAAMA DEMA Manuel Reyna Garza
Capitán 2/o. FAEAA (Ret.) Manuel Cervantes Ramos, 201st Squadron veteran
Capitan P.A. (Ret.) Jose Luis Pratt Ramos, 201st Squadron veteran
Capitan 1/o. P.A. (Ret.) Reynaldo Perez Gallardo, 201st Squadron veteran
Coronel P.A. (Ret.) Carlos Garduno Nunez, 201st Squadron veteran
Family of Tte. Col. FAPA (Ret.) Joaquin Ramirez Vilchiz, 201st Squadron veteran
Family of Capitan P.A. (Ret.) Miguel Moreno Arreola, 201st Squadron veteran
Family of General de Div. FAPA Fernando Hernandez Vega, 201st Squadron veteran
General de Division P.A (Ret.) Roberto Fierro Villalobos
Family of Teniente Mecanico Jesus Gutierrez Figueroa, 201st Squadron veteran
Family of Lieutenant Colonel Larry Dennis, USAF
Maestro Antonio Campuzano Rosales
Colonel (Ret) Michael Sampas, USMC
Mr Steve Blake, P-38 National Association
Mr Ed Leiser
Mr Dan Hagedorn
Mr Lin Hendrix
Mr Alberto Anido
Mr Ray Wagner
Mr Brewster C. Reynolds
Mr Sig Unander
Mr Victor Mancillas
Mr Dan Ford
Mr Barrett Tillman
Mr Christopher F. Shores
Mr Frank J. Olynyk
San Diego Aerospace Museum, San Diego, California
National Archives, Washington DC
United States Air Force Historical Research Agency
Smithsonian Air and Space Museum, Washington DC
Imperial War Museum, London
Royal Air Force Museum
Royal Canadian Air Force
French Air Force historical department
Philippines Air Force Historical Department
Japanese Self Defense Forces Historical Agency, Japan
Museo Militar de Aviación 'Teniente P.A. Jose Espinosa Fuentes' BAM#1 Fuerza Aérea Mexicana, Santa Lucia, Mexico state
Archivo General de la Nación, Mexico City.
Museo y Biblioteca de Tijuana BCN, Mexico
Main Public Library, San Diego, California
Sección Segunda, Cuartel General Fuerza Aérea Mexicana, Mexico D.F.
MacArthur Memorial, Norfolk, Virginia
Archivo de Cancelados, Secretaria de la Defensa Nacional, Mexico
Asociación Mexicana de Veteranos de la II Guerra Mundial A.C., Mexico
Agrupación de Sobrevivientes de la FAEM Escuadrón 201 A.C., Mexico
Philippines 1941-1945, the War in the Air (Facebook group)

And finally to my family, who had to put up with all the travel, researching and time on the computer, but in the end I always have their support to carry on. Love ya guys.


# ABOUT THE AUTHOR

SANTIAGO A. FLORES was born in San Diego, California. He was raised and educated in Tijuana, Baja California, Mexico. He started to research Mexican military aviation in 1972 after he discovered how little information was available on the subject. He has published over 220 articles on Mexican aviation and other aviation subjects in aviation magazines, on the internet and Facebook in Mexico and overseas, and has given conferences on the subject in Mexico and the United States. He served in the US Army, completing three overseas tours, including *Desert Storm* in 1991 and later twice in Afghanistan in support of Coalition forces after '9/11'. He was recognised for his efforts to expand general knowledge on Mexican military aviation history in 1999 with the award of the *Francisco Sarabia Conquistador del Cielo* Medal during Aeroexpo 1999 at Acapulco, Mexico, and in 2015 during the centennial of the birth of the country's military aviation by the Commander of the Mexican Air Force. He currently lives in San Diego, California, with his wife, Gaby, and daughters, Alison and Lorena.